Corporate Administrations and Rescue Procedures

Corporate Administrations and Rescue Procedures

Third Edition

William Trower, MA (Oxon)
One of Her Majesty's Counsel
of Lincoln's Inn

Adam Goodison, BA (Dunelm)
of Middle Temple

Matthew Abraham, LLB (UCL), BCL (Oxon)
of Lincoln's Inn

Andrew Shaw, MChem (Oxon)
of Lincoln's Inn

Bloomsbury Professional

Bloomsbury Professional
An imprint of Bloomsbury Publishing Plc

Bloomsbury Professional Ltd	Bloomsbury Publishing Plc
41–43 Boltro Road	50 Bedford Square
Haywards Heath	London
RH16 1BJ	WC1B 3DP
UK	UK

www.bloomsbury.com

**BLOOMSBURY and the Diana logo are trademarks of
Bloomsbury Publishing Plc**

© Bloomsbury Professional Ltd 2017

British Library Cataloguing-in-Publication Data

A catalogue record for this book is available from the British Library.

ISBN:	HB:	978 1 84766 568 3
	ePDF:	978 1 52650 238 4
	ePub:	978 1 52650 237 7

Typeset by Compuscript Ltd, Shannon
Printed and bound by CPI Group (UK) Ltd, Croydon, CR0 4YY

To find out more about our authors and books visit
www.bloomsburyprofessional.com. Here you will find extracts, author information, details of forthcoming events and the option to sign up for our newsletters

PREFACE

The Preface to the Second Edition of this book gave a general description of developments in the law of corporate insolvency between the production of the Cork Report in 1982 and the enactment of the Enterprise Act 2002. This legislation enacted Schedule B1 of IA 1986, which came into force on 15 September 2003. It signalled a shift in the approach to corporate rescue, abolishing administrative receivership in the vast majority of cases and introducing a substantially reformulated administration procedure to take its place. One of the principal reforms was the introduction of the right both of the holder of a floating charge and of the company and its directors to appoint an administrator out of court. The Second Edition was published shortly after these reforms were introduced, at which stage the impact of the legislation was still unclear. Since then, appointments without the intervention of the court have become the norm, and the number of reported decisions on some of the procedural aspects of administration has declined. However, taken overall, the introduction of what has become a court-supervised as opposed to a court-initiated procedure has not had any effect on the pace at which other new developments have been taking place. These have taken the form of many pieces of primary and secondary legislation, countless decisions of the courts on new areas of law and significant changes in practice.

Some of the new legislation has introduced provisions for special administration and rescue procedures in particular sectors, the most important of which have been the financial services sector; this has required the rewriting of Chapter 19. There has also been a proliferation of special administration regimes in other sectors, more especially where a public service is funded (anyway in part) by the provision of private finance. These special administration procedures are considered in a new Chapter 20. There have also been a number of significant general changes introduced by the Small Business, Enterprise and Employment Act 2015. These include new powers for administrators to commence fraudulent and wrongful trading proceedings and a new power to assign the statutory causes of action for fraudulent and wrongful trading and claims under sections 238, 239 and 244 of IA 1986. The 2015 Act also authorised the introduction of modernised decision making, deemed consent and opting-out procedures, the form of which has required a substantial rewriting of Chapter 4.

These procedural developments are dealt with in much greater detail in the most recent legislative change: the enactment of the Insolvency (England and Wales) Rules 2016, which completely replaced the Insolvency Rules 1986 with effect from 6 April 2017. They are an attempt to present the law in a more coherent and user-friendly form. Only time will tell whether this aim has been achieved, but it will take practitioners some time to familiarise themselves with the form of the new Rules and it is hoped that this book will be of some assistance to them in undertaking that task. For the most part the new Rules apply to all administrations, whether or not they commenced before the date on which they came into force, although Schedule 2 to the Rules identifies a limited number of aspects of a pre-April 2017 administration and CVA to which the Insolvency Rules 1986 will continue to apply. The reason for this approach is that the Rules are not intended to change the law to any significant extent – they are intended to consolidate and rationalise the existing law. The consequence is that it has proved possible to complete the Third Edition of this book with only very occasional reference to the Insolvency Rules 1986.

Amongst the other areas in which there have been significant developments since the Second Edition is that of cross-border insolvency, including the enactment of the UNCITRAL Model Law and the handing down of a number of appellate decisions referred to and discussed in Chapter 22. There have also been significant developments in the working out of an administrators' power and ability to make payments and distributions, most significantly with the decision of the Supreme Court in the *Nortel* and *Lehman* appeals, together with a number of other authorities, all of which are discussed in Chapter 15.

The Second Edition of this book included four appendices containing a number of sample agreements. These appendices no longer appear in this edition because we do not consider that the sample agreements have the same utility that they may have had when the First and Second Editions of this book were published. The appendices also included the statutory forms. They too have now been omitted, because one of the innovations introduced by the new Rules is to abolish all of the statutory forms apart from a small number which are intended to relate only to those aspects of bankruptcy and winding up which might impact on the work of the Official Receiver; none of them are designed to be used in administrations or a CVA.

The decision has also been made to remove the discussion of (and references to) the separate Scottish legislation which was included in the Second Edition of the book, most of which was contributed by David Sellar QC. This decision was made for the largely pragmatic reason that changes to the Scottish rules are pending but have been delayed, although it is understood that the Scottish Government intends to enact similar legislation to the Insolvency (England and Wales) Rules 2016 before the end of 2017. Some Scottish authority is referred to in the book, and it is hoped that the book will still be of some use to practitioners when considering principles which are also applicable north of the border.

There has been a change in the authorship of the Third Edition. Ian Fletcher and John Higham QC have both retired from the task. For this edition, the role of senior author has been undertaken by William Trower QC, who has been assisted by his co-authors Adam Goodison, Matthew Abraham and Andrew Shaw. Although parts of the book have been rewritten, much of it has simply been updated, and so the authors would like to express their continuing appreciation to Ian Fletcher and John Higham QC for the invaluable work which they both did on the earlier editions and which have continued to inform much of what is still included in the book.

We have endeavoured to state the law as at 6 April 2017, the date on which the Insolvency (England and Wales) Rules 2016 came into force.

William Trower QC
Adam Goodison
Matthew Abraham
Andrew Shaw

CONTENTS

Contents

Table of Statutes

Table of Statutory Instruments

Table of Cases

All references are to paragraph number

Table of Cases

Table of Cases

Table of Cases

Defined Terms

1994 Order	Insolvent Partnerships Order 1994, SI 1994 No 2421
Acquired Rights Directive	Council Directive 77/187/EEC of 14 February 1977 on the approximation of the laws of the Member States relating to the safeguarding of employees' rights in the event of transfers of undertakings, businesses or parts of businesses
BA 2009	Banking Act 2009
CA 1985	Companies Act 1985
CA 1989	Companies Act 1989
CA 2006	Companies Act 2006
CAA	Civil Aviation Authority
CDDA 1986	Company Directors Disqualification Act 1986
CBIR	Cross Border Insolvency Regulations 2006, SI 2006 No 1030
CGO	Central Gilts Office
COMI	Centre of main interests
CPR	Civil Procedure Rules 1998
CQC	Care Quality Commission
Credit Institutions Regulations	Credit Institutions (Reorganisation and Winding Up) Regulations 2004, SI 2004 No 1045
CVA	Company voluntary arrangement
EEA	European Economic Area
EC Insolvency Regulation	Council Regulation (EC) No 1346/2000 of 29 May 2000 on insolvency proceedings (OJ L60, 30/06/2000, 1–13)
EC Judgments Regulation	Council Regulation (EC) No 44/2001 of 22 December 2000 on jurisdiction and the recognition and enforcement of judgments in civil and commercial matters (OJ L12, 16/01/2001, 1–23)
EMIR Level 1 Regulation	Regulation (EU) No 648/2012 of the European Parliament and of the Council of 4 July 2012 on OTC derivatives, central counterparties and trade repositories

EMIR Level 2 Regulation	Commission Delegated Regulation (EU) No 149/2013 of 19 December 2012 supplementing Regulation (EU) No 648/2012 of the European Parliament and of the Council with regard to regulatory technical standards on indirect clearing arrangements, the clearing obligation, the public register, access to a trading venue, non-financial counterparties, and risk mitigation techniques for OTC derivatives contracts not cleared by a CCP
ERA 1996	Employment Rights Act 1996
FCA	Financial Conduct Authority
FCAR 2003	Financial Collateral Arrangements (No 2) Regulations 2003, SI 2003 No 3226
FMIR 1991	Financial Markets and Insolvency Regulations 1991, SI 1991 No 880
FMIR 1996	Financial Markets and Insolvency Regulations 1996, SI 1996 No 1469
FSCS	Financial Services Compensation Scheme
FSD	Financial support direction
FSMA 2000	Financial Services and Markets Act 2000
GEMA	Gas and Electricity Markets Authority
IA 1986	Insolvency Act 1986
IA 1994	Insolvency Act 1994
IA 2000	Insolvency Act 2000
ICAEW	Institute of Chartered Accountants of England and Wales
Insurers Regulations	Insurers (Reorganisation and Winding Up) Regulations 2004, SI 2004 No 353
IVA	Individual voluntary arrangement
LLP	Limited liability partnership
Model Law	UNCITRAL Model Law on Cross Border Insolvency
PPP	public private partnership
PRA	Prudential Regulation Authority
recast EC Judgments Regulation	Council Regulation (EC) No 1215/2012 of 12 December 2012 on jurisdiction and the recognition and enforcement of judgments in civil and commercial matters (OJ L351, 20/12/2012, 1–32)
recast Insolvency Regulation	Regulation (EU) 2015/848 of the European Parliament and of the Council of 20 May 2015 on insolvency proceedings (OJ L141, 05/06/2015, 19–72)

Recognition Requirements Regulations	Financial Services and Markets Act 2000 (Recognition Requirements for Investment Exchanges and Clearing Houses) Regulation 2001, SI 2001 No 995
Rules	Insolvency (England and Wales) Rules 2016, SI 2016 No 1024
SBEEA 2015	Small Business, Enterprise and Employment Act 2015
Settlement Finality Regulations	Financial Markets and Insolvency (Settlement Finality) Regulations 1999, SI 1999 No 2979
SFO	Serious Fraud Office
SRR	Special resolution regime
Transfer Regulations	Transfer of Undertakings (Protection of Employment) Regulations 2006, SI 2006 No 246
TULR(C)A 1992	Trade Union and Labour Relations (Consolidation) Act 1992
TUPE 1981	Transfer of Undertakings (Protection of Employment) Regulations 1981, SI 1981 No 1794

1 The appointment of an administrator

THE JURISDICTION TO APPOINT AN ADMINISTRATOR

1.1   An administrator of a company is a person appointed under Schedule B1 of the Insolvency Act 1986 ('IA 1986') to manage the company's affairs, business and property. A company enters administration when the appointment of an administrator takes effect and continues to be in administration during the period for which the appointment of an administrator has effect[1]. There are three separate means by which an appointment can be made. The first is by an order of the court, the second is by the holder of a qualifying floating charge and the third is by the company itself or its directors[2]. There are different procedures for each form of appointment. No person may be appointed as an administrator unless he is an authorised insolvency practitioner qualified to act in relation to the company[3]. Whether or not he is appointed by the court, the administrator of a company is an officer of the court[4]. Once appointed, it is the duty of the administrator:

(i)   to formulate proposals for achieving the purpose of administration;

(ii) to circulate those proposals to the company's creditors and members as soon as reasonably practicable (and in any event within eight weeks); and

(iii) to seek a decision on those proposals from the company's creditors within ten weeks of the date on which the company enters administration[5].

During the period for which the company is in administration, a moratorium is imposed on the company's creditors[6].

1.2   Where the court appoints an administrator[7], it makes an order in a prescribed form directing that, during the period for which the order is in force, the affairs, business and property of the company concerned shall be managed by an administrator, identified by name on the face of the order[8]. The order takes

---

1   Schedule B1 paragraph 1 of IA 1986.
2   Schedule B1 paragraph 2 of IA 1986.
3   Schedule B1 paragraph 6 of IA 1986. As to the qualification provisions, see Part XIII of IA 1986.
4   Schedule B1 paragraph 5 of IA 1986.
5   Schedule B1 paragraphs 49 and 51 of IA 1986. With effect from 6 April 2017, the decision is to be made in accordance with the procedures introduced by SBEEA 2015, as to which see further **CHAPTER 4** *post*.
6   Schedule B1 paragraph 43 of IA 1986.
7   Under Schedule B1 paragraph 13(1)(a) of IA 1986.
8   Rule 3.13(1)(f) of the Insolvency (England and Wales) Rules 2016 (SI 2016 No 1024) ("the Rules") and Schedule B1 paragraph 10 of IA 1986.

effect either from the time specified in the order, or, if no time is specified, from the time the order is made[9]. In the case of a company incorporated in England and Wales, the court for this purpose is the High Court or, alternatively, where the amount of the company's share capital, paid up or credited as paid up, does not exceed £120,000, the county court[10]. Where the appointment is made by the holder of a qualifying floating charge[11], or by the company or its directors[12], the appointment takes effect on the filing in court of a statutory form of notice of appointment and such other documents as may be prescribed[13].

1.3   The court may only make an administration order if it is satisfied that the company is or is likely to become unable to pay its debts and that an administration order is reasonably likely to achieve the purpose of administration[14]. Whether appointed by the court or appointed out of court, the proposed administrator must state in writing that, in his opinion, the purpose of administration is reasonably likely to be achieved[15]. The 'purpose of administration' is defined[16] to mean an objective specified in Schedule B1 paragraph 3 of IA 1986. This is a reference back to the fact that every administrator is under a duty to perform his functions with one of three objectives:

1   the objective of rescuing the company as a going concern;

2   the objective of achieving a better result for the company's creditors as a whole than would be likely if the company were wound up; or

3   the objective of realising property in order to make a distribution to one or more secured or preferential creditors.

The objectives are ranked in the order of priority listed above and, irrespective of the circumstances of his appointment, the administrator may only perform his functions towards the second or third objectives if he thinks that it is not reasonably practicable to achieve the objective or objectives ranking ahead in priority. While seeking to achieve the first and second objectives, the administrator must carry out his functions in the interests of the company's creditors as a whole[17]. It should be noted, however, that neither the order made by the court nor the proposed administrator's statement of opinion is required to specify the objective on which reliance is placed as forming the purpose of administration in any particular case. The administrator is also under a duty to perform his functions as quickly and efficiently as is reasonably practicable[18].

1.4   Subject to the provisions of section 426 of IA 1986[19], a company may only enter administration if it is a company within the meaning of Schedule B1 to IA 1986. Schedule B1 paragraph 111(1A) defines 'company' for the purpose

---

9   Schedule B1 paragraph 13(2) of IA 1986.
10   By virtue of the combined effect of sections 117 and 251 of IA 1986.
11   Under Schedule B1 paragraph 14 of IA 1986.
12   Under Schedule B1 paragraph 22 of IA 1986.
13   Schedule B1 paragraphs 19 and 31 of IA 1986.
14   Schedule B1 paragraph 11 of IA 1986.
15   Court appointments: Rules 3.2 and 3.7(1) of the Rules; appointments by holders of floating charge: Schedule B1 paragraph 18(3)(b) of IA 1986 and Rule 3.18(a) of the Rules; and appointments by company or directors: Schedule B1 paragraph 29(3)(b) of IA 1986 and Rule 3.26(a) of the Rules.
16   Schedule B1 paragraph 111(1) of IA 1986.
17   Schedule B1 paragraph 3(2) of IA 1986.
18   Schedule B1 paragraph 4 of IA 1986.
19   See **CHAPTER 22**.

of Schedule B1. It includes companies registered in England and Wales or Scotland under the Companies Act 2006 ('CA 2006') as well as other registered and unregistered undertakings covered by Article 3 of the EC Insolvency Regulation[20]. In *Panter v Rowellian Football Social Club*[21], the court held that it had no jurisdiction to appoint an administration over an unincorporated organisation. The court's jurisdiction to make an administration order in respect of a partnership is further considered in **CHAPTER 16**.

1.5 When a company is in administration, another administrator may not be appointed, unless the appointment is of a replacement or additional administrator by the original appointor or the court[22]. Thus, the holder of a qualifying floating charge cannot make an appointment once an appointment by the company takes effect and vice versa. In addition, it is provided[23] that a person may not be appointed as administrator of a company which is in liquidation. Thus, even in the exceptional case in which the court has power to appoint an administrator notwithstanding the fact that the company is already in liquidation, it must discharge the winding-up order and remove any voluntary liquidator as the case may be[24]. Special treatment is given to particular companies including financial institutions and insurers. When dealing with these companies it is important to follow the specific regimes in place for them[25]. See **CHAPTER 19** for the specialist regimes.

1.6 Subject to an exception in the case of applications made by the holder of a qualifying floating charge, it is a precondition of the making of an administration order that the court should be satisfied that the company is or is likely to become unable to pay its debts within the meaning of section 123 of IA 1986[26]. Likewise, an appointment by the company or its directors must be accompanied by a statutory declaration including a statement that the company is or is likely to become unable to pay its debts[27]. By section 123, a company is deemed unable to pay its debts:

(a) if a creditor (by assignment or otherwise) to whom the company is indebted in a sum exceeding £750 then due has served on the company, by leaving

---

20 Council Regulation (EC) No 1346/2000 of 29 May 2000 on insolvency proceedings. See eg *Thomas v Frogmore Real Estate Partners GP1 Ltd* [2017] EWHC 25 (Ch) for a review of the requirements under the EC Insolvency Regulation. There have been many cases in which the English court has made an administration order against a foreign company on the basis that its COMI was in the UK and so the presumption under Schedule B1 paragraph 111(1B) of IA 1986 was rebutted: eg *Re Collins & Aikman Corp Group* [2005] EWHC 1754 (Ch) (Germany), *Re Nortel Networks SA* [2009] EWHC 206 (Ch) (several European countries), *Re Hellas Telecommunications (Luxembourg) II SCA* [2009] EWHC 3199 (Ch) (Luxembourg), *Re European Directories (DH6) BV* [2010] EWHC 3472 (Ch) (Netherlands), *Re Northsea Base Investment Ltd* [2015] EWHC 121 (Ch) (Cyprus) and *Re Ronin Development Corporation* (7 October 2016, unreported) (USA).
21 [2011] EWHC 1301 (Ch).
22 Schedule B1 paragraph 7 of IA 1986.
23 By Schedule B1 paragraph 8(1) of IA 1986.
24 Schedule B1 paragraphs 37 and 38 of IA 1986 and Rule 3.14 of the Rules.
25 The case of *Re MTB Motors Ltd* [2010] EWHC 3751 (Ch) illustrated the need for proper investigation as to whether a company falls into one of the specialist regimes.
26 Schedule B1 paragraph 11(a) of IA 1986 (and see the definition at Schedule B1 paragraph 111(1) of IA 1986). The exception is provided for by Schedule B1 paragraph 35 of IA 1986 which relates to qualifying floating charge appointments.
27 Schedule B1 paragraphs 27(2)(a) and 30(a) of IA 1986. There is no equivalent requirement where the appointment is made by the holder of a qualifying floating charge.

it at the company's registered office, a written demand (in the prescribed form)[28] requiring the company to pay the sum so due and the company has for three weeks thereafter neglected to pay the sum or to secure or compound for it to the reasonable satisfaction of the creditor[29]; or

(b) if, in England and Wales, execution or other process issued on a judgment, decree or order of any court in favour of a creditor of the company is returned unsatisfied in whole or in part[30]; or

(c) if it is proved to the satisfaction of the court that the company is unable to pay its debts as they fall due[31]; or

(d) if it is proved to the satisfaction of the court that the value of the company's assets is less than the amount of its liabilities, taking into account its contingent and prospective liabilities[32].

1.7 In the case of an administration application made by the Financial Conduct Authority ('FCA') or the Prudential Regulation Authority ('PRA') pursuant to the powers given to it by section 359(1) of the Financial Services and Markets Act 2000 ('FSMA 2000'), it is additionally provided that[33]:

(a) a company or partnership will be unable to pay its debts if it is in default on an obligation to pay a sum due and payable under an agreement;

(b) an authorised deposit taker will be unable to pay its debts if it is in default on an obligation to pay a sum due and payable in respect of a relevant deposit; and

(c) an authorised reclaim fund will be unable to pay its debt if it is in default on an obligation to pay a sum payable as a result of a claim made by virtue of section 1(2)(b) or 2(2)(b) of the Dormant Bank and Building Society Accounts Act 2008.

1.8 In relation to inability to pay debts, a court must be satisfied on the balance of probabilities that the company is or is likely to become unable to pay its debts[34]. In *BNY Corporate Trustee Services Ltd v Eurosail-UK 2007-3BL plc*[35], the Supreme Court reviewed section 123(1)(e) and (2) of IA 1986 closely. The court held when determining whether the company was cash-flow solvent it will be important to take into account debts that fall due in the reasonably near future, although how far ahead would depend on the nature of the business and other circumstances. Beyond the reasonably near future, any attempt to apply a cash-flow test was speculative such that a comparison of present assets with present and future liabilities (discounted for contingencies and deferment), often called the balance sheet test, becomes the only sensible test. In an appropriate case, the court will hear expert evidence on the issue before reaching its decision[36].

1.9 The remaining pre-condition to establishing the court's jurisdiction to make an administration order is that the court must be satisfied that the making

28 Rules 7.2 and 7.3 of the Rules.
29 Section 123(1)(a) of IA 1986.
30 Section 123(1)(b) of IA 1986.
31 Section 123(1)(e) of IA 1986.
32 Section 123(2) of IA 1986.
33 Section 359(2), (3) and (4) of FSMA 2000.
34 *Re Colt Telecom Group plc (No 2)* [2002] EWHC 2815 (Ch).
35 [2013] UKSC 28.
36 *Re Colt Telecom Group plc* [2002] EWHC 2815 (Ch).

of the order is reasonably likely to achieve the purpose of administration[37]. In the case of out-of-court appointments, the equivalent requirement is that the proposed administrator must state in writing that in his opinion the purpose of administration is reasonably likely to be achieved[38].

1.10   In considering whether there is a reasonable likelihood that the purpose of administration will be achieved, the court no longer has to consider which particular objective is likely to be achieved nor does it have to specify any particular objective in any administration order it makes. Likewise, an out-of-court appointment does not have to identify any relevant objective. An administrator must have in mind all of the objectives and move down the hierarchy only if he is of the opinion that an objective is not reasonably practicable or that a better result can be achieved for the company's creditors by pursuing some other course.

THE PURPOSE OF ADMINISTRATION

1.11   As explained above, the 'purpose of administration' is defined to mean an objective specified in Schedule B1 paragraph 3 of IA 1986[39]. This is a reference back to the fact that every administrator is under a duty to perform his functions with the objective of:

(a)   rescuing the company as a going concern;

(b)   achieving a better result for the company's creditors as a whole than would be likely if the company were wound up; or

(c)   realising property in order to make a distribution to one or more secured or preferential creditors.

The administrator's first objective must be to rescue the company as a going concern. It is only if he thinks that that is not reasonably practicable, or that some other steps would achieve a better result for the company's creditors as a whole, that he can take those other steps. He is only permitted to perform his functions with the objective of realising property in order to make a distribution to one or more secured or preferential creditors, if he thinks that it is not reasonably practicable to achieve either of the first two objectives and if he does not unnecessarily harm the interests of the creditors as a whole[40]. It is only at this stage of the process that the administrator is no longer subject to the duty to perform his functions in the interests of the company's creditors as a whole[41].

1.12   The first objective of rescuing the company as a going concern can properly be characterised as the principal purpose of administration. As with the former concept of the survival of the company and the whole or some part of its undertaking as a going concern, the focus is on the rescue of the company as a legal entity, but the concept of the survival of a company's undertaking has been replaced by the concept of the rescue of a going concern. In practice,

---

37   Schedule B1 paragraph 11(b) of IA 1986.
38   Schedule B1 paragraphs 18(3)(b) and 29(3)(b) of IA 1986. This pre-condition applies whether the appointment is made by the holder of a qualifying floating charge, the company itself or the directors.
39   Schedule B1 paragraph 111(1) of IA 1986.
40   Schedule B1 paragraph 3(4) of IA 1986.
41   Schedule B1 paragraph 3(2) of IA 1986.

there is unlikely to be any real distinction between what was originally intended and what is now intended. What is envisaged is that, once the process of administration is complete, the company should emerge in a position to carry on trading as a going concern. It should be noted that there is no requirement for the going concern to be the same as the going concern before the company entered administration. The concept does, however, envisage the continued existence of a viable business capable of continuing to trade. The means by which that is achieved will be infinitely varied, but in appropriate cases will doubtless include the use of voluntary arrangements and schemes to provide for the compromise of liabilities, thereby permitting the company to carry on trading shorn of an unmanageable burden of debt.

1.13 The second objective of achieving a better result for the company's creditors as a whole than would be likely if the company were wound up is the equivalent of achieving a more advantageous realisation of the company's assets than would be effected on a winding up. It is, however, a test that is much broader in its formulation than the test applied under the old law[42], because it is not simply restricted to an advantageous realisation of assets. The concept of a better result lacks precision, but it presumably still demands a focus on the economic benefits for creditors, in the form of the dividend ultimately payable on their claims. Furthermore, it makes plain that a likely reduction in liabilities if the company enters administration may well justify an appointment if the effect is to increase that dividend. Under the former law there was real doubt as to whether a mere reduction in liabilities (eg in respect of tax) was sufficient to satisfy the jurisdictional test of achieving a more advantageous realisation of the company's assets than would be effected on a winding up; there is no longer any such doubt. When assessing the likelihood of a better result being achieved, the court or putative administrator is required to consider the company's creditors as a whole[43], which presumably means that he is required to disregard any special priority to which particular classes of creditor (eg secured or preferential) may be entitled. This is a very important aspect of the legislation because it makes plain that, until such time as he thinks that it is impracticable to rescue the company as a going concern or to achieve a better result for the creditors as a whole than would be likely if the company were wound up, an administrator must always have primary regard to the interests of the creditors as a body, rather than the special interests of the secured creditor by whom he may have been appointed. In practice, this should mean that it is only when there is no longer a real prospect of a dividend for unsecured creditors that the administrator will be free to perform his functions with the sole objective of making a distribution to the preferential or unsecured creditors.

1.14 The third and final objective is that of realising property in order to make a distribution[44] to one or more secured or preferential creditors. An administrator may only perform his functions with this objective if he thinks that it is not reasonably practicable to achieve either of the first two objectives. It reflects the task which had formerly been undertaken by an administrative receiver appointed by a debenture holder with fixed or floating security over the whole, or substantially the whole, of a company's property.

---

42 Under the old law the wording was 'the survival of the company, and the whole or any part of its undertaking, as a going concern'.

43 Schedule B1 paragraph 3(2) of IA 1986.

44 The power to distribute is a new one and, in the case of a distribution to secured or preferential creditors, may be exercised without the court's permission: Schedule B1 paragraph 65(3) of IA 1986.

APPLICATIONS TO COURT FOR THE MAKING OF AN ADMINISTRATION ORDER

1.15   An application for an administration order is made in a prescribed form of application[45] by[46]:

(a)   the company;

(b)   the directors of the company;

(c)   one or more creditors (including any contingent or prospective creditor or creditors[47]) of the company;

(d)   the justices' chief executive for a magistrates' court in the exercise of the power conferred by section 87A of the Magistrates' Courts Act 1980 (enforcement of fines imposed on companies);

(e)   a combination of the persons listed in (a) to (d) above.

1.16   By section 7(4)(b) of IA 1986, the supervisor of a company voluntary arrangement ('CVA') is also included amongst the persons who may apply to the court for an administration order to be made in relation to the company[48]. In the case of an authorised or former authorised person, an appointed representative or former appointed representative and a company that is carrying on or has carried on a regulated activity in contravention of the general prohibition within the meaning of FSMA 2000, the FCA and the PRA also have power to apply to the court for the making of an administration order[49]. Unlike a winding-up petition, in which the petitioner's *locus standi* must usually be determined before an order can be made, questions of status in relation to administration applications may be made on an urgent basis in circumstances where a dispute as to *locus standi* could frustrate the purpose of IA 1986 and prevent the order being made[50]. The issue of *locus standi* should normally be resolved before a final order is made[51]. Where an application is made by a creditor, the issue of standing may arise where there is a genuine dispute as to the existence of debt. In *Hammonds v Pro-fit USA Ltd*[52], the court held that a person was a 'creditor' within paragraph 12(1)(c) if he had a 'good arguable case' that a debt of sufficient amount was owing to him[53].

1.17   In the case of an application by a company, the resolution of the company in general meeting, or alternatively the consent of all the shareholders, is required before the application can be made. Similarly, in the case of a directors'

---

45   Rule 3.3 of the Rules.

46   Schedule B1 paragraph 12(1) of IA 1986.

47   Schedule B1 paragraph 12(4) of IA 1986. See generally *Re British American Racing (Holdings) Ltd* [2004] EWHC 2947 (Ch) regarding an application by a contingent creditor.

48   In which event the petition is treated as that of the company; see Rule 3.5 of the Rules.

49   Section 359(1) and (1A) of FSMA 2000 (as amended by Schedule 17 paragraph 55 of the Enterprise Act 2002).

50   *Re MTI Trading Systems Ltd* [1997] BCC 703 and (per the CA) [1998] BCC 400.

51   *Re MTI Trading Systems Ltd* [1997] BCC 703 and (per the CA) [1998] BCC 400.

52   [2007] EWHC 1998 (Ch), followed in *Fieldfisher LLP v Pennyfeathers Ltd* [2016] EWHC 566 (Ch).

53   Although it is worth noting that in *Thunderbird Industries plc v Simoco Digital UK Ltd* [2004] EWHC 209 (Ch) the court held that the practice in the winding up court should apply to administration applications. This is supported by the fact that there can be distributions to unsecured creditors in an administration with the effect that there is no material difference between such an administration and a liquidation.

petition, a resolution of the board of directors, or alternatively the assent of all such directors, is required[54]. If, however, the board of directors duly resolves to present a petition for an administration order, then it becomes the duty of all directors, including any dissentients, to take such steps as may be necessary to give effect to the resolution, and any director has authority to present the application on behalf of all of them[55]. Once made, an application of the directors becomes that of the company[56]. An application may be made by a company notwithstanding that there is no prospect of the members deriving any personal benefit from the making of the administration order[57]. An application may be made by the directors, and presumably by the company also, notwithstanding the appointment of a provisional liquidator[58].

1.18 In England and Wales, the application must comply with the matters set out in Rule 3.3 of the Rules and in particular contain the matters set out in Rule 3.3(2) of the Rules. The application must contain the following information:

1 The name of the application and a statement making it clear whether the application is being made by[59]–

   (a) the company,

   (b) the directors,

   (c) a single creditor,

   (d) a creditor on behalf of that creditor and others,

   (e) the holder of a qualifying floating charge,

   (f) the liquidator of the company,

   (g) the supervisor of a CVA, or

   (h) a designated officer of a magistrates' court.

2 If made by a creditor on behalf of that creditor and others, the application must contain the names of the others[60]. If the application is made by the holder of a qualifying floating charge, the application must contain details of the charge including the date of the charge, the date on which it was registered and the maximum amount, if any, secured by the charge[61].

3 In relation to all applications the application must contain–

   (a) particulars of the principal business carried on by the company[62];

   (b) a statement whether the company is an Article 1.2 undertaking[63];

   (c) a statement whether the proceedings flowing from the appointment will be main, secondary, territorial or non-EC proceedings and reference

---

54 Following the decision in *Minmar (929) Ltd v Khalastchi* [2011] EWHC 1159 (Ch) and *Baker v London Bar Co Ltd* [2011] EWHC 3398 (Ch) it is important to note that Schedule B1 paragraph 105 of IA 1986 does not apply to applications for an administration order or out of court appointments of administrators by directors.

55 *Re Equiticorp International plc* [1989] BCLC 597.

56 Rule 3.4 of the Rules.

57 *Re Land and Property Trust Co plc* [1991] BCLC 845.

58 See *Re Gosscott (Groundworks) Ltd* [1988] BCLC 363 per Mervyn Davies J at 366C. It should be noted that, in such circumstances, an out-of-court appointment may not be made: Schedule B1 paragraph 25(a) of IA 1986.

59 Rules 3.3(2)(a) and (b) of the Rules.

60 Rule 3.3(2)(c) of the Rules.

61 Rule 3.3(2)(d) of the Rules.

62 Rule 3.3(2)(f) of the Rules.

63 Rule 3.3(2)(g) of the Rules.

to the witness statement in support providing the reasons for the statement[64];

(d) the name and address of the proposed administrator[65];

(e) the address for service of the application[66]; and

(f) a statement that the applicant requests the court

(i) to make an administration order in relation to the company,

(ii) to appoint the proposed person to be administrator, and

(iii) to make such ancillary order as the applicant may request and such other order as the court thinks appropriate[67].

The application must be authenticated by the applicant or the applicant's solicitor and dated[68].

4 Except where the applicant is the holder of a qualifying floating charge making his application in reliance of Schedule B1 paragraph 35 of IA 1986, the application must contain a statement of the applicant's belief that the company is, or is likely to become, unable to pay its debts[69].

1.19 An application to court in England and Wales must be supported by a witness statement verified by a statement of truth[70]. If the application is to be made by the company, the witness statement must be made by one of the directors, the secretary of the company or the supervisor of a CVA and must state on whose behalf it is made[71]. If the application is to be made by the company's directors, a witness statement must be made by one of the directors or the secretary of the company[72]. In the case of an application by a creditor, the witness statement must be made by that creditor or a person acting under the authority of that creditor and in the case of an application by more than one creditor, a person acting under the authority of all of them, whether or not he himself is one of their number; the witness statement must state the nature of the maker's authority and his means of knowledge of the matters to which it relates[73]. The affidavit or witness statement should be sworn or signed by the time that the application is filed, so that there is at least some evidence in support of the act (the making of the application) which has an immediate effect on the rights of others[74].

1.20 The witness statement made in support of the application must contain[75] the following information:

(a) a statement of the company's financial position, specifying, to the best of the applicant's knowledge and belief, its assets and liabilities including contingent and prospective liabilities;

(b) details of any security known or believed to be held by creditors of the company, and whether in any case the security is such as to confer power

64 Rule 3.3(2)(h) of the Rules.
65 Rule 3.3(2)(j) of the Rules.
66 Rule 3.3(2)(k) of the Rules.
67 Rule 3.3(2)(l) of the Rules.
68 Rule 3.3(3) of the Rules.
69 Rule 3.3(2)(i) of the Rules.
70 Rule 3.6(1) of the Rules.
71 Rule 3.6(1)(a) of the Rules.
72 Rule 3.6(1)(b) of the Rules.
73 Rule 3.6(1)(c), (1)(d) and (2) of the Rules.
74 *Re West Park Golf & Country Club* [1997] 1 BCLC 20.
75 Rule 3.6(3) of the Rules.

on the holder to appoint an administrative receiver[76] or an administrator under Schedule B1 paragraph 14 of IA 1986. It must state whether any administrative receiver has been appointed;

(c) details of any insolvency proceedings in relation to the company including any petition that has been presented for the winding up of the company, so far as known to the applicant;

(d) where it is intended to appoint a number of persons as administrators, it must give details of the matters relating to the exercise of their functions and in particular which functions (if any) are to be exercised jointly and which functions (if any) are to be exercised by any or all of them[77];

(e) the reasons for the statement that the proceedings will be main, secondary, territorial or non-EC proceedings; and

(f) any other matters which, in the opinion of the applicant, will assist the court in deciding whether to make such an administration order (so far as lying within the knowledge or belief of the applicant)[78].

1.21 In the case of an application made by the holder of a qualifying floating charge in reliance on Schedule B1 paragraphs 35 or 37 of IA 1986, the applicant is required to give sufficient details to satisfy the court that he is entitled to make an appointment under Schedule B1 paragraph 14[79]. Where he satisfies the court that he is so entitled, the court may make an administration order whether or not it is satisfied that the company is unable to pay its debts[80]. Where the application is made under Schedule B1 paragraphs 37 or 38 of IA 1986 in relation to a company in liquidation, the witness statement must also provide details of the existing insolvency proceedings (including the name and address of the liquidator, the date the liquidator was appointed and by whom) and the reasons why it has subsequently been considered appropriate that an administration application should be made[81].

1.22 The application must also be supported by a statement from the proposed administrator(s) consenting to act[82]. The proposed administrator's statement and consent to act must contain the matters set out in Rule 3.2 of the Rules. The statement must contain the following.

(a) identification details for the company immediately below the heading[83];

(b) a certificate that the proposed administrator is authorised under the provisions of Part XIII of IA 1986 to act as an insolvency practitioner and details of the proposed administrator's IP number and regulatory body[84];

---

76 The power to appoint an administrative receiver of a company has been removed in all but a small number of exceptional cases by section 72A of IA 1986, as inserted by section 250 of the Enterprise Act 2002. Cf *Re Redman Construction Ltd* [2004] All ER (D) 146 (Jun).

77 By reference to Schedule B1 paragraph 100(2) of IA 1986.

78 In *Cornhill Insurance plc v Cornhill Financial Services Ltd* [1992] BCC 818, Dillon LJ, with whom the other members of the Court of Appeal agreed, stated, at 856D, that he had no doubt that those who apply ex parte for an administration order owe the court the usual duty of candour; see also *Astor Chemicals Ltd v Synthetic Technology Ltd* [1990] BCC 97, per Vinelott J at 107F and *Re Sharps of Truro Ltd* [1990] BCC 94. The need for frank disclosure was stressed by Chadwick J in *Re West Park Golf & Country Club* [1997] 1 BCLC 20.

79 Rule 3.6(4) of the Rules.

80 Schedule B1 paragraph 35(2) of IA 1986.

81 Rule 3.6(5) of the Rules.

82 Rule 3.7 of the Rules.

83 Rule 3.2(1)(a) of the Rules.

84 Rule 3.2(1)(b) to 3.2(1)(d).

(c) a statement that the proposed administrator consents to act as administrator of the company, details of any prior professional relationship that he has had with the company, and expressing his opinion that it is reasonably likely that the purpose of administration will be achieved in the particular case[85]; and

(d) the name of the applicant[86].

Where a number of persons are proposed to be appointed to act jointly or concurrently as the administrator of a company, each must make a separate statement and consent to act[87].

1.23   The administrator's opinion that there is a reasonable likelihood that the purpose of administration will be achieved is all that is required by the Rules. However, it remains the case that the court will sometimes find it difficult to exercise its discretion without more information being provided. In those cases, the evidential gap can be plugged by the evidence in support of the application containing a fuller description of other matters which will assist the court in deciding whether to make the order[88]. It will often be of great assistance to the court to be provided with an estimated cash flow forecast so that it can see the period for which the proposed source of funding will enable the company to continue to trade[89].

1.24   The application and all supporting documents must be filed with the court with a sufficient number of copies for service[90]. Each of the copies of the application delivered to the court is sealed and issued to the petitioner and the date and time of filing and the date and venue fixed for the hearing of the petition endorsed thereon[91]. After the application is filed, it is the duty of the petitioner to notify the court in writing of the existence of any insolvency proceedings[92] in relation to the company as soon as he becomes aware of them[93]. An administration application cannot be withdrawn without the leave of the court[94].

NOTIFICATION AND SERVICE OF THE APPLICATION

1.25   As soon as reasonably practicable after the making of an administration application, it is the duty of the applicant to give notice[95] of the application to:

(a) any person who has appointed an administrative receiver of the company, or who is, or may be entitled to appoint, an administrative receiver of the

---

85   Rules 3.2(1)(e), (1)(f) and (1)(h) of the Rules. There is no requirement for the statement to explain why the proposed administrator thinks that it is reasonably likely that the purpose of administration will be achieved: *Re Redman Construction Ltd* [2004] All ER (D) 146 (Jun).
86   Rule 3.2(1)(g) of the Rules.
87   Rule 3.2(3) of the Rules.
88   See Rule 3.6 of the Rules.
89   Likewise it will still be helpful for a statement of affairs to be prepared containing a comparison of estimated realisations on a going concern basis as against estimated realisations on a forced sale basis (see eg per Neuberger J in *Re C E King Ltd* [2000] 2 BCLC 297).
90   Rule 3.7(3) of the Rules.
91   Rule 3.7(4) of the Rules.
92   Including insolvency proceedings under the EC Insolvency Regulation.
93   Rule 3.10 of the Rules.
94   Schedule B1 paragraph 12(3) of IA 1986.
95   Which must be by way of service in accordance with Schedule 4 paragraph 3 of the Rules verified in accordance with Schedule 4 paragraph 6 of the Rules.

company or an administrator of the company under Schedule B1 paragraph 14 of IA 1986[96];

(b) any enforcement agent or other officer who to his knowledge is charged with distress or other legal process against the company or its property and any person who to his knowledge has distrained against the company or its property[97].

If the company is or has been an authorised person or appointed representative or is carrying on or has carried on a regulated activity in contribution of the general prohibition (as those expressions are used in FSMA 2000), the appropriate regulator (either the FCA or PRA) is entitled to be heard on the application[98]. Accordingly, it too should be notified of the application and served with the relevant papers.

1.26 In England and Wales, in addition to the persons who are required to be notified in accordance with Schedule B1 paragraph 12(2) of IA 1986[99], the application (together with any documents attached and the witness statement in support) is required to be served before the date fixed for the hearing[100]:

(a) on any administrative receiver who has been appointed;

(b) if there is pending any petition for the winding up of the company, on the petitioner and any provisional liquidator of the company;

(c) on any member state liquidator appointed in main proceedings in relation to the company;

(d) on the person proposed as administrator;

(e) on the company if the application is made by anyone other than the company; and

(f) on any supervisor of a CVA in relation to the company[101].

1.27 Service is effected on the company by delivering the application together with any documents attached and the witness statement in support to its registered office, or if such delivery is not practicable, by delivery to its last known principal place of business in England and Wales[102]. Service on any other person is effected by delivery of such documents to his 'proper address'[103]. In the case of a person who is an authorised or former authorised deposit taker, and who has appointed, or is or may be entitled to appoint, an administrative receiver or who is or may be entitled to appoint an administrator under Schedule B1 paragraph 14 of IA 1986, and who has not notified an address for service, the 'proper address' of that person is the address of an office of that person where, to the knowledge of the applicant, the company maintains a bank account, or where no such office is known to the applicant, the registered office of that person, or, if

---

96 Schedule B1 paragraph 12(2) of IA 1986.
97 Rule 3.9 of the Rules.
98 Section 362(2) of FSMA 2000.
99 As to which, see **PARAGRAPH 1.25** *ante*.
100 Rule 3.8(3) of the Rules.
101 Rule 3.8(3) of the Rules.
102 Schedule 4 paragraph 3(1)(a) of the Rules. In *Re Bezier Acquisition Ltd* [2011] EWHC 3299 (Ch), the court made it clear that the old Rule 2.8(2) did not contain a complete and exhaustive code as to the mode of service on a company. The old Rule 2.8(2), which permitted the court to direct an alternative manner of service is now found at Schedule 4, paragraph 1(5) of the Rules and applies to service of documents generally.
103 Schedule 4 paragraph 3(1)(a) of the Rules.

there is no such office, his usual or last known address[104]. Otherwise a person's 'proper address' is any which he has previously notified as his address for service[105]. If he has not notified any such address, then service may be effected by delivery to his usual or last known address[106]. Alternatively, service may be effected in such other manner as the court may direct[107].

1.28   Service is required to be verified by a certificate of service which must:

(a)   identify the application, the company and the applicant;

(b)   specify the court in which the application has been made, the date of the application was made, the court reference number, the date of the application, whether the copy served was sealed, the person who served it and the manner and date of service; and

(c)   be verified by a statement of truth.

Where substituted service has been ordered, the certificate must be accompanied by a sealed copy of the order for substituted service[108]. The certificate of service must be filed in court as soon as reasonably practicable after service, and in any event not less than the business day before the hearing of the application[109].

1.29   Under Schedule 5 paragraph 3 of the Rules, the court has power to extend or shorten the time for compliance with anything required or authorised to be done by the Rules. The time required for service of an administration application can therefore be abridged if necessary[110]. The court also has power pending the final determination of an administration application, to make an interim order[111]. Such an interim order may include an order for the appointment of a suitable person to take control of the property of the company and to manage its affairs pending the hearing[112]. Such an appointment is analogous to the appointment of a receiver of disputed property which is in jeopardy[113]. The court may make an interim order restricting the exercise of any powers of the directors of the company and may make provision conferring a discretion on the court or of a person qualified to act as an insolvency practitioner in relation to the company[114].

THE HEARING OF THE APPLICATION

1.30   Where all the persons required under the Rules to be served with the application consent to the making of an administration order, it will normally be possible to arrange for the application to be heard immediately or shortly

---

104   Schedule 4 paragraphs 3(3) and 3(4) of the Rules.
105   Schedule 4 paragraph 3(2) of the Rules.
106   Schedule 4 paragraph 3(2) of the Rules.
107   Schedule 4 paragraph 1(5) of the Rules.
108   Schedule 4 paragraph 6(2) of the Rules.
109   Rule 3.8(4) of the Rules.
110   See eg *Re a Company (No 00175 of 1987)* [1987] BCLC 467, *Re Gallidoro Trawlers Ltd* [1991] BCLC 411 and *Re Switch Services Ltd (In Administration)* [2012] Bus LR D91.
111   Schedule B1 paragraph 13(1)(d) of IA 1986.
112   *Re a Company (No 00175 of 1987)* [1987] BCLC 467 and *In re Switch Services Ltd* [2012] Bus LR D91.
113   *Re a Company (No 00175 of 1987)* [1987] BCLC 467 per Vinelott J at 471a–bb.
114   Schedule B1 paragraph 13(3) of IA 1986. The court's powers under Schedule B1 paragraph 13 are wide: see *SB Corporate Solutions Ltd v Prescott* [2012] Bus LR D91 (cf *Re Gallidoro Trawlers Ltd* [1991] BCLC 411).

following its filing[115]. In cases of great urgency, the court under the pre-Enterprise Act procedure was prepared to make an administration order upon an undertaking to present a petition[116]. Given that it is now possible for the company to make its own appointment without application to the court, there is no longer the same demand for the court to make orders on urgent but uncontested applications.

1.31   It should be noted, however, that where such an urgent application is required, the procedure will still represent a departure from the court's normal practice and the court will require to be satisfied that such departure is justified in all the circumstances[117]. In *Cornhill Insurance plc v Cornhill Financial Services Ltd*[118] the Court of Appeal emphasised the importance of the judge hearing an administration petition looking critically at what is proposed and, if necessary, notwithstanding the urgency, taking time for further consideration. Further, even though the court has power and may be prepared to expedite an application, it is unlikely, save in the most exceptional circumstances, to refuse to allow a party required to be served with the application, particularly one properly entitled to appoint an administrator or an administrative receiver, at least some limited time in which to consider whether to oppose the application and if so, to prepare such opposition or to make an appointment, if so entitled[119].

1.32   In other cases the application, once served, proceeds to a hearing in the normal way. At the hearing, any of the following may appear or be represented[120]:

(a)   the applicant;

(b)   the company;

(c)   one or more of the directors of the company;

(d)   any administrative receiver of the company;

(e)   any person who has presented a petition for the winding up of the company;

(f)   the person proposed for appointment as administrator;

(g)   any member state liquidator appointed in main proceedings in relation to the company;

(h)   any holder of a qualifying floating charge;

(i)   any supervisor of a CVA; and

(j)   with the permission of the court, any other person who appears to have an interest which justifies appearance.

In the case of a company which is or has been an authorised person[121] or an appointed representative[122] or is carrying on or has carried on a regulated activity[123]

---

115   *Re Chancery plc* [1991] BCLC 712 and *In re Halliwells LLP* [2010] EWHC 2036 (Ch); cf *Re Rowbotham Baxter Ltd* [1990] BCLC 397 per Harman J at 399C–D, approved by Dillon LJ in *Cornhill Insurance plc v Cornhill Financial Services Ltd* [1992] BCC 818 at 856F–H.

116   *Re Cavco Floors Ltd* [1990] BCLC 940; *Re Shearing and Loader Ltd* [1991] BCLC 764.

117   *Re Cavco Floors Ltd* [1990] BCLC 940 per Harman at 942d–e; *Re Chancery plc* [1991] BCLC 712 per Harman J at 713G.

118   [1992] BCC 818 per Dillon LJ at 856F–H.

119   Compare *Re a Company (No 00175 of 1987)* [1987] BCLC 467 per Vinelott J at 469e–h.

120   Rule 3.12(1) of the Rules. See also *Re Farnborough-Aircraft.com Ltd* [2002] EWHC 1224 (Ch).

121   Section 31(2) of FSMA 2000.

122   Section 39(2) of FSMA 2000.

123   Section 22 of FSMA 2000.

in contravention of the general prohibition[124], the FCA or the PRA (depending on which is appropriate) is also entitled to be heard[125].

1.33 Subject to the need to control multiple appearances by or multiple representation of persons having the same or similar interests[126], the court's power to grant leave to appear or to be represented to other interested persons, albeit at their own risk as to costs, is readily granted and secured and unsecured creditors and also contributories are regularly heard on administration applications. In the case of contributories, however, if it is apparent that the company is plainly insolvent on a 'balance sheet' basis and that they would have no interest in an immediate liquidation, the court may decline to hear them at all[127].

1.34 At the hearing, subject to being satisfied as to the jurisdictional requirements discussed above in the event that it is minded to make an administration order, the court has a discretion as to what order to make[128] and, in particular, may dismiss the application or adjourn the hearing conditionally or unconditionally. The court may also make an interim order or any other order it thinks appropriate, in which event the court should give directions as to the persons to whom, and how, notice of its order is to be given[129]. The court has an express power to treat the application as a winding-up petition[130] and to make any order which it could make under section 125 of IA 1986. If, however, there is an administrative receiver of the company (whether appointed before or after the making of the administration application[131]), the court is bound to dismiss an administration application in respect of the company unless:

(a) the person by or on behalf of whom the receiver was appointed consents to the making of the administration order; or

(b) the court thinks that if an administration order were made, the security by virtue of which the receiver was appointed would be–

   (i) liable to be released or discharged as a transaction at an undervalue or a preference under sections 238 to 240 of IA 1986,

   (ii) avoided as a floating charge under section 245 of IA 1986, or

   (iii) challengeable as a gratuitous alienation (under section 242 of IA 1986) or an unfair preference (under section 243 of IA 1986) or under any rule of law in Scotland[132].

1.35 The question of whether a receiver is an administrative receiver[133] may give rise to difficult questions of fact in some cases. In particular, it is unclear

---

124 Section 19 of FSMA 2000.
125 Section 362(2)(a) of FSMA 2000.
126 A point made in *Re Farnborough-Aircraft.com Ltd* [2002] EWHC 1224 (Ch).
127 *Re Chelmsford City Football Club (1980) Ltd* [1991] BCC 133.
128 Schedule B1 paragraph 13(1) of IA 1986.
129 Rule 3.15(3) of the Rules.
130 Schedule B1 paragraph 13(1)(e) of IA 1986.
131 Schedule B1 paragraph 39(2) of IA 1986.
132 Schedule B1 paragraphs 13(4) and 39(1) of IA 1986.
133 Ie in England, a receiver or manager of the whole or substantially the whole of a company's property appointed by or on behalf of the holders of any debentures of the company secured by a charge which as created was a floating charge or by such a charge and one or more other securities, or by a person who would be such a receiver or manager but for the appointment of some other person as the receiver of part of the company's property: section 29(2) of IA 1986. The definition of administrative receiver in section 29(2) of IA 1986 does not apply to Scotland but, section 251(1)(b) provides a definition which produces the same practical effect.

what test the court should apply in determining whether a receiver appointed over something less than the whole of a company's property has, nevertheless, been appointed over substantially the whole of that property. However, by virtue of the combined effect of Schedule B1 paragraphs 39 and 44(7) of IA 1986, unless his security is so open to attack, a person who at the date of presentation of the application either has appointed or is entitled to appoint an administrative receiver, is entitled to block the appointment of an administrator. This is unlikely to arise in practice as the effect of section 72A of IA 1986 is to reduce very considerably the number of persons entitled to appoint an administrative receiver, to those with qualifying floating charges created before 15 September 2003[134] and the exceptional categories of person listed in sections 72B to 72GA of IA 1986[135].

1.36   It is unclear to what extent the court, on the hearing of an application for the making of an administration order, would embark upon a detailed investigation as to whether a security by virtue of which an administrative receiver had been appointed was challengeable on the grounds set out above. Since administration proceedings were originally intended by Parliament to provide a temporary regime only and to fill a supposed lacuna in the law where there was no power to appoint an administrative receiver[136], it could be argued that the court should be unwilling to adjourn the hearing of an application for an administration order for any extended period to enable investigations to be made or disclosure to be given[137] and should only be prepared to exercise the jurisdiction not to dismiss an application for an administration order where an administrative receiver had been appointed, where it could readily and clearly be proved that the security, by virtue of which the administrative receiver had been appointed, could be successfully attacked on the grounds stated[138]. The position may be different where the question is whether the floating charge by which a purported administrative receiver was appointed was a qualifying floating charge and/or whether it was created on or before 15 September 2003. Any such issue would have to be determined in any event if there were to be a real question as to whether the holder of such a charge had or had not appointed an administrative receiver. It appears to be a curious omission that Schedule B1 paragraph 39 of IA 1986, like its predecessor, does not include among the circumstances in which the court can make an administration order notwithstanding the appointment of an administrative receiver the fact that the the security by virtue of which he was

---

134   See section 72A(4)(a) of IA 1986 and article 2 of the Insolvency Act 1986, section 72A (Appointed Date) Order 2003 (SI 2003 No 2095).

135   Ie appointments over companies in pursuance of certain capital market arrangements, appointments over certain project companies, appointments by virtue of market charges, system charges and collateral security charges and appointments over registered social landlords.

136   *Re Atlantic Computer Systems plc* [1992] Ch 505 per Nicholls LJ at 525F–G and 528B.

137   In the context of a dispute as to whether or not a company was insolvent, the court refused to order the disclosure sought by the petitioner in an attempt to bolster its case on that issue. Disclosure would only be ordered on an administration application in exceptional circumstances: *Highberry Ltd v Colt Telecom Group plc* [2002] EWHC 2503 (Ch) and *Hammond (A Firm) v Pro-Fit USA Ltd* [2007] EWHC 2941 (Ch).

138   See eg *Chesterton International Group plc v Deka Immobilien Inv GmbH* [2005] EWHC 656 (Ch). It is not thought that the court can proceed on the basis of a provisional view that the security may be capable of challenge under one or more of the provisions mentioned in Schedule B1 paragraph 39(1) of IA 1986. The use of the words 'liable' and 'challengeable' are thought to do no more than reflect the fact that once jurisdiction under any of sections 238–240, 242 and 243 of IA 1986 has been established, the court has a discretion as to the nature of the relief to be granted.

appointed is liable to be avoided against an administrator for non-registration under Part 25 of CA 2006.

1.37 Assuming that the jurisdictional requirements are satisfied, and that the court is not bound to dismiss the application, many factors may affect the exercise of the court's discretion whether to make an administration order. As already pointed out, one important consideration will inevitably be the degree of likelihood that the purpose of administration can be achieved. In this connection, it remains the case that a vitally important factor will be the extent to which funds will be available to finance the administration[139].

1.38 The court will take into account the interests of both secured and unsecured creditors and, where appropriate, members. The court will refuse to make an administration order where to do so would unfairly prejudice individual creditors or groups of creditors, as was the case in *Cornhill Insurance plc v Cornhill Financial Services Ltd*[140] where the object of the administration order, which was subsequently rescinded, was to seek to salvage the company's former business in the hands of another company to which it had been transferred, to freeze the company's indebtedness to a judgment creditor, to prevent the judgment creditor from realising the security held by it and to postpone the judgment creditor to other creditors who had been paid by the company to which the business had been transferred. In certain circumstances, however, the interests of secured creditors may carry less weight than those of others[141]. For example, where a creditor is fully secured and the company is solvent on a balance sheet basis[142], the secured creditor's desire for an administration order may be insufficient to outweigh the interests of members of the company who believe that their interests may be better served by the company not going into administration[143]. Where, however, it is plainly in the interests of the creditors for an administration order to be made, the court will still grant that relief even though the directors may have been motivated in making their application by extraneous considerations[144].

1.39 The court will also consider the likely attitude of creditors generally to any proposals an administrator is likely to put forward[145]. If it is clear that, whatever proposals an administrator puts forward, they are likely to be voted down at the initial creditors' meeting convened pursuant to Schedule B1 paragraph 53 of IA 1986, the court may decline to make an administration order[146]. There have been cases, however, in which the court has determined that an administration order ought to be made, notwithstanding the opposition of creditors amounting

---

139 See eg *Re Rowbotham Baxter Ltd* [1990] BCLC 397, a case under the former law and *Notoriety Films v Revenue and Customs Commissioners* [2006] EWHC 1998 (Ch).
140 [1992] BCC 818.
141 *Re Consumer and Industrial Press Ltd* [1988] BCLC 177 per Peter Gibson J at 181a.
142 Albeit suffering from cash flow problems sufficient to render it insolvent.
143 *Re Imperial Motors (UK) Ltd* [1990] BCLC 29. In many cases, of course, the secured creditor will be able to make an appointment out of court as the holder of a qualifying floating charge.
144 *Re Dianoor Jewels Ltd* [2001] 1 BCLC 450, where it was unsuccessfully alleged than an order should be set aside because it had been sought as part of an attempt to thwart ancillary relief proceedings between the controlling director of the company and his former wife and was therefore an abuse of process. See also *Thomas v Frogmore Real Estate Partners GP1 Ltd* [2017] EWHC 25 (Ch) (paragraph 51).
145 See eg *Re SCL Building Services Ltd* [1990] BCLC 98.
146 Cf *Re Arrows Ltd (No 3)* [1992] BCLC 555; see also *Re Land & PropertyTrust Co plc (No 2)* [1991] BCLC 849 (where Harman J at 854H concluded that in the light of opposition by creditors he had no jurisdiction to make an administration order), *Re West Park Golf & Country Club* [1997] 1 BCLC 20 and *Re Stallton Distribution Ltd* [2002] BCC 486.

to more than 50 per cent of the company's indebtedness[147], although in one of these cases that was largely because the court believed that the creditor was motivated by extraneous commercial considerations and was not satisfied that the creditor concerned would vote against the proposals when they came to be made. Similarly, the court may decline to make an administration order where the company is solvent on a balance sheet basis and where there is deadlock between its shareholders which the making of an administration order is unlikely to resolve[148]. In suitable cases, which should not occur as often as hitherto, given the tighter timetable within which administrations are now required to be conducted, the court may appoint an administrator but require him to report back to the court within a short period so that the court can consider whether to allow the administration to continue or to order that the administration shall cease to have effect and discharge the order[149]. In some cases, the court may require the administrator to hold a meeting of creditors before reporting back to the court, both within a relatively short period. This approach would be consistent with the duty that is imposed on every administrator to hold the initial creditors' meeting as soon as reasonably practicable and in any event within ten weeks[150].

1.40   As has been explained above, in the normal case the court has no power to appoint an administrator where the company is in liquidation[151]. The court does, however, have specific jurisdiction to appoint an administrator on the application of the holder of a qualifying floating charge notwithstanding the fact that the company is in compulsory liquidation[152]. It also has power to make an administration order on the application of a liquidator, whether the company is in voluntary or compulsory liquidation[153]. In both categories of case it is then obliged to discharge any winding-up order and specify which of the powers under Schedule B1 of IA 1986 are to be exercisable by the administrator[154]. In the case of a voluntary liquidation, the court must then make an order removing the liquidator from office[155]. In both categories of case it must provide for the release of the liquidator, the recovery of liquidation expenses and such ancillary matters as the court thinks fit[156]. It is thought that the circumstances in which a liquidator will consider it appropriate to apply for an administration order to be made against a company in liquidation will be very limited. As with the cases in which an application is made by the holder of a qualifying floating charge, such a move from liquidation to administration is only likely to be appropriate where the administration application is made within a very short period of time after the company goes into liquidation. As to the position of the holder of a qualifying floating charge, the jurisdiction is more likely to be useful in the rare cases in which an administration appointment is not made (for whatever reason) before a winding-up order is made. It is odd, however, that this jurisdiction does not appear to extend to permit an administration order to be made on the

---

147   *Re Structures and Computers Ltd* [1998] 1 BCLC 292 and *DKLL Solicitors v Revenue and Customs Commissioners* [2007] EWHC 2067 (Ch).
148   *Re Business Properties* (1988) 4 BCC 684.
149   Compare under the former law *Practice Statement (Administration order applications: content of independent reports)* [1994] 1 WLR 160.
150   Schedule B1 paragraph 51(2) of IA 1986.
151   Schedule B1 paragraph 8(1) of IA 1986.
152   Schedule B1 paragraph 37 of IA 1986.
153   Schedule B1 paragraph 38(1) of IA 1986.
154   Schedule B1 paragraphs 37(3) and 38(2) of IA 1986.
155   Rule 3.14(a) of the Rules, although an administration can only replace a voluntary liquidation on the application of a liquidator under Schedule B1 paragraph 38 of IA 1986.
156   For a full list see Rule 3.14(b)–(d) of the Rules.

application of the holder of a qualifying floating charge once a company has gone into voluntary liquidation. In that category of case, the ability of the holder of a qualifying floating charge to obtain the appointment of an administrator would appear to have been lost. It should be noted, however, that section 84 of IA 1986 provides that a company cannot go into voluntary liquidation without giving five days written notice to the holder of a qualifying floating charge[157].

1.41 If the court determines to make an administration order, there may yet be a dispute as to who should be appointed administrator. The court will normally be guided by the creditors' wishes, but where there is a dispute between different groups of creditors, the court will need to establish what is most conducive to the proper conduct of the administration[158]. In *Re Maxwell Communication Corpn plc*[159], there was a dispute between the directors and the creditor banks as to who should be appointed administrators. The judge appointed the administrators proposed by the banks on the basis that their firm had already engaged in an intensive investigation of the company's affairs and would be able to carry on the administration more cheaply, effectively and quickly as a result of their existing state of knowledge. The judge was reluctant to appoint an additional administrator from a different firm in view of the further expense and delay which would be caused by having to have co-operation between two different firms of accountants. The judge considered that any potential for a conflict of interest which might arise by virtue of the firm proposed by the banks having acted as auditors to a sub-subsidiary company was not, on the evidence before the judge, sufficiently great to warrant the appointment of the administrators proposed by the directors, either alone or jointly with the administrators proposed by the banks. In other cases where the potential conflict of interest is more apparent and more immediate, the court may be more ready to appoint an additional administrator from another firm[160]. The position of the holder of a qualifying floating charge has been given additional statutory protection. Where he proposes the appointment of an administrator other than the applicant's proposed appointee, the chargeholder is given a specific power to apply to court for the appointment of the person proposed by him[161]. There is then a statutory presumption that his proposed appointee will be appointed unless the court thinks it right to refuse the application because of the particular circumstances of the case[162]. The statutory presumption was presumably introduced as partial compensation for the removal (in all but the exceptional case) of the rights of banks and others with qualifying floating charges to thwart an administration application by the appointment of an administrative receiver. Presumably the exception to the presumption is to cover, amongst other circumstances, a situation in which the charge holder's proposed appointee is unable to be sufficiently impartial, a factor which is of particular importance in the light of the fact that administrators, unlike administrative receivers, are officers of the court with stricter duties to all creditors rather than primarily to their appointor. It should be noted, however, that the holder of a qualifying floating charge is also

---

157 Section 84(2A) and (2B) of IA 1986 as inserted by Schedule 1 paragraph 10 to the Enterprise Act 2002 (Insolvency) Order 2003 (SI 2003 No 2096).
158 See eg *GP Noble Trustees Ltd v Directors of Berkeley Berry Birch plc* [2006] EWHC 982 (Ch) and *Oracle (North West) Ltd v Pinnacle Services (UK) Ltd* [2008] EWHC 1920 (Ch) and *Med-Gourmet Restaurants Ltd v Ostuni Investments Ltd* [2010] EWHC 2834 (Ch).
159 [1992] BCLC 465.
160 See eg *Re Polly Peck International plc* (25 October 1990, unreported, Morritt J) and *Bank of Scotland plc v Targetfellow Properties Holdings Ltd* [2010] EWHC 3606 (Ch).
161 Schedule B1 paragraph 36(1) of IA 1986.
162 Schedule B1 paragraph 36(2) of IA 1986.

able to make its own appointment under Schedule B1 paragraph 14 of IA 1986, notwithstanding an application to the court[163]. Once such an appointment has been made the court cannot then make an administration order[164].

1.42   In the event that the court decides to make an administration order[165], the form of relief will be to order that during the period for which the order is in force, the affairs, business and property of the company are to be managed by the administrator or administrators named on the face of the order. The court has power to direct that its order should take effect at some time other than the time at which it is made[166]. Although the draftsman's description of this power contemplates a time before as well as a time after the making of the order, there are few circumstances in which it would be right for the court to direct that it should take effect from a time earlier than the time at which it is made[167]. Unlike the former law[168], the order will not identify the specific objectives which are anticipated as the purpose of administration with regard to the company. In the event that the court decides to appoint a number of persons to act as administrators, the order must specify which functions, if any, are to be exercised by the persons appointed acting jointly and which functions, if any, are to be exercised by any or all of the persons so appointed[169]. On the making of an administration order, the court must dismiss any outstanding petition for the winding up of the company[170] and any administrative receiver of the company must vacate office[171]. If an administrator is appointed in relation to a UK insurer, the court must immediately inform the FCA or the PRA of the appointment unless it was represented at all hearings in connection with the application[172]. In such a case, the administrator must also send to creditors and publish in the Official Journal of the EU certain prescribed information in relation to his appointment[173].

1.43   If the court makes an administration order, the costs of the applicant, and of any person appearing whose costs are allowed by the court, are payable as an expense of the administration[174]. It is thought that the costs to be paid as an

---

163   Ie the interim moratorium does not apply: Schedule B1 paragraph 44(7)(b) of IA 1986.
164   Schedule B1 paragraph 7 of IA 1986.
165   Rule 3.13 of the Rules sets out the contents of an order.
166   Schedule B1 paragraph 13(2) of IA 1986.
167   One circumstance in which such orders have been made is where there were formal deficiencies in an out-of-court appointment and an order was made having retrospective effect to the date on which everybody had originally assumed that the administrators were appointed: *In Re G-Tech Construction Ltd* [2007] BPIR 1275, *In re Derfshaw Ltd* [2011] EWHC 1565 (Ch) and *In re Frontsouth Witham Ltd* [2011] EWHC 1668 (Ch). The difficulties of such a course were explained in *In re Care Partnership Ltd* [2011] EWHC 2543 (Ch) and *In re Elgin Legal Ltd* [2016] EWHC 2523 (Ch).
168   Section 8(3) of IA 1986 in its original form.
169   Schedule B1 paragraph 100(2) of IA 1986 and Rule 3.13(2) if the Rules.
170   Schedule B1 paragraph 40(1)(a) of IA 1986. This does not apply to petitions presented under section 124A of IA 1986 or section 367 of FSMA 2000 (see Schedule B1 paragraph 40(2) of IA 1986).
171   Schedule B1 paragraph 41(1) of IA 1986. The consequences of an administrative receiver having to vacate office are considered in **CHAPTER 2** *post*.
172   Regulation 9 of the Insurers (Reorganisation and Winding Up) Regulations 2004 (SI 2004 No 353) as amended. The FCA or the PRA will then inform all member state regulators (regulation 10 of the Insurers (Reorganisation and Winding Up) Regulations 2004 (SI 2004 No 353) as amended).
173   Regulations 11 and 12 of the Insurers (Reorganisation and Winding Up) Regulations 2004 (SI 2004 No 353) as amended.
174   Rule 3.12(2) of the Rules. For expenses, see **CHAPTER 15** *post*.

expense will usually include the costs incurred by the proposed administrator in arriving at his conclusion that there is a reasonable likelihood that the purpose of administration will be achieved[175]. They should normally be paid promptly after the administration order has been made. Where there is a shortfall, the court has power to order how they should rank as against other expenses and they should normally take priority to other unsecured claims[176]. The court has a discretion as to whether to allow the costs of any party other than the applicant, particularly as regards those who appear by leave under Rule 3.12(1)(j) of the Rules[177]. Whether the court dismisses the application or makes an administration order, the court has a general discretion to make an order for costs against any party appearing or indeed against any other person[178]. Thus, where the court dismisses an application on behalf of the company, it retains a discretion to make an order for costs against the directors personally[179]. However, the court is unlikely to make an order for costs against directors personally where they have acted in good faith and on professional advice and with the support of independent reports[180]. Under the former law, it was established that if, on the dismissal of a petition for the making of an administration order, the court made a winding up order, the court may order the costs of the administration petition to be costs in the winding up[181]. Under the present law, the court has an express power to treat the administration application as a winding-up petition[182]. It follows that, where that course is taken, the costs incurred on the administration application can, if appropriate, be treated as costs of the winding up in the usual way.

APPOINTMENT OF AN ADMINISTRATOR BY THE HOLDER OF A QUALIFYING FLOATING CHARGE

1.44   The holder of a qualifying floating charge may appoint an administrator[183]. For a floating charge to qualify, the instrument by which it was created must fulfil one of three requirements. The instrument must either state that Schedule B1 paragraph 14 of IA 1986 applies to the floating charge, or it must purport to

---

175 Rule 3.12 of the Rules. This is the equivalent of costs incurred on the preparation of a Rule 2.2 report under the former law and cf *Re Shearing and Loader Ltd* [1991] BCLC 764.

176 *Re a Company (No 005174 of 1999)* [2000] 1 BCLC 593 (per Neuberger J). See further, Chapter 3 of the Rules.

177 Cf *Re Rowbotham Baxter Ltd* [1990] BCLC 397 per Harman J at 399B.

178 CPR Parts 44 and 47 apply to insolvency proceedings (including applications for an administration order) by Rule 12.41 of the Rules. The court may order costs of a person who has presented a winding-up petition which is dismissed on the making of an administration order: see *Irish Reel Productions Ltd v Capitol Films Ltd* [2010] EWHC 180 (Ch).

179 *Re Land and Property Trust Co plc (No 3)* [1991] 1 WLR 601 (where, however, Harman J accepted that it would only be in exceptional circumstances that the directors personally would be ordered to pay the costs of an administration petition; though the judge's decision to make an order for costs against the directors personally was reversed on appeal on the basis of additional evidence, the Court of Appeal affirmed the jurisdiction to make an order for costs against the directors personally, see *Land and Property Trust Co plc (No 2)* [1993] BCC 462); cf *Taylor v Pace Developments Ltd* [1991] BCC 406.

180 See *Land and Property Trust Co plc (No 2)* [1993] BCC 462.

181 *Re Gosscott (Groundworks) Ltd* [1988] BCLC 363 (where the judge allowed the company's costs of the administration petition down to the first hearing of the winding-up petition, having found that the administration petition was presented in good faith, reasonably and on professional advice). Cf *Re Fearman Ltd (No 2)* (1987) 4 BCC 141 and *Re Business Properties* (1988) 4 BCC 684.

182 Schedule B1 paragraph 13(1)(e) of IA 1986.

183 Schedule B1 paragraph 14 of IA 1986.

empower the holder to appoint an administrator, or it must purport to empower the holder to make an appointment which would constitute the appointment of an administrative receiver within the meaning of section 29(2) of IA 1986[184]. A person is the holder of a qualifying floating charge if he holds one or more debentures of the company secured by one or more qualifying floating charges which alone or together relate to the whole or substantially the whole of the company's property. He is also the holder of a qualifying floating charge if he is the holder of one or more debentures of the company secured by any number of different forms of security which together relate to the whole or substantially the whole of the company's property, so long as at least one of them is a qualifying floating charge[185].

1.45 To be the holder of a qualifying floating charge entitled to appoint an administrator, the charge itself must be a floating charge. The essence of a floating charge is that it is a charge, not on a particular asset, but on a fluctuating body of assets, which remain under the management and control of the chargor and which the chargor has the right to withdraw from the security despite the existence of the charge[186]. The floating charge must either itself relate to the whole or substantially the whole of the company's property or must, together with other charges, relate to the whole or substantially the whole of the company's property. The fact that the company does not in fact have any assets which are not the subject of a fixed charge should not, of itself, affect the question of whether the floating charge relates to the whole or substantially the whole of the company's property[187]. The position may, however, be different if, as a matter of both fact and the construction of the security, there is no property of the company to which the floating charge relates. Such a case would be highly unusual, because floating charges are usually drafted so as to catch all property not charged by way of fixed charge and a company will normally have some property (however small in value) which will be caught by it. For similar reasons, there has been little consideration of whether a charge relates to substantially the whole of a company's property. It is thought that the exclusion from the charged assets of anything more than property small in value and irrelevant to the conduct of the company's business will mean that the chargee will not be the holder of a qualifying floating charge.

1.46 There are a number of restrictions on the power of the holder of a qualifying floating charge to appoint an administrator. First, there are the general restrictions on the appointment of any administrator where a company is already in liquidation or administration. Secondly, an administrator may only be appointed under Schedule B1 paragraph 14 of IA 1986 while a floating charge

---

184 Schedule B1 paragraph 14(2) of IA 1986.
185 Schedule B1 paragraph 14(3) of IA 1986.
186 See Millett LJ in *Re Cosslett (Contractors) Ltd* [1998] Ch 495 at 510 approved by the Privy Council in *Agnew v IRC* [2001] UKPC 28, [2001] 2 AC 710 at 724 and by the House of Lords in *Smith (Administrator of Cosslett (Contractors) Ltd) v Bridgend County Borough Council* [2001] UKHL 58, [2002] 1 AC 336 at 352 and *Re Spectrum Plus Ltd (In Liquidation)* [2005] UKHL 41 (paragraph 111). See also the Court of Appeal discussion on the distinction between a floating charge and a legal possessory lien in: *Re Hamlet International plc (In Administration) Trident International Ltd v Barlow* [1999] 2 BCLC 506.
187 Cf *Re Croftbell Ltd* [1990] BCLC 844 where the court concluded that the lack of assets caught by a floating charge at the time of its creation did not mean that a receiver appointed under it was not an administrative receiver within the meaning of section 29 of IA 1986.

on which the appointment relies is enforceable[188]. Whether a floating charge is enforceable will depend on the terms of the instrument by which it was created, but this restriction is presumably designed to ensure that the holder of a qualifying floating charge can only appoint an administrator in the same circumstances that he could have appointed an administrative receiver before the coming into force of section 72A of IA 1986. Thus, it will often be necessary for the chargee to make demand so that the charge becomes enforceable on the failure by the chargor to comply with that demand[189]. Thirdly, an administrator may not be appointed under Schedule B1 paragraph 14 of IA 1986 if a provisional liquidator of the company has been appointed under section 135[190]. In those circumstances, the remedy of the holder of the qualifying floating charge is either to make an application for the discharge of the provisional liquidators on his undertaking to make an appointment under Schedule B1 paragraph 14 of IA 1986 or to apply for the appointment of an administrator under Schedule B1 paragraph 12(1)(c) and invite the court to dismiss the winding-up petition on which the provisional liquidator was appointed. Fourthly, an administrator may not be appointed under Schedule B1 paragraph 14 if an administrative receiver of the company is in office[191]. As with the restriction on appointment where a provisional liquidator has been appointed, this is designed to ensure that there is no conflict between competing office holders.

1.47 In addition to the appointment restrictions which apply in the case of all holders of a qualifying floating charge, there is an additional restriction where there is a prior qualifying floating charge to the one on which he relies. For these purposes, one floating charge is prior to another if it was created first or if it is to be treated as having priority in accordance with an agreement to which the holder of each floating charge was party[192]. Where there is such a prior qualifying floating charge, the person proposing to make an appointment under Schedule B1 paragraph 14 of IA 1986 may only do so if:

(a) he has first given at least two business days' written notice to the holder of any such prior charge; or

(b) the holder of any such prior charge has consented in writing to the making of the appointment[193].

This provision is to ensure that the holder of a prior qualifying floating charge is given an opportunity to make his own appointment should he choose to do so. The notice of intention to appoint must comply with Rule 3.16 and contain the matters set out in Rule 3.16(2). It should be noted that the provision for filing with the court a notice of intention to appoint an administrator brings into effect an interim moratorium equivalent to that which comes into effect on the making of an administration application[194]. There is no obligation on the holder of a qualifying floating charge to use any specific form of written notice, but if he wishes to bring the interim moratorium into effect, the notice must be in the

---

188 Schedule B1 paragraph 16 of IA 1986.
189 See eg *Bank of Baroda v Panessar* [1987] Ch 335. The time at which the charge must be enforceable is the time at which the appointment takes effect: *Fliptex Ltd v Hogg* [2004] EWHC 1280 (Ch).
190 Schedule B1 paragraph 17(a) of IA 1986.
191 Schedule B1 paragraph 17(b) of IA 1986.
192 Schedule B1 paragraph 15(2) of IA 1986.
193 Schedule B1 paragraph 15(1) of IA 1986.
194 Schedule B1 paragraphs 44(2), 44(5), 42 and 43 of IA 1986.

prescribed form which must be filed with the court at the same time as it is sent to the holder of any prior qualifying floating charge[195].

1.48   The appointment of an administrator by the holder of a qualifying floating charge under Schedule B1 paragraph 14 of IA 1986 takes effect when certain specific requirements are satisfied[196]. In particular, the appointing chargee must file with the court three copies of the notice of appointment in the prescribed form[197], the administrator's consent to act and either:

(a)   evidence that the appointer has given notice as required by paragraph 15(1)(a) of Schedule B1; or

(b)   copies of the written consent of all those required to give consent in accordance with paragraph 15(1)(b) of Schedule B1.

1.49   The court must apply the seal of the court to the copies and endorse them with the date and time of filing[198]. Rule 3.17 of the Rules sets out the contents of the notice. The notice must include a statutory declaration made by or on behalf of the appointing chargee that he is the holder of a qualifying floating charge in respect of the company's property, that each charge relied on is enforceable on the date of appointment and that the appointment is in accordance with Schedule B1[199]. Unlike an out-of-court appointment by the company, there is no requirement for the holder of a qualifying charge to include within his statutory declaration a statement that the company is or is unlikely to become unable to pay its debts. The statutory declaration must be made not more than five business days before filing the notice with the court[200]. The notice of appointment must identify the administrator and must be accompanied by the administrator's written statement consenting to act and expressing the opinion that the purpose of administration is reasonably likely to be achieved[201]. Evidence must also be filed with the court stating that appropriate notice has been given to, or consent has been received from, the holder of any prior floating charge[202]. Where more than one administrator has been appointed the notice must also be accompanied by a statement of which functions, if any, are to be exercised jointly and which are to be exercised by any or all of the persons appointed[203].

1.50   If the requirements identified above are not satisfied in any respect, the appointment will not have effect. This means that the purported administrator

---

195   Schedule B1 paragraph 44(3) of IA 1986 and Rule 3.16(4) of the Rules.
196   Schedule B1 paragraph 18 and 19 of IA 1986 and Rule 3.18(1) of the Rules. See also *Fliptex Ltd v Hogg* [2004] EWHC 1280 (Ch).
197   See Rule 3.17 of the Rules for the contents of the notice of appointment.
198   Schedule B1 paragraph 18(1) of IA 1986 and Rule 3.18(2) of the Rules. The sealing and endorsement requirements may assist in establishing that the filing of an out-of-court appointment constitutes the opening of insolvency proceedings for the purposes of the EC Insolvency Regulation.
199   Schedule B1 paragraph 18(2) of IA 1986. It is an offence to make a false statement in the statutory declaration which the person making it does not reasonably believe to be true: Schedule B1 paragraph 18(7) of IA 1986.
200   Schedule B1 paragraph 18(6) of IA 1986 and Rule 3.17(3) of the Rules.
201   Schedule B1 paragraph 18(3) of IA 1986 and Rules 3.17(1)(e) and 3.18(1)(a) of the Rules. The administrator's statement must be made in accordance with Rule 3.2 of the Rules, which is the same as required to be filed with an administration application. Thus it must include details of any prior professional relationship, the administrator's IP number and the name of his regulatory body. He may rely on information supplied by directors of the company unless he has reason to doubt its accuracy: Schedule B1 paragraph 18(4) of IA 1986.
202   Rule 3.17(1)(h) of the Rules.
203   Rule 3.17(2) of the Rules.

may have acted pursuant to an invalid appointment. In such circumstances, he may incur liabilities (for example, to third parties for breach of a warranty of authority or to the company itself for trespass). In any such circumstance, the court has power to order the appointing chargee to indemnify the person appointed against such liability if, but only if, it arises solely by reason of the appointment's invalidity[204]. This power is discretionary and is not available in any event where there is some reason for the liability arising other than the invalidity of the appointment. Furthermore, there is no reason why the parties should not make specific arrangements for indemnification which extend beyond those for which Schedule B1 paragraph 21 of IA 1986 makes provision nor is there any reason why the parties should not contract out of the statutory indemnity in an appropriate case. It is incumbent on any third party alleging the invalidity of an appointment to make any application without delay, otherwise he may be estopped from challenging the appointment at a later date[205].

1.51   The court must issue two of the sealed copies of the notice of appointment to the appointing chargee[206]. As soon as practicable after the requirements of Schedule B1 paragraph 18 of IA 1986 have been satisfied, the appointing chargee must notify the administrator and send one of the sealed copies to him[207]. The appointing chargee is also under a duty to send copies of the notice of appointment to any person making an administration application, and to the court in which the application is made, in any case in which he makes the appointment in reliance on Schedule B1 paragraph 14 of IA 1986 after receiving notice of the administration application[208]. This latter requirement is to ensure that the court does not then make an administration order without jurisdiction[209]. These notification requirements are important and non-compliance by the appointing chargee without reasonable excuse is an offence[210].

1.52   The holder of a qualifying floating charge may file a notice of appointment with the court notwithstanding that the court is not open for public business[211]. Rule 3.20 of the Rules makes specific provision for urgent appointments to take effect outside normal court opening hours and sets out the relevant procedure that must be followed. The following should be noted. The notice of appointment must be faxed to a designated fax number for that purpose or emailed, or attached to an email to a designated email address[212]. The notice of appointment must be in a special prescribed form[213]. This procedure is only available when the court is closed[214], but where a filing is properly made in accordance with Rule 3.20 of the Rules, it has the same effect for all purposes as a notice of appointment filed with the court specified as having jurisdiction in the case in accordance with Rule 3.18 of the Rules[215]. Furthermore, it is expressly

---

204   Schedule B1 paragraph 21 of IA 1986.
205   *Fliptex Ltd v Hogg* [2004] EWHC 1280 (Ch) per Peter Smith J (paragraph 36).
206   Rule 3.18(2) of the Rules.
207   Schedule B1 paragraph 20 of IA 1986 and Rule 3.18(3) of the Rules.
208   Rule 3.19(2) of the Rules.
209   Schedule B1 paragraph 7 of IA 1986.
210   Schedule B1 paragraph 20(b) of IA 1986.
211   Rule 3.20 of the Rules.
212   Rule 3.20(1) of the Rules. There is a duty on the Secretary of State to publish the fax number and email address on the Insolvency Service webpages and deliver notice of them to any person requesting them from the Insolvency Service.
213   Rule 3.21 of the Rules.
214   Rule 3.20(1) of the Rules.
215   Rule 3.22(1) of the Rules.

provided that the appointment will take effect from the date and time of the fax transmission or sending of the email[216]. There is a rebuttable presumption that such date and time that is recorded on the fax transmission report or hard copy of the email is the date and time at which the notice was filed[217]. Where this procedure is adopted, the appointor is required to notify the administrator as soon as reasonably practicable that the notice has been filed[218]. He is also under a duty to take to the court three copies of the faxed notice of appointment, together with the fax transmission report or hard copy email and all necessary supporting documents on the next day that the court is open for business[219]. He must include with those documents a statement providing details of the out-of-hours appointment and full reasons for the out-of-hours filing, including an explanation of why it would have been damaging to the company and its creditors not to have so acted[220]. If this is not done on the next day that the court is open for business, the administrator's appointment will cease to have effect[221]. The court must seal the copies and endorse them with both the date and time of the original fax transmission or email and the date of their subsequent filing[222]. The court must then return two of the three sealed copies of appointment to the appointing holder of a qualifying floating charge, who is under a duty, as soon as reasonably practicable, to send one to the administrator[223]. Although the court would appear to have jurisdiction to extend the time for compliance with the filing requirements[224], the circumstances in which such an order would be appropriate are exceptional. It is thought that the submission of documents out of time, but which would otherwise be in accordance with the requirements of Rule 3.20 of the Rules, will still constitute an appointment under Schedule B1 paragraph 14 of IA 1986, albeit one which takes effect from that time rather than the time of the original fax transmission or email.

APPOINTMENT OF AN ADMINISTRATOR BY THE COMPANY OR ITS DIRECTORS

1.53   The company and the directors of the company may appoint an administrator[225]. It is thought that, in the case of an appointment by a company, the resolution of the company in general meeting, or alternatively the consent of all the shareholders, will be required before the appointment can be made[226]. Similarly, in the case of a directors' appointment a resolution of the board of directors, or alternatively the assent of all such directors, will be required[227].

---

216 Rule 3.22(2) of the Rules. The appointer must ensure that the fax transmission report or the hard copy email complies with Rule 3.20(5) of the Rules. The appointer must also retain the fax transmission report or hard copy of the email: see Rule 3.20(6).
217 Rules 3.22(3) of the Rules.
218 Rule 3.20(7) of the Rules.
219 Rule 3.20(9) of the Rules.
220 Rule 3.20(9)(d) of the Rules.
221 Rule 3.22(2) of the Rules.
222 Rule 3.20(10) of the Rules.
223 Rule 3.20(11) and (12) of the Rules.
224 Schedule 5 paragraph 3 of the Rules.
225 Schedule B1 paragraph 22 of IA 1986.
226 See eg *Re Eiffel Steelworks Ltd* (unreported, 15 January 2005). Cf *Re Frontsouth (Witham) Ltd* [2011] EWHC 1668 (Ch).
227 See *Minmar (929) Ltd v Khalastchi* [2011] EWHC 1159 (Ch). In the case of a foreign company, see *In re Melodious Corp* [2015] EWHC 621 (Ch).

If the board of directors duly resolves to make an appointment it becomes the duty of all directors, including any dissentients, to take such steps as may be necessary to give effect to the resolution, and any director has authority to make the appointment on behalf of all of them[228], although a properly drawn resolution will empower one or more directors to sign the necessary documentation.

1.54 There are a number of restrictions on the power of the company or the directors to make an appointment. First, there are the general restrictions on the appointment of any administrator where a company is already in liquidation or administration. Secondly, there are a number of restrictions preventing appointments by the company or the directors for the 12-month period after the cessation of certain types of appointment and the ending of certain categories of arrangement and moratorium. Thus, an appointment may not be made under Schedule B1 paragraph 22 of IA 1986 during the period of 12 months beginning with the date on which an earlier appointment (a) by the company or directors, or (b) on an administration application made by the company or the directors, ceased to have effect[229]. Furthermore, an administrator may not be appointed by the company or the directors during the period of 12 months beginning with the date on which:

(a) any moratorium under Schedule A1 to IA 1986 ends without a voluntary arrangement being in force; or

(b) any voluntary arrangement ends if that arrangement was made during a Schedule A1 moratorium; or

(c) the arrangement ends prematurely within the meaning of section 7B of IA 1986[230].

Thirdly, subject to the provisions in Schedule B1 paragraph 25A, an administrator may not be appointed under Schedule B1 paragraph 22 of IA 1986 if a winding-up petition or an administration application has been presented and is not yet disposed of[231]. Thus, unlike an appointment by the holder of a qualifying floating charge, neither the company nor the directors can trump a winding-up petition or an administration application by third parties[232]. Fourthly, an administrator may not be appointed under Schedule B1 paragraph 22 of IA 1986 if an administrative receiver of the company is in office[233]. Fifthly, an administrator may not be appointed over certain persons (as described in section 362(1)(a) to (c) of FSMA 2000) without the consent of the appropriate regulator[234].

---

228 Cf *Re Equiticorp International plc* [1989] BCLC 597.
229 Schedule B1 paragraph 23 of IA 1986.
230 Schedule B1 paragraph 24 of IA 1986. For voluntary arrangements see **CHAPTER 11** *post* and for the Schedule A1 moratorium procedure see **CHAPTER 12** *post*.
231 Schedule B1 paragraph 25(a) and (b) of IA 1986. Schedule B1 paragraph 25A of IA 1986 permits an appointment if the winding up petition was presented after the filing of a notice of intention to appoint, unless the winding up petition was presented by the Secretary of State under section 124A or 124B of IA 1986 or by the FCA or PRA under section 367 of FSMA 2000.
232 In the case of appointments by holders of qualifying floating charges, and subject to the provisions of Schedule B1 paragraph 40(2), any winding-up petition is suspended (Schedule B1 paragraph 40(1)(b) of IA 1986) and, in the case of an administration application, the order cannot be made once an administrator has been appointed (Schedule B1 paragraph 7 of IA 1986).
233 Schedule B1 paragraph 25(c) of IA 1986.
234 See section 362A of FSMA 2000. There are contrasting views on whether failure to obtain the consent invalidates the appointment of the administrator. See eg *Re Ceart Risk Services Ltd* [2012] EWHC 1178 (Ch) (failure to obtain consent from the FSA (as it was then)).

1.55 Before making an out-of-court appointment, the company and the directors must give at least five business days' written notice to any person who is or may be entitled to appoint an administrative receiver of the company or an administrator under Schedule B1 paragraph 14 of IA 1986[235]. If notice of an intention to appoint is given then the notice must also be given to any enforcement agent or other officer who, to the knowledge of the person giving the notice, is charged with distress or other legal process against the company, any person known to have distrained against the company or its property, any supervisor of a CVA and the company itself (where the appointment is to be by the directors)[236]. Notice must be given by way of formal service as is required for service of an administration application[237]. The notice must identify the proposed administrator and be in the prescribed form[238]. The form of notice must include a statutory declaration, made by or on behalf of the intending appointor, that the company is or is likely to become unable to pay its debts, that the company is not in liquidation and that (so far as the person making the declaration is able to ascertain) the appointment is not prevented by the factors described in **PARAGRAPH 1.54** *ante*[239]. The notice must be accompanied by a copy of the resolution of the company or decision of the directors to make the appointment[240]. The notice and accompanying documents must be filed with the court as soon as reasonably practicable after notice has been given[241] and the statutory declaration must be made not more than five business days before filing[242]. It should be noted that, where there are persons to whom notice of intention to appoint is required to be given, the giving of such notice is a necessary pre-condition to the making of an appointment by the company or the directors. Appointment is only then possible once the five-day notice period has expired or once each person to whom notice has been given has consented in writing to the making of the appointment[243]. During the period between the filing in court of a notice of intention to appoint and either:

(a) the coming into effect of the appointment of an administrator, or

(b) the expiry of the ten business day period referred to in **PARAGRAPH 1.57** *post,*

---

235 Schedule B1 paragraph 26(1) of IA 1986. In order to do so, and thereby obtain the benefit of an interim moratorium, the directors must have a settled intention to appoint an administrator: *JCAM Commercial Real Estate Property XV Ltd v Davis Haulage Ltd* [2017] EWCA Civ 267.

236 Schedule B1 paragraph 26(2) and Rule 3.23(4) of the Rules. The notice of intention to appoint needs to be given to those prescribed under Schedule B1 paragraph 26(2) only if there is a floating charge holder entitled to notice under Schedule B1 paragraph 26(2). The question of whether a failure to comply with the notice requirements of Schedule B1 paragraph 26 invalidates the appointment of the administrator has been debated in many recent cases. The stance taken by the courts differs depending on which parties were not notified and the circumstances surrounding the failure to notify or any attempts to rectify the position: see eg *Adjei v Law for All* [2011] EWHC 2672 (ch) (failure to notify chargee), *Hill v Stokes plc* [2010] EWHC 3726 (failure to notify landlords who had distrained) and *Re Effile Steelworks Ltd* [2015] EWHC 511 (Ch) (failure to notify the company). There is a detailed review of the cases in *In Re M F Global (Overseas) Ltd* [2012] EWHC 1091 (Ch).

237 Rule 3.23(5) of the Rules.

238 Schedule B1 paragraph 26(3) of IA 1986. Rule 3.23 of the Rules sets out the content of the notice of intention to appoint.

239 Schedule B1 paragraph 27(2) of IA 1986. The statutory declaration must comply with Rule 3.23(6) of the Rules. It is an offence to make a false statement in the statutory declaration which the person making it does not reasonably believe to be true: Schedule B1 paragraph 27(4) of IA 1986.

240 Rule 3.23(2) of the Rules.

241 Schedule B1 paragraph 27(1) of IA 1986.

242 Schedule B1 paragraph 27(3)(b) of IA 1986 and Rule 3.23(6) of the Rules.

243 Schedule B1 paragraph 28 of IA 1986.

there is an interim moratorium in place equivalent to that which comes into effect on the making of administration application[244].

1.56   The actual appointment of an administrator by the company or the directors under Schedule B1 paragraph 22 of IA 1986 takes effect when certain specific requirements are satisfied[245]. The appointor must file at court three copies of the notice of appointment in the prescribed form, which must be sealed by the court and endorsed with the date and time of filing[246]. The procedure and the content of the notice of appointment differs depending on whether or not a notice of intention to appoint was given. In both instances the notice must include a statutory declaration made by or on behalf of the appointor that the company or the directors as the case may be are entitled to make the appointment, that the appointment is in accordance with Schedule B1 and that (so far as the person making the declaration can ascertain) the statements made and information given in the notice of intention to appoint remain accurate[247]. The statutory declaration must be made not more than five business days before filing with the court[248]. The notice of appointment must identify the administrator and must be accompanied by the administrator's written statement consenting to act and expressing the opinion that the purpose of administration is reasonably likely to be achieved[249]. Where more than one administrator has been appointed, the notice must also be accompanied by a statement of which functions, if any, are to be exercised jointly and which are to be exercised by any or all of the persons appointed[250].

1.57   There are different requirements, depending on whether or not notice of intention to appoint is required. Where it is required[251], no appointment can be made by the company or the directors unless the notification requirements have been complied with and either the five-day period has expired or written consent has been received by each person to whom notification was given[252]. Even then an appointment cannot be made after the period of ten business days beginning with the day on which the notice of intention to appoint was filed[253].

1.58   On filing with the court, the notice of appointment itself must be accompanied by the written consent of all persons to whom notice of intention to appoint was given, unless the period of notice (five business days) has expired[254]. Where no notice of intention to appoint was required, there is a

---

244   Schedule B1 paragraphs 44(4) and (5), 42 and 43 of IA 1986; see **PARAGRAPH 1.61** *ante*.
245   Schedule B1 paragraph 31 of IA 1986 and Rule 3.26 of the Rules.
246   Schedule B1 paragraph 29(1) and (5) of IA 1986 and Rule 3.26(1) of the Rules.
247   Schedule B1 paragraph 29(2) of IA 1986. It is an offence to make a false statement in the statutory declaration which the person making it does not reasonably believe to be true: Schedule B1 paragraph 29(7) of IA 1986.
248   Schedule B1 paragraph 29(6) of IA 1986 and Rules 3.24(3) and 3.25(4) of the Rules.
249   Schedule B1 paragraph 29(3) of IA 1986. The administrator's statement must be made in accordance with Rule 3.2 of the Rules, which is the same as required to be filed with an administration application. Thus it must include details of any prior professional relationship, the administrator's IP number and the name of his regulatory body. He may rely on information supplied by directors of the company unless he has reason to doubt its accuracy: Schedule B1 paragraph 18(4) of IA 1986.
250   Rules 3.24(2) and 3.25(3) of the Rules.
251   See **PARAGRAPH 1.55** *ante*.
252   Schedule B1 paragraph 28(1) of IA 1986.
253   Schedule B1 paragraph 28(2) of IA 1986, although a later appointment is a curable irregularity not a nullity: *In re Euromaster Ltd* [2012] EWHC 2356 (Ch).
254   Rule 3.26(1) of the Rules.

different prescribed form of notice of appointment[255] which includes a statutory declaration, made by or on behalf of the intending appointor, that the company is or is likely to become unable to pay its debts, that the company is not in liquidation and that (so far as the person making the declaration is able to ascertain) the appointment is not prevented by the factors described in **PARAGRAPH 1.54** *ante*[256]. In such a case, the notice of appointment itself must be accompanied by a copy of the resolution of the company or decision of the directors to make the appointment[257]. If any of the requirements for which provision is made by Schedule B1 paragraph 29 of IA 1986 are not satisfied before an administration order is made or an administrator is appointed by the holder of a qualifying floating charge, any attempted appointment by the company or the directors will not take effect[258].

1.59   As soon as practicable after the requirements of Schedule B1 paragraph 29 of IA 1986 have been satisfied, the appointor must notify the administrator and send one of the sealed copies to him[259]. Non-compliance by the appointor without reasonable excuse is an offence[260]. This obligation is disapplied in any case in which the attempted appointment of an administrator by the company or the directors does not take effect because of an appointment by the court or the holder of a qualifying floating charge before the time at which the company or the directors comply with the requirements of Schedule B1 paragraph 29 of IA 1986[261].

1.60   If the requirements identified in **PARAGRAPH 1.56** *ante* are not satisfied in any respect, the appointment will not have effect. It may be possible to characterise minor non-compliance as a formal defect or irregularity, in which event the appointment, which is probably a proceeding for these purposes[262], may have effect notwithstanding the defect[263]. In any other case, however, the purported administrator may have acted pursuant to an invalid appointment. In such circumstances, he may incur liabilities (eg to third parties for breach of a warranty of authority). In any such circumstance, the court has power to order the appointing chargee to indemnify the person appointed against such liability if, but only if, it arises solely by reason of the appointment's invalidity[264]. This power is discretionary and is not available in any event where there is some reason for the liability arising other than the invalidity of the appointment. Furthermore, there is no reason why the parties should not make specific arrangements for indemnification which extend beyond those for which Schedule B1 paragraph 34 of IA 1986 makes provision, nor is there any reason why the parties should not contract out of the statutory indemnity in an appropriate case.

---

255 Rule 3.25 of the Rules.
256 Schedule B1 paragraph 30(a) of IA 1986. This is the information that would have been included in the notice of intention to appoint had it been required.
257 Rule 3.26(2) of the Rules. Where notice of intention to appoint was required, these documents will have been filed already: Rule 3.23(1)(j) of the Rules.
258 Schedule B1 paragraph 33 of IA 1986.
259 Schedule B1 paragraph 32(a) of IA 1986 and Rule 3.26(4) of the Rules.
260 Schedule B1 paragraph 32(b) of IA 1986.
261 Schedule B1 paragraph 33(b) of IA 1986.
262 Notices of appointment out of court are filed at court and given a case number.
263 It may be possible to argue that it should not be invalidated because Rule 12.64 of the Rules applies.
264 Schedule B1 paragraph 34 of IA 1986.

THE EFFECT OF MAKING AN ADMINISTRATION APPLICATION OR FILING NOTICE OF INTENTION TO APPOINT

1.61 The effect of making an administration application or filing with the court a notice of intention to appoint under Schedule B1 paragraph 14 or 27(1) of IA 1986 is to impose an interim moratorium on the taking of steps against the company and its property[265]. In the case of an application to court, the period of the interim moratorium begins with the filing at court of the relevant documents[266] and ends with the granting or dismissal of the application or (where the order takes effect after the time at which it is made) the time at which it has effect[267]. In the case of any appointment out of court, the period of the interim moratorium begins with the filing in court of the notice of intention to appoint[268]. In the case of an intended appointment by the holder of a qualifying floating charge under Schedule B1 paragraph 14 of IA 1986, the period ends either at the time at which the appointment takes effect or at the expiry of five business days after the date of filing[269]. In the case of an intended appointment by the company or its directors under Schedule B1 paragraph 27(1) of IA 1986, the period ends either at the time at which the appointment takes effect or at the expiry of ten business days after the date of filing[270]. The time at which an appointment out of court takes effect is explained in more detail above. From the time at which the appointment takes effect the interim moratorium is replaced by the more permanent moratorium which lasts for the duration of the administration[271].

1.62 During the period of the interim moratorium, no resolution may be passed or order made for the winding up of the company[272]. The prohibition on the making of a winding-up order against the company does not apply to orders made on public interest petitions presented under section 124A of IA 1986 or to petitions presented by the FCA or PRA under section 367 of FSMA 2000[273]. In addition, the following steps[274] may not be taken except with the permission of

---

265   Schedule B1 paragraph 44(1), (2) and (4) of IA 1986.
266   An application is made when an administration application in accordance with Rule 3.3 of the Rules, together with the accompanying documents for which provision is made by Rules 3.2, 3.6 and 3.7, are filed at court under Rule 3.7 of the Rules.
267   Schedule B1 paragraph 44(1) of IA 1986. The court's power to provide for its order to take effect at some time other than the time the order is made is given by Schedule B1 paragraph 13(2)(a) of IA 1986.
268   Schedule B1 paragraphs 44(2) and 44(4) of IA 1986. In the case of an intended appointment by the holder of a qualifying floating charge, the notice must be in the prescribed form. If it is not, the interim moratorium will not take effect: Schedule B1 paragraph 44(3) of IA 1986. There can be no interim moratorium if there is no person to whom notice is required to be given under Schedule B1 paragraph 26(1) of IA 1986: *JCAM Commercial Real Estate Property XV Ltd v Davis Haulage Ltd* [2017] EWCA Civ 267 (paragraph 57).
269   Schedule B1 paragraph 44(2)(b) of IA 1986.
270   Schedule B1 paragraph 44(4)(b) of IA 1986 (ten days is the period specified in Schedule B1 paragraph 28(2) of IA 1986).
271   As to which, see **CHAPTER 2** *post*.
272   Schedule B1 paragraphs 42(2) and(3) and 44(5) of IA 1986.
273   Schedule B1 paragraph 42(4) and (5) of IA 1986.
274   Applied by the combined effect of Schedule B1 paragraphs 43(2)–(6) and 44(5) of IA 1986. It is important to note that Schedule B1 paragraph 43(6A) does not apply in relation to the interim moratorium by virtue of Schedule B1 paragraph 44(7)(c).

the court, which may be given subject to a condition or any other requirement in connection with what is described as the transaction[275]:

(a) no step may be taken to enforce security over the company's property;

(b) no step may be taken to repossess goods in the company's possession under a hire purchase agreement;

(c) a landlord, or other person to whom rent is payable[276], may not exercise a right of forfeiture by peaceable re-entry in relation to premises let to the company; and

(d) no legal process, including legal proceedings, execution, distress and diligence may be instituted or commenced against the company or its property[277].

1.63 There are, however, limitations upon the extent and effect of the interim moratorium imposed by Schedule B1 paragraph 44 of IA 1986. First, it does not come into effect where, at the time any application is made to the court, there is an administrative receiver of the company unless and until the person by or on whose behalf the administrative receiver was appointed consents to the making of an administration order[278]. Secondly, nothing in Schedule B1 paragraph 44 prevents or requires the permission of the court for the presentation of a petition for the winding up of the company on public interest grounds under section 124A of IA 1986, or by the Secretary of State under section 124B of IA 1986, or by the FCA or the PRA under section 367 of FSMA 2000[279]. It is not possible to present a winding up petition on any other basis without first obtaining the court's permission, but there is unlikely to be any need to do so (in any event where the interim moratorium is imposed on the making of an administration application) because the court has an express power to treat an administration application as a winding-up petition and proceed accordingly[280]. It appears that if the court is of the view that an administration application is bound to fail, it may, in an appropriate case, proceed directly to the appointment of a provisional liquidator of the company[281]. Thirdly, the interim moratorium does not prevent the appointment of an administrator by the holder of a qualifying floating charge[282] nor does it prevent the appointment of an administrative receiver of the company or the carrying out by such receiver (whenever appointed) of any of his functions[283]. It follows that the holder of a qualifying floating charge retains the ability to appoint his own administrator or (where permitted[284]) administrative

---

275 Schedule B1 paragraph 43(7) of IA 1986.
276 Schedule B1 paragraph 43(8) of IA 1986.
277 The latter provisions do not restrict the taking of proceedings by a recognised investment exchange or a clearing house with respect to market contracts for the purpose of its default rules, nor do they apply to prevent the enforcement of market charges.
278 Schedule B1 paragraph 44(6) of IA 1986. There is no equivalent provision where the company or its directors wish to appoint an administrator under Schedule B1 paragraph 22 of IA 1986, because any purported appointment in such circumstances would be prevented by Schedule B1 paragraph 25(c) and any notice of intention to appoint must include a statutory declaration that the appointment is not so prevented: Schedule B1 paragraph 27(2)(c) of IA 1986.
279 Schedule B1 paragraph 44(7)(a) of IA 1986.
280 Schedule B1 paragraph 13(1)(e) of IA 1986.
281 Using its powers under Schedule B1 paragraph 13(1)(e) of IA 1986. Cf *Re WF Fearman Ltd* (1988) 4 BCC 139.
282 Schedule B1 paragraph 44(7)(b) of IA 1986.
283 Schedule B1 paragraph 44(7)(c) and (d) of IA 1986.
284 See sections 72A–72G of IA 1986 and article 2 of the Insolvency Act 1986, Section 72A (Appointed Date) Order 2003 (SI 2003 No 2095).

receiver, notwithstanding the making of an administration application or the filing of notice of intention to appoint by the company or any other person having power to do so.

1.64 The precise effect of these restrictions, which are similar but not identical to those which are imposed following the making of an administration order, is discussed in fuller detail in **CHAPTER 2**. It is, however, apparent from the above that the very step of making an application or filing a notice of intention to appoint imposes a statutory moratorium on the company's creditors, subject only to creditors being able to apply to the court for permission to take any particular step which would otherwise be prohibited. Under the former law it was stressed that, as a result of the material impact that the mere making of an administration application is capable of having on the normal remedies available to a company's creditors (including its secured creditors), the court will be astute to ensure that its process is not abused and in an appropriate case will exercise its power to strike out an application that is bound to fail[285]. Likewise, it is now established that the interim moratorium will not be validly invoked if the directors file a notice of intention to appoint without a settled intention to make an appointment[286].

THE ADMINISTRATOR'S ELIGIBILITY FOR APPOINTMENT

1.65 There has been a reworking of the regulation of insolvency practitioners that has led to a substantially reformed regulatory framework. This has been introduced by both the Deregulation Act 2015 and the Small Business, Enterprise and Employment Act 2015. A full discussion of the reforms is outside the scope of this work, however the reader's attention is drawn to the introduction of two types of authorisation for insolvency practitioners: full and partial[287]. Partial authorisation means authorisation to act as an insolvency practitioner only in relation to companies or only in relation to individuals[288]. Full authorisation means authorisation to act as an insolvency practitioner in relation to companies, individuals and insolvent partnerships[289].

1.66 In order to be eligible for appointment as administrator, a person must be qualified to act as an insolvency practitioner in relation to the company[290]. To be qualified, the administrator must be an individual[291] who is appropriately

---

285 See eg *Re West Park Golf & Country Club* [1997] 1 BCLC 20.
286 *JCAM Commercial Real Estate Property XV Ltd v Davis Haulage Ltd* [2017] EWCA Civ 267, where the notice was filed in an attempt to obtain an interim moratorium pending the submission of proposals for a CVA.
287 Introduced by section 17 of the Deregulation Act 2015 and which was intended to increase the competition in the market for insolvency services.
288 Section 390A(1) of IA 1986.
289 Section 390A(1) of IA 1986.
290 Schedule B1 paragraph 6 of IA 1986.
291 Section 390(1) of IA 1986. It follows that the appointment is personal to the appointee; it is not an appointment of the firm in which the individual is a partner. This is the case even though the reason that a particular individual is proposed might be because of his membership of a particular firm and even though in many cases much of the work will be carried out by employees of the firm rather than the administrator himself: *Re Sankey Furniture Ltd* [1995] 2 BCLC 594.

authorised under section 390A of IA 1986[292]. In order to be qualified to act as an administrator of a company, an insolvency practitioner must ensure that there is in force at all such times security for the proper performance of his duties in accordance with the requirements of Part 3 of the Insolvency Practitioners Regulations 2005[293]. A person is not qualified to act as an administrator at any time if at that time:

(a)   he has been adjudicated bankrupt or sequestration of his estate has been awarded and (in either case) he has not been discharged; or

(b)   a moratorium period under a debt relief order applies in relation to him; or

(c)   he is subject to a disqualification order made or a disqualification undertaking accepted under the Company Directors Disqualification Act 1986; or

(d)   he lacks capacity (within the meaning of the Mental Capacity Act 2005) to act as an insolvency practitioner or is a patient within the meaning of section 329(1) the Mental Health (Care and Treatment) (Scotland) Act 2003 or has had a guardian appointed to him under the Adults with Incapacity (Scotland) Act 2000 (asp 4); or

(e)   there is a bankruptcy restriction order in force in respect of him[294].

A person who acts as the administrator of a company whilst he is not qualified to do so commits a criminal offence[295].

1.67   Quite apart from the statutory restrictions, an insolvency practitioner seeking appointment as an administrator must, as in any professional assignment, satisfy himself that he will not have to act in such a way that his judgment and objectivity will or might be seen to be improperly influenced or impaired by a lack of professional independence[296]. In particular, an administrator should not normally accept an appointment where there is a material professional relationship with the company over which he is to be appointed. The professional body of the practitioner concerned is likely to have similar principles in its own rules[297]. However, in the case of an appointment by the court, so long as full disclosure of any potential conflict of interest is made, the court will not take a narrow and technical view of whether or not it is appropriate for an administrator to act; it will consider what is in the best interests of the company's creditors as a whole[298].

---

292   Section 390(2) of IA 1986. The following professional bodies have been recognised under section 391 of IA 1986: The Chartered Association of Certified Accountants, The Insolvency Practitioners Association, The Institute of Chartered Accountants in England and Wales, The Institute of Chartered Accountants in Ireland, The Institute of Chartered Accountants of Scotland: see the Insolvency Practitioners (Recognised Professional Bodies) Order 1986 (SI 1986 No 1764) as amended.

293   SI 2005 No 524. See also section 390(3) of IA 1986. The security must provide for a general penalty sum of £250,000 and a specific penalty sum equal to the estimated value of the assets of the company up to a maximum of £5,000,000.

294   Section 390(4) of IA 1986.

295   Section 389(1) of IA 1986.

296   See the *Guide to Professional Conduct and Ethics for Persons Authorised by the Secretary of State to Act as Insolvency Practitioners.*

297   See eg the *ICAEW Code of Ethics*, which stresses the importance of integrity and objectivity in the acceptance and conduct of insolvency work.

298   See eg *Re Maxwell Communication Corpn plc* [1992] BCLC 465.

2 Effect of administration: the statutory moratorium

WINDING-UP PETITIONS AND RECEIVERSHIPS

2.1 There are a number of immediate consequences which flow from the company entering administration. Although in many respects different from each other in both concept and form, each of the consequences considered in this chapter is part of the statutory moratorium which is at the heart of the administration procedure. The purpose behind this moratorium is to give the administrator time to formulate and implement his proposals[1]. It should be stressed at the outset that whilst the statutory moratorium is an important prohibition of proceedings against the company or its property, it does not relieve a company of its contractual or other obligations; similarly, whilst there are limitations imposed on the enforcement of security and other property rights against the company, the legislation is not designed to deprive secured or other creditors of their proprietary rights simply to benefit other classes of creditors, for instance those whose claims against the company are wholly unsecured[2].

2.2 The first consequence of a company entering administration relates to winding-up proceedings. On the making of an administration order, winding-up petitions (other than public interest petitions under section 124A of IA 1986 and petitions under section 367 of FSMA 2000) must be dismissed[3]. The obligation to dismiss does not apply to an out-of-court appointment, although the petitioner will require permission to proceed[4] and no order can be made on such a petition unless the administration is brought to an end[5]. The dismissal of a winding-up petition is a judicial act; to that extent the dismissal is inevitable rather than automatically operative on the making of an administration order. However, although an order of the court is required, in practice the court will always dismiss any winding-up petition at the same time as it makes an administration order. Where an administrator is appointed by the holder of a qualifying floating charge, the court is required to suspend any winding-up petition[6]. The petition

---

1   *Re Atlantic Computer Systems plc* [1992] Ch 505 and *Mortgage Debenture Ltd v Chapman* [2016] EWCA Civ 103 (paragraph 13), per David Richards LJ.
2   *Re Atlantic Computer Systems plc* [1992] Ch 505, *Re P & C and R & T (Stockport) Ltd* [1991] BCLC 366 at 374, *Astor Chemicals Ltd v Synthetic Technology Ltd* [1990] BCLC 1 and *Barclays Mercantile Business Finance Ltd v Sibec Developments Ltd* [1992] 1 WLR 1253.
3   Schedule B1 paragraph 40(1)(a) and (2) of IA 1986.
4   Schedule B1 paragraph 43(6) of IA 1986.
5   Schedule B1 paragraph 42(3) of IA 1986.
6   Schedule B1 paragraph 40(1)(b) of IA 1986. There is no equivalent provision where the company or the directors make an appointment under Schedule B1 paragraph 22 of IA 1986.

can be resurrected after the administration is complete, to enable a winding-up order to be made if appropriate[7]. Section 127(2) of IA 1986 provides that, where a winding-up petition is suspended in these circumstances, the provisions of section 127(1) (providing for the avoidance of property dispositions post-commencement of a winding up) shall have no effect in respect of anything done by an administrator. This is consistent with the eventual making of a winding-up order on the original petition, thereby preserving an earlier date for the commencement of a subsequent liquidation[8]. Thereafter, throughout the period during which the company is in administration, no resolution may be passed and no order made for the winding up of the company, save for orders made on public interest petitions under section 124A of IA 1986 and petitions under section 367 of FSMA 2000[9]. The prohibitions against winding up are mandatory; unlike most other steps or proceedings against the company or its property[10] they cannot be overridden by the consent of the administrator or order of the court. The normal rule is therefore that the prohibitions serve to render administration incompatible with liquidation[11]. The only exception is where the court makes a winding-up order on a public interest petition under section 124A of IA 1986 or a petition under section 367 of FSMA 2000. In that event, the court can either order that the appointment of an administrator shall cease to have effect, or it can direct that the administrator continue in office[12]. If it directs a continuation in office it is empowered to give further directions as to which, if any, powers are to be exercisable by the administrator[13]; it may be a matter of some complexity to work out how a liquidator and an administrator will fulfil their respective functions without unnecessary conflict.

2.3 The second principal consequence of administration relates to administrative receivership. On the making of an administration order, any administrative receiver of the company must vacate office[14]. As is explained in **CHAPTER 1**, in the reducing category of case in which there is an administrative receiver of the company at all[15], the court is required to dismiss an administration application unless the appointing debenture holder consents to the appointment of an administrator or the security is open to challenge[16]. It follows that vacation of office by an administrative receiver in these circumstances will be very unusual and will only arise in the case of consent by his appointor or a successful challenge to the security under which he was appointed. There is no equivalent provision (viz requiring an administrative receiver to vacate office) where an appointment is made by the holder of a qualifying floating charge

---

7   This is what occurred in *In Re Portsmouth City Football Club Ltd* [2013] EWCA Civ 916.
8   The preservation for section 127 purposes of the earlier presentation of a winding-up petition was considered in *J Smiths Haulage Ltd* [2007] BCC 135 and *Harlow v Creative Staging Ltd* [2014] EWHC 2787 (Ch).
9   Schedule B1 paragraphs 42(1)–42(4) of IA 1986.
10 Schedule B1 paragraph 43 of IA 1986.
11 See eg Nicholls LJ in *Re Atlantic Computer Systems plc* [1992] Ch 505 at 525G–526A.
12 Schedule B1 paragraph 82 of IA 1986. It should be noted that, if any such petition comes to the attention of the administrator he is under a duty to apply to the court for directions, presumably to ensure that the court is thereby able to give proper consideration to the provisions of Schedule B1 paragraphs 82(3) and 82(4) of IA 1986.
13 Schedule B1 paragraph 82(4) of IA 1986.
14 Schedule B1 paragraph 41(1) of IA 1986.
15 Appointments can only be made in the categories of excepted case for which provision is made by sections 72B–72G of IA 1986 or where the relevant floating charge was created before 15 September 2003.
16 Schedule B1 paragraph 39.

under Schedule B1 paragraph 14 of IA 1986 or by the company or its directors under Schedule B1 paragraph 22. The reason for this is that an administrator may not be appointed under either of these provisions if an administrative receiver of the company is in office[17]. Once an administrator has been appointed no administrative receiver of the company may be appointed[18]. It follows that creditors with the right to appoint an administrative receiver must react quickly to any notice that an administration application or proposed appointment is pending if they do not wish to lose their own right to appoint an administrative receiver.

2.4   The third principal consequence of a company being in administration is that any receiver of part of the company's property[19] must vacate office if required to do so by the administrator[20]. It is submitted that like all discretions given to the administrator, the discretion to require a receiver to vacate office must be exercised in furtherance of the purpose of administration. It may, for example, be necessary for an administrator to force the removal of an uncooperative receiver, where he wishes to exercise his powers under Schedule B1 paragraphs 70 and 71 of IA 1986. Under the former law, it was not clear whether the statutory predecessor to Schedule B1 paragraph 41(2) was only applicable to the removal from office of a receiver already appointed before the date of the administration order. The view expressed in the first edition of this work was that appointments made after the date of the administration order, and therefore only capable of being made with the consent of the administrator or the leave of the court[21], could not be subject to reversal by the administrator under what was then section 11(2) of IA 1986. It was argued that, if they were so subject, an administrator disagreeing with the grant of leave by the court could have rendered it nugatory by immediately reversing its effect[22]. Under Schedule B1 paragraph 41(2), however, the ability of the administrator to require a receiver to vacate office applies 'where a company is in administration'. This form of words makes it much more difficult to argue that the administrator has no power to require a vacation of office where consent or permission has already been given, but any decision to do so could only be justified on the basis of a material change of circumstance since the time of the consent or permission as the case may be. There is also one other oddity, which may be a lacuna in the legislation. Where the whole of the company's property is charged by way of fixed charge, and there is no floating charge in the security documentation, any receiver will

---

17   Schedule B1 paragraphs 17(b) and 25(c) of IA 1986.
18   Schedule B1 paragraph 43(6A) of IA 1986 (as inserted by article 3 of the Enterprise Act 2002 (Insolvency) Order 2003 (SI 2003 No 2096)). An appointment of an administrative receiver would probably also constitute the enforcement of security which is prohibited by Schedule B1 paragraph 43(2) of IA 1986, but this prohibition, unlike the prohibition under Schedule B1 paragraph 43(6A) can be overridden by the consent of the administrator or the permission of the court.
19   And not therefore an administrative receiver.
20   Schedule B1 paragraph 41(2) of IA 1986. This paragraph does not apply to receivers appointed under a charge created or otherwise arising under a financial collateral arrangement within the meaning of regulation 8(2) of the Financial Collateral Arrangements (No 2) Regulations 2003 (SI 2003 No 3226).
21   See what was then section 11(3)(c) of IA 1986 and *Bristol Airport plc v Powdrill* [1990] Ch 744 at 761H–762A.
22   It was submitted that the question of whether or not an administrator, consenting to the appointment of a receiver, having reserved the right to require his removal should be determined by construction of the consent rather than by resort to what was then section 11(2) of IA 1986.

not be an administrative receiver[23], nor yet will he be subject to removal by the administrator under Schedule B1 paragraph 41(1), because he will not be a receiver of only part of the company's property. Such cases will, however, be extremely unusual.

2.5   On the vacation of office by an administrative receiver[24] or by a receiver of part of the company's property[25], his remuneration, defined so as to include any expenses properly incurred by him and any indemnity to which he is entitled out of the company's assets[26] are charged on and payable out of the property of the company in his custody or under his control at the time of vacation of office in priority to any security held by the person by or on whose behalf he was appointed[27]. This provision is made subject to the statutory moratorium contained in Schedule B1 paragraph 43 of IA 1986[28] and so any such receiver will have to seek the consent of the administrator or the permission of the court to enforce payment of any amounts secured by such a charge. It is clear that, whatever the nature of his appointor's security, a receiver vacating office pursuant to Schedule B1 paragraph 41 of IA 1986 will take ahead of him. What is less clear is the order of priority as between such a receiver and those (including the administrator himself) who may be entitled to the benefit of the similar statutory charges granted by Schedule B1 paragraph 99 of IA 1986 which arise upon the administrator vacating office. It is, however, thought that, as the charges granted by Schedule B1 paragraph 99 only give priority over security which, as created, was a floating charge[29] and that makes no mention of security granted by Schedule B1 paragraph 41, the usual rule providing for priority in accordance with the time of creation will apply and the receiver rather than the administrator will take first.

2.6   Where receivers vacate office under Schedule B1 paragraph 41 of IA 1986 they are no longer required to take any steps for the purpose of complying with their obligations[30] to pay preferential creditors[31]. This provision demonstrates a material difference between the intervention of winding up and the intervention of administration, but is a necessary consequence of the fact that the receivership has terminated, whilst on a winding up it continues, subject only to the removal for most purposes of the receiver's status as agent of the company[32]. It would also appear that where a receiver or administrative receiver appointed pursuant to a floating charge has vacated office pursuant to Schedule B1 paragraph 41, the administrator himself is under no positive duty to pay creditors whose claims would have been preferential in the receivership, although if he makes a distribution he is under a duty to make payments to preferential creditors in the administration[33]. Indeed, in the event that a voluntary

---

23   See section 29(2) of IA 1986.
24   Under Schedule B1 paragraph 41(1) of IA 1986.
25   Under Schedule B1 paragraph 41(2) of IA 1986.
26   It is thought that this will apply both to any contractual indemnity and to his right of indemnity at common law: *Re Glyncorrwg Colliery Co Ltd* [1926] Ch 951.
27   Schedule B1 paragraphs 41(3) and 41(4) of IA 1986 and section 45(3) of IA 1986.
28   Schedule B1 paragraph 41(4)(c) of IA 1986.
29   By express reference to Schedule B1 paragraph 70 of IA 1986.
30   Under sections 40 and 59 of IA 1986. Although Crown preference has now been abolished (section 251 of the Enterprise Act 2002), certain amounts owed to employees and pension schemes (Schedule 6 paragraphs 8–12 of IA 1986) remain preferential.
31   Schedule B1 paragraph 41(3)(b) of IA 1986.
32   Section 44(1)(a) of IA 1986: *Gosling v Gaskell* [1897] AC 575.
33   See Schedule B1 paragraph 65(2) of IA 1986 applying section 175 of IA 1986.

arrangement is entered into in the course of an administration or the company is wound up following the discharge of the administration order, different sets of preferential creditors may have priority[34]. It would therefore seem that the effect of a receiver vacating office under Schedule B1 paragraph 41 is to destroy the priority which preferential creditors would otherwise enjoy in the receivership pursuant to sections 40 and 59 of IA 1986[35].

THE ENFORCEMENT OF SECURITY

2.7   Schedule B1 paragraph 43 of IA 1986 makes substantive provision for the statutory moratorium. The courts demonstrated a desire to give a wide and purposive construction to its statutory predecessor (section 11(3) of IA 1986)[36], and a similar approach continues to be taken under the present law. This is consistent with the courts' resolve to construe the legislation in such a way as to maximise the prospects that the administrator is able to achieve the purpose for which he was appointed. Schedule B1 paragraphs 43(2) to (5) impose wide-ranging restrictions on the rights of secured creditors and owners of goods in the possession of the company. It prohibits the taking of any steps to enforce any security over the company's property[37], or to repossess goods in the possession of the company under any hire-purchase agreement[38], or to exercise a right of forfeiture by peaceable re-entry in relation to premises let to the company[39], except with the consent of the administrator or the permission of the court, subject (where the court gives permission) to such conditions or requirement as the court may impose[40].

2.8   The security to which Schedule B1 paragraph 43(2) of IA 1986 refers is defined to mean 'in relation to England and Wales, any mortgage, charge, lien or other security'[41]. The reference to 'other security' leaves room for the courts to construe the word as having its natural and ordinary meaning[42]. This is likely to include any right to sell an asset belonging to a debtor and appropriate the proceeds to payment of the debt[43]. In *Bristol Airport plc v Powdrill*[44], the Court of Appeal accepted the following definition as being no wider than the ordinary meaning of the word:

> 'Security is created where a person ("the creditor") to whom an obligation is owed by another ("the debtor") by statute or contract, in addition to the personal promise of the debtor to discharge the obligation, obtains rights

---

34   See section 387(2) and (3) of IA 1986.
35   It is submitted that Schedule B1 paragraph 70(2) of IA 1986 does not affect this conclusion.
36   See eg Sir Nicolas Browne-Wilkinson V-C in *Bristol Airport v Powdrill* [1990] Ch 744 at 758F–759B and Nicholls LJ in *Re Atlantic Computer Systems* [1992] Ch 505 at 526H–528H. See also *Re David Meek Access Ltd* [1994] 1 BCLC 680 at 686a–d and *In re Rhondda Waste Disposal Co Ltd* [2001] Ch 57 at 67 (paragraph 24).
37   Schedule B1 paragraph 43(2) of IA 1986.
38   Schedule B1 paragraph 43(3) of IA 1986: 'hire purchase agreement' is given an extended definition.
39   Schedule B1 paragraph 43(4) of IA 1986.
40   Schedule B1 paragraph 43(7) of IA 1986.
41   Section 248(b)(i) of IA 1986.
42   As happened in *Bristol Airport plc v Powdrill* [1990] Ch 744 at 760G.
43   See Lord Hoffmann in *Smith (Administrator of Cosslett (Contractors) Ltd) v Bridgend County Borough Council* [2001] UKHL 58 (paragraph 41).
44   [1990] Ch 744 at 760D.

exercisable against some property in which the debtor has an interest in order to enforce the discharge of the debtor's obligation to the creditor.'[45]

2.9   The court then went on to hold that a statutory right of detention[46] is a 'lien or other security' within the meaning of sections 11[47] and 248 of IA 1986. Adopting a similar approach, Harman J subsequently held[48] that the words 'other security' were wide enough to cover the proviso for re-entry conferred on a landlord under a lease, and that therefore, a peaceable exercise of that right could not be effected without the consent of the administrator or the leave of the court[49]. This conclusion was controversial from the outset on the basis, amongst others, that 'security' in section 11(3)(c) should have been given a legal rather than an economic meaning[50] and, in *Re Lomax Leisure Ltd*[51], Neuberger J declined to follow Harman J. The judge reached this conclusion with regret, but felt that he had little option in the light of the decision of the House of Lords in *Re Park Air Services, Christopher Moran Holdings Ltd v Bairstow*[52], in which Lord Millett had made clear that the definitions in section 248 of IA 1986 were not wide enough to render a landlord's right of re-entry a security for the purposes of that section. Although it is readily understandable why Neuberger J was driven to the conclusion he reached, it exposed an unfortunate lacuna in the legislation, because it enabled landlords to continue to exercise rights adverse to the interests of the insolvent estate, which would lead in some cases to the failure of what might otherwise have been a successful administration. The position has now been rectified. Schedule B1 paragraph 43(4) and (5) of IA 1986[53] prohibits any landlord or other person to whom rent is payable from exercising any right of forfeiture by peaceable re-entry (or in Scotland any right of irritancy) in relation to premises let to the company. As with the restriction on enforcement of security over the company's property, the prohibition against peaceable re-entry is subject to the consent of the administrator or the leave of the court.

2.10   Although, as yet, there is no authority on the point, it is not thought that the exercise of a contractual right of set-off amounts to the enforcement

---

45   Notwithstanding the width of this definition, it is submitted that the rights of purchasers under factoring or block discounting agreements, as against the debts purchased, are not subject to the provisions of Schedule B1 paragraph 43(2) of IA 1986; cf *Re George Inglefield Ltd* [1933] Ch 1 and *Lloyds and Scottish Finance Ltd v Cyril Lord Carpet Sales Ltd* [1992] BCLC 609. See also, *Welsh Development Agency v Export Finance Co Ltd* [1992] BCLC 148.

46   Although concerned only with the rights of an aerodrome authority under section 88 of the Civil Aviation Act 1982, the decision of the Court of Appeal would appear to be of general application to rights of detention conferred by other statutes: see per Sir Nicolas Browne-Wilkinson V-C in *Bristol Airport plc v Powdrill* [1990] Ch 744 at 760G–761B. For another case in which the Court of Appeal was concerned with proceedings which started as an application for leave to enforce a legal possessory lien, see *Re Hamlet International plc, Trident International Ltd v Barlow* [1999] 2 BCLC 506.

47   The statutory predecessor to Schedule B1 paragraph 43(2) of IA 1986.

48   In *Exchange Travel Agency Ltd v Triton Property Trust plc* [1991] BCLC 396.

49   Millett J in *Re Olympia &York Canary Wharf Ltd* [1993] BCLC 453 at 456 (albeit obiter) expressed his agreement with the decision in *Exchange Travel Agency Ltd v Triton Property Trust Ltd* [1991] BCLC 396 on this point. *Exchange Travel* was also followed in *Re a Debtor (No 162 of 1993), Doorbar v Alltime Securities Ltd (No 2)* [1995] 2 BCLC 513.

50   It is conceptually imprecise to regard the company's leasehold interest, which is by the act of re-entry destroyed, as property over which the landlord has security.

51   [2000] Ch 502.

52   [2000] 2 AC 172 at 186.

53   The lacuna was first closed by section 9 of the Insolvency Act 2000 which amended section 11(3) of IA 1986 to insert a new section 11(3)(ba).

of security over the company's property within the meaning of Schedule B1 paragraph 43(2) of IA 1986. A right of set-off does not give a security interest in the asset which the creditor seeks to extinguish by exercising his right; it is simply a personal right entitling the creditor to utilise his obligation to the company in discharge or reduction of the company's obligation to him. This is particularly so where the contractual right derives from the relationship between an insolvent company and its bank, and the bank relies on its right to combine a credit balance on one account with a debit balance on another. Whether the correct analysis is that the banker's right to combine is automatically operative in certain circumstances[54] or derives from an implied agreement[55] would seem to be irrelevant; the word 'security' should be given its natural meaning[56].

2.11   The property over which[57] the relevant security must subsist is defined to include:

> 'money, goods, things in action, land and every description of property wherever situated and also obligations and every description of interest whether present or future or vested or contingent, arising out of, or incidental to, property'[58].

2.12   The Court of Appeal, in *Bristol Airport plc v Powdrill*[59], considered that it was difficult to think of a wider definition and gave effect to the width of the definition by holding that a lessee's interest under a specifically enforceable chattel leasing agreement was property within the section. In that case the company had:

> 'at least an equitable right of some kind in that aircraft which falls within the statutory definition as being some description of interest … arising out of, or incidental to that aircraft'[60].

In so far as difficulty arises in the future on the meaning of the word 'property', it is likely to be in the context of whether a particular thing is an interest arising out of or incidental to property.

2.13   It is likely that the precise width of the words 'security' and 'property' will not be settled for some time. In these circumstances, the prudent course for any person with rights against a company in administration or its property is to seek the consent of the administrator or the permission of the court before seeking to exercise those rights. Although a refusal by a creditor to do an act at the request of an administrator which will lead to the loss of the relevant security[61] will not normally constitute a contempt of court pending a prompt application for leave[62], an administrator is an officer of the court and any act which could

---

54   *Halesowen Presswork and Assemblies Ltd v Westminster Bank Ltd* [1971] 1 QB 1 (in the Court of Appeal) and [1972] AC 785 (in the House of Lords), particularly per Lord Kilbrandon at 819, who stressed that two current accounts may be combined without the customer's consent.

55   Eg where the question is the terms of the implied agreement between a company and its bankers on the combination of a loan account debit balance and a current account credit balance: *Bradford Old Bank Ltd v Sutcliffe* [1918] 2 KB 833.

56   *Bristol Airport v Powdrill* [1990] Ch 744 at 760G.

57   For the purposes of Schedule B1 paragraph 43(2) of IA 1986.

58   Section 436 of IA 1986.

59   [1990] Ch 744 per Sir Nicolas Browne-Wilkinson V-C at 759D–G, approved by the Supreme Court in *Akers v Samba Financial Group* [2017] UKSC 6 (paragraphs 43 and 60).

60   [1990] Ch 744 per Sir Nicolas Browne-Wilkinson V-C at 759F.

61   Eg a refusal to deliver up property over which a lien is held.

62   *Bristol Airport plc v Powdrill* [1990] Ch 744 at 764F–H.

constitute an interference with his possession or right to possession is capable of amounting to a contempt[63]. It also seems that a breach of Schedule B1 paragraph 43(2) of IA 1986 (and presumably any of the other parts of the statutory moratorium) will give rise to a claim in damages[64].

2.14 The precise meaning of the prohibition against *taking steps* to enforce security or repossess goods in the company's possession was also subject to rigorous analysis in *Bristol Airport plc v Powdrill*[65]; in that case the relevant step was the enforcement of a lien. The Court of Appeal seems to have accepted that as a matter of ordinary English the taking of a step imports an overt act, or at least a positive act of reliance on his rights by the third party[66]. In most cases, it will be obvious whether or not a step has been taken, but whether the mere assertion of a lien by refusing to hand over possession to the administrator constituted the taking of a prohibited step raised particular difficulty[67]. The solution adopted by the Court of Appeal[68] was to hold that the holder of a lien does not take steps to enforce his lien until he expresses an *unqualified* refusal to hand over the goods to the administrator[69]. He will not express such an unqualified refusal if he asks for the administrator's consent to retain and makes a prompt application for leave under Schedule B1 paragraph 43(2) of IA 1986 in the event that consent is not then given[70].

2.15 As the Court of Appeal recognised, there is no reason why the same act should not both perfect the security and constitute a step in its enforcement[71]. This conclusion does, however, highlight the importance of whether a particular act is in fact an act of enforcement or whether it constitutes a dealing with or

---

63   *Re Sabre International Products Ltd* [1991] BCLC 470. Schedule B1 paragraph 5 of IA 1986 provides that he is an officer of the court whether or not he is appointed by the court.

64   *Euro Commercial Leasing Ltd v Cartwright & Lewis* [1995] 2 BCLC 618 at 623 in which a point that was common ground was recorded with apparent approval by Evans Lombe J. See also *Withers LLP v Rybak* [2011] EWCA Civ 1419 (paragraph 29).

65   [1990] Ch 744.

66   Per Woolf LJ at 768E: 'You are not taking steps to enforce a security unless by relying on the security you are preventing the administrator doing something to an aircraft or other chattel in which he has an interest which he would otherwise be entitled to do'.

67   *Bristol Airport plc v Powdrill* [1990] Ch 744: see also *Re Sabre International Products Ltd* [1991] BCLC 470.

68   See in particular the judgment of Woolf LJ in *Bristol Airport plc v Powdrill* [1990] Ch 744 at 768E–770B with which Sir Nicolas Browne-Wilkinson V-C agreed (at 767E).

69   Both Sir Nicolas Browne-Wilkinson V-C (at 762C–G) and Woolf LJ (at 769B–C) drew comfort from section 246(2) of IA 1986 which provides that in the context of that section a denial by the lien holder of a claim to possession by the office-holder constitutes enforcement of a lien. On this point, see also *Euro Commercial Leasing Ltd v Cartwright & Lewis* [1995] 2 BCLC 618 and *Re Carter Commercial Developments Ltd* [2002] BCC 803 (both cases on the enforcement a solicitor's lien over money in a client account). In the latter case, Jacob J explained that the lien holder required permission to hold the documents as soon as the company actually asked for their return.

70   Woolf LJ made clear that in case he was wrong in his construction of what was then section 11(3) of IA 1986, he would expect an administrator to give consent to detention under a statutory power (or by a lien holder) pending a speedy application to the court for leave. For a case in which the refusal to return detained goods was not qualified in the way suggested by Woolf LJ, see *Re Sabre International Products Ltd* [1991] BCLC 470. This is what happened in *Uniserve Ltd v Croxen* [2012] EWHC 1190 (Ch), where an application for permission to enforce a lien was made in response to an application by administrators for delivery up under section 234 of IA 1986.

71   Per Sir Nicolas Browne-Wilkinson V-C [1990] Ch 744 at 763H–764A and Woolf LJ at 769A–B, cited with approval by the Privy Council in *IMH Investments Ltd v Trinidad Home Developments Ltd* (Appeal No 49 of 2002) [2003] UKPC 85 (paragraph 38).

improvement of a relevant security[72]. Thus, where a creditor acquired a lien over an aircraft through the exercise post-administration of a contractual right to do so, that acquisition was not a breach of the statutory moratorium; the breach was the subsequent assertion of the lien without consent of the administrators or permission of the court[73]. This question might also arise on service of a notice to cause the crystallisation of a floating charge[74], although the occasions on which it will do so will now be rare[75]. In this context, it is not thought that, in the absence of specific provision in the documentation creating the security, the mere making of an administration order would itself constitute an event of crystallisation, unless, on the particular facts, and notwithstanding the administrator's principal obligation under Schedule B1 paragraph 3(1)(a) of IA 1986 to rescue the company as a going concern, the making of the administration order of itself caused the company to cease to trade as a going concern[76], thereby limiting the purpose of the administration to the second and third objectives[77]. The reason for this is that administration is not of itself incompatible with the continuance of the company's business; indeed quite the contrary, it is often to assist that trading that an order is made. Although there are arguments both ways it is thought that, in principle, the service of a notice to crystallise a floating charge cannot properly be said to be a step to enforce a security, but is merely the exercise of a contractual right to effect a change in the nature of the security, so that service of such a notice would not amount to a breach of Schedule B1 paragraph 43(2) of IA 1986[78].

2.16   A similar point was alluded to in *Barclays Mercantile Business Finance Ltd v Sibec Developments Ltd*[79]. In that case, Millett J regarded as difficult the question of whether the making of a demand for the return of goods so as to constitute a cause of action in conversion could in itself amount to the taking of a prohibited step to repossess goods in the company's possession, and declined to determine the point as its resolution was not necessary for his decision. With some diffidence, however, it is submitted that, provided the owner of the goods made it clear that in the event the demand was not complied with, he would seek the consent of the administrator or the permission of the court to take proceedings to recover the goods, the making of such a demand would not, in itself, constitute the taking of a step to repossess the goods. In any event, the point may well remain academic for the reason given by Millett J, namely the fact that an administrator who declines to allow an owner of goods in the company's possession to repossess the goods may be ordered, as an officer of the

---

72   Which would not seem to be a breach of Schedule B1 paragraph 43(2) of IA 1986.
73   *London Flight Centre (Stansted) Ltd v Osprey Aviation Ltd* [2002] BPIR 1115.
74   Such as was held to be effective in *Re Brightlife Ltd* [1987] Ch 200.
75   Because the definition of a floating charge in Schedule B1 paragraph 111(1) of IA 1986 is a charge which is a floating charge on its creation (confirming section 251 of IA 1986 which first defined a floating charge as being a charge which *as created* was a floating charge), thereby negating the consequences of *Re Brightlife Ltd* [1987] Ch 200 and making it impossible for a floating charge holder to improve his position under Schedule B1 paragraphs 70 and 71 of IA 1986.
76   Cf *Governments Stock and Other Securities Investments Co Ltd v Manila Rly Co* [1897] AC 81 at 86 and *Re Woodroffes (Musical Instruments) Ltd* [1986] Ch 366. The position may be different where the appointment is made out of court by the holder of a qualifying floating charge.
77   As to which see **CHAPTER 1**.
78   See the passage from the judgment of Millett J in *Re Olympia & York Canary Wharf Ltd* [1993] BCC 154.
79   [1992] 1 WLR 1253 at 1259.

court, to pay for the use of the goods or, alternatively, compensation for having wrongfully refused leave to repossess them, irrespective of whether or not he has committed the tort of conversion[80]. In *Re David Meek Plant Ltd*[81], Judge Weeks QC declined to decide a similar point, viz whether the mere service of a notice terminating a hire-purchase agreement would constitute a step in enforcing that security.

THE REPOSSESSION OF GOODS

2.17   Schedule B1 paragraph 43(3) of IA 1986 prohibits the taking of any steps to repossess goods in the company's possession under a hire purchase agreement[82], which includes[83] any conditional sale agreement[84], chattel leasing agreement[85] or retention of title agreement[86]. The word 'goods' is not given any special definition, but it is thought that given the context in which the word appears a court would gain assistance from the definition in section 61(1) of the Sale of Goods Act 1979, which is itself expressly incorporated into the Consumer Credit Act 1974[87]:

> '"goods" includes all personal chattels other than things in action and money, and in Scotland all corporeal moveables except money; and in particular "goods" includes emblements, industrial growing crops, and things attached to or forming part of the land which are agreed to be severed before sale or under the contract of sale and includes an undivided share in goods'.

2.18   For the purposes of determining whether or not goods are in the possession of the company, it is immaterial whether they remain on the company's premises or are entrusted to others or are sub-let to others as part of the company's trade. The only question is whether, as between the company and its supplier, the goods are in the possession of the company under a hire-purchase agreement (as defined)[88]. It should, however, be noted that this provision is:

> 'dealing with steps to repossess by a person who has let goods on hire purchase to the company, and possibly by somebody with a higher right than that person. The paragraph does not deal with a repossession which would not affect the company's enjoyment of the goods or the profit flowing to the company from them'[89].

---

80   [1992] 1 WLR 1253 per Millett J at 1259D–H.
81   [1994] 1 BCLC 680 at 684a.
82   Section 436 of IA 1986 provides that 'hire purchase agreement' has the same meaning as in the Consumer Credit Act 1974: see section 189 of that Act.
83   See the extended definition of 'hire purchase agreement' contained in Schedule B1 paragraph 111(1) of IA 1986.
84   Section 436 of IA 1986 provides that 'conditional sale agreement' has the same meaning as in the Consumer Credit Act 1974: see section189 of that Act.
85   'An agreement for the bailment or, in Scotland, the hiring of goods which is capable of subsisting for more than 3 months': section 251 of IA 1986.
86   'An agreement for the sale of goods to a company, being an agreement (a) which does not constitute a charge on the goods, but (b) under which, if the seller is not paid and the company is wound up, the seller will have priority over all other creditors of the company as respects the goods or any property representing the goods': section 251 of IA 1986. A more detailed description of the impact of retention of title agreements in an administration is given in CHAPTER 6.
87   By section 189 of that Act.
88   *Re Atlantic Computer Systems plc* [1992] Ch 505 at 531Aff.
89   *Re Atlantic Computer Systems plc* [1992] Ch 505 at 532E.

2.19   It is also irrelevant to the question whether Schedule B1 paragraph 43(3) of the IA 1986 would be infringed by a retaking of possession of the goods that the hire-purchase agreement pursuant to which the goods came into the company's possession has been terminated, whether prior to, on, or subsequently to the company entering into administration[90]. However, where the agreement in question had been terminated prior to the issue of an application for the making of an administration order, the fact that the owner was wrongfully prevented from re-taking possession of the goods following termination and prior to such issue may be a substantial factor warranting the grant of leave to the owner to retake possession of the goods[91].

THE INSTITUTION AND CONTINUATION OF LEGAL PROCESS

2.20   Schedule B1 paragraph 43(6) of IA 1986 prohibits the institution and continuance of 'legal process (including legal proceedings, execution, distress and diligence … against the company or property of the company'. The precise form of words has changed slightly, but it is not thought that there is any material distinction between the present formulation and the former law (section 11(3) (d) of IA 1986). It is plainly intended that the word 'legal process' might cover activity other than legal proceedings, execution, distress and diligence. Accordingly, the general meaning of that expression will be considered after a discussion of the activities which are expressly included within the meaning of legal process.

2.21   Under the former law, it was established that the word 'proceedings' had a narrow meaning and was limited to legal or quasi-legal proceedings, such as arbitrations[92], employment tribunal proceedings[93] and other formal dispute resolution processes[94]. It also applied to criminal proceedings[95]. The suggestion, however, that the prohibition on the commencement or continuation of proceedings extends to 'every sort of step against the company, its contracts or its property' has been found to be too wide a formulation[96]. It is also to be

---

90   *Re David Meek Access Ltd* [1994] 1 BCLC 680, per Judge Weeks QC at 686g, followed in *In re Business Environment Fleet Street Ltd* [2014] EWHC 3540 (Ch).

91   *Re David Meek Access Ltd* [1994] 1 BCLC 680 per Judge Weeks QC at 701c. Presumably, the same principle would apply where the appointment of an administrator was made out of court and the wrongful prevention occurred before any original notice of intention to appoint was filed.

92   *Bristol Airport plc v Powdrill* [1990] Ch 744 per Sir Nicholas Browne-Wilkinson V-C at 765E–F. Although, arbitrations were there described as '*quasi*-legal proceedings', it is submitted that they fall within the meaning of 'legal' proceedings as that expression is now used in Schedule B1 paragraph 43(6) of IA 1986.

93   See *Re Hartlebury Printers Ltd* [1992] ICR 559 and *Carr v British International Helicopters Ltd* [1994] 2 BCLC 474.

94   Eg adjudication schemes under the Housing Grants Construction and Regeneration Act 1996: *A Straume (UK) Ltd v Bradlor Developments Ltd* [2000] BCC 333 and *South Coast Construction Ltd v Iverson Road Ltd* [2017] EWHC 61 (TCC). See also *In re Frankice (Golders Green) Ltd; Hudson v The Gambling Commission* [2010] EWHC 1229 (Ch) where it was held that a licence review procedure was a legal process.

95   *In re Rhondda Waste Disposal Co Ltd* [2001] Ch 57. Cf *R v Dickson* [1991] BCC 719, a case on section 130(2) of IA 1986.

96   *Bristol Airport plc v Powdrill* [1990] Ch 744 per Sir Nicolas Browne-Wilkinson V-C at 766B–C. The approach of the Court of Appeal in *Bristol Airport* indicates that it is unlikely that 'proceedings' before an expert valuer or certifier such as those under consideration in *Arenson v Casson Beckman Rutley & Co* [1977] AC 405 (where the expert can be sued in negligence) are encompassed.

noted that the courts may be reluctant to construe the prohibition as extending to legal proceedings which are not against the company in any adversarial sense, particularly where the proceedings are themselves before the court in which the administration proceedings are pending[97]. Thus, it would appear that an application by a chargee for leave to register a charge out of time[98] is not 'proceedings against the company or its property'[99], nor are determinations by the Rail Regulator of an application made under section 17 of the Railways Act 1993[100]. On the other hand, notwithstanding what appears to have been a contrary view expressed by Harman J in *Re Synthetic Technology Ltd*[101], it is submitted that the presentation of a petition to wind up the company in administration clearly amounts to the institution of legal proceedings or other legal process against the company for which the prior consent of the administrator or the permission of the court is required[102].

2.22 Given the evident purpose of Schedule B1 paragraph 43(6) of IA 1986, the word 'execution' should be given the wide meaning of any process for enforcing or giving effect to the judgments and orders of the court and should not be restricted to the narrower meaning of the enforcement of judgments by public officers operating under writs of *fieri facias*, etc. Thus leave is required for an application to make a final charging order even after an interim charging order under CPR Part 73.4 has already been made[103]. Questions may, however, arise as to whether the institution or continuation of proceedings for or under an order for the examination of an officer of a corporate judgment debtor under CPR Part 71 would be prohibited without leave[104].

2.23 The final specific prohibition in Schedule B1 paragraph 43(6) of IA 1986 is that which prevents the institution or continuation of any distress of diligence against the company or its property. It is clear that the word 'distress' should be given its ordinary meaning. Attempts at first instance[105] to extend its meaning to what courts may regard as analogous rights of detention under other statutory provisions[106] have been firmly rejected by the Court of Appeal[107]:

'Distress is an ancient remedy and to a degree obsolescent. In my judgment in the absence of clear words in s.88 [of the Civil Aviation Act 1982] describing

---

97 See *Cook v Mortgage Debenture Ltd* [2016] EWCA Civ 103 (paragraph 16) and more generally. The Court of Appeal found that an application to join proceedings where no relief was sought against the company in administration does not fall within legal proceedings against the company.
98 Under section 859F of CA 2006.
99 *Re Barrow Borough Transport Ltd* [1990] Ch 227. This case illustrates the principle that the proceedings must be capable of being characterised as being *against* the company or its property, which may explain why *Air Ecosse Ltd v Civil Aviation Authority* (1987) 3 BCC 492 was correctly decided, albeit for the wrong reasons (cf *Biosource Technologies Inc v Axis Genetics plc* [2000] 1 BCLC 286 (per Ferris J)).
100 *Re Railtrack plc* [2002] 2 BCLC 755 at 768, although in that case the issue arose in the very special context of a railway administration order made under section 59 of the Railways Act 1993.
101 [1990] BCLC 378 at 382f–g.
102 See the comments in *Re Arucana Ltd* [2009] EWHC 3838 (Ch) (paragraphs 7 and 12).
103 *Clarke v Coutts & Co* [2002] EWCA Civ 943.
104 Cf *Fagot v Gaches* [1943] 1 KB 10 at 12.
105 By Harman J in *Bristol Airport plc v Powdrill* reported at first instance sub nom *Re Paramount Airways Ltd* [1990] BCC 130.
106 In that case under section 88 of the Civil Aviation Act 1982.
107 Per Sir Nicolas Browne-Wilkinson V-C in *Bristol Airport plc v Powdrill* [1990] Ch 744 at 765D–E.

the right to detain as being a right of distress, it would be wrong to treat it as such.'

2.24 The express prohibition against the institution or continuation of a distress would appear to represent a recognition by the draftsman that the words 'legal process' might not otherwise have covered the extra-judicial rights of the Crown, local authorities and landlords to distrain[108]. However, unless the institution or continuation of a distress covers no more than the seizure of goods and does not extend to their subsequent retention and sale[109], the completion by sale after administration of a distress levied by seizure before administration requires the permission of the court or the consent of the administrator. It would not therefore be safe for local authorities, landlords or the Crown to adopt such a course without first seeking either the consent of the administrator or the permission of the court under Schedule B1 paragraph 43(6) or a declaration as to their entitlement to proceed without leave.

2.25 Under the former law (section 11(3)(d) of IA 1986), there was conflicting authority on the meaning of the expression 'other legal process'. The word 'process' taken alone is capable of having a very wide meaning, which takes its colour from its context[110], but where it is used in the context of legal steps, the word is much more limited in meaning; so, for example, in the context of section 13 of the Bankruptcy Act 1869 it did not extend to the levying of distress[111]. In *Exchange Travel Agency Ltd v Triton Property Trust plc*[112], Harman J held that the exercise by a landlord of a right of re-entry under a lease was 'legal process' within the meaning of section 11(3)(d) of IA 1986. He concluded[113] that:

'it is a correct use of words to describe a landlord who has legal rights arising out of the privity of estate which he exercises by the process of peaceable re-entry as exercising "legal process"'.

2.26 Subsequently, in *Re Olympia & York Canary Wharf Ltd*[114], and after more extensive citation of authority on the meaning of the expression 'legal process' than was made available to Harman J, Millett J declined to follow *Exchange Travel Agency Ltd v Triton Property Trust plc*[115] on this point. The question for Millett J was whether the service of a notice electing to treat a contract with the company as terminated by the company's repudiatory breach was 'execution or other legal process' within the meaning of section 11(3)(d) of IA 1986. He concluded that 'legal process' was a well-known concept which together with legal proceedings embraced all steps in legal proceedings from the issue of initiating process to their final termination in the process of execution or other means of enforcement of a judgment, but did not extend to the taking of

---

108 As to 'legal process', see *Re Fanshaw and Yorston, ex p Birmingham and Staffordshire Gaslight Co* (1871) LR 11 Eq 615.
109 See *Re Memco Engineering Ltd* [1986] Ch 86 at 97dff. In the view of Mervyn Davies J, the phrase 'distraining or having distrained' expressed the notion of a continuing process.
110 See eg in another context *Nurse v Morganite Crucible Ltd* [1989] AC 692 at 701B (per Lord Griffiths); see also *Re Frankice (Golders Green) Ltd (in administration)* [2010] EWHC 1229 (Ch).
111 *Re Fanshaw and Yorston, ex p Birmingham and Staffordshire Gaslight Co* (1871) LR 11 Eq 615.
112 [1991] BCLC 396.
113 [1991] BCLC 396 at 401g/h.
114 [1993] BCC 154.
115 [1991] BCLC 396.

non-judicial steps. Accordingly, and consistent with the apparent inclination of Sir Nicolas Browne-Wilkinson V-C in *Bristol Airport plc v Powdrill*[116], he declared that service of a notice purporting to make time of the essence or to terminate a contract by reason of the company's repudiatory breach did not require the consent of the administrator or the leave of the court.

2.27 The question of what constitutes legal process has continued to prove a fertile ground for litigation under the post-Enterprise Act law. There is a helpful summary of the position in *Re Frankice (Golders Green) Ltd*[117] (per Norris J), where the court concluded that proceedings brought by the Gambling Commission before a regulatory panel amounted to legal process and there was no principle that regulatory proceedings will always fall outside the purview of the moratorium:

> '38. It is unnecessary to go through each of the decisions to analyse the relevant reasoning and indeed time does not permit. But the following description will suffice. First, it is clear that legal process and legal proceedings are not confined to claims by creditors against the company; they include claims against the company by third parties: *Biosource Technologies Inc v. Axis Genetics Plc*[118]. Second, it is plain that the legal process and legal proceedings are not confined to civil proceedings. Criminal proceedings are also caught by the moratorium, see *In Re Rhondda Waste Disposal Limited*[119], where a prosecution for breach of environmental regulations was permitted against the company, though the court plainly held that the criminal proceedings were caught by the moratorium. Thirdly, it is plain that the relevant legal process or legal proceedings are not confined to proceedings before a court of law. It covers proceedings before tribunals, before arbitrators and before statutory adjudicators.
>
> 39. The question is: what guidance do those single instances give in relation to the instant case? For my part, I have looked at the words "legal process ... against the company". I think the word "process" suggests something with a defined beginning and an ascertainable final outcome and which, in the interim, is governed by a recognisable procedure. I think the word "legal" indicates that that process must in some sense invoke the compulsive power of the law, and it suggests that the procedure must be quasi-legal in nature. One indicator of that might be that the process results in an appeal rather than, for example, reconsideration by means of judicial review, but I accept the submission of Mr Bompas that an appeal, of itself, does not determine whether a process is a legal or administrative one.'

2.28 A comparison of the judgment of Harman J in *Exchange Travel* with that of Millett J in *Olympia & York* remains instructive. Both judges agreed that what was then section 11 of IA 1986 should be construed in such a way that it gives effect to Parliament's intention of ensuring that an administrator is assisted in his attempts to achieve the statutory purpose or purposes for which he was appointed; to that extent both judgments follow the words of Sir Nicolas Browne-Wilkinson V-C in *Bristol Airport plc v Powdrill*[120]. Millett J, however,

116 [1990] Ch 744 at 766B–C;
117 [2010] 1 Bus LR 1608.
118 [2000] 1 BCLC 286.
119 [2001] Ch 57.
120 [1990] Ch 744 at 758F–G.

appears to have given greater recognition to the potential injustice which may be done to third parties if an unnecessarily wide construction is given to what is now Schedule B1 paragraph 43(6) of IA 1986 (formerly section 11(3)). Referring to subsections 11(3)(c) and (d) he said:

> 'They are not intended to interfere with the rights of creditors further than is required to enable the administrators to carry out their functions, and in particular they are not intended to interfere with the creditors' contractual rights to crystallise their rights or discharge their own contractual liabilities.'[121]

2.29   It should be noted that there is some room for argument that the conclusion reached under the former law in *Re Olympia & York Canary Wharf Ltd*[122] is no longer applicable because 'legal process' is now expressed to *include* amongst other things distress and diligence, which are not forms of judicial or quasi-judicial legal process[123]. It might therefore be said that a restrictive approach to the meaning of the expression is no longer appropriate. If such an argument were to be accepted it would be a retrograde step. It is submitted that the law based on *Re Olympia & York Canary Wharf Ltd*[124] and *Barclays Mercantile Business Finance Ltd v Sibec Developments Ltd*[125] strikes the correct balance between the interests of the insolvent estate and the interests of third parties in their dealings with the insolvent estate[126].

CONSENT BY THE ADMINISTRATOR: THE GRANT OF PERMISSION BY THE COURT

2.30   The prohibitions against enforcing security, repossessing goods, exercising rights of forfeiture and irritancy, and instituting or continuing legal process, legal proceedings, execution, distress and diligence are all subject to the consent of the administrator or the permission of the court[127]. Parliament intended that the consent of the administrator should be sought before any application is made to the court[128]. The Court of Appeal has stressed that the administrator should make his decision speedily and having regard to the considerations which the court would take into account[129], thereby hoping that the courts would not be swamped with applications for leave. The administrator should not use

---

121   [1993] BCC 154 at 158. This was an approach which Millett J has also adopted in *Barclays Mercantile Business Finance Ltd v Sibec Developments Ltd* [1992] 1 WLR 1253 at 1257D–F.
122   [1993] BCC 154.
123   That said, numerous cases have continued to follow the decision; see, for example, *Fulton v AIB Group (UK) Plc* [2014] NICh 8 and *Pan Ocean Co Ltd v Fibria Celulose S/A* [2014] EWHC 2124 (Ch).
124   [1993] BCC 154.
125   [1992] 1 WLR 1253.
126   The decision in *Re Olympia & York Canary Wharf Ltd* was applied in *Re Pan Ocean* [2014] EWHC 2124 (Ch) although in the context of the Cross-Border Insolvency Regulations 2006 (SI 2006 No 1030).
127   Schedule B1 paragraph 43 of IA 1986.
128   *Re Atlantic Computer Systems plc* [1992] Ch 505 at 542A. It seems that any division of the High Court can grant relief and it may be appropriate for the order to be made by the division in which proceedings are pending (*Joinery Plus Ltd v Laing Ltd* [2003] EWCH 439 (TCC), [2003] BPIR 890 at 919). In most cases, however, the more appropriate court will be the court with the conduct of the administration.
129   *Re Atlantic Computer Systems plc* [1992] Ch 505 at 529B–530A.

the power to give or withhold consent as a bargaining counter in negotiations in which he has regard only to the interests of the unsecured creditors[130], or presumably the secured or preferential creditors to whom he will be making a distribution where the only purpose of administration is the third objective[131]. Furthermore, if the court forms the view that any party has acted unreasonably in not agreeing terms (particularly where the amount involved is small), he is likely to be penalised in costs[132] and, in the case of an administrator, may be ordered to pay compensation where he has wrongfully withheld consent[133].

2.31 It should be noted that, whilst the court is expressly empowered[134] to impose a condition or requirement in connection with the relevant transaction, when it gives permission to enforce security, repossess goods, exercise rights of forfeiture and irritancy or institute or continue legal process, there is no such express power given to the administrator when giving consent. It is thought, however, that the explanation for this is that the draftsman wished to make clear that the court did have jurisdiction to impose conditions and other requirements, while the very concept of an administrator giving or withholding consent recognises that consent may be given or withheld on terms. What is clear from the *Atlantic* decision[135] is that the administrator is able to impose terms. It should also be noted that, after a period of some uncertainty[136], it now seems clear that permission can be granted with retrospective effect[137].

2.32 Notwithstanding its reluctance to be interpreted as having restricted the exercise of the wide discretion given to the courts by Parliament, the Court of Appeal[138] has set out general observations for cases where leave is sought to exercise existing proprietary and security rights against a company in administration. In making its observations, the Court of Appeal was motivated by a desire to assist administrators in determining whether or not they should give their consent under what is now Schedule B1 paragraph 43 of IA 1986 (formerly sections 11(3) and 11(4)) and if so on what terms. The observations, although directed at cases where lessors or owners are seeking to repossess, are

---

130 *Re Atlantic Computer Systems plc* [1992] Ch 505 at 529E–G. It follows from this that in reaching his decision on whether to consent to the commencement of proceedings, he should act with the responsibility that flows from his status as an officer of the court: *Re Polly Peck International plc (No 4)* [1998] 2 BCLC 185 at 196.

131 Schedule B1 paragraph 3(1)(c) of IA 1986.

132 *Bristol Airport plc v Powdrill* [1990] Ch 744 at 770B–D per Woolf LJ. For an example of such a case where a retention of title claimant was premature in the issue of proceedings, see *Re City Logistics Ltd* [2002] 2 BCLC 103.

133 See *Barclays Mercantile Business Finance Ltd v Sibec Developments Ltd* [1992] 1 WLR 1253 per Millett J at 1259E–1260B and **CHAPTER 5** *post*.

134 By Schedule B1 paragraph 43(7) of IA 1986.

135 *Re Atlantic Computer Systems plc* [1992] Ch 505: see also *Bristol Airport plc v Powdrill* [1990] Ch 744 at 763C–E.

136 Brought about by the decision in *In Re National Employers Mutual General Insurance Association Ltd* [1995] 1 BCLC 232.

137 See *Bank of Ireland v Colliers International UK plc* [2012] EWHC 2942 and *Fulton v AIB Group (UK) plc* [2014] NICh 8. The court may also grant leave after the administration has terminated (although only in rare circumstances): see *Gaardsoe v Optimal Wealth Management Ltd* [2012] EWHC 3266 (Ch).

138 In *Re Atlantic Computer Systems plc* [1992] Ch 505 at 541G–544C; the guidelines have been followed in Scotland: *Scottish Exhibition Centre Ltd v Mirestop Ltd* 1993 SLT 1034 and [1993] BCLC 1459 per Lord Morton of Shuna.

broadly applicable to many applications to enforce a security[139]. They can be summarised as follows:

(a) It is for the person seeking permission to make out his case[140].

(b) Permission should normally be given if the exercise of a proprietary right by a lessor or hirer, or the repossession of land or goods is unlikely to impede the achievement of the purpose of administration.

(c) Where the court cannot conclude that the exercise of a right would be unlikely to impede the achievement of the purpose of administration, it must balance the legitimate interests of the applicant and the legitimate interests of the other creditors of the company[141]. The Court of Appeal adopted the metaphor of 'scales and weights'[142], but it should be stressed that whilst the purpose of the prohibition is to assist the company to achieve the purpose of administration, the purpose of the power to give permission is to enable the court to relax the prohibition where it would be inequitable for it to apply.

(d) Great importance or weight will normally be given to the proprietary interests of the applicant[143]. An administration for the benefit of the unsecured creditors should not be conducted at the expense of those who are seeking to exercise proprietary rights save where that is unavoidable. Even then such conduct will usually be acceptable only to a limited extent. The same principle ought to apply where the balance is between the interests of the applicant and the interests of the secured creditors for whose primary benefit an administration may now be being conducted.

(e) It will normally be a sufficient ground for the grant of permission if significant loss[144] would be caused to the applicant by a refusal. If substantially greater loss would be caused to others by the grant of permission, or loss which is out of all proportion to the benefit which permission would confer on the applicant, that may outweigh the loss to the applicant caused by a refusal[145].

(f) In assessing the respective losses the court will have regard to matters such as the financial position of the company, its ability to pay sums

---

139 *Re Atlantic Computer Systems plc* [1992] Ch 505 at 543H–544A. The decision of the Court of Appeal is the starting point for any application for leave although one that involved a claim about proprietary interests: see for example *Funding Corp Discounting Ltd v Lexi Holdings plc* [2008] EWHC 985 (Ch), *Safe Business Solutions Ltd v Malcolm Cohen, Antony Newgate* [2017] EWHC 145 (Ch) and *South Coast Construction Ltd v Iverson Road Ltd* [2017] EWHC 61.

140 See also *Royal Trust Bank v Buchler* [1989] BCLC 130. This principle has also been applied on an application for leave to commence proceedings: *Re Divine Solutions (UK) Ltd* [2003] EWHC 1931 (Ch).

141 In *Re Atlantic Computer Systems plc* [1992] Ch 505, the Court of Appeal approved the approach of Peter Gibson J in *Royal Trust Bank v Buchler* [1989] BCLC 130 on this point. The approach of the Court of Appeal was in turn followed in *Re David Meek Access Ltd* [1993] BCC 175 and in subsequent cases such as *Re SSRL Realisations Ltd (In Administration)* [2015] EWHC 2590 (Ch).

142 Subject to the limitations expressed by the House of Lords in *Science Research Council v Nassé* [1980] AC 1028 at 1067.

143 Cf the approach of Sir Nicolas Browne-Wilkinson V-C in *Bristol Airport plc v Powdrill* [1990] Ch 744.

144 'Any kind of financial loss, direct or indirect, including loss by reason of delay, and may extend to loss which is not financial.' In *Re David Meek Access Ltd* [1993] BCC 175 at 189B–D, it was suggested that this statement 'may be putting the matter rather high' in that a refusal of leave to repossess almost inevitably may cause a lessor significant loss.

145 The Court of Appeal recognised the difficulties attendant on this formulation.

already accrued due to the applicant and sums continuing to accrue, the administrator's proposals, the period for which the administration has already been in effect and is expected to remain in place, the effect on the administration if permission were given, the effect on the applicant if leave were refused, the end result sought to be achieved by the administration, the prospects of that result being achieved and the history of the administration so far.

(g) An assessment of the degree of probability of each of the suggested consequences will often be necessary.

(h) The conduct of the parties is a material consideration. Where, as in *Bristol Airport plc v Powdrill*[146], the applicants had accepted benefits under the administration and only sought to enforce their security at a later stage, leave may be refused. It behoves an applicant to make its position clear at the outset of the administration and (if necessary) to apply to the court promptly[147].

(i) These considerations may be relevant both to the decision as to whether leave should be granted or refused and to a decision to impose conditions or other requirements.

(j) The court has power to achieve a result which has the effect of imposing terms on the company in administration as a condition of refusing leave under Schedule B1 paragraph 43 of IA 1986 either directly, by giving directions to the administrator as its officer, or indirectly, by granting permission to the applicant unless the administrator is prepared to take particular steps. As the Court of Appeal anticipated, such cases arise frequently; for example, where the court refuses permission on condition that the company pays current rent[148].

(k) On an application by a secured creditor for permission to enforce its security, an important consideration will be whether the applicant is fully secured. If it is, delay in enforcement is likely to be less prejudicial than cases where its security is insufficient.

(l) Where there is a dispute over the existence, validity or nature of security which the applicant is seeking to enforce, the court, on an application under Schedule B1 paragraph 43(2) of IA 1986, should only adjudicate on that issue if it raises a short point of law which it is convenient to determine without further ado. Otherwise the court need only be satisfied that the applicant has a seriously arguable case[149].

Subsequently, it has been held that if a creditor seeks to enforce a lien adventitiously acquired post-administration, the court would be highly likely to refuse permission on the grounds that enforcement would give an illegitimate priority to the lien holder who was not secured at the commencement of the administration[150].

---

146 [1990] Ch 744.
147 See also *Re Salmet International Ltd* [2001] BCC 796. Similarly, if an administrator has led a putative applicant to act to his detriment, permission may be granted.
148 'In most cases this should be possible, since if the administration order has been rightly made the business should generally be sufficiently viable to hold down current outgoings. Such a term may therefore be a normal term to impose'.
149 For a case in which the court gave a secured creditor leave to appoint a receiver notwithstanding a potential challenge under section 238 of IA 1986, see *Sinai Securities Ltd v Rosshill Properties* [2003] EWHC 910 (Ch) (Neuberger J).
150 *London Flight Centre (Stansted) Ltd v Osprey Aviation Ltd* [2002] BPIR 1115.

2.33 Many of these considerations will also apply when an applicant seeks permission to initiate or continue legal process under Schedule B1 paragraph 43(6) of IA 1986. There will, however, be additional factors to bear in mind, such as the strength and merits of the applicant's claim[151], whether the point is a short and simple one[152], the state of the proceedings and conduct of the parties[153] and whether the company is a necessary party to proceedings against it and others. In *Re Polly Peck International plc (No 4)*[154], the Court of Appeal decided that it was a pre-condition to the grant of leave that the putative claimant should have established a seriously arguable case. Similarly, if any question were to arise as to the court's jurisdiction to determine the issues raised in the proposed proceedings, that question should also be sufficiently established before the grant of leave. Furthermore, the mere fact that the company is in administration will not, of itself, enable the company to ignore its contractual obligations to others, whilst continuing to make use of the benefits which that self-same contract may have conveyed[155], and the court will not shrink from granting leave to seek injunctive relief in appropriate circumstances. In many respects, the position of an administrator is different from that of an administrative receiver[156], although the extent of the difference will now be dependent on the objective for which the administrator is primarily carrying out his functions. Thus, although there remains no true analogy between the position of a receiver and an administrator, because the administrator is appointed to manage the affairs of the company and not simply to realise the assets for the benefit of one of the creditors[157], the analogy is now closer than it was under the former law in the light of the fact that, once it is no longer reasonably practicable to achieve the first and second objectives, the administrator must perform his functions with the objective of realising property in order to make a distribution to one or more secured or preferential creditors[158]. It is important to note that where the applicant's claim is an ordinary money claim against the company it will only be in exceptional cases that the court will lift the moratorium[159]. Presumably, the fact that administration does not prevent time from running for the purposes of

---

151 See *Re Hartlebury Printers Ltd* [1992] ICR 559 at 570F–571C for a winding-up case where leave was sought under section 130 of IA 1986 and refused on the ground that the proposed proceedings had no legal merit.

152 See other winding-up cases: *MS Fashions Ltd v BCCI SA* [1992] BCC 571 at 575F and *New Cap Reinsurance Corpn Ltd v HIH Casualty and General Insurance Ltd* [2002] EWCA Civ 300. For a case in which leave was refused on the grounds (in any event in part) that highly complex proceedings would distract the administrators from achieving the statutory purposes, see *Biosource Technologies Inc v Axis Genetics plc* [2000] 1 BCLC 286. See also *Holdenhurst Securities plc v Cohen* [2001] 1 BCLC 460 at 463.

153 See *Ronelp Marine Ltd v STX Offshore and Shipbuilding Co Ltd* [2016] EWHC 2228 (Ch) where Norris J said that it was 'a factor of significant weight' that the proceedings in that case were already 'reasonably well advanced' when the application was made. He said that 'the nearer the outcome of the proceedings, the greater the weight to be attached to that factor' and *X-Fab Semiconductor Foundries AG v Plessey Semiconductors Ltd* [2014] EWHC 3190 (QB).

154 [1998] 2 BCLC 185, applying the test established by *Seaconsar Far East Ltd v Bank Markazi Jomhouri Islami Iran* [1994] 1 AC 438. The courts have adopted the approach under the CPR Part 24: see *Funding Corp Block Discounting Ltd v Lexi Holdings plc (in administration)* [2008] EWHC 985 (Ch).

155 *Astor Chemicals Ltd v Synthetic Technology Ltd* [1990] BCLC 1.

156 Cf *Airlines Airspares Ltd v Handley Page Ltd* [1970] Ch 193.

157 Per Vinelott J in *Astor Chemicals Ltd v Synthetic Technology Ltd* [1990] BCLC 1 at 12a–b.

158 Schedule B1 paragraph 3 of IA 1986.

159 See the comments of Patten J in *AES Barry Ltd v TXU Europe Energy* [2004] EWHC 1757 (Ch) (paragraph 24).

the Limitation Act 1980[160] means that a putative claimant would have a powerful case for leave to issue proceedings, if his claim was about to become statute barred. Depending on the circumstances, it would always be open to the court to restrict the grant of leave to the issue and service of a claim form, with further steps in the proceedings being stayed until such time as it was appropriate for them to be continued. Each case will depend on its own facts, but it is incumbent on the applicant to make out his case for leave which will normally require proper evidence of prejudice if leave is refused[161].

2.34 As the Court of Appeal in *Re Atlantic Computer Systems plc* pointed out[162], it would be unfortunate if the way in which the court exercised its discretion hardened into inflexible rules applicable to situations which arise regularly. In relation to proceedings which raise issues that go wider than the commercial interest of the putative claimant, the court is more likely to conclude that the balance comes down in favour of permission being granted[163]. Thus, in *Re Rhondda Waste Disposal Co Ltd*[164], the Court of Appeal concluded that the public interest in ensuring that prosecutions were permitted for serious breaches of the Environmental Protection Act 1990 outweighed the interests of the company's creditors. There will, of course, be other cases in which the public interest is protected by a conclusion that the process is not barred by Schedule B1 paragraph 43 of IA 1986 in the first place and so the exercise of the discretion does not even arise[165].

---

160 *Re Maxwell Fleet and Facilities Management Ltd* [2000] 1 All ER 464.
161 *Re Divine Solutions (UK) Ltd* [2003] EWHC 1931 (Ch).
162 [1992] Ch 505 at 528B–H.
163 Although a balancing exercise must still be undertaken: see *Hudson v The Gambling Commission* [2010] EWHC 1229 (Ch) in which the court held that the prejudice to the Gambling Commission did not outweigh the interests of the general body of creditors.
164 [2001] Ch 57.
165 *Re Railtrack plc* [2002] EWCA Civ 955.

3 Procedure following the appointment of an administrator

NOTIFICATION AND INFORMATION TO BE GIVEN BY THE ADMINISTRATOR

3.1   In the event that the court makes an administration order, it is required, as soon as reasonably practicable, to send two sealed copies of the order to the person who made the application, who is then required, as soon as reasonably practicable, to send one of the sealed copies to the person appointed as administrator[1]. Where an appointment is made by the holder of a qualifying floating charge or by the company or its directors, the court is required to issue to the person who made the appointment two copies of the notice of appointment sealed by the court and endorsed with the date and time of filing, one of which must be sent by him to the administrator as soon as reasonably practicable[2]. The administrator himself must then send to the company notice of his appointment and publish it as soon as reasonably practicable[3]. The administrator must also give notice of his appointment to the registrar of companies, which must be given within seven days of the date of any administration order or, in the case of an out-of-court appointment, within seven days of receiving notice of appointment under Schedule B1 paragraph 20 or 32 as the case may be[4]. He must also give notice to the following as soon as reasonably practicable after the date of any administration order or, in the case of an out-of-court appointment, the date he receives notice of his appointment under Schedule B1 paragraph 20 or 32 as the case may be[5]:

(a)   to any receiver or administrative receiver that may have been appointed;

(b)   if a winding-up petition is pending, to the petitioner and any provisional liquidator;

(c)   to any enforcement officer, enforcement agent or other officer who, to the administrator's knowledge, is charged with distress or other legal process against the company or its property;

---

1   Rule 3.15(1) and (2) of the Rules.
2   Rule 3.18(2) of the Rules.
3   Schedule B1 paragraph 46(2)(a), (b) and (8) of IA 1986 and Rules 3.27(1) and (2) of the Rules.
4   Schedule B1 paragraph 46(4) and (8) of IA 1986 and Rule 3.27(2) of the Rules. He must also give notice to any member state liquidator appointed in relation to the company: Rule 21.7 of the Rules.
5   Schedule B1 paragraph 46(5) of IA 1986. The persons to whom notice must be given are listed in Rule 3.27(3) of the Rules. The notice must contain the information set out in Rule 3.27 of the Rules. The court has power to disapply this notification obligation and to reduce or extend the period of time within which it must be done: Schedule B1 paragraph 46(7) of IA 1986.

(d) to any person who, to the administrator's knowledge has distrained against the company or its property;

(e) to any supervisor of a CVA.

3.2 As soon as reasonably practicable after his appointment, the administrator must also gazette and may advertise the appointment in such other manner as the administrator thinks fit[6]. In addition, as soon as reasonably practicable, the administrator must obtain a list of the company's creditors and, unless the court directs otherwise, must send notice of his appointment to each creditor of whose claim and address he is aware[7]. If an administrator without reasonable excuse fails to comply with his duties under Schedule B1 paragraph 46 of IA 1986, as described in this and the preceding paragraph, he commits an offence[8].

3.3 While a company is in administration, every business document (defined as invoices, orders for goods or services and business letters) issued by or on behalf of the company or the administrator, and all of the company's websites, must state the name of the administrator and that the affairs, business and property of the company are being managed by him[9]. If there is a contravention of this requirement, the company and any administrator or officer of the company who without reasonable excuse authorises or permits the contravention commits an offence[10]. It is prudent and normal practice to include in any such invoice, order or letter, if appropriate, a statement to the effect that the administrator contracts as agent of the company only and without personal liability[11].

STATEMENT OF AFFAIRS

3.4 As soon as reasonably practicable after his appointment, the administrator must require, by notice in the prescribed form, one or more of the persons mentioned below to provide to him a statement in the prescribed form as to the affairs of the company[12]. The statement is required to be verified by a statement of truth in accordance with the Civil Procedure Rules[13] by the persons required to submit it and must give particulars of the company's property, debts and liabilities, the names and addresses of its creditors, the securities held by them respectively, the dates on which each security was given and such other information as may be prescribed[14]. The persons who may be required by the administrator to submit a statement of affairs are described as 'relevant persons', who may be any person who is or has been an officer of the company, any person who took part in the company's formation at any time within one year before

---

6 Schedule B1 paragraph 46(2)(b) of IA 1986 and Rule 3.27(1) of the Rules.
7 Schedule B1 paragraph 46(3) of IA 1986. The form of notice is set out in Rule 3.27 of the Rules. The court's dispensing power is at Schedule B1 paragraph 46(7). In the case of the administration of an existing or former authorised person or appointed representative or company which is or has carried on a regulated activity in contravention of the general prohibition (as all those terms are used in FSMA 2000), notice must also be sent to the FCA or the PRA: section 362(3) of FSMA 2000.
8 Schedule B1 paragraph 46(9) of IA 1986.
9 Schedule B1 paragraph 45(1) and (3) of IA 1986.
10 Schedule B1 paragraph 45(2) of IA 1986.
11 As to which, see Schedule B1 paragraph 69 of IA 1986.
12 Schedule B1 paragraph 47(1) of IA 1986.
13 Schedule B1 paragraph 47(2)(a) of IA 1986.
14 Schedule B1 paragraph 47(2) of IA 1986. The statement of affairs must be in the form prescribed by Rule 3.30 of the Rules and must contain all particulars thereby required.

the date on which the company entered administration, any person employed by the company within that year and any person who is or has been within that year an officer or employee of a company which is, or has been during that year, an officer of the company[15]. For these purposes 'employment' includes employment under a contract for services[16]. If a person without reasonable excuse fails to comply with any requirement under Schedule B1 paragraph 47(1) of IA 1986, he commits an offence[17]. In addition, on the application of the administrator, the court may make such orders as it thinks necessary for the enforcement of the obligations of a person required to provide a statement of affairs[18].

3.5   Where the administrator determines to require a statement of the company's affairs to be made out and submitted to him, he must send a notice to each relevant person whom he determines appropriate requiring that person to prepare and submit the statement[19]. The notice is required[20] to inform each nominated person of:

(a)   the names and addresses of all others (if any) to whom the same notice has been delivered;

(b)   the requirement to deliver the statement of affairs to the administrator no later than 11 days after receipt of the notice requiring the statement of affairs; and

(c)   the effect of Schedule B1 paragraph 48(4) of IA 1986 (penalty for non-compliance) and section 235 of IA 1986 (duty to co-operate with the office-holder)[21].

The administrator must inform each nominated person to whom he has sent notice to provide a statement of affairs that a document for the preparation of the statement of affairs capable of completion in compliance with Rule 3.30 of the Rules will be supplied if requested[22].

3.6   The statement of affairs is required to contain the information set out in Rule 3.30 of the Rules and must be verified by a statement of truth by the relevant person (using the same document)[23]. The statement of affairs must be delivered to the administrator by the relevant person making the statement of truth (together with a copy of the statement of truth)[24]. The administrator may also require any other relevant person to submit an affidavit of concurrence, stating that he concurs in the statement of affairs, and, where the administrator does so, he must inform the person making the statement of affairs of that fact[25], and that person must then deliver a copy of the statement of affairs to all persons whom the administrator has required to make a statement of concurrence. A statement of concurrence must be submitted to the administrator within five business days of the day on which he received the statement of affairs (or such other period as the administrator may agree)[26]. It may be qualified in respect of

---

15   Schedule B1 paragraph 47(3) of IA 1986.
16   Schedule B1 paragraph 47(4) of IA 1986.
17   Schedule B1 paragraph 48(4) of IA 1986.
18   Rule 12.52(1)(a) of the Rules.
19   Rule 3.29(1) of the Rules.
20   By Rule 3.29(2)(b) of the Rules.
21   Rule 3.29(2)(b)(iii) of the Rules.
22   Rule 3.29(3) of the Rules.
23   Rules 3.30 of the Rules and Schedule B1 paragraph 47(2)(a).
24   Rule 3.29(4) of the Rules.
25   Rule 3.31(3) of the Rules. Rule 3.31(5) sets out the content of the statement.
26   Rule 3.31(6) of the Rules.

matters dealt with in the statement of affairs, where the maker of the statement of concurrence is not in agreement with the maker of the statement of affairs, where he considers the statement to be erroneous or misleading, or where he is without the direct knowledge necessary for concurring with it[27]. Every statement of concurrence must be verified by a statement of truth and be delivered to the administrator by the person who makes it, together with a copy[28]. Subject to the matters explained below, the administrator must send to the registrar of companies a copy of the statement of affairs and any statement of concurrence[29].

3.7   Where the administrator thinks disclosure of the whole or part of the statement of affairs would prejudice the conduct of the administration or might reasonably be expected to lead to violence against any person, he can apply to the court for an order that the statement or a specified part of it shall not be filed with the registrar of companies[30]. If the court makes such an order, the administrator must, as soon as reasonably practicable, deliver to the registrar of companies a copy of the order, the statement of affairs to the extent provided by the order and any statement of concurrence[31]. If a creditor seeks disclosure of a statement of affairs (or part thereof) in relation to which an order has been made under Rule 3.45 of the Rules, he may apply to the court for an order to that effect, which may be made subject to such conditions as to confidentiality, duration, scope of the order in the event of change of circumstances or other matters as the court thinks fit[32]. The application must be supported by written evidence in the form of a witness statement and the applicant must give the administrator at least three business days' notice of his application[33]. If there is a material change of circumstances rendering the limit on disclosure or any part of it unnecessary, the administrator is under a duty, as soon as reasonably practicable after the change, to apply to the court for the order or any part of it to be rescinded[34]. Where such an order is made, the administrator must, as soon as reasonably practicable, send to the registrar of companies a copy of the order and the statement of affairs to the extent provided by the order[35]. If a statement of proposals has by then been sent to creditors under Schedule B1 paragraph 49 of IA 1986, the administrator must also send a copy or summary of any statement of affairs that may have been filed after an order has been made under Rule 3.47(1) of the Rules[36].

3.8   The administrator may revoke a requirement on a relevant person to provide him with a statement of affairs or extend the 11-day period for the

---

27 Rule 3.31(5) of the Rules.
28 Rule 3.31(2) and (6) of the Rules.
29 Rule 3.32(1) of the Rules. By Rule 3.32(2) of the Rules, the administrator must not deliver to the registrar of companies with the statement of affairs any schedule required by Rule 3.30(6)(b) of the Rules. Where a member state liquidator has been appointed in relation to the company, copies of these documents must also be sent to him: Rule 21.7 of the Rules.
30 Rules 3.32(3) and 3.44 of the Rules. The power under Rule 3.45 of the Rules probably does not permit the court to limit disclosure of the statement of affairs to any member state liquidator appointed in relation to the company, in any event to the extent that an administrator is under a duty to communicate the information contained in it pursuant to Article 31 of the EC Insolvency Regulation.
31 Rule 3.45(3) of the Rules. Where a member state liquidator has been appointed in relation to the company, copies of these documents must also be sent to him: Rule 21.7 of the Rules.
32 Rules 3.46(1) and 3.46(4) of the Rules.
33 Rules 3.46(2) and 3.46(3) of the Rules. It is expressly provided (Rule 3.48(1) of the Rules) that CPR Part 31 (disclosure) shall not apply to any application under Rule 3.46 of the Rules.
34 Rule 3.47 of the Rules.
35 Rule 3.47(2) of the Rules.
36 Rule 3.48(2) of the Rules.

submission of the statement of affairs[37]. Such a power may be exercised at the administrator's own discretion or at the request of a nominated person[38]. If a release or extension of time is requested and it is refused by the administrator, the relevant person may apply to the court for it[39]. The court may, if it is satisfied that no sufficient cause is shown for the application, dismiss it without giving notice to any party other than the applicant[40]. Unless the application is dismissed, the court must fix a venue for the application to be heard[41]. The applicant must, at least 14 days before any hearing, send to the administrator a notice stating the venue accompanied by a copy of the application and of any evidence on which the applicant intends to rely[42]. The administrator may appear and be heard on the application and, whether or not he appears, may file a written report of any matters which he considers ought to be drawn to the court's attention[43]. If such a report is filed, a copy of it must be sent by the administrator to the applicant not later than five business days before the hearing[44]. Sealed copies of any order made on the application must be sent by the court to the applicant and the administrator[45]. On any such application, the applicant's costs must be paid by the applicant in any event, but the court may order that an allowance of all or part of them be payable as an expense of the administration[46].

3.9   The expenses of a nominated person which the administrator considers to have been reasonably incurred in making a statement of affairs or of a relevant person in making a statement of concurrence must be paid by the administrator as an expenses of the administration[47]. Any decision by the administrator that expenses were not reasonably incurred is subject to appeal to the court[48].

3.10   Although, as noted above, the administrator has power to relieve particular persons from the obligation to provide a statement of affairs[49], in view of the mandatory terms of Schedule B1 paragraph 47(1) of IA 1986 it is doubtful whether the administrator, or even the court, has power to dispense altogether with the requirement that a statement of affairs should be prepared following the appointment of an administrator[50].

THE ADMINISTRATOR'S PROPOSALS

3.11   An administrator must make a statement setting out proposals for achieving the purpose of administration[51]. The proposals may include a proposal

---

37   Schedule B1 paragraph 48(2) of IA 1986. The power to extend time may be exercised either before or after its expiry.
38   Rule 3.33(1) of the Rules.
39   Schedule B1 paragraph 48(3) of IA and Rule 3.33(2) of the Rules.
40   Rule 3.33(3) of the Rules.
41   Rule 3.33(4) of the Rules.
42   Rule 3.33(5) of the Rules.
43   Rule 3.33(6) of the Rules.
44   Rule 3.33(7) of the Rules.
45   Rule 3.33(8) of the Rules.
46   Rule 3.33(9) of the Rules.
47   Rule 3.34(1) of the Rules.
48   Rule 3.34(2) of the Rules.
49   Schedule B1 paragraph 48(2)(a) of IA 1986.
50   Cf Rule 3.35(h) of the Rules which contemplates the possibility that no statement of affairs may have been submitted at the time the administrator sends his proposals to creditors under Schedule B1 paragraph 49 of IA 1986.
51   Schedule B1 paragraph 49(1) of IA 1986.

for a voluntary arrangement under Part I of IA 1986[52] or a proposal for a compromise or arrangement to be sanctioned by the court under Part 26 of CA 2006[53]. IA 1986 and the Rules make provision for the contents of the statement of proposals. Schedule B1 paragraph 49(2)(b) of IA 1986 requires the statement to explain, where applicable, why the administrator thinks that the first or second objectives cannot be achieved[54], thus reinforcing the administrator's duty to give careful consideration before concluding that he is permitted to perform his functions with the third objective of realising property in order to make a distribution to one or more secured or preferential creditors. The administrator's statement of proposals made under Schedule B1 paragraph 49 (which is required by paragraph 49(4) to be delivered to the registrar of companies, creditors and members) must identify the proceedings and, in addition to the matters set out in paragraph 49, contain the following[55]:

(a) any other trading names of the company;

(b) details of the administrator's appointment[56];

(c) the names of the directors and secretary of the company and details of any shareholdings in the company which they may have;

(d) an account of the circumstances giving rise to the appointment of the administrator;

(e) the date the proposals are delivered to the creditors;

(f) if a statement of the company's affairs has been submitted–

  (i) a copy or summary of it, except so far as an order under Rule 3.45 or 3.46 limits disclosure of it, and excluding any schedule referred to in Rule 3.30(6)(b), or the particulars relating to individual creditors contained in any such schedule,

  (ii) details of who provided the statement of affairs, and

  (iii) any comments which the administrator may have upon the statement of affairs;

(g) if an order under Rule 3.45 or 3.46 has been made–

  (i) a statement of that fact, and

  (ii) the date of the order;

(h) if no statement of affairs has been submitted–

  (i) details of the financial position of the company at the latest practicable date (which must, unless the court orders otherwise, be a date not earlier than that on which the company entered administration), and

  (ii) an explanation as to why there is no statement of affairs;

(i) a full list of the company's creditors in accordance with Rule 3.35(2)[57];

---

52 Schedule B1 paragraph 49(3)(a) of IA 1986. See further, **CHAPTER 11** *post*.
53 Schedule B1 paragraph 49(3)(b) of IA 1986. See further, **CHAPTER 13** *post*.
54 Ie the objectives described in Schedule B1 paragraph 3(1)(a) (rescuing the company as a going concern) and Schedule B1 paragraph 3(1)(b) (achieving a better result for the company's creditors as a whole than would be likely if the company were wound up).
55 The list is contained in Rule 3.35(1) of the Rules.
56 Including: (i) the date of appointment, (ii) the person making the application or appointment, and (iii) where a number of persons have been appointed as administrators, details of the matters set out in Schedule B1 paragraph 100(2) relating to the exercise of their functions.
57 The list of creditors required must contain the details required by Rule 3.35(3) unless the creditor is an employee or former employee of the company or consumers claiming amounts paid in advance for the supply of goods and services, in which case the matters set out in Rule 3.35(5) must be set out.

(j) a statement of–

   (i) how it is envisaged the purpose of the administration will be achieved, and

   (ii) how it is proposed that the administration will end, including, where it is proposed that the administration will end by the company moving to a creditors' voluntary winding up:

   (aa) details of the proposed liquidator,

   (bb) where applicable, the declaration required by section 231, and

   (cc) a statement that the creditors may, before the proposals are approved, nominate a different person as liquidator in accordance with Schedule B1 paragraph 83(7)(a) and Rule 3.60(6)(b);

(k) a statement of either–

   (i) the method by which the administrator has decided to seek a decision from creditors as to whether they approve the proposals, or

   (ii) the administrator's reasons for not seeking a decision from creditors;

(l) the manner in which the affairs and business of the company–

   (i) have, since the date of the administrator's appointment, been managed and financed, including, where any assets have been disposed of, the reasons for the disposals and the terms upon which the disposals were made, and

   (ii) will, if the administrator's proposals are approved, continue to be managed and financed;

(m) a statement whether the proceedings are main, secondary, territorial or non-EC proceedings; and

(n) any other information that the administrator thinks necessary to enable creditors to decide whether or not to approve the proposals.

3.12 Except where the administrator proposes a CVA in relation to the company, the statement made by the administrator under paragraph 49 of Schedule B1 must also include[58]:

(a) to the best of the administrator's knowledge and belief, an estimate of the value of–

   (i) the prescribed part (whether or not the administrator might be required under section 176A to make the prescribed part available for the satisfaction of unsecured debts), and

   (ii) the company's net property (as defined by section 176A(6)); and

(b) a statement whether, the administrator proposes to make an application to the court under section 176A(5) and if so the reason for the application.

3.13 Where applicable the document containing the statement of proposals must include a statement of any pre-administration costs charged or incurred by the administrator or, to the administrator's knowledge, by any other person qualified to act as an insolvency practitioner in relation to the company[59]. Further, it must include where applicable a statement that the payment of any

---

58 Rule 3.35(6) of the Rules.
59 Rule 3.35(10)(a) of the Rules. See also Rule 3.36 of the Rules which sets out the contents of a statement of pre-administration costs required under Rule 3.35(10)(a) of the Rules.

unpaid pre-administration costs as an expense of the administration is subject to approval under Rule 3.52 of the Rules and not part of the proposals subject to approval under Schedule B1 paragraph 53 of IA 1986[60].

3.14   Under the former law it was very often the case that the administrator would seek the approval of creditors to his proposals in general terms only. Thus creditors were often asked to give their approval to proposals which simply authorised and required the administrator, for instance:

(a) to continue to manage the affairs of the company to achieve one or more of the stated purposes of the administration order;

(b) to sell all or any of the assets of the company as and when suitable offers were received from third parties for the benefit of creditors generally; and

(c) to report to the creditors' committee on a regular basis and to obtain its approval for significant disposals of assets where the administrator considered it appropriate.

3.15   In the light of the fact that the legislation is now very much more prescriptive than it was under the former law, administrators are no longer able to present proposals which are so general in form. In particular, Rule 3.35(1)(j) of the Rules, which requires the administrator to state how it is envisaged the purpose of administration will be achieved, imposes a positive duty on him to give a proper description of his intended administration strategy. While in practice, the nature of an administrator's proposals may be extremely varied, and the administrator will generally seek to preserve maximum flexibility in formulating them, the inherent benefit of flexibility should not be regarded as a reason for neglecting to give a proper description of how he proposes to achieve the purpose of administration.

3.16   Schedule B1 paragraph 73 of IA 1986 imposes certain limitations on the content of the administrator's proposals. It does so by stipulating that the proposals may not include any action[61] which affects the right of a secured creditor to enforce his security[62] or which would result in a preferential debt being paid otherwise than in priority to the non-preferential debts or which would result in an ordinary preferential debt being paid otherwise than in priority to any secondary preferential debt or which would result in one preferential creditor being paid a smaller proportion of an ordinary preferential debt than another or which would result in one preferential debt being paid a smaller proportion of a secondary preferential debt[63]. This prohibition does not apply[64] where the relevant creditor consents or where the act is included in proposals for a voluntary arrangement[65] or a scheme of arrangement[66] or where the act is included in proposals for a cross-border merger[67].

60   Rule 3.35(10)(b) of the Rules.
61   This form of words is presumably sufficiently wide to cover not just acts expressly set out in the proposals but also acts which the administrator may subsequently decide to commit on the basis of an authority given more generally.
62   Schedule B1 paragraph 73(1)(a) of IA 1986. For the meaning of security see **CHAPTER 2**.
63   Schedule B1 paragraph 73(1)(b), (bb), (c) and (d) of IA 1986.
64   Schedule B1 paragraph 73(2) of IA 1986.
65   Part I of IA 1986. See further, **CHAPTER 11**. In any such case, the protection for secured and preferential creditors is given by section 4(3) of IA 1986.
66   Part 26 of CA 2006. See further **CHAPTER 13**. In any such case, the protection for secured and preferential creditors would be obtained by the obligation to put them in a separate class for voting purposes.
67   Schedule B1 paragraph 73(2)(d) of IA 1986.

3.17   The provision which prevents the proposals authorising an administrator from acting so as to prejudice the position of preferential creditors is readily understandable. The prohibition against authorising any act which affects the right of a secured creditor to enforce his security gives rise to greater difficulties. The very fact that a company is in administration prevents a creditor from taking steps to enforce his security without the consent of the administrator or the permission of the court[68] and gives to the administrator power to dispose of assets subject to security without the consent of the secured creditor[69]. On the natural reading of Schedule B1 paragraph 73(1)(a) of IA 1986, the refusal of a secured creditor's request for consent to enforce and the exercise of a power to dispose of charged assets, would each constitute 'an action which affects the right of a secured creditor to enforce his security' and would thereby be prohibited from inclusion in the proposals[70]. If this is correct, the statutory stay will be of no effect and the powers under Schedule B1 paragraphs 70 and 71 cannot be exercised once the proposals have been approved. It is not thought that this can have been the intention of the legislature, because it would mean that the exercise of important administration powers would be severely curtailed. It is submitted that the restriction in Schedule B1 paragraph 73(1)(a) is directed at attempts to interfere either (a) with the secured creditor's right to receive the proceeds of enforcement of his security or (b) with a secured creditor's right to enforce his security other than by the operation of Schedule B1 paragraphs 43, 70 or 71 or any other statutory power.

3.18   As soon as is reasonably practicable, but in any event before the end of the period of eight weeks beginning with the day on which the company entered administration[71], the administrator must send his statement of proposals to the registrar of companies, to every creditor of the company other than an opted-out creditor[72] of whose claim and address he is aware and to every member of the company[73]. The court has power, on the application of the administrator, to vary this period of time (presumably by way of both extension and reduction)[74], although where it does so the administrator must give notice of the making of the order to all those to whom he is obliged to send his statement of proposals[75].

---

68   Schedule B1 paragraph 43(3) of IA 1986.
69   By order of the court in the case of assets charged by way of fixed charge (Schedule B1 paragraph 71 of IA 1986), but without any such order in the case of assets charged by way of floating charge (Schedule B1 paragraph 70 of IA 1986).
70   Whether expressly or by necessary implication.
71   Schedule B1 paragraph 49(5) of IA 1986. In an appropriate case, the court has jurisdiction to direct administrators not to send out proposals under Schedule B1 paragraph 49 of IA 1986, where the administration will end before the time has expired: *In re Coal Operations Ltd* [2013] EWHC 2581 (Ch).
72   Defined by section 248A of IA 1986 to be a creditor who, in accordance with the Rules, has elected to be an opted-out creditor. See also section 246C of IA 1986 as inserted by SBEEA 2015 which relates to creditors' ability to opt out of receiving certain notices and Rules 1.37 and 1.38 of the Rules, which set out how the opt-out takes place.
73   Schedule B1 paragraph 49(4) of IA 1986. In the case of the administration of an existing or former authorised person or appointed representative or company which is or has carried on a regulated activity in contravention of the general prohibition (as all those terms are used in FSMA 2000), the statement must also be sent to the appropriate regulator: section 362(3) of FSMA 2000. Where a member state liquidator has been appointed in relation to the company, copies of these documents must also be sent to him: Rule 21.7 of the Rules. If the administrator without reasonable excuse fails to comply with the requirements of Schedule B1 paragraph 49(5) of IA 1986, he commits an offence: Schedule B1 paragraph 49(7) of IA 1986.
74   Schedule B1 paragraphs 49(8) and 107 of IA 1986.
75   Rule 3.37(2) and (3) of the Rules.

The period may also be varied with the consent[76] of each secured creditor of the company and unsecured creditors[77]. In the case of a variation by consent (as opposed to one on application to the court), the time period may only be varied once, the consent cannot be used to extend a period by more than 28 days, it may not be used to extend a period which has already been extended by the court and it may not be used to extend a period after expiry[78]. Whether the company's unsecured creditors or preferential creditors consent is to be determined by the administrator seeking a decision from those creditors as to whether they consent[79]. In the case of the members of the company, he is to be taken to have complied with his obligation to send to them his statement of proposals by advertising in such manner as the administrator thinks fit, identifying the proceedings and containing the registered office of the company[80]. Where the administrator has made a statement that that the company has insufficient property to enable a distribution to be made to unsecured creditors other than by virtue of section 176A(2)(a) of IA 1986 consent is required from either each of the secured creditors or, if a distribution may be made to preferential creditors, each secured creditor and the preferential creditors of the company[81].

APPROVAL OF THE PROPOSALS

3.19   Except for the circumstances explained below, the administrator must seek a decision from the company's creditors as to whether they approve the statement of proposals[82]. The initial decision date for that decision must be within the period of ten weeks beginning with the day on which the company enters administration[83]. The statement of proposals delivered under Schedule B1 paragraph 49 must be accompanied by a notice to the creditors of the decision procedure[84] in accordance with Rule 15.8 of the Rules[85]. If the administrator seeks a decision using the deemed consent procedure[86], then the requirements in Rule 15.7 of the Rules also apply to the notice[87]. The new rules in relation

---

76   Which may be written or signified at a creditors' meeting: Schedule B1 paragraph 108(4) of IA 1986.
77   Schedule B1 paragraph 108 of IA 1986 as modified by SBEEA 2015.
78   Schedule B1 paragraph 108(5) of IA 1986. If the statement of proposals states that the administrator thinks that the company has insufficient property to enable a distribution to be made to unsecured creditors other than by virtue of section 176A(2) (the prescribed part provisions as to which see **CHAPTER 15**), the consent need only be given by each of the secured creditors and, where a distribution may be made to the preferential creditors: Schedule B1 paragraph 108(3) of IA 1986.
79   Schedule B1 paragraph 108 of IA 1986 as modified by SBEEA 2015.
80   Schedule B1 paragraph 49(6) of IA 1986 and Rule 3.37(1) of the Rules. The notice must be published as soon as reasonably practicable after the administrator sent his statement of proposals to creditors but no later than eight weeks (or such other period as may be agreed by the creditors or as the court may order) from the date that the company entered administration: Rule 3.37(1)(c) of the Rules.
81   Schedule B1 paragraph 108(3) of IA 1986.
82   Schedule B1 paragraph 51(1) of IA 1986.
83   Schedule B1 paragraph 51(2) of IA 1986. The initial decision date depends on whether the decision is initially sought by the deemed consent procedure or a qualifying decision procedure as discussed in **CHAPTER 4**: see Schedule B1 paragraph 51(3) of IA 1986.
84   Following the introduction of SBEEA 2015.
85   Rule 3.38(2) of the Rules.
86   See **CHAPTER 4**.
87   Rule 3.38(3) of the Rules. see **CHAPTER 4**.

to decisions made by creditors, as brought in both by virtue of the Rules and the Small Business, Enterprise and Employment Act 2015 ('SBEEA 2015'), are dealt with in detail at **CHAPTER 4** and apply to the approval of the administrators' proposals. As with the time period for sending out the proposals, the court has power, on the application of the administrator, to vary the time by which the initial decision date must take place[88]. Furthermore, the consent provisions in relation to varying the eight-week period for sending out the statement of proposals also apply to the ten-week period for the initial decision[89]. The administrator is under a duty to present a copy of his statement of proposals to the creditors and seek their decision[90]. If the administrator without reasonable excuse fails to comply with the requirements, he commits an offence[91].

3.20   Unless otherwise ordered by the court[92], the administrator must deliver a notice to every creditor setting out the details of the decision procedure in relation to the proposals[93].

3.21   The administrator is under no obligation to obtain a decision from the company's creditors where his statement of proposals states that he thinks[94] either:

(a)   that the company has sufficient property to enable each creditor of the company to be paid in full; or

(b)   that the company has insufficient property to enable a distribution to be made to unsecured creditors other than by virtue of section 176A(2)(a) of IA 1986[95]; or

(c)   that neither the first nor the second objective with which the administrator must perform his functions can be achieved[96].

Where the administrator has made a statement under Schedule B1 paragraph 52(1) and has not sought a decision on approval from creditors, the proposal will be deemed to have been approved unless a decision has been requested.

3.22   If requested to do so by creditors of the company whose debts amount to at least 10 per cent of the total debts of the company, the administrator is under a duty to seek a decision from the company's creditors[97]. For such a request to be effective it must contain the information set out in Rule 15.18(3) and must be delivered within eight business days of the date on which the administrator's

---

88   Schedule B1 paragraphs 51(4) and 107 of IA 1986. If the court extends the ten-week time period for which provision is made by Schedule B1 paragraph 51(2), the administrator must send out a notice in compliance with Rule 3.40 of the Rules.

89   Schedule B1 paragraph 108(1) of IA 1986.

90   Schedule B1 paragraph 51(1) of IA 1986.

91   Schedule B1 paragraph 51(5) of IA 1986.

92   Rule 15.12(1) of the Rules.

93   Rule 15.8 of the Rules. See also more generally **CHAPTER 4** on the requirements on a convener to provide notice of a decision procedure and venue.

94   Schedule B1 paragraph 52(1) of IA 1986.

95   A reference to the provisions dealing with the distribution of the prescribed part. See further **CHAPTER 15**.

96   Ie the objectives described in Schedule B1 paragraph 3(1)(a) of IA 1986 (rescuing the company as a going concern) and Schedule B1 paragraph 3(1)(b) of IA 1986 (achieving a better result for the company's creditors as a whole than would be likely if the company were wound up).

97   Schedule B1 paragraph 52(2) of IA 1986.

statement of proposals was sent out[98]. The request must include a statement of the purpose of the proposed meeting and either:

(a) a statement of the requesting creditor's claim or contributory's value, together with–

    (i) a list of the creditors concurring with the request, showing the amounts of their respective debts in the administration, and

    (ii) written confirmation of concurrence from each such creditor; or

(b) a statement of the requesting creditor's debt or contributory's value and that that alone is sufficient without the concurrence of other creditors or contributories[99].

3.23 An administrator must, not later than 14 days from receipt of a request, provide the requesting creditor with itemised details of the sum to be deposited as security for payment of the expenses of summoning and holding the meeting[100]. Unless the meeting resolves that the expenses of summoning and holding it should be paid out of the assets of the company as an expense of the administration, those expenses must be borne and paid by the requesting creditor[101]. The decision must be made within 28 days of either the administrator receiving the required sum requested or after the expiry of 14 days after the initial request if the administrator has failed to inform the requesting creditor or contributory of the sum required to be deposited as security[102].

3.24 As soon as reasonably practicable after the expiry of the period for the requisition of a decision, the administrator must deliver a notice of the date of deemed approval to the registrar of companies, the court and any creditor to whom the administrator has not previously delivered the proposal[103]. Where the administrator is required to seek a decision from the company's creditors under Rule 3.38 of the Rules, the administrator must at the same time deliver to the creditors a notice inviting them to decide whether a creditors' committee should be established if sufficient creditors are willing to be members of the committee[104].

CONSIDERATION OF THE PROPOSALS BY CREDITORS

3.25 The company's creditors may approve the administrator's proposals either without modification, or with modifications to which the administrator

---

98 Schedule B1 paragraph 52(2) of IA 1986 and Rule 15.18(2) of the Rules.
99 Schedule B1 paragraph 52(2) of IA 1986 and Rule 15.18(3) of the Rules.
100 Rule 15.19(1) of the Rules.
101 Rules 15.19(4) of the Rules. To the extent that any deposit is not required for the payment of expenses of summoning and holding the meeting (including presumably the case in which the meeting resolves that the expenses be paid out of the company's assets), the deposit must be repaid to the person who made it: Rule 15.19(7) of the Rules.
102 Schedule B1 paragraph 52(3) of IA 1986 and Rule 15.19(3). As with time periods for which provision is made in relation to the administrator's proposals, the court has power, on the application of the administrator, to vary time for holding this meeting (presumably by way of both extension and reduction): Schedule B1 paragraphs 52(4) and 107 of IA 1986. Unlike the time periods under Schedule B1 paragraphs 49, 50 and 51, this 28-day period cannot be varied using the creditors' consent procedure under Schedule B1 paragraph 108.
103 Rule 3.38(5) of the Rules. The notice must contain the information set out in Rule 3.38(6) of the Rules.
104 Rule 3.39(1) of the Rules.

consents[105]. See **CHAPTER 4** for detailed information about the procedure for creditors to make decisions.

3.26   After a decision has been made by the creditors the administrator must, as soon as is reasonably practicable, report any decision taken by filing at court, and sending to the registrar of companies a report[106]. Any such report must have annexed to it a copy of the proposals which were considered[107]. In addition, as soon as reasonably practicable the administrator must send the report (including, details of any modifications to the proposals that were approved) to the company's creditors[108] and every other person who received a copy of the original proposals[109]. It must also be sent to any member state liquidator both because he will be deemed to be a creditor for these purposes and because of the obligation to give notice to the court and the registrar of companies[110]. If the administrator fails without reasonable excuse to comply with any of these reporting or notification requirements he commits an offence[111].

3.27   If a report is given to the court that the creditors have failed to approve the administrator's proposals, the court may provide that the appointment of an administrator shall cease to have effect from a specified time, adjourn the hearing conditionally or unconditionally, make an interim order, make an order on a petition for winding up suspended by virtue of Schedule B1 paragraph 40(1)(b) of IA 1986, or make any other order (including an order making consequential provision) that the court thinks appropriate[112]. The court may have jurisdiction in an appropriate case to make an order directing that the administrator's proposals be put into effect notwithstanding opposition by a major creditor or to appoint new administrators[113]. In practice, it is incumbent upon the administrator to report to the court what he considers the appropriate course of action to be, and the court will give appropriate weight to those views[114]. The administrator's duties upon his appointment ceasing to have effect are described in **CHAPTER 17**.

APPROVAL OF REVISIONS

3.28   Where the administrator's proposals have been approved (with or without modifications) he is required to manage the affairs, business and property of

---

105 Schedule B1 paragraph 53(1) of IA 1986.
106 Schedule B1 paragraph 53(2) of IA 1986 and Rule 3.41(1) and (2) of the Rules.
107 Rule 3.41(3) of the Rules.
108 Given the wording of the old Rule 2.46(b), it is likely that 'company's creditors' in the new rule includes any creditors who did not receive notice of the meeting, but of whose claim the administrator has since become aware.
109 Rule 3.41(1) of the Rules.
110 Rules 21.7 of the Rules. Where appropriate the FCA or the PRA will also be entitled to notice: section 362(3) of FSMA 2000.
111 Schedule B1 paragraph 53(3) of IA 1986.
112 Schedule B1 paragraph 55 of IA 1986. In *Re BTR (UK) Ltd* [2012] BCC 864, the administrators declined to make an application to the court, but creditors did so and in the light of the rejection of the proposals, the court made a winding up order.
113 For the court's powers under the pre-Enterprise Act law see *Re Maxwell Communication Corpn plc* [1992] BCLC 465 per Hoffmann J at 467g–i and *Re Structures and Computers Ltd* [1998] 1 BCLC 292 at 298 per Neuberger J. Considered post-Enterprise Act in *DKLL Solicitors v Revenue and Customs Commissioners* [2007] EWHC 2067 (Ch).
114 *Re Stanleybet UK Investments Ltd* [2012] BCC 550.

the company in accordance with those proposals[115]. Where an administrator's proposals have been approved with or without modification at an initial creditors' meeting and he proposes to make a revision to those proposals which he thinks is substantial, he must send to each creditor of the company (who is not an opted-out creditor[116]) a statement of the proposed revision and seek a decision of the company's creditors as to whether they approve the proposed revision[117]. The statement of the proposed revision must be delivered to the creditors with a notice of the decision procedure in accordance with Rule 15.8[118]. The administrator must also, within five days of sending to creditors a statement of the proposed revisions, either send a copy of the statement to each member of the company of whose address he is aware, or publish a notice in such manner as the administrator thinks fit stating that the members may request in writing a copy of the proposed revision free of charge and state the address to which to write[119].

3.29 Any statement of revised proposals must include[120]:

(a) details of the court where the proceedings are[121] and the relevant court reference;

(b) the full name, registered address, registered number and any other trading names of the company;

(c) details relating to his appointment as administrator, including the date of appointment and the person making the application or appointment;

(d) the names of the directors and secretary of the company and details of any shareholdings in the company they may have;

(e) a summary of the original proposals and the reasons for proposing a revision;

(f) details of the proposed revision including details of the administrator's assessment of the likely impact of the proposed revision upon creditors generally or upon each class of creditor as the case may be;

(g) where a proposed revision relates to the ending of the administration by a creditors' voluntary liquidation and the nomination of a person to be the proposed liquidator of the company, details of the proposed liquidator, where applicable, the declaration required by section 231 of IA 1986 and a statement in accordance with Schedule B1 paragraph 83(7) of IA 1986 and Rule 3.60(6)(b) of the Rules that creditors may nominate a different person as the proposed liquidator; and

(h) any other information that the administrator thinks necessary to enable creditors to decide whether or not to vote for the proposed revisions.

---

115 Schedule B1 paragraph 68(1) of IA 1986.
116 Defined by section 248A of IA 1986 to be a creditor who, in accordance with the Rules, has elected to be an opted-out creditor. See also section 246C of IA 1986 as inserted by SBEEA 2015 which relates to creditors' ability to opt out of receiving certain notices and Rules 1.37 and 1.38 of the Rules which set out how the opt-out takes place.
117 Schedule B1 paragraphs 54(1) and (2) of IA 1986 and Rule 3.42(1) of the Rules. Where appropriate any member state liquidator, the FCA and the PRA will also be entitled to notice: Rule 21.7 of the Rules and section 362(3) of FSMA 2000.
118 Rule 3.42 of the Rules. The administrator may seek a decision using deemed consent in which case the requirements of Rule 15.7 will also apply to any notice given: see Rule 3.42(3) of the Rules.
119 Schedule B1 paragraphs 54(2)(c) and (3) of IA 1986 and Rules 3.42(4) and (5) of the Rules.
120 This list is set out in Rule 3.42(2) of the Rules.
121 Ie the court in which the administration order was made or the notice of appointment was filed.

The company's creditors may approve the proposed revision without modification or approve it with modification to which the administrator consents[122].

3.30   After a decision is reached in relation to any revision to the proposals, the administrator must, as soon as is reasonably practicable, deliver a report of the decision to the court and the registrar of companies[123]. In addition, as soon as reasonably practicable the administrator must deliver a report to the company's creditors (accompanied by a copy of the original statement of proposals and the revised statement of proposals if the administrator had not delivered notice of the decision procedure or deemed consent procedure to the creditor) and every other person to whom a copy of the original statement of proposals was delivered[124]. The report must contain the information set out in Rule 3.43(2) of the Rules. If the administrator fails without reasonable excuse to comply with any of these reporting or notification requirements he commits an offence[125].

3.31   If a report is given to the court that the creditors have failed to approve a revision of the administrator's proposals, the court has the same powers as on a failure by the creditors to approve the original statement of proposals. Where it proves impossible to implement the administrator's proposals as originally approved and where it is not possible to obtain the creditors' approval to a revision it is possible for the court to give directions to an administrator. The court has the power to direct the administrator in connection with any aspect of his management of the company's affairs, business and property[126], not just where the directions are consistent with the proposals or any revision, but also:

(a)   where the court thinks that the directions are required to reflect a change in circumstance since the proposals or any revision were approved; and

(b)   where the court thinks that the directions are desirable because of a misunderstanding about proposals or any revision to them[127].

PROGRESS REPORTS

3.32   The administrator is required to produce a progress report for the period of six months commencing on the date that the company entered administration, for every subsequent period of six months and for the period commencing with the date of his previous report and the date on which he ceases to act[128]. The report must include[129]:

(a)   identification details for the proceedings, which are likely to include details of the court where the administration application was made or where the notice of appointment was filed, and the relevant court reference number;

---

122   Schedule B1 paragraph 54(5) of IA 1986. It should be noted that usual requirements in relation to the decision procedure by creditors apply (as to which see **CHAPTER 4**).
123   Schedule B1 paragraph 54(6) of IA 1986 and Rule 3.43(1) of the Rules. The revised proposals must accompany the notice to the court (Rule 3.43(3) of the Rules, and must be delivered to the registrar of companies not later than five days after the report is delivered (Rule 3.42(6) of the Rules).
124   Rule 3.43 of the Rules. It must also be sent to any member state liquidator both because he will be deemed to be a creditor for these purposes and because of the obligation to give notice to the court and the registrar of companies: see Rule 21.7 of the Rules and where appropriate the FCA and the PRA will also be entitled to notice: section 362(3) of FSMA 2000.
125   Schedule B1 paragraph 54(7) of IA 1986.
126   Schedule B1 paragraphs 63 and 68(2) of IA 1986.
127   See further, **CHAPTER 5**.
128   Rules 18.2 and 18.6 of the Rules.
129   The list is set out in Rule 18.3 of the Rules.

(b) full details of the company's name, the address of its registered office and its registered number;

(c) identification and contact details for the administrator, the date of appointment, including any changes in office-holder[130] and, in the case of joint administrators, the report ought to (following the old rules) set out their functions as set out in the statement made for the purposes of Schedule B1 paragraph 100(2) of IA 1986[131];

(d) details of progress during the period of the report, including a summary account of receipts and payments;

(e) information relating to remuneration and expenses required by Rule 18.4 of the Rules;

(f) information relating to distributions required by Rules 18.10 to 18.13 of the Rules as applicable;

(g) details of what remains to be done; and

(h) any other relevant information for the creditors.

Where the administrator has ceased to act, the receipts and payments account must include a statement as to the amount paid to unsecured creditors by virtue of the application of section 176A of IA 1986 (prescribed part)[132].

3.33   The administrator must send a copy of the progress report, within one month of the end of the period covered by the report to the creditors (unless it is the final progress report), the court and the registrar of companies[133]. If the administrator makes default in complying with his obligations in respect of the progress report, he is liable to a fine and, for continued contravention, to a daily default fine[134].

---

130 A change in administrator is only required to be shown in the next report after the change: see Rule 18.3(3). Where the period of an administrator's appointment is extended, the next progress report after the date the extension is granted must contain details of the extension: see Rule 18.3(5) of the Rules. If the administrator is seeking the repayment of pre-administration expenses from a former administrator the change in administrator must continue to be shown until the next report after the claim is settled: see Rule 18.3(4) of the Rules.

131 Which functions, if any, are to be exercised by the persons appointed acting jointly and which functions if any are to be exercised by any or all of the persons appointed.

132 See Rule 18.3(2).

133 Rule 18.6(4) of the Rules. It must also be sent to any member state liquidator (Rules 21.7 of the Rules) and, where appropriate to the FCA or the PRA: section 362(3) of FSMA 2000.

134 Rule 18.6(5) of the Rules.

4 Decisions of creditors, creditors' committees and members

GENERAL

4.1　It is self-evident that those who stand to gain or lose most in the administration of an insolvent estate are its creditors. In the light of that consideration, IA 1986 provides a number of procedures by which the collective will of the creditors can be ascertained and implemented. Section 122 of the Small Business, Enterprise and Employment Act 2015 has introduced extensive change as regards the decision-making process of creditors, both in an administration and in the other insolvency processes, by introducing non-meeting decision-making processes, while also allowing a fall-back in certain defined circumstances for a meeting to take place. Thus the general default position is that there will be no actual creditors' meeting for a decision required by the Act or the Rules. In overall summary terms, there are now deemed consent procedures and qualifying decision procedures. A deemed consent procedure is where creditors are notified by the administrator of the intended decision, and unless 10 per cent of creditors by value object before the decision date stated in the notice, the decision is deemed made. If the 10 per cent threshold is met, the deemed consent procedure terminates without the decision having been made and the decision must be made by a qualifying decision procedure. As regards a qualifying decision procedure, these are listed in Rule 15.3 of the Rules, which states the prescribed decision procedures are:

(a) correspondence,

(b) electronic voting,

(c) a virtual meeting,

(d) a physical meeting, or

(e) any other decision-making procedure which enables all creditors who are entitled to participate in the making of the decision to participate equally.

4.2　Pursuant to section 246ZE of IA 1986 (inserted by section 122 of SBEEA 2015), physical meetings of creditors are prohibited and must not be used unless the creditors requisition a physical meeting, which can be made by any one of not less than 10 per cent by value of creditors, or 10 per cent by number of creditors, or ten creditors[1]. Of relevance in respect of administrations, it is now the position that the creditors' consideration of the proposals of the administrator pursuant to Schedule B1 paragraph 51 of IA 1986 are now carried

---

1　Section 246ZE(7) of IA 1986.

out by a deemed consent or decision procedure[2], and the decision of creditors pursuant to sections 3 to 6 of IA 1986 as to whether to approve a company voluntary arrangement are also carried out by decision (rather than by meeting)[3].

4.3 Creditors can opt out of receiving notices in insolvency proceedings, except that they will not be able to opt out of receiving notices relating to distributions or proposed distributions[4]. A creditor can elect to opt out at any time, and the election by the creditor must be by a notice in writing authenticated and dated by the creditor, to be delivered to the administrator. The opt out can be revoked at any time by the same procedure (notice to the administrator)[5].

THE STATUTORY PROVISIONS FOR DECISIONS OF CREDITORS AND CONTRIBUTORIES

4.4 Section 122 of SBEEA 2015 inserts sections 246ZE and 246ZF into IA 1986 which make general provision for decisions by creditors and contributories without a meeting being held[6].

4.5 The new section 246ZE of IA 1986 provides that the section applies where a person ('P') seeks a decision about any matter from a company's creditors or contributories. By subsection (2) the decision may be made by any qualifying decision procedure P thinks fit, except that it may not be made by a creditors' meeting or (as the case may be) a contributories meeting unless subsection (3) applies. Subsections (3) and (4) provide that a meeting must take place if at least the minimum number of creditors or (as the case may be) contributories make a request to P in writing that the decision be made by a creditors' meeting or (as the case may be) a contributories meeting. By subsection (7), the minimum number of creditors or contributories is either 10 per cent in value of the creditors or contributories, or 10 per cent in number of the creditors or contributories, or ten creditors or contributories. Subsection (5) allows a provision of the Act or the Rules, or the court to require a meeting to take place. A meeting is defined by subsection (9) as a meeting where the creditors or (as the case may be) contributories are invited to be present together at the same place (whether or not it is possible to attend the meeting without being present at that place). Rule 15.2(1) of the Rules provides that a 'physical meeting' means a meeting as described in section 246ZE(9), in contrast to a 'virtual meeting', which means a meeting where persons who are not invited to be physically present together may participate in the meeting including communicating directly with all the other

---

2   See Rule 3.38 of the Rules. See also Schedule B1, paragraphs 49–53 of IA 1986.
3   Schedule B1 paragraph 51(1)–(3) (as amended by Schedule 9 paragraph 10(5) of SBEEA 2015) and sections 3–6 of IA 1986 (as amended by Schedule 9 paragraphs 3–7 of SBEEA 2015).
4   Section 246C of IA 1986 (as amended by section 124 of SBEEA 2015). In addition to the prohibition on opt out regarding distributions, Rule 1.37 of the Rules also provides that an opt out does not apply to a notice which IA 1986 requires to be delivered to all creditors, without expressly excluding opted out creditors, a notice of a change in the office holder or the contact details for the office holder, notices of distribution, and a document which the Rules require to accompany a notice within sub-paragraphs (a)–(c) of Rule 1.37(2) of the Rules.
5   Rules 1.37–1.39 of the Rules (cf the minor amendment made to Rule 1.37(1) of the Rules by rule 5 of the Insolvency (England and Wales) (Amendment) Rules 2017 (SI 2017 No 366)).
6   Section 122 of SBEEA 2015 has effect, subject to transitional provisions, from 6 April 2017: see regulations 3, 4(a) and 5 of the Small Business, Enterprise and Employment Act 2015 (Commencement No 6 and Transitional and Savings Provisions) Regulations 2016 (SI 2016 No 1020).

participants in the meeting and voting (either directly or via a proxy holder). As regards qualifying decision procedures by Rule 15.3 of the Rules, the following decision procedures are prescribed as decision procedures: correspondence, electronic voting, a virtual meeting, a physical meeting or any other decision making procedure which enables all creditors who are entitled to participate in the making of the decision to participate equally[7]. Rules 15.4, 15.5 and 15.6 of the Rules make provision in turn for electronic voting, virtual meetings, and physical meetings.

4.6   The new section 246ZF of IA 1986 provides for a deemed consent procedure (which is a separate process to a qualifying decision procedure), which may be used where a company's creditors or contributories are to make a decision about any matter, unless a decision about the matter is required by virtue of IA 1986 or the Rules or any other legislation to be made by a qualifying decision procedure or if the court orders that a decision about the matter is to be made by a qualifying decision procedure.

4.7   By section 246Z(2) of IA 1986 any decision about remuneration of any person must be made by a qualifying decision procedure (rather than by a deemed consent procedure). By subsection (3) the deemed consent procedure is defined as where the relevant creditors (other than opted out creditors) or (as the case may be) the relevant contributories are given notice of the matter about which they are to make a decision, the proposed decision itself, the effect of subsections (4) and (5), and the procedure for objecting to the proposed decision. By subsection (4), if less than the appropriate number of relevant creditors or (as the case may be) relevant contributories object to the proposed decision in accordance with the procedure set out in the notice, the creditors (or as the case may be) the contributories are to be treated as having made the proposed decision. By subsection (6), the appropriate number of relevant creditors or relevant contributories is 10 per cent in value of those creditors or contributories, and 'relevant creditors' (by subsection (7)) means the creditors who, if the decision were to be made by a qualifying decision procedure, would be entitled to vote in the procedure (and subsection (8) makes similar provision as regards contributories). An 'opted out creditor' is defined by the new section 248A of IA 1986, inserted by section 124 of SBEEA 2015 (in force from 6 April 2017) as a person who is a creditor of the company and who in accordance with the Rules has elected (or is deemed to have elected) to be (and not to cease to be) an opted-out creditor in relation to the office-holder. Rule 15.7 of the Rules also makes further provision for the deemed consent procedure by providing further requirements for the contents of the deemed consent notice, the calculation of creditors' claims and the voting rights of creditors.

DECISIONS OF CREDITORS

4.8   The administrator is empowered to call a meeting of the members of the company and/or seek a decision on any matter from the company's creditors

---

7   'Attendance' and 'attend' are defined by Rule 1.2 of the Rules, as amended by rule 4 of the Insolvency (England and Wales) (Amendment) Rules 2017 (SI 2017 No.366). A person attends or is in attendance at a meeting who is present or attends remotely in accordance with Rule 15.6 of the Rules, or who participates in a virtual meeting, whether that person attends the meeting or virtual meeting in person, by proxy, or by corporate representative (in accordance with section 434B or 323 of CA 2006, as applicable).

at any time[8]. The administrator is required to seek a decision from the company's creditors on a matter if he is requested to do so by creditors of the company whose debts mount to at least 10 per cent of the total debts of the company or if he is directed to do so by the court[9]. If an administrator fails without reasonable excuse to seek a decision from the company's creditors on a matter as required he commits an offence[10]. A decision requested to be sought under Schedule B1 paragraph 56(1) of IA 1986 is a 'requisitioned decision' under Rule 15.18(1), and by Rule 15.18(3) of the Rules the request for a requisitioned decision must include a statement of the purpose of the proposed decision and either a statement of the requisitioning creditor's claim, together with a list of the creditors concurring with the request and the amounts of their respective claims or values and confirmation of concurrence from each creditor concurring, or a statement of the requesting creditor's debt and that that alone is sufficient without the concurrence of other creditors. By Rule 15.19 of the Rules, the convener must provide the requesting creditor with itemised details of the sum to be deposited as security for payment of the expenses of the procedure, not later than 14 days from receipt of a request for a requisitioned decision, and the convener is not obliged to initiate the decision procedure or deemed consent procedure until either the convener has received the required sum or the period of 14 days has expired without the convener having informed the requesting creditor of the sum required to be deposited as security. By Rule 15.19(3) of the Rules, a requisitioned decision must be made within 28 days of the date on which the earlier of the events specified in sub-paragraph (2) of Rule 15.19 occurs (the receipt by the convener of the required sum for expenses of the meeting procedure, or expiry of 14 days without the convener having informed the requisitioner of the required sum). Rule 15.19(4) to (6) of the Rules provide for the application of the deposited sum, and by sub-Rule (4) the expenses of the requisitioned decision must be paid out of the deposit (if any) unless the creditors decide that they are to be payable as an expense of the administration.

4.9 Where a member state liquidator has been appointed in relation to a company, he is entitled to participate by Rule 21.8 of the Rules.

NOTICES TO CREDITORS FOR DECISIONS, AND MEETINGS IF REQUISITIONED

4.10 Pursuant to Rule 15.2(b) of the Rules a 'decision procedure' means a qualifying decision procedure or a creditors' decision procedure as prescribed by Rule 15.3 of the Rules. By Rule 15.3 of the Rules, prescribed decision procedures are listed as correspondence, electronic voting, a virtual meeting, a physical meeting or any other decision-making procedure which enables all creditors who are entitled to participate in the making of the decision to participate equally.

---

8   Schedule B1 paragraph 62 of IA 1986 (as amended by Schedule 9 paragraph 10(23) of SBEEA 2015).
9   Schedule B1 paragraphs 56(1)(a) and (b) of IA 1986 (as amended by Schedule 9 paragraph 10(19) and (20) of SBEEA 2015).
10 Schedule B1 paragraph 56(2) of IA 1986 (as amended by Schedule 9 paragraph 10(20) of SBEEA 2015).

4.11   For electronic voting (defined as including any electronic system which enables a person to vote without the need to attend at a particular location to do so)[11], Rule 15.4 of the Rules provides that where the decision procedure uses electronic voting, then the notice delivered to creditors must give them any necessary information as to how to access the voting system, including any password required; and except where electronic voting is being used at a meeting, the voting system must be a system capable of enabling a creditor to vote at any time between the notice being delivered and the decision date; and in the course of a vote the voting system must not provide any creditor with information concerning the vote cast by any other creditor.

4.12   For virtual meetings, Rule 15.5 of the Rules provides that where the decision procedure uses a virtual meeting (defined as a meeting where persons who are not invited to be physically present together may participate in the meeting including communicating directly with all the other participants in the meeting and voting (either directly or via a proxy holder))[12] the notice delivered to creditors must contain any necessary information as to how to access the virtual meeting including any telephone number, access code or password required, and a statement that the meeting may be suspended or adjourned by the chair of the meeting (and must be adjourned if it is so resolved at the meeting).

4.13   For physical meetings, Rule 15.6 of the Rules provides that a request for a physical meeting may be made before or after the notice of the decision procedure or deemed consent procedure has been delivered, but must be made not later than five business days after the date on which the convener delivered the notice of the decision procedure or deemed consent procedure unless the Rules provide to the contrary. The convener must check the threshold requirements for calling physical meetings[13]. Where the threshold is met, the convener must summon the meeting by giving notice which complies with Rule 15.8 of the Rules as far as applicable and which must also contain a statement that the meeting may be suspended or adjourned by the chair of the meeting (and must be adjourned if it is so resolved at the meeting). The notice must also inform the creditors that as a result of the requirement to hold a physical meeting, the original decision procedure or the deemed consent procedure is superseded[14]. By Rule 15.6(5) of the Rules the convener must send the notice required by Rule 15.6(3) of the Rules not later than three business days after one of the thresholds requiring a physical meeting has been met or surpassed. By Rule 15.6(5) of the Rules the convener may permit a creditor to attend a physical meeting remotely[15] if the convener receives a request to do so in advance of the meeting; and must include in the notice of the meeting a statement explaining the convener's discretion to permit remote attendance.

4.14   Rule 15.8 of the Rules sets out the requirements for notices to creditors where a decision is sought by a decision procedure. The convener must deliver

---

11   Rule 15.2(1)(b) of the Rules.
12   Rule 15.2(1)(b) of the Rules.
13   Rule 15.6(2) of the Rules.
14   Rule 15.6(3) and (4) of the Rules.
15   Defined by Rule 15.6(7) of the Rules as meaning attending and being able to participate in the meeting without being in the place where the meeting is being held. Cf rule 4 of the Insolvency (England and Wales) (Amendment) Rules 2017 (SI 2017 No 366) (definition of 'attend' or 'attendance').

a notice to every creditor who is entitled to notice of the procedure[16]. The notice is required to contain the details specified in Rule 15.8(3) of the Rules which are:

'(a) identification details for the proceedings;

(b) details of the decision to be made or of any resolution on which a decision is sought;

(c) a description of the decision procedure which the convener is using, and arrangements, including the venue, for the decision procedure;

(d) a statement of the decision date;

(e) except in the case of a decision in relation to a proposed CVA or IVA, a statement of by when the creditor must have delivered a proof in respect of the creditor's claim in accordance with these Rules, failing which a vote by the creditor will be disregarded;

(f) a statement that a creditor whose debt is treated as a small debt in accordance with rule 14.31(1) must still deliver a proof if that creditor wishes to vote;

(g) a statement that a creditor who has opted out from receiving notices may nevertheless vote if the creditor provides a proof in accordance with paragraph (e);

...

(j) in the case of a decision in relation to a proposed CVA or IVA, a statement of the effects of the relevant provisions of the following–

  (i) rule 15.28 about creditors' voting rights,

  (ii) rule 15.31 about the calculation of creditors' voting rights, and

  (iii) rule 15.34 about the requisite majority of creditors for making decisions;

(k) except in the case of a physical meeting, a statement that creditors who meet the thresholds in sections 246ZE(7) or 379ZA(7) may, within five business days from the date of delivery of the notice, require a physical meeting to be held to consider the matter;

(l) in the case of a meeting, a statement that any proxy must be delivered to the convener or chair before it may be used at the meeting;

(m) in the case of a meeting, a statement that, where applicable, a complaint may be made in accordance with rule 15.38 and the period within which such a complaint may be made; and

(n) a statement that a creditor may appeal a decision in accordance with rule 15.35, and the relevant period under rule 15.35 within which such an appeal may be made.'

Where the decision procedure is a meeting, the notice must be accompanied by a blank proxy complying with Rule 16.3[17] of the Rules. Rule 15.8 of the Rules

---

16   Rule 15.8(2) of the Rules.
17   Rule 15.8(5) of the Rules.

can be disapplied if the court orders under Rule 15.12 of the Rules that notice of a decision procedure be given by advertisement only[18].

4.15   In fixing the venue for the decision procedure (including the resumption of an adjourned meeting), the convener must have regard to the convenience of those invited to participate[19]. Notice periods for decision procedures, and notices seeking deemed consent, are set out in a table in Rule 15.11 of the Rules so that, for example, for a decision of creditors in an administration, the persons to whom notice must be delivered are the creditors who had claims against the company at the date when the company entered administration (except for those who have subsequently been paid in full), and the minimum notice required is 14 days; for a proposed company voluntary arrangement, for a decision of the creditors, the default period of notice is 14 days, save that a seven-day period is provided for consideration of the proposal where a physical meeting is requisitioned[20] (and a seven-day period is required also for a notice for a decision on proposed modifications to the proposal from the company's directors under the moratorium provisions of Schedule A1 paragraph 31(7) of IA 1986). By Rule 15.12 of the Rules, the court may order that notice of the decision procedure is given by advertisement only, and in considering whether to make such order, the court must have regard to the relative cost of advertisement as against the giving of individual notices, the amount of assets available and the extent of the interest of creditors, members and contributories or any particular class of them. By Rule 15.13(5) of the Rules, the convener may gazette the decision procedure or the deemed consent procedure, in which case the details set out in Rule 15.13 of the Rules must be stated in the notice.

4.16   By Rule 15.9(1) of the Rules, in order to be counted in a decision procedure other than where votes are cast at a meeting, votes must be received by the convener on or before the decision date and in the case of a vote cast by a creditor, must be accompanied by a proof in respect of the creditor's claim unless it has already been given to the convener. By Rule 15.9(2) of the Rules, in an administration, a vote must be disregarded if a proof in respect of the claim is not received by the convener on or before the decision date or, in the case of a meeting, 4pm on the business day before the decision date unless under Rule 15.26 or 15.28(1)(b)(ii) of the Rules (as applicable) the chair is content to accept the proof later; or the convener decides, in the application of Chapter 8 of the Rules, that the creditor is not entitled to cast the vote. By Rule 15.9(3) of the Rules, for the decision to be made, the convener must receive at least one valid vote on or before the decision date.

4.17   By Rule 15.13 of the Rules, in an administration, where a decision is being sought by a meeting, the convener must gazette a notice of the procedure stating that a meeting of creditors or contributories is to take place, the venue for the meeting, the purpose of the meeting, the time and date by which, and place at which, those attending must deliver proxies and proofs (if not already delivered) in order to be entitled to vote, who is the convener in respect of the decision procedure and, if the procedure results from a request of one or more creditors,

---

18   Rule 15.8(6) of the Rules.
19   Rule 15.10 of the Rules.
20   See also Rule 2.31 of the Rules (and cf rule 7 of the Insolvency (England and Wales) (Amendment) Rules 2017 has amended Rule 2.31(3) of the Rules by substituting '(3) A notice summoning a meeting of the creditors must be delivered to the creditors at least seven days before the day fixed for the meeting.')

the fact that it was so summoned and the section of IA 1986 under which it was summoned.[21] The notice must be gazetted, before or as soon as reasonably practicable after notice of the meeting is delivered in accordance with the Rules, and information gazetted may also be advertised in such other manner as the convener thinks fit.[22] If the convener considers it is required, he may require the attendance at a creditors' meeting for a company voluntary arrangement or an administration of every present or former officer of the company, and in such event that person is required to attend the meeting.[23]

4.18   If a meeting of creditors is requisitioned and required, then Rules 15.20 to 15.27 of the Rules make provision for such meeting. By Rule 15.20(1) to (3) of the Rules, a meeting is not competent to act unless a quorum is in attendance, and a quorum in the case of a meeting of creditors is at least one creditor entitled to vote. Where the quorum Rules are satisfied by the attendance of the chair alone, or the chair and one additional person, but the chair is aware, either by virtue of proofs and proxies received or otherwise, that one or more additional persons would, if attending, be entitled to vote, the chair must delay the start of the meeting by at least 15 minutes after the appointed time of the meeting. By Rule 15.21 of the Rules, the chair of a meeting must be the convener, an appointed person (defined by Rule 1.2(2) and (3) of the Rules as a person appointed by an office holder other than the official receiver and who is qualified to act as an insolvency practitioner or is a person experienced in insolvency matters who is a member or employee of the office holder's firm or an employee of the office holder) or in cases where the convener is the official receiver, a person appointed by the official receiver. By Rule 15.22 of the Rules the chair has control over the proceedings at the meeting and may determine participation, intervention and what questions may be put to present or former officers of the company. By Rule 15.27 of the Rules, the chair may, without an adjournment, declare the meeting suspended for one or more periods not exceeding one hour in total (or, in exceptional circumstances, such longer total period during the same day at the chair's discretion). As regards adjournments, by Rule 15.23 of the Rules the chair may (and must if it is so resolved) adjourn a meeting for not more than 14 days, but subject to any direction of the court and to Rule 15.24 of the Rules[24]. By Rule 15.23(2) of the Rules, further adjournment under Rule 15.23 must not be to a day later than 14 days after the date on which the meeting was originally held (subject to any direction of the court). However, in a case relating to a proposed company voluntary arrangement, the chair may, and must if the meeting so resolves, adjourn a meeting held under Schedule A1 paragraph 29(1) of IA 1986 to a day which is not more than 14 days after the date on which the moratorium (including any extension) ends. Under Rule 15.25 of the Rules, in an administration, if no one attends to act as chair within 30 minutes of the time fixed for a meeting to start, then the meeting is adjourned to the same time and place the following week or, if that is not a business day, to the business day immediately following. If no one attends to act as chair within 30 minutes of the time fixed for the meeting after a second adjournment under Rule 15.25 of the Rules, then by Rule 15.25(2), the meeting comes to an end. By Rule 15.26

---

21   Rules 15.13(1) and (2) of the Rules.
22   Rule 15.13(3) and (4) of the Rules.
23   Rule 15.14(1) of the Rules. For the required notice periods, see Rule 15.14(4) of the Rules.
24   Rule 15.24 of the Rules provides that where a meeting proposes to remove a liquidator, and the liquidator or his nominee is the chair, the chair must not adjourn the meeting without the consent of at least one half (in value) of the creditors attending and entitled to vote.

of the Rules, where a meeting in an administration is adjourned, proofs may be used if delivered not later than 4pm on the business day immediately before resumption of the adjourned meeting, or later than that time where the chair is content to accept the proof.

PROXIES

4.19 Proxies are provided for by Rules 16.1 to 16.9 of the Rules. By Rule 16.2 of the Rules, a proxy is defined as a document made by a creditor, member or contributory[25] which directs or authorises another person (the proxy holder) to act as the representative of the creditor, member or contributory at a meeting or meetings by speaking, voting, abstaining or proposing resolutions[26]. By Rule 16.2(2) of the Rules, a proxy may be either a specific proxy which relates to a specific meeting, or a continuing proxy for the insolvency proceedings. By Rule 16.2(3) of the Rules, a specific proxy must direct the proxy holder how to act at the meeting by giving specific instructions, or authorise the proxy holder to act at the meeting without specific instructions, or contain both direction and authorisation, and by Rule 16.2(4) of the Rules, a proxy is to be treated as a specific proxy for the meeting which is identified in the proxy unless it states that it is a continuing proxy for the insolvency proceedings. By Rule 16.2(5) of the Rules a continuing proxy must authorise the proxy holder to attend, speak, vote or abstain, or to propose resolutions without giving the proxy holder any specific instructions how to do so. By Rule 16.2(6) of the Rules, a continuing proxy may be superseded by a proxy for a specific meeting or withdrawn by a written notice to the office holder. By Rules 16.2(7) and (8) of the Rules, a creditor, member or contributory may appoint more than one person to be proxy holder, but if so their appointment is as alternates, and only one of them may act as proxy holder at a meeting, and the proxy holder must be an individual. Rule 16.3 of the Rules provides and allows for the appointment by 'blank proxy' of a proxy by name or identity, such as appointing the chair of the meeting, or the official receiver[27].

---

25   It has been held that where a statute requires personal signature, as opposed to authorising an agent to sign on behalf of the principal creditor, an agent is not permitted to execute: *Wilson v Wallani* (1880) 5 Ex D 155. But see also *Re Diptford Parish Lands* [1934] Ch 151. The wording used in Rule 16.2 of the Rules would appear to allow an agent to execute on behalf of a principal, and as regards a company, execution by an agent on behalf of the company would be the ordinary course (see section 44(1)(b) and (2) of CA 2006).

26   A right to vote is considered to be property in English law, and a creditor or member may normally vote in his own interests and is not subject to fiduciary restraints in the exercise of the voting discretion: see *Eclairs Group Ltd v JKX Oil & Gas plc* [2015] UKSC 71 (paragraph 40). This is subject to Rule 16.7 of the Rules, which provides restrictions on a proxy holder voting for a resolution which would directly or indirectly place the proxy holder or any associate of the proxy holder in a position to receive any remuneration, fees or expenses from the insolvent estate or fix or change such remuneration.

27   Rule 1.2(2) of the Rules defines 'proxy' and 'blank proxy' and provides such words are to be interpreted in accordance with Part 16 of the Rules. The other references in the Rules to blank proxies are at Rule 2.26(1)(b) (where the nominee of a company voluntary arrangement invites the members to consider a proposal at a meeting, the notice to members must include a blank proxy); and Rule 15.8(5) (where a decision procedure is a meeting, the notice must be accompanied by a blank proxy complying with Rule 16.3); and see Rule 16.4(7) (the chair may require a proxy used at a meeting to be the same as or substantially similar to the blank proxy delivered for that meeting or to a blank proxy previously delivered which has been completed as a continuing proxy). Rule 16.3(2) of the Rules was substituted by rule 40(a) of the Insolvency (England and Wales) (Amendment) Rules 2017 (SI 2017 No 366).

A blank proxy, when completed with the details required by Rule 16.3(3)[28], becomes a proxy as described in Rule 16.2 of the Rules. The details required by Rule 16.3(3) of the Rules are the name and address of the creditor, member or contributory, either the name of the proxy holder or the identification of the proxy holder, and a statement that the proxy is either for a specific meeting which is identified in the proxy, or a continuing proxy for the proceedings; and if the proxy is for a specific meeting, instructions as to the extent to which the proxy holder is directed to vote in a particular way, to abstain or to propose any resolution[29]. Rule 16.3(4) of the Rules then goes on to provide that a blank proxy must not have inserted in it the name or description of any person as proxy holder or instructions as to how a person appointed as proxy holder is to act, and Rule 16.3(5) of the Rules provides that a blank proxy must have a note to the effect that the proxy may be completed with the name of the person or the chair of the meeting who is to be proxy holder.

4.20 As regards the use of proxies, Rule 16.4(1) of the Rules provides that a proxy for a specific meeting must be delivered to the chair before the meeting, while by Rule 16.4(2) of the Rules a continuing proxy must be delivered to the office-holder and may be exercised at any meeting which begins after the proxy is delivered. By Rule 16.4(3) of the Rules a proxy may be used at the resumption of the meeting after an adjournment, but if a different proxy is given for use at a resumed meeting, that proxy must be delivered to the chair before the start of the resumed meeting. By Rule 16.4(4) of the Rules, where a specific proxy directs a proxy-holder to vote for or against a resolution for the nomination or appointment of a person as office-holder, the proxy-holder may, unless the proxy states otherwise, vote for or against (as the proxy-holder thinks fit) a resolution for the nomination or appointment of that person jointly with another or others. By Rule 16.4(5) of the Rules, a proxy-holder may propose a resolution which is one on which the proxy-holder could vote if someone else proposed it, and by Rule 16.4(6) of the Rules where a proxy gives specific directions as to voting, this does not, unless the proxy states otherwise, prohibit the proxy-holder from exercising discretion how to vote on a resolution which is not dealt with by the proxy. By Rule 16.4(7) of the Rules, the chair may require a proxy used at a meeting to be the same as or substantially similar to the blank proxy delivered for that meeting or to a blank proxy previously delivered which has been completed as a continuing proxy.

4.21 Rule 16.5 of the Rules provides for the exercise of proxies by the chair. Pursuant to Rule 16.5(1) of the Rules, where a proxy appoints the chair (however described in the proxy) as proxy-holder the chair may not refuse to be the proxy-holder. Rule 16.5(2) of the Rules provides that where the office-holder is appointed as proxy-holder, but another person acts as chair of the meeting, that other person may use the proxies as if that person were the proxy-holder. Rule 16.5(3) of the Rules provides that where, in a meeting of creditors in an administration the chair holds a proxy which requires the proxy-holder to vote for a particular resolution and no other person proposes that resolution, the chair must propose it unless the chair considers that there is good reason for

---

28 As amended by rule 40(c) of the Insolvency (England and Wales) (Amendment) Rules 2017 (SI 2017 No 366).
29 Rule 16.3(c), as amended by rule 40(c) of the Insolvency (England and Wales) (Amendment) Rules 2017 (SI 2017 No 366).

not doing so, and by Rule 16.5(4) of the Rules that if the chair does not propose such a resolution, the chair must as soon as reasonably practicable after the meeting deliver a notice of the reason why that was not done to the creditor, member or contributory. By Rule 16.9 of the Rules, a person authorised to represent a corporation (other than as a proxy holder) at a meeting of creditors or contributories must produce to the chair the instrument conferring the authority or a copy of it certified as a true copy by two directors, or a director and the secretary or by a director in the presence of a witness who attests the director's signature. Such instrument conferring the authority must have been executed in accordance with section 44(1) to (3) of CA 2006 unless the instrument is the constitution of the corporation.

4.22   Under Rule 16.6 of the Rules, a person attending a meeting is entitled, immediately before or in the course of the meeting, to inspect proxies and associated documents delivered to the chair or to any other person in accordance with the notice convening the meeting, and the proxies can be inspected at all reasonable times on any business day by a creditor (in the case of proxies used at a meeting of creditors) and a director (in the case of corporate insolvency proceedings). Rule 16.6(2) of the Rules provides for the retention of the proxies by the chair or the office holder. The right of inspection is subject to the law on confidentiality of documents as provided by Rule 1.58 of the Rules.

4.23   In the case of the administration of an existing or former authorised person or appointed representative or company which is or has carried on a regulated activity in contravention of the general prohibition (as all those terms are used in FSMA 2000), the FCA or the PRA is entitled to appoint a person to take part in creditors' decision making[30].

CREDITORS' ENTITLEMENT TO VOTE

4.24   Although each creditor must be given notice of any decision to be made by creditors and is entitled to vote, the extent to which he can influence the outcome of the decision will depend on his entitlement to vote and the value of his vote. The value of the creditor's right includes claims whether they are present or future, certain or contingent, ascertained or sounding only in damages (see Rules 14.2(1) and 14.1(5) of the Rules), and by Rule 14.1(3) of the Rules a debt in relation to an administration means, subject to Rule 14.1(4) (liability in tort)[31], any debt or liability to which the company is subject at the relevant date, any debt or liability to which the company may become subject after the relevant date by reason of any obligation incurred before that date, and any interest provable as mentioned in Rule 14.23 of the Rules. The relevant date provisions are found in Rule 14.1(3)(a) and (b) of the Rules and mean in the case of an administration which was not immediately preceded by a winding up, the date on which the company entered administration, and in the case of an administration which was immediately preceded by a winding up, the date on which the company went into liquidation.

---

30   Section 362(5) of FSMA 2000.
31   By Rule 14.1(4) of the Rules, a tortious claim is a provable debt if the cause of action has accrued at the relevant date, or if all the elements necessary to establish the cause of action exist at that date except for actionable damage.

4.25 In an administration[32] Rule 15.28 of the Rules provides that a creditor is entitled to vote in a decision procedure or to object to a decision proposed using the deemed consent procedure only if the creditor has (subject to Rule 15.29 of the Rules, which concerns the scheme manager's voting rights in a winding up of an authorised deposit taker) delivered to the convener a proof of the debt claimed in accordance with Rule 15.28(3), including any calculation for the purposes of Rule 15.31 or 15.32 of the Rules, and the proof was received by the convener not later than the decision date, or in the case of a meeting, 4pm on the business day before the meeting, or in the case of a meeting, later than 4pm on the business day before the meeting deadline where the chair is content to accept the proof and the proof has been admitted for the purposes of entitlement to vote. By Rule 15.28(3) of the Rules, a debt is claimed in accordance with Rule 15.28 if it is claimed as due from the company to the person seeking to be entitled to vote or in relation to a member state liquidator, claimed to be due to creditors in proceedings in relation to which that liquidator holds office.

4.26 By Rule 15.28(2) of the Rules, in the case of a meeting, a proxy-holder is not entitled to vote on behalf of a creditor unless the convener or chair has received the proxy intended to be used on behalf of that creditor. By Rule 15.28(4) of the Rules the convener or chair may call for any document or other evidence to be produced if the convener or chair thinks it necessary for the purpose of substantiating the whole or any part of a claim. By Rule 15.28(5) of the Rules, in a decision relating to a proposed company voluntary arrangement, every creditor, secured or unsecured, who has notice of the decision procedure is entitled to vote in respect of that creditor's debt. By Rule 15.28(6) of the Rules, where a decision is sought in an administration under paragraph 3.52(3) (b) (pre-administration costs), 18.18(4) (remuneration: procedure for initial determination in an administration) or 18.26(2) (first exception: administrator has made statement under Schedule B1 paragraph 52(1)(b) of IA 1986), creditors are entitled to participate to the extent stated in those paragraphs.

4.27 Rule 15.30 of the Rules provides for voting rights in an administration where there is overlap between the claims of creditors and claims made by member state liquidators and provides by sub-Rule (1) that where a creditor in an administration is entitled to vote under Rule 15.28(1) of the Rules, and has made the claim in other proceedings, votes on a resolution in a decision procedure, and a member state liquidator casts a vote in respect of the same claim, only the creditor's vote is to be counted. Whereas by sub-Rule (2), where in an administration a creditor has made a claim in more than one set of other proceedings and more than one member state liquidator seeks to vote in respect of that claim, the entitlement to vote in respect of that claim is exercisable by the member state liquidator in the main proceedings, whether or not the creditor has made the claim in the main proceedings. By sub-Rule (3) 'other proceedings' means main, secondary or territorial proceedings in another member state.

4.28 As regards the valuation of votes and requisite majorities, the requisite majorities for a creditors' decision is provided for in Rule 15.34 of the Rules, which provides that a decision is made by creditors when a majority (in value) of those voting have voted in favour of the proposed decision, except where

---

[32] But not including a CVA for which separate provision is made by Rule 15.28(5) of the Rules. The test for identifying a creditor entitled to vote on (and therefore capable of being bound by) a CVA is different from the test of whether a creditor would have a provable debt: *Re T&N Ltd* [2005] EWHC 2870 (Ch).

Rule 15.34 provides otherwise. By Rule 15.34(2) of the Rules[33], in the case of an administration, a decision is not made if those voting against it:

(a) include more than half in value of the creditors to whom notice of the decision procedure was delivered; and

(b) are not, to the best of the convener or chair's belief, persons connected with the company.

4.29   By Rule 15.34(3) of the Rules each of the following decisions in a proposed CVA is made when three-quarters or more (in value) of those responding vote in favour of it, namely:

(a) a decision approving a proposal or a modification;

(b) a decision extending or further extending a moratorium; or

(c) a decision bringing a moratorium to an end before the end of the period of any extension.

4.30   By Rule 15.34(4) of the Rules, in a proposed CVA a decision is not made if more than half of the total value of the unconnected creditors vote against it. By Rule 15.34(5) of the Rules, it provides that for the purposes of paragraph (4), the presumption (provided by Rule 15.34(5)(a) of the Rules) is that a creditor is unconnected unless the convener or chair decides that the creditor is connected with the company, and (by Rule 15.34(5)(b) of the Rules), in deciding whether a creditor is connected, reliance may be placed on the information provided by the company's statement of affairs or otherwise in accordance with the Rules; and (by Rule 15.34(c) of the Rules), the total value of the unconnected creditors is the total value of those unconnected creditors whose claims have been admitted for voting.

4.31   By Rule 15.33(1) of the Rules, the convener or chair in respect of a decision procedure must ascertain entitlement to vote and admit or reject claims accordingly. By Rule 15.33(2) of the Rules the convener or chair may admit or reject a claim in whole or in part, and by Rule 15.33(3) of the Rules, if the convener or chair is in any doubt whether a claim should be admitted or rejected, the convener or chair must mark it as objected to and allow votes to be cast in respect of it, subject to such votes being subsequently declared invalid if the objection to the claim is sustained. The convener's or chair's decision is, by Rule 15.35(1) of the Rules, subject to appeal to the court by a creditor, or by a contributory. By Rule 15.35(2) of the Rules, in a proposed company voluntary arrangement, an appeal against a decision may also be made by a member of the company. By Rule 15.35(3) of the Rules, if the decision is reversed or varied, or votes are declared invalid, the court may order another decision procedure to be initiated or make such order as it thinks just but, in a company voluntary arrangement, the court may only make an order if it considers that the circumstances which led to the appeal give rise to unfair prejudice or material irregularity. By Rule 15.35(4) of the Rules, an appeal under Rule 15.35 of the Rules may not be made later than 21 days after the decision date, save that this does not apply in a proposed company voluntary arrangement, where instead an appeal may not be made after the end of the period of 28 days beginning with the day in a proposed company voluntary arrangement, on which the first

---

[33]   Amended by rule 39 of the Insolvency (England and Wales) (Amendment) Rules 2017 (SI 2017 No 366).

of the reports required by section 4(6) or Schedule A1 paragraph 30(3) of IA 1986 was filed with the court. By Rule 15.35(6) of the Rules, the convener or chair who made the decision is not personally liable for costs incurred by any person in relation to an appeal under Rule 15.35 of the Rules unless the court makes an order to that effect (and under Rule 15.35(7) of the Rules, the court may not make an order under paragraph (6) if the person who made the decision in a winding up by the court is the official receiver or a person nominated by the official receiver).

4.32   By Rule 15.31(1) of the Rules, votes are calculated according to the amount of each creditor's claim in an administration, as at the date on which the company entered administration, less any payments that have been made to the creditor after that date in respect of the claim, and less any adjustment by way of set-off which has been made in accordance with Rule 14.24 of the Rules or would have been made if that Rule were applied on the date on which the votes are counted. Votes are calculated in a proposed CVA at the date the company went into liquidation where the company is being wound up; at the date the company entered into administration (less any payments made to the creditor after that date in respect of the claim) where it is in administration; at the beginning of the moratorium where a moratorium has been obtained (less any payments made to the creditor after that date in respect of the claim), or if none of these apply, then votes are calculated at the decision date.

4.33   By Rule 15.31(2) of the Rules, a creditor may vote in respect of a debt of a liquidated or unascertained amount if the convener or chair decides to put upon it an estimated minimum value for the purposes of entitlement to vote and admits the claim for that purpose. By Rule 15.31(3) of the Rules, a proviso to this is made so that in relation to a proposed company voluntary arrangement, a debt of an unliquidated or unascertained amount is to be valued at £1 for the purposes of voting unless the convener or chair or an appointed person decides to put a higher value on it.

4.34   By Rule 15.31(4) of the Rules, where a debt is wholly secured its value for voting purposes is nil. By Rule 15.31(5) of the Rules, where a debt is partly secured its value for voting purposes is the value of the unsecured part. A proviso is provided to this by Rule 15.31(6) of the Rules which provides that, however, the value of the debt for voting purposes is its full value without deduction of the value of the security in the following cases, namely where the administrator has made a statement under Schedule B1 paragraph 52(1)(b) of the Rules and the administrator has been requested to seek a decision under paragraph 52(2); and where, in a proposed company voluntary arrangement, there is a decision on whether to extend or further extend a moratorium or to bring a moratorium to an end before the end of the period of any extension.

4.35   Rules 15.31(7) to (9) of the Rules provide:

- by sub-Rule (7) that no vote may be cast in respect of a claim more than once on any resolution put to the meeting; and for this purpose (where relevant), the claim of a creditor and the claim of any member state liquidator in relation to the same debt are a single claim;
- by sub-Rule (8) that a vote cast in a decision procedure which is not a meeting may not be changed; and
- by sub-Rule (9) that sub-Rule (7) does not prevent a creditor or member state liquidator from voting in respect of less than the full value of an

entitlement to vote; or casting a vote one way in respect of part of the value of an entitlement and another way in respect of some or all of the balance of that value.

4.36 Article 32(2) of the EC Regulation on insolvency proceedings[34] ('the EC Insolvency Regulation') (which continues to apply to insolvency proceedings falling within the scope of this Regulation and which have been opened before 26 June 2017)[35] provides that the liquidators in the main and any secondary proceedings[36] shall lodge in other proceedings claims which have already been lodged in the proceedings for which they were appointed, provided that the interests of creditors in the latter proceedings are served thereby, subject to the right of creditors to oppose that or to withdraw the lodgement of their claims where the law applicable so provides. Further, by Article 32(3) of the EC Insolvency Regulation, the liquidator in the main or secondary proceedings shall be empowered to participate in other proceedings on the same basis as a creditor, in particular by attending creditors' meetings. The Rules provide for the member state liquidator's participation in creditor decision procedures by Rules 15.30 and 21.8 of the Rules. The recast EC Regulation on insolvency proceedings[37] ('the recast Insolvency Regulation') (which applies only to insolvency proceedings opened from 26 June 207)[38] provides similar provisions (to the former Article 32 of the EC Insolvency Regulation) on the exercise of creditors' rights by Article 45 of the recast Insolvency Regulation.

4.37 A single creditor, such as a bank or trust company, may be a creditor in more than one capacity, for example as trustee for its own account, or as trustee for two parties wishing to vote differently. In such circumstances it is permissible for such creditor to split the voting claim, by voting one part in favour and another part against any particular proposal[39].

4.38 Rule 15.32 of the Rules provides for the calculation of voting rights in special cases. By sub-Rule (1) in an administration, a creditor under a hire-purchase agreement is entitled to vote in respect of the amount of the debt due and payable by the company on the date on which the company entered administration. By sub-Rule (2), in calculating the amount of any debt for the purpose of sub-Rule (1), no account is to be taken of any amount attributable to the exercise of any right under the relevant agreement so far as the right has become exercisable solely by virtue of the making of an administration application, a notice of intention to appoint an administrator or any matter arising as a consequence of the notice, or the company entering administration. By sub-Rule (3) any voting rights which a creditor might otherwise exercise in respect of a claim in a creditors' voluntary winding up or a winding up by the court of an authorised deposit-taker are reduced by a sum equal to the amount

---

34 Council Regulation (EC) No 1346/2000 of 29 May 2000 on insolvency proceedings (OJ L60, 30/06/2000, 1–13).

35 As provided by Article 84(1) and (2) of Regulation (EU) 2015/848 of the European Parliament and of the Council of 20 May 2015 on insolvency proceedings (OJ L141, 05/06/2015, 19–72).

36 'Member State liquidator' is defined by Rule 1.2(2) as meaning a person falling within the definition of liquidator in Article 2(b) of the EC Insolvency Regulation appointed in proceedings to which the EC Insolvency Regulation applies in a member state other than the United Kingdom.

37 Regulation (EU) 2015/848 of the European Parliament and of the Council of 20 May 2015 on insolvency proceedings (OJ L141, 05/06/2015, 19–72).

38 See Article 84(1) and (2) of the recast Insolvency Regulation.

39 *Re Polly Peck International plc* [1991] BCC 503.

of that claim in relation to which the scheme manager, by virtue of its having delivered a statement under Rule 15.29 of the Rules, is entitled to exercise voting rights.

4.39 There is no provision in Rules 15.28 to 15.35 of the Rules dealing with the valuation of foreign currency claims for decision or meeting purposes. However, Rule 14.21(1) of the Rules, when dealing with proofs of debt, provides that a proof for a debt incurred or payable in a foreign currency must state the amount of the debt in that currency, and by sub-Rule (2) provides that the office-holder must convert all such debts into sterling at a single rate for each currency determined by the office-holder by reference to the exchange rates prevailing on the relevant date. There is an appeal process to the court provided by Rules 14.21(4) and (5) of the Rules.

EXCLUSION OF CREDITORS

4.40 Rules 15.36 to 15.38 of the Rules provide for the eventuality where a creditor for some reason is unable to take part or attend a decision-making process such as a virtual meeting, and these Rules give the excluded person certain rights. By Rule 15.36(1) of the Rules an 'excluded person' is defined as a person who has taken all steps necessary to attend a virtual meeting or has been permitted by the convener to attend a physical meeting remotely under the arrangements which have been put in place by the convener of the meeting, but do not enable that person to attend the whole or part of that meeting. By Rule 15.36(2) of the Rules, where the chair becomes aware during the course of the meeting that there is an excluded person, the chair may continue the meeting or declare the meeting void and convene the meeting again or declare the meeting valid up to the point where the person was excluded and adjourn the meeting. By Rule 15.36(3) of the Rules, where the chair continues the meeting, the meeting is valid unless the chair decides in consequence of a complaint under Rule 15.38 of the Rules to declare the meeting void and hold the meeting again; or the court directs otherwise. By Rule 15.38(4) of the Rules, without prejudice to sub-Rule (2), where the chair becomes aware during the course of the meeting that there is an excluded person, the chair may, at the chair's discretion and without an adjournment, declare the meeting suspended for any period up to one hour.

4.41 By Rule 15.37(1) of the Rules, a creditor who claims to be an excluded person may request an indication of what occurred during the period of that person's claimed exclusion. By Rule 15.37(2) of the Rules a request under sub-Rule (1) should be made in accordance with sub-Rule (3) as soon as reasonably practicable, and in any event, not later than 4pm on the business day following the day on which the exclusion is claimed to have occurred. By Rule 15.37(3) of the Rules, a request under sub-Rule (1) must be made to the chair where it is made during the course of the business of the meeting; or to the convener where it is made after the conclusion of the business of the meeting. Under Rule 15.37(4) of the Rules, where satisfied that the person making the request is an excluded person, the person to whom the request is made under sub-Rule (3) must deliver the requested indication to the excluded person as soon as reasonably practicable, and in any event, not later than 4pm on the business day following the day on which the request was made under sub-Rule (1).

4.42   Rule 15.38 provides for complaints to be made by excluded persons. By Rule 15.38(1) a person who is, or claims to be, an excluded person may make a complaint, and by Rule 15.38(1)(b) a person who attends the meeting and claims to have been adversely affected by the actual, apparent or claimed exclusion of another person may also make a complaint. By Rule 15.38(2), the complaint must be made to the appropriate person who is the chair, where the complaint is made during the course of the meeting; or to the convener, where it is made after the meeting. By Rule 15.38(3), the complaint must be made as soon as reasonably practicable and, in any event, no later than 4pm on the business day following the day on which the person was, appeared or claimed to be excluded; or where an indication is sought under Rule 15.37, the day on which the complainant received the indication. By Rule 15.38(4), the appropriate person must, as soon as reasonably practicable following receipt of the complaint consider whether there is an excluded person. Where satisfied that there is an excluded person, the appropriate person must consider the complaint and, where satisfied that there has been prejudice, take such action as the appropriate person considers fit to remedy the prejudice.

4.43   Rules 15.38(5) to (9) of the Rules then provide a resolution process to remedy the exclusion, if material to the vote. By Rule 15.38(5) of the Rules it is provided that Rule 15.38(6) of the Rules applies where the appropriate person is satisfied that the complainant is an excluded person and a resolution was voted on at the meeting during the period of the person's exclusion; and the excluded person asserts how he intended to vote on the resolution. Rule 15.38(6) of the Rules provides that where the appropriate person is satisfied that if the excluded person had voted as he intended it would have changed the result of the resolution, then the appropriate person must, as soon as reasonably practicable, count the intended vote as having been cast in that way; amend the record of the result of the resolution; where notice of the result of the resolution has been delivered to those entitled to attend the meeting, deliver notice to them of the change and the reason for it; and where notice of the result of the resolution has yet to be delivered to those entitled to attend the meeting, the notice must include details of the change and the reason for it. By sub-Rule (7), where satisfied that more than one complainant is an excluded person, the appropriate person must have regard to the combined effect of the intended votes. By sub-Rule (8), the appropriate person must deliver notice to the complainant of any decision as soon as reasonably practicable. Rule 15.38(9) of the Rules provides for a court remedy by permitting a complainant who is not satisfied by the action of the appropriate person to apply to the court for directions and any application must be made no more than two business days from the date of receiving the decision of the appropriate person.

MINUTES OF CREDITORS' AND CONTRIBUTORIES' DECISIONS

4.44   Rule 15.40 of the Rules provides for the record of a decision made by decision procedure (and thus a decision of creditors or contributories, in contrast to a decision of members, which is provided for by Rule 15.41 of the Rules and CA 2006). By Rule 15.40(1) of the Rules, the convener or chair must cause a record of the decision procedure to be kept, and by Rule 15.40(2) of the Rules, in the case of a meeting, the record must be in the form of a minute of the meeting. By sub-Rule (3), the record must be authenticated by the convener or chair and be retained by the officeholder as part of the records of the insolvency proceedings in question. By sub-Rule (4), the record must identify the proceedings, and must include:

(a) in the case of a decision procedure of creditors, a list of the names of the creditors who participated and their claims;

(b) in the case of a decision procedure of contributories, a list of the names of the contributories who participated;

(c) where a decision is taken on the election of members of a creditors' committee or liquidation committee, the names and addresses of those elected;

(d) a record of any change to the result of the resolution made under Rule 15.38(6) (changing a resolution because of the exclusion of an excluded person whose vote was material) and the reason for any such change; and

(e) in any case, a record of every decision made and how creditors voted.

4.45 By Rule 15.40(5) of the Rules, where a decision is sought using the deemed consent procedure, a record must be made of the procedure, authenticated by the convener, and must be retained by the office-holder as part of the records of the insolvency proceedings in question. By sub-Rule (6), this record under sub-Rule (5) must identify the proceedings, state whether or not the decision was taken, and contain a list of the creditors or contributories who objected to the decision, and in the case of creditors, their claims. By sub-Rule (7), a record under Rule 15.40 of the Rules must also identify any decision procedure (or the deemed consent procedure) by which the decision had previously been sought.

CREDITORS' COMMITTEE

Formation of creditors' committee

4.46 By Rule 3.39(1) of the Rules, where the administrator is required to seek a decision from the company's creditors under Rule 3.38 of the Rules (the reference to the administrator being required by Schedule B1 paragraph 51 of IA 1986 to seek approval from the company's creditors of the statement of proposals made under Schedule B1 paragraph 49 of IA 1986), the administrator must at the same time deliver to the creditors a notice inviting them to decide whether a creditors' committee should be established if sufficient creditors are willing to be members of the committee. Pursuant to Schedule B1 paragraph 57(1) of IA 1986, the company's creditors may, in accordance with the Rules, establish a creditors' committee. By Rule 17.3(1) of the Rules, a creditors' committee in an administration must have at least three members but not more than five members. By Rule 3.39(2) of the Rules, the notice inviting creditors to form a creditors' committee must also invite nominations for membership of the committee, such nominations to be received by the administrator by a date to be specified in the notice. By Rule 3.39(3) of the Rules, the notice must state that any nominations must be delivered to the administrator by the specified date and can only be accepted if the administrator is satisfied as to the creditor's eligibility under Rule 17.4 of the Rules. By Rule 3.39(4) of the Rules, a notice under Rule 3.39 must also be delivered to the creditors at any other time when the administrator seeks a decision from creditors and a creditors' committee has not already been established at that time. The eligibility criteria for serving on the creditors' committee is set out in Rule 17.4(2) of the Rules, which provides that a creditor is eligible to be a member of such a committee if the person has proved for a debt, the debt is not fully secured and neither the proof has been wholly disallowed for voting purposes, or the proof has been wholly rejected for the purpose of distribution or dividend. By Rule 17.4(3) of the Rules, no person can be a member of a committee as both a creditor and a contributory. By Rule 17.4(4) of the Rules, a body corporate may be a member of a creditors' committee, but it cannot act otherwise than by a representative appointed under Rule 17.17 of the Rules (committee members' representatives).

4.47   By Rule 17.5(1) of the Rules, where the creditors decide that a creditors' committee should be established, the convener or chair of the decision procedure (if not the administrator) must as soon as reasonably practicable deliver a notice of the decision to the administrator and where a decision has also been made as to membership of the committee, inform the administrator of the names and addresses of the persons elected to be members of the committee. By Rule 17.5(2) of the Rules, before a person may act as a member of the committee that person must agree to do so. By Rule 17.5 (3) of the Rules, a person's proxy-holder attending a meeting establishing the committee or, in the case of a corporation, its duly appointed representative, may give such agreement (unless the proxy or instrument conferring authority contains a statement to the contrary). By Rule 17.5(4) of the Rules, where a decision has been made to establish a committee but not as to its membership, the administrator must seek a decision from the creditors (about creditor members of the committee). By Rule 17.5(5) of the Rules, the committee is not established (and accordingly cannot act) until the administrator has delivered a notice of its membership in accordance with Rule 17.5(9) of the Rules (notice to the registrar or companies). By Rule 17.5(6) of the Rules, the notice must contain a statement that the committee has been duly constituted, identification details for any company that is a member of the committee, the full name and address of each member that is not a company, and by Rule 17.5(7) of the Rules the notice must be authenticated and dated by the office-holder. By Rule 17.5(8) of the Rules, the notice must be delivered as soon as reasonably practicable after the minimum number of persons required by Rule 17.3 of the Rules have agreed to act as members and been elected. By Rule 17.5(9) of the Rules, the administrator must also, as soon as reasonably practicable, deliver the notice to the registrar of companies.

4.48   Its principal functions comprise assisting the administrator in discharging his own functions[40] and acting in relation to him in such manner as may be agreed from time to time[41]. The committee also has a number of specific powers and duties. It is empowered in certain circumstances to apply for the appointment of a replacement administrator[42] and in the case of an administrator appointed by a qualified floating charge holder under Schedule B1 paragraph 14 of IA 1986, or an administrator appointed by the company or the directors under Schedule B1 paragraph 22 of IA 1986, the creditors committee may provide the discharge of the administrator at a time appointed by resolution of

---

40   Ie managing the affairs, business and property of the company: Schedule B1 paragraph 59 of IA 1986.

41   Rule 17.2 of the Rules.

42   Where an administrator appointed by the court dies, resigns, is removed from office or vacates office: Schedule B1 paragraph 91(1) of IA 1986. See further, **PARAGRAPH 17.36** *post*.

the creditors' committee (provided the administrator has not made a statement pursuant to Schedule B1 paragraph 52(1)(b) of IA 1986 that the company has insufficient property to enable a distribution to be made to unsecured creditors other than by virtue of the prescribed part provisions set out in section 176A of IA 1986). By Rule 3.52(1) of the Rules, where the administrator has made a statement of pre-administration costs under Rule 3.35(10)(a) of the Rules, the creditors' committee may determine whether and to what extent the unpaid pre-administration costs set out in the statement are approved for payment. The creditors' committee is also entitled by Rule 3.63(1) to (3) and (4)(b) of the Rules to be notified of the administrator's intention to resign. By Rule 3.65(1) and (2)(c) of the Rules, the creditors' committee must also be served with any application made under Schedule B1 paragraph 88 of IA 1986 to remove the administrator from office. By Rule 14.13 of the Rules, with the permission of the creditors' committee, the administrator may divide any property, which from its peculiar nature or other special circumstances cannot be readily or advantageously sold in its existing form among the company's creditors according to its estimated value[43]. The creditors' committee also plays an important role in the fixing of the administrator's remuneration by Rules 18.18 and 18.24 to 18.28 of the Rules. Further, the views of the creditors' committee will often be regarded by the court as an informed reflection of the likely views of the company's creditors as a whole[44], although the extent to which the views of the committee are truly representative of the creditors as a whole will obviously depend on the facts. It has been said that the court should only direct the administrators to act contrary to a vote of the committee in exceptional circumstances[45].

4.49 Pursuant to Schedule B1 paragraph 57(3) of IA 1986, a creditors' committee may require the administrator to attend on the committee at any reasonable time of which he is given at least seven days' notice and to provide the committee with information about the exercise of his functions. By Rule 17.22 of the Rules, the notice delivered to the administrator requiring his attendance must be accompanied by a copy of the resolution and must be authenticated by a member of the committee. By Rule 17.22(3) of the Rules, a member's representative may authenticate the notice for the member. By Rule 17.22(4) of the Rules, the meeting at which the administrator's attendance is required must be fixed by the committee for a business day, and must be held at such time and place as the administrator-holder determines. By Rule 17.22(5) of the Rules, where the administrator so attends, the committee may elect one of its number to be chair of the meeting in place of the administrator or an appointed person.

OPERATION OF CREDITORS' COMMITTEE

4.50 By Rule 17.27 of the Rules, it is provided that the acts of a creditors' committee are valid notwithstanding any defect in the appointment, election

---

43 See also Rule 18.10 of the Rules.
44 See eg *Re Smallman Construction Ltd* [1989] BCLC 420, *Re WBSL Realisations 1992 Ltd* [1995] 2 BCLC 576 at 579 and *Re Exchange Travel (Holdings) Ltd* [1993] BCLC 887 (in which the committee was separately represented on the administrators' contested application for their release).
45 *Re C E King Ltd* [2000] 2 BCLC 297 at 306.

or qualifications of a member of the committee or a committee member's representative or in the formalities of its establishment.

4.51   By Rule 17.17(1) of the Rules a member of the committee may, in relation to the business of the committee, be represented by another person duly authorised by the member for that purpose. By Rule 17.17(2) of the Rules, a person acting as a committee member's representative must hold a letter of authority entitling that person to act (either generally or specifically) and authenticated by or on behalf of the committee member. By Rule 17.17(3) of the Rules, a proxy or an instrument conferring authority (in respect of a person authorised to represent a corporation) is to be treated as a letter of authority to act generally (unless the proxy or instrument conferring authority contains a statement to the contrary). By Rule 17.17(4) of the Rules, the chair at a meeting of the committee may call on a person claiming to act as a committee member's representative to produce a letter of authority, and may exclude that person if no letter of authority is produced at or by the time of the meeting or if it appears to the chair that the authority is deficient. By Rule 17.17(5) of the Rules, a committee member may not be represented by another member of the committee, or by a person who is at the same time representing another committee member or by a body corporate or by an undischarged bankrupt, or by a person whose estate has been sequestrated and who has not been discharged, or by a person to whom a moratorium period under a debt relief order applies or by a person who is subject to a company director's disqualification order or a company director's disqualification undertaking, or by a person who is subject to a bankruptcy restrictions order (including an interim order), a bankruptcy restrictions undertaking, a debt relief restrictions order (including an interim order) or a debt relief restrictions undertaking. By Rule 17.17(6) of the Rules, where a representative authenticates any document on behalf of a committee member the fact that the representative authenticates as a representative must be stated below the authentication.

4.52   By Rule 17.7(1) of the Rules, the administrator must deliver or file a notice if there is a change in membership of the committee which, by Rule 17.7(2) of the Rules, must contain the date of the original notice in respect of the constitution of the committee and the date of the last notice of membership given (if any), a statement that the notice of membership replaces the previous notice, identification details for any company that is a member of the committee, the full name and address of any member that is not a company, a statement whether any member has become a member since the issue of the previous notice and the identification details for a company or otherwise the full name of any member named in the previous notice who is no longer a member and the date the membership ended. By Rule 17.7(3) of the Rules, the notice must be authenticated and dated by the office-holder and by Rule 17.7(4) of the Rules must, as soon as reasonably practicable, be delivered to the registrar of companies.

4.53   Where there is a vacancy among the creditor members of a creditors' committee or where the number of creditor members of the committee is fewer than the maximum allowed, Rule 17.8 of the Rules applies, which provides by Rule 17.8(2) of the Rules that a vacancy need not be filled if the administrator and a majority of the remaining creditor members agree, and if the total number of creditor members does not fall below three. By Rule 17.8(3) of the Rules the administrator is given discretion to appoint a creditor, who is qualified under Rule 17.4 of the Rules to be a member of the committee, to fill a vacancy or as an additional member of the committee, if a majority of the remaining creditor members of the committee (provided there are at least two) agree to the appointment and if the creditor agrees to act. By Rule 17.8(4) of the Rules, alternatively, the administrator may seek a decision from creditors to appoint a creditor (with that creditor's consent) to fill the vacancy. By Rule 17.8(5) of the Rules, where the vacancy is filled by an appointment made by a decision of creditors which is not convened or chaired by the administrator, the convener or chair must report the appointment to the administrator.

4.54 As regards resignation or termination of membership, by Rule 17.10 of the Rules a member of a committee may resign by informing the administrator in writing. By Rule 17.11 of the Rules, a person's membership of a committee is automatically terminated if that person becomes bankrupt (in which case the person's trustee in bankruptcy replaces the bankrupt as a member of the committee), if that person is a person to whom a moratorium period under a debt relief order applies, if that person neither attends nor is represented at three consecutive meetings (unless it is resolved at the third of those meetings that this Rule is not to apply in that person's case), if that person has ceased to be eligible to be a member of the committee under Rule 17.4 of the Rules, or if that person ceases to be a creditor or is found never to have been a creditor. By Rule 17.12 of the Rules, a creditor member of a committee can be removed by a decision of the creditors through a decision procedure, save that by Rule 17.12(2) of the Rules at least 14 days' notice must be given of a decision procedure for removal.

4.55 By Rule 17.14(1) of the Rules, meetings of the committee are required to be held when and where determined by the administrator. By Rule 17.14(2) of the Rules, the administrator must call a first meeting of the committee to take place within six weeks of the committee's establishment, and by Rule 17.14(3) of the Rules, after the calling of the first meeting, the administrator is required to call a meeting if so requested by a member of the committee or a member's representative (with the meeting then to be held within 21 days of the request being received by the administrator), and for a specified date, if the committee has previously resolved that a meeting be held on that date. By Rule 17.14(4) of the Rules, the office-holder must give five business days' notice of the venue of a meeting to each member of the committee (or a member's representative, if designated for that purpose), except where the requirement for notice has been waived by or on behalf of a member (and the waiver, by Rule 17.14(5) of the Rules may be signified either at or before the meeting). By Rule 17.15 of the Rules, the chair at a meeting of a committee must be the administrator or an appointed person. By Rule 17.16 of the Rules, as regards a quorum, a meeting of a committee is duly constituted if due notice of it has been delivered to all the members, and at least two of the members are in attendance or represented.

4.56 By Rule 17.20(1) of the Rules, remote attendance is possible for meetings where the administrator considers it appropriate, so that a meeting may be conducted and held in such a way that persons who are not present together at the same place may attend it. By Rule 17.20(2) of the Rules, a person attends such a meeting who is able to exercise that person's right to speak and vote at the meeting, and by Rule 17.20(3) of the Rules it is provided that a person is able to exercise the right to speak at a meeting when that person is in a position to communicate during the meeting to all those attending the meeting any information or opinions which that person has on the business of the meeting. By Rule 17.20(4) of the Rules, a person is able to exercise the right to vote at a meeting when that person is able to vote, during the meeting, on resolutions or determinations put to the vote at the meeting, and that person's vote can be taken into account in determining whether or not such resolutions or determinations are passed at the same time as the votes of all the other persons attending the meeting. By Rule 17.20(5) of the Rules, where such a meeting is to be held the administrator must make whatever arrangements the administrator considers appropriate to enable those attending the meeting to exercise their rights to speak or vote and verify the identity of those attending the meeting and to ensure the security of any electronic means used to enable attendance. By Rule 17.20(6) of the Rules, a requirement in the Rules to specify a place for the meeting may be satisfied by specifying the arrangements the administrator proposes to enable persons to exercise their rights to speak or vote where in the reasonable opinion of the administrator a meeting will be attended by persons who will not be present together at the same place and it is unnecessary or inexpedient to specify a place for the meeting. By Rule 17.20(7) of the Rules, in making the arrangements referred to in sub-Rule (6) and in forming the opinion referred to, the administrator must have regard to the legitimate interests of the committee members or their representatives attending the meeting in the efficient despatch of the business of the meeting. By Rule 17.20(8) of the Rules, where the notice of a meeting does not specify a place for the meeting the administrator must specify a place for the meeting if at least one member of the committee requests him to do so in accordance with Rule 17.21 of the Rules.

4.57 Rule 17.21 of the Rules provides for where a member of the committee requests that a place for a meeting should be specified. By Rule 17.21(2) of the Rules, the request must be made within three business days of the date on which the administrator delivered the notice of the meeting in question. By Rule 17.21(3) of the Rules, where the administrator considers that the request has been properly made in accordance with Rule 17.21 of the Rules, the administrator must deliver notice to all those previously given notice of the meeting that it is to be held at a specified place, and as to whether the date and time are to remain the same or not and must fix a venue for the meeting, the date of which must be not later than seven business days after the original date for the meeting, and must give three business days' notice of the venue to all those previously given notice of the meeting. By Rule 17.21(5) of the Rules, where the administrator has specified a place for the meeting in response to a request under Rule 17.20(8) of the Rules, the chairman of the meeting must attend the meeting by being present in person at that place.

4.58 Voting rights and resolutions of the committee are dealt with by Rules 17.18 and 17.19 of the Rules. By Rule 17.18(1) of the Rules, at a meeting of the committee, each member (whether the member is in attendance or is represented by a representative) has one vote, and by Rule 17.18(2) of the Rules, a resolution is passed when a majority of the members attending or represented have voted in favour of it. By Rule 17.18(3) of the Rules, every resolution passed must be recorded in writing and authenticated by the chair, either separately or as part of the minutes of the meeting, and the record must be kept with the records of the proceedings.

4.59 Resolutions can be passed by correspondence by Rule 17.19 of the Rules. Rule 17.19(1) of the Rules provides that the administrator may seek to obtain the agreement of the committee to a resolution by delivering to every member (or the member's representative designated for the purpose) details of the proposed resolution. By Rule 17.19(2) of the Rules, the details must be set out in such a way that the recipient may indicate agreement or dissent and where there is more than one resolution may indicate agreement to or dissent from each one separately. By Rule 17.19(3) of the Rules, a member of the committee may, within five business days from the delivery of details of the proposed resolution, require the administrator to summon a meeting of the committee to consider the matters raised by the proposed resolution. By Rule 17.19(4) of the Rules, in the absence of such a request, the resolution is passed by the committee if a majority of the members (excluding any who are not permitted to vote by reason of Rule 17.25(4)) deliver notice to the administrator that they agree with the resolution. By Rule 17.19(5) of the Rules a copy of every resolution passed in this way, and a note that the agreement of the committee was obtained, must be kept with the records of the proceedings.

4.60 The administrator is required to defray out of the assets of the company the reasonable travelling expenses of the members of the committee or their representatives directly incurred in relation to their attendance at meetings of the committee or otherwise on the business of the committee, provided there is a six-week gap since the previous meeting (unless the meeting is summoned by the administrator)[46]. The members of the committee are not entitled to reimbursement of any other expenses[47]. Rule 3.51(2)(g) of the Rules provides expressly for necessary disbursements by the administrator in the course of the administration, including any expenses incurred by members of the creditors' committee or their representatives and allowed for by the administrator under Rule 17.24 of the Rules.

CONFLICTS OF INTEREST

4.61 During his membership of the committee, a member is likely to come into possession of information confidential to the company. Pursuant to Rule 1.58 of the Rules, where an administrator considers that a document forming part of the records of the insolvency proceedings should be treated as confidential or is of such a nature that its disclosure would be prejudicial to the conduct of the proceedings or might reasonably be expected to lead to violence against any person, the administrator may decline to allow it to be inspected by a person who would otherwise be entitled to inspect it, including members of a creditors' committee, subject to direction of the court[48]. Membership of the creditors' committee does not prevent a person from dealing with the company while the company is in administration[49], provided that any transactions in the course of such dealings are in good faith and for value[50]. A statutory remedy is given to any person interested to make application to the court to set aside any such

---

46   Rule 17.24(1) and (2) of the Rules.
47   It is thought that there may be cases in which it would be proper for the administrator to procure the company to pay expenses of members of the committee, even though he may be under no strict obligation to do so.
48   Rule 1.58(2), (3) and (4) of the Rules.
49   *A fortiori* once the appointment of an administrator has ceased to have effect.
50   Rule 17.26(2) of the Rules.

transaction which appears not to be in good faith[51] and for value[52]. The court has power to set aside a transaction and make such other order about the transaction as it thinks just including an account or compensation[53].

4.62   Similarly, where a member of a creditors' committee has an interest in any particular matter which is adverse to the interests of the company or the insolvent estate as a whole, he may have to withdraw from discussion of that matter, and it may be inappropriate for the administrator to provide him with any information relating to it. Indeed, as a fiduciary[54], it is up to the member himself to ensure that he does nothing which has the effect of putting his other interests in conflict with, or ahead of, his interests as a representative of the insolvent estate. In a difficult case, it is always open to the administrator to apply to the court for directions[55].

MEETINGS OF MEMBERS

4.63   Save where it is sought to achieve the approval of a voluntary arrangement under Part I of IA 1986 or the sanctioning of a compromise or scheme of arrangement under Part 26 of CA 2006, an administrator will rarely need to summon meetings of the members of a company subject to administration proceedings[56]. Nevertheless, pursuant to Schedule B1 paragraph 62 of IA 1986[57], an administrator has power to call a meeting of members of the company to which he has been appointed[58].

4.64   As regards company meetings, Rules 15.41 to 15.46 of the Rules supplement the provisions of CA 2006 and general provisions of English law, or relevant local law as applicable. Rule 15.41(1) of the Rules provides that unless IA 1986 or the Rules provide otherwise, a company meeting must be called and conducted, and records of the meeting must be kept in accordance with the law of England and Wales, including any applicable provision in or made under CA

---

51   It is thought that where a transaction involved the misuse of confidential information, the requirement of good faith would not be satisfied.
52   There is no definition of what would constitute value for these purposes (cf section 238(4) of IA 1986), but the wording is similar to section 42 of the Bankruptcy Act 1914 (now repealed).
53   Rule 17.26(3) of the Rules.
54   *Re F T Hawkins & Co Ltd* [1952] Ch 881, which concerned a committee of inspection in a winding up. See also *Re Geiger* [1915] 1 KB 439 at 447 and *Re Bulmer* [1937] Ch 499.
55   Under Schedule B1 paragraph 63 of IA 1986.
56   Although the members will normally have no commercial interest in an administration, their shares being worthless, nevertheless the formal requirements are that a public company must hold an annual general meeting within six months of its accounting reference date (being the financial year end) pursuant to section 336(1) of CA 2006. Private companies are not required to hold an annual general meeting, but they may choose to do so, or would need to do so if their Articles require an annual general meeting. The exception to private companies not having to hold an annual general meeting is in respect of traded companies, which by section 366 of CA 2006 is required to hold an annual general meeting within nine months of the year end.
57   As amended by Schedule 9 paragraph 10(23) of SBEEA 2015.
58   One such circumstance in which it used to be necessary to obtain the shareholders' resolution, even in administration, concerned substantial property transactions (the acquisition of substantial non-cash assets by or from directors) (see the former section 320 of the repealed CA 1985 and cases such as *Demite Ltd v Protect Health Ltd* [1998] BCC 638 (a receivership case but the same principle used to apply in an administration). Now, the provisions of sections 190–196 of CA 2006 apply, and by section 193 of CA 2006, approval of members is not required for an arrangement entered into by a company which is being wound up (unless it is in a members' voluntary winding up) or is in administration.

2006, in the case of a company incorporated either in England and Wales, or one incorporated outside the United Kingdom other than in an EEA state. By Rule 15.41(1)(b) of the Rules, unless IA 1986 or the Rules provide otherwise, a company meeting of a company incorporated in an EEA state other than the United Kingdom must be called and conducted, and records of the meeting must be kept in accordance with the law of that state applicable to meetings of the company. By Rule 15.41(2) of the Rules, for the purpose of Rule 15.41 of the Rules, reference to a company meeting called and conducted to resolve, decide or determine a particular matter includes a reference to that matter being resolved, decided or determined by written resolution of a private company passed in accordance with section 288 of CA 2006.

4.65   By Rule 15.41(3) of the Rules, in an administration, in summoning any company meeting the administrator must have regard to the convenience of the members when fixing the venue, and the chair of the meeting must be either the administrator or an appointed person.

4.66   Section 246A of IA 1986 allows for remote attendance at a meeting of members. By section 246A(3), where the convener thinks it appropriate, the meeting of members may be conducted and held in such a way that persons who are not present together at the same place may attend it. By section 246A(4), where a meeting is conducted and held in the manner referred to in section 246A(3), a person attends the meeting if that person is able to exercise any rights which that person may have to speak and vote at the meeting[59]. By section 246A(6), it is the duty of the convener of the meeting to make whatever arrangements he considers appropriate to enable those attending the meeting to exercise their rights to speak or vote, and to ensure the identification of those attending the meeting and the security of any electronic means used to enable attendance. By section 246A(7), where in the reasonable opinion of the convener a meeting will be attended by persons who will not be present together at the same place, and it is unnecessary or inexpedient to specify a place for the meeting, any requirement under IA 1986 or the Rules to specify a place for the meeting may be satisfied by specifying the arrangements the convener proposes to enable persons to exercise their rights to speak or vote. By section 246A(9), a request can be made for the convener to specify a place for the meeting if members with not less than 10 per cent of the total voting rights of all members having at the date of the request a right to vote at the meeting request it.

4.67   The Rules on remote attendance are set out in Rules 15.42 and 15.43 of the Rules. By Rule 15.42(1) of the Rules, when a meeting is to be summoned and held in accordance with section 246A(3), the convener must notify all those to whom notice of the meeting is being given of the ability of a person claiming to be an excluded person to request an indication in accordance with Rule 15.45 of the Rules, the ability of a person within Rule 15.46(1) of the Rules to make

---

[59]   Section 246A(5) of IA 1986 provides that, for the purposes of section 246A, a person is able to exercise the right to speak at a meeting when that person is in a position to communicate to all those attending the meeting, during the meeting, any information or opinions which that person has on the business of the meeting, and the subsection also provides that, for the purposes of section 246A, a person is able to exercise the right to vote at a meeting when that person is able to vote, during the meeting, on resolutions put to the vote at the meeting and that person's vote can be taken into account in determining whether or not such resolutions are passed at the same time as the votes of all the other persons attending the meeting.

a complaint in accordance with that Rule, and in either case, the period within which a request or complaint must be made.

4.68   By Rule 15.43 of the Rules, if a request is made under section 246A(9)(b) to require the convener to specify a place for the meeting, then by Rule 15.43(2) of the Rules the request must be accompanied by a list of the members making or concurring with the request and their voting rights, and from each person concurring, confirmation of that person's concurrence. By Rule 15.43(3) of the Rules, the request must be delivered to the convener within seven business days of the date on which the convener delivered the notice of the meeting in question. By Rule 15.43(4) of the Rules, where the convener considers that the request has been properly made in accordance with IA 1986 and with Rule 15.43 of the Rules, the convener must deliver notice to all those previously given notice of the meeting that it is to be held at a specified place, and as to whether the date and time are to remain the same or not, and the convener must set a venue (including specification of a place) for the meeting, the date of which must be not later than 28 days after the original date for the meeting, and the convener must deliver at least 14 days' notice of that venue to all those previously given notice of the meeting. By Rule 15.43(5) of the Rules, where the convener has specified a place for the meeting in response to a request of the requisite number of members, the chair of the meeting must attend the meeting by being present in person at that place.

4.69   There are similar provisions applying to members who are 'excluded persons' as discussed in respect of creditors above. As regards members, Rule 15.44(1) of the Rules provides that an 'excluded person' means a person who has taken all steps necessary to attend a company meeting under the arrangements which have been put in place by the convener of the meeting under section 246A(6) of IA 1986, but do not enable that person to attend the whole or part of that meeting. By Rule 15.44(2) of the Rules, where the chair becomes aware during the course of the meeting that there is an excluded person, the chair may continue the meeting, or declare the meeting void and convene the meeting again, or declare the meeting valid up to the point where the person was excluded and adjourn the meeting. By Rule 15.44(3) of the Rules, where the chair continues the meeting, the meeting is valid unless the chair decides in consequence of a complaint under Rule 15.46 of the Rules to declare the meeting void and hold the meeting again, or unless the court directs otherwise. Rule 15.44(4) of the Rules provides that, without prejudice to sub-Rule 15.44(2), where the chair becomes aware during the course of the meeting that there is an excluded person, the chair may, in the chair's discretion and without an adjournment, declare the meeting suspended for any period up to one hour.

4.70   Rules 15.45 and 15.46 of the Rules provide for an excluded person to obtain information, and for a complaint process. By Rule 15.45(1) of the Rules, a person who claims to be an excluded person may request an indication of what occurred during the period of that person's claimed exclusion. By Rule 15.45(2) of the Rules, the request must be made as soon as reasonably practicable, and in any event, not later than 4pm on the business day following the day on which the exclusion is claimed to have occurred, and the request (by Rule 15.45(3) of the Rules) must be made to the chair where it is made during the course of the business of the meeting, or to the convener where it is made after the conclusion of the business of the meeting. By Rule 15.45(4) of the Rules, where satisfied that the person making the request is an excluded person, the person to whom the request is made under Rule 15.45(3) of the Rules must deliver the requested indication to the excluded person as soon as reasonably practicable, and in any event, not later than 4pm on the business day following the day on which the request was made under Rule 15.45(1) of the Rules.

4.71 The complaint process is provided for in Rule 15.46 of the Rules, which provides that a person may make a complaint who is, or claims to be, an excluded person or who attends the meeting and claims to have been adversely affected by the actual, apparent or claimed exclusion of another person. By Rule 15.46(2) of the Rules, the complaint must be made to the chair, where the complaint is made during the course of the meeting, or to the convener, where it is made after the meeting. By Rule 15.46(3) of the Rules, the complaint must be made as soon as reasonably practicable and, in any event, no later than 4pm on the business day following the day on which the person was, appeared or claimed to be excluded, or where an indication is sought under Rule 15.45 of the Rules, the day on which the complainant received the indication.

4.72 By Rule 15.46(4) of the Rules, upon receipt of the complaint, the chair or the convener must, as soon as reasonably practicable following receipt of the complaint, consider whether there is an excluded person; where satisfied that there is an excluded person, consider the complaint; and where satisfied that there has been prejudice, take such action as the appropriate person considers fit to remedy the prejudice. By Rule 15.46(5) and (6) of the Rules, where the chair or convener is satisfied that the complainant is an excluded person and that a resolution was voted on at the meeting during the period of the person's exclusion and that the excluded person asserts how the excluded person intended to vote on the resolution, and where the chair or convener is satisfied that if the excluded person had voted as that person intended it would have changed the result of the resolution, then the chair or convener must, as soon as reasonably practicable count the intended vote as having been cast in that way, must amend the record of the result of the resolution, must where notice of the result of the resolution has been delivered to those entitled to attend the meeting, deliver notice to them of the change and the reason for it, and must where notice of the result of the resolution has yet to be delivered to those entitled to attend the meeting, include in the notice details of the change and the reason for it. By Rule 15.46(7) of the Rules, where satisfied that more than one complainant is an excluded person, the chair or convener must have regard to the combined effect of the intended votes. By Rule 15.46(8) of the Rules, the chair or convener must deliver notice to the complainant of any decision as soon as reasonably practicable. By Rule 15.46(9) of the Rules, a complainant who is not satisfied by the action of the chair or the convener may apply to the court for directions and any application must be made no more than two business days from the date of receiving the decision of the chair or convener.

5 Powers, duties, status and liabilities of an administrator

THE PURPOSES FOR WHICH AN ADMINISTRATOR'S POWERS MAY BE EXERCISED

5.1 Under IA 1986, an administrator is given wide powers to manage the affairs, business and property of the company to which he has been appointed. Not only does the administrator have a wide range of specific powers set out in Schedule 1 to IA 1986[1], but it is further expressly provided by Schedule B1 paragraph 59(1) that he may do 'anything necessary or expedient for the management of the affairs, business and property of the company'. Each of the specific powers set out in Schedule 1 is expressed to be without prejudice to the generality of paragraph 59(1)[2]. The similar form of words under the pre-Enterprise Act 2002 law[3] meant that any power of the directors before the making of the administration order was within the powers of the administrator after the order has been made[4] and this remains the case.

5.2 Two limitations, however, must be noted at the outset. First, notwithstanding the width of the management powers conferred on an administrator by IA 1986, it must be borne in mind that in carrying out his functions, the administrator acts as agent of the company[5] so that, *prima facie*, the administrator has no greater power than the company itself as his principal. Thus, it was held in *Re Home Treat Ltd*[6] that an administrator had no power to commit the company to ultra vires acts, ie acts outside the capacity of the company as described by its constitution. Notwithstanding that section 39 of CA 2006 provides that the validity of acts done by a company are not to be called into question on the ground of lack of capacity by reason of anything in the company's constitution, an administrator still should not commit the company to ultra vires acts without having obtained the prior directions of the court. Although any such transaction, in the case of a company which is not a charity, would appear to be binding and enforceable at the suit of both the company itself and the counterparties to such a transaction, an administrator who caused the company to enter into an ultra vires transaction without having obtained appropriate directions would appear to be in breach of duty to the company.

1   Schedule B1 paragraph 60 of IA 1986.
2   Schedule B1 paragraph 59(2) of IA 1986.
3   Section 14(1)(a) of IA 1986.
4   *Denny v Yeldon* [1995] 1 BCLC 560 at 564, a case in which the power in issue was procuring the amendment of the company's pension scheme trust deed.
5   Schedule B1 paragraph 69 of IA 1986.
6   [1991] BCLC 705 per Harman J at 706i–707b.

5.3   Secondly, the administrator must perform his functions with the objective of:

(a)   rescuing the company as a going concern; or

(b)   achieving a better result for the company's creditors as a whole than would be likely if the company were wound up; or

(c)   realising property in order to make a distribution to one or more secured or preferential creditors[7].

It is also fundamental to an administration under IA 1986 that following his appointment an administrator should make a statement setting out his proposals under Schedule B1 paragraph 49 of IA 1986 for achieving the purpose of administration. Once those proposals have been approved by the creditors, with or without modification, the administrator is required to manage the affairs, business and property of the company in accordance with those proposals as from time to time revised[8]. Under the pre-Enterprise Act 2002 law, pending the approval of the administrator's proposals, his powers should not have been exercised for any purpose other than those specified in the administration order; although, even then, if he acted towards the achievement of some other purpose, while he might have been acting improperly, he would not have been acting without power to do so[9]. The present position is different. Neither a court order nor a notice of appointment will identify the specific objective for which an administrator must perform his functions. What is required by Schedule B1 paragraphs 3 and 4 of IA 1986 is that he must perform his functions towards the achievement of each objective in a statutory order of priority and as quickly and efficiently as is reasonably practicable.

5.4   The first objective with which the administrator must perform his functions is that of rescuing the company as a going concern[10]. It is only if he thinks that it is not reasonably practicable to achieve that objective that he is permitted to turn his attention to the objective of achieving a better result for the company's creditors as a whole than would be achieved if the company were wound up without first being in administration[11]. In performing his function with either of these two objectives, the administrator is under a statutory duty to act in the interests of the company's creditors as a whole[12]. This applies irrespective of the circumstances of his appointment or the identity of his appointor. The administrator is only permitted to perform his functions with the objective of realising property in order to make a distribution to one or more secured or preferential creditors if he thinks that it is not reasonably practicable to achieve either of the other objectives[13]. At this stage his duty to perform his functions in the interests of the company's creditors as a whole is qualified: it is replaced by a duty not unnecessarily to harm the interests of the creditors of the company as a whole[14].

---

7   Schedule B1 paragraph 3(1) of IA 1986, defined as the purpose of administration (Schedule B1 paragraph 111(1) of IA 1986).
8   Schedule B1 paragraph 68(1) of IA 1986.
9   *Denny v Yeldon* [1995] 1 BCLC 560.
10   Schedule B1 paragraph 3(1)(a) of IA 1986.
11   Schedule B1 paragraphs 3(1)(b) and 3(3) of IA 1986.
12   Schedule B1 paragraph 3(2) of IA 1986.
13   Schedule B1 paragraph 3(4) of IA 1986.
14   Schedule B1 paragraphs 3(2) and 3(4)(b) of IA 1986.

COURT DIRECTIONS

5.5   Schedule B1 paragraph 68(2) of IA 1986 expressly provides that the administrator must comply with any directions given by the court in connection with his management of the company's affairs, business and property. Such directions may be given, *inter alia*, upon the making of any administration order[15] or on the application of the administrator under Schedule B1 paragraph 63 of IA 1986. They can also be given on the application of a creditor or any other person with a legitimate interest in the directions sought[16]. There are now, however, statutory restrictions on the timing and nature of any directions that the court may give[17]. Thus, such directions may only be given where no proposals have been approved under Schedule B1 paragraph 53, or where the directions are consistent with any proposals or revision, or where the court thinks that the directions are desirable in order to reflect a change in circumstances or because of a misunderstanding about the proposals or any revision to them. It follows that the court has no power to give directions to an administrator to do something inconsistent with the proposals unless the direction is required in order to reflect a change of circumstances. It also follows that the legislation contemplates that where he wishes to do something inconsistent with the proposals the administrator will normally have to obtain a revision to them under Schedule B1 paragraph 54 of IA 1986, using one of the decision procedures set out at Rule 15.3 of the Rules or, if appropriate, the deemed consent procedure described by Rule 15.7 of the Rules[18]. Nonetheless, in principle, even prior to approval of his proposals, an administrator's statutory powers are fully exercisable notwithstanding the absence of any specific or general direction from the court[19]. For a time, this principle seems to have been lost sight of. In a series of decisions[20] it was either assumed or actually decided that the leave of the court was required for the exercise of certain of the administrator's statutory powers before the approval of his proposals under what is now Schedule B1 paragraph 49 (formerly section 23) of IA 1986. However, after a comprehensive review of the authorities it was eventually confirmed that, properly construed, section 17 of IA 1986 empowered an administrator to exercise all of his statutory powers (and in particular to sell

---

15   Schedule B1 paragraph 13(1)(f) of IA 1986.

16   Thus, under the pre-Enterprise Act 2002 law and notwithstanding the absence of any express statutory provision directly authorising the same, the court had power to give directions to an administrator on the application of a creditor: see *Re Mirror Group (Holdings) Ltd* [1992] BCC 972 per Sir Donald Nicholls V-C at 976G–H, or on the application of the owner of goods held by the administrator, see *Barclays Mercantile Business Finance Ltd v Sibec Developments Ltd* [1992] 1 WLR 1253 per Millett J at 1259E–F; cf *Re Atlantic Computer Systems plc* [1992] Ch 505 at 540D–541C.

17   Schedule B1 paragraph 68(3) of IA 1986.

18   By section 246ZE of IA 1986, a physical meeting of creditors may not be held unless requested in writing by at least 10 per cent by value of the company's creditors.

19   Cf *Re Charnley Davies Ltd (No 2)* [1990] BCLC 760 at 767C–E. This follows from the fact that, with effect from his appointment, an administrator is required to perform his functions with the objectives set out in Schedule B1 paragraph 3 of IA 1986, those functions being the doing of anything necessary or expedient for the management of the affairs, business and property of the company. A similar passage in the first edition of this work (dealing with the position under the pre-Enterprise Act 2002 law) was cited with approval by Neuberger J in *Re T & D Industries plc* [2000] 1 BCLC 471 at 482.

20   The concern arose in the context of the sale of the whole of the company's business and undertaking, eg *Re Montin Ltd* [1999] 1 BCLC 663, *Re Osmosis Group Ltd* [1999] 2 BCLC 329 and *Re P D Fuels Ltd* [1999] BCC 450.

all or any of the company's assets) at any stage of the administration[21]. Schedule B1 paragraph 68 now makes it clear that a direction from the court is never a necessary pre-requisite to the exercise by the administrator of any of his statutory powers[22].

5.6 On the other hand, the administrator should be astute not to frustrate the consideration of his proposals by the company's creditors. Where, therefore, an administrator proposes to dispose of in effect the entirety of the company's assets and undertaking prior to obtaining the creditors' decision on whether to accept or reject his proposals, there will be occasions on which he would be wise to seek the directions of the court first[23]. While, however, the court will be sympathetic to such an application where a point of principle is at stake or where the proposal is either contentious or contrary to the administration strategy set out in the evidence, such an application is not one that should be made as a matter of course[24].

5.7 The power to apply for directions pursuant to Schedule B1 paragraphs 63 and 68 of IA 1986 is, of course, exercisable by the administrator at any time during the period for which the appointment of an administrator has effect and may be exercised both after as well as before the administrator's proposals have been approved by the company's creditors[25]. The power is often exercised in order to determine the status of property held by the company in administration or to determine competing claims to such property. Thus, for instance, where an administrator wishes to make use of another party's goods for the purpose of the administration and cannot agree terms, he can apply to the court for directions[26]. If he fails to do so, it is open to the owner to apply to the court to direct the administrator to hand over the goods and to pay compensation in the meantime[27]. If the administrator wrongfully retains goods of another otherwise than for the proper purposes of the administration, for example to use them as a bargaining counter, the court has power to direct the administrator personally to pay compensation for having wrongfully refused consent to repossess them without any right of recoupment against the company's assets[28]. An administrator may also wish to consider applying to the court for directions prior to exercising, or refraining from exercising, his powers, where the creditors' committee or a significant creditor or group of creditors has indicated its opposition to the course of action proposed by the administrator[29]. Under the pre-Enterprise Act 2002

---

21 *Re T & D Industries plc* [2000] 1 BCLC 471 (although he should not act so as to avoid consideration of his proposals unless it is necessary for him to so).
22 *Re Transbus International Ltd* [2004] EWHC 932 (Ch).
23 Cf *Re NS Distribution Ltd* [1990] BCLC 169; *Re Consumer and Industrial Press Ltd* (No 2) (1987) 4 BCC 72; but see also the discussion by the Court of Appeal in *O'Connell v Rollings* [2014] EWCA Civ 639 (paragraphs 78–80).
24 *Re T & D Industries plc* [2000] 1 BCLC 471, in which Neuberger J stressed that an application will not normally be appropriate where there is no opportunity for an *inter partes* hearing at which the advantages and disadvantages of the proposal can be properly argued.
25 It may also be exercised where the creditors have failed to approve the administrator's proposals.
26 *Barclays Mercantile Business Finance Ltd v Sibec Developments Ltd* [1992] 1 WLR 1253 per Millett J at 1259E–G.
27 *Barclays Mercantile Business Finance Ltd v Sibec Developments Ltd* [1992] 1 WLR 1253 per Millett J at 1259E–G.
28 *Barclays Mercantile Business Finance Ltd v Sibec Developments Ltd* [1992] 1 WLR 1253 per Millett J at 1259E–G; see also per Millett J at 1259H–1260B.
29 For example, the various 'waterfall' applications concerning the distribution of the solvent estate of Lehman Brothers International (Europe).

law, the court had an exceptional jurisdiction, to authorise the administrator to implement alternative (and even inconsistent) proposals to those which have been approved by the company's creditors where it was not commercially practicable to call a further meeting of creditors and where it had proved impossible to implement the original proposals as approved[30]. This jurisdiction now exists in a different form[31], in that it can only be exercised where the proposed course is consistent with the approved proposals, or a direction of the court is needed to reflect a change of circumstance or misunderstanding. In practice, these are circumstances in which the old jurisdiction would have been exercised and are little more than a statutory codification of it. In all cases, the administrator should attempt to set out in his application, as specifically as possible, the directions he seeks, if appropriate, specifying alternatives[32].

5.8   Even if requested to do so, the court may decline to give directions to an administrator, particularly where the court is being asked to make in effect a commercial judgment where not all interested parties are represented before the court and where the evidence may not necessarily be complete[33]. In such circumstances, the court may leave it to the administrator to exercise his own judgment leaving open the possibility of a subsequent claim against him for breach of duty or a subsequent application under Schedule B1 paragraph 74 of IA 1986[34]. It is only in the clearest case that the court would be prepared to second-guess a matter which the administrator is far better equipped to determine[35].

SPECIFIC POWERS OF AN ADMINISTRATOR

5.9   Schedule 1 to IA 1986 sets out a large number of specific powers of an administrator[36]. The same powers are conferred upon an administrative receiver[37], although the circumstances in which an administrative receiver can still be appointed are now restricted[38]. The powers in question are as follows:

(a)   to take possession of, collect and get in the property of the company and, for that purpose, to take such proceedings as may seem to an administrator expedient;

(b)   to sell or otherwise dispose of the property of the company by public auction or private contract or, in Scotland, to sell, hire out or otherwise to dispose of the property of the company by public roup[39] or private bargain;

(c)   to raise or borrow money and to grant security therefor over the property of the company;

---

30   *Re Smallman Construction Ltd* [1989] BCLC 420.
31   Schedule B1 paragraph 68(3) of IA 1986.
32   *Re Synthetic Technology Ltd* [1990] BCLC 378.
33   Cf *Re N S Distribution Ltd* [1990] BCLC 169 per Harman J at 170c–171g and see *Re T & D Industries plc* [2000] 1 BCLC 471, 483 applied in *Re Ciro Citterio Menswear plc* [2002] EWHC 897 (Ch), *Re Transbus International Ltd* [2004] EWHC 932 (Ch) and *Re M F Global UK Ltd* [2014] EWHC 2222 (Ch).
34   See **CHAPTER 14** *post*.
35   *MTI Trading Systems Ltd v Winter* [1998] BCC 591, *Re C E King Ltd* [2000] 2 BCLC 297 and *BLV Realty Group II Ltd* [2009] EWHC 2994 (Ch).
36   Schedule B1 paragraph 60 of IA 1986.
37   Section 42(1) of IA 1986.
38   Sections 72A–GA of IA 1986.
39   'Roup' is the traditional Scottish term for 'auction'; sale by such auction is very rare in practice.

(d) to appoint a solicitor or accountant or other professionally qualified person to assist him in the performance of his functions;

(e) to bring or defend any action or other legal proceedings in the name and on behalf of the company;

(f) to refer to arbitration any question affecting the company;

(g) to effect and maintain insurances in respect of the business and property of the company;

(h) to use the company's seal;

(i) to do all acts and to execute in the name and on behalf of the company any deed, receipt or other document;

(j) to draw, accept, make and endorse any bill of exchange or promissory note in the name and on behalf of the company;

(k) to appoint any agent to do any business which he is unable to do himself or which can more conveniently be done by an agent and to employ and dismiss employees;

(l) to do all such things (including the carrying out of works) as may be necessary for the realisation of the property of the company;

(m) to make any payment which is necessary or incidental to the performance of his functions[40];

(n) to carry on the business of the company;

(o) to establish subsidiaries of the company;

(p) to transfer to subsidiaries of the company the whole or any part of the business and property of the company;

(q) to grant or to accept a surrender of a lease or tenancy of any of the property of the company and to take a lease or tenancy of any property required or convenient for the business of the company;

(r) to make any arrangement or compromise on behalf of the company;

(s) to call up any uncalled capital of the company;

(t) to rank and claim in the bankruptcy, insolvency, sequestration or liquidation of any person indebted to the company and to receive dividends, and to accede to trust deeds for the creditors of any such person;

(u) to present or defend a petition for the winding up of the company;

(v) to change the situation of the company's registered office; and

(w) to do all other things incidental to the exercise of the foregoing powers.

Most significantly the powers include the power to carry on the company's business for the purpose of administration. An administrator is therefore free of the limitations which inhibit a liquidator from carrying on a company's business.

5.10 It should be noted that among such powers is the power to present or to defend a petition for the winding up of the company. Any such petition will be the petition of the company acting by the administrator[41]. Save where the company is restored to solvency or where a voluntary arrangement under section 1 of IA 1986[42]

---

40 The extent to which an administrator can make payments to creditors is considered in **CHAPTER 15** *post*.

41 Rule 7.27(1) of the Rules; by Rule 7.4(2) of the Rules, an administrator is a 'relevant office-holder'.

42 **CHAPTER 11** *post*.

or a scheme of arrangement under Part 26 of CA 2006[43] is approved or sanctioned, an administrator will always have to give consideration to the question of whether it is appropriate for the company to be wound up. However, as there is now power to make a distribution in an administration[44] and for the company to be dissolved without first going into liquidation[45], it is no longer the case that a winding up will be the normal exit route from an administration in all other circumstances. Furthermore, where liquidation is the appropriate way forward, it is no longer the case that a winding up can only follow on the making of a winding-up order on a petition presented to the court. It is now possible for the administrator to procure a voluntary winding up as if a resolution to that end had been passed[46]. The various exit routes from administration are considered in greater detail in **Chapter 17** *post*.

5.11   An administrator has express power under Schedule B1 paragraph 61 of IA 1986 to remove any director of the company and to appoint a director of it, whether or not to fill a vacancy. He may also call a meeting of the members or creditors of the company[47]. If, however, the removal of a particular director amounts to a breach of contract by the company, the company will be liable in damages to the director concerned for any loss suffered by him as a result of such breach[48]. Nevertheless, the power to appoint and remove directors provides the administrator with a valuable weapon with which to enforce, if necessary, the provision in Schedule B1 paragraph 64 that the company or its officers may not exercise a management power without the consent of the administrator. A management power is widely defined to mean a power which could be exercised so as to interfere with the exercise of the administrator's powers, whether that management power is conferred by an enactment or an instrument. The consent of the administrator, may be general or specific. The relationship between the administrator and the company's officers is considered in more detail in **Chapter 7** *post*.

5.12   The administrator is required to exercise the power to seek a decision from the company's creditors if he is requested, in accordance with the Rules, to do so by creditors whose debts amount to at least 10 per cent of the total debts of the company, or if he is directed to do so by the court[49]. The administrator

43   **Chapter 13** *post*.
44   Schedule B1 paragraph 65 of IA 1986.
45   Schedule B1 paragraph 84 of IA 1986 and **paragraph 17.24ff** *post*. It used to be thought that in the absence of a formal petition, there was no power to make a winding-up order on an application by the administrator to the court for directions: *Re Brooke Marine Ltd* [1988] BCLC 546 and *Re SyntheticTechnology Ltd* [1990] BCLC 378 at 382; cf *Re Charnley Davies Business Services Ltd* (1987) 3 BCC 408, although this was thrown into doubt by *Lancefield v Lancefield* [2002] BPIR 1108, 1111, an insolvent partnership case in which *Re Brooke Marine Ltd* (above) and *Re Synthetic Technology Ltd* (above) do not appear to have been cited. The decision in *Lancefield v Lancefield* has been applied subsequently, and it now seems clear that the court does have jurisdiction to wind up a company in the absence of a winding up petition provided that one or more of the circumstances in section 122 of IA 1986 have been met: *Re Graico Property Co Ltd* [2016] EWHC 2827 (Ch).
46   Schedule B1 paragraph 83 of IA 1986.
47   Schedule B1 paragraph 62 of IA 1986.
48   Compare *Southern Foundries (1926) Ltd v Shirlaw* [1940] AC 701 and *Shindler v Northern Raincoat Co Ltd* [1960] 1 WLR 1038. See also *Astor Chemicals Ltd v Synthetic Technology Ltd* [1990] BCLC 1, *P & C and R & T (Stockport) Ltd* [1991] BCLC 366 and *Barclays Mercantile Business Finance Ltd v Sibec Developments Ltd* [1992] 1 WLR 1253, considered in more detail in **Chapters 6** and **7** *post*. However, if an administrator acting in good faith and in the course of his duties causes a company in administration to breach a pre-administration contract, he will not be liable for the tort of inducing breach of contract (*Lictor Anstalt v MIR Steel UK Ltd* [2011] EWHC 3310 (Ch)).
49   Schedule B1 paragraph 56(1) of IA 1986.

also has a specific power[50] which he must exercise if the company's creditors decided that he must[51], to apply to the court for an order that the appointment of an administrator of the company shall cease to have effect. The exercise of this power is considered in **CHAPTER 17** *post*.

5.13   The administrator's powers are exercisable without the sanction of any creditors' committee appointed pursuant to Schedule B1 paragraph 57 of IA 1986. In this respect, the exercise of the administrator's powers is less circumscribed than the exercise of the more limited powers of a liquidator[52]. Where, however, a proposed exercise of his powers by an administrator is opposed by the creditors' committee, the administrator may wish to consider applying to the court for directions[53].

POWER TO DEAL WITH CHARGED PROPERTY

5.14   In addition to the specific powers mentioned above, an administrator is also given power under Schedule B1 paragraphs 70, 71 and 72 of IA 1986 to deal with property of the company which is subject to a floating charge or other security and with goods in the possession of the company under a hire-purchase agreement, which is defined by Schedule B1 paragraph 111(1) of IA 1986 to include a conditional sale agreement, chattel leasing agreement or a retention of title agreement. The word 'security' is defined[54] as meaning, in relation to England and Wales, any mortgage, charge, lien or other security[55]. It should be noted that these provisions do not apply to market charges as defined by section 173(1) of CA 1989[56], collateral security within the meaning of the Settlement Finality Regulations[57] or charges created or otherwise arising under a financial collateral arrangement within the meaning of FCAR 2003[58].

5.15   Schedule B1 paragraph 70 of IA 1986 deals with property which is subject to a charge which is a floating charge on its creation[59]. Schedule B1 paragraph 71 of IA 1986 deals with property which is subject to any other security[60]. With

---

50   Schedule B1 paragraph 79 of IA 1986.
51   Schedule B1 paragraph 79(2)(c) of IA 1986.
52   Cf sections 165 and 167 of and Schedule 4 to IA 1986 for the position in a winding up.
53   See **PARAGRAPHS 5.5–5.8** *ante*.
54   See section 248 of IA 1986.
55   For wide definitions of the meaning of 'security', see *Bristol Airport plc v Powdrill* [1990] Ch 744, per Sir Nicolas Browne-Wilkinson V-C at 760D and *Smith (Administrator of Cosslett (Contractors) Ltd) v Bridgend County Borough Council* [2002] UKHL 58, [2002] 1 BCLC 77 at 91h; see also **PARAGRAPH 2.7FF** *ante*.
56   These provisions apply in a modified form to some categories of market charge.
57   SI 1999 No 2979.
58   SI 2003 No 3226.
59   See the definition of floating charge in Schedule B1 paragraph 111(1) of IA 1986.
60   For the distinction between a fixed and a floating charge, see, *inter alia*, *Re Yorkshire Woolcombers Association Ltd* [1903] 2 Ch 284, affd *sub nom Illingworth v Houldsworth* [1904] AC 355; *Evans v Rival Granite Quarries Ltd* [1910] 2 KB 979; *Siebe Gorman & Co Ltd v Barclays Bank Ltd* [1979] 2 Lloyds 142; *Re Brightlife Ltd* [1987] Ch 200; *Re Atlantic Computer Systems plc* [1992] Ch 505; *Re Atlantic Medical Ltd* [1993] BCLC 386; *William Gaskell Group Ltd v Highley* [1993] BCC 200; *Re CCG International Enterprises Ltd* [1993] BCLC 1428; *Re G E Tunbridge Ltd* [1995] 1 BCLC 34 (a case arising in an administration); *Re Pearl Maintenance Services Ltd* [1995] 1 BCLC 449; *Royal Trust Bank v National Westminster Bank plc* [1996] 2 BCLC 682; *Re ASRS Establishment Ltd* [2000] 2 BCLC 631; *Chalk v Kahn* [2000] 2 BCLC 361; *Agnew v IRC* [2001] UKPC 28; *Smith (Administrator of Cosslett Contractors Ltd) v Bridgend County BC* [2002] UKHL 58; *Re Spectrum Plus Ltd* [2004] EWHC 09 (Ch); and *Re Harmony Care Homes* [2009] EWHC 1961 (Ch).

respect to property subject to a charge which is a floating charge on its creation, Schedule B1 paragraph 70(1) of IA 1986 provides that the administrator may dispose of or take action relating to such property as if it were not subject to the charge; no prior court order is necessary. Schedule B1 paragraph 70(2) goes on to provide that where property is disposed of in reliance on that power, the holder of the floating charge shall have the same priority in respect of any property of the company directly or indirectly representing the property disposed of as he had in respect of the property disposed of. Presumably, in this context, the use of the word priority connotes the priority to which the chargeholder is entitled over other creditors of the company, whether secured or unsecured, as regards payment of the debt due to him. This priority, however, is itself subject to the priority afforded to debts or liabilities incurred under contracts entered into or contracts of employment adopted by an administrator in the carrying out of his functions and to the administrator's own claims for remuneration and other expenses incurred by him[61]. Unlike a disposal of property subject to other forms of security, the chargeholder is not given a statutory right to receive the market value of the relevant property.

5.16   The priority given to the claims of preferential creditors over the claims of debenture holders secured by a charge which, as created, was a floating charge, has been preserved. This result appears to follow from the combined effect of:

(a)   section 754 of CA 2006, which applies in relation to companies registered in England and Wales, *inter alia*, where, with the consent of the administrator or the court, the debenture holder takes possession of property comprised in the debenture in the course of an administration;

(b)   section 4(4) of IA 1986, which applies to protect the position of preferential creditors where in the course of an administration a voluntary arrangement is agreed;

(c)   section 175 of IA 1986, which gives priority to the payment of preferential debts, *inter alia*, where the company is being wound up following administration; and

(d)   Schedule B1 paragraph 65(2) of IA 1986 which applies section 175 of IA 1986 in relation to any distribution made by an administrator as it applies in a winding up.

This last provision imposes a statutory duty on administrators to pay preferential creditors out of floating charge assets before accounting to the chargeholder for any surplus if, but only if, he is exercising his power to make a distribution. It should be noted, however, that whereas for the purposes of sections 4(4) and 175 and Schedule B1 paragraph 65(2) of IA 1986, the company's preferential creditors will be ascertained as at the date the company enters administration[62], if in the course of an administration, a debenture holder is allowed to take possession, then for the purpose of section 754 of CA 2006, the preferential debts will fall to be ascertained as at the date upon which possession is taken[63]. Presumably, therefore, where the administrator proposes to allow a chargeholder to take possession of assets subject to the security which, as created, was a floating charge, before doing so he should ensure that adequate provision has

---

61   See Schedule B1 paragraph 99(3) and (4) of IA 1986, considered in greater detail in **PARAGRAPH 5.26FF, PARAGRAPH 7.4FF** and **CHAPTER 15** *post*.

62   See section 387(2)(a), (3)(a), (3)(aa), (3)(ab), (3)(ba) and (3A) of IA 1986.

63   Section 754(3) of CA 2006.

been made to enable payment to be made of the preferential debts of the company ascertained as at the date of the administration. Further, the administrator should not normally allow the chargeholder to take possession if that would result in two different sets of preferential creditors having to be paid at the expense of other unsecured creditors[64].

5.17 Where the relevant property is subject to a security, other than one which is a floating charge on its creation, the administrator can only dispose of the property, without the consent of the holder of the security on the making of an order by the court enabling him to dispose of the property as if it were not subject to the security[65]. Likewise, where the relevant property comprises goods in the company's possession under a hire-purchase agreement, conditional sale agreement, chattel leasing agreement or retention of title agreement[66], the administrator can only dispose of the property, without the consent of the owner of the goods, on the making of an order by the court enabling the administrator to dispose of the goods as if all the rights of the owner under the agreement were vested in the company[67]. The court can only make orders under Schedule B1 paragraphs 71(1) and 71(2) of IA 1986 on the application of the administrator and if it thinks that the disposal of the property or goods concerned would be likely to promote the purpose of administration in respect of the company[68].

5.18 Where the administrator applies to the court for an order under Schedule B1 paragraph 71 or 72 of IA 1986, the court fixes a venue for the hearing of the application and the administrator is thereupon required as soon as reasonably practicable to give notice of the venue to the holder of the security or the owner of goods under the relevant agreement as the case may be[69]. The application would be subject to the normal procedures of the court in which the application is made. If an order is made, the court is required to send two sealed copies to the administrator and the administrator is required to send one of them to the holder of the security or the owner under the relevant agreement[70]. The administrator is also required to send a copy of the order to the registrar of companies before the end of the period of 14 days starting with the date of the order[71]. If he fails, without reasonable excuse, to send a copy of the order to the registrar of companies before the end of the period of 14 days starting with the date of the order, he commits an offence[72].

5.19 The power of the court to make such an order is exercisable in order to promote the achievement of the purpose of administration and is not dependent upon the existence of a dispute between the administrator and the holder of the security or the owner of the goods as to the latter's rights or a dispute as

---

64 Debts which would be preferential under section 754 of CA 2006 upon a chargeholder taking possession which accrue due after the company enters administration are likely, in many instances, to amount to administration expenses which in any event the court would direct the administrator to pay in priority to other debts and which would have priority pursuant to Schedule B1 paragraph 99 of IA 1986 and see also Rule 3.50 of the Rules: see **PARAGRAPH 5.26FF, PARAGRAPH 7.4FF** and **CHAPTER 15** *post*.

65 Schedule B1 paragraph 71(1) of IA 1986.

66 For the meaning of these terms, see **PARAGRAPH 2.17** *ante*.

67 Schedule B1 paragraph 72(1) of IA 1986. Before an order can be made under this provision, the court must be satisfied that the property is in the possession of the company (*Re Business Environment v Fleet Street Ltd* [2014] EWHC 3540 (Ch)).

68 Schedule B1 paragraphs 71(2) and 72(2) of IA 1986.

69 Rule 3.49(2) and (3) of the Rules. For the meaning of venue see Rule 1.2 of the Rules.

70 Rule 3.49(4) and (5) of the Rules.

71 Schedule B1 paragraphs 71(5) and 71(6) of IA 1986 and Rule 3.49(5)(b) of the Rules.

72 Schedule B1 paragraphs 71(6) and 72(5) of IA 1986.

to the value of the property in question[73]. In the exercise of its discretion, the court carries out a balancing test between the prejudice that would be felt by the secured creditor, if an order is made, against the prejudice that would be felt by those interested in the promotion of the purpose of administration in relation to the company, if it is not[74]. In the exercise of its discretion, the court may decline to make an order under Schedule B1 paragraph 71 or 72 of IA 1986 prior to consideration by creditors of the administrator's proposals, where the effect of making the order would be to pre-empt any decision the creditors might take[75].

5.20 Though giving an administrator a right to obtain an order for the sale of property subject to a fixed security or goods subject to a hire purchase or other agreement, Schedule B1 paragraphs 71 and 72 of IA 1986 are designed to preserve the rights of priority of the secured creditor, or the owner of the goods concerned, to the net proceeds of sale, or what would otherwise have been the net proceeds of sale, after the costs of realisation. Thus, it must be a condition of an order under both paragraphs that the net proceeds of the disposal, and any additional money required to be added to the net proceeds to produce the amount determined by the court as the net amount which would be realised on a sale of the property or goods at market value[76], are to be applied towards discharging the sums secured by the security or payable under the hire-purchase or other agreement relating to the goods[77]. Presumably, the sums 'payable' under a hire-purchase or other agreement relating to goods disposed of by an administrator pursuant to an order under Schedule B1 paragraph 72, are not limited to sums due and owing to the owner at the date of disposal but include all sums payable under the agreement whether at the date of disposal of the goods or thereafter. Even so, this may cause injustice to the owner of goods leased to the company under a leasing agreement where the goods in question would be of significant value to the owner at the end of the lease. It is thought that in such a case the court would not authorise the disposal of the goods by the administrator without making it a further condition of the order that the owner should be fully compensated for the loss to him of the value of the goods. Where an order under Schedule B1 paragraph 71 relates to more than one security, the net proceeds of the disposal, and such sums as may be required to make good any such deficiency, must be applied towards discharging the sums secured by the securities in the order of their priorities[78].

5.21 Thus, Schedule B1 paragraphs 71 and 72 give the administrator valuable powers which, subject to the obtaining of an appropriate order, will allow him to realise the company's encumbered assets in conjunction with its unencumbered assets, whilst retaining for the secured creditor concerned his right to receive

---

73 *Re ARV Aviation Ltd* [1989] BCLC 664 per Knox J at 667h–668c.
74 *Re ARV Aviation Ltd* [1989] BCLC 664 per Knox J at 668h–I, applied in *Re Capitol Films Ltd* [2010] EWHC 3223 (Ch) and *O'Connell v Rollings* [2014] EWCA Civ 639.
75 Cf *Re Consumer and Industrial Press Ltd (No 2)* (1988) 4 BCC 72 and *O'Connell v Rollings* [2014] EWCA Civ 639.
76 'Market value' is defined to mean the amount which would be realised on a sale of property in the open market by a willing vendor: Schedule B1 paragraph 111(1) of IA 1986. For value in the context of section 238 of IA 1986, see **PARAGRAPH 8.33** *post*. On an application under Schedule B1 paragraph 72 of IA 1986 in *Stanley Holmes & Sons Ltd v Davenham Trust plc* [2007] EWCA Civ 1568, the Court of Appeal held that a judge ought to have made a finding of fact as to market value and not simply split the difference between two competing valuations.
77 Schedule B1 paragraphs 71(3) and 72(3) of IA 1986. The net proceeds of sale includes all proper costs, charges and expenses reasonably incurred in the preservation and realisation of an asset, including the administrator's remuneration (*Townsend v Biscoe* (10 August 2010, unreported)).
78 Schedule B1 paragraph 71(4) of IA 1986.

from his security what he would have realised had he been allowed to realise the secured property himself[79]. The secured creditor's security is preserved not only in respect of the principal sum secured by the security but also in respect of all interest properly payable thereunder and, subject to the discretion of the court, his costs of any such realisation by the administrator, including the costs of the application for an order under Schedule B1 paragraphs 71 and 72 of IA 1986 itself[80]. What would not appear to be preserved, however, is the secured creditor's right to retain his security in circumstances in which it would have been contrary to his interests for a postponed right to redemption to be accelerated[81]. In such circumstances, once the court has concluded that a sale is required, the proceeds of realisation must be used to discharge the security.

5.22 However, these provisions do not appear to give the court jurisdiction to empower an administrator to deal with book debts of the company subject to a valid fixed charge in favour of a creditor[82], save by way of an assignment for value, eg in favour of a debt factoring company. In the case of any such assignment, the secured creditor would in any event retain his right to be paid the proceeds of any such assignment and thus it is considered unlikely that the court would normally be prepared to make an order under Schedule B1 paragraph 71(1) of IA 1986 with respect to book debts which were subject to a valid fixed charge. The existence of a possibly valid fixed charge on book debts may therefore be of considerable concern to an administrator notwithstanding the provisions of Schedule B1 paragraph 71, particularly if the charge purports to extend to future book debts, including book debts arising in the course of an administration. It follows that the existence of such a fixed charge on book debts may have a considerable impact upon the funding of an administration.

5.23 Where there is a dispute between the administrator and the secured creditor or the owner of the goods concerned as to the net amount which would be realised on a sale of the relevant property or goods in the open market by a willing vendor, the court can make an order under Schedule B1 paragraphs 71 or 72 of IA 1986 as the case may be at the same time as directing an enquiry into the market value of the property[83]. Schedule B1 paragraphs 71 and 72 do not, however, enable the court to make an order permitting the administrator to realise charged property and to retain the proceeds until such time as it is decided whether or not to make a formal challenge to the validity of the security concerned[84]. If the administrator wishes to challenge the security it is incumbent on him to issue proceedings and, if necessary, to seek interlocutory relief in those proceedings[85].

---

79 *Re ARV Aviation Ltd* [1989] BCLC 664 per Knox J at 668f–g and cf *Re Capitol Films Ltd* [2010] EWHC 3223 (Ch).
80 *Re ARV Aviation Ltd* [1989] BCLC 664 per Knox J at 669c–g.
81 Eg where he is fully secured and has lent with the benefit of a particularly advantageous interest rate.
82 The difficulty of obtaining such a charge is now well illustrated by *Agnew v IRC* [2001] UKPC 28 but see *Re Spectrum Plus Ltd* [2004] EWHC 9 (Ch).
83 *Re ARV Aviation Ltd* [1989] BCLC 664 per Knox J at 669h–670a and see also *O'Connell v Rollings* [2014] EWCA Civ 639.
84 *Re Newman Shopfitters (Cleveland) Ltd* [1991] BCLC 407 per Judge O'Donoghue at 409g–i.
85 *Re Newman Shopfitters (Cleveland) Ltd* [1991] BCLC 407 per Judge O'Donoghue at 409g–i. In *Arthur D Little Ltd (in administration) v Ableco Finance LLC* [2002] EWHC 701 (Ch), the court dealt with the question of whether a charge was void for non-registration under what was then section 395 of CA 1985 on an urgent application under Part 8 of the CPR, to enable the administrator to then make an application under what was then section 15(2) of IA 1986 in the event that the charge was found to be valid.

STATUS AND LIABILITIES OF THE ADMINISTRATOR

5.24   In exercising his functions an administrator is deemed to act as the company's agent[86]. Thus, unless the contract provides otherwise, contracts entered into by the administrator as agent on behalf of the company are binding upon the company but not upon the administrator personally[87]. In so far as transactions undertaken by an administrator are concerned, it is provided[88] that persons dealing with the administrator in good faith and for value need not inquire whether the administrator is acting within his powers.

5.25   However, even in the absence of any personal contractual liability on the part of the administrator, upon his ceasing to be an administrator sums payable in respect of debts or liabilities arising out of contracts entered into[89] by him or a predecessor of his are charged on and payable out of property of which he had custody or control immediately before the time he ceased to be administrator[90]. Likewise, any liability for wages or salary arising under a contract of employment adopted by him[91] or a predecessor of his are charged on and payable out of property of which he had custody or control immediately before the time he ceased to be administrator[92]. Any such sums are payable in priority to any security which was a floating charge on its creation[93]. An enforceable statutory charge[94] is accordingly created in favour of third parties contracting with the administrator as agent on behalf of the company and employees whose contracts of employment are adopted by him[95]. Furthermore, prior to an administrator vacating office, the court may in any event direct the administrator to pay particular debts of the company as expenses of the administration, even though the administrator has incurred no personal liability for such debts[96].

5.26   The reference to sums payable in respect of a debt or liability arising out of a contract entered into by an administrator or by any predecessor of his would appear to extend to all debts and liabilities incurred whilst the administrator holds office arising out of such contracts. Thus a liability incurred in the course of an administration for damages for wrongful repudiation of a contract entered into by an administrator *prima facie* will be secured by the statutory

---

86   Schedule B1 paragraph 69 of IA 1986. However, not every action taken by the administrator will be in his capacity as the company's agent: cf *SNR Denton UK LLP v Kirwan* [2013] ICR 101 and *Wright Hassall LLP v Morris* [2012] EWHC 188 (Ch).
87   See *Re Atlantic Computer Systems plc* [1992] Ch 505 at 526d–e.
88   By Schedule B1 paragraph 59(3) of IA 1986.
89   Including employment contracts: see *Re Paramount Airways Ltd (No 3)* [1993] BCC 662 per Evans-Lombe J at 669G.
90   Schedule B1 paragraph 99(4) of IA 1986.
91   For the meaning of the word adopted see **PARAGRAPH 7.6FF** *post*.
92   Schedule B1 paragraph 99(5) of IA 1986.
93   Schedule B1 paragraphs 99(3)(b) and 99(4)(b) of IA 1986; see also Schedule B1 paragraph 70 of IA 1986.
94   In the absence of agreement, such a charge would appear not to be enforceable without an order of the court. Potential difficulties may arise where the assets charged are insufficient to discharge the liabilities secured, although Rule 3.51 of the Rules (as to which see further **PARAGRAPH 15.33FF** *post*) provides for statutory order of priority in respect of administration expenses.
95   See **PARAGRAPH 7.4FF** *post*. Presumably the statutory charge is also created in favour of the Inland Revenue as security for the obligation to make payment of PAYE and the primary Class 1 National Insurance contributions payable in respect of adopted employment contracts, as to which see: *IRC v Lawrence* [2001] 1 BCLC 204.
96   See further **PARAGRAPH 15.33FF** *post*.

charge under Schedule B1 paragraph 99(4) of IA 1986 and have priority over the administrator's remuneration and expenses[97]. A liability arising out of a contact entered into prior to the administration will not, however, be secured by this statutory charge, even though it may relate to a period during which the company is in administration unless the administrator has incurred the liability in the course of the administration, in which case the liability will be treated as if it were an expense of the administration.[98] It appears that it is possible for an administrator to agree with a third party contracting with the company to exclude the operation of the statutory charge[99]. Further, where an administrator ceases to be in office, sums payable under contracts entered into by the administrator or a predecessor of his may still be charged on any property of the company in his custody or under his control at that time pursuant to Schedule B1 paragraph 99(3) as an expense, albeit if the charge under Schedule B1 paragraph 99(4) had been successfully excluded, such sums would not enjoy priority over the administrator's remuneration and other expenses[100]. The statutory charge in favour of employees whose contracts of employment are adopted by an administrator is considered in **CHAPTER 7** *post*[101].

5.27   As regards torts committed by an administrator whilst acting as such, the administrator will bear personal liability for such torts applying general common law principles[102] and the company itself may also be liable applying normal agency principles. It would seem, however, that where an administrator does incur personal liability in tort, the court has a discretion as to the extent to which the administrator will be allowed to indemnify himself out of the assets in his custody or under his control[103]. In exercising that discretion, the court will be concerned with the question of whether the tort in respect of which the indemnity is sought can be regarded as wrongful as against the company or secured or other creditors in whose interests the administrator is acting[104].

5.28   In consequence of the administrator's position as agent of the company, it is unlikely, at least as the law presently stands, that the administrator could be held to be personally liable for the tort of knowingly causing or inducing the company of which he was administrator to breach a contract to which the company was party[105]. In *Welsh Development Agency v Export Finance Co Ltd*[106], the Court of Appeal, by a majority, held that a receiver was not liable

---

97   Cf *Amble Assets LLP v Longbenton Foods Ltd* [2011] EWHC 3774 (Ch), where a provision that the return of a deposit under a contract for the sale of property by the administrators would rank as an unsecured claim, not an administration expense, was upheld.
98   *Re Games Station Ltd* [2014] EWCA Civ 180; cf *Laverty v British Gas Trading Ltd* [2014] EWHC 2721 (Ch).
99   *Amble Assets LLP v Longbenton Foods Ltd* [2011] EWHC 3774 (Ch). See further **PARAGRAPH 7.14** *post*.
100   Cf *Re Paramount Airways Ltd (No 3)* [1993] BCC 662 at 675H; the effect of Schedule B1 paragraph 99(3) of IA 1986 is considered in **PARAGRAPH 15.31FF** *post*.
101   See **PARAGRAPH 7.4FF** *post*.
102   *Rainham Chemical Works Ltd v Belvedere Fish Guano Co* [1921] 2 AC 465; *Performing Right Society Ltd v Ciryl Theatrical Syndicate Ltd* [1924] 1 KB 1; *C Evans & Sons Ltd v Spritebrand Ltd* [1985] 1 WLR 317; *Williams v Natural Life Health Foods Ltd* [1998] 1 WLR 830; *MCA Records Inc v Charly Records Ltd* [2001] EWCA Civ 1441; and *Standard Chartered Bank v Pakistan National Shipping Corpn* [2002] UKHL 43.
103   See *Barclays Mercantile Business Finance Ltd v Sibec Developments Ltd* [1992] 1 WLR 1253 per Millett J at 1260A–B.
104   *Lipe Ltd v Leyland DAF Ltd* [1994] 1 BCLC 84 at 88d–f.
105   Particularly if the administrator was acting in good faith: *Lictor Anstalt v MIR Steel UK Ltd* [2014] EWHC 3316 (Ch).
106   [1992] BCLC 148.

for the tort of inducing a breach of contract by the company to which he had been appointed, applying the principle that an agent could not be liable for inducing a breach of his principal's contract. However, Dillon LJ[107] (with whom on this point Ralph Gibson LJ[108] considered himself effectively bound) and Staughton LJ considered the rule to be anomalous[109]. It is submitted, however, that the position of an administrator is indistinguishable from that of a receiver on this point. Whether the rule giving rise to the administrator's apparent immunity from suit on this ground would withstand scrutiny by the Supreme Court may be open to question. It is submitted that, in principle, a better ground for defending a claim brought against an administrator for having induced a breach of contract by the company would be justification based on the administrator's duty to manage the affairs, business and property of the company for the purpose of administration[110].

5.29   The question might also arise whether a third party, entering into a transaction with a company in administration which the third party knew to be inconsistent with a prior contractual obligation of the company, could be liable for the tort of knowingly causing or procuring a breach of contract[111]. Irrespective of the personal liability, if any, of the administrator, it is submitted, however, that provided such a third party did not have actual knowledge that in causing the company to enter into the transaction in question the administrator was exercising his powers as administrator in bad faith or for an improper purpose, the third party would be able to rely upon the defence of justification to any claim in tort which might be brought against him[112].

5.30   It has been held that, as well as being an agent of the company, the administrator is also an 'officer of the company', in any event for certain purposes[113]. On this basis it is possible to make a prospective order under section 1157 of CA 2006 relieving the administrator from any liability for negligence, default, breach of duty or breach of trust, on the grounds that the administrator had acted and was acting honestly and reasonably and ought fairly to be excused[114].

THE ADMINISTRATOR AS AN OFFICER OF THE COURT

5.31   An administrator is also an officer of the court, whether or not he is appointed by the court[115]. This has the consequence, at least in England and

---

107   [1992] BCLC 148 at 173b–c.
108   [1992] BCLC 148 at 179h–i.
109   [1992] BCLC 148 at 191c–d.
110   See *BLV Realty Organization Ltd v Batten* [2009] EWHC 2994 (Ch), where it was held that the wrongful termination of a contract with a single creditor might, nonetheless, be in the interests of the creditors as a whole and thus would not constitute unfair harm for the purposes of Schedule B1 paragraph 74 of IA 1986.
111   See eg *British Motor Trade Association v Salvadori* [1949] Ch 556.
112   Cf *Edwin Hill & Partners v First National Finance Corpn plc* [1989] 1 WLR 225.
113   *Re Home Treat Ltd* [1991] BCLC 705 in relation to what was then section 727 of CA 1985, applied in *Re Powertrain Ltd* [2015] EWHC 3998 (Ch), where Newey J held that a liquidator was an offer of the company and so entitled to relief under section 1157 of CA 2006.
114   *Re Home Treat Ltd* [1991] BCLC 705.
115   Schedule B1 paragraph 5 of IA 1986. For the position under the pre-Enterprise Act 2002 law see *Re Atlantic Computer Systems plc* [1992] Ch 505 per Nicholls LJ at 529F–530A. As an officer of the court, it also seems likely that an administrator will be a public authority for the purposes of section 6 of the Human Rights Act 1998 (cf *Re Malcolm* [2004] EWHC 339 (Ch)).

Wales, that he is subject to the rule in *Re Condon, ex p James*[116], pursuant to which officers of the court are required to do the fullest equity. The scope of the rule however was considerably qualified by Walton J in *Re Clark (a bankrupt)*[117] where the learned judge held that for the rule to be applicable the following conditions have normally to be satisfied:

(a) there must be some form of enrichment of the insolvent estate;

(b) the claimant must not be in a position to submit an ordinary proof of debt (in the context of an administration, in any event prior to any notice of proposed distribution[118] being given, the claimant would presumably have to demonstrate that he was not simply an unsecured creditor with claims arising out of events pre-dating the administration);

(c) the circumstances must be such that an honest man who would be personally affected by the result would be bound to admit that it would be unfair that he should keep the property and/or money concerned and that his claim had no merits[119];

(d) the rule is applicable only to the extent necessary to nullify the enrichment of the estate.

5.32 In practice, therefore, the specific application of the rule in *ex p James*[120] may be somewhat limited in the context of administrations. What, on the other hand, is clear is that the court has power to give directions to an administrator as an officer of the court as to the manner in which the administration is to be conducted not only on the administrator's own application but also on application by a creditor or member, whether for permission to take any of the steps specified in Schedule B1 paragraph 43 of IA 1986[121] or generally[122]. It has been said, in the context of applications for permission under what is now Schedule B1 paragraph 43, that whilst there are 'no hard-and-fast principles' in the 'interim temporary regime' constituted by an administration, an administrator is to be expected to behave responsibly, to give reasons for his decisions and not to use his position as an administrator as a bargaining counter in which he has regard

---

116 (1874) 9 Ch App 609. He will be subject to the rule even where the only objective with which he acts is that of realising property in order to make a distribution to one or more secured creditors (Schedule B1 paragraph 3(1)(c) of IA 1986) and in that respect his position is more circumscribed than the position of an administrative receiver: cf *Triffit Nurseries v Salads Etcetera Ltd* [2000] 1 BCLC 761 at 773.

117 [1975] 1 WLR 559.

118 Rule 14.28 of the Rules. See **PARAGRAPH 15.8** *post*.

119 In many cases, the need to satisfy this requirement would bring an applicant within Schedule B1 paragraph 74 of IA 1986; see **CHAPTER 14** *post*.

120 (1874) 9 Ch App 609.

121 For an administration case in which the court considered the application of the rule in *ex p James*, see *Re Japan Leasing (Europe) plc* [1999] BPIR 911 and, on an administrator's application for directions, see *Re Mark One (Oxford St) plc* [2000] 1 BCLC 462 (NB the actual decision in *Japan Leasing* was disapproved by the Supreme Court in *Re D&D Wines International Ltd; Angove's Pty Ltd v Bailey* [2016] UKSC 47 but without reference to the *ex p James* point). Sir Terence Etherton C held that the rule did not apply in *In re London Scottish Finance Ltd* [2013] EWHC 4047 (Ch). The application of the rule was also argued, but no ruling was given, in *Re CE King Ltd* [2000] 2 BCLC 297 and *Re Niagara Mechanical Services International Ltd* [2000] 2 BCLC 425. In *Re Nortel Companies* [2013] UKSC 52, the Supreme Court held that the rule in *ex p James* could not justify the contention that an administrator could be ordered to change the statutory ranking of a particular debt simply because the ranking appeared unattractive. See also *Re Farepak Food and Gifts Ltd* [2006] EWHC 3272 (Ch).

122 See *Re Mirror Group (Holdings) Ltd* [1992] BCC 972.

only to the interests of unsecured creditors[123]. The same principle will apply even where the only objective with which the administrator acts is that of realising property in order to make a distribution to one or more secured creditors. If, however, an administrator wrongfully refuses a creditor or the owner of goods in the company's possession consent pursuant to Schedule B1 paragraph 43(2) or 43(3) to enforce his security or to repossess such goods, the court may direct him to pay compensation to the creditor or the owner of the goods concerned, in an appropriate case without a right of recoupment against the company's assets[124].

5.33   As an officer of the court, an administrator must exercise his powers, including the powers to grant consent under Schedule B1 paragraph 43 of IA 1986 and to make payments necessary or incidental to the performance of his duties, speedily and responsibly, having regard to any orders the court might be expected to make on a formal application for directions[125]. If he fails to do so he may be penalised in costs[126] or, as previously noted, ordered to pay compensation[127]. The obligation to act speedily and responsibly established under the former law is now given express statutory force by Schedule B1 paragraph 4 of IA 1986 which obliges an administrator to perform all of his functions as quickly and efficiently as is reasonably practicable.

5.34   Finally, it may be noted that as an administrator is an officer of the court, deliberate and unjustified interference with the management by the administrator of the affairs, business and property of a company or his custody or control of its property may constitute a contempt of court[128].

DUTIES OF AN ADMINISTRATOR

5.35   On his appointment the administrator of a company is required to take custody or control of all property to which he thinks the company is entitled[129]. As already noted, he is also required to manage the affairs, business and property of the company in accordance with:

(a)   any proposals approved under Schedule B1 paragraph 53 of IA 1986;

(b)   any revision of those proposals which is made by him and which he does not consider substantial; and

(c)   any revision of those proposals approved under Schedule B1 paragraph 54 of IA 1986[130].

5.36   As an agent of the company appointed to carry out specific functions by the court, it would appear that the administrator owes fiduciary duties to the

---

123 See *Re Atlantic Computer Systems plc* [1992] Ch 505 at 527G–530A; see also **PARAGRAPH 2.30**FF.
124 *Barclays Mercantile Business Finance Ltd v Sibec Developments Ltd* [1992] 1 WLR 1253 per Millett J at 1259E–1260B.
125 *Re Atlantic Computer Systems plc* [1992] Ch 505 at 529C–530A.
126 *Re Atlantic Computer Systems plc* [1992] Ch 505 at 529C–530A.
127 See **PARAGRAPH 5.32** *ante*.
128 Cf *Re Henry Pound, Son and Hutchins* (1889) 42 Ch D 402 per Kay J at 491; see also *Re Paramount Airways Ltd* [1990] BCC 130 per Harman J at 141H–142B.; although alluded to, this point was not expressly addressed in the Court of Appeal (*Bristol Airport plc v Powdrill* [1990] Ch 744 at 764E–H.) See also *Re Sabre International Products Ltd* [1991] BCLC 470.
129 Schedule B1 paragraph 67 of IA 1986.
130 Schedule B1 paragraph 68(1) of IA 1986. For the administrator's proposals, see **PARAGRAPH 3.11**FF *ante*. For revisions to those proposals, see **PARAGRAPH 3.28**FF *ante*.

company[131] to act in good faith, to exercise his powers for proper purposes, not to make any secret profit from his position as administrator[132] and not to place himself in a position whereby his duties as administrator and his personal interests or any duties owed by him to third parties conflict[133]. In this respect, the position of an administrator would appear to be comparable to that of a liquidator[134]. Although any transaction entered into by an administrator in breach of the 'self-dealing' rule will be voidable at the instance of the company, a third party dealing with the administrator in good faith and for value will not be affected by constructive knowledge of any breach of his fiduciary duties by the administrator[135].

5.37 In addition, an administrator owes the company a duty to exercise reasonable skill and care in the conduct of the administration. The administrator's duty of care to the company was accepted, albeit without contrary argument, by Millett J in *Re Charnley Davies Ltd (No 2)*[136] and would appear to be implicit in the provisions of Schedule B1 paragraph 75 of IA 1986, which preserves the right on the part of the official receiver, another administrator, the liquidator or any creditor or contributory of the company, to bring proceedings against an existing, purported or former administrator of the company for any misfeasance or breach of any fiduciary or other duty[137] in relation to the company, notwithstanding that the administrator has been discharged under Schedule B1 paragraph 98 of IA 1986[138]. Thus, it would seem that an administrator owes a duty to the company to take reasonable care not only in selling the company's assets, but in choosing the time at which to sell the assets[139]. He will also be at risk if he permits the company to continue trading at a loss[140]. Once the administrator is performing his functions with the objective of realising property in order to make a distribution to one or more secured or preferential creditors, the position may be different. In such a case, his duty to act in the interests of the company's creditors as a whole is modified, but the objective

---

131 For a reference to remedies for breach of fiduciary duty committed by an administrator see Schedule B1 paragraph 75(3) of IA 1986.

132 Thus, an administrator's remuneration must be fixed by the creditors or the court: Rules 18.18 and 18.23 of the Rules.

133 In the context of group insolvencies, it might be in the interests of creditors of the various group companies for there to be a common office-holder notwithstanding that this might give rise to conflicts of interest; the courts have acknowledged that a pragmatic approach might be required, ie managing these conflicts rather than avoiding them altogether: *Sisu Capital Fund v Tucker* [2005] EWHC 2170 (Ch).

134 See eg *Silkstone and Haigh Moor Coal Co v Edey* [1900] 1 Ch 167, *Re R Gertzenstein Ltd* [1937] Ch 115 and *Re Corbenstoke Ltd (No 2)* [1990] BCLC 60.

135 Schedule B1 paragraph 59(3) of IA 1986.

136 [1990] BCLC 760 at 775d–776a.

137 For breaches of other duties see: *Re Westlowe Storage and Distribution Ltd* [2000] 2 BCLC 590.

138 The power to proceed against a former administrator after he has been discharged from liability under Schedule B1 paragraph 98 of IA 1986 is only exercisable with the permission of the court: Schedule B1 paragraph 75(6) of IA 1986. See also section 212(4) of IA 1986.

139 *Re Charnley Davies Ltd (No 2)* [1990] BCLC 760 (per Millett J at 775f–g); cf the position of an administrative receiver: see *Downsview Nominees Ltd v First City Corpn Ltd* [1993] AC 295, *Medforth v Blake* [2000] Ch 86 and *Silven Properties Ltd v Royal Bank of Scotland plc* [2003] EWCA Civ 1409, although even in the case of receivership the borderline between these two duties is far from clear (*Lloyds Bank plc v Cassidy* [2002] EWCA Civ 1427, [2003] BPIR 424 at 440 per Mance LJ).

140 *Re Centralcrest Engineering Ltd* [2000] BCC 727.

of realisation must still be achieved in a manner that does not unnecessarily harm the interests of the company's creditors as a whole[141]. It is thought that in performing this duty the administrators will be in a similar position to that of the receivers whose duties were described in *Medforth v Blake*[142]. Whatever the objective with which the administrator is bound to perform his functions, it must be appreciated that it is not for every error of judgment that an administrator will be found to have acted in breach of his duty of care. A complaint that he has failed to take reasonable care is a complaint of professional negligence. In the words of Millett J: 'the administrator is not to be judged by the standards of the most meticulous and conscientious member of his profession but by those of the ordinary, skilled practitioner. In order to succeed the claimant must establish that the administrator has made an error which a reasonably skilled and careful practitioner would not have made'[143].

5.38   The circumstances in which an administrator may become liable to individual creditors is very much more circumscribed. An individual creditor does of course have the right to apply to the court under Schedule B1 paragraph 74 of IA 1986 if he considers that the administrator is acting or has acted so as unfairly to harm his interests or is proposing to act in such manner. In such an event, if satisfied as to the merits of the petitioner's complaint, the court has a discretionary power to intervene[144]; but acting unfairly does not appear to be the same concept as negligence[145] or, indeed, breach of duty. Similarly, as already noted, an individual creditor may be able to bring proceedings under Schedule B1 paragraph 75 of IA 1986 against an existing, former or purported administrator, but in such a case the creditor's complaint is one of breach of duty owed by the administrator to the company.

5.39   It is conceivable that an individual unsecured creditor might be able to bring a claim for breach of a specific statutory duty on the part of an administrator[146], but to do so the creditor would have to overcome the burden of establishing that the particular statutory duty concerned was imposed for the benefit or protection of a particular class of which the creditor forms part[147], which may be very difficult for it to do[148]. It is also possible that an administrator, when he comes to realise property which is subject to a security which was

---

141 Schedule B1 paragraphs 3 and 4 of IA 1986.
142 [2000] Ch 86.
143 *Re Charnley Davies Ltd (No 2)* [1990] BCLC 760 per Millett J at 775h–776a.
144 See *BLV Realty Organization Ltd v Batten* [2009] EWHC 2994 (Ch) and *Holgate v Reid* [2013] EWHC 4630 (Ch) and see also **PARAGRAPH 14.1**FF *post*.
145 For the position under the pre-Enterprise Act 2002 law, see *Re Charnley Davies Ltd (No 2)* [1990] BCLC 760, per Millett J at 782–784. For a summary of the meaning of 'unfairly harm' at Schedule B1 paragraph 74(1)(b) of IA 1986 see *Four Private Investment Funds v Lomas* [2008] EWHC 2869 (Ch) (paragraphs 34–39).
146 Cf, in the case of a liquidator, *Pulsford v Devenish* [1903] 2 Ch 625, *James Smith & Sons (Norwood) Ltd v Goodman* [1936] Ch 216 and *A & J Fabrications Ltd v Grant Thornton* [1998] 2 BCLC 227 (explained in *Kyrris v Oldham* [2003] EWCA Civ 1506) and, in the case of directors, *Peskin v Anderson* [2001] 1 BCLC 372.
147 See eg *Lonrho Ltd v Shell Petroleum Co Ltd (No 2)* [1982] AC 173, especially per Lord Diplock at 185D–F and *RCA Corpn v Pollard* [1983] Ch 135; cf *IRC v Goldblatt* [1972] Ch 498.
148 For a voluntary arrangement case in which the Court of Appeal concluded that the statutory scheme taken as a whole indicated that there was no private law claim for breach of statutory duty available against the supervisor of a voluntary arrangement see *King v Anthony* [1998] 2 BCLC 517.

a floating charge on its creation (pursuant to his powers under Schedule B1 paragraph 70 of IA 1986), may owe a duty to the holder of the security to take reasonable care to obtain a proper price[149]. In the context of dealings with property subject to other forms of security, the provisions of Schedule B1 paragraphs 71(3) and 72(3) of IA 1986 will normally render otiose the existence of any common law duty of care[150]. Subject however to such possibilities, it was established under the pre-Enterprise Act 2002 law that, given the nature of the office of an administrator and the purposes for which he is appointed, which may not necessarily be coincidental with the immediate commercial interests of individual creditors, it is neither just nor reasonable that an administrator should owe duties of care in relation to his conduct of the administration to individual creditors and it is submitted that, at least in general, no such duties are owed under the present law either[151]. The proper remedy is for a claim to be made under Schedule B1 paragraph 75 of IA 1986 to pay compensation or to restore assets to the company for the benefit of the creditors as a whole. The position may be different, however, where an administrator is performing his functions with the objective of realising property in order to make a distribution to one or more secured or preferential creditors[152]. He can only perform his functions towards this objective if he thinks that it is not reasonably practicable to achieve either of the other two statutory objectives, and, where he does so, he must not unnecessarily harm the interests of the creditors of the company as a whole[153]. It is thought that, so long as it is not alleged that the administrator should have done something which might unnecessarily have harmed the interests of the creditors of the company as a whole, there is room in principle for the imposition of a duty of care to the individual secured and preferential creditors for whose benefit he is realising the company's property[154].

---

149 Cf *Cuckmere Brick Co Ltd v Mutual Finance Ltd* [1971] Ch 949, *Downsview Nominees Ltd v First City Corpn Ltd* [1993] AC 295 and *Medforth v Blake* [2000] Ch 86; presumably such a duty would also be enforceable at the suit of a surety who was entitled to be subrogated to the security in question; cf *Standard Chartered Bank v Walker* [1982] 3 All ER 938. On the other hand, the absence, in the case of assets subject to a charge which as created was a floating charge, of any express provision comparable to Schedule B1 paragraph 71(3) of IA 1986 and the provisions of Schedule B1 paragraphs 70(1), 99(3) and 99(4) could arguably negative the existence of any such duty. A creditor entitled to such security could presumably apply for relief under Schedule B1 paragraph 74(1) in the event that a sale or proposed sale by the administrator of assets subject to such security or the terms of any such sale harmed his interests.

150 The question of the administrator's personal liability could, however, arise where the company's assets were insufficient to make up any deficiency between the net proceeds of sale and the amount for which the property in question would have been realised on a sale in the open market by a willing vendor.

151 *Kyrris v Oldham* [2003] 2 BCLC 35, upheld on appeal at [2003] EWCA Civ 1506 in which an attempt by unsecured creditors to sue administrators of a partnership for professional negligence was struck out; cf *Knowles v Scott* [1891] 1 Ch 717, *Re HIH Casualty & General Insurance Ltd* [2005] EWHC 2125 (Ch) (paragraphs 116–126) (and not reversed on this point on appeal) where David Richards J considered that where a liquidator caused loss to a creditor by disregarding his personal rights (for example, by not paying a distribution in relation to an unsecured claim for which the creditor has proved and where the proof has not been rejected), then the creditor has a personal claim against the liquidator for breach of statutory duty.

152 Schedule B1 paragraph 3(1)(c) of IA 1986.

153 Schedule B1 paragraph 3(4) of IA 1986.

154 See the claims which were not struck out in *Kyrris v Oldham* [2003] EWCA Civ 1506.

SPECIFIC DUTIES OF AN ADMINISTRATOR

5.40   In addition, a number of specific duties are cast upon an administrator by IA 1986 and the Rules:

(a)   to seek a decision from the company's creditors on a matter if requested, in accordance with the Rules, to do so by creditors of the company whose debts amount to 10 per cent of the total debts of the company, or if directed to do so by the court[155];

(b)   to ensure that invoices, orders for goods or services, business letters and order forms (described as business documents), whether in hard copy, electronic or any other form, that are issued by or on behalf of the company or the administrator contain the name of the administrator and state that the affairs, business and property of the company are being managed by him[156];

(c)   to advertise and to notify the company, creditors, the registrar of companies and other prescribed persons of his appointment as administrator[157];

(d)   to require the submission to him of a statement of affairs of the company[158];

(e)   to send to the registrar of companies and all creditors (other than opted-out creditors) and members known to the administrator a statement of his proposals for achieving the purpose of administration and to seek a decision from the company's creditors as to whether they approve the administrator's proposals[159];

(f)   where he proposes a substantial revision to his proposals, to summon a creditor's meeting and present to it a copy of the proposed revision[160];

(g)   to prepare and send to the company's creditors, the court and the registrar of companies a progress report for every period of six months from the time at which the company enters administration[161];

(h)   to apply to the court for the appointment of an administrator of the company to cease to have effect if he thinks that the purpose of administration cannot be achieved or that the company should not have entered administration or if he is required to do so by a decision of the company's creditors or (in the case of an appointment by the court) if he thinks that the purpose of administration has been sufficiently achieved in relation to the company[162];

(i)   to send notice of dissolution to the registrar of companies, the court and each creditor of whose claim he is aware, if he thinks that the company has no property which might permit a distribution to its creditors[163].

5.41   The administrator is required to maintain a separate record of the matters relating to the administration[164], which he is required to produce for inspection

---

155 Schedule B1 paragraph 56 of IA 1986; see **PARAGRAPH 4.8FF** *ante*.
156 Schedule B1 paragraph 45 of IA 1986; see **PARAGRAPH 3.3** *ante*.
157 Schedule B1 paragraph 46 of IA 1986 and Rule 3.27 of the Rules; see **PARAGRAPHS 3.1 AND 3.2** *ante*.
158 Schedule B1 paragraph 47 of IA 1986; see **PARAGRAPH 3.4FF** *ante*.
159 Schedule B1 paragraphs 49–53 of IA 1986; see **PARAGRAPH 3.11FF** *ante*.
160 Schedule B1 paragraph 54 of IA 1986; see **PARAGRAPH 3.28FF** *ante*.
161 Rule 18.6 of the Rules; see **PARAGRAPH 3.32FF** *ante*.
162 Schedule B1 paragraph 79(2) and (3) of IA 1986; see **PARAGRAPH 17.7FF** *post*.
163 Schedule B1 paragraph 84 of IA 1986; see **PARAGRAPH 17.24** *post*.
164 Regulation 13 of the Insolvency Practitioners Regulations 2005 (SI 2005 No 524).

by his authorising body or its representative on the giving of reasonable notice or the Secretary of State[165].

5.42 In addition, amongst the specific statutory duties of an administrator, it is his duty under the Company Directors Disqualification Act 1986 ('CDDA 1986') to report on the conduct of the company's directors. Under section 7A of CDDA 1986, the administrator must prepare a report about the conduct of each person who was a director of the company on the insolvency date[166] or at any time during the period of three years ending with that date and send this conduct report to the Secretary of State within three months of the insolvency date unless an extension is granted. In addition, if new information[167] comes to the attention of the administrator, he must send that information to the Secretary of State as soon as reasonably practicable. Under section 7(4) of CDDA 1986, the Secretary of State or the official receiver may also require the administrator or former administrator:

(a) to furnish him with such information with respect to any person's conduct as a director of the company, and

(b) to produce and permit inspection of such books, papers and other records relevant to that person's conduct as such a director, as they may reasonably require for the purpose of any application to disqualify that person under section 6 of CDDA 1986 or in order to determine whether such a disqualification order should be made.

5.43 By virtue of section 22(4) of CDDA 1986, 'director' includes any person occupying the position of director, by whatever name called, and by virtue of sections 6(3C) and 7A(12), the court's power to disqualify and the administrator's duty to report relate to any shadow director. 'Shadow director' means a person in accordance with whose directions or instructions the directors of the company are accustomed to act (but so that a person is not deemed a shadow director by reason only that the directors act on advice given by him in a professional capacity in accordance with instructions, a direction, guidance or advice given by him in the exercise of a statutory function or in accordance with guidance or advice given by him in his capacity as a Minister of the Crown) (section 22(5) of CDDA 1986). Although it was suggested[168] that the terms 'de facto director' and 'shadow director' are mutually exclusive, the extension of the concept of de facto directorship means that this is not the case[169]. A person will be a shadow director if he has real influence in the corporate affairs of the company, even if that influence does not extend over the whole field of its corporate activities[170]; however, there must at least be a pattern of conduct in which the de jure directors were accustomed to act[171] in accordance with the instructions of the shadow[172]. There is no need for the de jure directors to act in a subservient role to the alleged

---

165 Regulation 15 of the Insolvency Practitioners Regulations 2005.
166 In the case of an administration, the 'insolvency date' is the date on which the company entered administration: section 7A(10)(d) of CDDA 1986.
167 'New information' is information which an office-holder considers should have been included in a conduct report prepared in relation to the company, or would have been so included had it been available before the report was sent: section 7A(6) of CDDA 1986.
168 *Re Hydrodam (Corby) Ltd* [1994] 2 BCLC 180 at 183 (per Millett J).
169 *Revenue and Customs Commissioners v Holland* [2010] UKSC 51.
170 *Secretary of State for Trade and Industry v Deverell* [2000] 2 BCLC 133 (paragraph 35).
171 The mere giving of instructions is not enough: *Ultraframe (UK) Ltd v Fielding* [2005] EWHC 1638 (Ch) (paragraph 1278).
172 *Secretary of State for Trade and Industry v Becker* [2002] EWHC 2200 (Ch).

shadow director, nor is it necessary for their discretion to be surrendered to him. Whether what occurred constitutes a direction or instruction must be objectively ascertained on all the evidence, but non-professional advice is capable of coming within the statutory definition[173].

5.44   These provisions are supplemented by the Insolvent Companies (Reports on Conduct of Directors) Rules 2016[174], which make provision for the method by which reports and new information under section 7A of CDDA 1986 are to be sent to the Secretary of State[175]. If the administrator without reasonable excuse fails to comply with his obligations under section 7A(4) and (5) he is liable to a fine not exceeding £1,000 and, for continued contravention, to a daily default fine not exceeding £100[176]. The rules further provide for the enforcement by direct order of the court of the administrator's obligations under section 7(4) of CDDA 1986 and specifically provide that any such order may provide that all the costs of and incidental to the application for any such order shall be borne by the person to whom the order is directed[177].

5.45   A further reporting duty is imposed on all administrators by FSMA 2000. Where a company is in administration within the meaning of Schedule B1 to IA 1986, the administrator is obliged[178] to report to the appropriate regulator[179] without delay if he thinks that the company is carrying on a regulated activity[180] in contravention of the general prohibition[181] or a credit-related activity in contravention of section 20 of FSMA 2000. The duty does not arise, however, if the administration arises out of an order made on an application made by the PRA or the FCA and the regulator's application depended on a contravention by the company of the general prohibition[182].

5.46   In the context of the duties of an administrator it is also appropriate to note that, pursuant to sections 120 and 121 of the Pensions Act 1995, an insolvency practitioner appointed to a company (including an administrator) with an occupational pension scheme must give notice to the board of the Pension Protection Fund, the Pensions Regulator and the trustees or managers of the pension scheme within 14 days of the date on which the company entered administration or the date on which the administrator became aware of the existence of the pension scheme, whichever is later[183]. The administrator must also issue notices as to whether or not it is possible to rescue such a pension scheme[184].

5.47   Finally, it may be noted that where a company in administration incurs, whether before or after the appointment of an administrator, any liability

---

173   *Secretary of State for Trade and Industry v Deverell* [2000] 2 BCLC 133.
174   SI 2016 No 180.
175   Rules 4, 6 and 7 of SI 2016 No 180.
176   Rule 8 of SI 2016 No 180.
177   Rule 3 of SI 2016 No 180.
178   Section 361(2) of FSMA 2000.
179   In the case of a PRA-regulated activity, the PRA and the FCA and in all other cases the FCA: section 361(2A) of FSMA 2000.
180   See section 22 of FSMA 2000.
181   See section 19 of FSMA 2000.
182   Section 361(3) of FSMA 2000.
183   Regulation 4 of the Pension Protection Fund (Entry Rules) Regulations 2005 (SI 2005 No 590). The notice must be in writing and contain the information stipulated by regulation 4(1) of SI 2005 No 590.
184   Sections 122, 123 and 148 of the Pensions Act 1995.

to a third party against which it is insured under a contract of insurance, the company's rights against the insurer under the contract in respect of the liability are transferred to and vest in the third party to whom the liability was incurred[185]. However, the third party may not enforce those rights against the insurer until the company's liability to the third party has first been established, whether by a declaration in proceedings brought against the insurer, a judgment, an award in an arbitration or by agreement[186]. It is the duty of the administrator, at the request of any person claiming that the company is under a liability to him, to provide certain information for the purpose of ascertaining whether any rights have been so transferred to and vested in him and for the purpose of enforcing such rights, if any[187]. In particular, pursuant to such duty the administrator may be required to allow all contracts of insurance and other relevant documentation in his control to be inspected and copies thereof to be taken[188]. Within 28 days of receipt of such a notice the administrator must either provide the information requested or give notice that he is unable to provide such information together with the reasons why[189].

185 Sections 1(1), (2) and 6(2) of the Third Parties (Rights Against Insurers) Act 2010.
186 Sections 1(3), (4) and 2 of the Third Parties (Rights Against Insurers) Act 2010.
187 Section 11 and Schedule 1 to the Third Parties (Rights Against Insurers) Act 2010.
188 Schedule 1 to the Third Parties (Rights Against Insurers) Act 2010.
189 Schedule 1 paragraph 2 of the Third Parties (Rights Against Insurers) Act 2010.

6 Contracts

GENERAL

6.1   Administration does not have any effect on the legal personality of the company, nor does it, of itself, have any effect on a third party's contractual obligations to the company; nor (without more) does it terminate contracts to which the company is a party. In this context it should be noted that there is no general principle that contracts of agency are terminated on the insolvency of the agent: each case will depend on its own facts[1]. A contract, however, will very often provide for its termination, or for the obligations or rights of one or other of the parties to come to an end if it enters administration[2], but even where an agency agreement is terminated on the grounds of administration[3], there is no reason in principle why the agent's rights under the agreement (eg to collect monies received by it after the date of termination) should not continue, so that the monies so received form part of the insolvent estate and are not held on trust for the principal. However, this will not be the situation if there is a simple revocation of the agency without more, and, in the normal case, an agency will be revocable even if it is expressed to be irrevocable[4]. Subject to the possible exception described below, there would seem to be no objection to a provision terminating a contract on the grounds that a party has entered administration, although there will be instances in which there is some uncertainty as to whether or not the relevant termination clause extends to administration[5]. Nor, in the absence of any express provision, does administration of itself constitute a repudiatory breach of contract by the company. This is of particular significance in the case of contracts which are executory[6] at the date the company enters administration. It will be a question of fact in each case as to whether the company, acting for these purposes through the administrator, has evinced an intention no longer to perform[7].

6.2   There is a well-established rule that a contractual term is void if it provides for the qualification or determination of an existing interest on bankruptcy[8] or

---

1   *Triffit Nurseries v Salads Etcetera Ltd* [2000] 1 BCLC 761 (a receivership case).
2   It will, of course, be a question of construction as to whether notice is required before termination or whether it happens automatically.
3   Or any other form of insolvency procedure.
4   *In re D&D Wines International Ltd; Angoves Pty Ltd v Bailey* [2016] UKSC 47.
5   *In re MF Global UK Ltd (in special administration)* [2012] EWHC 3068 (Ch), in which the issue arose in relation to the appointment of administrators under the Investment Bank Special Administration Regulations 2011 (SI 2011 No 245).
6   Ie a contract in which obligations remain to be performed on both sides.
7   For a case in which a lessee failed to establish that a lessor in administration had repudiated an agreement to lease see: *Re Olympia and York Canary Wharf Ltd (No 2)* [1993] BCC 159.
8   *Ex p Mackay* (1873) 8 Ch App 643, *Ex p Williams* (1877) 7 Ch D 138 and *Re Johns, Worrell v Johns* [1928] 1 Ch 737.

winding up[9]. Until recently it was unclear whether what has come to be called the anti-deprivation principle was also applicable to administration. It has now been established that it is[10], because the public policy which engages the principle is aimed at preventing attempts to withdraw an asset on bankruptcy, liquidation or administration thereby reducing the value of the insolvent estate to the detriment of creditors. This whole area of the law has now been reconsidered by the Supreme Court in the case of *Belmont Park Investments Pty Ltd v BNY Corporate Trustee Services Ltd*[11], which established that there are two distinct rules, although they are both part of a more general principle that parties cannot contract out of the insolvency legislation. The first rule is the anti-deprivation principle itself[12], which is aimed at preventing attempts to withdraw an asset on formal insolvency (including administration) thereby reducing the value of the insolvency estate to the detriment of creditors. The second is the principle that it is contrary to public policy to contract out of the *pari passu* distribution rule. The basis for avoidance in this instance is that it would run counter to the fundamental principle of *pari passu* distribution amongst all of the creditors of the bankrupt or the company as the case may be[13]. Any attempt to contract out of that principle is contrary to public policy and is void[14]. The position is more complex in relation to the anti-deprivation principle, because the relevant provision will not be struck down if it was entered into in good faith and has a legitimate commercial basis[15].

6.3   On the appointment of an administrator, one of his first acts will be to assess the extent to which he can and should continue essential contracts. In approaching that task, he must first consider whether the continuation of a contractual relationship with a particular counter-party will assist in furthering the purpose of administration. If he forms the view that it will not, it is incumbent on him to assess whether he can then procure the company to determine the contract with less damage to the achievement of that purpose than would occur if the contract was to be continued. In carrying out that exercise, the administrator will have to bear in mind the likelihood of any order being made under Schedule B1 paragraph 43 of IA 1986 on any application for permission to enforce security, to repossess goods or to institute proceedings against the company. Clearly the possibility, or probability, of a counter-party being successful on any such application, or achieving the imposition of onerous terms[16] as a condition of the court refusing permission to take the relevant step, is likely to have a considerable bearing upon the administrator's assessment both of the benefits of continuing a particular contract and of the advantage, if any, to be gained by seeking to determine it. The administrator should also bear in mind the likely or possible outcome of any proceedings against the company for which permission is given pursuant to Schedule B1 paragraph 43(6)(b) of IA 1986.

---

9   *Re Apex Supply Co Ltd* [1942] Ch 108 and *British Eagle Airlines Ltd v Cie Nationale Air France* [1975] 1 WLR 758 (per Lord Cross at 779) both proceed on the assumption that the rule in bankruptcy applies to winding up.

10   *Belmont Park Investments Pty Ltd v BNY Corporate Trustee Services Ltd* [2011] UKSC 38.

11   [2011] UKSC 38.

12   First characterised as such by Neuberger J in *Money Markets International Stockbrokers Ltd v London Stock Exchange Ltd* [2002] 1 WLR 1150.

13   *Ex p MacKay* (1873) 8 Ch App 643 and *British Eagle Airlines Ltd v Cie Nationale Air France* [1975] 1 WLR 758. *Farmers' Mart Ltd v Milne* 1914 SC (HL) 84.

14   *British Eagle Airlines Ltd v Cie Nationale Air France* [1975] 1 WLR 758 at 780H.

15   *Belmont Park Investments Pty Ltd v BNY Corporate Trustee Services Ltd* [2011] UKSC 38 (paragraphs 102–106).

16   Pursuant to the power under Schedule B1 paragraph 43(7) of IA 1986.

6.4   In this context, the decision of Vinelott J in *Astor Chemicals Ltd v Synthetic Technology Ltd*[17], a case where the administrator of a manufacturing company sought to determine an exclusive distributorship agreement, is particularly instructive. The court will not simply permit the administrator to disregard the company's contractual obligations to third parties, as might happen in a receivership[18]. In particular, in determining applications for interlocutory relief, the court will consider whether or not an injunction should be granted against the company by applying normal principles of the balance of damage and convenience[19], giving such weight as may be appropriate to the company's insolvency or likely insolvency and the possibility of the company in administration being forced into liquidation. In many cases such considerations will be of the greatest significance, but may not necessarily sway the court from granting appropriate injunctive relief against the company in all circumstances, particularly where an award of damages against the company is likely to turn out to be an inadequate remedy[20].

6.5   Similarly, in *Re P & C and R &T (Stockport) Ltd*[21], Scott J accepted the proposition that in general an administration order does not constitute authority for an administrator to break the company's contracts. He went on to hold, however, that on the facts of that particular case the company's counter-party (its joint venturer) had no equity to compel the company to perform its contractual obligations, notwithstanding the fact that the administrator's proposals contemplated that the company would seek to develop and realise property vested in it pursuant to the joint venture agreement. Each of these two decisions is consistent with the general proposition that the administration, of itself, does not affect substantive rights: it merely has procedural consequences on the enforcement of those rights[22].

6.6   In determining how to proceed, the administrator may also have to take into account the impact of Schedule B1 paragraph 99(4) and (5) of IA 1986, which provide that, where a person ceases to be an administrator any sums payable in respect of debts or liabilities arising out of a contract entered into by him (or his predecessor) or in respect of any liabilities arising under contracts of employment adopted by him (or his predecessor) shall be charged on and payable out of any property of the company in his custody or under his control in priority to any charge arising under Schedule B1 paragraph 99(3)[23] and to any security which as created was a floating charge[24]. It will be noted, however, that a clear distinction is drawn between the adoption of contracts of employment and the entering into of new contracts. The continuation of existing contracts other than employment contracts is not covered by this provision, though where

17   [1990] BCLC 1.
18   *Airlines Airspares Ltd v Handley Page Ltd* [1970] Ch 193, unless the plaintiff is asserting a proprietary right ranking ahead of the debenture holder: *Freevale Ltd v Metrostore (Holdings) Ltd* [1984] Ch 199. See also *Land Rover Group v UPF (UK) Ltd (in administrative receivership)* [2002] EWHC 3183 (QB).
19   *American Cyanamid Co v Ethicon Ltd* [1975] AC 396.
20   Thus in *Astor Chemicals Ltd v Synthetic Technology Ltd* [1990] BCLC 1, Vinelott J granted an interlocutory injunction against the company.
21   [1991] BCLC 366.
22   *Barclays Mercantile Business Finance Ltd v Sibec Developments Ltd* [1992] 1 WLR 1253 at 1257, cited with approval in *Re David Meek Plant Ltd* [1994] 1 BCLC 680, 685b.
23   Ie a charge for his remuneration and any expenses properly incurred by him.
24   Within the meaning of Schedule B1 paragraph 70 of IA 1986. See also Schedule B1 paragraph 111(1) of IA 1986 for the definition of 'floating charge'.

an administrator causes the company in administration to continue to take the benefit of an existing contract, he may in any event be directed, as an officer of the court, to discharge sums payable under such contracts[25]. The possibility of such a direction must also therefore be taken into account by the administrator.

RETENTION OF TITLE AGREEMENTS

6.7   As in the insolvency of any trading company, an administrator is likely to be faced with claims by suppliers that goods in the possession of the company at the commencement of the administration are goods to which, notwithstanding delivery to the company, title has been retained by the supplier[26]. One of the administrator's tasks will be to establish whether a retention of title clause has in fact been incorporated into the relevant contract. This is often a difficult question on which legal advice and statements from the company's management will be necessary. Once incorporation has been established, however, a simple well-drafted retention of title clause will, without more, be good protection for a supplier[27]. In some circumstances, that protection may extend to goods in the hands of a sub-purchaser[28]. It will only, however, be good protection if the purchaser takes appropriate steps to protect his own interests. Thus, it is perfectly possible that, on the true construction of the relevant clause, the purchaser in administration will continue to be entitled to sell goods to sub-purchasers, even where it has not acquired title to those goods, until such time as notice terminating that entitlement is given by the seller; it will not necessarily be the case that the administration of the purchaser will have the effect of terminating that entitlement[29].

6.8   A retention of title clause will often give a supplier rights of self-help to recover the goods supplied. The supplier may also allege that with effect from the commencement of the administration any express or implied licence to deal with those goods has been terminated[30]. In such a case any dealing by the administrator in a manner contrary to the true owner's rights is likely to constitute a conversion. For his part, an administrator attempting to achieve the purpose of administration will wish to ensure that he has free use of the company's trading stock; that stock will nearly always include goods to which claim has been made by retention of title creditors. Parliament has resolved the conflict between the interests of supplier and company in administration by imposing restrictions on the exercise of the suppliers' contractual rights and his rights to take proceedings, whilst protecting the market value of his proprietary rights in the goods supplied.

---

25 *Barclays Mercantile Business Finance Ltd v Sibec Developments Ltd* [1992] 1 WLR 1253 at 1260.
26 See *Clough Mill Ltd v Martin* [1985] 1 WLR 111 and *Armour v Thyssen Edelstahlwerke AG* [1991] 2 AC 339, in which the House of Lords confirmed that Scots law on retention of title was the same as English law.
27 See *Clough Mill Ltd v Martin* [1985] 1 WLR 111 and *Armour v Thyssen Edelstahlwerke AG* [1991] 2 AC 339, in which the House of Lords confirmed that Scots law on retention of title was the same as English law.
28 *Re Highway Foods International Ltd* [1995] 1 BCLC 209.
29 *Sandhu v Jet Star Retail Ltd* [2011] EWCA Civ 459.
30 Cf the failure to exercise that right in *Sandhu v Jet Star Retail Ltd* [2011] EWCA Civ 459.

6.9   The restriction on the supplier's contractual rights is that the statutory moratorium[31] is extended to goods in the possession of the company under a retention of title agreement. The moratorium will not prevent the supplier from terminating a contractual right to deal with the goods once the company has entered administration[32], but the supplier must seek the court's permission to exercise his rights of self-help or to take proceedings for the recovery of the goods[33]. It is thought that the word 'repossess' should be given a wide meaning in this context and should cover even products which may have been manufactured from the supplier's goods and others[34], and which have not therefore technically ever been in the supplier's possession. Any other construction would frustrate the underlying purpose of the restriction on the exercise of a supplier's rights, although in practice he will rarely succeed in establishing an interest in manufactured goods into which his own materials have been incorporated.

6.10   The protection of the rights of a supplier to the goods is given by Schedule B1 paragraph 72 of IA 1986[35]. This is considered in more detail elsewhere, but, if the administrator wishes to avoid possible proceedings for conversion[36], he must seek the consent of the owner of the goods or the permission of the court before disposing of goods supplied under a retention of title agreement. The court must[37] make it a condition of any order giving leave to dispose of the goods that the net proceeds of the disposal or, if greater, the net market value, are applied towards discharging the sums payable under the retention of title agreement. Such a condition will obviously restrict the freedom of the administrator to use the proceeds of stock supplied under a retention of title agreement as working capital for the company's continued trading. It will be a question of judgment in each case as to whether the administrator disposes of goods alleged to have been supplied under a retention of title agreement without application to the court and risks proceedings for conversion or applies to the court under Schedule B1 paragraph 72[38]. It is usual for an administration sale to be only of such right title and interest as the company has in the property sold which transfers the risk to the purchaser, but it is also prudent for the sale agreement to exclude any claim (whether for contribution or otherwise) by the purchaser against the company or the administrator, which might derive from claims against the purchaser by the true owner[39].

6.11   As well as retaining title to the goods themselves, suppliers often attempt to claim rights in the proceeds of resales by the company to third parties. In some

---

31   Under Schedule B1 paragraph 43 of IA 1986. For the purposes of this provision, a retention of title agreement is included within the definition of 'hire purchase agreement': Schedule B1 paragraph 111(1) of IA 1986.

32   *Barclays Mercantile Business Finance Ltd v Sibec Developments Ltd* [1992] 1 WLR 1253.

33   See *Fashoff (UK) Ltd v Linton* [2008] EWHC 537 (Ch) for a case in which an application to lift the statutory moratorium to permit enforcement of a retention of title clause failed on the grounds of delay.

34   *Clough Mill Ltd v Martin* [1985] 1 WLR 111 at 119E–120F (per Robert Goff LJ).

35   For the purposes of this provision as well, a retention of title agreement is included within the definition of 'hire purchase agreement': Schedule B1 paragraph 111(1) of IA 1986.

36   *Clough Mill Ltd v Martin* [1985] 1 WLR 111 and see the detailed explanation of the law of conversion in this area in *Blue Monkey Gaming Ltd v Hudson* (16 June 2014, unreported, HHJ McCahill QC at paragraphs 386ff).

37   Schedule B1 paragraph 72(3)(b) of IA 1986.

38   The correct course is normally to seek the court's protection under paragraph 72 (see eg *Hachette UK Ltd v Borders (UK) Ltd* [2009] EWHC 3487 (Ch)), but in practice this is often not done.

39   See *Mir Steel UK Ltd v Morris* [2012] EWCA Civ 1397.

cases, the supplier will also seek to argue that he has obtained a proprietary interest in goods which constitute the product of a manufacturing process conducted by the company or even an amalgamation of the goods supplied by him and others of the company's suppliers. An administrator will have to consider whether he should give effect to any such attempt to obtain priority over the company's ordinary unsecured creditors; in most cases such an attempt will be unsuccessful on the grounds that the supplier rights in manufactured product or the proceeds of sale of the goods constituted an unregistered charge[40].

6.12 Although it is now clear that a clause simply retaining title to particular goods until those or other goods have been paid for does not require registration[41] as a charge[42], unless it is part of a wider transaction designed to secure repayment of monies lent[43], it will be very difficult for a supplier to arrange matters so that he obtains rights to trace into the proceeds of sale of goods which have not been paid for without registering that right as a charge[44]. It is only if the supplier can establish a fiduciary relationship, under which the company was selling on his behalf, rather than on its own account, that he has any prospect of success[45]. Otherwise, he is likely simply to have been granted by the company a proprietary interest in an asset belonging to the company, namely the debt due from the third party purchaser; such a grant by the company is almost certain to be by way of charge[46]. In the context of an ordinary commercial transaction, the court will be most reluctant to find that the true nature of the relationship between the parties was fiduciary in form.

6.13 The supplier will encounter similar difficulties if he attempts to obtain property rights in new goods into which the goods he has supplied have been incorporated or subsumed[47]. The reason is similar to the reason why it is difficult for him to lay claim to the proceeds of resale of goods to a third party; the supplier is not laying claim to an asset, which continues to belong to him. The asset is, in substance, a new asset in respect of which he has been granted proprietary rights by the company; those rights are almost certain to be by way of charge.

SET-OFF

6.14 Any right to set off a liability to an insolvent company against a liability owed by that company is of considerable importance to third parties.

---

40 For receivership cases in which such an attempt failed, see *In Re Peachdart Ltd* [1984] Ch 131 and *Ian Chisholm Textiles Ltd v Griffiths* [1994] 2 BCLC 291 and for a similar liquidation case see *Modelboard Ltd v Outer Box Ltd* [1992] BCC 945. Section 859H(3) of CA 2006 now provides that an unregistered charge is void (so far as any security on the company's property or undertaking is conferred by it) against an administrator.
41 Within the meaning of and as contemplated by s.859A of CA 2006.
42 *Clough Mill Ltd v Martin* [1985] 1 WLR 111 and *Armour v Thyssen Edelstahlwerke AG* [1991] 2 AC 339.
43 *Re Curtain Dream plc* [1990] BCLC 925.
44 See eg *Re Andrabell Ltd* [1984] 3 All ER 407, *Tatung (UK) Ltd v Galex Telesure Ltd* (1988) BCC 325, *E Pfeiffer Weinkellerei-Weineinkauf GmbH & Co v Arbuthnot Factors Ltd* [1988] 1 WLR 150.
45 See eg *Re Andrabell Ltd* [1984] 3 All ER 407.
46 *Compaq Computer Ltd v Abercorn Group Ltd* [1993] BCLC 602 and *Modelboard Ltd v Outer Box Ltd* [1993] BCLC 623.
47 *Hendy Lennox (Industrial Engines) Ltd v Grahame Puttick Ltd* [1984] 1 WLR 485, *Borden (UK) Ltd v Scottish Timber Products Ltd* [1981] Ch 25, *Re Peachdart Ltd* [1984] Ch 131 and *Ian ChisholmTextiles Ltd v Griffiths* [1994] 2 BCLC 291.

The Insolvency Act itself makes no express provision for set-off in any of the corporate insolvency procedures; insolvency set-off is dealt with in the Rules. Furthermore, the only corporate insolvency process in respect of which the mandatory and self-executing provisions of the set off provisions in the Rules[48] are always applied from the outset, is winding up[49]. In this context, however, it should be noted that, where a liquidation is immediately preceded by an administration, sums due from the company to another party are not to be taken into account for set-off purposes if, at the time they became due, the company was in administration or that other party had notice that an administration application was pending or notice of intention to appoint had been given[50]. The statutory set off provisions in an administration[51] are limited in their application to the circumstance in which an administrator has given notice of his intention to make a distribution under Rule 14.29 of the Rules[52]. It follows that, until such time as it is intended to make a distribution, administration set-off must be approached from the same starting point as set-off between solvent entities even though one of the parties to the set-off will, *ex hypothesi*, be insolvent or likely to become insolvent. It also follows that, prior to the making of a distribution, the normal principles of set-off in equity and under the Statutes of Set-Off[53] govern the position, although those dealing with a company in administration will wish to take into account the likelihood that a right to an insolvency set-off may arise at some stage in the future[54]. It is not proposed to consider the normal principles in any detail[55], but a summary and some of the practical consequences of the principles are set out below.

6.15   A set-off is a right to appropriate an obligation to another person in discharge or reduction of that person's obligation to the person asserting the set-off. There must be a mutuality, that is unity of identity and interest[56], as between creditor and debtor. At common law, set-off is only available where the claim sought to be set off is in respect of a liquidated debt or a money demand which can be readily and without difficulty ascertained[57]. A debtor of the company cannot set off against his personal liability to the company any liability of the company to him qua trustee for another. Similarly, a debtor cannot set off against his liability to the company, any liability of the company to him arising

---

48   Which provides for the setting off of mutual credits, mutual debts and other mutual dealings.
49   Rule 14.25 of the Rules applies where a company 'goes into liquidation'.
50   Any such debt (which as a matter of definition must be a liability of the company: Rule 14.1(3) of the Rules) is excluded from the definition of 'mutual dealings' by Rule 14.25(6) of the Rules.
51   Rule 14.24 of the Rules.
52   A further analysis of this provision is in **CHAPTER 15** *post*.
53   2 Geo.2, c.22, s.13, and 8 Geo.2, c.24, sections 1 and 5.
54   Ie under Rules 14.24 or 14.25 of the Rules. For a description of the practical reasons why administration and liquidation differ on this point see paragraph 2.6 of the Financial Markets Law Committee's November 2007 paper on Administration Set-Off and Expenses (Issue 108).
55   For a detailed treatment of set-off see Philip R Wood, *English and International Set-Off* (1989); S Rory Derham, *Derham on the Law of Set-Off* (4th edn, 2010); Louise Gullifer (ed), *Goode on Legal Problems of Credit and Security* (5th edn, 2014); and Sheelagh McCracken, *The Banker's Remedy of Set-Off* (4th edn, 2017).
56   Eg neither a trustee nor an agent can set off a claim owed in his personal capacity against a claim owing in his fiduciary capacity.
57   See eg *Stooke v Taylor* (1880) 5 QBD 569, *Hanak v Green* [1958] 2 QB 9, *Axel Johnson Petroleum AB v MG Mineral Group AG* [1992] 1 WLR 270 and *B Hargreaves Ltd v Action 2000 Ltd* [1993] BCLC 1111. Unliquidated claims can, however, be set off in equity.

out of separate transactions which accrued due after he acquired notice of the assignment of or the crystallisation of a floating charge over the debt he owes[58]. However, administration of itself, in contrast to the crystallisation of a floating charge, effects no change in the identity of the parties beneficially entitled to debts due to the company. It is thought therefore that, subject to the rights of creditors holding fixed or crystallised security over the company's debts, if any, a debtor to a company in administration who, following the entry of the company into administration, takes an assignment[59] of debts owed by the company will be able to set off the assigned debts against his own debt to the company[60], in any event so long as the company does not go into liquidation and the administrator does not make a distribution in the exercise of his powers under Schedule B1 paragraph 65 of IA 1986. The effectiveness of such a device may, of course, have a considerable impact upon an administrator's ability to realise the company's assets in so far as they comprise substantial debts due to the company. It should be noted, however, that a debtor who has taken that course since 15 September 2003 will be taking a much greater risk than had hitherto been the case. The reason for that is that he will be unable to utilise the debt due from the company as a set-off in any administration distribution or in any subsequent liquidation, because the provisions of Rules 14.24 and 14.25 of the Rules now require any such claims against the company to be left out of the account taken under those Rules.

6.16   In the case of unliquidated cross-claims, equitable set-off will be available, provided that the cross-claim by the debtor against the company arises out of the same transaction or series of transactions as have given rise to the debt owed to the company, and the debtor is able to show that there is some equitable ground sufficient to impeach the company's title to its demand[61]. It is thought that, at least where the cross-demands arise out of the same transaction or series of transactions, there would normally be sufficient equity in the fact that the company was insolvent (while the debtor was unable to rely on the wider terms of Rule 14.24 or 14.25 of the Rules) to ensure that set-off was allowed. That will not necessarily be the case, however, particularly if the company in administration sues on a dishonoured cheque[62].

6.17   The question of whether a particular right of set-off operates as a defence to a claim made other than in judicial proceedings[63], or is only capable of being raised as a procedural defence in legal proceedings[64], is of importance. Where

---

58   *Re Pinto Leite & Nephews, ex p Visconde des Olivaes* [1929] 1 Ch 221, *NW Robbie & Co Ltd v Witney Warehouse Co Ltd* [1963] 1 WLR 1324 and *Business Computers Ltd v Anglo-African Leasing Ltd* [1977] 1 WLR 578; cf *Biggerstaff v Rowatt's Wharf Ltd* [1896] 2 Ch 93 and *Christie v Taunton, Delmard, Lane & Co* [1893] 2 Ch 175.

59   No doubt at a significant discount from their true value.

60   Cf the position in a receivership, see *NW Robbie & Co Ltd v Witney Warehouse Co Ltd* [1963] 1 WLR 1324, and in a liquidation, see Rule 14.25 of the Rules and cf *Re Eros Films Ltd* [1963] Ch 565.

61   See eg *Newfoundland Government v Newfoundland Rly Co* (1888) 13 App Cas 199, *Hanak v Green* [1958] 2 QB 9, *Business Computers Ltd v Anglo-African Leasing Ltd* [1977] 1 WLR 578 and *Dole Dried Fruit and Nut Co v Trustin Kerwood Ltd* [1990] 2 Lloyd's Rep 309; cf, however, *Henriksen Rederi A/S v PHZ Rolimpex* [1974] QB 233.

62   *Isovel Contracts Ltd v ABB Building Technologies Ltd* [2002] 1 BCLC 390.

63   Ie is a self-help remedy: eg a banker's right to combine accounts: see *Halesowen Presswork and Assemblies Ltd v Westminster Bank Ltd* [1971] 1 QB 1 at 34 (per Lord Denning MR).

64   See eg *Talbot v Frere* (1878) 9 Ch D 568 at 573 and *Sovereign Life Assurance Co v Dodd* [1892] 2 QB 573 at 577.

the company in administration has the right to exercise a remedy of self-help[65], the administrator may seek to exercise his right and refuse the counter-party permission to sue to enable his claim against the company to be properly formulated. It is thought that in those circumstances the court would normally give leave for the counter-party to issue proceedings against the company. This will not always be the case, however, because the court will have to balance the interests of the counter-party against those of the company and its creditors as a whole in achieving the purpose of administration. Occasionally, the balance may come down in favour of permission being refused[66].

---

65 Eg forfeiture of a lease for non-payment of rent or withdrawal of a vessel for non-payment of hire: per Lord Denning MR in *The Nanfri* [1978] QB 927 at 974.
66 Cf the approach of the Court of Appeal in *Re Atlantic Computer Systems plc* [1992] Ch 505 on an application under what was then s.11 of IA 1986.

7 Administration as it affects officers of the company and its employees

EFFECT ON OFFICERS OF THE COMPANY AND THEIR POWERS

7.1   The appointment of an administrator does not, of itself, cause the officers of a company (ie the directors and the secretary) to cease to hold office. However, both in law and in practice, the position of the officers of a company the day before the company enters administration and their position on the day after are very different. The officers of the company are still subject to the normal requirements of company law to make appropriate returns to the registrar of companies and also to deal with such matters as the preparation of the company's accounts[1]. However, the role of the officers is diminished in practical terms because from the time of his appointment, the administrator, acting as deemed agent for the company, with power to do all such things as may be necessary for the management of its affairs, business and property, is effectively in charge of the company's affairs[2]. The officers of the company are of course entitled to resign from their offices as directors or secretary as the case may be, though, in the case of employed directors or an employed secretary, their position as officers of the company is to be distinguished from their position under their respective contracts of employment with the company to which different considerations may apply[3].

7.2   Consideration has been focused in the past upon the powers of directors and the company secretary following the appointment of a receiver. The general position is that in the event of a receivership the directors and the secretary of a company continue to be entitled to exercise their powers as such provided that no action which they take in any way prejudices or impedes the actions of the receiver in carrying out his functions[4]. However, perhaps as a result of the difficulties which have been faced by receivers, IA 1986 provides expressly that any power conferred on the company or its officers, whether by any enactment (eg CA 2006) or any instrument (eg the memorandum or articles of association), which could be exercised in such a way as to interfere with the exercise by the administrator of his powers is not exercisable except with the consent of the administrator, which

---

1   These duties are not in practice enforced.
2   Schedule B1 paragraphs 59–69 of IA 1986.
3   The effect of the company entering administration upon contracts of employment is considered in **PARAGRAPH 7.4FF** *post*.
4   See *Newhart Developments Ltd v Co-operative Commercial Bank Ltd* [1978] QB 814 and *Tudor Grange Holdings Ltd v Citibank NA* [1992] Ch 53.

may be given either generally or in relation to particular cases[5]. Directors are not, therefore, entitled to interfere with the running of the company's affairs save with the consent of the administrator. Given that IA 1986 places the duty to manage the company's affairs, business and property upon the administrator[6], it is unusual for an administrator to give a general consent to the continued exercise by directors of their powers. However, there may often be cases in which an administrator would and should be prepared to devolve some power to one or more officers of the company for specific purposes. The approach to be adopted will clearly vary according to the circumstances of the particular case but administrators should always bear in mind that the wholesale replacement of a company's existing management will inevitably increase the cost of administration proceedings and may not necessarily be either conducive to the purpose of administration or in the interests of creditors generally. If necessary, it is always open to the administrator to apply to the court for directions as to the extent to which he should permit the directors to continue to exercise their powers[7].

7.3   Occasionally, in a receivership, one or more of the directors of the company may attempt to interfere with the receiver's conduct of the company's affairs. In the case of administrations, such concerns have been addressed directly in that the administrator is empowered to remove any director of the company[8]. The administrator is also empowered to appoint any person to be a director of the company, whether to fill a vacancy or otherwise[9] (although it is unlikely that such an appointment would be made or accepted other than in exceptional circumstances). As previously noted, however[10], the removal of a director may amount to a breach of contract by the company for which the company may be liable in damages.

POSITION OF EMPLOYEES

7.4   In contrast to the position in a compulsory liquidation, the general rule is that the appointment of an administrator of a company will not operate to terminate the contracts of employment of the company's employees[11]. To that extent, the appointment of an administrator is analogous to the appointment of a receiver out of court[12]. The position of an administrator in relation to contracts of employment is, however, somewhat different from that of a receiver. Though, *prima facie*, the receiver is personally liable on any contract of employment which is adopted by him in the performance of his functions[13], IA 1986 does

---

5   Schedule B1 paragraph 64 of IA 1986.
6   Schedule B1 paragraph 68 of IA 1986.
7   Schedule B1 paragraph 63 of IA 1986. It would be open to the court to give such a direction on the application of the administrators at the time that the company enters administration, particularly in circumstances where the question of the division of responsibilities between the proposed administrator and the directors is addressed as part of any application for appointment.
8   Schedule B1 paragraph 61(a) of IA 1986.
9   Schedule B1 paragraph 61(b) of IA 1986.
10   See also **PARAGRAPH 7.15** *post*.
11   *Powdrill v Watson* [1995] 2 AC 394 at 448E–G.
12   In *Re Mack Trucks (Britain) Ltd* [1967] 1 WLR 780 and *Nicoll v Cutts* [1985] 1 BCC 99427.
13   Sections 37(1), 44(1) and 57(2) of IA 1986. In the case of an administrative receiver, any such personal liability is now limited in relation to contracts of employment adopted on or after 15 March 1994 to 'qualifying liabilities': see sections 44(1)(b), (2A), (2B), (2C) and (2D) and 57(2), (2A), (2B) and (2C) of IA 1986. For a general discussion of the differences between the respective positions of an administrator and an administrative receiver see: *Powdrill v Watson* [1995] 2 AC 394.

not provide for an administrator to be personally liable in respect of employees' contracts of employment. The present position is, rather, that, upon the administrator ceasing to hold office, debts or liabilities arising under contracts of employment adopted by the administrator or a predecessor administrator are to be charged on and paid out of any property of the company in his custody or under his control at that time, in priority both to the administrator's own claims for his remuneration and expenses and to any security over such property which as created was a floating charge[14]. Any liability to make a payment under this provision is restricted to a liability to pay wages or salary, which includes holiday pay, sickness pay, payment in lieu of holiday and contributions to an occupational pension scheme[15]. It is also, however, expressly provided that action taken within the period of 14 days after an administrator's appointment shall not be taken to amount to or contribute to any such adoption[16].

7.5 In addition, debts or liabilities incurred whilst an administrator holds office, under contracts, including contracts of employment[17], entered into by the administrator or a predecessor of his in the carrying out of his or the predecessor's functions, are also, on the administrator ceasing to hold office, to be charged on any property of the company in his custody or under his control at that time and to enjoy the same degree of priority as liabilities arising under adopted contracts of employment[18]. Since an administrator is most unlikely to wish to incur personal liability on contracts entered into by him, this latter provision appears to be directed, at least primarily, at contracts, including contracts of employment, which an administrator enters into as agent[19] on behalf of the company. Thus there is a clear distinction to be drawn between existing contracts of employment which an administrator adopts and new contracts of employment into which an administrator enters on behalf of the company following his appointment.

7.6 The meaning of the word 'adopted' was the subject of consideration in *Powdrill v Watson*[20]. Evans-Lombe J, at first instance, came to the conclusion that the use of the verb 'adopt' did not import the voluntary assumption by the administrator of personal liability for an employee's contract but simply referred to the administrator having 'procured the company to continue to carry out' the employment contract in question[21]. This conclusion appears to be consistent with the apparently intended objective of the similarly worded sections 37(1), 44(1) and 57(2) of IA 1986, applying to receivers, namely the statutory reversal of the decision in *Nicoll v Cutts*[22]. Evans-Lombe J's decision was subsequently upheld in the Court of Appeal[23]. In the Court of Appeal, Dillon LJ, who delivered the leading judgment, stated that if administrators wished to use a company's existing staff they had either to adopt the existing contracts or to negotiate new contracts which did not amount to sham contracts[24]. If administrators continued substantially after the 14-day period of grace to continue to employ staff and to

14 Schedule B1 paragraph 99(4) and (5) of IA 1986.
15 Schedule B1 paragraph 99(6) of IA 1986.
16 Schedule B1 paragraph 99(5)(a) of IA 1986.
17 See eg *Powdrill v Watson* [1994] 2 BCLC 118 per Evans-Lombe J at 125i.
18 Schedule B1 paragraphs 99(4) and (5) of IA 1986.
19 Ie pursuant to Schedule B1 paragraph 69 of IA 1986. For an administrator's agency in this context see *Re a Company (No 005174 of 1999)* [2000] 1 BCLC 593 at 602g–h.
20 [1994] 2 BCLC 118 (Evans Lombe J, Court of Appeal) and [1995] 2 AC 394.
21 [1994] 2 BCLC 118 at 127h.
22 [1985] BCLC 322.
23 [1994] 2 BCLC 118 at 134.
24 [1994] 2 BCLC 118 at 140a.

pay them in accordance with their previous contracts, administrators would be held impliedly to have adopted their contracts of employment[25]. Dillon LJ also indicated that an administrator would be taken to have adopted a contract of employment:

(a) where, after the expiry of 14 days from his appointment, he stated that he was keeping on the employee in question or the labour force or a section of it of which the employee was a member;

(b) where, though saying nothing, he continued to use the employee's labour; or

(c) where he did some other act constituting a recognition of the continuation of the contract, eg paying the employee's salary, giving sick leave, allowing holidays[26].

Leggatt LJ stated that the word 'adopted' in relation to contracts of employment simply meant 'the continuance of which is expressly or impliedly accepted'[27].

7.7   The House of Lords[28] took a slightly different approach. Lord Browne-Wilkinson first explained that the mere continuation of the employment by the company does not lead inexorably to the conclusion that the contract has been adopted by the administrator[29], but then appeared to state that, if the employee has continued in employment for more than 14 days after the appointment of an administrator, there is no escape from the conclusion that the whole contract of employment has been adopted[30]. The apparent inconsistency in these two statements was considered by Laddie J in *Re Antal International Ltd*[31], in which the judge explained that the critical issue is whether the administrator has engaged in conduct which amounts to an election to continue the employees' contracts. In the case of *Powdrill v Watson*[32], it was doubtless the case that a mere continuation of the employment did amount to an election to continue to employ. That was not the case in the unusual circumstances of *Re Antal International Ltd*[33] itself where the administrator only became aware of the existence of the relevant employees (based in France) more than 14 days after their appointment, and took steps to terminate their employment immediately he did so.

7.8   At first instance in *Powdrill v Watson*, Evans-Lombe J had also held[34], albeit *obiter*, that it was permissible by an appropriately worded notice to contract out of the 'effect of adoption of contracts of employment', though for a notice to have such effect the notice would need to make clear to the recipient what right it was of the employee which the administrator was purporting to exclude. The Court of Appeal expressly reserved for a future occasion the question whether in the case of a new contract of employment an administrator could effectively exclude the operation of the provisions which are now contained in Schedule B1

25   [1994] 2 BCLC 118 at 139h.
26   [1994] 2 BCLC 118 at 140g, approving a passage to this effect in relation to receivers in Goode *Principles of Corporate Insolvency Law* (Sweet & Maxwell, 1990).
27   [1994] 2 BCLC 118 at 145a.
28   [1995] 2 AC 394.
29   [1995] 2 AC 394 at 448G.
30   [1995] 2 AC 394 at 449H–450A and 452C–D.
31   [2003] EWHC 1339 (Ch).
32   [1995] 2 AC 394.
33   [2003] EWHC 1339 (Ch).
34   [1994] 2 BCLC 118 at 129j–130b, following an earlier unreported decision of Harman J which dealt with the position of administrative receivers under section 44 of IA 1986 (*Re Specialised Mouldings Ltd* 13 February 1987, unreported).

paragraph 99(4) of IA 1986[35]. This issue was not decided by the House of Lords. Lord Browne-Wilkinson expressly limited his conclusion to a finding that a unilateral attempt by an administrator to avoid adoption while still allowing the employees to work for the company did not avoid an adoption[36].

7.9   It was further held in *Powdrill v Watson*[37] that where an administrator adopted an employment contract the statutory charge extended to all debts and liabilities becoming due under such a contract whilst the administrator was acting as such. This also extends to the PAYE and National Insurance payable on any such liability[38]. On this basis, the charge therefore secured not only remuneration for periods of employment whilst the company was in administration but also all the contractual debts or liabilities accruing due under a contract of employment at the date of its termination, if occurring whilst the company was in administration, including, in that case, accrued holiday pay entitlement, sums payable in lieu of notice, damages for wrongful dismissal, accrued bonuses and sums payable by the employer in respect of pension contributions. In particular, there was no requirement that the liability to pay such sums should be directly attributable to the period during which the administrator held office. On the other hand, it was also decided at first instance that the charge securing liabilities under adopted contracts of employment did not secure statutory employment rights or entitlements not forming part of an employee's contractual rights or entitlements such as sums payable for compensation for unfair dismissal[39].

7.10   In view of what were widely perceived, in particular by insolvency practitioners, to be the commercial consequences of the decisions at first instance and in the Court of Appeal in *Powdrill v Watson*[40], emergency legislation was enacted by Parliament in the form of IA 1994 amending, *inter alia*, the original form of section 19 of IA 1986[41], the predecessor to Schedule B1 paragraph 99 of IA 1986. The present legislation provides that, where there are liabilities arising under contracts of employment adopted by the administrator, the liabilities secured by the statutory charge are limited to amounts payable by way of wages or salary and no account is to be taken of any sums payable by reference to anything done or which occurs before the adoption of the contract[42]. Wages or salary payable in respect of a period of holiday or absence from work through sickness or other good cause and contributions to an occupational pension scheme are deemed, for this purpose, to be wages or salary in respect of services rendered in that period. A sum payable in lieu of holiday is deemed to be wages or salary payable in respect of services rendered in the period by reference to which the holiday entitlement arose[43].

7.11   In *Re Allders Department Stores Ltd*[44] the administrators of Allders applied for directions as to whether statutory liabilities for redundancy or unfair

35   Then section 19(5) of IA 1986; see [1994] 2 BCLC 118 at 141d–g and 145f.
36   [1995] 2 AC 394 at 452C–D.
37   [1995] 2 AC 394.
38   *IRC v Lawrence* [2001] 1 BCLC 204.
39   [1994] 2 BCLC 118 at 132e. On this basis, claims for a statutory redundancy payment also fall outwith the statutory charges for which Schedule B1 paragraph 99(4) of IA 1986 provides.
40   [1994] 2 BCLC 118. The consequences were considered to be even more serious for administrative receivers personally liable on contracts of employment adopted by them.
41   The bill received Royal Assent on 23 March 1994, approximately one month after the Court of Appeal's decision.
42   The form of words now contained in Schedule B1 paragraph 99(5)(b) of IA 1986.
43   Schedule B1 paragraph 99(6) of IA 1986.
44   [2005] EWHC 172 (Ch).

dismissal were to be paid as an expense of the administration within Rule 2.67(1)(f) of the Insolvency Rules 1986[45]. Lawrence Collins J held that they were not[46]. Subsequently in *Re Huddersfield Fine Worsteds Ltd*[47] Peter Smith J considered whether protective awards under section 189 of the Trade Union and Labour Relations (Consolidation) Act 1992 ('TULR(C)A 1992') and awards of pay in lieu of notice should fall within Schedule B1 paragraphs 99(4) to 99(6) of IA 1996. Peter Smith J distinguished the decision in *Re Allders Department Stores Ltd* and held that such payments were wages and salary for the purposes of Schedule B1 paragraph 99 of IA 1986. However, when the same issue came before Etherton J in *Re Ferrotech Ltd*[48], he held that protective awards under TULR(C)A 1992 and awards of pay in lieu of notice did not fall within paragraph 99 of IA 1986, *inter alia* because giving priority to such payments would seriously undermine the rescue culture that underlay the administration regime. On conjoined appeals of these two cases[49], the Court of Appeal agreed that for such payments to fall within Schedule B1 paragraph 99 of IA 1986 would be to undermine the rescue culture and held that protective awards under section 189 of TULR(C)A 1992 did not arise *under* a contract of employment and so did not fall within this provision. The Court of Appeal further accepted that there were four principal categories of payment in lieu of notice[50] and of these only the first category, namely, where an employer gives proper notice of termination, tells the employee that he need not work his notice period and pays a lump sum attributable to this period, fell within Schedule B1 paragraph 99 of IA 1986 because such payments were wages within the normal meaning of that word.

7.12 Thus, in broad terms, the statutory charge now only secures wages or salary or contributions to an occupational pension scheme to which an employee is entitled under his contract of employment and which are attributable to services rendered after the adoption of his contract of employment whilst the administrator remains in office. In particular, sums payable in lieu of notice[51] or by way of damages for wrongful dismissal do not constitute qualifying liabilities. It should be noted that in any event the court has power to direct payment forthwith of sums due under a contract of employment as an administration expense, notwithstanding that the administrator remains in office so that the statutory charge has not yet arisen[52]. In practice, of course, an administrator may, in any event, be obliged to pay the remuneration of those employees whose continued services he requires for the purposes of the administration.

7.13 As regards new contracts of employment into which an administrator enters after his appointment as agent of the company, the statutory charge

---

[45] The equivalent provision in the Rules is at Rule 3.51.
[46] [2005] EWHC 172 (Ch) (paragraph 24). Lawrence Collins J fortified himself in reaching this conclusion by observing that leading practitioner texts, including the second edition of this work, considered that statutory employment claims were unsecured claims: [2005] EWHC 172 (Ch) (paragraph 25).
[47] [2005] EWHC 1682 (Ch).
[48] [2005] EWHC 1848 (Ch).
[49] *Re Huddersfield Fine Worsteds Ltd* [2005] EWCA Civ 1072.
[50] As identified by the House of Lords in *Delaney v Staples* [1992] 1 AC 687.
[51] Save to the extent that they are paid where an employer has given proper notice of termination, tells the employee he need not work his notice and pays the employee a lump sum attributable to this period: see **PARAGRAPH 7.11** *ante*.
[52] See eg *Powdrill v Watson* [1994] 2 BCLC 118 per Dillon LJ at 142a. The court also has a discretion to direct the payment of interest upon such sums, see *Powdrill v Watson* [1994] 2 BCLC 118 per Dillon LJ at 143h.

conferred by Schedule B1 paragraph 99(4) of IA 1986 is not confined in its operation to wages and salary referable to what occurs after the date of adoption, and accordingly, the extent of the debts and liabilities thereby secured will be all liabilities arising out of the contract. It may, of course, occur that an administrator, apart from taking on new employees, may wish to renegotiate the terms upon which the company's existing workforce is employed, for instance, to reduce the level of remuneration and benefits payable thereunder. Such renegotiated contracts, if not amounting to sham contracts[53] or mere variations of the existing contracts, may constitute new contracts of employment for the purpose of Schedule B1 paragraph 99(4) of IA 1986. If so, unless the administrator can successfully exclude the operation of the statutory charge, the benefits to be derived from such renegotiation may turn out to be illusory since the liabilities secured by Schedule B1 paragraph 99(4) are not confined to qualifying liabilities and may be substantially more extensive.

7.14   It therefore becomes important to consider whether it is possible to contract out of the rights conferred by Schedule B1 paragraph 99(4) of IA 1986. As noted above[54], in *Powdrill v Watson*[55], Evans-Lombe J appears to have accepted that contracting out was possible. In so doing, he followed Harman J in the earlier unreported case of *Re Specialised Mouldings Ltd*[56] in rejecting an argument that such contracting out was only possible where IA 1986 expressly so provided, ie in the case of new contracts entered into by receivers[57]. Evans-Lombe J nevertheless acknowledged the strength of the argument to the contrary. Further, though the Court of Appeal left open the question whether it was possible to contract out of the provisions now contained in Schedule B1 paragraph 99 of IA 1986, Dillon LJ expressly stated that the decision in *Re Specialised Mouldings Ltd* could not rank as a helpful authority. Dillon LJ also specifically declined to consider the possible application to what was then section 19(5) of IA 1986 of the principle applied by the House of Lords in *Salford Union Guardians v Dewhurst*[58] that it was not possible to contract out of a mandatory statutory requirement[59]. The point was not dealt with by the House of Lords[60]. Given the present state of the authorities, it must remain an open question whether it is possible to contract out of the effect of Schedule B1 paragraph 99(4) of IA 1986 in an employment context. Administrators seeking to renegotiate existing contracts of employment, as well as those entering into new contracts generally, cannot therefore safely assume either that such contracting out is possible or that it will be held to be effective. Furthermore, in practice, the issue of whether or not it is possible to contract out is more likely to be effective (if it ever is) in the case of individually negotiated arrangements with members of senior management as opposed to a workforce as a whole.

---

53   [1994] 2 BCLC 118 at 140a: it is not entirely clear what Dillon LJ meant when he referred to 'sham contracts'. A sham was described by Diplock LJ in *Snook v London and West Riding Investments Ltd* [1967] 2 QB 786 as meaning 'acts done or documents executed by parties to the "sham" which are intended to give to third parties or to the court the appearance of creating between the parties legal rights and obligations different from the actual legal rights and obligations (if any) which the parties intended to create'.

54   See **PARAGRAPH 7.8** *ante*.

55   [1994] 2 BCLC 118.

56   (13 February 1987, unreported).

57   See sections 37(1)(a), 44(1)(b) and 57(2) of IA 1986.

58   [1926] AC 619.

59   [1994] BCLC 118 at 141b–g.

60   [1995] 2 AC 394.

7.15   An administrator's approach in relation to a company's employees will be determined by reference to the principal objective with which he is performing his functions. Against that background, the administrator will have to determine at an early stage whether the company's employees are likely to be required in the conduct of the administration and, if so, which of the company's employees are likely to be required and for how long. Accordingly, an administrator may well decide to dispense with the services of the company's employees or some of them either immediately or shortly after the company enters administration. Even where the administrator decides that the purpose of administration will not be served by a particular employee or employees generally being dismissed with immediate effect, an executive director or any employee occupying a senior executive position may be able to claim that the abrogation of his role in the management of the company's affairs constitutes a repudiation of his contract of employment and further that such repudiation amounts to a constructive dismissal of him. Provided that his contract of employment had not been adopted by the administrator, any claim by an existing director or employee for damages for wrongful dismissal is likely to be an unsecured claim against the company[61]. On the other hand, such claims, if of sufficient magnitude, may be a potential problem for an administrator seeking to obtain approval by the creditors of a company voluntary arrangement.

RIGHTS OF EMPLOYEES AS PREFERENTIAL CREDITORS

7.16   As already noted, though, generally speaking, an administrator has no specific responsibility for discharging either in whole or in part the liabilities of the company to preferential creditors the priority of the claims of preferential creditors is effectively preserved in an administration. In particular, employees and ex-employees of an insolvent company may rank as preferential creditors in respect of certain debts owing at the 'relevant date'. In the case of a voluntary arrangement, the relevant date will be the date on which the arrangement takes effect unless the approval is obtained in the course of an administration, in which case the relevant date will be the date on which the company entered administration[62]. There are also a number of complex provisions, which relate back a winding-up to the date on which the company entered administration for the purposes of determining the relevant date[63]. Furthermore, the date that the company entered administration is now the relevant date whenever the question of a creditor's preferential status may arise in an administration[64] (eg in relation to distributions[65]).

7.17   The debts which are preferential debts for the purposes of a formal insolvency under IA 1986 are set out in section 386 and Schedule 6 thereto (read in conjunction with Schedule 4 to the Pension Schemes Act 1993). These debts include, *inter alia*:

(a)   so much of any amount which is owed by the company to an existing or former employee and is payable by way of remuneration in respect of the

---

61   Assuming that the administrator has not entered into a fresh contract of employment with him which falls within the provisions of Schedule B1 paragraph 99(4) of IA 1986.
62   Section 387(2) of IA 1986.
63   Section 387(3) of IA 1986.
64   Section 387(3A) of IA 1986.
65   Under Schedule B1 paragraph 65 of IA 1986. See further, **CHAPTER 15** *post*.

whole or any part of the period of four months up to the relevant date; priority is enjoyed only to the extent that such unpaid remuneration does not exceed the maximum amount prescribed by order of the Secretary of State[66];

(b) any amount owed by way of accrued holiday remuneration in respect of any period of employment before the relevant date to an employee whose employment has been terminated, whether before, on or after that date[67]; and

(c) so much of any sum owed in respect of money advanced for the purpose as has been applied for the payment of a debt which, if it had not been paid, would have been a debt falling within (a) and (b) above[68].

7.18   For the purpose of determining its preferential status, an amount is to be regarded as payable by way of remuneration in respect of any period if it is paid as wages or salary, whether for time or piecework or earned wholly or partly by way of commission in respect of services rendered in that period[69]. It does not include remuneration payable to a director by way of fees. Remuneration payable in respect of a period of holiday or of absence from work through sickness or other good cause is deemed to be wages or salary in respect of services rendered in that period[70].

7.19   Other statutory entitlements of employees are also deemed to be remuneration in respect of the period for which they are payable and therefore potentially preferential[71]. These entitlements are as follows:

(a) guaranteed payments under Part III of the Employment Rights Act 1996 ('ERA 1996') (employee without work to do);

(b) any payment for time off under section 53 (time off to look for work or arrange training) or 56 (time for ante-natal care) of ERA 1996 or under section 169 of TULR(C)A 1992 (time off for carrying out trade union duties, etc);

(c) remuneration on suspension on medical grounds, or on maternity grounds, under Part VII of ERA 1996;

(d) remuneration under a protective award under section 189 of TULR(C)A 1992 (redundancy dismissal with compensation)[72].

CLAIMS AND ENTITLEMENTS FOLLOWING DISMISSAL

7.20   It is likely that during the course of an administration, employees of the company will be dismissed by the administrator, either immediately on appointment or thereafter. Such dismissals of employees effected in the course of administration proceedings are likely to give rise to entitlements arising under the employment protection legislation, or at common law, or both. It had been held at employment tribunal level that statutory employment proceedings within the jurisdiction of an employment tribunal could be commenced and continued against a company in administration without the consent of the administrator or leave of the court, by way of exception to the general rule under what is now

66   Schedule 6 paragraph 9 of IA 1986: the present limit is £800: see the Insolvency Proceedings (Monetary Limits) Order 1986 (SI 1986 No 1996).
67   Schedule 6 paragraph 10 of IA 1986.
68   Schedule 6 paragraph 11 of IA 1986.
69   Schedule 6 paragraph 13(1)(a) of IA 1986.
70   Schedule 6 paragraph 15(a) of IA 1986, ie including statutory sick pay.
71   Schedule 6 paragraph 13(1)(b) and (2) of IA 1986.
72   See **PARAGRAPH 7.42**FF *post*.

Schedule B1 paragraph 43(6) of IA 1986[73]. This decision was overruled by the Employment Appeal Tribunal in *Carr v British International Helicopters Ltd*[74] which held that the consent of the administrator or the leave of the court was required for the commencement of such proceedings, although in the ordinary case such consent or leave would often be granted[75].

Redundancy payments

7.21   An employee who has completed at least two years' continuous employment or more and who is dismissed by reason of redundancy will (subject to certain statutory exceptions) be entitled to a statutory redundancy payment[76]. An employee will be taken to be dismissed by reason of redundancy where the dismissal is attributable wholly or mainly to:

(a)   the cessation or intended cessation of the business for the purposes of which the employee was employed, either completely or at the place where the employee was employed; or

(b)   the cessation or diminution, or expected cessation or diminution, of the requirements of that business for employees to carry out work of a particular kind, either completely or at the place where the employee was employed[77].

7.22   The amount of a statutory redundancy payment is based on the employee's age, length of employment and gross average wage, expressed as a weekly amount. The employee will be entitled to:

(a)   one and a half weeks' pay for each year of continuous employment consisting wholly of weeks in which the employee was not below the age of 41;

(b)   one week's pay for each year of continuous employment consisting wholly of weeks in which the employee was below the age of 41 but not below the age of 22;

(c)   half a week's pay for each year of continuous employment not falling within (a) or (b) above excluding any period prior to the employee's eighteenth birthday[78].

7.23   The maximum number of years of continuous employment which count is 20 (the last 20 being the ones which will count)[79]; and there is also a statutory limit on the maximum amount of a 'week's pay' counting for the purposes of the calculation. This last amount is reviewed annually. The maximum as from 6 April 2016 is £479 per week[80]. An employee's claim for an unpaid statutory

---

73   *MSF v Parkfield Castings, a division of Parkfield Group plc (in liquidation)* (COIT case no 22180/90, unreported).
74   [1993] BCC 855. It was held, however, that employment tribunal proceedings commenced without such leave or consent did not constitute a nullity, but should be stayed pending application for the administrator's consent or the leave of the court for the continuation of the proceedings.
75   [1993] BCC 855; cf *Re Hartlebury Printers Ltd (in liquidation)* [1992] ICR 559 where Morritt J refused to grant leave for the commencement or continuation of employment tribunal proceedings commenced against the company where the claim made in the proceedings was readily demonstrated to be without any merit.
76   Sections 135 and 155 of ERA 1996.
77   Section 139(1) of ERA 1996.
78   Section 162(1) of ERA 1996.
79   Section 162(3) of ERA 1996.
80   Section 227(1) of ERA 1996 and the Employment Rights (Increase of Limits) Order 2016 (SI 2016 No 288).

redundancy payment does not rank as a preferential claim, but it is a claim in respect of which application may be made for payment out of the National Insurance Fund[81].

Unfair dismissal

7.24 An employee of a company who is dismissed by the administrator of the company and who has, by the effective date of termination of his employment, completed at least two years' continuous employment[82], may bring a complaint of unfair dismissal before an employment tribunal[83]. In order to resist such a claim, it is necessary for the employer to show the reason for the dismissal (or the principal reason if more than one) and that it was one of a number of substantial potentially fair reasons for dismissal set out in the legislation or some other substantial reason of a kind such as to justify dismissal[84]. If the employer discharges this burden, the employment tribunal must go on to consider whether in the circumstances the employer acted reasonably or unreasonably in treating the reason as a sufficient reason for dismissing the employee[85].

7.25 The substantial reason most likely to be relevant in the case of a company in administration is redundancy[86]. A dismissal by the administrator, albeit for the reason of redundancy, will be held to be automatically unfair where the employee has been selected for redundancy for reasons relating to membership or non-membership of a trade union[87] (in which case no period of qualifying employment is required)[88], for reasons relating to the employee taking leave for family reasons[89], or for reasons relating to the employee's activities in connection with health and safety at work[90].

7.26 A redundancy dismissal which is not automatically unfair may nevertheless be held to be unreasonable and therefore unfair in the circumstances where the administrator has:

(a) selected the employee for dismissal using unfair criteria or applied fair criteria in an unfair fashion[91];

(b) failed to give the employee advance warning of redundancy or to consult with the employee or has otherwise handled the redundancy in an unfair manner[92] (eg by failing to consider whether the employee instead of being dismissed could be offered alternative employment[93]).

---

81 Section 166 of ERA 1996.
82 Section 108 of ERA 1996. Where the period of continuous employment began before 6 April 2012, this time period is one year: Unfair Dismissal and Statement of Reasons for Dismissal (Variation of Qualifying Period) Order 2012 (SI 2012 No 989).
83 Section 111 of ERA 1996.
84 Section 98(1) and (2) of ERA 1996.
85 Section 98(4) of ERA 1996. Cf *Airbus UK Ltd v Webb* [2008] EWCA Civ 49.
86 Section 98(2)(c) of ERA 1996.
87 Sections 152 and 153 of TULR(C)A 1992.
88 Section 154 of TULR(C)A 1992.
89 Section 99 of ERA 1996.
90 Section 100 of ERA 1996.
91 Section 188(3) of TULR(C)A 1992. See *Williams v Compair Maxam Ltd* [1982] ICR 156, EAT. See also **PARAGRAPH 7.42FF** *post*.
92 See *Polkey v A E Dayton Services Ltd* [1988] ICR 142.
93 *Vokes Ltd v Bear* [1974] ICR 1; *Stacey v Babcock Power Ltd* [1986] ICR 221.

7.27   The usual remedy in the case of a successful complaint of unfair dismissal is an award of compensation. An employment tribunal award of compensation must consist of a basic award and a compensatory award[94]. The basic award is calculated in the same way as a statutory redundancy payment, taking account of the employee's age, period of continuous employment (subject to a maximum of 20 years counting) and gross average wage, expressed as a weekly amount (subject to a statutory ceiling for calculation purposes) save that the exclusion of periods of continuous employment whilst the employee was under the age of 18 does not apply[95]. The compensatory award is of such amount as the employment tribunal considers just and equitable in all the circumstances, having regard to the loss sustained by the employee in consequence of his dismissal in so far as that loss is attributable to the employer's action[96]. It will take account of loss of salary or wages and of fringe benefits (including pensions) and other elements such as loss of statutory employment rights[97]. The employee is subject to a duty to mitigate such loss and the compensation award will be diminished to the extent that the employee succeeds or ought to have succeeded in this regard[98]. Where the employment tribunal finds that the dismissal was to any extent caused or contributed to by action of the employee, it is required to reduce the award by such proportion as it considers just and equitable having regard to that finding[99]. Where there is a finding of unfair dismissal due to a procedural defect when the dismissal was for a potentially fair reason then an award may be reduced to take account of the fact that the employee may have been dismissed in any event. The compensatory award is subject to a statutory maximum, which is subject to annual review and with effect from 6 April 2016 stands at £78,962[100].

7.28   An employment tribunal award for compensation does not constitute a preferential claim against the company's assets. There is, however, a distinction between the basic award and the compensatory award. An employee in whose favour a basic award is made against an insolvent company may apply to the Secretary of State for the amount of the award to be paid to him from the National Insurance Fund[101]. By contrast, the compensatory award comprises only an unsecured claim against the company's assets.

Wrongful dismissal

7.29   Where the administrator dismisses the employee in breach of contract, eg in the case of a contract terminable by notice, by failing to give the stipulated notice, or, where the notice period has not been expressly agreed, reasonable notice at common law (being in either case not less than the employee's statutory minimum notice entitlement) or by prematurely terminating the employee's fixed-term contract, the employee will have a common law claim for breach of the employment contract or 'wrongful dismissal'. A claim for damages will lie

---

94   Section 118 of ERA 1996.
95   Section 119 of ERA 1996.
96   Section 123(1) of ERA 1996.
97   *Norton Tool Co Ltd v Tewson* [1972] ICR 501 approved by the House of Lords in *Dunnachie v Kingston upon Hull City Council* [2004] UKHL 36.
98   Section 123(4) of ERA 1996.
99   Section 123(6) of ERA 1996.
100 Section 124 of ERA 1996 and the Employment Rights (Increase of Limits) Order 2016 (SI 2016 No 288).
101 Section 184(1)(d) of ERA 1996.

which will be based on the employee's loss of salary or wages and contractual benefits over the notice period (having regard to the minimum periods of notice prescribed by legislation)[102] or the residue of the contractual term, subject to the employee's duty to mitigate his loss.

7.30   Any award of damages will rank as an unsecured claim against the company's assets[103]. However, where the company is insolvent, the employee may apply to the Secretary of State for a payment from the National Insurance Fund in respect of the employee's statutory minimum notice entitlement[104].

PAYMENTS OUT OF THE NATIONAL INSURANCE FUND

7.31   An employee of a company in administration who is dismissed may, in consequence of the company being insolvent, apply to the Secretary of State for certain payments to be made to him out of the National Insurance Fund[105].

Redundancy payments

7.32   As mentioned in **PARAGRAPH 7.23** *ante*, such application may be made in respect of an unpaid redundancy payment. If, on an application made to him in writing by the relevant employee, the Secretary of State is satisfied that:

(a)   the employee is entitled to the payment, and

(b)   the employer is insolvent[106] and the whole or part of the payment remains unpaid, the Secretary of State is required to pay to the employee the amount of the payment or the unpaid part as the case may be[107]. Following such payment, all rights to recover the payment from the company pass to the Secretary of State[108].

Statutory maternity pay

7.33   An employee who is entitled to statutory maternity pay and is unable to obtain payment of it (including by reason of insolvency) may apply to the Secretary of State for payment of the relevant amount out of the National Insurance Fund[109]. Again, following such payment, all rights to recover the payment from the company pass to the Secretary of State.

---

102   Section 86(1) of ERA 1996.
103   Unless the contract of employment was adopted by the administrator or was entered into by him after the company entered administration: see **PARAGRAPH 7.4FF** *ante*.
104   Section 184(1)(b) of ERA 1996.
105   Sections 182–186 of ERA 1996.
106   An employer is taken to be insolvent where a company is in administration: section 183 of ERA 1996.
107   Section 182 of ERA 1996.
108   Section 189 of ERA 1996.
109   Regulations 7 and 30 of the Statutory Maternity Pay (General) Regulations 1986 (SI 1986 No 1960). Employees entitled to statutory paternity pay or statutory adoption pay may apply to HMRC for payment of the relevant amount (regulation 43 of the Statutory Paternity Pay and Statutory Adoption Pay (General) Regulations 2002 (SI 2002 No 2822)).

Other debts

7.34   An employee who has been dismissed from the service of a company in administration may also apply to the Secretary of State for payment of certain other debts[110]. The Secretary of State is obliged to make a payment in respect of the debt claimed on being satisfied that the employer has become insolvent, that the employee's employment has terminated and that on 'the appropriate date'[111] the employee was entitled to be paid the whole or part of the debt concerned.

7.35   The debts in respect of which a claim may be made are:

(a)   arrears of pay in respect of one or more (but no more than eight) weeks[112] (such arrears being deemed to include a guarantee payment, remuneration on suspension on medical grounds[113], remuneration on suspension on maternity grounds[114], payment for time off for trade union duties or for seeking alternative employment following notice of redundancy, and remuneration under a protective award)[115];

(b)   any amount which the company is liable to pay to the employee for any period of statutory minimum notice or for any failure to give such notice[116];

(c)   any holiday pay for a period or periods of holiday not exceeding six weeks in all, to which the employee became entitled during the 12 months ending on 'the appropriate date'[117];

(d)   any basic award of compensation for unfair dismissal[118];

(e)   reasonable sum for reimbursement of the whole or part of any fee or premium paid by an apprentice or articled clerk[119].

Where the amount of the debt is referable to a period of time, the maximum amount payable to an employee in respect of each category of debt (ie (a) to (e) above), for any one week (or proportionately less for a period of less than a week), is fixed by the Secretary of State by order[120].

7.36   The expression 'the appropriate date' means, in relation to arrears of pay (other than remuneration under a protective award) and to holiday pay, the date on which the company became insolvent[121]. In relation to a protective award or a basic award of compensation for unfair dismissal, the expression means the latest of:

(a)   the date on which the employer became insolvent;

(b)   the date of termination of the employee's employment; and

(c)   the date on which the award was made[122].

---

110   Sections 182 and 184 of ERA 1996.
111   Sections 182(c) and 185 of ERA 1996.
112   Section 184(1)(a) of ERA 1996.
113   Defined at section 64 of ERA 1996.
114   Defined at section 66 of ERA 1996.
115   Section 184(2) of ERA 1996.
116   Section 184(1)(b) of ERA 1996.
117   Section 184(1)(c) of ERA 1996.
118   Section 184(1)(d) of ERA 1996.
119   Section 184(1)(e) of ERA 1996.
120   Section 186 of ERA 1996 (see SI 2016 No 288; the present limit is £479 per week).
121   Section 185(a) of ERA 1996.
122   Section 185(b) of ERA 1996.

In relation to any other claim, the expression means the later of (a) and (b) above[123]. Therefore, the Secretary of State will only pay in respect of arrears of pay or holiday pay by reference to the period up to the company becoming insolvent[124].

7.37 Where a claim for arrears of wages, holiday pay or any amount which the company is liable to pay in respect of a period of statutory minimum notice for any week exceeds the maximum amount referred to in **PARAGRAPH 7.35** *ante*, the Secretary of State is entitled to reduce the claim to the statutory amount and then to deduct any tax and National Insurance payments due upon that amount[125].

7.38 The procedure for making claims on the National Insurance Fund is that the employee should first apply to the administrator for payment. Having ascertained the amount properly payable, the administrator should prepare and send to the Secretary of State a statement of the amounts appearing to him to be payable to the applicant[126]. The Secretary of State will make the payment and can in fact do so in the absence of the statement if he is satisfied that he does not need the statement in order to determine the amount of the debt owed and unpaid[127]. Following such payment, all rights to recover the payment from the company pass to the Secretary of State[128].

Unpaid pension contributions

7.39 A claim may also be submitted to the Secretary of State for a payment in respect of unpaid relevant contributions to an occupational pension scheme. Application may be made by the person 'competent to act in respect of the occupational or personal pension scheme' who will generally be its trustee or trustees. The Secretary of State is required to make a payment upon being satisfied that at the time when the employer became insolvent[129] there were 'relevant contributions' to the scheme which were unpaid by the employer[130].

7.40 'Relevant contributions' are contributions payable by the employer on his own account and employees' contributions which have been deducted by the employer from pay but not paid into the scheme[131]. The payment which may be claimed in respect of contributions payable by the employer on his own account is the smallest of the following:

(a) the balance of the contributions payable by the employer and unpaid in respect of the 12 months preceding the employer's insolvency;

(b) the amount certified by an actuary as necessary to meet the scheme's liability on dissolution to pay the benefits provided by the scheme to or in respect of the employees of the employer;

---

123 Section 185(c) of ERA 1996.
124 Ie in the case of an administration, the date upon which the company enters administration: section 183(3)(a) of ERA 1996.
125 *Morris v Secretary of State for Employment* [1985] ICR 522.
126 Section 187(1) of ERA 1996.
127 Section 187(2) of ERA 1996.
128 Including any right to receive the payment as a preferential debt of the company: section 189(2) of ERA 1996, in which event, as against the employee concerned, the Secretary of State is entitled to priority over any other preferential debts owed to the employee.
129 Section 124(1) of Pension Schemes Act 1993.
130 Section 124(2) of Pension Schemes Act 1993.
131 Section 124(2) of Pension Schemes Act 1993.

(c) 10 percent of the total remuneration paid or payable to those employees for the 12 months preceding the employer's insolvency[132].

The payment in respect of employees' contributions is limited to the amount of such contributions deducted from pay during the 12 months preceding the employer's insolvency[133].

7.41 A statement by the administrator (or other 'relevant officer') to the Secretary of State as to the amount of relevant contributions appearing to have been unpaid on the date of the employer's insolvency is normally a prerequisite of payment (and the administrator must provide such a statement on request)[134] but the Secretary of State may make a payment without such a statement if he is satisfied that he does not need one in order to determine the amount of unpaid relevant contributions[135]. Following payment, all rights to recover the payment from the employer pass to the Secretary of State[136].

CONSULTATION WITH REPRESENTATIVES ABOUT PROPOSED REDUNDANCIES

7.42 An employer proposing to dismiss on grounds of redundancy 20 or more employees within 90 days is subject to statutory obligations[137] to consult with representatives and for this purpose to provide specified information to the representatives. Where the employees are of a description in respect of which a trade union is recognised, representatives will mean representatives of the trade union[138], otherwise it will mean employee representatives who are either elected or in some circumstances appointed[139]. The statutory obligation to consult continues to apply after the company enters administration which does not of itself displace the need for compliance[140].

7.43 There are specific timing requirements in relation to the obligation to consult:

(a) where it is proposed to dismiss as redundant 100 or more employees, consultation must begin at least 45 days before the first dismissal occurs;

(b) where it is proposed to dismiss as redundant 20 or more but fewer than 100 employees, consultation must begin at least 30 days before the first dismissal occurs[141].

---

132 Section 124(3) of Pension Schemes Act 1993.
133 Section 124(5) of Pension Schemes Act 1993.
134 Section 125(1) of Pension Schemes Act 1993.
135 Section 125(5) of Pension Schemes Act 1993.
136 Section 127 of Pension Schemes Act 1993.
137 Section 188 of TULR(C)A 1992. In *USDAW v Ethel Austin Ltd* [2013] ICR 1300, it was held that the words 'at one establishment' should be deleted from section 188 as a matter of construction in order for this provision to comply with Council Directive 98/59/EC and to avoid a fact-sensitive approach when considering whether the requirements of section 188 had been met.
138 Section 188(1B)(a) of TULR(C)A 1992.
139 Section 188(1B)(b) of TULR(C)A 1992.
140 *Re Hartlebury Printers Ltd (in liquidation)* [1992] ICR 559; see further, however, **PARAGRAPH 7.48** *post*.
141 Section 188(1A) of TULR(C)A 1992.

7.44   The purpose of consultation is to give the employees the opportunity of contributing to the decision-making process and to give their views on issues such as selection for redundancy and timing. It follows that any consultation does not meet the statutory requirement if it begins after employees have been given notice of dismissal for redundancy. On the other hand, it is thought that an employer can give notice of dismissal once the process of consultation has begun provided that it is made clear that the notice may be withdrawn if agreement is reached as a result of the consultation.

7.45   To facilitate the process of consultation, the statute requires that the appropriate representatives be given information on the following points:

(a)   the reasons why the redundancies are proposed;

(b)   the number and descriptions of the employees affected;

(c)   the total number of employees of the relevant descriptions employed at the establishment in question;

(d)   the selection criteria;

(e)   method of carrying out the dismissals;

(f)   the proposed method of calculating the amount of any redundancy payments to be made;

(g)   the number of agency workers working for and under the supervision of the employer;

(h)   the parts of the employer's undertaking in which those agency workers are working; and

(i)   the type of work those agency workers are carrying out[142].

This information has to be supplied in writing. The consultation is required to include consultation about ways of avoiding the dismissals, reducing the numbers of employees to be dismissed and mitigating the consequences of the dismissals. It is to be undertaken by the employer with a view to reaching agreement with the employee's representatives[143].

7.46   Where an employer fails to comply with its obligation, an employee, employee representative, or recognised trade union may complain to an employment tribunal[144] on behalf of the employees who have been dismissed as redundant or whom it is proposed will be dismissed as redundant and in respect of whom the employer has failed to comply with its obligations[145]. A protective award requires payment to the employees concerned of remuneration for a period from the earlier of:

(a)   the date when the first dismissal takes effect (irrespective of when the dismissed employee actually leaves); and

(b)   the date when the award is made,

and continuing for such period as the employment tribunal considers just and equitable, but it shall not exceed 90 days[146]. An employer is not entitled to

---

142   Section 188(4) of TULR(C)A 1992.
143   Section 188(2) of TULR(C)A 1992.
144   Section 189(1) of TULR(C)A 1992.
145   Section 189(3) of TULR(C)A 1992.
146   Section 189(4) of TULR(C)A 1992.

deduct from sums due under a protective award sums paid to the employee under the contract of employment in respect of the same period[147]. A complaint must be presented within three months of the last relevant dismissal. An employment tribunal may, however, entertain a complaint presented after the three-month period if it is satisfied that it was not reasonably practicable for the claim to be presented within the three-month period[148].

7.47 An employee who is in employment during the protected period and who:

(a) is fairly dismissed for a reason other than redundancy;

(b) unreasonably terminates his employment;

(c) unreasonably refuses an offer of alternative employment by the employer; or

(d) accepts an offer of alternative employment but unreasonably terminates or gives notice under his new contract,

will not be entitled to a protective award in respect of any period during which he would have remained in the company's employment but for such dismissal, termination or refusal[149].

7.48 The statute gives a defence to a complaint of failure to comply with the consultation requirements where the employer is able to show that there were 'special circumstances' which rendered it not reasonably practicable for the employer to comply with the consultation requirements[150]. It is specifically provided that where the decision leading to a dismissal is that of a person who controls the employer, directly or indirectly, the failure of that person to supply the requisite information to the transferor is not a 'special circumstance'[151]. It is also well established that insolvency does not, of itself, amount to 'special circumstances' and that it is necessary for an employment tribunal to examine the particular circumstances in order to determine whether they are 'special'[152]. Thus while, as previously indicated[153], the appointment of an administrator of itself does not constitute a special circumstance, the combination of the appointment and the other circumstances of the case considered in the light of the duties and responsibilities of the administrator may constitute special circumstances[154]. An example of 'special circumstances' would be a sudden and unforeseen event necessitating the closure of the business[155], as distinct from where the closure was the result of a gradual decline in business. The burden of proof of 'special circumstances' lies on the administrator, who must also prove the company took such steps towards compliance as were reasonably practicable[156].

147 Section 190(3) of TULR(C)A 1992 which permitted such deductions was repealed by section 34(3) of the Trade Union Reform and Employment Rights Act 1993.
148 Section 189(5) of TULR(C)A 1992, in which event the complaint must have been presented within such time as the tribunal considers reasonable.
149 Section 191 of TULR(C)A 1992.
150 Section 188(7) of TULR(C)A 1992.
151 Section 188(7) of TULR(C)A 1992.
152 *Re Hartlebury Printers Ltd* [1992] ICR 559; *Clarks of Hove Ltd v Bakers Union* [1978] ICR 1076.
153 See **PARAGRAPH 7.42** *ante*.
154 *Re Hartlebury Printers Ltd* [1992] ICR 559.
155 *Union of Shop, Distributive and Allied Workers v Leancut Bacon Ltd (in liquidation)* [1981] IRLR 295, EAT.
156 Section 189(6) of TULR(C)A 1992.

NOTIFICATION OF PROPOSED REDUNDANCIES TO THE DEPARTMENT OF EMPLOYMENT

7.49 An administrator proposing to dismiss several employees by reason of redundancy may be subject to a duty to notify the Department for Business, Innovation and Skills in writing of his proposal: there is a prescribed form for the purpose[157]. The obligation will arise where the administrator:

(a) proposes to make 100 or more employees at one establishment redundant within 90 days or less;

(b) proposes to make 20 or more employees redundant within such a period.

In case (a) above, notification must be given at least 45 days before the first dismissal takes effect, and in case (b) above at least 30 days beforehand[158]. A copy of the notification must be given to any representatives to be consulted[159]. Where 'special circumstances' render full compliance with this obligation not reasonably practicable the administrator must take such steps to comply as are reasonably practicable in the circumstances[160]. Ignorance of the requirement does not constitute a 'special circumstance'[161]. Failure to comply is a criminal offence, which may result in conviction and a fine of up to level five on the standard scale for magistrates' courts[162].

SALE OF THE BUSINESS OR ASSETS

7.50 The achievement of the purpose of administration may necessitate or involve the sale of the company's business in whole or in part. The administrator will endeavour to effect any such sales on a going concern basis subject always to the objective with which he is performing his functions and the approval of his proposals by creditors. However, careful consideration is required both by the administrator and by any purchaser of the implications of the Transfer of Undertakings (Protection of Employment) Regulations 2006 (as amended) (the 'Transfer Regulations')[163]. The Transfer Regulations replaced the Transfer of Undertakings (Protection of Employment) Regulations 1981 ('TUPE 1981')[164], which were introduced to bring the laws of the United Kingdom into compliance with a European Union Directive (known as the 'Acquired Rights Directive')[165]. The European Court itself has considered the application of the Acquired Rights Directive in the context of insolvency. The European Court has drawn a distinction between insolvency procedures initiated for the purpose of winding up a company in order to distribute its assets and the situation where the procedures are intended to facilitate the sale of the company's business as an ongoing entity. The European Court has held that the Acquired Rights Directive

---

157 Section 193(4) of TULR(C)A 1992.
158 Section 193(1) and (2) of TULR(C)A 1992.
159 Section 193(6) of TULR(C)A 1992.
160 Section 193(7) of TULR(C)A 1992.
161 *Secretary of State for Employment v Helitron Ltd* [1980] ICR 523.
162 Section 194(1) of TULR(C)A 1992.
163 SI 2006 No 246.
164 SI 1981 No 1794.
165 Council Directive 77/187/EEC of 14 February 1977 on the approximation of the laws of the Member States relating to the safeguarding of employees' rights in the event of transfers of undertakings, businesses or parts of businesses, as now amended by Directive 98/50.

is not applicable to the former but is applicable to the latter[166]. In most cases, administration proceedings would appear to fall into the latter category[167].

7.51 The Transfer Regulations apply to the 'transfer' of an 'undertaking' or 'business'[168]. The Transfer Regulations will also apply to the transfer of part of an undertaking or business[169].

7.52 What is transferred need only be something in the nature of a stable 'economic entity'[170] which is resumed or continued by the transferee after the transfer and which retains an identity of its own after the transfer[171]. This approach has been adopted in the United Kingdom[172].

7.53 The Transfer Regulations also apply to a service provision change whereby:

(a) activities cease to be carried out by a person ('a client') on his own behalf and are carried out instead by another person on the client's behalf ('a contractor');

(b) activities cease to be carried out by a contractor on a client's behalf (whether or not those activities had previously been carried out by the client on his own behalf) and are carried out instead by another person ('a subsequent contractor') on the client's behalf; or

(c) activities cease to be carried out by a contractor or a subsequent contractor on a client's behalf (whether or not those activities had previously been carried out by the client on his own behalf) and are carried out instead by the client on his own behalf[173].

For a service provision change to have occurred, activities carried out by different contractors before and after the provision change had to be carried out for the same client[174].

7.54 In practical terms, in deciding whether a particular transaction involves the transfer of an undertaking, consideration should be given to such matters as:

(a) the type of undertaking or business in question;

(b) whether goodwill has been assigned (often regarded as a key indicator in favour of there having been a transfer of an undertaking but not a conclusive one against);

---

166 *d'Urso v Ercole Marelli Elettromeccanica General SpA: C-369/88* [1993] CMLR 513.
167 Cf *OTG Ltd v Barke* [2011] IRLR 272.
168 Regulation 3(1)(a) of the Transfer Regulations.
169 Regulation 3(1)(a) of the Transfer Regulations.
170 An 'economic entity is defined at Regulation 3(2) of the Transfer Regulations as 'an organised grouping of resources which has the objective of pursuing an economic activity, whether or not that activity is central or ancillary'.
171 *Spijkers v Gebroeders Benedik Abbatoir CV: C-24/85* [1986] 2 CMLR 296.
172 See, for example, *Whitewater Leisure Management Ltd v Barnes* [2000] IRLR 456.
173 Regulation 3(1)(b) of the Transfer Regulations. The Transfer Regulations do not apply to a service provision change where the activities concerned consist wholly or mainly of the supply of goods to the client: regulation 3(3) of the Transfer Regulations.
174 *Hunter v McGarrick* [2012] EWCA Civ 1399. See also *SNR Denton UK LLP v Kirwan* [2013] ICR 101, where the Employment Appeal Tribunal held that there had not been a service provision change where an in-house solicitor whose functions included dealing with various service contracts was dismissed and the service contracts were disposed of by solicitors engaged by the administrators.

(c) whether the benefit and burden of current contracts with suppliers or customers are transferred;

(d) whether intellectual property rights are transferred (patents, copyrights, licences);

(e) whether any trade name is transferred;

(f) whether the transferor is to give any restrictive covenants in favour of the transferee (this being a means of protecting goodwill);

(g) whether the tangible assets of a business, such as premises and stock, are transferred;

(h) whether or not the majority of the employees of a business are taken over by the new employer;

(i) the degree of similarity between the activities carried on before and after the transaction and the period, if any, for which those activities are suspended[175].

7.55 In order for the Transfer Regulations to apply there must be a 'transfer' of the undertaking concerned. A 'transfer' for these purposes is not limited to a sale. A transfer may take place by two or more transactions and irrespective of whether any property is transferred by the transferor to the transferee[176]. Examples (some drawn from decisions of the European Court) of transfers other than on sale are:

(a) where a landlord starts running a business after the lessee's default, which has been held to amount to a transfer to the landlord of the business carried on at the premises[177];

(b) the expiry of a lease of premises at which a business had been carried on followed by the grant by the landlord of a new lease, which has been held to amount to the transfer of the business to the new lessee[178];

(c) the grant of a new 'in store' franchise to replace that granted to a previous franchisee[179];

(d) agreement whereby the owner of a business entrusts the responsibility for providing a canteen service to his staff to an outside contractor who assumes the obligations of an employer vis-à-vis the employees engaged in the provision of the canteen service[180].

7.56 If a sale or other transfer takes place to which the Transfer Regulations apply (termed a 'relevant transfer'), the following consequences will result:

1 The contracts of employment of the employees who are employed in the undertaking immediately prior to its transfer[181] and whose contracts of employment with the transferor would otherwise have been terminated by the transfer will have effect after the transfer as if originally made between the employees and the transferee[182] (an employee's contract will not be

---

175 See, *inter alia, Spijkers v Gebroeders Benedik Abbatoir CV: C-24/85* [1986] 2 CMLR 296 and *Rask and Christensen v ISS Kantineservice A/S: C-209/91* [1993] IRLR 133.

176 Regulation 3(6) of the Transfer Regulations.

177 *Landsorganisationen i Danmark v Ny Molle Kro: C-287/86* [1989] ICR 330.

178 *Foreningen af Arbejdsledere i Danmark v Daddy's Dance Hall A/S: C-324/86* [1988] IRLR 315.

179 Cf *Robert Seligman Corpn v Baker* [1983] ICR 770.

180 *Rask and Christensen v ISS Kantineservice A/S* [1993] IRLR 133.

181 Regulation 4(3) of the Transfer Regulations.

182 Regulation 4(1) of the Transfer Regulations.

automatically transferred if the employee informs the transferor that he or she objects to the transfer for reasons not falling within sub-paragraph (4) below; but in that event the transfer will terminate the contract without the transferor being treated as having dismissed the employee in question so that the employee will be unable to claim either unfair dismissal or a redundancy payment[183]).

2   Employees who are so transferred have continuity of employment for all purposes, and all rights and claims which they had against their previous employer may be claimed and asserted against the transferee[184].

3   Any employee[185] who is dismissed either by the transferor before the transfer or by the transferee after it and in whose case the transfer or a reason connected with it is the reason or principal reason for the dismissal is deemed automatically to have been unfairly dismissed[186] unless an 'economic, technical or organisational reason' entailing changes in the workforce is the reason or principal reason for the dismissal (in which case the dismissal will not be automatically fair but will be deemed to have been for a 'substantial reason' and therefore capable of being justified as fair)[187].

4   An employee whose employment is automatically transferred may claim constructive dismissal if there occurs a substantial change in the employee's 'working conditions' to his material detriment[188]. The employee in this case may resign and claim constructive dismissal prior to the transfer and in anticipation of such a breach[189].

7.57   The consequences set out in the preceding paragraph have obvious disadvantages from the point of view of a purchaser of the business of a company in administration where employees are involved. Employees with qualifying service whose contracts of employment are transferred to a purchaser might be disappointed at not receiving any redundancy payments but their employment and their continuity of employment are preserved. The administrator, on the other hand, may be relieved of the administrative burden of processing employees' claims against the National Insurance Fund but otherwise the amount for which he is able to realise the company's business is likely to be reduced to the detriment of the company's secured creditors and also, very possibly, its unsecured creditors.

7.58   The introduction of TUPE 1981 had a very significant effect on the conduct of receivership sales. By the time IA 1986 was enacted, however, a practice had developed of making employees of a business about to be sold to a purchaser redundant shortly before (sometimes only a few hours before) the sale was effected. The efficacy of this procedure in avoiding the effect of TUPE 1981 in such circumstances was apparently upheld by the Court of Appeal, which, in *Secretary of State for Employment v Spence*[190], held that employment contracts were not automatically transferred to a transferee of a business under the express wording at regulation 5 of TUPE 1981 unless the employees were employed

---

183   Regulation 4(7) and (8) of the Transfer Regulations.
184   Regulation 4(2) of the Transfer Regulations.
185   Whether or not employed in the undertaking in question: Regulation 7(4) of the Transfer Regulations.
186   Regulation 7(1) of the Transfer Regulations.
187   Regulation 7(2) and (3) of the Transfer Regulations.
188   Regulation 4(9) of the Transfer Regulations.
189   *University of Oxford v Humphreys* [2000] IRLR 183.
190   [1987] QB 179.

in that business 'immediately before the transfer'[191]. In so holding, the Court of Appeal took the view that the contract of employment had to be subsisting at the moment of the transfer of the undertaking in order to be subject to the express provisions of the Regulations. The effect of this was that in *Spence* itself, employees who had been dismissed prior to the transfer were not employed in the business immediately before the transfer and their contracts of employment were not, therefore, transferred to the transferee.

7.59 The effect of TUPE 1981 underwent further analysis, however, in the speeches of the members of the House of Lords in *Litster v Forth Dry Dock and Engineering Co Ltd*[192]. The position in *Litster* was that the Forth Dry Dock Co Ltd had gone into receivership in September 1983. The purchaser proposed to purchase all the assets of the company from the receivers and to take a new lease of the dock which the company had occupied. The purchaser insisted on the employees of the company in receivership being dismissed so as to avoid taking on liability for them. It was, accordingly, arranged between the purchaser and the receiver that all the employees would be dismissed approximately one hour before completion of the sale. Following completion, the purchaser re-employed only a small number of the dismissed employees. The employees complained to the employment tribunal that they had been unfairly dismissed. The employment tribunal found that the reason for their dismissal was one connected with the transfer, and that dismissal was thus unfair and that the liability for such unfair dismissal had been transferred to the purchaser. The Employment Appeal Tribunal upheld the employment tribunal's decision, but thereafter the Court of Session allowed an appeal by the purchaser. The dismissed employees then appealed to the House of Lords which held that:

(a) the UK courts were under a duty to give a purposive construction to TUPE 1981 so as to accord with the decisions of the European Court on the corresponding provisions of the Acquired Rights Directive to which TUPE 1981 was intended to give effect;

(b) in order for the purposes of the Acquired Rights Directive to be given effect, it was necessary to construe the reference in regulation 5(3) of TUPE 1981 to employees employed 'immediately before the transfer' as extending by implication to employees 'who would have been so employed if they had not been unfairly dismissed within the meaning of Regulation 8(1) (ie unfairly dismissed before the transfer for a reason connected with the transfer);

(c) accordingly, where the dismissal of the employees had taken place before the business transfer for a reason connected with the transfer which was not justified for economic, technical or organisational reasons, the liability for the employees' rights and claims, including those for unfair dismissal, had been transferred to the purchaser[193].

7.60 The result of *Litster*[194] appears to be that any arrangements reached in the course of negotiations with a purchaser as to the dismissal of members of the company's workforce by an administrator are likely to involve liability

---

191 See especially the wording of regulation 5(3) of TUPE 1981. See also *Secretary of State for Trade and Industry v Lassman* [2000] ICR 1109.
192 [1990] 1 AC 546.
193 *Secretary of State for Employment v Spence* [1987] QB 179 was held however to have been correctly decided on the basis that on the particular facts of that case the employees had not been unfairly dismissed within the meaning of regulation 8(1) of TUPE 1981.
194 [1990] 1 AC 546.

on the part of the purchaser for employees' contractual and statutory rights unless it can be established that the dismissal was for an economic, technical or organisational reason relating to the conduct of the business itself entailing changes in the workforce[195]. Even if such a reason can be established, a dismissal may still, on the facts, be held to be an unfair dismissal[196], although in that event the liability for unfair dismissal would appear to remain with the company and not to be transferred to the purchaser[197]. As a matter of practice therefore, administrators on being appointed should seek to determine at an early date what the optimum size of the company's work force should be and, if appropriate, effect redundancies early on in the administration. Redundancies in such circumstances may be more capable of being justified by reason of 'economic, technical or organisational reasons' entailing changes in the workforce, thus avoiding any dismissal being deemed automatically unfair[198] and with the consequent transfer of liability under the Transfer Regulations.

7.61 The Transfer Regulations also require both the transferor and the transferee of an undertaking respectively to provide specified information to either the representatives of a trade union recognised by them in relation to their respective employees who may be affected by any transfer or appointed or elected employee representative where no trade union is recognised[199]. The information to be provided is as follows:

(a) the fact that the transfer is to take place, when, approximately, and why;

(b) the 'legal, economic and social implications' of the transfer for the affected employees;

(c) the measures which the employer envisages taking in relation to those employees (if there are none, that fact must be stated); and

(d) if the employer is the transferor, any measures which the transferee envisages taking in relation to those employees transferring to its employment (if there are none, that fact must be stated)[200].

In order to enable the transferor to discharge its obligation under regulation 13(2) of the Transfer Regulations, the transferee is obliged to give the transferor such information at such time as will enable the transferor to do so[201].

7.62 The information must be given to the appropriate representatives long enough before the transfer to enable consultations to take place with the representatives[202]. It might therefore be expected that there would be an obligation on the part of an employer to consult with the appropriate representatives

---

195 Cf *Wheeler v Patel* [1987] ICR 631. Cf *Longden v Ferrari Ltd* [1994] BCC 250, EAT, where it was held that on the facts neither the proposed transfer of the company's business nor a reason connected with it was the reason or principal reason for the dismissal of the applicant employees by administrative receivers effected while negotiations for the sale of the business were pending.

196 Ie if the employment tribunal concludes that in the circumstances the employer acted unreasonably in treating the reason as a sufficient reason for dismissal: see section 98(4) of Employment Rights Act 1996.

197 See *Litster* [1990] 1 AC 546.

198 Under regulation 7(1) of the Transfer Regulations. For a case in which a dismissal by an administrator was for economic reasons, see *Honeycombe 78 Ltd v Cummins* (10 December 1999, unreported), EAT.

199 Regulation 13(3) of the Transfer Regulations.

200 Regulation 13(2) of the Transfer Regulations.

201 Regulation 13(4) of the Transfer Regulations.

202 Regulation 13(2) of the Transfer Regulations.

whenever a transfer is proposed. This is not so. The duty to consult, as opposed to the duty to supply information, only arises where and if an employer envisages taking measures in connection with the transfer in relation to employees of his who may be affected thereby[203]. Where consultation with representatives is required, it must take place 'with a view to seeking their agreement to measures to be taken'[204]. During the course of consultation, the employer must consider and reply to any representations made by the employee's representatives and if those representations are rejected, state why[205].

7.63 The Transfer Regulations provide that if there are special circumstances which render it not reasonably practicable for an employer to perform its statutory duty with regard to information and consultation, the employer must take all such steps towards complying as are reasonable in the circumstances[206]. This exception may be of assistance to administrators but, by analogy with the provisions concerning consultation in circumstances of redundancy, the fact that the company has entered administration does not, of itself, amount to a special circumstance[207].

7.64 In most circumstances in which an administrator will be involved with the transfer of an undertaking, the company in administration will be the transferor. Its obligations with regard to information and consultation will fall to be carried out by the administrator. However, as appears from **PARAGRAPHS 7.61 AND 7.62** *ante*, a transferee is similarly obliged to provide the prescribed information to the appropriate representatives by it in relation to its own employees who may be affected by the transfer and to consult with those representatives if it envisages taking any 'measures' in relation to those employees as a result of the transfer.

7.65 If there has been a failure to inform or to consult, an employee, employee representative, or a trade union, as appropriate, may present a complaint to an employment tribunal[208]. If the tribunal finds the complaint to be well founded, it will make a declaration to that effect and may award compensation to be paid to the employees affected[209]. The amount of compensation which may be awarded is such as the employment tribunal considers to be just and equitable, having regard to the seriousness of the failure of the employer to comply with his duty, subject to a limit of 13 weeks' pay per employee[210]. A 'week's pay' for these purposes is, unlike a statutory redundancy payment, or a basic award for unfair dismissal, not subject to a statutory ceiling[211].

7.66 Where an employee complains of a failure to inform or to consult and the transferor contends that the reason for such failure was the fact that the transferee failed to supply the information which it was required to provide to the transferor concerning measures which the transferee intended to take after the transfer[212], the transferor may serve a notice to that effect on the transferee

---

203 Regulation 13(6) of the Transfer Regulations: see *Institution of Professional Civil Servants v Secretary of State for Defence* [1987] IRLR 373.
204 Regulation 13(6) of the Transfer Regulations.
205 Regulation 13(7) of the Transfer Regulations.
206 Regulation 13(9) of the Transfer Regulations.
207 See **PARAGRAPHS 7.42 AND 7.48** *ante*.
208 Regulation 15(1) of the Transfer Regulations.
209 Regulation 15(7) and (8) of the Transfer Regulations.
210 Regulation 16(3) of the Transfer Regulations.
211 Cf **PARAGRAPHS 7.22, 7.23 AND 7.27** *ante*.
212 See **PARAGRAPH 7.61** *ante*.

which will have the effect of making the transferee a party to the proceedings[213]. Where such a failure on the part of the transferee is established, the employment tribunal may order that the award of compensation be paid by the transferee rather than the transferor[214].

7.67 If the transferor has, prior to a transfer, recognised any trade union in relation to employees who will be affected by the transfer, the transferee will be deemed, following the transfer, to have recognised that trade union, provided that the undertaking or part of the undertaking maintains an identity distinct from the remainder of the transferee's undertaking[215]. Similarly, the Transfer Regulations provide that any collective agreement between the transferor and any trade union recognised by it in relation to employees employed in the undertaking transferred is inherited by the transferee[216]. It should be noted that any terms of a collective agreement which have been incorporated in an individual employee's contract of employment will, upon a transfer to which the Transfer Regulations apply, become binding as between the employee and the transferee by virtue of regulation 4. However, where the contract of employment incorporates provisions of collective agreements, the rights, powers, duties and liabilities in relation to any provision of a collective agreement are not transferred by the Transfer Regulations provided that:

(a) the provision of the collective agreement is agreed after the date of the transfer; and

(b) the transferee is not a participant in collective bargaining for the provision[217].

Insolvency provisions

7.68 The Transfer Regulations removed the exception relating to 'hivedowns' provided by regulation 4 of TUPE 1981 and replaced it with insolvency provisions that were provided for by the Acquired Rights Directive 2001[218]. Under these provisions, if at the time of the relevant transfer the transferor is subject to relevant insolvency proceedings[219] then Part XI Chapter VI and Part XII of ERA 1996 shall apply in the case of a relevant employee[220], irrespective of the fact that the qualifying requirement that the employee's contract has been terminated has not been met[221]. Liability for the sums payable to the relevant

---

213 Regulation 15(5) of the Transfer Regulations.
214 Regulation 15(7) of the Transfer Regulations.
215 Regulation 6 of the Transfer Regulations.
216 Regulation 5 of the Transfer Regulations.
217 Regulation 4A of the Transfer Regulations.
218 Council Directive 98/50/EC of 29 June 1998 amending Directive 77/187/EEC on the approximation of the laws of the Member States relating to the safeguarding of employees' rights in the event of transfers of undertakings, businesses or parts of businesses.
219 Defined at regulation 8(6) of the Transfer Regulations as 'insolvency proceedings which have been opened in relation to the transferor not with a view to the liquidation of the assets of the transferor and which are under the supervision of an insolvency practitioner'.
220 A 'relevant employee' is defined at regulation 8(1) of the Transfer Regulations as an employee of the transferor either whose contract transfers to the transferee by virtue of the Transfer Regulations; or whose employment with the transferor is terminated before the relevant transfer if the transfer is the sole or principal reason for the dismissal (cf regulation 7(1) of the Transfer Regulations).
221 Regulation 8(3) of the Transfer Regulations. Cf *Pressure Cookers Ltd v Molloy* [2011] BCC 894.

employee under these provisions shall not be transferred under regulation 4 of the Transfer Regulations[222].

7.69 Further, where the transferor is subject to relevant insolvency proceedings[223], the Transfer Regulations shall not prevent the transferor or the transferee (or an insolvency practitioner) and appropriate representatives of assigned employees agreeing to permitted variations of the employee's contract of employment[224]. A permitted variation is where:

(a) the sole or principal reason for it is the transfer itself or a reason connected with the transfer that is not an economic, technical or organisational reason entailing changes in the workforce; and

(b) it is designed to safeguard employment opportunities by ensuring the survival of the undertaking, business or part of the undertaking or business that is the subject of the relevant transfer[225].

7.70 Where the transferor is the subject of bankruptcy proceedings or any analogous insolvency proceedings which have been instituted with a view to the liquidation of the assets of the transferor and are under the supervision of an insolvency practitioner, then regulations 4 and 7 of the Transfer Regulations do not apply[226]. However, in *OTG Ltd v Barke*[227], the Employment Appeal Tribunal held that an administration was not capable of constituting such insolvency proceedings and thus regulation 8(7) of the Transfer Regulations would never apply to companies in administration.

---

222 Regulation 8(5) of the Transfer Regulations. Cf **PARAGRAPHS 7.21–7.23 AND 7.31–7.38** *ante*.
223 A relevant insolvency proceeding is defined at regulation 8(6) of the Transfer Regulations.
224 Regulation 9(1) of the Transfer Regulations.
225 Regulation 9(7) of the Transfer Regulations.
226 Regulation 8(7) of the Transfer Regulations.
227 [2011] BCC 608. This approach was confirmed by the Court of Appeal in *Key2Law Surrey LLP v De'Antiquis* [2011] EWCA Civ 1567.

8 Statutory rights and remedies available to administrators

GENERAL

8.1   An administrator, as office-holder[1], is given the benefit of a number of statutory rights and remedies to assist him in the carrying out of his functions and duties. These rights and remedies are partly designed to ensure that the impact of commercial pressure which might otherwise be available to particular creditors is reduced and partly to assist in ensuring that the general principle of equal treatment of all creditors according to their legitimate rights is observed. In a number of respects, these rights and remedies are modified or excluded in relation to market contracts as defined by section 155 of CA 1989[2], collateral security within the meaning of the Settlement Finality Regulations[3] and charges created or otherwise arising under a financial collateral arrangement within the meaning of the Financial Collateral Arrangements (No 2) Regulations 2003[4].

8.2   Where the administrator is considering the exercise of one or more of the statutory remedies, it may be appropriate for the company to be placed into liquidation before proceedings are instituted. Such a course will, in any event, be necessary where the application for the remedy cannot be said to be in furtherance of the purpose of administration[5]. The reason for this is that an administrator is required[6] to carry out his functions in accordance with the proposals approved under Schedule B1 paragraph 53 of IA 1986 (or any revision of those proposals), which must be directed towards achieving the purpose of administration[7]. In particular, the nature of a preference claim[8] is such that it may sometimes be inappropriate for an administrator to pursue such proceedings before the intervention of a liquidation, although proceedings commenced by an administrator can always be continued by a liquidator[9].

---

1   Sections 233, 233A, 234, 235, 236, 238, 239, 244, 245 and 246 of IA 1986.
2   See further, **CHAPTER 18** *post*.
3   SI 1999 No 2979.
4   SI 2003 No 3226.
5   Schedule B1 paragraph 3 of IA 1986.
6   By Schedule B1 paragraph 68 of IA 1986.
7   Schedule B1 paragraph 49(1) of IA 1986.
8   Under section 239 of IA 1986.
9   As occurred in *Re Exchange Travel (Holdings) Ltd (No 3)* [1996] 2 BCLC 524.

SUPPLIES OF GAS, WATER, ELECTRICITY AND TELECOMMUNICATIONS SERVICES

8.3   Section 233[10] of IA 1986 provides for the terms which it is lawful for certain suppliers[11] of gas, water, electricity, telecommunication services or specified electronics goods or services[12] to impose as a condition of continuing their supplies to a company when it has entered administration. Section 233 of IA 1986 does not of itself impose any duty on the relevant supplier to continue making supplies, nor does it contain any express restriction on the right of the supplier to disconnect the service provided. Subject always to the terms of any particular contract, suppliers of goods or services not caught by section 233 of IA 1986 will not normally be bound to continue to make supplies to a company in administration which has defaulted in making payment due for goods or services already supplied[13].

8.4   If an administrator, as an office-holder[14], requests (or concurs in a request for) the supply of services from any of the relevant suppliers, that supplier is not entitled to make it a condition of the giving of the supply, and is not entitled to do anything which has the effect of making it a condition of the giving of the supply, that outstanding charges in respect of supplies made before the date on which the company entered administration[15] are paid[16]. It is, however, lawful for the supplier to make it a condition of the giving of the supply that the administrator personally guarantees any charges in respect of the supply[17].

8.5   The general significance of the provision is that it removes the right of the supplier to use a demand to pay outstanding arrears as a commercial bargaining tool when negotiating a continuation of the supply with the administrator. However, in commercial terms, the dividing line between the simple disconnection of the supply for non-payment and the doing of something which has the effect of making it a condition of the giving of the supply that outstanding charges are paid, is a thin one.

---

10   The scope of section 233 of IA 1986 was significantly increased by the Insolvency (Protection of Essential Supplies Order) 2015 (SI 2015 No 989), which came into effect on 1 October 2015 and extended the categories of suppliers to which section 233 applies.

11   Including landlords who supply utilities to tenants.

12   The supplies to which this provision applies are set out at section 233(3), (3A) and (5) of IA 1986. In *Official Receiver v Sahaviriya Steel Industries UK Ltd* [2015] EWHC 2877 (Ch), HHJ Pelling QC held that there was a serious issue to be tried as to whether section 233 of IA 1986 had extra-territorial effect and permitted service out of the jurisdiction of an application for an order under section 233 of IA 1986 that the company's Thai parent restore access to an essential IT system.

13   *Leyland DAF Ltd v Automotive Products plc* [1994] 1 BCLC 245; see also *Re Edwards, ex p Chalmers*(1872–73) LR 8 Ch App 289.

14   Section 233(1) of IA 1986.

15   Section 233(4)(a) of IA 1986.

16   Section 233(2)(b) of IA 1986.

17   Section 233(2)(a) of IA 1986. In *Laverty v British Gas Trading Ltd* [2014] EWHC 2721 (Ch), Sir Terence Etherton C held that the provisions of section 233 of IA 1986 were relevant to the question of whether or not supply of gas and electricity under deemed contracts arising under the Gas Act 1986 and the Electricity Act 1989 respectively were provable debts or administration expenses. The Chancellor considered that while section 233 of IA 1986 was not determinative of the issue, it weighed against charges under such deemed contracts being administration expenses; in particular, it was unclear why Parliament had felt it necessary to provide a specific guarantee mechanism in section 233 of IA 1986 if deemed contracts were to be treated as contracts made by an administrator or liquidator and thus charges under them were to be treated as expenses of the administration or liquidation.

GETTING IN THE COMPANY'S PROPERTY

8.6   An administrator, as office-holder[18], is entitled to apply to the court for an order requiring any person who has in his possession or control any property, books, papers or records to which the company appears to be entitled to pay, deliver, convey, surrender or transfer such property, books, papers or records to him[19]. This power may only be used to enable the administrator to perform his statutory functions[20]. Although the analogous power in a compulsory liquidation is exercisable by the liquidator on behalf of the court[21], there is no such delegation of power in an administration; the administrator must apply to the court for relief before the proposed respondent comes under a direct obligation to comply with any request for delivery up.

8.7   The procedure is a useful means by which an administrator can seek the delivery up of the company's property. Under the analogous provision in the pre-1986 legislation[22], the courts showed themselves reluctant to permit what was regarded as an essentially summary procedure to be used for the resolution of disputes[23]. This reluctance rendered the provision of little practical use.

8.8   The courts now appear to be prepared to give the provision[24] a wider construction and the existence of a dispute between the company and the person in possession of the property will not of itself render inappropriate an application under section 234 of IA 1986[25]. The court has wide powers[26] to make such orders on an application under IA 1986 as it could have made if the proceedings had been commenced by writ[27]. It remains the case, however, that there will be many disputes which, whilst falling within the terms of section 234, are inappropriate for summary determination by the Companies Court or other courts in the exercise of their insolvency jurisdiction[28]. Further, the court will not allow an administrator to make an application under section 234 where

---

18   Section 234(1) of IA 1986.

19   Section 234(2) of IA 1986.

20   See *Sutton v GE Capital Commercial Finance Ltd* [2004] EWCA Civ 315, which concerned a request by an administrative receiver that a firm of solicitors deliver up documents to assist the debenture holder in an action against at third party. The Court of Appeal held that this was outside the administrative receiver's functions, which were to get in, protect and realise the mortgaged property for the benefit of the company and its creditors and not to assist the debenture holder in litigation.

21   Rule 7.78 of the Rules.

22   Section 551 of CA 1985.

23   *Re Palace Restaurants Ltd* [1914] 1 Ch 492 at 500 (decided under section 164 of the Companies (Consolidation) Act 1908).

24   Section 234 of IA 1986.

25   *Re London Iron and Steel Co Ltd* [1990] BCLC 372, approved by the Court of Appeal in *Smith (administrator of Cosslett (Contractors) Ltd) v Bridgend County Borough Council* [2000] 1 BCLC 775 at 783 and not disapproved in the House of Lords [2001] UKHL 58.

26   Under Part 12 of the Rules.

27   *Re London Iron and Steel Co Ltd* [1990] BCLC 372 at 376f. Thus, it has been used in conjunction with an application under section 236 of IA 1986 (*Re Brook Martin & Co (Nominees) Ltd* [1993] BCLC 328); to initiate process for the recovery of money over which solicitors were asserting a lien (*Euro Commercial Leasing Ltd v Cartwright & Lewis* [1995] 2 BCLC 618); to recover a substantial tangible asset (*Smith (administrator of Cosslett (Contractors) Ltd) v Bridgend County Borough Council* [2001] UKHL 58) and even by one office-holder against another to obtain delivery up of the company's books and records (*Re First Express Ltd* [1992] BCLC 824).

28   The procedures and the practices of the Companies Court are unsuited to the resolution of complex commercial litigation.

proceedings by the company in its own name for similar relief would be liable to be stayed by reason of the company having agreed to submit any dispute relating to the subject matter of the proposed application to the exclusive jurisdiction of a foreign court[29]. It is also now established that section 234 is an inappropriate procedure for claiming damages or other compensation when property in respect of which the administrator would have been entitled to an order for delivery up under that section has been disposed of[30]. In such circumstances, the appropriate remedy will be to procure the company to advance such claim as it may have for damages in conversion[31]. In exercising its discretion under section 234 of IA 1986, the court will need to be satisfied that the interests of other persons in the property sought by the administrator are protected[32].

8.9 Where an application is made under section 234 of IA 1986, it should be made on notice unless the following two conditions are met:

(a) giving the respondent an opportunity to be heard would cause injustice to the administrator by reason of delay or action which the respondent or others are likely to take before the order is made; and

(b) the court is satisfied that any damage which the respondent may suffer because of the order can be compensated under a cross-undertaking or that the risk of uncompensatable loss is clearly outweighed by the risk of injustice to the administrator if the order is not made[33].

8.10 An administrator is given protection where he seizes or disposes of property which is not property of the company if, at the time of the seizure or disposal he believes and has reasonable grounds for believing that he is entitled to seize or dispose of that property[34]. In such an event, he is not liable to any person in respect of any loss or damage resulting from the seizure or disposal except in so far as the loss or damage may be caused by the administrator's own negligence[35]. He is also granted a lien over the property, or the proceeds of its sale, for such expenses as were incurred in connection with the seizure or disposal[36]. Although the word 'property' is generally defined in wide terms[37], an administrator's protection under this provision is restricted to the seizure or disposal of tangible property and does not extend to choses in action[38] which cannot sensibly be said to have been seized.

8.11 It is important to distinguish between the requirement that the administrator should act reasonably[39], and the exclusion of liability for loss and

---

29 See *Re Leyland Daf Ltd* [1994] 1 BCLC 264, upheld in the Court of Appeal at [1994] 2 BCLC 106.
30 *Smith (administrator of Cosslett (Contractors) Ltd) v Bridgend County Borough Council* [2000] 1 BCLC 775, not disapproved in the House of Lords [2001] UKHL 58.
31 *Smith (administrator of Cosslett (Contractors) Ltd) v Bridgend County Borough Council* [2001] UKHL 58 (paragraph 32).
32 *Uniserve v Croxen* [2012] EWHC 1190 (Ch).
33 *Re First Express Ltd* [1992] BCLC 824 at 828.
34 Section 234(3) and (4) of IA 1986.
35 Section 234(4)(a) of IA 1986.
36 Section 234(4)(b) of IA 1986.
37 Section 436 of IA 1986: '"property" includes money, goods, things in action, land and every description of property wherever situated and also obligations and every description of interest, whether present or future or vested or contingent, arising out of, or incidental to, property'.
38 *Welsh Development Agency v Export Finance Co Ltd* [1992] BCLC 148 at 171a, 179h and 190i. See also *Stewart v Engel* [2000] 2 BCLC 528 at 533g–534c and *OBG v Allen* [2007] UKHL 21.
39 Section 234(3)(b) of IA 1986.

damage other than that caused by the administrator's own negligence[40]. Even if the administrator had reasonable grounds for believing that he was entitled to seize or dispose of the property in question, he will not be excused from liability for loss caused by his own negligence. The precise ambit of this provision is unclear. If, for example, the administrator's original seizure was reasonable, is there nevertheless room for a duty of care to the true owner? If there is such a duty, it may be that an administrator's subsequent carelessness in ignoring clear evidence of title gives the claimant a remedy for damage flowing from the continuing unlawful retention, even though the original seizure was reasonable.

8.12   It has been said that the main purpose of the section is to protect an office-holder who deals with property which appears to belong to the company but which in fact belongs to a third party[41]. Thus, in practice, the most common application of the protection will be when an administrator disposes of goods supplied to the company under a retention of title clause of which he is not aware at the time of disposal. In many cases, this will constitute a wrongful interference for which the administrator would be personally liable[42] without proof of negligence. In showing that he had reasonable grounds for believing that he was entitled to seize or dispose of the property, it will normally be prudent for an administrator to take advice on the merits of adverse claims of which he is aware. Where, however, the allegation is that the administrator has converted by keeping (ie by failing to comply with a lawful demand for the delivery up of a chattel to the person with an immediate right to possession), and the person with the immediate right to possession has suffered loss as a result of the conversion, it is not thought that section 234 of IA 1986 will provide any protection; the mere act of keeping would not appear to be a seizure or a disposal[43].

DUTIES TO CO-OPERATE WITH THE ADMINISTRATOR

8.13   Section 235 of IA 1986 imposes an obligation on certain categories of person to give to the administrator, as office-holder[44], such information concerning the company and its promotion, formation, business, dealings, affairs or property as the administrator may reasonably require[45]. The same individuals are also under an obligation to attend on the administrator at such time as he may reasonably require[46]. The categories of person are[47]:

(a)   present and past officers of the company[48];

---

40   Section 234(4)(a) of IA 1986.
41   *Stewart v Engel* [2000] 2 BCLC 528 at 534b.
42   See eg *Clough Mill Ltd v Martin* [1985] 1 WLR 111 which was formulated as a claim in conversion.
43   Cf *Euromex Ventures Ltd v BNP Paribas Real Estate Advisory and Property Management UK Ltd* [2013] EWHC 3007 (Ch), where Newey J held that section 234 of IA 1986 did provide a defence to a conversion claim in relation to assets sold by the administrators.
44   Section 235(1) of IA 1986 applying the provisions of section 234(1) of IA 1986.
45   Section 235(2)(a) of IA 1986.
46   Section 235(2)(b) of IA 1986.
47   Section 235(3) of IA 1986.
48   Defined to include directors, managers and secretaries: section 251 of IA 1986. As to past officers, see: *Re Recover Ltd* [2003] EWHC 536 (Ch). A company's auditor will probably be an officer: *Sasea Finance Ltd v KPMG* [1998] BCC 216 at 222–223 and *Mutual Reinsurance Co Ltd v Peat Marwick Mitchell & Co* [1997] 1 BCLC 1.

(b) those who have taken part in the formation of the company at any time within one year before the date on which the company entered administration[49];

(c) present employees and individuals employed by the company[50] within one year before the date on which the company entered administration; and

(d) where an officer of the company is or has been[51] another company, present and past employees and officers of that other company, so long as they were employees or officers within one year before the date on which the company entered administration.

Section 235 of IA 1986 does not limit the ability of the office-holder to have whomever he pleases present at an interview he has requested under that provision, but he may only question the interviewee about the company of which he is administrator[52].

8.14 An individual who, without reasonable excuse, fails to comply with an obligation imposed upon him by section 235 of IA 1986, commits an offence[53]. In addition, the administrator[54] may apply to the court[55] for such relief as may be necessary for the enforcement of obligations imposed by section 235. The court has a general discretion as to the nature of the relief to be granted in any particular case and may also order the person against whom any order is made to bear the costs of any application[56]. In practice, if an administrator has difficulties in persuading an individual to attend on him under section 235[57], it will normally be more effective to seek relief under section 236 of IA 1986[58] than an order under Rule 12.52 of the Rules.

PRIVATE EXAMINATIONS

8.15 An administrator, as office-holder[59], is entitled to apply to the court for orders[60] against officers of the company[61], any person known or suspected to have in his possession any property of the company or supposed to be indebted

---

49 Described as the 'effective date'; see section 235(4)(a) of IA 1986.
50 Including employment under a contract for services.
51 Within one year before the date on which the company entered administration.
52 *Re Bernard Madoff Investment Securities LLC* [2009] EWHC 442 (Ch).
53 See section 235(5) of IA 1986. It is also evidence that would justify a finding of unfitness to be concerned in the management of a company for the purposes of CDDA 1986: *Secretary of State for Trade and Industry v McTighe (No 2)* [1996] 2 BCLC 477 at 489 and see also *Re Brampton Manor (Leisure) Ltd* [2009] EWHC 1796 (Ch).
54 Described as 'the competent person': Rule 12.52(2)(d) of the Rules.
55 Under Rule 12.52(1)(e) of the Rules.
56 Rule 12.52(3) of the Rules.
57 Or providing information by any other means, as to which see: *Re Arrows Ltd (No 4)* [1995] 2 AC 75, 101.
58 See **PARAGRAPH 8.15**FF post. But see *Re Westminster Properties Management Ltd* [2000] 1 WLR 2230 for a case in which information was obtained by the use of the section 235 powers rather than a formal examination under section 236 of IA 1986.
59 Section 236(1) of IA 1986 applying the provisions of section 234(1) of IA 1986. Only the administrator can apply and the court will be circumspect to prevent a creditor from attempting to procure such an examination for its own benefit: *Re James McHale Automobiles Ltd* [1997] 1 BCLC 273.
60 Under section 236 of IA 1986.
61 Section 236(2)(a) of IA 1986. Defined to include directors, managers and secretaries: section 251 of IA 1986. A company's auditor will probably be an officer: *Sasea Finance Ltd v KPMG* [1998] BCC 216 at 222–23 and *Mutual Reinsurance Co Ltd v Peat Marwick Mitchell & Co* [1997] 1 BCLC 1.

to the company[62] and any person whom the court thinks capable of giving information concerning the promotion, formation, business, dealings, affairs or property of the company[63]. The purpose of the jurisdiction is to assist the office-holder, who comes to his task with no knowledge of the company's affairs[64], in discovering facts and matters concerning the affairs of the company[65] and to enable the office-holder more effectively to discharge his functions[66]. Those functions will include the gathering of information to enable him to report to the Secretary of State under CDDA 1986[67].

8.16   The powers given to an administrator by section 236 of IA 1986 are of considerable practical importance and often significantly improve the administrator's prospects of achieving the purpose for which he was appointed. Thus in *In re Pantmaenog Timber Co Ltd*[68], Lord Hope said that it was self-evident that the powers are conferred on, amongst others, administrators for the better discharge of their functions. In *British and Commonwealth Holdings plc v Spicer and Oppenheim*[69], the House of Lords approved the following passage from the judgment of Buckley J in *Re Rolls Razor Ltd*[70] as being equally applicable to administration:

'The powers conferred by section 268[71] are powers directed to enabling the court to help a liquidator to discover the truth of the circumstances connected with the affairs of the company, information of trading, dealings, and so forth, in order that the liquidator may be able, as effectively as possible, and, I think, with as little expense as possible ... to complete his function as liquidator, to put the affairs of the company in order and to carry out the liquidation in all its various aspects, including, of course, the getting in of any assets of the company available in the liquidation. It is, therefore, appropriate for the liquidator, when he thinks that he may be under a duty to try to recover something from some officer or employee of a company, or some other person who is, in some way, concerned with the company's affairs, to be able to discover, with as little expense as possible and with as much ease as possible, the facts surrounding any such possible claim.'

8.17   Even though one of the purposes which most clearly justifies the making of an order is to reconstitute in the mind of the office-holder the state of the company's knowledge, the power of the court to grant relief under section 236 of IA 1986 is not limited to obtaining documents or other information needed for that purpose[72]. Subject to the question of oppression to the proposed

---

62   Section 236(2)(b) of IA 1986.
63   Section 236(2)(c) of IA 1986.
64   *Cloverbay Ltd v BCCI* [1991] Ch 90 at 102D.
65   *Re Castle New Homes Ltd* [1979] 1 WLR 1075 at 1080; *Re JT Rhodes Ltd* [1987] BCLC 77; *Re Embassy Art Products Ltd* [1988] BCLC 1 at 7i; *Re Esal (Commodities) Ltd* [1989] BCLC 59 at 73a; *Re Cloverbay Ltd* (1989) 5 BCC 732 at 738G.
66   *Re Rolls Razor Ltd* [1968] 3 All ER 698 at 700; *Re Spiraflite Ltd* [1979] 1 WLR 1096 at 1100C; *Re Esal Commodities Ltd* [1989] BCLC 59 at 64d–h, 69i–70c; *Cloverbay Ltd v BCCI* [1991] Ch 90 at 105F and *Re Pantmaenog Timber Co Ltd* [2003] UKHL 49, [2003] 3 WLR 767 at 770.
67   *Re Polly Peck International plc, ex p Joint Administrators* [1994] BCC 15 at 16, approved by Lord Millett in *Re PantmaenogTimber Co Ltd* [2003] UKHL 49, [2003] 3 WLR 767 at 785.
68   [2003] UKHL 49, [2003] 3 WLR 767 at 770.
69   [1993] AC 426 at 438.
70   [1968] 3 All ER 698 at 700.
71   The predecessor provision to section 236 of IA 1986.
72   *British and Commonwealth Holdings plc v Spicer and Oppenheim* [1993] AC 426 at 439C–D, although this may be a factor in deciding whether the order is oppressive: see **PARAGRAPH 8.22**FF *post*.

examinee[73], the principal question for the court is whether the administrator reasonably requires the relief sought in order to carry out his functions[74]. In considering that question (but not of course in balancing his need against any oppression to the examinee), the court will give appropriate weight to the views of the administrator[75]. In a large and complex insolvency, the court will not need much persuading that anyone involved ought to be ready to co-operate with the office holder[76], all the more so if their involvement was intimate in relation to the question to be investigated[77]. If, however, the administrator does not have a reasonable need for the relevant information, he will not be entitled to the relief, irrespective of any oppression to the examinee, nor will he be entitled to any relief if its grant would expose the examinee to criminal proceedings[78]. Put another way, the power under section 236 of IA 1986 may only be invoked for a legitimate purpose in relation to the company concerned and it will be abusive for it to be used for a purpose foreign to the functions of the administrator in relation to that company[79].

8.18 The court is empowered to make three different types of order under section 236 of IA 1986:

1   The court may summon the examinee to appear before it for examination[80]. The venue[81] must be specified in the order and the appearance must not be less that 14 days from the date of the order[82].

2   The court may order the examinee to submit a witness statement to the court containing an account of his dealings with the company[83]. The order must specify the matters to be dealt with in the witness statement[84] and the time within which it is to be submitted to the court[85].

3   The court may require an examinee to produce any books, papers or other records in his possession or under his control relating to the company or concerning the promotion, formation, business, dealings, affairs or property of the company[86]. The order must specify the time and manner of compliance[87].

---

73   Considered in more detail in **PARAGRAPH 8.22**FF *post.*
74   *British and Commonwealth Holdings plc v Spicer and Oppenheim* [1993] AC 426 at 439.
75   For a consideration of this question, see *Re Rolls Razor Ltd (No 2)* [1970] Ch 576 at 592; *Re Spiraflite Ltd* [1979] 1 WLR 1096 at 1100; *Cloverbay Ltd v BCCI SA* [1991] Ch 90 at 104C, 106G–107G; *Re British & Commonwealth Holdings plc (Nos 1 & 2)* [1992] Ch 342 at 371H–372B, CA; *Sasea Finance Ltd v KPMG* [1998] BCC 216, 220F; *Re Trading Partners Ltd* [2002] 1 BCLC 655 at 668h and *Re Alocasia Ltd* [2014] EWHC 1134 (Ch) (paragraph 53).
76   *Re Bank of Credit and Commerce International SA (No 7)* [1994] 1 BCLC 455 at 461.
77   *Re Bank of Credit and Commerce International SA (No 12)* [1997] 1 BCLC 526.
78   *Re Galileo Group Ltd* [1999] Ch 100 at 111 (proceedings under section 82 of the Banking Act 1987).
79   *Re PantmaenogTimber Ltd* [2003] UKHL 49, [2003] 3 WLR 767 at 784 (per Lord Millett).
80   Section 236(2) of IA 1986. At the examination only the administrator (or his solicitors or counsel) may ask questions: *Re Maxwell Communications Corpn plc (No 3)* [1995] 1 BCLC 521 at 534.
81   Ie the time, date and place: Rule 1.2 of the Rules.
82   Rule 12.19(1) and (2) of the Rules, (subject to the court's power to extend or abridge time pursuant to Rule 12.9).
83   Sections 236(3) and (3A) of IA 1986.
84   Rule 12.19(3)(a) of the Rules.
85   Rule 12.19(3)(b) of the Rules.
86   Section 236(3) of IA 1986. The court cannot grant relief unless it is satisfied that the documents to which the order is directed do in fact relate to the company or its property: *Re Mid East Trading Ltd* [1998] 1 BCLC 240.
87   Rule 12.19(4) of the Rules.

8.19 A provision similar to section 236 of IA 1986, section 25 of the Bankruptcy Act 1914, has been construed[88] to exclude from its provisions persons outside the jurisdiction of the court and in *In re M F Global UK Ltd*[89], David Richard J held that the same approach should be taken in relation to section 236 of IA 1986. However, in *Re Omni Trustees Ltd (No 2)*[90], HHJ Hodge QC noted that *Re Mid East Trading Ltd*[91] had not been cited to David Richards J and accepted that there were structural differences between section 25 of the Bankruptcy Act 1914 and section 236 of IA1986: in particular, there was a crucial difference between on the one hand, requiring a respondent to attend court for examination, and on the other requiring a respondent to submit documents or an account of his dealings. HHJ Hodge QC therefore held that section 236(3) of the Act did have extra-territorial effect and a court could require a respondent resident outside the jurisdiction to submit an account of his dealings with the company, or to produce any books, papers or other records in his possession or under his control relating to the company. It now seems settled though that section 236(2) of IA 1986, authorising the court to summon persons to appear before it, does not have extra-territorial effect. The court is, however, empowered to order any such person to be examined elsewhere in the United Kingdom or outside the United Kingdom[92]. It will not make such an order unless it is satisfied that it will be enforced by the courts of the jurisdiction in which the proposed examinee is then resident[93].

8.20 An application for an order under section 236 of IA 1986 may be made without notice[94]. The application must be accompanied by a brief statement of the grounds on which it is made[95]. The statement is not normally served on the examinee and he is not entitled to see it as of right[96]. The court does, however, have a discretion to permit inspection by any person[97] and, in the case of an application by the examinee to set aside the order, the court will exercise that discretion in favour of disclosure where it will or may be unable fairly and properly to dispose of that application if part of the evidence is withheld from the examinee, unless the administrator can show a more powerful reason for refusing to order disclosure[98]. If there are not good reasons[99] for applying without notice, the application should be made on notice to the proposed examinee[100].

---

88   *Re Tucker* [1990] Ch 148.
89   [2015] EWHC 2319 (Ch).
90   [2015] EWHC 2697 (Ch).
91   [1998] 1 BCLC 240.
92   Section 237(3) of IA 1986.
93   *Re Tucker* [1990] Ch 148 and see also *MF Global UK Ltd* [2015] EWHC 2319 (Ch), in which David Richard J held that section 237(3) of IA 1986 was independent of section 236 and could have extra-territorial effect but that it was necessary that there be available procedural machinery by which the respondent could be compelled to comply with an order to give evidence.
94   Rule 12.18(2) of the Rules. The same practice on an application for a public examination was approved in *Re Casterbridge Properties Ltd* [2002] BPIR 428 at 440.
95   Rule 12.18(1)(b) of the Rules.
96   Rule 12.21(3)(d) of the Rules.
97   Rule 12.21(2) and (3) of the Rules.
98   *Re British and Commonwealth Holdings plc (Nos 1 & 2)* [1992] Ch 342 at 355D, 366H–368A, 387B/C. This point was not subject to challenge in the House of Lords. For a case in which inspection was not permitted, see *Re Anglo American Insurance Co Ltd* [2003] BPIR 793.
99   Such as the need to maintain the confidentiality of the statement of the administrator in support of the application or to avoid the delay which a with-notice hearing would entail.
100 See *Re Maxwell Communication Corpn plc (No 3)* [1995] 1 BCLC 521 at 528 and *Re PFTZM Ltd* [1995] 2 BCLC 354.

8.21 Where there is confidential material which the administrator would not wish to have disclosed to an examinee, the practice which should now be adopted is for an administrator to file a report in two parts. The main part will contain that part of the report which is not confidential and will also include an explanation as to why any confidential annexure should be kept confidential; the second part will be the confidential annexure itself[101]. Adherence to this practice will greatly assist the resolution of disputes about disclosure of material on the basis of which orders under section 236 of IA 1986 are made. The present position is contrary to the practice which existed before the coming into force of IA 1986[102].

8.22 The court will not make an order under section 236 of IA 1986, and will refuse to order an examinee to answer specific questions, where (in either case) to do so would be unduly oppressive. Similarly, where an order has been made without notice, the court will discharge or vary it on the application of the examinee if, after balancing the requirements of the administrator to obtain the information against the possible oppression to the person from whom the information is sought, that is the appropriate course to take[103]. It follows that in most cases the only issue in dispute between a proposed examinee and the administrator will be whether the order is oppressive and if so whether any oppression is outweighed by the administrator's need for the relief sought.

8.23 In conducting the balancing exercise, the court will take into account all the circumstances of the case, and so precedent provides an uncertain guide to the result in any particular case. The following points appear, however, to have been established as being relevant factors for the court to take into account when exercising its discretion:

1 Whether the examination is more likely to make the examinee vulnerable to future claims is relevant, particularly where the proposed examinee may be accused of fraud[104], although there is no longer a practice that the existence or absence in the mind of the administrator of a settled intention to sue is conclusive[105]. It remains the case that section 236 of IA 1986 is directed at assisting the administrator in carrying out his functions; it is not designed to give him advantages other litigants do not possess, even though that may be the practical effect of any order made.

---

101 *Re British and Commonwealth Holdings plc (No 2)* [1992] Ch 342 at 356A–D.
102 For cases on the old practice, see *Re Gold Co* (1879) 12 Ch D 77; *Re Rolls Razor Ltd (No 2)* [1970] Ch 576 at 586; *Re Bletchley Boat Co Ltd* [1974] 1 WLR 630 at 633 and *Re Aveling Barford Ltd* [1989] 1 WLR 360 at 366.
103 See the approach adopted and approved by Sir Nicolas Browne-Wilkinson V-C in *Cloverbay Ltd v Bank of Credit and Commerce International SA* [1991] Ch 90 at 99 and the House of Lords in *British and Commonwealth Holdings plc (No 2) v Spicer and Oppenheim* [1993] AC 426 at 439 (per Lord Slynn of Hadley).
104 See eg the facts in *Cloverbay Ltd v Bank of Credit and Commerce International SA* [1991] Ch 90, the judgments in which were reconsidered at length and approved by the Court of Appeal in *Shierson v Rastogi* [2002] EWCA Civ 1624, in which Peter Gibson LJ stressed (at 600) that it is still oppressive to require a defendant accused of serious wrongdoing to prove the case against himself on oath: the question is whether that oppression is outweighed by the office-holder's need to know.
105 *Re British and Commonwealth Holdings plc (Nos 1 and 2)* [1992] Ch 342 at 370H–371B, CA and [1993] AC 426 at 436C, HL; *Cloverbay Ltd v Bank of Credit and Commerce International SA* [1991] Ch 90 at 101E–H, 106D–G, 109B–H; *Shierson v Rastogi* [2002] EWCA Civ 1624, [2003] 1 WLR 586, 605D–F. Cf *Re Anglo American Insurance Co Ltd* [2003] BPIR 793 and *Re James McHale Automobiles Ltd* [1997] 1 BCLC 273.

2 Whilst there may be cases in which it is proper for an administrator to issue a claim form to prevent a limitation period from expiring while he proceeds with private examinations to enable him to determine whether or not to proceed with the action, such a course will be scrutinised by the court with great care and may amount to an abuse of process[106].

3 The case for making an order against an officer or employee of the company will usually be stronger than the case for making an order against a third party[107]. The reason for this is that such persons will have owed contractual and fiduciary duties to the company whose affairs are being managed by the administrator, and are subject to statutory duties[108] to assist the administrator.

4 An order for the oral examination of a witness is much more likely to be oppressive than an order for the production of documents[109]. In an appropriate case[110], the court may require the examinee to be served with a questionnaire to answer before an examination is held[111]. Similarly, in a complex case, the court may order the administrator to give the examinee advance notice of the areas of questioning in order to save time and costs.

5 The extent of the logistical difficulties likely to be encountered by the proposed examinee in complying with the order is capable of being a relevant consideration[112].

6 If the information sought by the administrator was within the knowledge of the company prior to administration, that will add weight to the administrator's application[113], although it does not follow that if it was not, the administrator will fail[114].

7 It is not appropriate to use an application for relief under section 236 of IA 1986 in the context of a disputed proof of debt[115], as the proper procedure is

---

106 *Re Sasea Finance Ltd* [1998] 1 BCLC 559.

107 *Cloverbay Ltd v Bank of Credit and Commerce International SA* [1991] Ch 90, 102H; *Re British and Commonwealth Holdings plc (Nos 1 and 2)* [1992] Ch 342, 372B and *Shierson v Rastogi* [2002] EWCA Civ 1624. Indeed, others having a close relationship with the company (eg former shareholders) are more likely to be the subject of section 236 orders, than mere witnesses: *Re Bank of Credit and Commerce International SA (No 12)* [1997] 1 BCLC 526. See also *Re Westmead Consultants Ltd* [2002] 1 BCLC 384.

108 Under section 235 of IA 1986.

109 *Cloverbay Ltd v Bank of Credit and Commerce International SA* [1991] Ch 90, 103C–E; *Re British and Commonwealth Holdings plc (Nos 1 & 2)* [1992] Ch 342 at 372C–D; where documents contain information of a confidential or sensitive nature, the court may be prepared to permit redaction in an appropriate case: eg *In re Gallileo Group* [1999] Ch 100 at 114F–G and *Re Trading Partners Ltd* [2002] 1 BCLC 655 at 670a–b.

110 Particularly if there is no impropriety alleged against the proposed examinee.

111 See *Re Rolls Razor Ltd (No 2)* [1970] Ch 576 at 595E–596D and *Re Norton Warburg Holdings Ltd* [1983] BCLC 235; contrast *Re Bishopgate Investment Management Ltd* (15 July 1992, unreported, Hoffman J), *Re Maxwell Communications Corpn plc (No 3)* [1995] 1 BCLC 521 and *Re Bank of Credit and Commerce International SA (No 12)* [1997] 1 BCLC 526. An examination was held not to be appropriate in *Re Westmead Consultants Ltd* [2002] 1 BCLC 384, amongst other reasons because the proposed examinee had already supplied a witness statement.

112 *British and Commonwealth Holdings plc v Spicer and Oppenheim* [1993] AC 426 at 439H–440A and *Re Bank of Credit and Commerce International SA (No 12)* [1997] 1 BCLC 526.

113 *Re British and Commonwealth Holdings plc (Nos 1 and 2)* [1992] Ch 342 at 375E–376A (CA) and [1993] AC 426, 435C–437B.

114 See **PARAGRAPH 8.17** *ante*.

115 *Bellmex International Ltd v British American Tobacco Ltd* [2001] 1 BCLC 91: a principle which is now of relevance to administrations in the light of the new proof and distribution provisions (see **CHAPTER 15** post).

for the proof to be rejected if insufficient evidence is adduced to justify its admission.

8.24 Although an examinee who is under a statutory duty to co-operate with the administrator under section 235 of IA 1986 cannot rely on the privilege against self-incrimination as a ground for refusing to answer questions posed in an examination under section 236 of IA 1986[116], it may be oppressive to require him to answer when criminal proceedings are pending[117]. In this context, the court will be astute to ensure that the actual conduct of the examination is not conducted in a manner that is unfair[118]. Nevertheless, the fact that an examinee is facing criminal proceedings is not an absolute bar to a private examination proceeding[119] and in an appropriate case the administrator's requirements may outweigh any potential oppression to the examinee. This is so notwithstanding that the administrator may be obliged to supply a copy of the transcript to the Serious Fraud Office pursuant to a requirement imposed under section 2 of the Criminal Justice Act 1987[120]. In *Soden v Burns*[121] the Secretary of State was compelled to disclose transcripts of interviews conducted by his inspectors in an investigation under section 432 of CA 1985, provided that the relevant witnesses were given an adequate opportunity to object.

8.25 If an examinee is required to attend before the court for examination, a reasonable sum in respect of his travelling expenses must be tendered[122] and it is usual for this to be done at the time of service of the order. Any other costs falling on the examinee are in the discretion of the court[123]. *Prima facie*, the administrator's costs of any proceedings are paid out of the company's assets[124]. Where, however, it appears that an examination was made necessary because information had been unjustifiably refused by the examinee, the court may order that the costs of the examination be paid by him[125]. This provision obviously gives the administrator an incentive to invite an examinee to provide the information sought on a voluntary basis before he applies to invoke the court's jurisdiction. It should be noted, however, that the jurisdiction to order the

---

116 *Re Jeffrey S Levitt Ltd* [1992] BCLC 250; *Bishopsgate Investment Management Ltd v Maxwell* [1993] Ch 1. It appears to be an open question whether examinees not subject to any duty to co-operate under section 235 of IA 1986 may invoke the privilege against self-incrimination, although the description of the effect of *Bishopsgate Investment Management Ltd v Maxwell* (above) given by Lord Browne-Wilkinson in *Hamilton v Naviede* [1995] 2 AC 75 at 93–9 draws no such distinction.

117 See *Re Arrows Ltd (No 2)* [1992] BCLC 1176 and the cases there cited.

118 *Shierson v Rastogi* [2002] EWCA Civ 1624, [2003] 1 WLR 586 at 601. It is plain that breaching a duty of confidence is also no reason to refuse to answer although the possibility of a breach will be a factor in determining whether the question must be answered and if so on what terms: *Re Richbell Strategic Holdings Ltd* [2000] 2 BCLC 794 at 800.

119 Cf *Re British and Commonwealth Holdings plc (No 2)* [1992] Ch 342, 378C–E and see *Re Arrows Ltd (No 2)* [1992] BCLC 1176 at 1188c–d (the decision in which was upheld by the Court of Appeal: [1994] 1 BCLC 355).

120 *Hamilton v Naviede* [1995] 2 AC 75.

121 [1996] 1 WLR 1512.

122 Rule 12.22(4) of the Rules.

123 Rule 12.22(4) of the Rules; orders for the payment of costs (other than travelling expenses) incurred by an examinee are unusual and only made in exceptional circumstances: see *Re Aveling Barford Ltd* [1989] 1 WLR 360 and *Re Cloverbay Ltd* (1989) 5 BCC 732. Such an exceptional case was the costs of disclosing documents by Bank of America to the liquidators of BCCI described in the second judgment in *Re Bank of Credit and Commerce International SA (No 12)* [1997] BCC 561 at 576ff.

124 Rule 12.22(3) of the Rules.

125 Rule 12.22(1) of the Rules.

examinee to pay the costs of the examination is different from the jurisdiction[126] to order the examinee to pay the costs of the application for an examination. In the latter case, there is no need to establish an unjustifiable refusal to provide information – a serious risk of non-cooperation is sufficient[127].

8.26 Any order under section 236 of IA 1986 must be served on the examinee as soon as reasonably practicable[128]. Where an examinee, without reasonable excuse, fails to attend before the court for examination[129] or where there are reasonable grounds for believing that a proposed examinee has absconded or is about to abscond with a view to avoiding his appearance before the court[130], the court may cause a warrant to be issued for the arrest of the examinee and for the seizure of any books, papers, records, money or goods in his possession[131]. This power can only be exercised for the purpose of bringing the examinee and anything within his possession before the court[132]. Although in practice the court will ensure that the examinee is brought before a registrar or judge forthwith, the court does have power to authorise a person arrested under such a warrant to be kept in custody and for anything seized under such a warrant to be held until the examinee is brought before the court or until such other time as the court may order[133]. The court also has a general jurisdiction to grant such injunctive relief as may be appropriate to ensure compliance with the relief it has granted under section 236 of IA 1986, including orders restraining an examinee from leaving the jurisdiction[134].

8.27 If it appears to the court, on consideration of any evidence obtained under section 236 of IA 1986[135], that any person has in his possession any property of the company, the court may order[136] that person to deliver that property to the administrator on such terms as the court thinks fit. There is a similar provision for the payment of amounts in whole or partial discharge of debts due to the company[137]. In practice, it is highly unlikely that the court would make any such order against any person other than the examinee then before it, but it seems that section 237 is wide enough to cover third parties, and could in principle be used to obtain urgent orders for delivery up (without prejudice to the holder's right to apply to discharge the order) in order to preserve property in jeopardy[138].

---

126 Under Rule 12.22(2) of the Rules.
127 *Miller v Bain* [2002] BCC 899 at 905.
128 Rule 12.19(5) of the Rules. The requirement for personal service in Rule 9.3(5) of the Insolvency Rules 1986 no longer exists.
129 Section 236(4)(a) of IA 1986.
130 Section 236(4)(b) of IA 1986.
131 Section 236(5) of IA 1986. For a Northern Ireland case on the issue of a warrant under the equivalent process in connection with a public examination, see *Re H G Holden (Contracts) Ltd* [2002] NICh 2.
132 Section 236(5) of IA 1986.
133 Section 236(6) of IA 1986.
134 *Re Oriental Credit Ltd* [1988] Ch 204 and *Morris v Murjani* [1996] 1 WLR 848. See also *Re Bank of Credit and Commerce International SA (No 7)* [1994] 1 BCLC 455, in which the examinee domiciled abroad was required to give security as a condition of being permitted to leave the jurisdiction and *Daltel Europe Ltd v Makki (No 1)* [2004] EWHC 726 (Ch), in which the passport of a prospective examinee was seized.
135 Presumably whether by witness statement, in documentary form or pursuant to an oral examination.
136 On the application of the administrator: section 237(1) of IA 1986.
137 Section 237(2) of IA 1986.
138 Cf CPR Part 25.1(1).

8.28 The written record of any examination, any answers given to interrogatories and any witness statement submitted in compliance with an order of the court are not filed in court[139] and are not available for inspection (without order of the court) by any person other than the administrator[140]. Although required to seek the leave of the court to obtain access to transcripts relating to matters relevant to investigations under section 2 of the Criminal Justice Act 1987, the Director of the Serious Fraud Office will nearly always be entitled to the grant of such leave[141]. As section 433 of IA 1986 now protects the deponent from use being made in criminal proceedings of the transcript taken in any examination conducted under section 236 of IA 1986, it is difficult to think of any circumstance in which the court might properly order an administrator not to make disclosure to the SFO if properly served[142]. However, in the absence of specific statutory powers of inspection, it seems that the court will only give leave to other third parties to inspect such documents if they can show that inspection is for the benefit of the administration[143]. Although in *Re Arrows Ltd (No 4)*[144] the Court of Appeal and the House of Lords both criticised the width of the public interest immunity on which Millett J based his decision in *Re Barlow Clowes Gilt Managers Ltd*[145], it is thought that this should remain the correct approach where the third party seeking inspection does not rely on statutory powers such as those afforded to the Director of the Serious Fraud Office[146].

8.29 Where an oral examination has been held, and possibly where there has simply been an informal examination under threat of section 236 of IA 1986, the written record may be used, in civil proceedings, as evidence against the respondent of any statement made by him in the course of his examination[147]. It seems[148] that even if documents inspected by an administrator pursuant to an order made under section 236 were disclosed by mistake, the court will only restrain further use of the material in circumstances analogous to those in which it will undo the consequences of mistaken disclosure made in the course of discovery[149], ie where the recipient must have known that the disclosure was made by mistake and in cases of fraud. In the light of the decision of the

---

139 Rule 12.21(1) of the Rules.
140 Or anyone else who could have applied for an order under section 236 of IA 1986: Rule 12.21(2) of the Rules. It should be noted that only the administrator (or his solicitors or counsel) may conduct the examination: *Re Maxwell Communications Corpn plc (No 3)* [1995] 1 BCLC 521, 534, in which an unsuccessful application was made to permit part of the examination to be conducted by a US attorney.
141 *Hamilton v Naviede* [1995] 2 AC 75, 104–106.
142 If the court were to order an administrator not to make disclosure, that would amount to a reasonable excuse for non-compliance with a notice under section 2 of the Criminal Justice Act 1987: *Hamilton v Naviede* [1995] 2 AC 75, 104.
143 *Re Barlow Clowes Gilt Managers Ltd* [1992] Ch 208 at 218A, a liquidation case, but it is thought that the principle is the same. For a further application of the principle, see: *Re Esal (Commodities) Ltd* [1989] BCLC 59. Cf *Re Polly Peck International plc, ex p Joint Administrators* [1994] BCC 15.
144 [1993] Ch 452 at 468 and [1995] 2 AC 75 at 102.
145 [1992] Ch 208.
146 See *Hamilton v Naviede* [1995] 2 AC 75 at 102.
147 Rule 12.20(6) of the Rules and s.433(1) of IA 1986 and see *Hamilton v Naviede* [1995] 2 AC 75 at 101.
148 *Re a Company (No 009296 of 1990)* [1992] BCC 510.
149 For which, see *Guinness Peat Properties Ltd v Fitzroy Robinson Partnership* [1987] 1 WLR 1027.

European Court of Human Rights in *Saunders v the United Kingdom*[150], the former ability of the prosecuting authorities to use statements made under section 236 in criminal proceedings against an examinee has been prohibited[151]. The prohibition against the use of information obtained under compulsion does not, however, extend to director's disqualification proceedings[152].

TRANSACTIONS AT AN UNDERVALUE

8.30   Where the company has at a relevant time[153] entered into a transaction with any person at an undervalue[154], an administrator, as office-holder[155], is entitled to apply for such order as the court thinks fit for restoring the position to what it would have been if the company had not entered into that transaction[156]. A company enters into a transaction with a person at an undervalue if it makes a gift to that person or otherwise enters into a transaction with that person on terms that provide for the company to receive no consideration[157] or if it enters into a transaction with that person for a consideration the value of which, in money or money's worth, is significantly less than the value, in money or money's worth, of the consideration provided by the company[158]. For the purposes of IA 1986, the word 'transaction' is defined[159] to include 'a gift, agreement or arrangement'. The word 'transaction' requires there to be some element of dealing between the parties to the transaction[160]. It is thought that the use of the word 'arrangement' indicates that the question of whether the transaction was legally enforceable is

---

150   (1997) 23 EHRR 313. The ruling in this case was followed by the ECtHR in *Kansal v United Kingdom* (2004) 39 EHRR 31.

151   Section 433(2) of IA 1986, as inserted by section 59 of the Youth Justice and Criminal Evidence Act 1999. The prohibition is subject to exceptions in relation to certain offences under IA 1986 and the Rules and also in cases in which questions relating to the statement are asked in the criminal proceedings by or on behalf of the defendant. See also, *Shierson v Rastogi* [2002] EWCA Civ 1624, [2003] 1 WLR 586 at 602.

152   Under section 6 of CDDA 1986: *Re Westminster Property Management Ltd* [2000] 1 WLR 2230 (a case on section 235 of IA 1986, but the same principle applies).

153   For the meaning of relevant time see **PARAGRAPH 8.34** *post* and section 240 of IA 1986.

154   Section 238(2) of IA 1986. The fact that the transaction must be 'entered into' by the company was stressed in *Re Brabon* [2001] 1 BCLC 11, a bankruptcy case brought under section 423 of IA 1986 in which some of the impugned transactions were transfers by the bankrupt's mortgagee, not the bankrupt himself.; see also *Re Ovenden Colbert Printers Ltd* [2013] EWCA Civ 1408. In a section 423 context, the position may be different if the transaction was effected by a mortgagee at the instance of mortgagors acting with the purpose of prejudicing another third party: *Department for Environment, Food and Rural Affairs v Feakins* [2002] BPIR 281.

155   Section 238(1)(a) of IA 1986.

156   Section 238(3) of IA 1986. Section 241(1) of IA 1986 provides examples of the types of order which the court is empowered to make by the very wide terms of section 238(3): see also **PARAGRAPHS 8.36 AND 8.37** *post*.

157   Section 238(4)(a) of IA 1986.

158   Section 238(4)(b) of IA 1986. Millett J's analysis of the requirements of section 238(4)(b) in *In re MC Bacon Ltd (No 1)* [1990] BCLC 324 at 340 was approved by the House of Lords in *Phillips v Brewin Dolphin Bell Lawrie Ltd* [2001] UKHL 2, a case in which Lord Scott also explained (at 156) that where the consideration provided by the company is the sale or transfer of an asset, its value will be prima facie not less than the amount that a reasonably well informed purchaser is prepared in arms' length negotiations to pay for it (see also *Re Brabon* [2001] 1 BCLC 11).

159   By section 436 of IA 1986.

160   *Clarkson v Clarkson* [1994] BCC 921 and *Re Taylor Sinclair (Capital) Ltd* [2001] 2 BCLC 176.

irrelevant[161]. It will often be the case, of course, that a director who participates in any such transaction will be guilty of a misfeasance[162].

8.31   If the transaction provides for no consideration to pass to the company, it will fall foul of section 238(4)(a) of IA 1986 even if the recipient provided valuable consideration to a third party sufficient, as a matter of general principle, to render the company contractually bound[163]. Furthermore, the critical question is not the value of what was given by the recipient: it is rather the value of what was received by the company, whether what was received came from the recipient or from some other source[164]. The word transaction[165] is sufficiently wide to enable (and indeed require) the court to consider a transaction as a whole[166], so that if the company receives consideration or value as part of an arrangement of which any payment, transfer or disposition by the company forms another part, that may give the recipient sufficient protection. Furthermore, in considering whether a transaction involving a transfer of charged property at an undervalue should be set aside at the suit of an office-holder appointed over the transferor, the court will only consider the value of the equity of redemption in fact lost by the transferor as a result of the transaction[167].

8.32   The question of whether the value (in money or money's worth) of the consideration received by the company is *significantly less* than the value (in money or money's worth) of the consideration given by the company is one which has given rise to difficulty. In many cases, it will be obvious that the consideration is significantly less, but where it is not, it will be appropriate to bear in mind the purpose for which the provision was enacted. Section 238 of IA 1986 is designed to prevent an insolvent company from depleting its assets prior to the intervention of formal insolvency proceedings[168]. If the depletion effected by the transaction is, in the context of the transaction, insignificant, it will not fall foul of section 238[169]. If, however, the difference in value can be said to be other than immaterial or insubstantial and particularly, if the transaction involves a substantial element of bounty, the transaction will be vulnerable[170]. One area which has proved a fertile source of litigation is the grant of agricultural tenancies for the purpose of prejudicing the interests of the mortgagee of the transferor's freehold interest[171]. In that context, the court must reach a conclusion on the true value and then assess what is significantly less. It is inappropriate to

---

161   Cf the discussion of the word 'arrangement' in another context in *Re British Basic Slag Ltd's Agreements* [1963] 1 WLR 727.
162   Eg *Re Barton Manufacturing Co Ltd* [1999] 1 BCLC 740.
163   See eg *Re Wyvern Developments Ltd* [1974] 1 WLR 1097.
164   *Phillips v Brewin Dolphin Bell Lawrie Ltd* [2001] UKHL 2.
165   See **PARAGRAPH 8.30** *ante*.
166   Cf *Agricultural Mortgage Corpn v Woodward* [1995] 1 BCLC 1 at 11d, *Phillips v Brewin Dolphin Bell Lawrie Ltd* [2001] UKHL 2 and *Damon v Widney plc* [2002] BPIR 465 (a preference case).
167   *Re Brabon* [2001] 1 BCLC 11 at 37.
168   See Sir Donald Nicholls V-C in *Re Paramount Airways Ltd* [1993] Ch 223 at 230B–G and Millett J in *Re M C Bacon Ltd* [1990] BCLC 324 at 340. See also *Re Lewis's of Leicester Ltd* [1995]1 BCLC 428 at 439b.
169   In *Menzies v National Bank of Kuwait SAK* [1994] BCC 119, the consideration alleged to have been provided by the company was held to have been non-existent.
170   Cf *Re Kumar (a bankrupt)* [1993] BCLC 548. See also *Re Ciro Citterio Menswear plc* [2002] EWHC 293 (Ch) in which a loan without interest was held to be a sufficient undervalue.
171   Therefore cases under section 423 of IA 1986 (see **PARAGRAPH 8.40**FF *post*) rather than section 238, but the question of the consideration given from and to the company is the same: see the decisions of the CA in *Agricultural Mortgage Corpn v Woodward* [1995] 1 BCLC 1 and *National Westminster Bank plc v Jones* [2001] EWCA Civ 1541.

take a range of values within which legitimate disagreement is permissible and then to make a further reduction to an amount that is significantly less than the lower end of that range[172]. That does not however mean that in every case it is necessary to ascribe a precise figure to both the incoming and outgoing value[173].

8.33 It appears that the requirement that the consideration should be capable of being valued in money or money's worth is critical. So, in *MC Bacon Ltd*[174], Millett J held that the grant by a company of a charge or debenture as security for *its own* indebtedness cannot be a transaction at an undervalue[175], because the loss by the company of the right to apply the proceeds of its assets otherwise than in payment of the secured debt is not something capable of valuation in monetary terms. By the same token, the company's *net* assets have not been depleted; all that has happened is that the order of priority as between its creditors has been adjusted. *Prima facie*, this principle would not apply to the giving by the company of collateral security, because the company would then be divesting itself of an asset[176] in return for the grant of consideration to another. Much would then depend on whether it could be argued that the consideration given to the other was (indirectly) valuable consideration received by the company. This may, for example, be the case where charges are given by the company as security for the indebtedness to the recipient of a parent, subsidiary or co-subsidiary of the company[177]. Further, in *Hill v Spread Trustee Ltd*[178] Arden LJ, relying on dicta of Lords Hoffmann and Millett in *Buchler v Talbot*[179] to the effect that a chargeholder has a proprietary interest in the property charged, doubted the reasoning in *MC Bacon Ltd* but did not have to decide the point. There will also be cases in which the basic question of valuing the consideration given and received by the company is a difficult task[180]. Although any such difficulty is not of itself a reason for attributing no value, where the consideration can be characterised as speculative, it is for the recipient seeking to rely on it to establish its value[181]. In an appropriate case it may be necessary to take into account events that occur after the date of the transaction in valuing the consideration received by the company[182].

---

172 *National Westminster Bank plc v Jones* [2001] EWCA Civ 1541, [2002] 1 BCLC 55 at 61h–62b, approving the judge's approach at [2001] 1 BCLC 98 at 122–123.

173 *Ramlort Ltd v Reid* [2004] EWCA Civ 800 (paragraph 103). See also *Stanley v TMK Finance Ltd* [2010] EWHC 3349 (Ch).

174 [1990] BCLC 324 at 341, approved by Balcombe LJ in *Menzies v National Bank of Kuwait SAK* [1994] BCC 119 at 129 and followed in *Department for Environment, Food and Rural Affairs v Feakins* [2005] EWCA Civ 1513.

175 It may, however, be a preference (see **PARAGRAPH 8.46FF** *post*).

176 The property charged less the value of the equity of redemption.

177 See eg the judgment of Pennycuick J in *Charterbridge Corpn Ltd v Lloyds Bank Ltd* [1970] Ch 62, described as a 'powerful judgment' by Slade LJ in *Rolled Steel Products (Holdings) Ltd v British Steel Corpn* [1986] Ch 246 at 294.

178 [2006] EWCA Civ 542. Arden LJ also rejected a submission that the grant of security could not be a transaction for no consideration because it did not deplete the debtor's assets and noted that in *M C Bacon Ltd* 1990] BCLC 324, Millett J had been careful to point out that the security before him had not been given without consideration because it was given in exchange for forbearance by the creditor.

179 [2004] UKHL 9 (paragraphs 29 and 51).

180 For a case in which the court conducted a detailed examination of the true value of what the transferor lost, see *National Westminster Bank plc v Jones* [2001] 1 BCLC 98, approved by the CA at [2001] EWCA Civ 1541.

181 *Phillips v Brewin Dolphin Bell Lawrie Ltd* [2001] UKHL 2 (paragraph 27).

182 *Ibid*, a principle considered by Sir Andrew Morritt V-C in *Re Thoars* [2002] EWHC 2416 (Ch) in holding that post-transaction events may be relevant to the value of the consideration both

8.34   A transaction at an undervalue is only capable of challenge[183] if it was entered into during the period of two years ending with what is described as the onset of insolvency, being the date on which any administration application was made[184], the date on which any notice of intention to appoint was filed at court or the date on which the appointment takes effect[185]. It is also capable of challenge if it was entered into at a time between the making of any administration application and the making of an administration order on that application and at a time between the filing with the court of any notice of intention to appoint and the making of an appointment under Schedule B1 paragraph 14 or 22 of IA 1986[186]. Where the transaction was entered into during the period of two years ending with the onset of insolvency, the administrator must establish that the company was then unable to pay its debts within the meaning of section 123 of IA 1986[187], or became unable to pay its debts[188] in consequence of the transaction[189]. There is a rebuttable presumption that the company was then unable (or became unable) to pay its debts, where the transaction was entered into by the company with a person connected[190] with the company[191].

8.35   The court is not permitted to make any order under section 238 of IA 1986 if the respondent establishes that the company entered into the transaction in good faith and for the purpose of carrying on its business[192] and that at the time it did so there were reasonable grounds for believing that the transaction would benefit the company[193]. It appears that whether the company acted in good faith[194] will depend upon the subjective question of whether the directors in fact believed that the transaction would benefit the company[195], while the requirement that there should be reasonable grounds for the requisite belief imposes an objective standard. It seems that the onus of establishing each component part of this protection is on the respondent[196]. Where the defence is

---

given and received by the company and for the purpose of both reducing and increasing that value. In the event, the principle was not applied at trial (*Ramlort Ltd v Reid* [2004] EWCA Civ 800 (paragraphs 65 and 66)).

183   As having been made at a relevant time within the meaning of section 238(2) of IA 1986.

184   In the case in which section 238 of IA 1986 applies by reason of an administration order: section 240(1)(a) and (3)(a) of IA 1986.

185   In the case in which section 238 applies by reason of an administrator being appointed under Schedule B1 paragraphs 14 or 22 of IA 1986: section 240(3)(b) of IA 1986. There is a similar relation back of the onset of insolvency in a case where a company goes into liquidation following conversion of administration into winding up by virtue of Article 37 of the EC Regulation: section 240(3)(d) of IA 1986.

186   Section 240(1)(c) and (d).

187   Section 240(2)(a) of IA 1986.

188   Within the meaning of section 123 of IA 1986.

189   Section 240(2)(b) of IA 1986.

190   Ie a director or shadow director of the company, or an associate (as to which see section 435 of IA 1986) of such a director or shadow director or an associate of the company: section 249 of IA 1986.

191   Section 240(2) of IA 1986. For a case in which the connected person succeeded in rebutting the presumption see: *Re Ciro Citterio Menswear plc* [2002] EWHC 293 (Ch).

192   Section 238(5)(a) of IA 1986.

193   Section 238(5)(b) of IA 1986.

194   For the meaning of 'good faith' in section 42 of the Bankruptcy Act 1914 see *Re Windle* [1975] 1 WLR 1628 at 1634.

195   Cf Lord Greene MR in *Re Smith & Fawcett Ltd* [1942] Ch 304 at 306.

196   For a case where this was achieved, see *Sinai Securities Ltd v Rosshill Properties Ltd* [2003] EWHC 910 (Ch).

not made out, there will often be an additional claim against the directors who procured the transaction for misfeasance or breach of duty[197].

8.36   As has been mentioned in **PARAGRAPH 8.30** *ante*, the jurisdiction of the court extends to making such order as the court thinks fit for restoring the position to what it would have been if the company had not entered into that transaction[198]. It would appear that this does not require the court to restore the exact position which existed before the transaction was entered into, but it must restore the position so far as is practicable, if necessary, where the transaction is made up of more than one component part, setting aside one component and not the other or others of them[199]. Without limiting the generality of the court's powers, section 241(1) of IA 1986 enables the court to order:

(a) the vesting in the company of any property transferred as part of the transaction, or any property or money representing such property[200];

(b) the release or discharge (in whole or in part) of any security given by the company[201];

(c) the payment in respect of benefits received from the company of such sums to the administrator as the court thinks fit[202];

(d) the imposition of new or revived obligations on any guarantor or surety whose obligations were released (in whole or in part) under the relevant transaction[203];

(e) the provision of security for the discharge of any obligation imposed by or arising under the order and the imposition of a charge for the same purpose including directions that the priority of the security or charge shall be the same as any security or charge released or discharged under or by the transaction[204].

8.37   The court has a discretion to refuse relief. For example, in *Claridge's Trustee in Bankruptcy v Claridge*[205], which concerned a claim under the equivalent provision in bankruptcy (section 339 of IA 1986), Sales J held that there had been a transaction at an undervalue but did not make a restorative

---

197   *Re Barton Manufacturing Co Ltd* [1999] 1 BCLC 740, although if proceedings under section 212 of IA 1986 are thought to be desirable, the company would have first to be placed into liquidation.

198   Section 238(3) of IA 1986. The fact that the precise nature of the relief granted is discretionary was stressed by Neuberger J in *National Westminster Bank plc v Jones* [2001] 1 BCLC 98 at 121a–b.

199   Cf *Chohan v Saggar* [1993] BCLC 661 and [1994] 1 BCLC 706 at 713 in which the similar, but not identical, provisions contained in section 423(2) of IA 1986 were considered: see **PARAGRAPH 8.42** *post*. See also the relief granted in *Phillips v Brewin Dolphin Bell Lawrie Ltd* [2001] UKHL 2 and the discussion of principle in *Walker v W A Personnel Ltd* [2002] BPIR 621 at 634 (in which the court explained that there was no presumption one way or the other as to whether compensation would be ordered or a re-vesting order made). This discussion has now been approved by the Court of Appeal in *Ramlort Ltd v Reid* [2004] EWCA Civ 800 (paragraph 125).

200   Sections 241(1)(a) and 241(b) of IA 1986.

201   Section 241(1)(c) of IA 1986.

202   Section 241(1)(d) of IA 1986.

203   Section 241(1)(e) of IA 1986.

204   Section 241(1)(f) of IA 1986.

205   [2011] EWHC 2047 (Ch). See also *4Eng v Harper* [2009] EWHC 2633 (Ch), where in the context of a claim under section 423 of IA 1986, Sales J explained the circumstances where a change of position defence would be available.

order because he found that the transferee had changed position in good faith as a result of the funds received from the bankrupt; and in *Re MDA Investment Management Ltd*[206], Park J found that there had been a transaction at an undervalue but refused to restore the position to what it would have been but for the transaction because he held that this would have made the company in liquidation worse off. However, of itself, delay by an administrator in bringing proceedings under section 238 of IA 1986 is not a relevant reason for refusing relief which would otherwise be due[207].

8.38 The proceeds of an action brought by an administrator under section 238 of IA 1986 are not to be treated as part of the company's net property available for satisfaction of the claims of the holders of any floating charge over the assets of the company[208]. The administrator may assign his right of action (including the proceeds of any action) under section 238 of IA 1986 to a third party[209].

8.39 The court may make an order under section 238 of IA 1986 which affects the property of, or imposes an obligation on, any person whether or not he is the person with whom the company entered into the transaction[210]. There is, however, no power to make such an order against a person, who did not himself enter into a transaction with the company, where property was acquired or a benefit was received by him in good faith and for value[211]. There is a rebuttable presumption that a person has not acted in good faith if he was connected with or was an associate of either the company or the person with whom the company entered into the transaction[212]. The presumption will also apply if the third party had notice[213] both of the fact that the company had entered into the transaction at an undervalue and either that an administration application has been made, or that an administration order had been made or that a copy of notice to appoint an administrator under Schedule B1 paragraphs 14 or 22 has been filed or that notice of the appointment of an administrator has been filed under Schedule B1 paragraph 18 or 29[214]. Orders under section 238 can be made against persons resident or domiciled abroad[215]; the words 'any person' are to be given a wide meaning. Accordingly, in an appropriate case, leave to serve the originating process out of the jurisdiction[216] will be granted. However, the absence of any sufficient connecting factors with the jurisdiction may justify the court declining to grant relief, even against a respondent who has been duly served within the jurisdiction[217]. It should be noted that such applications are probably proceedings relating to the winding up of insolvent companies or other legal persons and

---

206 [2003] EWHC 2277 (Ch).
207 *Stonham v Ramrattan* [2010] EWHC 1033 (Ch); this case concerned a claim in bankruptcy under section 339 of IA 1986.
208 Section 176ZB of IA 1986.
209 Section 246ZD of IA 1986.
210 Section 241(2) of IA 1986.
211 Section 241(2) of IA 1986.
212 Section 241(2A) of IA 1986. In any event, the onus of proving good faith is on the third party: *Re Sonatacus Ltd* [2007] EWCA Civ 31.
213 Which presumably means both actual knowledge and constructive notice.
214 Section 241(3) and (3A) of IA 1986.
215 *Re Paramount Airways Ltd* [1993] Ch 223, approved by the Supreme Court in *Bilta (UK) Ltd v Nazir (No 2)* [2015] UKSC 23 (paragraph 214).
216 Under CPR Part 6: see Schedule 4 paragraph 1 of the Rules.
217 Re Paramount Airways Ltd [1993] Ch 223 at 239F–240G, applied in In re Banco Nacional de Cuba [2001] 1 WLR 2039 at 2058.

so fall outside the Brussels Regulations[218]. It seems that a claim to set aside a transaction at an undervalue will be a claim upon a specialty for the purposes of section 8 of the Limitation Act 1980. It follows that a 12-year limitation period will apply from the date the cause of action was complete (ie the appointment of an administrator), unless on the particular facts of the case it is a claim to recover a sum of money, in which event the period will be six years[219].

TRANSACTIONS DEFRAUDING CREDITORS

8.40   An administrator may also have to consider the provisions of section 423 of IA 1986, which gives the court wide-ranging powers to grant relief when a transaction at an undervalue[220] is entered into for the purpose of putting assets beyond the reach of actual or potential claimants or otherwise prejudicing their interests in relation to their claims against the company. It is unlikely that an administrator will often wish to have recourse to section 423, because the type of transaction under attack is identical to that referred to in section 238 of IA 1986 and the administrator has the added burden of proving that the purpose for which the company entered into the transaction was to put assets beyond the reach of actual or potential claimants or creditors or otherwise prejudicing their interests[221]. The principal advantage of a claim under section 423 is that there is no time limit within which the transaction must have occurred[222] and, accordingly, if the requisite state of mind can be established, the provision may be of assistance in an appropriate case. It should also be noted that, where a victim of the relevant transaction is bound by a voluntary arrangement, the supervisor has *locus standi* to apply for relief under section 423[223]. Furthermore, the court has power to grant leave to serve proceedings under section 423 out of the jurisdiction if it falls within paragraph 3.1 of CPR Practice Direction 6B[224].

8.41   Subject to proving that the company entered into the relevant transaction for the purpose of putting assets beyond the reach of actual or potential claimants or otherwise prejudicing their interests, the question of whether a particular transaction is capable of being challenged under section 423 of IA 1986 is governed by the same principles which determine the question of whether a transaction is a transaction at an undervalue[225]. For these purposes, a company enters into a transaction with a person at an undervalue if it makes a gift to

---

218   (EC) No 44/2001 and (EU) No 1215/2012. See *UBS AG v Omni Holding AG* [2000] 2 BCLC 310 at 317, which related to the Civil Jurisdiction and Judgments Act 1982.

219   Because the then section 9 of the Limitation Act 1980 would be applicable: *Re Priory Garage (Walthamstow) Ltd* [2001] BPIR 144.

220   See **PARAGRAPH 8.30**FF *ante*.

221   Section 423(3) of IA 1986. Note however that in *Re Ayala Holdings Ltd* [1993] BCLC 256 at 265d–g, Chadwick J thought it arguable that the requirement of having to prove such purpose only applied where an order was sought against the debtor; *sed quaere*. In reversing Chadwick J's decision, albeit on a different point, the members of the Court of Appeal expressed disagreement with Chadwick J (see *Menzies v National Bank of Kuwait SAK* [1994] BCC 119 at 126H–127D, 129G–H and 130B).

222   Cf the need for a transaction vulnerable under section 238 of IA 1986 to have occurred at a 'relevant time': see **PARAGRAPH 8.34** *ante*.

223   Section 424(1)(b) of IA 1986.

224   *In re Banco Nacional de Cuba* [2001] 1 WLR 2039 applied in *Erste Group Bank AG v JSC 'VMZ Red October'* [2015] EWCA Civ 379.

225   See **PARAGRAPH 8.30**FF *ante*.

that person or otherwise enters into a transaction with that person on terms that provide for the company to receive no consideration[226], or if it enters into a transaction with that person for a consideration the value of which, in money or money's worth, is significantly less than the value, in money or money's worth, of the consideration provided by the company[227]. Protective provisions analogous to those introduced by section 238(5) of IA 1986 for transactions at an undervalue[228] are not of course relevant to transactions vulnerable to section 423; this is not surprising given that it is difficult to see how a transaction entered into for the purpose of putting assets beyond the reach of actual or potential claimants or creditors could ever be entered into in good faith and for the purpose of carrying on the company's business.

8.42   The question of the company's motive, intention or purpose in entering into the relevant transaction does, however, give rise to more difficult questions. It is clear that even though in many cases, proof of the requisite purpose will be indicative of dishonesty, it is not necessary for an administrator (or other applicant) to establish dishonesty or fraud[229]. All he must establish is that the transaction was entered into for the purpose of putting assets beyond the reach of actual or potential claimants or creditors or of otherwise prejudicing their interests in relation to their claims against the company. So, as was the case in *Arbuthnot Leasing International Ltd v Havelet Leasing Ltd (No 2)*[230], the mere fact that the company was advised by solicitors and counsel to enter into the transaction does not prevent the transaction from being vulnerable under section 423[231], although there will obviously be cases in which the facts that the debtor company was acting on the advice of professionals will mean that no inference of nefarious purpose can be drawn[232]. Furthermore, it seems that an applicant must only establish that a substantial motivating purpose of the company in entering into the transaction was to remove assets from the reach of actual or potential claimants or creditors or of otherwise prejudicing their interests in relation to their claims against the company. It must be a purpose of substance and not merely a consequence[233], but the applicant does not need to establish that it was the sole purpose, nor even the dominant purpose as was once thought to be the case[234]. Even if the company knows that the transaction alone will not prejudice a person's interests, this will not be enough to escape liability under

---

226   Section 423(1)(a) of IA 1986.
227   Section 423(1)(c) of IA 1986.
228   See **PARAGRAPH 8.35** *ante*.
229   *Arbuthnot Leasing International Ltd v Havelet Leasing Ltd (No 2)* [1990] BCC 636 at 644B–E and *Chohan v Saggar* [1992] BCC 306 at 323A/B.
230   [1990] BCC 636. See also *National Westminster Bank plc v Jones* [2001] EWCA Civ 1541 and for a case in which an iniquitous purpose was not established because the relevant transaction was part of the reorganisation of a state banking sector, see: *In Re Banco Nacional de Cuba* [2001] 1 WLR 2039 at 2056.
231   Nor will it necessarily be a defence if the transaction was effected by a mortgagee at the instance of mortgagors acting with the purpose of prejudicing another third party: *Department for Environment, Food and Rural Affairs v Feakins* [2002] BPIR 281.
232   *The Law Society v Southall* [2001] EWCA Civ 2001, where the advice was given by accountants for fiscal reasons.
233   *IRC v Hashmi* [2002] EWCA Civ 981, applied in *Kubiangha v Ekpenyong* [2002] EWHC 1567 (Ch), [2002] 2 BCLC 597 at 601.
234   See the discussion in *Royscott Spa Leasing Ltd v Lovett* [1995] BCC 502 and *Re Brabon* [2001] 1 BCLC 11. See also *Chohan v Saggar* [1992] BCC 306 at 323B–C; *Moon v Franklin* [1996] BPIR 196 at 204; *Midland Bank plc v Wyatt* [1997] 1 BCLC 242 at 254; *Re* Schuppan (No 2) [1997] 1 BCLC 256 at 271; and Jyske Bank Ltd v Spjeldnaes [1999] 2 BCLC 101 at 120.

section 423 of IA 1986: it is entry into the transaction, not the transaction itself, which has to have the necessary purpose[235].

8.43   Once a company has entered administration, the most appropriate person to initiate proceedings under section 423 of IA 1986 is the administrator. There is, however, provision[236] for any 'victim of the transaction' to make, with the leave of the court[237], an application for relief. For these purposes, a victim of the transaction would appear to be wider than the definition at section 423(5) of IA 1986[238]. However, where the company which entered into the transaction[239] is in administration, any application under section 423 (whether brought by the administrator or a victim) is treated as being made on behalf of every victim of the transaction[240]. This would appear to mean that the court ought to take into account the position and interests of all victims of the transaction whether or not they appear on the application and any relief granted ought not (without more) to favour the interests of the victim who makes the application at the expense of other victims who do not. Indeed, section 423 appears to contemplate that, in any such case, a distribution mechanism in the form of a mini-winding up may be brought into play with the appointment of a receiver to administer it if necessary[241]. In the case of a company which was carrying on a regulated activity at the time of the transaction, an application can be made by the FCA or the PRA, so long as a victim of the transaction was a party to an agreement the making or performance of which constituted or was part of a regulated activity carried on by the company[242]. Such applications are to be treated as if made on behalf of every victim of the relevant transaction[243].

8.44   Where the court is satisfied that the company has entered into a transaction falling within section 423 of IA 1986, it may make such order as it thinks fit for restoring the position to what it would have been if the transaction had not been entered into and protecting the interests of the persons who are victims of the transaction[244]. So far as practicable, the order must seek both to restore the position to what it would have been and to protect the interests of victims of the transaction[245]. Without limiting the generality of the court's powers, section 425(1) of IA 1986 enables the court to order:

(a)   the vesting in any person, either absolutely or for the benefit of all the victims of the transaction, of any property transferred as part of the transaction or any property or money representing such property[246];

235   *Hill v Spread Trustee Co Ltd* [2006] EWCA Civ 542 (paragraph 102).
236   Section 424(1)(a) of IA 1986. On the test the court will apply on considering whether or not to grant leave see *Re Simon Carves Ltd* [2013] EWHC 685 (Ch) (paragraph 27).
237   It is thought that on any application for leave, the court will take into account the views of the administrator and whether or not he wishes to initiate proceedings challenging the same transaction: see *Re Ayala Holdings Ltd* [1993] BCLC 256.
238   *Fortress Value Recovery Fund I LLC v Blue Sky Special Opportunities Fund LP* [2013] EWHC 14 (Comm) and see also *Hill v Spread Trustee Co Ltd* [2006] EWCA Civ 542. Victims are not limited to creditors of the debtor: *Clydesdale Financial Services v Smailes* [2009] EWHC 3190 (Ch).
239   Described in section 423(5) of IA 1986 as 'the debtor'.
240   Section 424(2) of IA 1986.
241   *In Re Banco Nacional de Cuba* [2001] 1 WLR 2039 at 2058.
242   Section 375 of FSMA 2000.
243   Section 375(2) of FSMA 2000.
244   Section 423(2) of IA 1986.
245   See the cases cited in the footnotes to **PARAGRAPH 8.36** *ante*.
246   Section 425(1)(a) and (b) of IA 1986.

(b) the release or discharge (in whole or in part) of any security given by the company[247];

(c) the payment in respect of benefits received from the company of such sums to such other person as the court thinks fit[248];

(d) the imposition of such new or revised obligations as the court thinks appropriate on any guarantor or surety whose obligations were released (in whole or in part) under the relevant transaction[249];

(e) the provision of security for the discharge of any obligation imposed by or arising under the order and the imposition of a charge for the same purpose including directions that the priority of the security or charge shall be the same as any security or charge released or discharged by the transaction[250].

8.45 However, whilst the court can make an order under section 423 of IA 1986 affecting the property of or imposing an obligation on any person, whether or not he is the person with whom the company entered the transaction[251], it cannot make an order against a person, who did not enter into a transaction with the company, where property was acquired or a benefit was received by him in good faith, for value and without notice of the relevant circumstances[252]. Like a claim to set aside a transaction at an undervalue, it seems that a claim under section 423 of IA 1986 will be a claim upon a specialty for the purposes of section 8 of the Limitation Act 1980. It follows that a 12-year limitation period will apply from the date the cause of action was complete (ie the appointment of an administrator), unless on the particular facts of the case it is a claim to recover a sum of money, in which event the period will be six years[253].

PREFERENCES

8.46 Where the company has at a relevant time[254] given a preference to any person[255], an administrator, as office-holder[256], is entitled to apply for such order as the court thinks fit for restoring the position to what it would have been if the company had not given that preference[257]. A company gives a preference to any person if it does anything or suffers anything to be done which has the effect of putting a creditor or surety for any of the company's debts or other liabilities[258] into a position which in the event of the company going into insolvent liquidation will be better than the position he would have been in if that thing had not been

---

247 Section 425(1)(c) of IA 1986.
248 Section 425(1)(d) of IA 1986.
249 Section 425(1)(e) of IA 1986.
250 Section 425(1)(f) of IA 1986.
251 Section 425(2) of IA 1986.
252 Section 425(2) of IA 1986. The relevant circumstances are the circumstances by virtue of which an order under section 423 may be made in respect of the transaction: section 425(3) of IA 1986. Strangely, the Insolvency (No 2) Act 1994 does not amend section 425(2) and (3) of IA 1986 as it amends section 241(2) and (3) of IA 1986: see **PARAGRAPH 8.39** *ante*.
253 Hill v Spread Trustee Co Ltd [2006] EWCA Civ 542.
254 For the meaning of 'relevant time' see **PARAGRAPH 8.34** *ante* and section 240 of IA 1986.
255 Section 239(2) of IA 1986.
256 Sections 239(1) and 238(1)(a) of IA 1986.
257 Section 239(3) of IA 1986. Section 241(1) of IA 1986 provides examples of the types of order which the court is empowered to make by the very wide terms of section 239(3) of IA 1986.
258 Section 239(4)(a) of IA 1986.

done[259]. This form of words obviously extends beyond the simple making of a payment in discharge of a creditor's debt. Thus, it includes the giving of security to secure an existing debt[260], the retrospective conversion of an interest-free loan to the company into an interest-bearing loan[261] and a company's declaration that it holds certain assets on trust for a creditor[262].

8.47 A preference given to a person connected with the company[263], otherwise than by reason only of being its employee, is capable of challenge[264] if it was given during the period of two years ending with what is described as the onset of insolvency, being the date on which any administration application was made[265], the date on which any notice of intention to appoint was filed at court or the date on which the appointment takes effect[266]. This period is reduced to six months where the preference is not also a transaction at an undervalue and the person preferred is not a connected person[267]. It is also capable of challenge if it was entered into at a time between the making of any administration application and the making of an administration order on that application and at a time between the filing with the court of any notice of intention to appoint and the making of an appointment under Schedule B1 paragraph 14 or 22 of IA 1986[268]. Where the preference was given during either the period of six months or the period of two years ending with the onset of insolvency, the administrator must establish that the company was then unable to pay its debts within the meaning of section 123 of IA 1986[269], or became unable to pay its debts[270] in consequence of the preference[271]. Unless the preference was also a transaction at an undervalue entered into with a person connected with the company, there is no presumption that this condition is satisfied in the case of a preference[272].

8.48 The court is not permitted to make any order under section 239 of IA 1986 unless the company which gave the preference was influenced in deciding to give it by a desire[273] to put the creditor or surety into a position which in the

---

259 Section 239(4) of IA 1986. It is insufficient that at the time it was given, the alleged preference merely might have improved the position of the person to whom it was given; see *Re Ledingham-Smith (a bankrupt)* [1993] BCLC 635 per Morritt J at 640i–641c.

260 *Re Mistral Finance Ltd* [2001] BCC 27 and cf *Re Fairway Magazines Ltd* [1993] BCLC 643.

261 *Re Shapland Inc* [2000] BCC 106 at 110.

262 *Re Thirty-Eight Building Ltd* [1999] 1 BCLC 416.

263 Ie a director or shadow director of the company, or an associate (as to which, see: section 435 of IA 1986) of such a director or shadow director or an associate of the company: section 249 of IA 1986.

264 As having been made at a relevant time within the meaning of section 239(2) of IA 1986.

265 In the case in which section 239 applies by reason of an administration order: section 240(1) (a) of IA 1986 and section 240(3)(a) of IA 1986.

266 In the case in which section 239 applies by reason of an administrator being appointed under Schedule B1 paragraphs 14 or 22 of IA 1986: section 240(3)(b) of IA 1986.

267 Section 240(1)(b) of IA 1986.

268 Section 240(1)(c) and (d) of IA 1986.

269 Section 240(2)(a) of IA 1986.

270 Within the meaning of section 123 of IA 1986.

271 Section 240(2)(b) of IA 1986.

272 Section 240(2) of IA 1986.

273 *Prima facie*, it is the state of mind of the directors of the company with which the court will be concerned, but, in an appropriate case, the court will look at the mind of any other person responsible for procuring the preference: cf *El Ajou v Dollar Land Holdings plc* [1994] BCC 143. In *Re M C Bacon Ltd* [1990] BCLC 324 at 336c–d Millett J referred to 'those who made the decision'. See also *Re Shapland Inc* [2000] BCC 106, 109.

event of the company going into insolvent liquidation[274] would be better than the position he would have been in if that thing had not been done[275]. There is a rebuttable presumption that this requirement is satisfied where the recipient of the preference is a person connected with the company[276], otherwise than by reason only of being its employee[277]. It seems that, even where all of the beneficiaries of a preferred pension trust are connected with the company, the presumption will not apply if the same cannot be said of all of the trustees[278]. In other cases the burden of proof lies upon the administrator[279]. It should be noted that the effect of the need to establish that the company was influenced by a desire to prefer the creditor or surety concerned may be that, where more than one creditor or surety was preferred by the same act, a claim will not lie against all of them[280]. It is the decision to give a preference, rather than the giving of the preference pursuant to that decision, which must be influenced by the desire to prefer[281].

8.49 The test is no longer whether the administrator has established a dominant intention to prefer[282]; the question is whether the company had a desire to prefer and whether that desire influenced the company in giving the preference[283]. It follows that, in practice, the administrator will have to show that the company positively wished to improve the position of the creditor or surety in the event of its own insolvent liquidation. It also follows that, in practice, the court will always have jurisdiction to grant relief under section 239 of IA 1986 where the desire to prefer was an operative influence on the mind of the company; this will be the case even though the requisite desire may not have been the only factor which influenced the company in giving the preference[284]. The question of whether or not the company was influenced by a desire to prefer is of course a pure question of fact. Thus, although it used to be the law that payment to a

---

274 NB: the state of mind must anticipate liquidation, not administration, although, in most cases, this is likely to amount to the same thing.
275 Section 239(5) of IA 1986.
276 Ie a director or shadow director of the company, or an associate (as to which, see section 435 of IA 1986) of such a director or shadow director or an associate of the company: section 249 of IA 1986. *Re Fairway Magazines Ltd* [1993] BCLC 643 was a case in which the presumption was successfully rebutted, while *Re Exchange Travel (Holdings) Ltd (No 3)* [1996] 2 BCLC 524 (upheld on appeal: 24 March 1998, unreported, CA) and *Re Conegrade Ltd* [2002] EWHC 2411 (Ch) were cases in which it was not.
277 Section 239(6) of IA 1986 and see *Re Beacon Leisure Ltd* [1992] BCLC 565, *Re Fairway Magazines Ltd* [1993] BCLC 643 and *Re Brian D Pierson (Contractors) Ltd* [2001] 1 BCLC 275.
278 Re Thirty-Eight Building Ltd [1999] 1 BCLC 416.
279 Cf Re Ledingham-Smith (a bankrupt) [1993] BCLC 635.
280 *Re Agriplant Services Ltd* [1997] 2 BCLC 598 at 605.
281 *Re Stealth Construction Ltd* [2011] EWHC 1305 (Ch). In *Wills v Corfe Joinery Ltd* [1998] 2 BCLC 75 the relevant transaction was effected pursuant to an antecedent agreement and Lloyd J held the relevant time for determining the company's state of mind was at the time of the transaction, not the antecedent agreement because this was when the decision to repay the creditors in preference to others was made.
282 Cf the old law where it was necessary for a liquidator to establish that the preference was made with the dominant intention of preferring the respondent over the company's other creditors: *Peat v Gresham Trust Ltd* [1934] AC 252.
283 See the analysis of Millett J in *Re M C Bacon Ltd* [1990] BCLC 324 at 335c–336d and the summary of Mummery J in *Re Fairway Magazines Ltd* [1993] BCLC 643 at 649.
284 Per Millett J in *Re M C Bacon Ltd* [1990] BCLC 324 at 336b–d. See also *Re Fairway Magazines Ltd* [1993] BCLC 643 at 649e.

creditor applying pressure for payment could not be a preference[285], it is not thought that this principle can still be applied in the same terms[286]. Furthermore, the mere fact that the directors may not have appreciated that the company was in fact insolvent does not mean that they might not have been influenced by the requisite desire, if they suspected that it might in the future become so[287]. Indeed, the mere fact that the directors were optimistic about the company's future prospects will not necessarily rebut any applicable presumption that they were influenced by a desire to prefer[288]. If, however, what turns out to have been an act of preference was motivated by a genuine desire to stabilise the company during a period of difficult trading, it is unlikely that an officeholder will establish that the directors were influenced by any desire to prefer[289].

8.50   As has been mentioned in **PARAGRAPH 8.46** *ante*, the jurisdiction of the court extends to making such order as the court thinks fit for restoring the position to what it would have been if the company had not given the preference[290]. This does not require the court to restore the exact position which existed before the transaction was entered into, but to restore the position so far as is possible[291]. Without limiting the generality of the court's powers, section 241(1) of IA 1986 enables the court to order:

(a) the vesting in the company of any property transferred in connection with the preference, or any property or money representing such property[292];

(b) the release or discharge (in whole or in part) of any security given by the company[293];

(c) the payment in respect of benefits received from the company of such sums to the administrator as the court thinks fit[294];

(d) the imposition of new or revived obligations on any guarantor or surety whose obligations were released (in whole or in part) by the giving of the preference[295];

(e) the provision of security for the discharge of any obligation imposed by or arising under the order and the imposition of a charge for the same purpose including directions that the priority of the security or charge shall be the same as any security or charge released or discharged by the giving of the preference[296].

---

285 Eg *Re FLE Holdings Ltd* [1967] 1 WLR 1409, although the practical effect of such pressure may be that the giving of the preference was not *in fact* influenced by a desire to prefer: see *Re Ledingham-Smith (a bankrupt)* [1993] BCLC 635.

286 But see paragraph 1256 of the Report of the Review Committee on Insolvency Law and Practice (the Cork Report) (Cmnd 8558).

287 *Re Exchange Travel (Holdings) Ltd (No 3)* [1996] 2 BCLC 524 at 541, approved by the Court of Appeal on a stay application [1997] 2 BCLC 579 at 594, although the judgment on the appeal itself (24 March 1998) is unreported.

288 *Re Conegrade Ltd* [2002] EWHC 2411 (Ch).

289 *Re Lewis's of Leicester Ltd* [1995] 1 BCLC 428 at 438.

290 Section 239(3) of IA 1986.

291 This means that neither the company nor the recipient should be left any better or worse off than if the transaction had not been entered into: *Damon v Widney plc* [2002] BPIR 465 at 470 and see the cases cited at **PARAGRAPH 8.36** *ante*.

292 Sections 241(1)(a) and 241(1)(b) of IA 1986.

293 Section 241(1)(c) of IA 1986.

294 Section 241(1)(d) of IA 1986.

295 Section 241(1)(e) of IA 1986.

296 Section 241(1)(f) of IA 1986.

8.51 *Statutory rights and remedies available to administrators*

The proceeds of an action brought by an administrator under section 239 of IA 1986 are not to be treated as part of the company's net property available for satisfaction of the claims of the holders of any floating charge over the assets of the company[297]. The administrator may assign his right of action (including the proceeds of any action) under section 239 of IA 1986 to a third party[298].

8.51 The court may make an order under section 239 of IA 1986 which affects the property of, or imposes any obligation on, any person whether or not he is the person to whom the company gave the preference[299]. There is, however, no power to make an order prejudicing any interest in property or requiring any person who received a benefit from the preference to pay any sum to the administrator, so long as the respondent was not himself the person to whom the preference was given, and so long as the property was acquired or the benefit was received by him in good faith and for value[300]. There is a rebuttable presumption that a person has not acted in good faith if he was connected with or was an associate of either the company or the person to whom the company gave the preference[301]. The presumption will also apply if the third party had notice[302] both of the circumstances which amounted to the giving of the preference and either that an administration application has been made, or that an administration order had been made or that a copy of notice to appoint an administrator under Schedule B1 paragraph 14 or 22 has been filed or that notice of the appointment of an administrator has been filed under Schedule B1 paragraph 18 or 29[303]. Orders under section 239 of IA 1986 can be made against persons resident or domiciled abroad[304]; the words 'any person' are to be given a wide meaning. Accordingly, in an appropriate case, leave to serve the originating process out of the jurisdiction will be granted[305]. As in the case of transactions at an undervalue, the absence of any sufficient connecting factors with the jurisdiction may justify the court declining to grant relief, even in the case of a respondent who has been duly served within the jurisdiction[306]. It should be noted that such applications are probably proceedings relating to the winding up of insolvent companies or other legal persons and so fall outside the Brussels Regulations[307]. Like a claim to set aside a transaction at an undervalue or a claim under section 423 of IA 1986, it seems that a preference claim will be a claim upon a specialty for the purposes of section 8 of the Limitation Act 1980. It follows that a 12-year limitation period will apply from the date the cause of action was

---

297 Section 176ZB of IA 1986.
298 Section 246ZB of IA 1986.
299 Section 241(2) of IA 1986.
300 Section 241(2) of IA 1986. For these purposes, the relevant circumstances are the circumstances under which any order under section 239 of IA 1986 could be made in respect of the transaction if an administration order were made in relation to the company: section 241(3) of IA 1986. See also *Re Sonatacus Ltd* [2007] EWCA Civ 31.
301 Section 241(2A) of IA 1986. In any event, the onus of proving good faith is on the third party: *Re Sonatacus Ltd* [2007] EWCA Civ 31.
302 Which presumably means both actual knowledge and constructive notice.
303 Section 241(3) and (3A) of IA 1986.
304 *Re Paramount Airways Ltd* [1993] Ch 223, approved by the Supreme Court in *Bilta (UK) Ltd v Nazir (No 2)* [2015] UK SC 23 (paragraph 214).
305 Under CPR Part 6: see Schedule 4 paragraph 1 of the Rules.
306 *Re Paramount Airways Ltd* [1993] Ch 223 at 239F–240F, applied (in the context of section 423 of IA 1986) in *Re Banco Nacional de Cuba* [2001] 1 WLR 2039 at 2058.
307 (EC) No 44/2001 and (EU) No 1215/2012. See *UBS AG v Omni Holding AG* [2000] 2 BCLC 310 at 317, which related to the Civil Jurisdiction and Judgments Act 1982.

complete (ie the appointment of an administrator), unless on the particular facts of the case it is claim to recover a sum of money, in which event the period will be six years[308].

EXTORTIONATE CREDIT TRANSACTIONS

8.52   Where the company has been a party to a transaction for or involving the provision of credit[309] to the company and the transaction was entered into during the period of three years ending with the date on which the company entered administration and is or was extortionate[310], an administrator, as office-holder[311], is entitled to apply for relief under section 244 of IA 1986. A transaction is extortionate if, having regard to the risk accepted by the person providing the credit, the terms were such as to require grossly exorbitant payments to be made[312] in respect of the provision of credit or otherwise grossly contravened ordinary principles of fair dealing[313]. With the exception of the degree of risk accepted by the provider of the credit, section 244 does not require the court to have regard to any particular factors when determining whether the transaction was extortionate[314], but it is thought that most of the factors set out in section 138 of the Consumer Credit Act 1974 (since repealed)[315] will be material on an application under section 244[316].

8.53   Where an application is made under section 244 of IA 1986, there is a rebuttable presumption that the transaction is or was extortionate[317] and so the onus of proof on this issue is shifted to the creditor to prove the negative[318].

8.54   The court has wide powers under section 244(4) of IA 1986 to relieve the company from the burden of an extortionate credit transaction[319]. It may include provision setting aside the whole or any part of any obligation created by the transaction[320], varying the terms of the transaction or the terms on which security is held[321], requiring any party to the transaction to repay to the administrator any sums paid by the company[322], requiring any person to surrender to the administrator any property held by way of security for the transaction[323] and

---

308 *Re Priory Garage (Walthamstow) Ltd* [2001] BPIR 144.
309 Although 'credit' is not defined in IA 1986, section .9(1) of the Consumer Credit Act 1974 provides that 'credit' for the purposes of that Act includes a cash loan and any other form of financial accommodation.
310 Section 244(2) of IA 1986.
311 Sections 244(1) and 238(1)(a) of IA 1986.
312 Whether unconditionally or in certain contingencies.
313 Section 244(3) of IA 1986.
314 In a commercial transaction where interest rates are spelled out at the outset, the test for showing that a transaction was 'extortionate' would be very stringent: *White v Davenham Trust Ltd* [2010] EWHC 2748 (Ch) (paragraph 50).
315 By Schedule 1 paragraph 1 of the Consumer Credit Act 2006.
316 Cf *St George's Property Services (London) Ltd* [2011] EWCA Civ 858 (paragraph 10). Section 138 of the Consumer Credit Act 1974 was, of course, drafted with the position of an individual debtor, and not a corporate debtor, in mind.
317 Section 244(3) of IA 1986.
318 This reflects the approach adopted in section 171(7) of the Consumer Credit Act 1974.
319 These powers may be exercised concurrently with any powers exercisable in relation to the transaction as a transaction at an undervalue: section 244(5) of IA 1986.
320 Section 244(4)(a) of IA 1986.
321 Section 244(4)(b) of IA 1986.
322 Section 244(4)(c) of IA 1986.
323 Section 244(4)(d) of IA 1986.

directing accounts to be taken[324]. The proceeds of an action brought by an administrator under section 244 of IA 1986 are not to be treated as part of the company's net property available for satisfaction of the claims of the holders of any floating charge over the assets of the company[325]. The administrator may assign his right of action (including the proceeds of any action) under section 244 of IA 1986 to a third party[326].

AVOIDANCE OF FLOATING CHARGES

8.55   Where a company has entered administration[327], any floating charge on the company's undertaking or property which, as created, was a floating charge, and which was created at a relevant time[328], is invalid, except to the extent of the value of so much of the consideration for the creation of the charge as consists of money paid to the company, goods or services supplied to the company, the discharge or reduction of any debt of the company or agreed interest payable on such consideration[329].

8.56   A charge which, as created, was a floating charge is vulnerable[330] if it was created in favour of any person at a time in the period of 12 months ending with what is described as the onset of insolvency, being the date on which any administration application was made[331], the date on which any notice of intention to appoint was filed at court or the date on which the appointment takes effect[332]. It is also capable of challenge if it was entered into at a time between the making of any administration application and the making of an administration order on that application and at a time between the filing with the court of any notice of intention to appoint and the making of an appointment under Schedule B1 paragraph 14 or 22 of IA 1986[333]. Where the person in whose favour the charge was created was not connected with the company at the time of creation[334] and the charge was created during the 12-month period prior to the onset of insolvency, the administrator must establish that the company was then unable to pay its debts within the meaning of section 123 of IA 1986[335], or became unable to pay its debts[336] in consequence of the transaction under which the charge was created[337]. The period for which a floating charge is vulnerable

---

324 Section 244(4)(e) of IA 1986.
325 Section 176ZB of IA 1986.
326 Section 246ZD of IA 1986.
327 Sections 238(1), 245 and 251 of IA 1986.
328 See section 245(3) of IA 1986 and **PARAGRAPH 8.56** *post.*
329 Section 245(2) of IA 1986.
330 As having been created at a relevant time: section 245(2) of IA 1986.
331 In the case in which section 245 of IA 1986 applies by reason of an administration order: section 245(3)(b) of IA 1986 and section 245(5)(a) of IA 1986.
332 In the case in which section 245 of IA 1986 applies by reason of an administrator being appointed under Schedule B1 paragraphs 14 or 22 of IA 1986: section 245(5)(b) of IA 1986 as amended by Schedule 17 paragraph 31 of the Enterprise Act 2002.
333 Section 245(3)(b) and (c) of IA 1986.
334 Ie not a director or shadow director of the company, nor an associate (as to which see section 435 of IA 1986) of such a director or shadow director or an associate of the company: section 249 of IA 1986 and see *Unidare v Cohen* [2005] EWHC 1410 (Ch).
335 Section 245(4)(a) of IA 1986.
336 Within the meaning of section 123 of IA 1986.
337 Section 245(4)(b) of IA 1986.

is extended to two years prior to the onset of insolvency[338] where it is created in favour of a person connected with the company[339]. The administrator is not obliged to establish that the company was or became insolvent in consequence of the transaction in question where the beneficiary of the charge was connected with the company at the time of its creation[340].

8.57 In appropriate cases the court may have to embark upon a valuation of the consideration for the creation of the charge in order to determine the extent of the validity of the charge. Section 245(6) of IA 1986 gives some guidance in relation to the value of goods and services; their value is the amount in money, which, at the time they were supplied, could reasonably have been expected to be obtained for supplying them in the ordinary course of business. The court is required to make this judgment as if the supply was made on the same terms (apart from the consideration) as those on which they were supplied to the company.

8.58 To be valid for these purposes, the consideration for the creation of the charge must have been provided at the same time as or after the creation of the charge. Whatever the position may have been under the old law[341], the requirements of consideration and contemporaneity are clearly separate under section 245 of IA 1986[342]. Furthermore, it has now been held by the Court of Appeal[343] that the test of contemporaneity should be strictly applied. In a case where there has been an agreement to execute a debenture which itself creates a present equitable right to a security[344], the insistence upon a strict application of the test is unlikely to cause difficulties provided the moneys in question have been advanced[345] in consideration of the charge. However, in a case where an agreement to execute a debenture does not create any such present equitable right, moneys advanced[346] at any time prior to the formal execution of the debenture will not fall within the exception to section 245 of IA 1986 so as to validate the charge *pro tanto*, unless the interval is so short that it can be regarded as *de minimis*, for example a coffee break[347]. Thus it would now seem that where the advance of moneys precedes the creation of a charge by a matter of a day or days, the advance will not be secured by a floating charge which is otherwise invalid under section 245 of IA 1986[348].

---

338 Section 245(3)(a) of IA 1986.
339 Ie a director or shadow director of the company, or an associate (as to which, see section 435 of IA 1986) of such a director or shadow director or an associate of the company: section 249 of IA 1986 and see *Unidare v Cohen* [2005] EWHC 1410 (Ch).
340 Section 245(4) of IA 1986.
341 Section 617 of CA 1985, *Re Columbian Fireproofing Co Ltd* [1910] 2 Ch 120 and *Re F & E Stanton Ltd* [1929] 1 Ch 180.
342 *Power v Sharp Investments Ltd* [1994] 1 BCLC 111, CA.
343 *Power v Sharp Investments Ltd* [1994] 1 BCLC 111, per Sir Christopher Slade at 122c–124a and Ralph Gibson LJ at 128i–129e.
344 Thereby triggering the running of time within which a resulting charge must be registered.
345 Or goods or services or other consideration provided.
346 Or goods or services or other consideration provided.
347 *Power v Sharp Investments Ltd* [1994] 1 BCLC 111 per Sir Christopher Slade and Ralph Gibson LJJ not following *Re Columbian Fireproofing Co Ltd* [1910] 2 Ch 120 and *Re F & E Stanton Ltd* [1929] 1 Ch 180 on this point.
348 Presumably the decision of Mummery J on this point, in *Re Fairway Magazines Ltd* [1993] BCLC 643, a case which involved a delay of one month between the initial advance and the execution of the debenture and which was decided prior to the decision of the Court of Appeal in *Power v Sharp Investments Ltd* [1994] 1 BCLC 111, must be regarded as erroneous.

8.59 Further under the old law[349], the payment of money to the company had to have been made in substance for the benefit of the company[350]. Thus, a transaction which in substance amounted merely to the substitution of a secured for an unsecured debt, and which was therefore of benefit to one creditor only at the expense of others, constituted insufficient consideration so as to validate the charge[351]. It was, and appears to remain, the case that a transaction at a relevant time whereby an insolvent company creates a floating charge over its assets so as to secure an existing debt or debts will be caught by section 245[352]. However, in the light of the provisions of section 245(2)(b) of IA 1986, which provides that the consideration sufficient to validate the charge, *pro tanto*, may consist of the discharge or reduction of any debt of the company, it is submitted that on this point the authorities under the former law may be of limited assistance in construing section 245[353]. It is submitted that the provisions of section 245(2)(b) make it plain that the discharge of prior unsecured indebtedness of the company owed to third parties can and does now amount to sufficient consideration so as to validate, *pro tanto*, a floating charge and that there is no requirement that the assets available to unsecured creditors should be swelled. The point which appears to remain unresolved, and which was apparently not argued in *Re Fairway Magazines Ltd*[354], is whether it makes any difference that the debt of the company in question which is discharged had been previously guaranteed by the persons in whose favour the floating charge is created. It is submitted that it is at least arguable that it does not and that cases such as *Re Orleans Motor Co Ltd*[355], where a guarantor, in return for a floating charge, has discharged indebtedness owed by the company to the holder of the guarantee, may now turn upon whether or not the transaction in question amounted to a preference under sections 239 and 243 of IA 1986 rather than section 245 itself[356].

---

349 See section 617 of CA 1985 and its predecessors.
350 See *Re Matthew Ellis Ltd* [1933] Ch 458, *Re Destone Fabrics Ltd* [1941] Ch 319 and *Re G T Whyte & Co Ltd* [1983] BCLC 311; cf *Re Orleans Motor Co Ltd* [1911] 2 Ch 41, *Re Hayman, Christy and Lilly Ltd* [1917] 1 Ch 283 and *Re Ambassadors (Bournemouth) Ltd* (1961) 105 Sol Jo 969.
351 See *Re Matthew Ellis Ltd* [1933] Ch 458, *Re Destone Fabrics Ltd* [1941] Ch 319 and *Re G T Whyte & Co Ltd* [1983] BCLC 311; cf *Re Orleans Motor Co Ltd* [1911] 2 Ch 41, *Re Hayman, Christy & Lilly Ltd* [1917] 1 Ch 283 and *Re Ambassadors (Bournemouth) Ltd* (1961) 105 Sol Jo 969.
352 *Re Orleans Motor Co Ltd* [1911] 2 Ch 41, *Re Matthew Ellis Ltd* [1933] Ch 458 and *Re G T Whyte & Co Ltd* [1983] BCLC 311.
353 It is true that in *Re Fairway Magazines Ltd* [1993] BCLC 643 at 652b–653, Mummery J appears to have followed the former authorities in holding that the general purpose of the provision was to prevent a company, on its last legs, from creating a floating charge to secure moneys which do not go to swell the assets of the company in question and become available for creditors. However, no argument on the effect of section 245(2)(b) of IA 1986 appears to have been addressed to Mummery J on this point, and, in so far as Mummery J referred to the necessity that the consideration provided should go to swell the assets of the company in question, he appears to have overlooked the fact that the dictum of Parker J in *Re Orleans Motor Company Ltd* [1911] 2 Ch 41 to that effect was disapproved by the Court of Appeal in *Re Matthew Ellis Ltd* [1933] Ch 458.
354 *Re Fairway Magazines Ltd* [1993] BCLC 643.
355 *Re Orleans Motor Co Ltd* [1911] 2 Ch 41.
356 In *Re Fairway Magazines Ltd* [1993] BCLC 643 Mummery J rejected the claim in so far as it was based on alleged preference. Whilst no argument appears to have been addressed to Mummery J on the effect of section 245(2)(b) of IA 1986, it is respectfully submitted that, to the extent that the floating charge in question was held to be invalid, the case was wrongly decided.

8.60   It is thought that where a payment has been made in discharge of the secured liability before the company entered administration, the payment will not be recoverable under section 245 of IA 1986 even though the charge might have been vulnerable in the subsequent administration[357]. Where under section 245 a floating charge is invalid in whole or in part, the invalidity would appear to arise only upon the company entering administration, in which event the appropriate course is for the administrator to seek a declaration of invalidity and repayment of any amounts recovered by the holder of the charge since that time[358]. In view of the fact that, for present purposes, section 245 only applies once a company enters administration[359], it is doubtful whether the section allows an administrator to recover from the holder of a floating charge sums recovered by him at any time prior to the company actually entering administration[360]. However, where a floating charge is considered to be potentially vulnerable under section 245, an applicant for an administration order may be able to apply for an interim order preventing the making of payments to the holder of the floating charge[361].

AVOIDANCE OF CHARGES FOR NON-REGISTRATION

8.61   By section 874 of CA 2006 (in relation to charges created before 6 April 2013) and by section 859H of CA 2006 (in relation to charges created on or after 6 April 2013)[362] most (but not all) charges created by a company registered in England and Wales are void against, *inter alios*, an administrator unless the prescribed particulars of the charge and the instrument[363] by which it was created or evidenced are delivered to or received by the registrar of companies within 21 days of the date of its creation[364]. On the true construction of sections 874 and 859H, the avoidance of the charge against the administrator operates as an avoidance as against the company in administration and not just the administrator himself[365]. The charge is only void so far as any security on the company's property of undertaking is conferred by it, and the avoidance does not affect any underlying obligation on the company to repay the money secured by the charge[366].

---

357   For a decision to this effect under the old law, see *Mace Builders (Glasgow) Ltd v Lunn* [1987] BCLC 55.
358   See the procedure adopted in *Power v Sharp Investments Ltd* [1994] 1 BCLC 111.
359   See sections 238(1) and 245(1) of IA 1986.
360   Cf Schedule B1 paragraphs 44(7)(c) and (d) of IA 1986. NB: in administration proceedings there is no equivalent of section 129(2) of IA 1986, pursuant to which a compulsory liquidation is deemed to have commenced at the time of the presentation of the petition for winding up; *Power v Sharp Investments Ltd* [1994] 1 BCLC 111.
361   Cf Schedule B1 paragraph 39(1)(c) of IA 1986.
362   The provisions of section 404 of CA 1985 still apply to charges created before 1 October 2009.
363   Or a certified copy of the instrument in the case of charges created on or after 6 April 2013 (sections 859A and 859B of CA 2006).
364   In *Hounslow Badminton Association v Registrar of Companies* [2013] EWHC 2961 (Ch) Vos J held that particulars of a charge had been validly delivered to the registrar of companies, notwithstanding that the company had been dissolved at the time of delivery.
365   *Smith (Administrator of Cosslett (Contractors) Ltd) v Bridgend County Borough Council* [2001] UKHL 58.
366   Sections 874(3) and 859H(4) of CA 2006 and see eg *Re Monolithic Building Co Tacon v Monolithic Building Co* [1915] 1 Ch 643.

8.62 The charges to which section 874 of CA 2006 applies[367] are a charge for the purpose of securing any issue of debentures[368], a charge on uncalled share capital of the company, a charge which if created by an individual would require registration as a bill of sale[369], a charge on land or any interest in land[370], a charge on book debts[371], a floating charge on the company's undertaking or property, a charge on calls made but not paid, a charge on a ship or aircraft or any share in a ship and a charge on goodwill or any intellectual property[372]. The word charge is to be read as including a mortgage[373]. The courts will look at the true nature of the transaction; the description which the parties choose to adopt is not conclusive[374]. Where a legal possessory lien confers no proprietary right independent of the right to retain possession, it will not be a floating charge, even where it includes a right to sell the relevant chattels[375]. In relation to charges created on or after 6 April 2013, section 859A of CA 2006 adopts an inclusive definition of a charge and consequently section 859H of CA 2006 applies to all charges except a charge in favour of a landlord on a cash deposit given as security in connection with the lease of land, a charge created by a member of Lloyd's to secure its obligations in connection with its underwriting business at Lloyd's and a charge excluded from the application of section 859A by or under any other Act[376]. Section 859H also applies to a charge securing a series of debentures[377].

8.63 The question of whether an agreement for the sale of goods incorporating a retention of title clause constitutes a registrable charge has caused some difficulty. It is now clear that a clause simply retaining title to particular goods until those or other goods have been paid for does not require registration[378], unless it is part of a wider transaction designed to secure repayment of moneys lent[379]. It will, however, be very difficult for a supplier so to arrange matters that he obtains rights to trace into the proceeds of sale of goods which have not been paid for without registering that right as a charge[380]. He will encounter

---

367 See section 860(7) of CA 2006.
368 This is probably limited to the issue of a series of individual debentures: *Automobile Association (Canterbury) Inc v Australasian Secured Deposits Ltd* [1973] 1 NZLR 417.
369 For an example of such a case, see *Re Sugar Properties (Derisley Wood) Ltd* [1988] BCLC 146.
370 But not a charge on rent or any other periodical sum issuing out of land. The holding of debentures entitling the holder to a charge on land is not to be treated as an interest in land: section 861(1) of CA 2006.
371 Which does not include the deposit of a negotiable instrument to secure the payment of any book debts: section 861(3) of CA 2006.
372 For these purposes, intellectual property means any patent, trade mark, service mark, registered design, copyright or design right or any licence under or in respect of any such right: section 861(4) of CA 2006.
373 Section 861(5) of CA 2006.
374 *Re Curtain Dream plc* [1990] BCLC 925, but cf *Lloyds and Scottish Finance Ltd v Cyril Lord Carpet Sales Ltd* [1992] BCLC 609, *Welsh Development Agency v Export Finance Co Ltd* [1992] BCLC 148 and *Orion Finance Ltd v Crown Financial Management Ltd* [1996] 2 BCLC 78.
375 *Re Hamlet International plc,Trident International Ltd v Barlow* [1999] 2 BCLC 506.
376 Section 859A of CA 2006.
377 Sections 859H and 859B of CA 2006.
378 *Clough Mill Ltd v Martin* [1985] 1 WLR 111 and *Armour v Thyssen Edelstahlwerke AG* [1991] 2 AC 339.
379 *Re Curtain Dream plc* [1990] BCLC 925.
380 See eg *Re Andrabell Ltd* [1984] 3 All ER 407, *Tatung (UK) Ltd v Galex Telesure Ltd* (1989) 5 BCC 325, *E Pfeiffer Weinkellerei-Weineinkauf GmbH & Co v Arbuthnot Factors Ltd* [1988] 1 WLR 150, *Compaq Computer Ltd v Abercorn Group Ltd* [1993] BCLC 602 and *Modelboard Ltd v Outer Box Ltd* [1993] BCLC 623.

similar difficulties if he attempts to obtain property rights in new goods into which the goods he has supplied have been incorporated or subsumed[381]. In both cases, the reason for this difficulty is that the property in respect of which the supplier asserts rights pending payment of the purchase price is different from the property originally supplied. In the case of the proceeds of resale, the new property is the debt due from the sub-purchaser to the purchaser and in the case of property manufactured with, *inter alia*, the goods originally supplied, the original goods will usually have lost their separate identity.

8.64   The duty under section 874 of CA 2006 to deliver to the registrar of companies the prescribed particulars of a charge is on the company, although any person interested may also apply for registration[382]. The duty is discharged, and accordingly any charge will not be avoided, if the relevant particulars are delivered to or received by the registrar of companies; it does not matter that the decision of the registrar not to register may have been erroneous[383]. In relation charges created on or after 6 April 2013 the position is different because section 859A of CA 2006 does not impose a positive duty on the company to deliver the prescribed particulars of the charge to the registrar. For charges created before, on or after 6 April 2013, the registrar's certificate that the requirements as to registration have been satisfied is conclusive[384].

8.65   If there has been a failure to register the charge within the 21 days allowed, it is necessary to apply to the court for an order extending time for registration[385]. The court must be satisfied that the failure was 'accidental, or due to inadvertence or to some other sufficient cause, or is not of a nature to prejudice the position of creditors or shareholders of the company, or that on other grounds it is just and equitable to grant relief'[386]. In practice, and subject to the court, in any order extending time, making express provision to protect the position of any supervening chargeholders, this is not usually difficult to establish[387], unless the company is insolvent and in imminent danger of liquidation or administration.

8.66   It has long been established that the supervention of an insolvent liquidation almost invariably leads to the court refusing an extension of time for registration[388], although where a liquidation is merely imminent the company's insolvency and the imminence of the liquidation are simply factors (albeit often powerful ones), which the court takes into account when determining whether or not to grant relief[389]. Unless there is clear evidence that liquidation of the

---

381   *Hendy Lennox (Industrial Engines) Ltd v Grahame Puttick Ltd* [1984] 1 WLR 485, *Borden (UK) Ltd v Scottish Timber Products Ltd* [1981] Ch 25, *Re Peachdart Ltd* [1984] Ch 131, *Modelboard Ltd v Outer Box Ltd* [1993] BCLC 623 and *Ian Chisholm Textiles Ltd v Griffiths* [1994] BCC 96.
382   Sections 860(3) of CA 2006.
383   As a result of *Slavenburg's Bank NV v Intercontinental Natural Resources Ltd* [1980] 1 WLR 1076, a case decided under the provisions of CA 1985, in difficult cases, the registrar used to issue a letter confirming that an attempt to register had been made.
384   Sections 869(6) and 859I(6) of CA 2006 and see *Re C L Nye Ltd* [1971] Ch 442, *R v Registrar of Companies, ex p Central Bank of India* [1986] QB 1114 and *Exeter Trust Ltd v Screenways Ltd* [1991] BCC 477.
385   Under sections 873 or 859F of CA 2006.
386   Under sections 873 or 859F of CA 2006, and see **PARAGRAPH 8.68** *post*.
387   But evidence of the reason for the failure must be adduced: see *Re Telomatic Ltd* [1993] BCC 404.
388   This is, however, a matter of discretion rather than jurisdiction: *Re Ashpurton Estates Ltd* [1983] Ch 110 and see *Re R M Arnold & Co Ltd* [1984] BCLC 535.
389   *Re Braemar Investments Ltd* [1989] Ch 54.

company is not imminent[390], the court should always make its order subject to a proviso, such as contained in the order in *Re LH Charles & Co Ltd*[391], giving the company liberty to apply to discharge the order within a specified period after a winding up becoming effective on or before a specified date[392]. If the jurisdiction to extend time under section 873 or 859F of CA 2006 has been established, it will often be appropriate for the court to grant relief subject to the proviso, even where liquidation is highly likely[393]. Refusal of any relief will normally only be justified if it can be seen that any liquidator would be bound to obtain an order to set aside the leave to register out of time[394]. Irrespective of the imminence of an insolvency, the order should also include a proviso[395] that it is without prejudice to the rights of parties acquired during the period between the date of the charge's creation and the date of actual registration[396].

8.67 The approach long adopted in the case of an insolvent liquidation has now been applied in the context of an administration. In *Re Barrow Borough Transport Ltd*[397], Millett J concluded that where an administration order was made for the purposes of the company's survival and the whole or some part of its business as a going concern, there may be no reason why an extension of time for registration should not be granted, so long as that purpose remained capable of achievement. Where, however, the purpose of administration in relation to a particular company no longer includes the objective of its survival, justice will normally require that no extension of time should be granted. As was highlighted in *Barclays Bank plc v Stuart Landon Ltd*[398], the real question is whether third parties either:

(a) have acquired vested rights in the charged property during the period prior to the late registration being effected; or

(b) have acted to their detriment in the belief that there was no charge.

If either is the case, the indulgence ought not to be granted to the chargee, but otherwise it generally should be. These conclusions demonstrate the applicability of the principles enunciated in the liquidation cases to imminent administrations and to cases where an administration order has already been made.

UNENFORCEABILITY OF LIENS

8.68 Where a company has entered administration[399], a lien or other right to retain possession of any of the books, papers or other records of the company is

---

390 Which should come from a director or the company secretary.
391 [1935] WN 15.
392 For a case in which the Court of Appeal stressed the importance of this proviso, see *Exeter Trust Ltd v Screenways Ltd* [1991] BCLC 888. See also *Ali v Top Marques Car Rental Ltd* [2006] EWHC 109 (Ch).
393 Although see *Rehman v Chamberlain* [2011] EWHC 2318 (Ch) for an example of a case where extension would have been refused.
394 *Barclays Bank plc v Stuart Landon Ltd* [2001] EWCA Civ 140.
395 *Re Joplin Brewery Co Ltd* [1902] 1 Ch 79.
396 *Watson v Duff, Morgan and Vermont (Holdings) Ltd* [1974] 1 WLR 450. Although this will normally only affect questions of priority between secured creditors, that is not necessarily the case: *Barclays Bank plc v Stuart Landon Ltd* [2001] EWCA Civ 140, [2001] 2 BCLC 316 at 320; see also *Re Telomatic Ltd* [1993] BCC 404 at 409.
397 [1990] Ch 227.
398 [2001] EWCA Civ 140.
399 Section 246(1)(a) of IA 1986.

unenforceable to the extent that its enforcement would deny possession of any books, papers or records to the administrator[400]. This provision is designed to facilitate the management of the company's affairs by removing an impediment to the immediate access to documents which an administrator requires to enable him to fulfil his functions. It seems that section 246 of IA 1986 is directed at the administrator's exercise of the company's proprietary claims to recovery of its books, papers and records[401]; it is not concerned with the question of whether an administrator is entitled to have access to the information contained in documents which both belong to and are in the possession of a third party[402].

8.69　An administrator cannot invoke section 246 of IA 1986 where the lien is on documents which give a title to property and are held as such[403]. Property has a wide meaning[404] and the documents of title referred to are capable of including debentures, charges, leases and share certificates[405]. It has been decided[406] that the words 'held as such' do not mean that the document must be held so as to confer on the holder of the document a proprietary interest in the underlying property; all they require is for the holder to establish that the circumstances, manner or capacity in which the documents are held, are such as to give rise to a lien[407]. It should be noted, however, that even in the case of documents of title over which a lien is held, an administrator may be able to obtain an order for their production under section 236 of IA 1986, though such an order would in any event be without prejudice to and would not destroy the lien[408].

FRAUDULENT TRADING

8.70　One of the changes introduced by SBEEA 2015 was to give an administrator the power to commence fraudulent trading proceedings, seeking a contribution to the company's assets from any person, who was knowingly party to the carrying on of the business of the company with intent to defraud creditors of the company or creditors of any other person, or for any fraudulent purpose[409]. The power to apply to the court for relief under section 246ZA of IA 1986 is the same as the power given to a liquidator by section 213 of IA 1986[410], and was introduced to ensure that a company did not have to go into liquidation simply to enable such proceedings to be brought. This section came into force

---

400　Section 246(2) of IA 1986.
401　Eg under s.234 of IA 1986.
402　See *Re Aveling Barford Ltd* [1989] 1 WLR 360 at 364H–365A.
403　Section 246(3) of IA 1986. See *Re Carter Commercial Developments Ltd* [2002] BCC 803.
404　Section 436 of IA 1986: 'property' includes money, goods, things in action, land and every description of property wherever situated and also obligations, whether present or future or vested or contingent, arising out of, or incidental to, property.
405　See eg *Brereton v Nicholls* [1993] BCLC 593 at 594h–595a.
406　By Morritt J in *Brereton v Nicholls* [1993] BCLC 593.
407　Morritt J recognised that this construction was tautologous, but dismissed the argument that the protection of section 246(3) of IA 1986 was limited to cases where the holder had acquired a proprietary interest as doing greater violence to the wording of the section.
408　See *Re Aveling Barford Ltd* [1989] 1 WLR 360.
409　Section 246ZA of IA 1986, as inserted by section 117(2) of SBEEA 2015.
410　Section 213 of IA 1986 is the statutory successor to section 332 of CA 1948 and section 630 of CA 1985, although under the former law applications could also be made by creditors and contributories and the remedy was a declaration of personal responsibility for all or any of the company's debts and liabilities not a contribution to its assets: cf *In re Cyona Distributors Ltd* [1967] Ch 889.

on 1 October 2015[411], and the transitional provisions apply its terms to the carrying on of any business of the company on or after 1 October 2015[412], with the consequence that pre-October 2015 business activity cannot be taken into account as part of the carrying on of the company's business with the necessary fraudulent intent. It follows that it will still be necessary for a company to go into liquidation where business activity prior to that date is a component of any fraudulent trading claim that an administrator may wish to bring.

8.71   Proof of an intent to defraud or a fraudulent purpose requires proof of actual dishonesty involving real moral blame[413]; the test involves subjective dishonesty importing either an actual intent to defraud creditors or a reckless indifference as to whether or not they were defrauded[414]. It is possible to establish liability where the business of the company was carried on with intent to defraud a single creditor[415], but liability will not arise merely because a creditor of a company has been defrauded in the course of the carrying of its business[416]. It is not sufficient to establish that a company carried on business while it was insolvent[417]. Where this limb of the section is made out the administrator will then have to establish that the respondent was knowingly a party to such carrying on of the business. The acts of participation can take many different forms, but what is always required is participation with knowledge of the fraudulent purpose. This will be established where the participant shut his eyes to the obvious[418], and it may be attributed to a corporate respondent where the individual with the requisite knowledge was the individual with authority to deal with the company on its behalf[419]. Once the elements of the liability have been established, the contribution to the company's assets must reflect the loss which has been caused by the carrying on of the business in which the respondent participated and it is wrong in principle to add a punitive element[420]. The persons against whom relief for fraudulent trading can be sought include persons outside the jurisdiction[421]. It is thought that the six-year limitation period runs from the time that the company enters administration[422]. The proceeds of an action brought by an administrator under section 246ZA of IA 1986 are not to be treated as part of the company's net property available for satisfaction of the claims of the holders of any floating

---

411 Small Business, Enterprise and Employment Act 2015 (Commencement No 2 and Transitional Provisions) Regulations 2015 (SI 2015 No 1689).
412 Schedule 1 paragraph 15 of the Small Business, Enterprise and Employment Act 2015 (Commencement No 2 and Transitional Provisions) Regulations 2015 (SI 2015 No 1689).
413 *Re Patrick and Lyon Ltd* [1933] Ch 786, 790, and this will be established where a company incurs credit with no good reason for thinking that funds will become available to enable it to pay its debts: *R v Grantham* [1984] QB 675, 682.
414 *Bernasconi v. Nicholas Bennett & Co* [2000] BCC 921 (paragraph 14).
415 *In re Gerald Cooper Chemicals Ltd* [1978] Ch 262 and *Morphitis v Bernasconi* [2003] EWCA Civ 289 (per Chadwick LJ at paragraph 46). For a case in which the defrauded creditor was HMRC see *Re Todd (Swanscombe) Ltd* [1990] BCC 125.
416 *Morphitis v Bernasconi* [2003] EWCA Civ 289.
417 *Re Augustus Barnett & Son Ltd* (1986) 2 BCC 98904.
418 *In re BCCI SA; Morris v State Bank of India* [2003] EWHC 1868 (Ch) (paragraph 11), followed by Roth J in *In re Overnight Ltd (No 2); Goldfarb v. Higgins* [2010] EWHC 613 (Ch).
419 *Bank of India v Morris* [2005] EWCA Civ 693 (paragraphs 129 and 130).
420 *Morphitis v Bernasconi* [2003] EWCA Civ 289 (paragraphs 53–55).
421 *Bilta (UK) Ltd v Nazir (No 2)* [2013] EWCA Civ 968 (paragraph 90).
422 Six years from the date on which the company went into liquidation was held to be the limitation period for a claim brought by a liquidator under section 213 of IA 1986 in *In Re Overnight Ltd* [2009] EWHC 601 (Ch).

charge over the assets of the company[423]. The administrator may assign his right of action (including the proceeds of any action) under section 246ZA of IA 1986 to a third party[424].

WRONGFUL TRADING

8.72   Another of the changes introduced by SBEEA 2015 was to give an administrator the power to commence wrongful trading proceedings, seeking a contribution to the company's assets from any person, who is or has been a director of the company and who (at a time he was a director) knew or ought to have concluded that there was no reasonable prospect that the company would avoid entering insolvent administration or going into insolvent liquidation[425]. Like the fraudulent trading provisions, the power to apply to the court for relief under section 246ZB of IA 1986 derives from similar powers given to a liquidator, in this case by section 214 of IA 1986, and was introduced to ensure that a company did not have to go into liquidation simply to enable such proceedings to be brought[426]. It came into force on 1 October 2015[427], and the transitional provisions apply its terms to the carrying on of any business of the company on or after 1 October 2015[428]. Presumably this means that any time prior to that date cannot be taken into account as a time at which the director knew or ought to have reached the relevant conclusion. It follows that it may still be necessary for a company to go into liquidation where the administrator considers that there is a sustainable claim which relates back to a point in time prior to 1 October 2015.

8.73   Wrongful trading was introduced as a new cause of action in 1986. Proceedings are often not straightforward[429] and the jurisdictional requirements are more difficult to satisfy than might appear at first sight to be the case. The first matter which must be established is that the company has entered insolvent administration, a state of affairs which is satisfied where it enters administration at a time when its assets are insufficient for the payment of its debts and other liabilities and the expenses of the administration[430]. Where a company has entered administration, this will normally be the case, but it is to be noted that it is different from the test of whether the company 'is or is likely to become unable to pay its debts' within the meaning of Schedule B1 paragraphs 11(a) and 27(2)(a) of IA 1986. The second matter is that the respondent must have been a director of the company at the relevant time[431]. The third matter is that

---

423   Section 176ZB of IA 1986.
424   Section 246ZD of IA 1986 as inserted by section 118 of SBEEA 2015, which applies where a company went into administration on or after 1 October 2015: Schedule 1 paragraph 16 of the Small Business, Enterprise and Employment Act 2015 (Commencement No 2 and Transitional Provisions) Regulations 2015 (SI 2015 No 1689) .
425   Section 246ZB of IA 1986, as inserted by section 117(3) of SBEEA 2015.
426   For a case where this was a factor see *Re Integral Ltd* [2013] EWHC 164 (Ch).
427   Small Business, Enterprise and Employment Act 2015 (Commencement No 2 and Transitional Provisions) Regulations 2015 (SI 2015 No 1689).
428   Schedule 1 paragraph 15 of the Small Business, Enterprise and Employment Act 2015 (Commencement No 2 and Transitional Provisions) Regulations 2015 (SI 2015 No 1689).
429   For a striking example see *In re Continental Assurance Co of London plc* [2007] 2 BCLC 287.
430   Section 246ZB(6)(a) of IA 1986.
431   Section 246ZB(2)(c) of IA 1986 and by section 246ZB(7) of IA 1986 director includes shadow director (ie a person on whose instructions the directors of the company are accustomed to act: section 251 of IA 1986).

the administrator must identify the time at which he contends that the respondent knew or ought to have concluded that the company would not avoid insolvent administration or liquidation. For this purpose, the facts which a director ought to have known and the conclusions which he ought to have reached are those which would be known, ascertained or reached by a reasonably diligent person having the knowledge, skill and experience both that he might reasonably be expected to have had[432] and that he did in fact have[433]. If the directors have taken advice from professionals, their contemporaneous views on the prospects of the company's survival will often be relevant and sometimes determinative[434]. The court will be careful not to apply hindsight when making that assessment[435], but wilfully blind optimism will be sufficient to establish liability[436]. It should also be noted that it is not sufficient to establish that the respondent director knew that the company was insolvent at a particular point in time, because it is commonplace for companies to have a reasonable prospect of trading out of their difficulties[437].

8.74 Even where the administrator establishes that there was a moment in time before administration at which the director concerned knew or ought to have concluded that there was no reasonable prospect that the company would avoid insolvent administration or liquidation, it is a defence for him to establish that thereafter he took every step that he ought to have taken with a view to minimising the loss to the company's creditors[438]. These are such steps as ought to have been taken by a reasonably diligent person having the knowledge skill and experience both that he might reasonably be expected to have had and that he did in fact have[439]. This is a high hurdle for the directors to surmount, and it is not sufficient for the directors simply to show their actions after the relevant date were aimed at reducing the company's net deficit; the position of all creditors must be taken into account[440]. The level of contribution is at the discretion of the court, but as a matter of basic principle it should be quantified by reference to the loss which the company sustained as a result of the continued trading after the date at which the respondent ought to have concluded that it should go into administration (or liquidation)[441]. It is thought that the six-year limitation period runs from the time that the company enters administration[442]. The proceeds of

---

432 As to which see eg *Re Produce Marketing Consortium Ltd (No 2)* [1989] BCLC 520 and *Re Robin Hood Centre plc, Brooks v Armstrong* [2015] EWHC 2289 (Ch) and on appeal at [2016] EWHC 2893 (Ch).
433 Section 246ZB(4) of IA 1986.
434 *Re Ralls Builders Ltd* [2016] EWHC 243 (Ch) (paragraph 206).
435 *In re Hawkes Hill Publishing Ltd* [2007] BCC 937 (paragraphs 38 and 47).
436 *Roberts v Frohlich* [2011] EWHC 257 (Ch) (paragraphs 95 and 112).
437 *In re Hawkes Hill Publishing Ltd* [2007] BCC 937 (paragraph 28) and *Re Ralls Builders Ltd* [2016] EWHC 243 (Ch) (paragraph 168).
438 Section 246ZB(3) of IA 1986.
439 Section 246ZB(4) of IA 1986.
440 *Re Ralls Builders Ltd* [2016] EWHC 243 (Ch) (paragraphs 243–251).
441 *Re Ralls Builders Ltd* [2016] EWHC 243 (Ch) (paragraphs 241 and 242).
442 Six years from the date on which the company went into liquidation was held to be the limitation period for a wrongful trading claim brought by a liquidator under section 214 of IA 1986 in *Re Farmizer (Products) Ltd* [1997] 1 BCLC 589.

an action brought by an administrator under section 246ZB of IA 1986 are not to be treated as part of the company's net property available for satisfaction of the claims of the holders of any floating charge over the assets of the company[443]. The administrator may assign his right of action (including the proceeds of any action) under section 246ZB of IA 1986 to a third party[444].

443 Section 176ZB of IA 1986.
444 Section 246ZD of IA 1986 as inserted by section 118 of SBEEA 2015, which applies where a company went into administration on or after 1 October 2015: Schedule 1 paragraph 16 of the Small Business, Enterprise and Employment Act 2015 (Commencement No 2 and Transitional Provisions) Regulations 2015 (SI 2015 No 1689). This changes the law as discussed by the Court of Appeal in *Re Oasis Merchandising Services Ltd* [1998] Ch 170 and see also *In Re Longmeade Ltd* [2016] EWHC 356 (Ch) (paragraphs 74–83) and *In Re Ralls Builders Ltd* [2016] EWHC 243 (Ch) (paragraph 235).

9 The administrator's task

(Originally contributed by PricewaterhouseCoopers LLP)

INTRODUCTION

9.1   One of the administrator's primary duties is to prepare and issue to the company's creditors proposals for achieving the purpose of administration[1].

9.2   Immediately on his appointment the administrator is faced with a two-fold task. He must:

(a)   formulate practical proposals for achieving the purpose of administration, which will involve considering which of the three objectives detailed in Schedule B1 paragraph 3 of IA 1986 he is seeking to achieve; and

(b)   manage the company's affairs in such a way as to avoid that objective becoming frustrated and to protect the interests of the creditors. In practice, a proposed administrator is well recommended already to have formulated his broad strategy and the likely exit from administration prior to his appointment.

9.3   The administrator's initial priority will be to obtain as much information as possible on the company's financial and trading position and, if the business is to be continued, on the market in which it operates. He may already have much of the information needed and have formed a view on the way in which he will seek to achieve the purpose of administration, and if he was appointed by the court he will have received a copy of the evidence in support of the application containing a statement of the company's financial position[2]. However, this task may be more difficult if he is appointed with very little prior knowledge about the company (although he will have to have sufficient knowledge to enable him to confirm, prior to being appointed, that he is of the opinion that the purpose of administration is reasonably likely to be achieved)[3].

FINANCIAL INFORMATION

9.4   The basic information on the company's financial position will come from its own books of account. It may be necessary to bring those books up to

---

1   Schedule B1 paragraph 49 of IA 1986.
2   Rules 3.3(2) and 3.6(3) of the Rules.
3   Schedule B1 paragraphs 18(3) and 29(3) of IA 1986 and Rule 3.2(1)(h) of the Rules.

date. Even in the best-run companies, the accounting records may not reflect the current financial position completely. At any given moment, there may be supplies obtained for which invoices have not yet been received from the suppliers (particularly for continuous supplies such as electricity and telecommunication services) and invoices received but not yet posted. The administrator will want to make sure that all transactions relating to the period before his appointment have been posted in the books, if only to ensure that they are differentiated from transactions after the date of the order.

9.5 If the company's undertaking is to be continued, the administrator will wish to establish the extent to which existing liabilities need to be paid in order to maintain the business's viability. In most cases, existing liabilities will simply rank as claims against the company, to be handled in accordance with the proposals eventually approved by the creditors[4], but the administrator may make 'duress' payments if he thinks that it is likely to assist in achieving the purpose of administration[5].

9.6 Goods bought subject to reservation of title must be identified. If the company has not yet paid for them, and the reservation of title has been properly incorporated in the supply contract and is not void as an unregistered charge, the goods will still be the property of the seller[6]. They cannot be used during the administration unless the company pays for them[7].

9.7 Leased equipment may be essential to the company's business. As already noted[8], the administrator cannot simply ignore the rights of the owners of leased equipment to recover their property in the event of non-payment of accrued rentals. When considering the company's financial position, the administrator will therefore generally assume that some payment will have to be made for leased equipment. The amount to be paid may be a matter for negotiation, though an administrator should not use his position as a bargaining counter to be used solely in the interests of a particular class of creditors[9].

9.8 The company may have other contractual rights which terminate either on a failure to pay sums due under the contract or on the company entering administration. Examples include:

(a) leases of land and buildings;

(b) ship charters;

(c) licences to use patented processes or trade marks;

(d) permission to use copyright material; and

(e) insurance.

Arrangements will have to be made with the other parties concerned if the company is to continue utilising such rights during the course of the administration.

---

4   As to the position of certain public service suppliers, see section 233 of IA 1986 and **PARAGRAPHS 8.3–8.6** *ante*.
5   Schedule B1 paragraph 66 of IA 1986. See further, **PARAGRAPH 15.1FF** *post*.
6   See **PARAGRAPHS 6.7–6.13** and **PARAGRAPH 8.65** *ante*.
7   Under Schedule B1 paragraph 72 of IA 1986, the administrator can apply to the court for an order authorising him to dispose of the goods but any such order will be conditional on payment to the supplier of so much of the net proceeds of sale as are necessary to discharge the sums payable under the retention of title agreement. See further, **PARAGRAPHS 5.14–5.24** *ante*.
8   See **PARAGRAPH 2.24FF** and **PARAGRAPHS 5.14–5.25FF** *ante*.
9   *Re Atlantic Computer Systems plc* [1992] Ch 505 at 529 E–G.

9.9 Most insolvency practitioners are covered by one or other of the 'open cover' insurance schemes available in the United Kingdom market. These provide automatic insurance cover even if the company has failed to pay the premiums on its existing policies but, obviously, the premiums for the administration period must be paid as an expense of the administration.

9.10 Except perhaps in retail businesses, the debts due to a company normally represent an important part of its assets. Unless the debts have been factored, practically all of a company's trading receipts will relate to invoices raised a month or two earlier. When a company becomes insolvent the insolvency practitioner dealing with it can often rely on cash receipts from debtors to generate most of the funds needed to keep the business going in the short term.

9.11 If book debts are purportedly subject to a fixed charge, the administrator will need to determine or obtain directions as to whether the fixed charge is valid, or whether it is invalid by reason of the chargeholder not having sufficient control over the purportedly charged assets[10]. If the charge is valid, the chargeholder cannot enforce the charge directly[11], but, on the other hand, the administrator cannot use the proceeds[12]. The administrator will have to come to a suitable arrangement with the chargeholder if he wishes to use the receipts from debtors to finance the ongoing business. The chargeholder might be prepared to allow the receipts to be used in the business if the company grants him acceptable additional security. The debts will also be unavailable to the administrator if, as is increasingly likely to be the case following the decision in *Re Spectrum Plus Ltd*, they have been factored or discounted and thus no longer form part of the assets of the company.

9.12 It may be possible to release funds by disposing of other assets which are not essential to the business. Few companies have Van Goghs in their boardrooms but there may be unused machines or unnecessary executive jets.

FINANCIAL PROJECTIONS

9.13 Once the basic financial information has been assembled, the administrator will be able to prepare cash-flow projections for the company. These projections will indicate the expected future cash receipts and payments and show the resulting cash balances or deficits at various future dates. They will normally be prepared on a computer spreadsheet so that they can be rapidly recalculated using a series of different assumptions and recalculated in future when the actual results for a particular period are known. The period covered by the initial projections will vary from case to case. There may be a detailed projection for the three months beginning with the appointment of the administrators and a less detailed projection covering the nine-month period to the automatic end of the administration. If the administrator applies to court for an extension, or the creditors grant one, a further cash-flow projection will be required.

---

10   See *Re Spectrum Plus Ltd* [2005] UKHL 41.
11   Schedule B1 paragraph 43(2) of IA 1986: see further, **PARAGRAPH 2.7**FF *ante*.
12   Schedule B1 paragraph 71 of IA 1986: see further, **PARAGRAPH 5.14**FF *ante*.

9.14 A simple cash-flow projection, assuming there is no fixed charge over debts, would look something like this:

	Jan 7 £000	Jan 14 £000	Jan 21 £000	Jan 28 £000
Expected receipts				
From debtors	90	90	70	70
From sales during administration	—	—	—	20
	90	90	70	90
	Jan 7 £000	Jan 14 £000	Jan 21 £000	Jan 28 £000
Expected payments				
Raw materials	—	40	40	40
Wages and salaries	60	60	60	60
Electricity	—	—	—	10
Delivery costs	6	6	6	6
Legal fees	—	—	15	—
	66	106	121	116
	Jan 7 £000	Jan 14 £000	Jan 21 £000	Jan 28 £000
Opening bank balance	0	24	8	−43
Closing bank balance	24	8	−43	−69

This shows a positive bank balance at the end of the first two weeks, but this is mainly due to the fact that existing stocks of raw materials make it unnecessary to buy any raw material in the first week. The projection indicates that finance of £43,000 will be required at the end of the third week, rising to £69,000 at the end of the fourth week.

9.15 The administrator can attempt to find sources for that finance, take steps to reduce or eliminate the need for finance, or do both at the same time. This might for example be achieved by:

(a) a reduction in production;

(b) the consequent sale of a surplus machine; and

(c) the negotiation of additional credit from suppliers.

9.16 The administrator will use his cash-flow projections to see what finance will be required if trading is to be continued and to gauge the effects of the alternative courses of action open to him. He will also need to ensure that the cash available to him from time to time will be sufficient to meet the commitments entered into by him when payment becomes due. At this stage, the projections can be no more than estimates. If the business is continued, the projections will have to be updated and compared against the actual results at frequent intervals. Any material divergences between the two must be investigated so that corrective action can be taken or the projections revised where necessary.

9.17 Even if the cash-flow projections indicate that there will be sufficient cash available to enable trading to continue, the administrator needs separately to consider whether the business would be operating at a loss if it continues. Any trading losses will in effect be financed by assets which would otherwise have been available to meet the claims of creditors and the administrator may be at risk of action from creditors unless this dissipation of assets is carefully monitored and justified[13].

SHOULD THE BUSINESS BE CONTINUED?

9.18   The financial projections will indicate whether it is financially possible to continue the company's business. The administrator may have to negotiate loan facilities to provide the necessary finance. If he concludes that it is impossible to keep the business going, the administrator will have to consider whether this makes it impossible to achieve the purpose of administration, or whether the company should not have entered administration. In either of those cases, he must apply to the court for an order that his appointment as administrator ceases to have effect[14]. In practice, the point should have been considered before his appointment.

9.19   If the business can be continued, the next question is 'should the business be continued?'. In view of the hierarchy of objectives with which an administrator must perform his functions[15], in most administrations there will be a presumption that the business will be continued. Even if the administrator has decided that he is not going to achieve the primary objective of rescuing the company as a going concern, his objective must be to achieve a better result for the creditors as a whole than if the company was wound up, unless he thinks that is not reasonably practicable. In practice, this is likely to be achieved by continuing the business so it can be sold as a going concern. In the long run, it will not be worthwhile saving the company and its business unless the business can be made profitable, or at least break even. If the business continues to make losses indefinitely, the company will inevitably become insolvent again.

9.20   To determine whether the business can be made profitable, the administrator will have to establish the cause or causes of the past losses. In some cases, the reason for the losses will be easy to spot and easy to isolate. Few companies suffer a sudden and unique trading disaster[16], but there will be some (eg uninsured trading losses incurred while a hotel company is waiting for its premises to be rebuilt following a fire). Far more common are losses caused by:

(a)   diversification into a field for which the management does not have the necessary expertise;

(b)   the premature or injudicious introduction of a new product line;

(c)   a failure to recognise that an old product line has become unprofitable; and

(d)   attempts to make extraordinary profits through deals which have not gone as expected (such as currency speculation).

---

13   See further, **PARAGRAPH 9.23** *post.*
14   Schedule B1 paragraph 79 of IA 1986.
15   Schedule B1 paragraph 3 of IA 1986. See further, **PARAGRAPHS 5.3 AND 5.4** *ante.*
16   Even an insolvency caused by the failure of one or more major customers may simply be a symptom of poor management judgment and poor credit control, or of a general malaise in the industry.

9.21 In other cases the administrator and his staff and advisers will have to make sufficient enquiries and conduct wider research to pinpoint the causes of the loss and decide whether corrective action can be taken. This may involve, for example:

(a) a review of the market in which the company operates;

(b) a comparison of the company's products and marketing with those of its major competitors;

(c) a review of its production and distribution systems;

(d) a review of its management and accounting systems, with particular attention to costing, management information and internal controls; and

(e) an assessment of the personnel needed to run the company's business effectively.

The administrator will be well advised at the very least to meet all the executive directors of the company and meet or seek the views of the company secretary and/or the company's professional advisers if the company secretary discharges relatively nominal functions.

9.22 It is advisable to enter any suggested reorganisation plans into the computer model set up to calculate the financial projections. The administrator will then be able to gauge their likely financial effects more accurately. For example, reducing production may eliminate the need for finance in the first few months and it may also reduce losses. If the discontinued production accounts for the whole of the losses (ie the administrator can identify and abandon all the loss-making product lines), the business will return to making profits.

9.23 Even if the business cannot be made profitable, so that it is not possible to rescue the company as a going concern, it may still be useful to keep the business going, either to complete current contracts or work in progress, which may mitigate large claims against the company, or with a view to sale as a going concern, which may achieve substantially better realisations than on a break-up sale and will avoid claims from employees who are transferred with the business. The administrator will have to assess the business's possible attractions to a purchaser. It may have products which could be profitable if manufactured in the course of a larger operation. The company may have a brand name with a good reputation, which other companies in the same field would be willing to buy. Companies in allied trades might like to acquire the business in order to obtain access to its customers. Someone wishing to move into the company's market might find it cheaper and quicker to buy the company's business rather than start from scratch himself.

9.24 If the administrator concludes that it would not be in the interests of the creditors to keep the business going, he will have to decide whether this means that it is impossible to achieve the purpose of administration. If it does, he must apply to the court for an order that his appointment as administrator cease to have effect[17], but he may still be able to achieve the third objective of realising property in order to make a distribution to one or more secured or preferential creditors.

---

17 Schedule B1 paragraph 79 of IA 1986.

BUSINESS PRACTICALITIES

9.25 As mentioned earlier, the administrator and his staff and advisers will not be concentrating solely on financial matters. The market in which the company operates is important. The company may be able to organise its production line more efficiently. It may be able to reduce its stock levels through the use of 'just in time' techniques. It may have expertise for which others would be prepared to pay a premium.

9.26 Financial factors are not the only ones which determine whether or not the business can be continued. Does the company have the human and physical resources it needs to trade effectively? Will it be able to keep them? Is it complying fully with the applicable regulations, such as those on product labelling, health and safety, waste and pollution control, data protection and vehicle licensing?

9.27 Which of the non-financial factors has the greatest importance will depend on the type of industry in which the company is engaged and the company's own particular circumstances. The administrator must quickly assess the contracts and resources essential to the business and ensure they are secured. In the case of a company managing leisure centres on behalf of local authorities, for example, the most urgent task will be to see whether the appointment of administrators or some other event has brought any of the management contracts to an end and, if so, to try to negotiate terms under which the company will continue to provide management services. In the case of a manufacturing company, the most urgent task may be to obtain continued supplies of raw materials notwithstanding the company's failure to pay for earlier supplies. The attitude of the suppliers may be driven by that of their credit insurers.

9.28 All businesses need staff. The company's employees will inevitably have insecurities about their future employment even if the administrator expects to be able to rescue the company as a going concern. Communication channels are important and it is usual for representatives of the administrator to visit each site where the company has operations, if that is practicable, to explain to the staff there both the practical situation and their employment protection rights[18] and to address their concerns. It may be necessary for the administrator to pay any pre-administration arrears of pay by way of duress payment to retain the services of key employees.

9.29 If redundancies do become necessary as a result of reorganisation of the business, the selection of staff for redundancy must be carried out according to the procedures agreed between the company and any recognised trade union or, where there are no agreed procedures, in accordance with other recognised principles. The selection must always be based on objective criteria. Even though the company is in administration, efforts must be made to comply as far as possible with the obligations to give prior notice of pending redundancies to any recognised trade union and to the Redundancy Payments Service, and to consult. As a protective measure, some insolvency practitioners give notice of pending redundancies immediately upon appointment[19]. Redundancies should

---

18   These rights are discussed in more detail in **CHAPTER 7** *ante*.
19   The obligations of a company in administration as regards proposed redundancies are considered in more detail in **PARAGRAPHS 7.42–7.49** *ante*.

be handled as sensitively as possible, not only for the sake of those being made redundant but also to avoid alienating or demoralising staff who remain.

9.30 Particular care must be taken when dealing with businesses which can only be operated under the supervision or responsibility of someone who has specified qualifications or who has been registered for the purpose. Examples include:

(a) public houses, where the manager may hold the licence to sell alcohol;

(b) chemists' shops, where medicines can only be dispensed in the presence of a pharmacist; and

(c) nursing homes, which must have a qualified matron approved by and registered with the local authorities.

9.31 The administrator will need to check:

(a) which assets, if any, are leased or on hire-purchase;

(b) which goods, if any, are subject to reservation of title; and

(c) whether any leases or other contracts have terminated because of the appointment of administrators or because of some default brought about by the company's insolvency.

If any are identified, the administrator will have to take steps to negotiate terms for the continued use of the assets, buy the goods, remedy the breach or negotiate a renewal of the contract. That is, of course, assuming these things are needed. There may be advantages in allowing owners to recover goods which are of little commercial use or value.

9.32 The administrator will also want to establish which assets are surplus to requirements. This will happen as part of the review of the business and any reorganisation planning. The administrator may sell surplus assets provided he can do so without prejudicing the objective of the administration but if he does so prior to issuing his proposals, he will have to include in his proposals the reasons why he has done so and the terms on which the assets were disposed of[20].

9.33 Many companies are scrupulous about complying with the regulations affecting their industries. Others adopt a cavalier attitude. Most fall between the two extremes, generally complying with the regulations but with occasional lapses. Since many of the relevant statutes and regulations impose criminal liability on both the company and its responsible officer, for his own protection the administrator must check that the company is complying with them. Asking the directors whether they are complying with all relevant regulations will practically always produce the answer 'Yes'. It is therefore better to find out which regulations are relevant to the company's operations and review the company's compliance with them. The company's employees may know what lapses, if any, are occurring. The administrator's staff can and should bear the regulations in mind when they are walking round the premises. Are there any potentially dangerous machines without safety guards? Are fire exits clearly marked and clear of obstructions? How does the company dispose of its waste? If the administrator discovers that the company is failing to comply with some aspect of the applicable regulations he must, of course, take steps to make sure

---

20 Rule 3.35(1)(l) of the Rules and see **PARAGRAPH 3.11** ante.

it complies in future. This may require changes to the operating methods and financial projections.

MANAGING THE COMPANY'S AFFAIRS

9.34 It is usually assumed that the administrator ousts the directors from the control of the company's business. Indeed, this frequently happens in practice. As already noted, however[21], administrators may prefer to leave the existing management structure in place, subject to their own general oversight. The advantages of this are that it reduces disruption and leaves the day-to-day management of the business under the control of those who know it best.

9.35 In other cases, the administrator may decide to work directly through the company's senior management, with the directors' management roles, in effect, being undertaken by the administrator and the senior members of his staff. If he and his senior staff do not have the necessary expertise, the administrator can engage the services of an appropriate consultant or exercise his power to appoint a suitably qualified and experienced person as an additional director[22].

9.36 The company's management information systems will have to be reviewed to determine whether or not they are adequate for the changed circumstances in which the company finds itself. It may be necessary to increase the reporting frequency. The administrator's financial projections must be built into the system and continually revised. The administrator will wish to be provided with copies of the management information (or access to it if it is computer-based). He must make sure the information is monitored and that any problems or potential problems are identified and tackled as early as possible.

9.37 The directors will retain their statutory powers and duties as directors (as opposed to managers), subject to the overriding principle that they cannot exercise their powers in any way which would interfere with the exercise of the administrator's powers unless he consents[23]. In theory, their continuing duties include the duty to submit an annual return[24] and audited accounts to the registrar of companies[25]. By concession, the registrar will not require the directors to submit these if the company is in administration.

FORMULATING THE PROPOSALS

9.38 The administrator must satisfy himself that any proposals he prepares are in the creditors' interests (or where he is pursuing the third objective of realising property in order to make a distribution to one or more secured or preferential

---

21 See **PARAGRAPH 7.2** *ante*.
22 Schedule B1 paragraph 61 of IA 1986. The terms of such an appointment will have to be considered carefully, particularly as the new director is being appointed to a company known to be insolvent.
23 Schedule B1 paragraph 64 of IA 1986.
24 Section 854 of CA 2006.
25 Section 441 of CA 2006 (subject to small company and micro entities exemptions in any event).

creditors that they do not unnecessarily harm their interests)[26] and that the creditors can be expected to accept them. He will therefore need to consider all the possible options to see which are most likely to achieve the purpose of administration, starting with the primary objective of rescuing the company as a going concern, and then if necessary working down through the hierarchy of objectives set out in Schedule B1 paragraph 3 of IA 1986. The administrator may have difficult decisions as to the strategy to follow, and in determining what is the best result for creditors. The creditors may not consider a rescue involving a possible higher dividend later to be a better result than a sale of the assets resulting in a lower, but certain and quicker, dividend.

9.39   To identify all the possible alternatives the administrator needs experience, business sense and imagination. For example, if the business is sound but needs further finance he will have to consider the ways in which the finance could be raised. Are the current shareholders prepared to introduce additional funds? Is the issue of loan stock feasible? Can some of the existing liabilities be converted to equity and, if so, on what terms? Is financial assistance available from the government or a governmental body? Could a sale and lease-back of major assets be arranged?

9.40   The administrator's proposals must include his proposals for achieving the purpose of administration and for ending the administration as well as the factual information prescribed by the Rules.[27] Perhaps the most important information to be given is that relating to the proposed management and finance of the company's business in the future and 'any other information that the administrator thinks necessary to enable creditors to decide whether or not to approve the proposals'[28]. It is essential that creditors are given the information needed to show that the proposals are practical and in their interests. The information given, and the amount of detail included, will vary from case to case. Creditors may find it helpful if the administrator refers briefly to possible alternatives and the reasons for their rejection.

9.41   The proposals will provide the legal framework in which the company's affairs are to proceed in the future. They must be clear and unambiguous. They need to be both:

(a) sufficiently flexible to allow the scheme put forward by the administrator to continue if circumstances do not quite turn out as originally envisaged; and

(b) sufficiently well defined to enable the scheme to be terminated if the actual results are substantially different from those the creditors expected when they voted in favour.

To use the example commonly cited, what happens if the proposals provide that creditors shall be paid 27 pence in the pound but it only proves possible to pay 26 pence?

---

26   Schedule B1 paragraph 3 of IA 1986. There may be some cases where the creditors' interests are governed more by sentiment or sympathy rather than the financial outcome. The creditors of a local football club, for example, may prefer to accept less than they would get on liquidation in order to see the club continue.

27   Schedule B1 paragraph 49 of IA 1986 and Rule 3.35 of the Rules.

28   Rule 3.35(1)(l) and (n); see **paragraph 3.11**FF *ante*.

9.42 *The administrator's task*

9.42 Ultimately the administrator will need to ask himself: 'Are these proposals which I would accept if I were a creditor?'. To this end he will need to determine not only what is commercially practical in the circumstances but what realistically creditors may be prepared to accept. It is in this context that his professional judgment is likely to be most at a premium.

10 Sale of assets in an administration and related matters

INTRODUCTORY CONSIDERATIONS

10.1 As has been noted earlier[1], the administrator must lay before a meeting of the company's creditors his proposals for achieving the purpose of the administration. The underlying policy is for the administrator's proposals to have been formulated after the administrator has had an opportunity of reviewing in detail the financial affairs of the company, bearing in mind the purpose of the administration. In cases where it was proposed to realise the company's assets in whole or in part, it was commonplace for the administrator to seek general approval to sell assets of the company for the best obtainable consideration and on the best possible terms without seeking specific approval for the sale of particular assets or the terms of particular sales. This approach gave administrators a considerable degree of flexibility, but it also led to a number of larger administrations extending over a considerable period of time whilst the administrator sought to realise the company's assets. Whether this was intended when IA 1986 came into force is doubtful, but the practice became widespread and established. With the introduction of Schedule B1 to IA 1986, much more detailed information was required to be given to creditors[2]. In practice, while the new arrangements are much more prescriptive and designed to require more specific information from the administrator, the degree of flexibility formerly available to him has not been significantly curtailed.

10.2 In exercising his powers, the administrator is deemed to act as the company's agent[3]. The duties of an administrator as such have already been considered in **CHAPTER 5** *ante*. It is, however, quite clear that, in relation to the disposal of a company's assets, whether on an individual basis or generally, an administrator owes a duty to the company to exercise reasonable care. This duty not only extends to the manner and conduct of any sale but appears also to extend to the timing of such sale.

PRE-PACKAGED ASSET SALES

10.3 A practice which has proved controversial in a number of instances is what has come to be called a pre-pack asset sale, in which the whole (or sometimes a

---

1 **CHAPTER 3** *ante.*
2 See the position now set out in Rule 3.35 of the Rules.
3 Schedule B1 paragraph 69 of IA 1986.

freestanding part) of the company's business and undertaking is sold to a purchaser immediately after an administrator is appointed but without the approval or even knowledge of the company's creditors. In the early years of administration it was well recognised that, prior to the holding of the meeting of creditors to consider his proposals, it was possible for an administrator to proceed with the sale of particular assets, but it was thought that he should not, without specific directions from the court, sell such part of the company's property as would effectively frustrate consideration of his proposals by the creditors. However, in *Re T & D Industries plc*[4] it was decided that an administrator has power to exercise all of his statutory powers (and in particular to sell all or any of the company's assets) at any stage of the administration whether or not his proposals have been approved by the creditors or the court. Furthermore the court made clear that it would not normally be appropriate for the court to give any direction on a sale, unless there is a point of principle at stake or a dispute with an opportunity for an *inter partes* hearing[5].

10.4   This approach, which was clearly correct as a matter of principle, gave added impetus, to pre-pack asset sales, ie sales completed immediately after the appointment of administrators in cases in which it has been possible to carry out the preparatory sales work before the appointment. There are a number of good commercial reasons why a pre-pack sale may be desirable or even necessary. In particular, it is often thought that they are an efficient means for preserving the value of a company's going-concern business, particularly where the nature of that business is dependent on activities which are sensitive to the stigma or consequences of insolvency. However, although pre-pack sales have real benefits in facilitating business rescue, they are controversial both because they exclude creditor involvement in the sale process and because they have sometimes given rise to the abusive sale of businesses to connected parties at an undervalue. These concerns led to the promulgation with effect from January 2009 of a Statement of Insolvency Practice[6] (SIP 16) to deal with pre-packaged sales in administrations. SIP 16 has been amended twice since, the latest version having come into effect on 1 November 2015.

10.5   The basic approach which an administrator must adopt is to differentiate clearly between his role in providing advice to the company before any formal appointment and his functions and responsibilities following appointment, and the separate characteristics of those roles must be clearly explained to the directors and the creditors. He is then required to provide creditors with something called an SIP 16 statement which must comprise sufficient information such that a reasonable and informed third party would conclude that the pre-pack was appropriate and that the administrator had due regard to the creditors' interests. In the case of a pre-pack sale to a connected party, the level of detail in the SIP

---

4   [2000] 1 WLR 646 and *Re Transbus International Ltd* [2004] EWHC 932 (Ch) (although he should not act so as to avoid consideration of his proposals unless it is necessary for him to do so). See also *In re Kayley Vending Ltd* [2009] EWHC 904 (Ch). This approach has been described with approval by the Court of Appeal in *O'Connell v Rollings* [2014] EWCA Civ 639 (paragraph 79).

5   For a case in which relief authorising a pre-pack sale was granted, see *In re Hellas Telecommunications (Luxembourg) II SCA* [2009] EWHC 3199 (Ch). See also *Re Kayley Vending Ltd* [2009] EWHC 904 (Ch).

6   SIP 16 was commissioned and approved by the regulators' Joint Insolvency Committee and has been adopted by each of the regulators and the Insolvency Service.

statement may need to be greater, but SIP 16 itself contains a lot of detail on the information which may need to be disclosed. SIP 16 also has a section which sets out the key compliance standards which an administrator is required to fulfil during the various stages of the pre-pack process, being:

(a) the pre-appointment period in which preparatory work was carried out;

(b) the marketing process;

(c) the post-appointment period in which the administrator had to consider the manner of the disposal; and

(d) the process of disclosure to creditors once the disposal has taken place.

There is then an Appendix with guidance both on the marketing essentials and what should be included in the SIP 16 statement.

10.6 SIP 16 also contains a number of specific provisions where a pre-pack sale is made to a connected person. In particular a pre-pack pool of independent experts has been established for the purpose of expressing an opinion on the purchase of a business and/or its assets by connected parties. If viewed favourably, the pool member will issue a response to the effect that it is not in his opinion unreasonable to proceed. Any opinion from the pre-pack pool should then be included within the SIP 16 statement. There are also provisions for viability statements intended to explain what the purchasing entity will do differently in order that the business will not fail; that too should be included with the SIP 16 statement. This is all intended to increase the level of information available to creditors so that they have an informed opportunity to consider the position when the proposals are put before them[7]. The sale itself is unlikely to be vulnerable to any challenge thereafter, but where there are legitimate grounds for complaint, it may well have an effect on whether or not it is appropriate for the administrator to remain in office[8], and whether the company should go into liquidation, and if so who should be appointed to be the liquidator.

ASSET SALES: GENERAL

10.7 In larger administrations, the company may have been in discussions for several weeks or longer with its bankers with a view to some form of financial restructuring being effected. Valuations of assets prepared in the course of such discussions may have been prepared either on a going concern basis or on a break-up basis. Especially where there has been poor performance in a particular sector of the economy, administrators should approach such valuations of assets with care, particularly bearing in mind the provenance of such valuations and the purposes for which they were prepared.

10.8 In cases where the administrator is considering the disposal of the company's assets, he will invariably require formal valuations to be prepared. The administrator should ensure that he obtains proper valuations from experienced

---

7   The administrators' proposals are required in any event to include the reasons for the disposal of any assets and the terms upon which the disposals were made: Rule 3.35(1)(l)(i) of the Rules.

8   *Clydesdale Financial Services Ltd v Smailes* [2009] EWHC 1745.

valuers of the relevant assets. It is usual to obtain valuations[9] on two different bases:

1   *Open market value with existing use.* This is the best price at which an unconditional sale of the assets for immediate payment might reasonably be expected on the date of the valuation to be achievable, assuming–

    (a)   a willing seller;

    (b)   a willing buyer without any special reason for interest in the assets;

    (c)   a reasonable period of marketing, given the nature of the property; and

    (d)   that the existing use of the assets continues.

2   *Forced sale value.* This is the best price at which an unconditional sale of the assets for immediate payment might reasonably be expected on the date of the valuation to be achievable, assuming–

    (a)   a willing buyer without any special reason for interest in the assets;

    (b)   a seller who has imposed a time limit for completion which does not allow a reasonable period of marketing; and

    (c)   that the existing use of the assets does not necessarily continue.

In the case of a forced sale valuation the time limit imposed for completion is obviously critical.

10.9   If a disposal of assets is thought by an administrator to be appropriate, it will be important for the administrator to ensure that any sale is properly and appropriately advertised and that adequate information about the assets available for sale is given to as many potential purchasers as possible. An advertisement of the sale of particular assets in a relatively small locality may be entirely appropriate for one administration whereas a worldwide advertisement may be appropriate for the sale of assets of a company whose area of operations has extended over many countries. The administrator should also ensure that potential purchasers are given appropriate facilities for viewing and inspecting the assets, if in tangible form.

10.10   It is usual for the administrator to prepare an information brochure which is sent to all prospective purchasers of assets. The information brochure will typically contain relevant details of each of the individual assets available for sale as well as information about the business of the company including relevant financial information. It is important, however, for the administrator to insert in the information brochure a suitable form of disclaimer, so that the onus in relation to any possible sale falls squarely on the purchaser. Such a disclaimer might be in a form similar to the following:

'The following particulars are set out as a general outline only for the guidance of intending purchasers or their advisers and do not constitute either in whole or in part an offer or contract. All references to descriptions, dimensions, references to condition and necessary permissions for use and occupation and other details, while given in good faith and believed to be correct, should not be relied upon as statements or representations of fact by intending purchasers or their advisers, all of whom should satisfy themselves by inspection or otherwise as to the accuracy of such references. No warranty or

---

9   There is a definition of 'market value' in Schedule B1 paragraph 111(1) of IA 1986.

representation whatsoever is given as to the accuracy of any such references. The administrator acts only as agent of the company and without personal liability.'

The administrator should be careful in preparing his information brochure to ensure compliance with any relevant statutory provisions such as those of FSMA 2000 and the Enterprise Act 2002 applicable to an offer for sale of shares in a subsidiary company.

FUNDING ARRANGEMENTS

10.11 It has sometimes proved possible to combine a corporate voluntary arrangement in relation to a company with a sale of its assets or alternatively with a sale of the shares in the company, though in the latter instance it will be the shareholders rather than the company who will be the vendors. In these, and in other, circumstances, the administrator may be able to reach an understanding with a potential purchaser for the funding of the company or its business pending the approval of the administrator's proposals by the creditors or of a corporate voluntary arrangement by the company and its creditors or the fulfilment of any other necessary pre-conditions to the completion of any sale[10]. The mechanics for the transaction may, for instance, envisage that the purchaser, subject to agreed terms and conditions, provides the funding requirements of the company until the approval by the creditors of the administrator's proposals or a proposed corporate voluntary arrangement, the proposed purchaser being entitled to retain all of the trading profits during the relevant period while at the same time bearing all of any trading losses. It is sometimes provided that if for any reason the administrator's proposals are not approved by the creditors and the company, then the purchaser will receive back any monies advanced by him in the intervening period less the amount of any losses incurred or plus the amount of profits earned during such period. In this connection, it is important to establish in advance the basis on which any such profits or losses are to be computed, eg using accounting principles and bases consistent with those used by the company in the calculation of its profits or losses in, for example, the last three accounting periods.

10.12 A funding agreement entered into in the course of an administration will normally provide for the funder in such circumstances to be responsible to the administrator for the outgoings and day-to-day liabilities of the business. Usually, it will be possible to calculate the approximate amount of such monthly outgoings and the administrator should require payment in advance of such amount with provision being made for any excess to be met by the funder. The funding agreement should provide for appropriate adjustments to be made as between the administrator and the funder at the end of the period of the funding.

10.13 Arrangements between an administrator and a funder may be expressed to be subject to the directions of the court. This may be a sensible precaution as an administrator will wish to avoid fettering his powers to the prejudice of the overall outcome of the administration. Further, although the administrator may in principle be prepared to act in accordance with the reasonable instructions

---

10 This discussion does not consider funding by entities other than a prospective purchaser, eg banks and/or venture capitalists.

of the funder during the funding period, power should always be reserved to the administrator to refuse to act in accordance with the wishes of the funder, if to do so, in the administrator's opinion, would prejudice the position of the administrator or the conduct of the administration. It may, in addition, be necessary to obtain the consent to any funding agreement of the holder of any fixed charge over the company's book or other debts paid or payable in the course of the administration.

10.14 In making arrangements with a funder, an administrator will normally insist on a widely drawn indemnity to protect him and the company in administration from any losses, costs, liabilities and expenses arising out of the carrying on of the business during the funding period. The funding agreement will also invariably exclude any personal liability on the part of the administrator as well as confirming the absence of warranties or representations to the funder on the part of both the administrator and the company[11].

10.15 Whilst a funding agreement may be intended to provide the framework enabling a business to continue to trade pending an eventual sale of the company or its business to the funder, it is nevertheless important to provide in the funding agreement for the circumstances in which the agreement should terminate. In any given situation, the particular provisions will vary, but the following may typically be found in the termination provisions of a funding agreement:

(a) termination upon seven days' or longer written notice by the funder to the administrator;

(b) termination forthwith upon the discharge of the administration order, the insolvency of the funder, impossibility of performance by the funder, failure by the funder to perform its obligations under the funding agreement or upon the making of a court order directing the administrator to terminate the funding agreement;

(c) termination upon completion of the sale and purchase of the shares of the company in administration or of the business being funded by the funder.

TERMS OF ASSET SALES

10.16 Each sale of assets by a company in administration will inevitably contain its particular terms but a number of core provisions are likely to appear in most agreements for the sale of assets by a company in administration. Such core provisions are described in the following paragraphs.

10.17 Any sale of assets of a company in administration will normally be a sale by the company itself, albeit that the administrator negotiates and authorises any such sale under the powers given to him under Schedule 1 to IA 1986. The administrator acts as the company's agent[12]. It is normally desirable, however, specifically to designate the company in administration as the vendor so that, save to the extent expressly provided, if any, obligations under the sale agreement do not fall upon the administrator personally. It should, however, be borne in mind that any obligations undertaken by the company in administration under any such sale agreement may be recoverable against and charged on the assets in the

---

11 Administrators are invariably insistent upon excluding all potential personal liability, however remote.

12 Schedule B1 paragraph 69 of IA 1986.

administrator's custody or under his control[13] or otherwise directed by the court to be paid as expenses of the administration.

10.18 Though administrators generally seek to exclude any personal liability under sale agreements, it may not always be possible for them to do so, eg in cases where the administrator personally is required to carry out particular steps. In such circumstances, it is desirable from the point of view of the administrator to seek to ensure that any personal liability of the administrator for breach of any contractual obligation is appropriately limited and that a time limit is imposed within which any such liability may be enforced.

10.19 Recitals are normally inserted in a sale agreement setting out the details of the appointment of the administrator whether by order of the court or otherwise. If acting for a purchaser, it is prudent to seek to obtain a copy of the order of the court appointing the administrator or other relevant documentation relating to the appointment of the administrator. Under Schedule B1 paragraph 59(3) of IA 1986, a person dealing with the administrator in good faith and for value is not concerned to enquire whether the administrator is acting within his powers.

10.20 A definitions clause will normally contain definitions of, *inter alia*, the various assets to be sold, the date for completion and the date with effect from which the sale is to be regarded as having taken place, if different.

10.21 The consideration specified in the agreement will often be a fixed aggregate amount. It may well be desirable to allocate the consideration as against particular assets so that the administrator will be able to demonstrate that the amount obtained for a particular asset bears reasonable comparison with any valuation of the assets that has been obtained. The amount obtained for any particular asset may also be important in determining the amount to which the holder of any security over the asset is entitled although the holder of a security, other than one which as created was a floating charge, will normally in any event have the protection of Schedule B1 paragraph 71 of IA 1986. The purchaser also may be concerned to ensure that appropriate amounts are allocated against particular assets, eg for the purposes of stamp duty or capital allowances.

10.22 An administrator will normally seek to ensure that a sale agreement contains a clause providing that the purchaser, having inspected the assets as they stand, takes the same in the condition in which they are and that no warranty or assurance is given or implied as to the description, condition, quality or fitness of such assets. It is usual also expressly to record that such provisions are fair and reasonable in all the circumstances of a sale of assets by a company in administration and that the purchaser:

(a) has been afforded a full opportunity to inspect the assets in question;

(b) relies on its own inspection, investigation and analysis;

(c) has made such inspection, investigation and analysis; and

(d) acknowledges the intervention of administration and the constraints on selling necessarily imposed in such circumstances[14].

10.23 From the administrator's perspective, it is highly desirable to provide in the sale agreement that the company in administration sells such right, title and

---

13   Schedule B1 paragraph 99(4) of IA 1986.
14   Cf sections 6, 7 and 21 of the Unfair Contract Terms Act 1977.

interest as the company has in the assets as at the date of transfer[15]. Such assets will be sold by the company subject to any subsisting reservation of title claims, charges, liens, encumbrances or other third party rights. In this connection, if there is known to be a possible retention of title claim, suitable arrangements may have to be made in case the claim is upheld. Whilst an administrator will normally take steps to ensure that the company has an unchallengeable title to the assets which it is sought to sell, where possible, the normal practice is to put the responsibility upon the purchaser to satisfy itself as to title. It is normal to insert in the sale agreement a clause to the effect that any failure by the vendor to pass any title, right or interest to or in any of the assets is not to be a ground enabling the purchaser to rescind or to treat the vendor as in breach of the sale, or to claim a reduction of the purchase price.

TAX CONSIDERATIONS

10.24   Save for the case of the sale of shares in respect of which no VAT will be payable[16], it should be borne in mind that VAT may be payable on the sale of assets[17] unless it can be shown that the sale is of a business or a part of a business capable of separate operation which is being sold as a going concern. In the latter event, by reason of the provisions of the Value Added Tax (Special Provisions) Order 1995[18] and subject to compliance with the requirements set out in article 5 thereof, liability for VAT will not arise. In this connection, the ultimate intentions of the transferee as to the type of goods or services that it proposes to supply following completion of the sale agreement are irrelevant[19]. The vital consideration is whether the transferee has been put into possession of a business which was a going concern at the time of transfer[20]. However, even in the case of purchases of a going concern, tax may in certain circumstances be payable to the extent that a particular sale includes an assignment of certain interests in or rights over land[21]. In cases of doubt, where prior clearance for HM Customs and Excise cannot be obtained, it is prudent practice that VAT should be charged and should be recovered at completion from the purchaser. In addition, it is advisable to record in the sale agreement that the consideration is exclusive of VAT (if any); otherwise the purchaser may seek to claim that the consideration was VAT inclusive and thereby leave the administrator with a potential liability for an apparent VAT element on the sale. If VAT is payable, the company as vendor must deliver to the purchaser a VAT invoice to enable the purchaser to recover the VAT in due course[22].

---

15   Otherwise the company will be unable to exclude the provisions of section 12 of the Sale of Goods Act 1979 or section 8 of the Supply of Goods (Implied Terms) Act 1973; see sections 6(1) and 20(1) of the Unfair Contract Terms Act 1977.

16   Share sales are exempt supplies: section 31 and Schedule 9 Group 5 to the Value Added Tax Act 1994.

17   The usual rules will of course apply to the supply of zero-rated goods (section 30 of the Value Added Tax Act 1994) and to exempt supplies (section 31 of the Value Added Tax Act 1994).

18   SI 1995 No 1268.

19   *Customs and Excise Comrs v Dearwood Ltd* [1986] STC 327, although immediate intentions are: *Customs and Excise Comrs v Padglade Ltd* [1995] STC 602.

20   *Customs and Excise Comrs v Dearwood Ltd* [1986] STC 327.

21   Article 5(2) of SI 1995 No 1268.

22   Regulation 13 of the Value Added Tax Regulations 1995 (SI 1995 No 2518).

10.25 Stamp duty land tax will normally be payable on the value of the consideration for freehold and leasehold properties[23]. The rate, however, is reduced to nil where the amount or value of the consideration is £150,000 or less (for non-residential property) and the transaction effected by the relevant instrument does not form part of a larger transaction or a series of transactions in respect of which the amount or value, or aggregate amount or value, of the consideration exceeds £150,000[24]. Stamp duty is payable at the rate of 0.5 per cent on the value of the consideration for transfers of stock and marketable securities[25]. Where, however, the assets in question are sold to an associated company, ie where one of the parties to the transaction is the beneficial owner of not less than 75 per cent of the issued share capital of the other, relief from stamp duty is available under section 42 of the Finance Act 1930 (stamp duty) and Schedule 7 Part 1 of the Finance Act 2003 (stamp duty land tax). The relief, together with the reduced rate payable on transfers of marketable securities, may enable an administrator to effect a stamp duty saving where the assets of the company in administration are transferred to a subsidiary company which is later sold to a third-party purchaser albeit that anti-avoidance provisions charge stamp duty/stamp duty land tax if the company is transferred out of the group within three years[26]. Stamp duty on share transfers following upon the sale of shares in a subsidiary may in any event be negligible if the sale has been effected for a nominal consideration. It may in certain circumstances, however, be necessary for the value of the business sold to be adjudicated upon by the stamp duty office[27]. In the absence of any agreement to the contrary, stamp duty is payable by the purchaser[28].

EMPLOYEES AND PENSION MATTERS

10.26 The position of employees has already been considered in **CHAPTER 7** *ante*. Especially in view of the decision of the House of Lords in *Litster v Forth Dry Dock and Engineering Co Ltd*[29], it is very important that the administrator obtains a full indemnity from the purchaser of an undertaking in respect of the potential claims of employees whose contracts of employment are effectively transferred to the purchaser.

10.27 As part of the overall arrangements for the sale of a business, the purchaser, if an established company of any size, may wish (if it is possible to do so), to make suitable arrangements to transfer the accrued benefits of employees of the business being sold under the pension scheme of the company in administration to the pension scheme operated by the purchaser. It is very important to note, however, that the assets belonging to a pension scheme are not assets of the company in administration[30]. Nonetheless, any surplus arising after all proper benefits have been provided for, may form an asset available to

---

23 Sections 42 and 55 of the Finance Act 2003.
24 Section 55 of the Finance Act 2003.
25 Schedule 13 to the Finance Act 1999 and section 125 of Finance Act 2003.
26 Section 111 of the Finance Act 2002 and Schedule 7 paragraph 3 of the Finance Act 2003.
27 See *Western Abyssinian Mining Syndicate Ltd v IRC* (1935) 14 ATC 286.
28 Sections 14(4) and 15B of the Stamp Act 1891 and section 85 of the Finance Act 2003.
29 [1990] 1 AC 546.
30 However, an administrator is under a duty to satisfy himself that at least one of the trustees of the company's pension scheme is an independent person.

the administrator subject to the terms of the relevant pension documentation. The scheme rules may provide for any such surplus to be paid over to the company in administration as the employer under the pension scheme documentation, or the fate of the surplus may be within the discretion of the trustees or, indeed, there may be other possibilities. It is therefore of importance to establish at an early stage the provisions in the relevant pension scheme documentation to enable a view properly to be taken. In practice this does not happen very often because it is unusual to find an overfunded pension scheme, and the restrictions on returning any surplus are stringent[31]. Since it is often impossible to finalise the pensions aspects of a sale before completion, it is sometimes agreed that if the trustees of the pension scheme of the company in administration are agreeable, and subject to the purchaser becoming an 'employer' for the purposes of such scheme within a period of not more than 12 months from the completion date, then subject to Inland Revenue approval, the trustees of such pension scheme will discuss with the trustees of the purchaser's pension scheme appropriate transfer values for those employees whose rights and entitlements are to be transferred to the purchaser's pension scheme. Although an administrator may not be directly affected by such pension arrangements, it may be appropriate for the administrator to consent to the arrangements in a formal deed of adherence.

CHANGE OF NAME

10.28 In many administrations and particularly larger cases, the company name will be perceived by a purchaser as a valuable asset in an on-going business. For this reason, arrangements are often made as part of an agreement for the purchaser to be entitled to use the name of the company in administration. However, the following points should be noted in such circumstances:

(a) Any change of name of a company can either be effected under a power given in the company's articles or will require the members of the company to pass an appropriate special resolution[32]. The cost of convening the necessary extraordinary general meeting may or may not be an acceptable cost to a purchaser who would normally be expected to meet such costs. In the case of a listed public company in administration, the cost is unlikely to be acceptable.

(b) On the other hand, the prospective purchaser of the business of a trading subsidiary may only wish to use the corporate name of that subsidiary. If the subsidiary is a wholly owned subsidiary of the company in administration, the administrator as administrator of the parent company will be in a position to procure the passing of the appropriate special resolution at relatively little cost.

10.29 If the sale is to a purchasing company controlled by directors or former directors of the company in administration, and there is a possibility that the company in administration will thereafter go into insolvent liquidation, there may be issues for the directors arising out of the prohibited name provisions of IA 1986. These will apply if they are directors of a purchasing company which has a name that is so similar to the company's name as to suggest an association with it. Where they do apply, those directors will commit an offence and expose themselves to the potential for personal liability under section 217 of IA 1986.

---

31 Section 37 of the Pensions Act 1995, section 251 of the Pensions Act 2004 and the Occupational Pension Schemes (Payments to Employer) Regulations 2006 (SI 2006 No 802).
32 Section 77 of CA 2006.

11 Voluntary arrangements

INTRODUCTION

11.1   This chapter considers the procedures for the approval and implementation of a voluntary arrangement under Part I of IA 1986. A voluntary arrangement is a composition in satisfaction of the company's debts or a scheme of arrangement of its affairs providing for a person who is qualified to act as an insolvency practitioner or authorised to act as a nominee[1] in relation to the voluntary arrangement ('the nominee') to act in relation to the voluntary arrangement either as trustee or otherwise for the purpose of supervising its implementation[2]. It is no longer the case that one of the specific statutory purposes for which a company goes into administration is the approval of a voluntary arrangement under Part I of IA 1986[3]. It remains the case, however, that it is often desirable for the statutory stay imposed either by the company being in administration or by the imposition of a moratorium under Schedule A1 to IA 1986[4] to be in place before a voluntary arrangement is proposed[5]. Neither form of stay is, however, a necessary precursor to a proposal for a voluntary arrangement and the procedures differ according to whether the administrator of a company is promulgating the proposal or the proposal is promulgated by the directors of the company[6]. The procedures are different again where the proposed voluntary

---

1   For the authorisation requirements of acting as an insolvency practitioner whether as nominee or administrator see sections 388–389A of IA 1986.
2   Section 1(1) and (2) of IA 1986, as amended by Schedule 2 paragraph 2 of the Insolvency Act 2000.
3   Until 15 September 2003, when the provisions of Schedule B1 to IA 1986 (introduced by the Enterprise Act 2002) came into force, one of the purposes for which an administration order could be granted was the approval of a voluntary arrangement (s.8 (3)(b) of IA 1986). Contrast with the provisions in force since 15 September 2003 at Schedule B1 paragraph 3(1) of IA 1986 where the current purposes of administration are set out, being rescuing the company as a going concern, achieving a better result for the company's creditors that would be likely if the company were wound up or realising property in order to make a distribution to one or more secured or preferential creditors.
4   As inserted by Schedule 1 to the Insolvency Act 2000. For the moratorium procedures for an eligible company, see **CHAPTER 12** *post.*
5   For a case in which an adjournment of a winding-up petition was refused where an attempt to promulgate a voluntary arrangement was not protected by an administration order, see *Re Piccadilly Property Management Ltd* [1999] 2 BCLC 145 and compare *Re Dollar Land (Feltham) Ltd* [1995] 2 BCLC 370. For a case where the Commercial Court granted a stay of proceedings pending the scheme company promulgating a scheme, see *Re Vietnam Shipbuilding Industry Groups* [2013] EWHC 2476 (Ch) (paragraph 25).
6   Section 1(3) of IA 1986.

arrangement is sought with the assistance of a moratorium under section 1A of IA 1986[7]. In the unusual case in which it is proposed that some person other than the administrator should act as nominee, the procedure is the same as that in which the proposal is promulgated by the directors, substituting the administrator for the directors. Once a company is in administration, the directors have no power to make a proposal under Part I of IA 1986[8]. This chapter includes references to the new Insolvency (England and Wales) Rules 2016. These new 2016 Rules came into force on 6 April 2017 (and replaced the Insolvency Rules 1986 referred to in earlier editions of this work). The 2016 Rules provide for transitional and savings provisions in Schedule 2 of the 2016 Rules. By Rule 5 of Schedule 2, where on or after the commencement date (6 April 2017) a creditors' or contributories' meeting is to be held as a result of a notice issued before 6 April 2017 in relation to a meeting for which provision is made by the 1986 Rules or the 1986 Act, or where a meeting is to be held as a result of a requisition by a creditor or contributory made before that date, the new decision-making procedures contained in Part 15 of the 2016 Rules do not apply, and the 1986 Rules relating to the following continue to apply, namely:

- the requirement to hold the meeting,
- the notice and advertisement of the meeting,
- the governance of the meeting,
- the recording and taking minutes of the meeting,
- the membership and formalities of establishment of liquidation and creditors' committees where the resolution to form the committee is passed at the meeting,
- the office holder's resignation or removal at the meeting,
- the office holder's release,
- the fixing of the office holder's remuneration,
- requests for further information from creditors,
- the handover of assets to a supervisor of a voluntary arrangement where the proposal is approved at the meeting,
- the notice of the appointment of a supervisor of a voluntary arrangement where the appointment is made at the meeting,
- claims that remuneration is or that other expenses are excessive, and
- complaints about exclusion at the meeting.[9]

As regards the transitional provisions for where a CVA moratorium under Schedule A1 of IA 1986 is proposed, Rule 9 of Schedule 2 to the 2016 Rules provides that where, before 6 April 2017, the directors of a company submit to the nominee the documents required under Schedule A1 paragraph 6(1) of IA 1986, the 1986 Rules relating to moratoria continue to apply to that proposed voluntary arrangement. The rest of this chapter refers to the 2016 Rules (in place of the former 1986 Rules).

---

7   In such cases, the procedures are provided for by Schedule A1 to IA 1986 and Rules 2.11–2.24 of the 2016 Rules.
8   Section 1(1) of IA 1986.
9   Schedule 2, Rule 5(1) and (2) of the Rules.

11.2   Section 1(4) of IA 1986 provides that 'company' for the purposes of Part I (sections 1 to 7B) means:

(a)   a company registered under the Companies Act 2006 in England and Wales (or Scotland)[10],

(b)   a company incorporated in an EEA State other than the United Kingdom, or

(c)   a company not incorporated in an EEA State but having its centre of main interests in a member state other than Denmark.

Section 1(5) of IA 1986 provides, in relation to a company, that 'centre of main interests' has the same meaning as in the EC Insolvency Regulation and, in the absence of proof to the contrary, it is presumed to be the place of its registered office (within the meaning of the EC Insolvency Regulation)[11]. The same definition of 'a company' is used both in respect of voluntary arrangements and an administration[12].

11.3   As regards English and Welsh registered companies under the Companies Act, since section 1(4)(a) of IA 1986 confines voluntary arrangements to companies registered under the Companies Act 2006, this means that companies incorporated in the United Kingdom otherwise than under the Companies Act are excluded, such as companies incorporated by Royal Charter[13], or under special public, private or local Acts of Parliament or corporations sole[14]. It would appear also that entities such as trade unions, friendly societies, cooperative societies or other bodies formed under the Industrial and Provident Societies Acts 1965 to 2002 and the Co-operative and Community Benefit Societies and Credit Unions Act 2010 are also excluded[15].

11.4   The reference to 'a company' in section 1(4)(b) and (c) of IA 1986 is to an entity with its own separate legal personality. In *O'Neill v Phillips*[16] Lord Hoffmann referred to a company as 'an association of persons for an economic purpose'. This description of a company was accepted and applied in *Re Hellas Telecommunications (Luxembourg) II SCA*[17] where the court accepted that a *société en commandite par actions* incorporated under the laws of Luxembourg with characteristics under that law of a combination of a joint stock company and a limited partnership which had a separate legal personality, a constitution and shareholders, was a 'company' within, Schedule B1 paragraph 111(1A)(b) of IA 1986 (a company incorporated in an EEA State other than the UK).

---

10   Section 1(1) of the Companies Act 2006.
11   The present section 1(4) and (5) were introduced with effect from 13 April 2005 by the Insolvency Act 1986 (Amendment) Regulations 2005 (SI 2005 No 879) (save section 1(4)(a) was updated from 1 October 2009 by Schedule 1 paragraph 71 of the Companies Act 2006 (Consequential Amendments, Transitional Provisions and Savings) Order 2009 (SI 2009 No 1941) to take account of the Companies Act 2006.
12   Schedule B1 paragraph 111(1A) of IA 1986.
13   Cf *Re The Salvage Association* [2003] EWHC 1028, where Blackburne J decided, applying the provisions of section 1(4) in force prior to 13 April 2005, that an association incorporated by Royal Charter could be the subject of a voluntary arrangement.
14   Such as the office of the Archbishop of Canterbury.
15   See *Re Devon and Somerset Farmers Ltd* [1994] Ch 57 (industrial and provident society was not a company for the purposes of administrative receivership). See also *Re Dairy Farmers of Britain Ltd* [2009] EWHC 1389 (Ch) where a declaration was granted that an industrial and provident society was not a 'company' within section 72A of IA 1986, so it was lawful for receivers to be appointed and the prohibition in section 72A did not apply.
16   [1999] 1 WLR 1092 at 1098G.
17   [2009] EWHC 3199 (Ch).

11.5 Industrial and provident societies are permitted to utilise a company voluntary arrangement,[18] as can building societies[19] and also NHS Foundation Trusts[20].

11.6 A proposed voluntary arrangement shall not have effect in relation to an EEA insurer (ie a non-UK insurer subject to regulation in another EU state) if the decision to approve the arrangement under section 4 of IA 1986 was taken after 20 April 2003[21]. Likewise, a proposed voluntary arrangement shall not have effect in relation to an EEA credit institution if the decision to approve the arrangement under section 4 of IA 1986 was taken after 5 May 2004[22].

11.7 There are many different forms that a voluntary arrangement can take depending, amongst other matters, on the extent of the company's insolvency, the nature of its business and the source of available assets. There are, however, a number of general points that can be made on the form of an arrangement. First and foremost, it must qualify as a composition or scheme. A composition in satisfaction of a company's debts is an agreement by which a creditor accepts or is required to accept the payment of a lesser sum or other consideration in exchange for the forbearance to sue for the full amount of his debt. A scheme of arrangement is a broader concept. Any form of moratorium is capable of being a scheme, so long as it does not amount to the creditors giving up everything in return for nothing[23]. Secondly, a voluntary arrangement operates as an agreement[24] between the company and those who are bound by operation of section 5(2) of IA 1986[25]. It follows that it will always be a question of construction of the arrangement itself as to whether or not it has any particular effect[26]. Ordinary principles of construction[27] will have to be applied to the

---

18   Industrial and Provident Societies and Credit Unions (Arrangements, Reconstructions and Administration) Order 2014 (SI 2014 No 229) with effect from 6 April 2014.
19   Section 90a of the Building Societies Act 1986.
20   Section 53 of the National Health Service Act 2006.
21   Regulation 4(6) of the Insurers (Reorganisation and Winding Up) Regulations 2004 (SI 2004 No 353).
22   Regulation 3(6) of the Credit Institutions (Reorganisation and Winding Up) Regulations 2004 (SI 2004 No 1045).
23   *IRC v Adam & Partners Ltd* [2001] 1 BCLC 222 at 231 explaining *Re NFU Development Trust Ltd* [1972] 1 WLR 1548; *Re T&N Ltd (No 3)* [2006] EWHC 1447 (Ch) (paragraph 53).
24   But not an agreement for the purposes of section 203 of the Employment Rights Act 1996: see *Re Britannia Heat Transfer Ltd* [2007] BPIR 1038.
25   In contrast to a scheme of arrangement made under sections 895–899 of the Companies Act 2006 (which can be used to bind and provide for a particular class of creditor rather than all creditors), a voluntary arrangement under sections 1–7B of IA 1986 will bind all creditors who were entitled to vote in the qualifying decision procedure by which the creditors' decision to approve the voluntary arrangement was made (s.5 (2) of IA 1986 as amended by Schedule 9 paragraph 6(2) of SBEEA 2015)). Cf *Re T&N Ltd* [2005] EWHC 2870 (Ch) ('creditor' for purposes of a CVA), and *Re T&N Ltd (No 3)* [2006] EWHC 842 (Ch), paragraphs 16 and 17.
26   *Johnson v Davies* [1999] Ch 117 and *Whitehead v Household Mortgage Corpn* [2002] EWCA Civ 1657, [2003] BPIR 1482 at 1488. See also *Appleyard Ltd v Ritecrown Ltd* [2007] EWHC 3515 (Ch); *Tucker & Spratt v Gold Fields Mining LLC* [2009] EWCA Civ 173; *Re Energy Holdings (No 3) Ltd* [2010] EWHC 788 (Ch); *Re Sixty UK Ltd* [2009] EWHC 3866 (Ch); *Oakrock Ltd v Travelodge Hotels Ltd* [2015] EWHC 30.
27   See *ICS Ltd v West Bromwich BS* [1998] 1 WLR 896 at 912H and 913; *BCCI SA v Ali* [2001] UKHL 8, [2001] 1 AC 251 at 259F–G; *Mannai Investment Co Ltd v Eagle Star Life Assurance Co Ltd* [1997] AC 749 at 771B; *Rainy Sky SA v Kookmin Bank* [2011] UKSC 50 (paragraph 19); *AG of Belize v Belize Telecom* [2009] UKPC 10 (paragraph 16). See also *Tucker and Spratt (joint supervisors of Energy Holdings (No 3) (in liquidation)) v Gold Fields Mining LLC* [2009] EWCA Civ 173, where the Court of Appeal considered the proper construction of the Claims Date clause and whether a creditor who lodged its claim late was barred.

question of whether any particular term is expressed[28] or to be implied into the arrangement, although the court will sometimes adopt a practical approach to construction to ensure that if there is careless and clumsy drafting it does not frustrate the underlying purpose of the arrangement[29]. Thus, the question of whether or not a debt is released will depend on the true construction of the arrangement[30], as will such matters as the terms, if any, on which any assets may be held on trust for the creditors[31], whether the arrangement provides a mechanism for subsequent variation[32] or the circumstances in which it is to come to an end and the effect of a termination[33]. It should be noted that, although it will often be the case that a moratorium on creditors' claims will be implied into a scheme that makes no express provision[34], there may be schemes in which no such implication is justified[35]. It follows that, if a moratorium is intended, it should be expressly included.

PROCEDURE WHERE THE ADMINISTRATOR IS THE NOMINEE

11.8   Where a company is in administration and, as is the normal case, the administrator is himself the nominee who it is proposed should supervise the

---

28   In *Alman v Approach Housing Ltd* [2001] 1 BCLC 530 there was no express stay of proceedings in the relevant CVA, and Rimer J rejected an argument that a stay of proceedings should be implied as a term of the arrangement (paragraphs 7–17).

29   *Welsby v Brelec Installations Ltd* [2000] 2 BCLC 576 at 585, applied in *County Bookshops Ltd v Grove* [2002] EWHC 1160, [2003] 1 BCLC 479 at 488. In *Re Pinson Wholesale Ltd* [2008] BCC 112 HH Judge Norris QC held a term should be implied into an arrangement to enable the joint supervisors to be fairly remunerated.

30   *Johnson v Davies* [1999] Ch 117 in which it was concluded that on the true construction of the arrangement, there was a moratorium and not a release sufficient to discharge the liability of a co-debtor, although the Court of Appeal rejected an argument based on *R A Securities Ltd v Mercantile Credit Co Ltd* [1995] 3 All ER 581 that a voluntary arrangement could never have the effect of releasing a co-debtor; see further *Lloyds Bank plc v Ellicott* [2002] EWCA Civ 133. See also *Prudential Assurance Co Ltd v PRG Powerhouse Ltd* [2007] EWHC 1002 (Ch); *Re T&N Ltd (No 3)* [2006] EWHC 1447 (Ch); *Re Lehman Bros International (Europe) (in administration) (No 2)* [2009] EWCA Civ 1161 (paragraphs 63 and 83); *Re La Seda de Barcelona SA* [2010] EWHC 1364 (Ch); *Mourant & Co Trustees Ltd v Sixty UK Ltd (in administration)* [2010] EWHC 1890 (Ch). Note also *Re Telewest Communications plc (No 1)* [2004] EWHC 924 (Ch) (paragraph 58).

31   *Re Bradley-Hole* [1995] 1 WLR 1057 and *Welburn v Dibb Lupton Broomhead* [2002] EWCA Civ 1601, [2003] BPIR 768 at 775–6.

32   *Raja v Rubin* [2000] Ch 274, in which the Court of Appeal (especially per Clarke LJ at 290) stressed the desirability of a voluntary arrangement making express provision for variation. See also *Re Cape plc* [2006] EWHC 1316 (Ch) where David Richards J held the court had jurisdiction to sanction a scheme of arrangement which contained provision for future amendment either of the scheme itself or of agreements or other documents to be made pursuant to the scheme.

33   *Re N T Gallagher & Son Ltd* [2002] EWCA Civ 404, in which the Court of Appeal reviewed the authorities on the circumstances in which the intervention of a liquidation might terminate a trust established by a voluntary arrangement and require the supervisor to hand over to the liquidator the assets held on trust for the purposes of the arrangement.

34   *Sea Voyager Maritime Inc v Bielecki* [1999] 1 BCLC 133 at 150. In *El Ajou v Stern* [2006] EWHC 3067 (Ch) Kitchin J held that terms should be implied into an individual voluntary arrangement that creditors subject to the IVA would take no steps to enforce while the IVA subsisted, and that if the IVA was completed (and had not failed) creditors would accept whatever was distributed to them in full and final settlement of their debts (paragraph 31). The creditor was therefore disallowed from enforcing his interest claim by bankruptcy proceedings subsequent to the IVA.

35   *Alman v Approach Housing Ltd* [2001] 1 BCLC 530.

implementation of the voluntary arrangement, his proposal, as well as setting out the terms of the proposed arrangement, is required[36]:

(a) to identify the company, and explain why the proposer thinks a CVA is desirable, and explain why the creditors are expected to agree to a CVA, and be authenticated and dated by the proposer;[37]

(b) so far as within the administrator's knowledge, to set out as required by Rule 2.3 of the Rules:

    (i) the company's assets, with an estimate of their respective values;

    (ii) which assets are charged and the extent of the charge;

    (iii) which assets are to be excluded from the CVA;

    (iv) particulars of any property to be included in the CVA which is not owned by the company, including details of who owns such property, and the terms on which it will be available for inclusion;

(c) to set out the nature and amount of the company's liabilities (so far as within the administrator's immediate knowledge), and how the company's liabilities are proposed to be met, modified, postponed or otherwise dealt with by means of the CVA, and in particular:

    (i) how preferential creditors and creditors who are, or claim to be, secured will be dealt with;

    (ii) how creditors who are connected with the company[38] will be dealt with;[39]

(d) to set out relevant details as regards either the nominee or the supervisor;

(e) to state whether any, and if so what, guarantees have been given in respect of the company's debts, specifying which of the guarantors are persons connected with the company[40], and to state whether any, and if so what, guarantees are proposed to be offered for the purposes of the CVA and, if so, by whom and whether security is to be given or sought;

(f) to state the proposed duration of the voluntary arrangement;

(g) to state the proposed dates of distributions to creditors, with estimates of their amounts;

(h) to state whether the proceedings will be main, territorial or non-EC proceedings with reasons;

(i) to state how the business of the company will be conducted during the CVA;

(j) to state details of any further proposed credit facilities for the company, and how the debts so arising are to be paid;

(k) to state the manner in which funds held for the purposes of the CVA are to be banked, invested or otherwise dealt with pending distribution to creditors;

(l) to state how funds held for the purpose of payment to creditors, and not so paid on the termination of the CVA, will be dealt with;

(m) to state any other matters that the proposer considers appropriate to enable members and creditors to reach an informed decision on the proposal.

---

36 By Rules 2.2 and 2.3 of the Rules.
37 Rule 2.2 of the Rules.
38 See sections 249, 251 and 435 of IA 1986.
39 In respect of companies not in administration, there are provisions in Rules 2.3(1)(f)(iii) and (iv) for disclosure of the potential for claims under sections 238, 239, 244 and 245, and how the company will be indemnified if there are circumstances giving rise to such claims.
40 See sections 249, 251 and 435 of IA 1986.

11.9   The administrator is also required to state in the proposal the following, in so far as known[41]:

(a)   an estimate of:

    (i)   the value of the prescribed part (whether or not the administrator might be required under section 176A of IA 1986 to make the prescribed part available for the satisfaction of unsecured debts),

    (ii)   the value of the company's net property (as defined by section 176A(6) of IA 1986);

(b)   a statement as to whether the administrator proposes to make an application to the court under section 176A(5) of IA 1986 and, if so, the reasons for the application;

(c)   details of the nature and amount of the company's preferential creditors.

11.10   Where the nominee is the administrator, and once he has prepared his proposal, he must fix a time, date and venue for meetings of the company and creditors to consider the proposal[42]. The Rules concerning the consideration of the proposal by the members and the creditors are set out in Rules 2.25 to 2.36 of the Rules, and Parts 15 and 16 of the Rules. The different rules for the consideration of members on the one hand, and creditors on the other hand, are as follows.

11.11   As regards the members, the administrator (as nominee) must deliver to every person whom the nominee believes to be a member a notice which must identify the proceedings, state the venue for the meeting, state the effect of Rule 2.35 of the Rules about members voting rights, state the effect of Rule 2.36 of the Rules about the requisite majority of members for passing resolutions, and state the effect of Rule 15.35 of the Rules about rights of appeal, and be accompanied by a copy of the proposal, a copy of the statement of affairs, or if the nominee thinks fit a summary including a list of creditors with the amounts of their debts, and details of each resolution to be voted on.[43] The notice under Rule 2.25(2) of the Rules summoning the meeting of the company must be delivered at least 14 days before the day fixed for the meeting to all the members and to every officer or former officer whose presence the nominee thinks is required and all other directors of the company, and every officer or former officer who receives such a notice stating that the nominee thinks that person's attendance is required is required to attend the meeting[44]. Where in accordance with the Act or the Rules the members are invited to consider a proposal, the consideration is presumed to have duly taken place even if not everyone to whom the notice is to be delivered receives it[45]. The chair of the meeting must be the nominee or an appointed person[46]. A member is entitled to vote according to the rights attaching to the member's shares in accordance with the articles of the company[47]. A member's shares include any other interest that person may have as a member of the company[48]. The value of a member's vote is determined by reference to the number of votes conferred on that member by the company's articles[49]. The requisite majorities of members

---

41   Rule 2.3(3) of the Rules.
42   Section 3(2) of IA 1986.
43   Rule 2.25(3) of the Rules.
44   Rule 2.30 of the Rules.
45   Rule 2.32 of the Rules.
46   Rule 2.34 of the Rules.
47   Rule 2.35(1) of the Rules.
48   Rule 2.35(2) of the Rules.
49   Rule 2.35(3) of the Rules.

to pass the resolution is provided by Rule 2.36 of the Rules, which provides that a resolution is passed by members by correspondence or at a meeting of the company when a majority (in value) of those voting have voted in favour of it. This is subject to any express provision to the contrary in the articles. A resolution is not passed by correspondence unless at least one member has voted in favour of it[50].

11.12 As regards creditors, the administrator (as nominee) must invite the creditors to consider the proposal by way of a decision procedure[51], and must deliver to each creditor a notice in respect of the decision procedure which complies with Rule 15.8 of the Rules (notices to creditors of decision procedure) so far as is relevant[52]. Notice of the decision procedure, and notices seeking deemed consent, must be delivered pursuant to Rule 15.11 of the Rules with a minimum notice period of seven days for consideration of the proposal where a physical meeting is requisitioned, and in other cases a minimum of 14 days. The notice to creditors must also be accompanied by a copy of the proposal, a copy of the statement of affairs, or if the nominee thinks fit a summary including a list of creditors with the amounts of their debts, and must state how a creditor may propose a modification to the proposal and how the nominee will deal with such a proposal for modification[53]. The decision date for the creditors' decision procedure may be on the same day as, or on a different day to, the meeting of the company[54], although the creditors' decision on the proposal must be made before the members' decision and the members' decision must be made not later than five business days after the creditors' decision[55]. Rule 2.31 of the Rules applies where the creditors requisition a physical meeting to consider a proposal (with or without modification) in accordance with section 246ZE of IA 1986 and Rule 15.6 of the Rules, and specifies that the meeting must take place within 14 days of the date on which the prescribed proportion of creditors have required the meeting to take place, with notice of at least seven days required for a physical meeting under this rule[56].

---

50 Rules 2.36(1), (2) and (3) of the Rules. Although section 246ZE of IA 1986 (inserted by section 122 of SBEEA 2015) abolishes the requirement to hold meetings in company insolvency, and provides a process for decision making by creditors and contributories, it appears that a meeting of members is still required for a resolution for the commencement of a CVA (save where the correspondence exception provided by Rule 2.36 can be effected) because Part 15, Chapter 12 of the Rules provides that unless IA 1986 or the Rules provide otherwise, a company meeting must be called and conducted and records of the meeting must be kept in accordance with the law of England and Wales, including any applicable provision in or made under CA 2006 in the case of a company incorporated in England and Wales or outside the UK other than in an EEA State; and in accordance with the law of that state applicable to meetings of the company in the case of a company incorporated in an EEA state other than the UK: see the Rules as to company meetings as now included at Part 15, Chapter 12 of the Rules. Cf also sections 3(2) and 4(1) of IA 1986, and Rule 2.25(1) of the Rules where a meeting of the company is specified, in contrast to Rule 2.25(2) of the Rules which refers to the creditors considering the proposal 'by way of a decision procedure'.
51 Decision procedures are those referred to in Part 15, Chapter 2. See **CHAPTER 4**.
52 Rule 2.25(4) of the Rules.
53 Rule 2.25(5) of the Rules.
54 Rule 2.28(1) of the Rules.
55 Rule 2.28(2) and (3) of the Rules.
56 Rule 2.31(1), (2) and (3) of the Rules. The Insolvency (England and Wales) (Amendment) Rules 2017 (SI 2017 No 366) substituted a new Rule 2.31(3) to provide '(3) A notice summoning a meeting of the creditors must be delivered to the creditors at least seven days before the day fixed for the meeting.')

11.13 Where the proposal is made by the directors or where the administrator is not the intended nominee, the directors or the administrator should submit to the nominee the document setting out the terms of the proposed voluntary arrangement[57], and a statement of the company's affairs containing particulars of its creditors and of its debts and other liabilities and of its assets and the other information as required by Rules 2.3(1) and (2) and 2.6 of the Rules[58]. The proposal may be amended with the nominee's agreement in writing where the nominee is not the administrator and the nominee's report has not been filed with the court under section 2(2) of IA 1986[59]. A nominee who consents to act must deliver a notice of that consent to the proposer as soon as reasonably practicable after the proposal has been submitted to the nominee under section 2(3) of IA 1986[60], and the notice must state the date the nominee received the proposal[61]. Pursuant to section 2(2) of IA 1986, the nominee shall, within 28 days (or such longer period as the court may allow) after he is given notice of the proposal for a voluntary arrangement, submit a report to the court stating whether, in his opinion, the proposed voluntary arrangement has a reasonable prospect of being approved and implemented, whether, in his opinion, the proposal should be considered by a meeting of the company and by the company's creditors and if, in his opinion, it should, the date on which and time and place at which he proposes a meeting of the company should be held[62].

11.14 Where the nominee fails to submit a report to the court as required by section 2 of IA 1986 or has died, the court may, on the application of the administrator or the directors as the case may be, direct that the nominee be replaced by another person qualified to act as an insolvency practitioner or authorised to act as a nominee[63]. Where it is impracticable or inappropriate for the nominee to continue to act as such, the court may, on the application of the administrator or the directors or the nominee as the case may be, direct that the nominee be replaced as such by another person qualified to act as an insolvency practitioner in relation to the voluntary arrangement[64]. If the applicant is not the nominee, the applicant who intends to apply to the court under section 2(4) of IA 1986 for the nominee to be replaced must deliver a notice that such an application is intended to be made to the nominee at least five business days before filing the application with the court[65]. If the nominee makes an application under section 2(4) of IA 1986, the nominee must deliver a notice that such an application is intended to be made to the person intending to make the proposal, or the proposer, at least five business days before filing the application with the court[66]. The court can only make a replacement appointment where the replacement nominee has

57   Section 2(3) of IA 1986.
58   The nominee can require the proposer to provide further information as set out in Rule 2.8 of the Rules.
59   Rule 2.2(2) and (3) of the Rules.
60   Rule 2.4(2) of the Rules.
61   Rule 2.4(3) of the Rules.
62   Section 2(2) of IA 1986 (as amended by Schedule 9 Part 1 of SBEEA 2015 which provides for insertion of section 2(2)(b) and (c) into IA 1986), and Rule 2.9 of the Rules.
63   Section 2(4) of IA 1986. In the case of a moratorium, the replacement of the nominee is dealt with by Schedule A1 paragraph 28 of IA 1986.
64   Section 2(4)(b) of IA 1986.
65   Rule 2.10(1) of the Rules.
66   Rule 2.10(2) of the Rules.

filed at court a statement indicating his consent to act and that he is a qualified insolvency practitioner or an authorised person in relation to the company[67].

11.15 Where the nominee reports to the court that the proposal should be considered by a meeting of the company and by the company's creditors[68], the nominee is required to summon a meeting of the company to consider the proposal for the time, date and place proposed in his report and to seek a decision from the company's creditors as to whether they approve the proposal[69]. The requirements for notification of the meeting to members or creditors, and the requirements of the rules as to consideration of the proposal are the same as those set out in PARAGRAPHS **11.11** AND **11.12** *ante*.

MEETING OF THE COMPANY AND DECISION-MAKING PROCESS OF THE CREDITORS

11.16 Section 3(3) and (4) of IA 1986 provides that a decision of the company's creditors as to whether they approve the proposal is to be made by a qualifying decision procedure, and notice of the qualifying decision procedure must be given to every creditor of the company of whose claim and address the person seeking the decision is aware[70]. However, no meeting will now take place if a creditors' decision procedure is used, unless the creditors requisition a physical meeting to consider the proposal (with or without modification) in accordance with section 246ZE of IA 1986 and Rule 15.6 of the Rules. Where the nominee is inviting the creditors to consider the proposal by a decision procedure, the decision date must be not less than 14 days from the date of delivery of the notice and not more than 28 days from the date the nominee's report is filed with the court under Rule 2.9 of the Rules[71]. The decision date for the creditors' decision procedure may be on the same day as, or on a different day to, the meeting of the company, but the creditors' decision on the proposal must be made before the members' decision, and the members' decision must be made not later than five business days after the creditors' decision[72].

11.17 The chair of a meeting in respect of a voluntary arrangement must be the nominee or an appointed person[73]. Proxies are now provided for by

---

67 Rule 2.10(3) of the Rules.
68 Section 3(1) of IA 1986, as amended by Schedule 9 paragraph 3(2) of SBEEA 2015. Cf *Re a Debtor (No 83 of 1988)* [1990] 1 WLR 708 (when considering whether an interim order ought to be extended in the context of a proposed individual voluntary arrangement, the court decided it was pointless to extend the interim order because there was no point in holding any creditors meeting in circumstances where it was apparent that the 75% required majority could not be achieved).
69 Section 3(1) of IA 1986 (as amended by Schedule 9 paragraph 3 of SBEEA 2015).
70 Section 3(3) and (4) of IA 1986 (as amended by Schedule 9 paragraph 3(4) of SBEEA 2015). In the case of a moratorium, see Schedule A1 paragraph 29(2) of IA 1986. Where the company is in administration and a voluntary arrangement is proposed, section 362(3) of FSMA 2000 entitles the FCA to be served with any document required to be sent to a creditor of the company and section 362(5) of FSMA 2000 entitles the FCA to appoint a person to attend any meeting of creditors summoned under any enactment and to make representations as to any matter for decision at such a meeting.
71 Rule 2.27 of the Rules.
72 Rule 2.28(1), (2) and (3) of the Rules.
73 Rule 2.34 of the Rules.

Part 16 of the Rules. Pursuant to Rule 16.5(1) of the Rules, where a proxy appoints the chair (however described in the proxy) as proxy-holder, the chair may not refuse to be the proxy holder. Pursuant to Rule 16.7(1) and (2) of the Rules, a proxy holder must not vote for a resolution which would directly or indirectly place the proxy holder or any associate of the proxy holder in a position to receive any remuneration, fees or expenses from the insolvent estate or fix or change the amount of or the basis of any remuneration, fees or expenses receivable by the proxy holder or any associate of the proxy holder out of the insolvency estate, unless the proxy specifically directs the proxy holder to vote in that way.

11.18 Rule 2.30 of the Rules specifies that a notice under Rule 2.25(2) of the Rules summoning a meeting of the company must be delivered at least 14 days before the day fixed for the meeting to all the members and to every officer or former officer of the company whose presence the nominee thinks is required, and to all other directors of the company. Every officer or former officer who receives such a notice stating that the nominee thinks that person's attendance is required, is required to attend the meeting[74].

11.19 By section 4(1) and (1A) of IA 1986[75], where under section 3 of IA 1986 a meeting of the company is summoned to consider the proposed voluntary arrangement and the company's creditors are asked to decide whether to approve the proposed voluntary arrangement, they may approve the voluntary arrangement with or without modifications. The modifications may include one conferring the functions proposed to be conferred on the nominee on another person qualified to act as an insolvency practitioner or authorised to act as nominee in relation to the voluntary arrangement, but they cannot include a modification by virtue of which the proposal ceases to be a proposal for a composition in satisfaction of the company's debts, or a scheme of arrangement of its affairs or which seeks to dispense with the requirement that a qualified insolvency practitioner or authorised nominee should supervise the voluntary arrangement[76]. If in response to a notice inviting members to consider the proposal by correspondence or creditors to consider the proposal other than at a meeting, a member or creditor proposes that a person other than the nominee be appointed as supervisor, that person's consent to act and confirmation of being qualified to act as an insolvency practitioner in relation to the company must be delivered to the nominee by the deadline in the notice of the decision by correspondence or by the decision date (as the case may be)[77]. If, at either a meeting of the company or the creditors to consider the proposal, a resolution is moved for the appointment of a person other than the nominee to be supervisor, the person moving the resolution must produce to the chair at or before the meeting:

(a) confirmation that the person proposed as supervisor is qualified to act as an insolvency practitioner in relation to the company;

(b) that person's written consent to act (unless that person is present at the meeting and there signifies consent to act)[78].

---

74 Rule 2.30(1) and (2) of the Rules.
75 As amended and inserted by Schedule 9 Part 1 of SBEEA 2015.
76 Section 4(2) of IA 1986.
77 Rule 2.33(1) of the Rules.
78 Rule 2.33(2) of the Rules.

11.20 It is provided by section 4(3) and (4) of IA 1986 (and, in the case of a moratorium by Schedule A1 paragraph 31(4), (5) and (6) of IA 1986) that neither the meeting of the company, nor the decision of the creditors may approve[79]:

(a) except with the concurrence[80] of the creditor concerned, any proposal or modification which affects the right of a secured creditor[81] to enforce his security[82]; or

(b) except with the concurrence of the preferential creditor concerned, any proposal or modification under which:

   (i) any preferential debt of the company is paid otherwise than in priority to non-preferential debts[83], or any ordinary preferential debt of the company is to be paid otherwise than in priority to any secondary preferential debts that it may have; or

   (ii) a preferential creditor is to be paid an amount in respect of an ordinary preferential debt that bears to that debt a smaller proportion than is borne to another ordinary preferential debt by the amount that is to be paid in respect of that other debt[84] or a preferential creditor of the company is to be paid an amount in respect of a secondary preferential debt that bears to that debt a smaller proportion than is borne to another secondary preferential debt by the amount that is to be paid in respect of that other debt.

11.21 Section 386 of IA 1986 provides for categories of preferential debts, and specifies that a reference to the preferential debts of a company is to the debts listed in Schedule 6 to IA 1986. A reference to the 'ordinary preferential debts' of a company is to the preferential debts listed in any of Schedule 6 paragraphs 8 to 15B of IA 1986. A reference to the 'secondary preferential debts' of a company is to the preferential debts listed in Schedule 6 paragraph 15BA or 15BB of IA 1986. Section 387 of IA 1986 explains references in Schedule 6 to 'the relevant date', being the date which determines the existence and amount of a preferential debt. By section 387(2), for the purposes of section 4 of IA 1986

---

79 As amended by Schedule 9 Part 1 of SBEEA 2015.

80 Prior to the Rules, it used to be that if a secured creditor voted for a voluntary arrangement that had, on its true construction, the effect of affecting his rights to enforce his security, he will have concurred for the purposes of section 4(3) of IA 1986: *Khan v Permayer* [2001] BPIR 95. However, since Rule 15.31(4) of the Rules bars any vote by a fully secured creditor, because it provides that where a debt is wholly secured its value for voting purposes is nil, the position as now provided under the Rules may well not be as set out in *Khan v Permayer*.

81 'Secured creditor' is defined by section 248(1) of IA 1986 as 'a creditor of the company who holds in respect of his debt a security over the property of the company'. This includes an execution creditor with the benefit of a walking possession agreement (*Peck v Craighead* [1995] 1 BCLC 337). 'Property' is defined by section 436 of IA 1986.

82 'Security' is defined by section 248(2) of IA 1986 as meaning, in relation to England and Wales, any mortgage, charge, lien or other security. See also *Bristol Airport v Powdrill* [1990] Ch 744 at 760D and *Smith (Administrator of Cosslett (Contractors) Ltd) v Bridgend County Borough Council* [2001] UKHL 58, [2002] 1 BCLC 77 at 88.

83 Section 4(4)(a) of IA 1986. If, unusually, the arrangement involves the discharge by the purchaser of a business of certain non-preferential debts in circumstances in which there is no commensurate reduction in the cash price paid for the acquisition of that business, the mere fact that some unsecured creditors will thereby receive more than the preferential creditors will not lead to a breach of section 4(4)(a) of IA 1986: *IRC v Wimbledon Football Club Ltd* [2004] EWCA Civ 655.

84 Section 4(4)(b) of IA 1986.

(meetings to consider a company voluntary arrangement), the relevant date in relation to a company which is not being wound up is:

- if the company is in administration, the date on which it entered administration; and

- if the company is not in administration, the date on which the voluntary arrangement takes effect.

11.22 It seems that, if there is an infringement of these provisions (in any event so far as the preferential debts are concerned), the arrangement will not be invalid, although there will have been a material irregularity for the purposes of section 6(1)(b) of IA 1986[85].

11.23 In the case of a proposed voluntary arrangement relating to a UK insurer, which includes a composition in satisfaction of any insurance debts and a distribution to creditors of some or all of the assets of the insurer in the course of or with a view to terminating the whole or any part of its business, the meeting of the company, and the creditors' decision, cannot approve any proposal or modification under which any insurance debt of the company is to be paid otherwise than in priority to such of its debts as are not insurance debts or preferential debts[86].

11.24 Soon after IA 1986 came into force, there was a question as to whether a landlord's right to forfeit a lease or to peaceable re-entry was the right of a secured creditor to enforce a security. Although a series of cases either assumed or expressly held that the right was such a security right[87], after a comprehensive review of the authorities, Neuberger J held in *Lomax Leisure Ltd*[88] that the exercise of the right to forfeit a lease for non-payment of rent could not be regarded as the enforcement of a security for the purposes of the statutory moratorium that comes into force when a company goes into administration (Schedule B1 paragraph 43(4) of IA 1986 now prevents a landlord to peaceably re-enter without the consent of the administrator). This case at first instance, and further Court of Appeal authority, shows that an arrangement may compromise not only the claim of a landlord for rent, but also the right to forfeit, (depending on the proper construction of the arrangement)[89].

11.25 As referred to above, the decision date for the creditors' decision procedure may be on the same day as, or on a different day to, the meeting of the company, but the creditors' decision on the proposal must be made before the members' decision.[90] Where a physical meeting of creditors is requisitioned

---

85   *IRC v Wimbledon Football Club Ltd* [2004] EWCA Civ 655.
86   Section 4(4A) of IA 1986, as inserted in the case of UK insurers by regulation 33 of the Insurers (Reorganisation and Winding Up) Regulations 2004 (SI 2004 No 353).
87   See in particular *Doorbar v Alltime Securities Ltd* [1996] 1 WLR 456 at 466, *March Estates plc v Gunmark Ltd* [1996] 2 BCLC 1. See *Re The Cotswold Company Ltd* [2009] EWHC 1151 (Ch). The issue is no longer relevant in the context of administration, because of the provisions of Schedule B1 paragraph 43(4) of IA 1986.
88   [2000] Ch 502, approving the approach of Lightman J in *Razzaq v Pala* [1997] 1 WLR 1336, in which Lightman J confessed that he had changed his mind since his own previous decision in *March Estates plc v Gunmark Ltd* [1996] 2 BCLC 1.
89   *Thomas v Ken Thomas Ltd* [2006] EWCA Civ 1504 (over-ruling comments in *Re Naeem* [1990] 1 WLR 48 and in *March Estates plc v Gunmark* [1996] 2 BCLC 1 where Hoffmann J and Lightman J respectively had held that a CVA could not affect the right of forfeiture of a landlord).
90   Rule 2.28(1) and (2) of the Rules.

in accordance with Rule 2.31 of the Rules, section 246ZE of IA 1986 and Rule 15.6 of the Rules, the chair will have the power under Rule 15.23(1) of the Rules to adjourn the meeting for not more than 14 days, subject to any direction of the court and to Rule 15.24 of the Rules (adjournment of meeting to remove a liquidator). The chair must adjourn if the creditors so resolve. Further adjournment under Rule 15.23(1) and (2) of the Rules must not be to a day later than 14 days after the date on which the meeting was originally held (subject to any direction of the court). The chair of a meeting may, without an adjournment, declare the meeting suspended for one or more periods not exceeding one hour in total (or, in exceptional circumstances, such longer total period during the same day at the chair's discretion)[91]. The power to adjourn the meeting of the company will be determined either by the powers of adjournment in relation to company meetings under CA 2006, or by the law of the state applicable to meetings of the company in the case of a company incorporated in an EEA state other than the UK[92].

11.26 If, for the purpose of obtaining the approval of the members or creditors of a company to a proposal for a voluntary arrangement, any officer of the company makes a false representation or fraudulently does or omits to do anything, he commits an offence for which he is liable to imprisonment, or a fine, or both[93]. Shadow directors are officers for this purpose[94], as, presumably, are administrators[95]. If it appears to the nominee or supervisor that any past or present officer of the company has been guilty of an offence in connection with a voluntary arrangement that has taken effect under section 4A or Schedule A1 paragraph 36 of IA 1986[96], he must forthwith report the matter to the appropriate authority[97] and provide it with such information and access to documents as it may require[98]. If proceedings are then instituted by a prosecuting authority, the nominee, supervisor and every officer and agent of the company past and present comes under a duty to give all assistance in connection with the prosecution which he is reasonably able to give[99].

MAJORITIES

11.27 The majority required for the creditors' decision to approve the proposal or a modification is a majority of three-quarters or more (in value) of those responding voting in favour of it[100], and a decision is not made if more than

---

91   Rule 15.27 of the Rules.
92   Rule 15.41(1) and (2) of the Rules.
93   Section 6A of IA 1986. The offence is committed whether or not the arrangement is approved: section 6A(2) of IA 1986.
94   Section 6A(3) of IA 1986.
95   Cf *Re Home Treat Ltd* [1991] BCLC 705.
96   Or a moratorium that has been obtained for the company.
97   In England, the Secretary of State: section 7A(2) of IA 1986.
98   Section 7A(1) and (2) of IA 1986.
99   Section 7A(8) of IA 1986. Agents include bankers, solicitors and auditors and the reference to the prosecuting authority is to the DPP or the Secretary of State in England. The court is empowered to direct compliance with section 7A(8) on application made by the prosecuting authority (s.7A(9) of IA 1986).
100 Rule 15.34(3) of the Rules. Save for decisions such as approval of a CVA, the default position for creditors' decisions requires the approval of a majority (in value): Rule 15.34(1) of the Rules.

half of the total value of the unconnected creditors vote against it[101]. Rule 15.31 of the Rules provides for the calculation of voting rights and provides by Rule 15.31(1)(d) of the Rules that in a proposed CVA votes are calculated according to the amount of each creditor's claim:

- at the date the company went into liquidation where the company is being wound up;

- at the date the company entered into administration (less any payments made to the creditor after that date in respect of the claim) where it is in administration;

- otherwise at the decision date.

11.28 The Rules relating to creditors voting rights are contained in Part 15, Chapter 8 of the Rules. These provide as follows:

- In a decision relating to a proposed CVA, every creditor, secured or unsecured, who has notice of the decision procedure is entitled to vote in respect of that creditor's debt: Rule 15.28(5) of the Rules[102].

- However, as regards a secured claim, Rule 15.31(4) of the Rules provides that where a debt is wholly secured, its value for voting purposes is nil. Rule 15.31(5) of the Rules provides that where a debt is partly secured its value for voting purposes is the value of the unsecured part.

- In relation to a proposed CVA, a debt of an unliquidated or unascertained amount is to be valued at £1 for the purposes of voting unless the convener or chair or an appointed person decides to put a higher value on it: Rule 15.31(3) of the Rules[103].

- The convener or chair in respect of a decision procedure must ascertain entitlement to vote and admit or reject claims accordingly: Rule 15.33(1) of the Rules.

---

101 Rule 15.34(4) of the Rules. Under Rule 15.34(5) of the Rules, for the purposes of subs.(4), a creditor is unconnected unless the convener or chair decides that the creditor is connected with the company; in deciding whether a creditor is connected reliance may be placed on the information provided by the company's statement of affairs or otherwise in accordance with the Rules; and the total value of the unconnected creditors is the total value of those unconnected creditors whose claims have been admitted for voting.

102 There is no statutory definition of 'creditor' for the purposes of a company voluntary arrangement, since Rule 14.1(3) of the Rules defines a 'debt' for the purposes of winding up and administration (and not for CVAs). Future debts are capable of being debts within a CVA: see *Doorbar v Alltime Securities Ltd* [1996] 1 WLR 456; *Re Cancol Ltd* [1995] BCC 1133; *Re Sweatfield Ltd* [1997] BCC 744. Claims for unliquidated damages can be creditor claims: *Beverley Group plc v McClue* [1995] BCC 751. On business rates and CVAs, see *Kaye v South Oxfordshire District Council* [2013] EWHC 4165 (Ch). A CVA can exclude certain creditors: see *Burford Midland Properties Ltd v Marley Extrusions Ltd* [1994] BCC 604. In appropriate circumstances the court can direct someone to be a creditor alongside CVA creditors: see *Re FMS Financial Management Services Ltd* (1989) 5 BCC 191. See also *Re T&N Ltd* [2005] EWHC 2870 (Ch) for a detailed review of contingent debts in the context of a CVA (at paragraphs 32–68).

103 Contrast with the ordinary rule for creditors' decisions as stated in Rule 15.31(2), where a CVA proposal is not relevant (a creditor may vote in respect of a debt of an unliquidated or unascertained amount if the convener or chair decides to put upon it an estimated minimum value for the purpose of entitlement to vote and admits the claim for that purpose). On the valuation of claims by the chairman, see *Re Newlands (Seaford) Educational Trust* [2006] EWHC 1511 (Ch); and see in respect of unliquidated claims *Leighton Contracting (Qatar) WLL v Simms* [2011] EWHC 1735 (Ch).

- The convener or chair may admit or reject a claim in whole or in part: Rule 15.33(2) of the Rules.

- If the convener or chair is in any doubt whether a claim should be admitted or rejected, the convener or chair must mark it as objected to and allow votes to be cast in respect of it, subject to such votes being subsequently declared invalid if the objection to the claim is sustained: Rule 15.33(3) of the Rules[104].

11.29 An appeal process against the decision of the convener or chair under Part 15, Chapter 8 of the Rules, is provided by Rule 15.35 of the Rules. By Rule 15.35(1) of the Rules, a decision of the convener or chair is subject to appeal to the court by a creditor. By Rule 15.35(2) of the Rules, in a proposed CVA, an appeal against such a decision may also be made by a member of the company. In a proposed CVA, the appeal must be made within 28 days beginning with the day on which the first of the reports required by section 4(6) of IA 1986 was filed with the court (the chair's report of the result of the meeting and decision to the court). The person who made the decision subject to appeal (who will presumably be the chair) is not personally liable for costs incurred by any person in relation to an appeal unless the court makes an order to that effect[105]. If the court on hearing the appeal reverses or varies the decision on the vote, or if votes admitted to vote are declared invalid, by Rule 15.35(3) of the Rules the court may order another decision procedure to be initiated or make such order as it thinks just but, in a CVA the court may only make an order if it considers that the circumstances which led to the appeal give rise to unfair prejudice or material irregularity (ie here picking up the references to unfair prejudice or material irregularity as referred to in section 6(1) of IA 1986).

EFFECT OF A DECISION APPROVING THE ARRANGEMENT

11.30 If, in accordance with the Rules, a decision approving a voluntary arrangement has been made under section 4 of IA 1986, either by the meeting of the company summoned under section 3 of IA 1986 and by the company's creditors pursuant to section 3, or if the voluntary arrangement has been approved by the company's creditors[106] under section 3, that decision will have effect in accordance with its terms[107]. Thus section 4A of IA 1986 removes the ability of the company meeting to cause a voluntary arrangement to be rejected where the arrangement has been approved by the creditors. Elsewhere in IA 1986 and the Rules, this provision is described as giving rise to a state of affairs in which the decision approving the voluntary arrangement has effect under section 4A of IA 1986. If, however, the decision taken by the creditors differs from that taken by the meeting of the company, a member of the company may apply to the court no later than 28 days after the date of the later of the creditors' or the company's

---

104 See *Re a Debtor (No 222 of 1990) ex p Bank of Ireland* [1992] BCLC 137 and *Harmony Carpets v Chaffin-Laird* [2000] BPIR 61.
105 Rule 15.35(6) of the Rules.
106 Section 4A(2), (3), (4)(a) and (6)(a) were amended by Schedule 9 Part 1 of SBEE 2015 (to provide for a creditors' decision, rather than a creditors' meeting).
107 Section 4A(1) and (2) of IA 1986.

meeting[108]. On any such application, the court is empowered to order that the decision of the company's meeting shall have effect instead of the decision of the creditors' or to make such other order as it thinks fit[109]. It is thought that the court would only interfere if the member was able to show a legitimate or tangible interest, such as where the company might have been solvent, but the effect of the approval was to deprive him of such value as his shares may have had[110]. Where a member of a regulated company applies to the court for such relief, the appropriate regulator is entitled to be heard on the application[111]. The appropriate regulator means, where the regulated company is a PRA regulated company within the meaning of Schedule A1 paragraph 44 of IA 1986, the FCA and the PRA; and in any other case, the FCA[112].

11.31   Where a decision approving a voluntary arrangement has effect under section 4A of IA 1986, the arrangement takes effect as if made by the company at the time the creditors decided to approve the voluntary arrangement and binds every person who, in accordance with the Rules was entitled to vote in the qualifying decision procedure by which the creditors' decision to approve the voluntary arrangement was made or would have been so entitled if he had had notice of it, as if he were a party to the voluntary arrangement[113].

11.32   There is no specific provision dealing with the position of joint debtors or co-obligors, or sureties, in England and Wales. It might have been thought that any release of the company would only be by operation of law and so would not have the effect of releasing any other person[114]. It is now clear, however, that the mere fact that the company has been discharged from liability on a joint debt or other obligation pursuant to a voluntary arrangement under Part I of IA 1986 will not of itself release a joint debtor or co-obligor or surety. In each case, it is a question of construction of the terms of the arrangement itself[115]. Does the release of a joint liability contain, either expressly or by necessary implication[116],

---

108   Section 4A(3) and (4) of IA 1986 and, in the case of a moratorium, Schedule A1 paragraph 36(3) and (4) of IA 1986. See also Rule 2.28 (timing of creditors' decision in relation to the meeting of the company).
109   Section 4A(6) of IA 1986 and, in the case of a moratorium, Schedule A1 paragraph 36(5) of IA 1986.
110   Cf *Re Chesterfield Catering Co Ltd* [1977] Ch 373; *Re Rica GoldWashing Co* (1879) 11 Ch D 36; *Re Pimlico Capital Ltd* [2002] EWHC 878 (Ch)
111   Section 4A(5) of IA 1986.
112   Section 4A(5A) of IA 1986.
113   Section 5(1) and (2) of IA 1986 (as amended by Schedule 9 Part 1 of SBEEA 2015). The position is thus similar to the position of creditors bound by a scheme of arrangement under Part 26 of CA 2006, ie actual notice does not have to be established for a creditor to be bound. Prior to 1 January 2003 a creditor was not bound by a CVA unless notified. Section 5(1) and (2) of IA 1986 was amended from 1 January 2003 (by Schedule 2 paragraph 6 of the Insolvency Act 2000) so that creditors were bound whether or not notified. (Cf also the amendments to section 5(2) and (4)(a) as inserted by Schedule 9 Part 1 of SBEEA 2015 regarding creditors' decisions rather than creditors' meeting, and including a reference to the report to the court under section 4 (6A).)
114   See, for example, *Dane v Mortgage Insurance Corpn Ltd* [1894] 1 QB 54 at 63. Cf *Prudential Assurance Co Ltd v PRG Powerhouse Ltd* [2007] EWHC 1002 (Ch) (paragraph 41) (whether payment of a dividend to a creditor pursuant to a CVA has automatically as a matter of law discharged the liability of a third party co-debtor or surety).
115   See, for example, the analysis of the relevant clauses as carried out in *Prudential Assurance Co Ltd v PRG Powerhouse Ltd* [2007] EWHC 1002 (Ch) (paragraphs 40–70).
116   For a case on implied reservation of rights, see *Koutrouzas v Lombard Natwest Factors Ltd* [2002] EWHC 1084 (QB).

a reservation of rights against the company's joint or joint and several debtor?[117] It follows that the effect of the approval of a voluntary arrangement, on the obligations of a former tenant of leasehold property which has been assigned to the company, will also depend on the terms of the arrangement itself[118]. It may also be the case, however, that the reservation of rights against a co-debtor or surety can be found outside the terms of the arrangement itself[119].

CONSEQUENTIAL MATTERS

11.33   Pursuant to the provisions of section 4(6) and (6A) of IA 1986[120], after the conclusion of the company's meeting, and the decision of the creditors, the person who sought the decision (presumably normally the chairman) must report the decision to the court, and immediately after reporting to the court, give notice of the creditors' decision to such persons as may be prescribed. Records of the decision as set out in Rule 15.40 of the Rules must be kept by the convener or chair.

11.34   Pursuant to section 5(1) and (3) of IA 1986, where a decision approving a voluntary arrangement has effect under section 4A of IA 1986, the court may:

(a)   provide for the appointment of an administrator to cease to have effect; and/or

(b)   give such directions with respect to the conduct of the administration as it thinks appropriate for facilitating the implementation of the voluntary arrangement.

However, section 5(4) of IA 1986 specifically provides that an order providing for the appointment of an administrator to cease to have effect cannot be made before the end of the period of 28 days beginning with the first day on which each of the reports required by section 4(6) and (6A) of IA 1986 has been made to the court, or at any time when an application under section 6 of IA 1986 or an appeal in respect of such application is pending, or at any time in the period within which such an appeal may be brought.

CHALLENGES TO THE VOLUNTARY ARRANGEMENT

11.35   Under section 6 of IA 1986 (or, in the case of a moratorium, Schedule A1 paragraph 38 of IA 1986), any person entitled, in accordance with the Rules, to vote at the meeting of the company or in the relevant qualifying decision procedure (where the relevant qualifying decision procedure is defined by section 6(1A) as the qualifying decision procedure in which the company's creditors

---

117   *Johnson v Davies* [1999] Ch 117; *Lloyds Bank plc v Ellicott* [2002] EWCA Civ 1333; and *Whitehead v Household Mortgage Corpn* [2002] EWCA Civ 1657.

118   *RA Securities Ltd, the Mercantile Credit Co Ltd* [1995] 3 All ER 381 and *March Estates plc v Gunmark Ltd* [1996] 2 BCLC 1 as explained in *Johnson v Davies* [1999] Ch 117 (although in the light of the Landlord and Tenant (Covenants) Act 1995, there will be many cases in which the former tenant's liability to the landlord will have been extinguished on assignment). See also *Prudential Assurance Co Ltd v PRG Powerhouse Ltd* [2007] EWHC 1002 (Ch) (paragraph 56).

119   *Greene King plc v Stanley* [2001] EWCA Civ 1966.

120   As amended by, Schedule 9 paragraph 4 of SBEEA 2015.

decide whether to approve a voluntary arrangement)[121], and any person who would have been entitled, in accordance with the Rules, to vote in the relevant qualifying decision procedure[122] if he had had notice of it, and the administrator, the nominee (if other than the administrator) or any person who has replaced the nominee[123], may apply to the court on the grounds:

(a) that a voluntary arrangement which has effect under section 4A of IA 1986 unfairly prejudices the interests of a creditor, member[124] or contributory of the company; and/or

(b) that there has been some material irregularity at or in relation to the meeting of the company, or in relation to the relevant qualifying decision procedure[125].

11.36 Any such application must be made within a period of 28 days beginning with the first day on which each of the reports required by section 4(6) and (6A) has been made to the court or, in the case of a person who would have been entitled to vote at the relevant qualifying decision procedure if he had had notice of it within the period of 28 days beginning with the day on which he became aware that the relevant qualifying decision procedure had taken place[126]. In the case of a person who would have been entitled to vote in the creditors' decision if he had had notice of it, any such application, so long as it is made on the ground that the voluntary arrangement prejudices his interests, can be made after the arrangement ceased to have effect, unless it came to an end prematurely[127]. Where on such an application the court is satisfied as to either of the grounds, it may:

(a) revoke or suspend any decision approving the voluntary arrangement which has effect under section 4A of IA 1986; or

(b) in the case of an allegation of material irregularity, revoke or suspend any decision taken which has effect under section 4A of IA 1986; and/or

---

121 Section 6(1A) was inserted by Schedule 9 Part 1 of SBEEA 2015.

122 The provisions inserting reference to the relevant qualifying decision procedure were inserted by Schedule 9 Part 1 of SBEEA 2015.

123 See sections 2(4) and 4(2) of IA 1986. In the case of a moratorium, the express reference to a replacement nominee has been excluded, presumably because 'nominee' is defined by Schedule A1 paragraph 1 of IA 1986 to include 'any person for the time being carrying out the functions of a nominee under this Schedule'.

124 Defined in section 250 of IA 1986 as extending to any person 'to whom shares in the company have been transferred or transmitted by operation of law'.

125 Section 6(1) and (2) of IA 1986 (as amended by Schedule 9 Part 1 of SBEEA 2015 to take account of the decision of creditors being made without an actual meeting taking place (and, in the case of a moratorium, Schedule A1 paragraph 38(1) and (2) of IA 1986). It is thought that the applicant would have to show a legitimate or tangible interest, so a member cannot apply in respect of alleged unfair prejudice to creditors: cf *Re Chesterfield Catering Co Ltd* [1977] Ch 373; *Re Rica Gold Washing Co* (1879) 11 Ch D 36; *Re Pimlico Capital Ltd* [2003] EWHC 878 (Ch). The FCA and PRA may also apply under section 6 of IA 1986 as provided by section 356 of FSMA 2000.

126 Section 6(3) of IA 1986 (as amended by Schedule 9 Part 1 of SBEEA 2015 (and, in the case of a moratorium, Schedule A1 paragraph 38(3) of IA 1986). The court has no power to extend this time limit: *Re Bournemouth and Boscombe Athletic Club Ltd* [1998] BPIR 183 and see also *IRC v Adam & Partners Ltd* [1999] 2 BCLC 730. Compare the position in an individual voluntary arrangement where there is such a power: *Tager v Westpac Banking Corpn* [1997] 1 BCLC 313 and see also *Plant v Plant* [1998] 1 BCLC 38.

127 Section 6(3) of IA 1986. An arrangement comes to an end prematurely if, when it ceases to have effect, it has not been fully implemented in respect of all persons bound by the arrangement by virtue of an entitlement to vote at the meeting (ie excluding those who were bound without having notice of the meeting): section 7B of IA 1986.

(c) give a direction to any person for the summoning of a further company meeting to consider any revised proposal, and direct any person to seek a decision from the company's creditors (using a qualifying decision procedure) as to whether they approve any revised proposal the person who made the original proposal may make, or in a case where there has been a material irregularity, to seek a decision from the company's creditors (using a qualifying decision procedure) as to whether they approve the original proposal[128].

11.37 The court also has an express power to give such further supplemental directions as it thinks fit, including directions with the respect to things done under the voluntary arrangement since it took effect[129]. Where an application is made for a new meeting to consider a revised proposal, the test for the court is whether that proposal is serious and viable[130]. Where the court has directed the summoning of further meetings or a decision process to consider a revised proposal and it is then satisfied that the person who made the original proposal does not intend to submit a revised proposal, it must then revoke the direction and revoke or suspend any decision approving the voluntary arrangement which has effect under section 4A of IA 1986[131].

11.38 In order to sustain a complaint of unfair prejudice under section 6 of IA 1986 or, in the case of a moratorium, Schedule A1 paragraph 38 of IA 1986, the applicant must demonstrate unfair prejudice brought about by the terms of the voluntary arrangement itself[132]. The fact that other creditors of the same type as the applicant have voted in favour of a voluntary arrangement does not prevent a creditor from asserting successfully that he has been unfairly prejudiced, and the actionable unfairness may be prejudicial to the interests of a class even if the whole class does not complain[133]. A creditor must establish that any unfairness affects him in his capacity as such, whether he is a creditor for a liquidated, unliquidated, certain or contingent claim; any extraneous interest he may have

---

128 Section 6(4) of IA 1986 (as amended by Schedule 9 Part 1 of SBEEA 2015 (and, in the case of a moratorium, Schedule A1 paragraph 38(4) of IA 1986). Whether the court simply revokes or suspends the approval given, orders a new meeting or makes no order will depend on the nature of the prejudice or irregularity and in particular whether the court is satisfied as to whether a new meeting would or might make any difference.

129 Section 6(6) of IA 1986 (and, in the case of a moratorium, Schedule A1 paragraph 38(8) of IA 1986). Presumably, this power extends to doing anything to reverse or mitigate the effects of the prejudice or the irregularity, so long as it does not have an unfair impact of the position of third parties, whether or not they are themselves bound by the voluntary arrangement.

130 *Re a Debtor (No 101 of 1999) (No 2)* [2001] BPIR 996.

131 Section 6(5) of IA 1986 (and, in the case of a moratorium, Schedule A1 paragraph 38(5) of IA 1986).

132 *Re a Debtor (No 87 of 1993) (No 2)* [1996] 1 BCLC 63 at 86; *Inland Revenue Commissioners v The Wimbledon Football Club* [2004] EWCA Civ 655 (paragraph 18); *Sisu Capital Fund Ltd v Tucker* [2005] EWHC 2170 (Ch) (paragraphs 68–78). Cf *Re a Debtor (No 259 of 1990)* [1992] 1 WLR 226 per Hoffmann J at 228H–229F. For a case in which an application was dismissed because (amongst other matters) the alleged prejudice was caused by collateral matters and not the terms of the arrangement itself, see: *Swindon Town Properties Ltd v Swindon Town Football Co Ltd* [2003] BPIR 253. See also, *Re Primlaks (UK) Ltd (No 2)* [1990] BCLC 234 and *Re Naeem (a bankrupt) (No 18 of 1988)* [1990] 1 WLR 48. In *Somji v Cadbury Schweppes plc* [2001] 1 WLR 615 at 629, the Court of Appeal decided that it did not need to conclude whether this line of authority was correct, but seems to have considered that it probably was. See also *Sisu Capital Fund Ltd v Tucker* [2005] EWHC 2170 (Ch) (paragraph 70).

133 *Re Primlaks (UK) Ltd (No 2)* [1990] BCLC 234 per Harman J at 236g–237d and *Sea Voyager Maritime Inc v Bielecki* [1999] 1 BCLC 133.

must be excluded from consideration[134]. A voluntary arrangement may provide unequal or differential treatment of creditors of the same class, and this will not of itself constitute unfairness, although it may give cause to inquire and require an explanation[135]. Depending on the circumstances, differential treatment may be necessary to ensure fairness[136], although in *Prudential Assurance Co Ltd v PRG Powerhouse Ltd*[137], an attempt to strip guarantees given in favour of landlords in a proposal of a tenant was held to be unfairly prejudicial to the relevant landlords and the CVA was set aside[138]. In determining whether or not there is unfairness, it is necessary to consider all the circumstances[139] and, in particular, the alternatives available and the practical consequences of a decision to confirm or reject the arrangement, and thus a simple comparison with what would happen in a liquidation or other comparative process, such as a scheme of arrangement, is not necessarily determinative of unfair prejudice[140]. It has been held that unfairness may be assessed by a comparative analysis from a number of different angles, including what have been described as vertical and horizontal comparisons, with the vertical comparison being between the CVA or the position on winding up, and the horizontal comparison being the comparison with other creditors or classes of creditors[141]. It is not for the court to speculate on whether the terms of a proposed voluntary arrangement which were put forward by an office holder were the best that could have been obtained, or whether it would have been better if it had not contained all of the terms which it did contain. Unless the court is satisfied that better terms or some other compromise would have been on offer, the comparison must be between the proposed compromise and no compromise at all judging matters as of the date of the vote on the arrangement. If an administrator or liquidator puts forward a proposal which he considers to be fair then, unless it is established that he acted other than in good faith or that he is partisan to the interests of some only of the creditors, the court should not speculate about what other proposals might have gained acceptance and been capable of implementation (an essential element, since there is not much point in gaining approval unless the resulting arrangement can be implemented). The statutory scheme envisages that different creditors might have different views on whether an arrangement should be approved and provides for the minority to be bound by the majority, subject

---

134 *Doorbar v Alltime Securities Ltd (Nos 1 and 2)* [1996] 1 WLR 456 and *Sea Voyager Maritime Inc v Bielecki* [1999] 1 BCLC 133, a case in which the court found that a creditor had been unfairly prejudiced to the extent that the voluntary arrangement interfered with its rights against insurers under the Third Parties (Rights Against Insurers) Act 1930.

135 *Inland Revenue Commissioners v The Wimbledon Football Club Ltd* [2004] EWCA Civ 655 (paragraph 18(2)); *Sisu Capital Fund Ltd v Tucker* [2005] EWHC 2170 (Ch) (paragraph 69). See also *RCC v Portsmouth City FC* [2010] EWHC 2013 (Ch) and *RCC v Football League Ltd* [2012] EWHC 1372 (Ch).

136 *Inland Revenue Commissioners v The Wimbledon Football Club Ltd* [2004] EWCA Civ 655 (paragraph 18(4)).

137 [2007] EWHC 1002 (Ch).

138 See also *Mourant v Sixty UK Ltd* [2010] EWHC 1890 (Ch).

139 *Prudential Assurance Co Ltd v PRG Powerhouse Ltd* [2007] EWHC 1002 (Ch) (paragraph 74).

140 *In Re a Debtor (No 101 of 1999)* [2001] 1 BCLC 54; *Inland Revenue Commissioners v The Wimbledon Football Club Ltd* [2004] EWCA Civ 655 (paragraph 18(3)); *Sisu Capital Fund Ltd v Tucker* [2005] EWHC 2170 (Ch) (paragraph 71). *Re Portsmouth City Football Club (in admin)* [2010] EWHC 2013 (Ch) (paragraphs 65–71). *Prudential Assurance Co Ltd v PRG Powerhouse Ltd* [2007] EWHC 1002 (Ch) (paragraph 95).

141 See *Prudential Assurance Co Ltd v PRG Powerhouse Ltd* [2007] EWHC 1002 (Ch) (paragraph 75). And see *Re Portsmouth City Football Club (in admin)*, *HMRC v Portsmouth City Football Club Ltd* [2010] EWHC 2013 (Ch) (paragraph 41).

to the protection of the minority in cases of unfair prejudice. This concept is aimed at disproportionate prejudice on one side or the other. If the reasonable and honest man, in the same position as an applicant alleging unfair prejudice, might reasonably have approved the voluntary arrangement which is challenged, then the challenge fails[142].

11.39 The concept of material irregularity is directed primarily at procedural considerations although it is not limited to what occurred at the meeting itself. It is wide enough to apply to the situation where there has been a material misrepresentation, non-disclosure or other irregularity in relation to the proposal or statement of affairs presented to the meeting at which the voluntary arrangement was approved[143]. It seems, however, that the court will only interfere with an administrator's judgment about what material should be placed before the creditors if it is a decision to which no reasonable insolvency practitioner could come[144]. For an irregularity to be material there must be some indication that it made a difference to the result[145], although it may be sufficient to show that, on an objective assessment, the irregularity would be likely to have made a material difference to the way in which the creditors would have considered and assessed the terms of the proposal[146]. However, a failure to give notice of a meeting to approve a voluntary arrangement to a creditor whose vote could not have altered the outcome, for example, because the creditor's vote would in any event have been required to have been left out of assessment, is not of itself, it would seem, an irregularity that is material[147]. Other examples of material irregularities are failures to deal with a proxy properly[148] and an attempt to modify a secured or preferential creditor's rights in breach of the provisions of section 4(3) or (4) of IA 1986[149]. It should be noted that the only route to challenge an approved voluntary arrangement is under section 6 of IA 1986, or as regards voting rights to follow the process as set out in Rule 15.38 of the Rules by way of complaint to the appropriate person who is the chair, where the

---

142 *Sisu Capital Fund Ltd v Tucker* [2005] EWHC 2170 (Ch) (paragraphs 73–76). And see *Re T&N Ltd* [2004] EWHC 2361 (paragraph 81).

143 *In Re a Debtor (No 87 of 1993) (No 2)* [1996] 1 BCLC 63 and *Fender v IRC* [2003] EWHC 3543 (Ch). *Sisu Capital Fund Ltd v Tucker* [2005] EWHC 2170 (Ch) (paragraphs 79–81). In *Goldstein v Bishop & Barnett* [2016] EWHC 2187 (Ch) Warren J held there was a material irregularity in relation to the approval of an individual voluntary arrangement where the debtor failed properly to disclose proceedings against him before the Solicitors Disciplinary Tribunal, and in *National Westminster Bank v Kapoor* [2011] EWCA Civ 1083, it was a material irregularity to take into account a debt which had been collusively assigned to avoid the impact of the equivalent of what is now Rule 15.34(2)–(7) of the Rules.

144 In *Re Trident Fashions plc* [2004] EWHC 293 (Ch) (see paragraphs 38 and 45–46 per Lewison J).

145 In *Doorbar v Alltime Securities Ltd* [1996] 1 WLR 456 the Court of Appeal proceeded on this basis. *Sisu Capital Fund Ltd v Tucker* [2005] EWHC 2170 (Ch) (paragraph 81).

146 *Fender v IRC* [2003] EWHC 3543 (Ch), [2003] BPIR 1304 at 1309 applying *Somji v Cadbury Schweppes plc* [2001] 1 WLR 615 at 626 (a case which, on this point, was concerned with material omissions within the meaning of section 276(1)(b) of IA 1986). See also *Re Trident Fashions plc* [2004] EWHC 293 (Ch).

147 *Re Cardona* [1997] BCC 697.

148 *Peck v Craighead* [1995] 1 BCLC 337 and *Narandar-Girdhar v Bradstock* [2016] EWCA Civ 88.

149 In the case of a moratorium, Schedule A1 paragraph 31(4) of IA 1986. Cf *Re a Debtor (No 259 of 1990)* [1992] 1 WLR 226 per Hoffmann J at 229F–230A. As to the position of preferential creditors see *Inland Revenue Commissioners v The Wimbledon Football Club Ltd* [2004] BCC 638. In *Newlands (Seaford) Educational Trust* [2006] EWHC 1511 (Ch) a challenge to the chairman's decision on valuation of a claim failed (Sir Andrew Morritt).

complaint is made during the course of the meeting, or the convener, where it is made after the meeting, or if not satisfied by the action of the appropriate person, by application to the court for directions under Rule 15.38(9) of the Rules. It is not open to a creditor to allege that the approval of the voluntary arrangement was void (for example, because of a secret deal between the company and some of the creditors)[150]. Furthermore, no irregularity at or in relation to a meeting summoned under section 3 of IA 1986 invalidates a decision taken at such a meeting, unless the court grants relief under section 6[151].

11.40 Where, on an application under section 6 of IA 1986, the court makes an order revoking or suspending the approval of the voluntary arrangement, Rule 2.40 of the Rules applies and the applicant for the order must deliver a sealed copy of it to the proposer and the supervisor (if different).[152] If the order includes a direction by the court under section 6(4)(b) for the summoning of further meetings for a matter to be considered further, the applicant for the order must deliver a notice that the order has been made to the person who is directed to take such action.[153] The proposer must then[154]:

- as soon as reasonably practicable deliver a notice that the order has been made to all of those persons to whom a notice to consider the matter was delivered or who appear to be affected by the order;

- within five business days of delivery of a copy of the order (or within such longer period as the court may allow), deliver (if applicable) a notice to the court advising that it is intended to make a revised proposal to the company and its creditors, or to invite reconsideration of the original proposal.

The applicant for the order must deliver a copy of the order to the registrar of companies within five business days of the making of the order with a notice which must contain the date on which the voluntary arrangement took effect[155].

IMPLEMENTATION OF THE VOLUNTARY ARRANGEMENT

11.41 Where the decision approving a voluntary arrangement has effect under section 4A of IA 1986 and the supervisor is not the same person as the proposer, the proposer must, as soon as reasonably practicable, do all that is required to put the supervisor in possession of the assets included in the voluntary arrangement[156]. Where the company is in administration and the supervisor is not the same person as the administrator, the supervisor must before taking possession of the assets included in the voluntary arrangement, deliver to the administrator an undertaking to discharge the balance referred to in Rule 2.39(3) of the Rules out of the first realisation of assets, and upon taking possession of the assets included in the voluntary arrangement, discharge such balance.[157]

---

150 *Somji v Cadbury Schweppes plc* [2001] 1 WLR 615.
151 Section 6(7) of IA 1986 and, in the case of a moratorium, Schedule A1 paragraph 38(9) of IA 1986. In the case of a moratorium, the decision will have been made under Schedule A1 paragraph 29 of IA 1986.
152 Rule 2.40(2) of the Rules.
153 Rule 2.40(4) of the Rules.
154 Rule 2.40(5) of the Rules.
155 Rule 2.40(6) of the Rules.
156 Rule 2.39(1) of the Rules.
157 Rule 2.39(2) of the Rules.

The balance referred to in Rule 2.39(3) of the Rules is any balance due to the administrator by way of fees or expenses properly incurred and payable under IA 1986 or the Rules, and on account of any advances made in respect of the company, together with interest on such advances at the rate specified in section 17 of the Judgments Act 1838 at the date on which the company entered administration[158].

11.42 By Rule 2.39(4) of the Rules, the administrator is granted a charge on the assets included in a voluntary arrangement in respect of any sums comprising such balance, subject only to the deduction from realisations by the supervisor of the proper costs and expenses of such realisations. By Rule 2.39(5) of the Rules, the supervisor must from time to time out of the realisation of assets discharge all guarantees properly given by the administrator for the benefit of the company and to pay all the administrator's expenses.

11.43 By Rule 2.43 of the Rules, the fees and expenses that may be incurred for the purposes of the voluntary arrangement are fees for the nominee's services agreed with the company (or, as the case may be, the administrator) and disbursements made by the nominee before the decision approving the voluntary arrangement takes effect under section 4A of IA 1986 or in a moratorium Schedule A1 paragraph 36 of IA 1986, and fees or expenses which are sanctioned by the terms of the voluntary arrangement or where they are not sanctioned by the terms of the voluntary arrangement would be payable, or correspond to those which would be payable, in an administration or winding up[159]. Where the remuneration of the nominee or the supervisor is fixed on the basis of time spent, Rule 2.45 of the Rules provides for persons to whom information must be provided giving the details required by Rule 2.45(5) of the Rules in relation to the remuneration.

11.44 The court has a continuing role after the voluntary arrangement has effect under section 4A of IA 1986 whether or not the company remains in administration. In particular, if any of the company's creditors or any other person is dissatisfied by any act, omission or decision of the supervisor, he may apply to the court and the court can confirm, reverse or modify the supervisor's decision, can give the supervisor directions or make such other order as it thinks fit[160]. This power is similar to the power given to the court to control a trustee in bankruptcy[161] and is an echo of the power given to the court to control the acts, omissions and decisions of the supervisor of an individual voluntary arrangement[162]. It gives a wide discretion, but one that should only be exercised on the application of a person who can show that he has some substantial interest adversely affected by the act, omission or decision of which complaint is made[163]. So, for example, it is not uncommon for an arrangement to contain express

---

158 Rule 2.39(3) of the Rules.
159 Rule 2.43 of the Rules.
160 Section 7(3) of IA 1986 and, in the case of a moratorium, Schedule A1 paragraph 39(3) and (4) of IA 1986 (in which case the voluntary arrangement will have taken effect under Schedule A1 paragraph 29 of IA 1986). The existence of this statutory power means that there is no private law claim for breach of statutory duty available against the supervisor of a voluntary arrangement, who is apparently to be treated as an officer of the court: *King v Anthony* [1998] 2 BCLC 517.
161 Section 303 of IA 1986.
162 Section 263(3) of IA 1986.
163 *Holdenhurst Securities plc v Cohen* [2001] 1 BCLC 460.

provision for a creditor to apply under section 7(3) of IA 1986 or Schedule A1 paragraph 39(3) of IA 1986 where there is a dispute over the amount for which a supervisor intends to admit a creditor to proof[164]. The court's power to control a supervisor is expressed in different terms from those used to describe the court's power to control an administrator[165] or a liquidator[166], but it is thought that in the same way that an outsider to the liquidation cannot be a person aggrieved by the act of a liquidator[167], so, in all but the rarest case, a person dissatisfied by the act of a supervisor must be someone who claims in or through the estate administered by the supervisor[168]. He should not be able to use section 7(3) of IA 1986 or Schedule A1 paragraph 39(3) of IA 1986 if his interest is adverse to that of the insolvent estate[169]. It should be noted that the section does not permit the court to give directions for the variation of a voluntary arrangement where the arrangement itself makes no provision for the means by which its terms can be varied[170].

11.45 The supervisor may also seek the court's directions in relation to any particular matter arising under the voluntary arrangement[171]. The matter on which direction is sought must arise *under* the arrangement[172], a form of words that is different from and apparently narrower than the statutory power given to an administrator to seek directions in connection with his functions[173]. The most obvious type of circumstance in which it would be appropriate for a supervisor to seek directions is where there are uncertainties as to the true construction of the arrangement or to the manner in which it would be appropriate for the supervisor to exercise any discretion given to him by the arrangement. There is also no reason why a voluntary arrangement should not require the supervisor to seek the direction of the court as to how to proceed in certain defined circumstances. The supervisor is also included amongst the persons given power to apply to the court for the making of a winding-up order or an administration order[174], a power that is exercisable irrespective of whether or not the arrangement itself makes express provision for the circumstances in which it should be exercised. Most of the statutory powers given to administrators and liquidators are not given to supervisors of a voluntary arrangement.

---

164 See eg *Re Millwall Football and Athletic Club (1985) plc* [1998] 2 BCLC 272.
165 Where the application can only be made by a creditor or member and the issue is whether an act or omission of the administrator is unfairly harmful to the creditor or member concerned (Schedule B1 paragraph 74 of IA 1986 discussed in **CHAPTER 14** *post*).
166 Where the question is whether a person is a person aggrieved by the act or decision of the liquidator (s.168(5) of IA 1986).
167 *Mahomed v Morris* [2000] 2 BCLC 536.
168 See the bankruptcy case of *Port v Auger* [1994] 1 WLR 862, in which Harman J also expressed the view that the test of whether a person could be treated as dissatisfied for the purpose of this provision is different from the old test of whether a person was a person aggrieved for the purposes of the statutory predecessor to section 303 of IA 1986.
169 The special right of the FCA and PRA to apply to the court and to be heard on any application (in relation to existing and former authorised persons and appointed representatives) is governed in the case of a moratorium by Schedule A1 paragraph 44(13) and (14) of IA 1986 and in other cases by section 356(1) and (3) of FSMA 2000.
170 *Re Alpa Lighting* [1997] BPIR 341 and *Raja v Rubin* [2000] Ch 274.
171 Section 7(4)(a) of IA 1986 and, in the case of a moratorium, Schedule A1 paragraph 39(5)(a) of IA 1986.
172 A point that was stressed in *Raja v Rubin* [2000] Ch 274.
173 Schedule B1 paragraph 63 of IA 1986.
174 Section 7(4)(b) of IA 1986 and, in the case of a moratorium, Schedule A1 paragraph 39(5)(b) of IA 1986. For a strange case in which Harman J rejected an attempt to strike out a supervisor's petition, see *Re Leisure Study Group Ltd* [1994] 2 BCLC 65.

The principal exception is that a supervisor is empowered to apply for relief under section 423 of IA 1986 in any case where a victim of the transaction is bound by a voluntary arrangement[175].

11.46   The court has a general power to appoint a qualified insolvency practitioner (or person authorised to act as supervisor) either in substitution for or in addition to an existing supervisor or to fill a vacancy in any case in which it is expedient to do so and it is inexpedient, difficult or impracticable for the appointment to be made without the assistance of the court[176]. The application can be made by any creditor of the company or by the former or retiring supervisor. In an exceptional case, it can also be made by the regulator responsible for removing the supervisor's qualification to act[177]. It is presumably the case that similar principles would be applied to an application to substitute a supervisor as are applicable in an application to remove an administrator. It should be noted that section 7(6) of IA 1986 (and, in the case of a moratorium, Schedule A1 paragraph 39(7) of IA 1986) expressly contemplates the appointment of an additional supervisor, a power now reflected by new provisions dealing with the appointment of additional administrators[178].

11.47   Where the voluntary arrangement authorises or requires the supervisor to carry on the business of the company, to realise assets of the company or otherwise to administer or dispose of any of its funds, he is required to keep accounts and records[179]. The accounts and records which must be kept are of the supervisor's acts and dealings in, and in connection with, the voluntary arrangement, including in particular records of all receipts and payments of money[180]. The supervisor must preserve any such accounts and records which were kept by any other person who has acted as supervisor of the voluntary arrangement and in the supervisor's possession[181]. The supervisor must deliver reports on the progress and prospects for the full implementation of the voluntary arrangement once every 12 months to the registrar of companies, the company, the creditors bound by the voluntary arrangement, to the members (unless the court dispenses this requirement under Rule 2.41(10) of the Rules), and if the company is not in liquidation, to the company's auditors (if any) for the time being[182]. The Secretary of State has power to require the production and audit of a supervisor's accounts and records in relation to the voluntary arrangement and copies of reports and summaries in compliance with Rule 2.41 of the Rules[183]. The supervisor must provide such further information and assistance as the Secretary of State requires for the purposes of audit[184].

---

175   Section 424(1)(b) of IA 1986. This will include a supervisor under a moratorium voluntary arrangement because the arrangement will still have been approved under Part I of IA 1986: see section 1A of IA 1986.
176   Section 7(5) and (6) of IA 1986 and, in the case of a moratorium, Schedule A1 paragraph 39(6) of IA 1986.
177   *Re Stella Metals* [1997] BCC 626.
178   Schedule B1 paragraph 103 of IA 1986.
179   Rule 2.41(1) of the Rules.
180   Rule 2.41(2) of the Rules.
181   Rule 2.41(3) of the Rules.
182   Rule 2.41(4)–(7) and (10) of the Rules.
183   Rule 2.42(1) of the Rules.
184   Rule 2.42(2) of the Rules.

VARIATION AND TERMINATION OF A VOLUNTARY ARRANGEMENT

11.48 The power to vary a voluntary arrangement depends entirely on the terms of the arrangement itself. There is nothing to prevent the creditors from binding themselves to a process for varying the original arrangement, although the variation clause will be subject to careful scrutiny to ensure that it is not repugnant to the essence of the arrangement[185]. If no such term is included, the only means by which an arrangement can be varied is by the unanimous agreement of all those bound: the court has no power to intervene[186]. Where the original arrangement does not contain adequate provision for variation, there is no reason in principle why the rights of those bound should not in effect be varied by a further voluntary arrangement, although in any such case it would have to be proposed and approved in accordance with the provisions of Part I of IA 1986 in the normal way.

11.49 As to termination, in the first instance, it is a matter of construction of the arrangement itself as to when it has come to an end[187]. Depending on the terms contained in the voluntary arrangement, it may come to an end after the expiry of a fixed period of time, or on the commencement of a winding up, or when the assets within the arrangement have been realised and distributed, or when a particular trading activity has ceased, or on the occurrence of some other event. When the arrangement comes to an end it ceases to have effect for the purposes of binding those persons who have hitherto been bound by virtue of section 5(2)(b) of IA 1986[188]. Under the law prior to the Insolvency Act 2000, the circumstances in which an arrangement may come to an end were the subject of a number of reported cases, particularly where a liquidation or bankruptcy intervened[189]. At one stage it was thought that the normal rule was that the making of a winding-up order on a petition presented by a post-arrangement creditor or the directors would not serve to terminate the arrangement or require the assets to be handed to the liquidator, but that the contrary would be the case where the petition is presented by a supervisor in exercise of his powers under section 7(4)(b) of IA 1986[190]. The Court of Appeal[191] in 2002 reviewed the earlier cases and determined that, in the absence of provision to the contrary in the voluntary arrangement itself, the trust established by the arrangement will survive the

---

185 *Re Broome, Thomson v Broome* [1999] 1 BCLC 356.
186 *Raja v Rubin* [2000] Ch 274.
187 *Re N T Gallagher & Son Ltd* [2002] EWCA Civ 404. The Rules provide for the proposal itself to spell out the duration of the arrangement (Rule 2.3(o) of the Rules).
188 The concept of a voluntary arrangement ceasing to have effect appears in sections 5(2A) and 7B of IA 1986, introduced by Schedule 2 of the Insolvency Act 2000.
189 *Re Bradley-Hole* [1995] 1 WLR 1097, *Davis v Martin-Sklan* [1995] 2 BCLC 483, *Re Halson Packaging Ltd* [1997] 2 BCLC 280, *Re Arthur Rathbone Kitchens Ltd* [1997] BPIR 194, *Re Excalibur Airways Ltd* [1998] 1 BCLC 436, *Kings v Cleghorn* [1998] BPIR 463, *Re Maple Engineering Ltd* [2000] BCC 93, *Welsby v Brelec Installations Ltd* [2000] 2 BCLC 576 and *Re Kudos Glass Ltd* [2001] 1 BCLC 390.
190 Eg *Re Excalibur Airways Ltd* [1998] 1 BCLC 436 at 439. In the case of a moratorium, the power is given by Schedule A1 paragraph 39(5)(b) of IA 1986.
191 *Re N T Gallagher & Son Ltd* [2002] EWCA Civ 404, [2002] 2 BCLC 133 at 149, applied in *Oakley Smith v Greenberg* [2002] EWCA Civ 1217 and *Welburn v Dibb Lupton Broomhead* [2002] EWCA Civ 1601.

intervention of a liquidation, whatever its foundation. Likewise, there is no reason in principle why the voluntary arrangement itself may not continue after the intervention of a liquidation[192], although it will be a matter of construction as to what remains to be done under the arrangement, whether, for example, creditors under the arrangement are barred from proving in the liquidation and whether the supervisor has anything to do apart from administering such of the assets as may continue to be held on the trusts of the arrangement notwithstanding the liquidation. A company may also resolve to go into voluntary liquidation notwithstanding the approval of a voluntary arrangement, so that, even though such a resolution may be a breach of the terms of the arrangement, the resolution itself will be valid[193].

11.50 It should be noted that a member state liquidator is empowered to apply to court for the conversion under Article 37 of the EC Insolvency Regulation of a voluntary arrangement into a winding up if this is in the interests of the creditors in the main proceedings. Where he does so he must make and file a witness statement in support of the application[194] which must state:

(a) that main proceedings have been opened in relation to the company in another member state;

(b) the witness's belief that conversion would be in the interests of the creditors in the main proceedings;

(c) the witness' opinion as to whether the company ought to enter voluntary or compulsory winding up; and

(d) all such other matters as would in the opinion of the applicant assist the court in deciding whether or not to make an order and what, if any, consequential provisions to include[195].

11.51 Where a voluntary arrangement comes to an end, whether by being fully implemented or by being terminated, the supervisor comes under certain additional reporting obligations[196]. Not more than 28 days after the final completion or termination[197] of a voluntary arrangement, the supervisor must send to all creditors and members who are bound by it, the registrar of companies, the court[198] and any member state liquidator[199], notice that the arrangement has been fully implemented or terminated (as the case may be). The notice must be accompanied by a copy of a report summarising all receipts and payments and explaining in relation to the arrangement any departure from the terms of the arrangement as they originally took effect or, in the case of termination, why the arrangement has terminated, and should include (if applicable) a statement as to the amount paid to any unsecured creditors by virtue of section 176A of IA 1986[200]. A supervisor may not vacate office until after the copies of the notice

---

192 *Re N T Gallagher & Son Ltd* [2002] EWCA Civ 404, [2002] 2 BCLC 133 at 149, applied in *Oakley Smith v Greenberg* [2002] EWCA Civ 1217 and *Welburn v Dibb Lupton Broomhead* [2002] EWCA Civ 1601.
193 *Re Arthur Rathbone Kitchens Ltd* [1997] 2 BCLC 280.
194 Rule 21.2(2) of the Rules.
195 Rule 21.2 of the Rules.
196 Rule 2.44 of the Rules.
197 It is thought that a voluntary arrangement will have 'terminated' whenever it ceases to have effect without having been fully implemented.
198 Rule 2.44 of the Rules.
199 Included by virtue of Rule 21.7 of the Rules.
200 Rule 2.44(2) of the Rules.

and report have been delivered to the registrar of companies and filed with the court[201].

11.52   The requirements of CA 2006 continue to apply to a company within a company voluntary arrangement. In *Re TXU Europe Group plc*[202], where there was a surplus left after payment of creditors, and thus shareholders were entitled to the surplus, Newey J held that in making any distributions to shareholders the supervisors must comply with the requirements as to return of capital as provided by CA 2006, which would only be permitted if the company went into liquidation.

---

201   Rule 2.44(4) of the Rules.
202   [2011] EWHC 2072 (Ch).

12 Moratoriums for small companies

INTRODUCTION

12.1 It was a perceived weakness of the provisions of Part I of IA 1986 when originally enacted, whereby directors could propose a voluntary arrangement for a company, that there was no provision for obtaining a moratorium while the proposal for the voluntary arrangement was being considered (other than by applying for an administration order). In the case of small companies in particular, the costs of administration proceedings were considered significantly to reduce the benefits to creditors of a voluntary arrangement, if approved. On the other hand, in the absence of a moratorium, creditors were free to proceed against the company and its assets and so to jeopardise the prospects of a voluntary arrangement succeeding.

12.2 To meet this perceived weakness, IA 2000, introduced a new moratorium procedure which is available where the directors of an eligible company intend to make a proposal for a voluntary arrangement[1]. In such a case, the provisions of a new Schedule A1 to IA 1986 apply so as to govern:

(a) which companies are eligible for the new moratorium procedure;

(b) the procedure for obtaining such a moratorium;

(c) the effects of such a moratorium; and

(d) the procedure applicable in relation to the approval and implementation of a voluntary arrangement where such a moratorium is or has been in force[2].

This chapter considers what companies are eligible, the procedure for obtaining a moratorium and its effect. The procedure in relation to the approval and implementation of a voluntary arrangement where a moratorium is in place is considered in **CHAPTER 11** *ante*, which also deals with procedure applicable where either no moratorium is in place or the company is in administration.

ELIGIBLE COMPANIES

12.3 The basic requirement for eligibility for the moratorium procedure is that in the year ending with the date of filing[3], or in the financial year of the company which ended last before that date, the company satisfied two or more

---

1 See section 1A(1) of IA 1986 as introduced by section 1 and Schedule 1 of IA 2000.
2 Section 1A(2) of IA 1986.
3 See **PARAGRAPH 12.13** *post*.

of the requirements for being a small company specified by section 382(3) of CA 2006[4]. Those requirements are:

(a) that the company's turnover should be not more than £10.2m;

(b) that the company's assets should total not more than £5.1m; and

(c) that the company should employ not more that 50 employees[5].

As an additional exception, a parent company is not eligible unless the group headed by it qualifies as a small group or a medium sized group in relation to the financial year of the company which ended last before the date of filing[6]. 'Group' has the same meaning as in Part 15 of CA 2006, (as provided for by section 474(1) of CA 2006). A group qualifies as small in relation to a financial year if it so qualifies under section 383(2) to (7) of CA 2006, and qualifies as medium sized in relation to a financial year if it so qualifies under section 466(2) to (7) of CA 2006[7]. The qualifying conditions for a small group as provided by section 383(4) of CA 2006 are met by a group in a year in which it satisfies two or more of the following conditions, namely an aggregate turnover of not more than £10.2m net or £12.2m gross, an aggregate balance sheet total of not more than £5.1m net or £6.1m gross, or an aggregate number of employees of not more than 50[8]. The qualifying conditions for a medium-sized group as provided by section 466(4) of CA 2006 are met by a group in a year in which it satisfies two or more of the following requirements, namely an aggregate turnover of not more than £36m net or £43.2m gross, an aggregate balance sheet total of not more than £18m net or £21.6m gross, or an aggregate number of employees of not more than 250[9]. Section 467 of CA 2006 excludes certain companies from being treated as medium sized, such exclusions being a public company, a company that has permission under Part 4 of FSMA 2000 to carry on a regulated activity, carries on insurance market activity or is a member of an ineligible group. A group is ineligible if any of its members is a public company, a body corporate (other than a company) whose shares are admitted to trading on a regulated market, a person (other than a small company) who has permission under Part 4A of FSMA 2000 to carry on a regulated activity, a small company that is an authorised insurance company, a banking company, an e-money issuer, a MiFID investment firm, a UCITS management company or a person who carries on insurance market activity[10].

12.4 There are, also, a number of specific exclusions of companies which might otherwise be eligible[11]. The exclusions are as follows:

(a) companies which effect or carry out contracts of insurance which are not exempt in relation to that activity from the general prohibition within the meaning of section 19 of FSMA 2000;

(b) companies which have permission to accept deposits under Part IV of FSMA 2000 or which have a liability in respect of a deposit accepted in accordance with the Banking Act 1979 or Banking Act 1987;

---

4 Schedule A1 paragraphs 2(1) and 3 of IA 1986.
5 For the purpose of determining whether the requirements have been met, the provisions of section 382 (4), (5) and (6) of CA 2006 apply, see paragraph 3(3) of Schedule A1 to IA 1986.
6 See Schedule A1 paragraph 3(4) of IA 1986.
7 See Schedule A1 paragraph 3(5) of IA 1986.
8 Section 383(4) of CA 2006.
9 Section 466(4) of CA 2006.
10 Section 467 of CA 2006.
11 Schedule A1 paragraph 2(1) and (2) of IA 1986 (as amended by article 29 of the Financial Services and Markets Act 2000 (Consequential Amendments) Order 2002 (SI 2002 No 1555)).

(c) companies which are party to a market contract or any whose property is subject to a market charge or a system charge[12]; and

(d) companies which are participants in a payment or securities settlement system which has been designated under Part II of the Financial Markets and Insolvency (Settlement Finality) Regulations 1999[13] or any whose property is subject to a collateral security charge within the meaning of those regulations[14].

12.5 In addition, a company is excluded from being eligible for a moratorium if, on the date of filing[15]:

(a) the company is in administration;

(b) a winding-up order has been made or the company is in voluntary liquidation;

(c) there is an administrative receiver of the company;

(d) a voluntary arrangement has effect in relation to the company;

(e) there is a provisional liquidator of the company;

(f) a moratorium has been in force for the company at any time in the period of 12 months ending with the date of filing and either no voluntary arrangement had effect at the time that moratorium ended or a voluntary arrangement which had effect at any time during the 12-month period has come to an end prematurely[16];

(g) an administrator appointed by the company or its directors under Schedule B1 paragraph 22 of IA 1986 has held office in the period of 12 months ending with the date of filing; or

(h) a voluntary arrangement in relation to the company which had effect pursuant to a proposal made by an administrator or liquidator had come to an end prematurely and, during the 12 months ended with the date of filing, an order has been made under section 5(3)(a) of IA 1986 staying the winding-up proceedings or providing for the appointment of the administrator to cease to have effect[17].

12.6 A company is also excluded from being eligible for a moratorium if, at the date of filing:

(a) it is party to a capital market arrangement[18];

(b) it is a project company of a public-private partnership (PPP) project which includes step-in rights[19]; or

(c) it has incurred a liability under an agreement of £10m or more[20].

---

12 See **CHAPTER 18** *post.*
13 SI 1999 No 2979.
14 See **CHAPTER 18** *post.*
15 Schedule A1 paragraph 4(1) of IA 1986.
16 For the circumstances in which a voluntary arrangement comes to an end prematurely, see **CHAPTER 11** *ante.*
17 Schedule A1 paragraph 4 of IA 1986.
18 Schedule A1 paragraph 4A of IA 1986. An arrangement will be a capital market arrangement if it meets the criteria set out in paragraph 4A and one or more of those in paragraph 4D.
19 Schedule A1 paragraph 4B of IA 1986. The expressions 'project company', 'public-private partnership project' and 'step-in rights' are defined in paragraphs 4H, 4I and 4J.
20 Schedule A1 paragraph 4C of IA 1986. Liability includes a present or future liability whether in either case it is certain or contingent. It also includes a liability to be paid wholly or partly in foreign currency (in which event the sterling equivalent is calculated as at the time when the liability was incurred). Where the liability is a contingent liability under a guarantee, indemnity or security provided on behalf of another person, the amount of the liability is the full amount of the liability in relation to which the guarantee, indemnity or security is provided.

These exclusions were introduced by the Insolvency Act 1986 (Amendment) (No 3) Regulations 2002[21] and reflect the exceptional cases in which the holder of a qualifying floating charge can still appoint an administrative receiver of the company[22].

OBTAINING AND EXTENDING A MORATORIUM

12.7   The procedures for obtaining a moratorium are set out in section 1A of IA 1986, and Schedule A1 of IA 1986 and Rules 2.11 to 2.24 of the Rules. Where the directors of an eligible company intend to make a proposal for a voluntary arrangement, they may take steps to obtain a moratorium for the company[23] and they are required to submit to the nominee a document setting out the terms of the proposed voluntary arrangement, a statement of the company's affairs containing such particulars of its creditors and of its debts and other liabilities and of its assets as may be prescribed and any other information necessary to enable the nominee to make his report which the nominee requests[24].

12.8   The proposal for the company voluntary arrangement and the statement of affairs must contain the same information as with a non-moratorium voluntary arrangement, as set out in **CHAPTER 11** *ante*[25].

12.9   The statement of affairs must be made up to a date not earlier than two weeks before the date of the proposal[26]. However the nominee may allow the statement to be made up to an earlier date (but not more than two months before the proposal) where that is more practicable[27], and if this occurs, the nominee's statement to the directors on the proposal must explain why[28]. The statement of affairs must be verified by a statement of truth made by at least one director[29]. The nominee, the directors or any person appearing to the court to have an interest, may apply to the court for a direction that specified information be omitted from the statement of affairs as delivered to the creditors where disclosure of that information would be likely to prejudice the conduct of the voluntary arrangement or might be expected to lead to violence against any person[30].

12.10   Within 28 days of the submission to him of the document setting out the terms of the proposed voluntary arrangement, the nominee is required to submit a statement to the directors indicating whether or not in his opinion:

(a) the proposed voluntary arrangement has a reasonable prospect of being approved and implemented;

(b) the company is likely to have sufficient funds available to it during the proposed moratorium to enable it to carry on the business proposed to be carried on during the moratorium; and

---

21   SI 2002 No 1990.
22   As to which, see sections 72A–72H of IA 1986.
23   Section 1A(1) of IA 1986.
24   Schedule A1 paragraph 6(1) of IA 1986.
25   Rules 2.3, 2.6 and 2.11 of the Rules.
26   Rule 2.11(2) of the Rules.
27   Rule 2.11(3) of the Rules.
28   Rule 2.11(4) of the Rules.
29   Rule 2.11(5) of the Rules.
30   Rule 2.12 of the Rules.

(c)   the proposed voluntary arrangement should be considered by a meeting of the company and by the company's creditors[31].

In forming his opinion, the nominee is entitled to rely upon the information submitted to him unless he has reason to doubt its accuracy[32]. The statement must include the name and address of the nominee and be authenticated and dated by the nominee, and must explain as regards the nominee's opinions stated pursuant to Schedule A1 paragraph 6(2) why the nominee has formed that opinion, and if the nominee is willing to act, be accompanied by a statement of the nominee's consent to act in relation to the proposed voluntary arrangement (which consent must include the name and address of the nominee, state that the nominee is qualified to act as an insolvency practitioner in relation to the company and be authenticated and dated by the nominee)[33].

12.11   Provided that the nominee is satisfied as to the matters on which he is required to report, the directors then obtain the moratorium by filing with the court:

(a)   a document setting out the terms of the proposed voluntary arrangement;

(b)   a statement of the company's affairs containing the prescribed particulars or information;

(c)   a statement that the company is eligible for the moratorium;

(d)   a statement from the nominee that he has consented to act; and

(e)   the nominee's statement that, in his opinion the proposed voluntary arrangement has a reasonable prospect of being approved and implemented, the company is likely to have sufficient funds available to it during the proposed moratorium to enable it to carry on its business and that the proposed voluntary arrangement should be considered by a meeting of the company and by the company's creditors[34].

The documents must be filed, together with four copies of a schedule listing them, not later than ten business days after the nominee's opinion under Schedule A1 paragraph 7(1) of IA 1986 was submitted to the directors[35]. The court must endorse the copies of the schedule with the date on which the documents were filed and deliver three copies of the endorsed schedule to the directors[36].

12.12   To protect against steps taken to obtain a moratorium triggering the appointment of a receiver or an administrative receiver, Schedule A1 paragraph 43 of IA 1986 provides that a provision in an instrument creating a floating charge is void if it provides for obtaining a moratorium or anything done with a view to obtaining a moratorium to be either:

(a)   an event causing the floating charge to crystallise or causing restrictions which would not otherwise apply to be imposed on the disposal of the property by the company; or

(b)   a ground for the appointment of a receiver.

---

31   Schedule A1 paragraph 6(2) and (4) of IA 1986, as amended by Schedule 9 paragraph 9(3) of SBEEA 2015; Rule 2.13(1) and (2).

32   Schedule A1 paragraph 6(3) of IA 1986.

33   Rule 2.13(2)–(4) of the Rules.

34   Schedule A1 paragraph 7 of IA 1986, as amended by Schedule 9 paragraph 9(3) of SBEEA 2015.

35   Rule 2.14(4)(b) and (5) of the Rules.

36   Rule 2.14(6) of the Rules.

12.13 The moratorium comes into force on the filing of the documents referred to in the preceding paragraphs[37] and ends with the later of the day on which the company meeting summoned under Schedule A1 paragraph 29 of IA 1986 is first held, and the day on which the company's creditors decide whether to approve the proposed voluntary arrangement, unless extended, subject to the provisions of Schedule A1 paragraph 8(3) to (4) of IA 1986[38]. By Schedule A1 paragraph 8(3) of IA 1986 the definition of the 'initial period' means the period of 28 days beginning with the day on which the moratorium comes into force[39]. By paragraph 8(3A), if the company meeting has not first met before the end of the initial period, the moratorium ends at the end of that period, unless before the end of that period it is extended under Schedule A1 paragraph 32 of IA 1986. By Schedule A1 paragraph 8(3B) of IA 1986, if the company's creditors have not decided whether to approve the proposed voluntary arrangement before the end of the initial period the moratorium ends at the end of that period, unless before the end of that period the moratorium is extended under Schedule A1 paragraph 32 of IA 1986 or a meeting of the company's creditors is summoned in accordance with section 246ZE of IA 1986. Where a meeting of creditors takes place, the moratorium ends with the day on which the meeting of the company's creditors is first held, unless it is extended under Schedule A1 paragraph 32 of IA 1986[40]. By Schedule A1 paragraph 8(4) of IA 1986[41], the moratorium ends at the end of the initial period if the nominee has not before the end of that term summoned a meeting of the company, and sought a decision from the company's creditors as required by Schedule A1 paragraph 29(1) of IA 1986. However, the moratorium may end earlier if the nominee withdraws his consent to act[42], if the court so orders on application made under paragraph 26, 27 or 40 of Schedule A1 of IA 1986[43], or by virtue of a decision at one or both of the meetings of the company summoned under Schedule A1 paragraph 29 of IA 1986 or the company's creditors[44]. If it has not otherwise come to an end, the moratorium ends at the end of the day on which a decision to approve the voluntary arrangement takes effect[45].

12.14 When a moratorium comes into force, the directors are required to notify the nominee forthwith[46] and deliver as soon as reasonably practicable after delivery to the directors by the court of the endorsed copies (of the documents required to be filed pursuant to Schedule A1 paragraph 7(1) of IA 1986) two copies of the schedule to the nominee and one to the company[47]. When the moratorium comes into force, the nominee shall, in accordance with the rules

---

37 Schedule A1 paragraph 8(1) of IA 1986.
38 Schedule A1 paragraph 8(2) of IA 1986, as amended by Schedule 9 paragraph 9(4) of SBEEA 2015. As to the extension of the moratorium, see **PARAGRAPH 12.15** *post*.
39 Schedule A1 paragraph 8(2)–(4) of IA 1986 is inserted by paragraph 9(4) of Schedule 9 to SBEEA 2015.
40 Schedule A1 paragraph 8(3C) of IA 1986 (as inserted by paragraph 9(4) of Schedule 9 to SBEEA 2015).
41 As inserted by paragraph 9(4) of Schedule 9 to SBEEA 2015.
42 See **PARAGRAPH 12.37** *post*.
43 See **PARAGRAPHS 12.39, 12.40 AND 12.42** *post*.
44 Schedule A1 paragraph 8(6) of IA 1986 (as amended by paragraph 9(5) of Schedule 9 to SBEEA 2015). Presumably, therefore, the decision by a creditors' meeting not to approve a proposed voluntary arrangement or to adjourn without agreeing to extend the moratorium (see **PARAGRAPH 12.15** *post*) will bring the moratorium to an immediate end.
45 Schedule A1 paragraph 8(7) of IA 1986.
46 Schedule A1 paragraph 9(1) of IA 1986.
47 Rule 2.15(1) of the Rules.

advertise the coming into force of the moratorium and to notify the registrar of companies, the company and any creditor who has presented a winding-up petition before the beginning of the moratorium, provided the petition has not been dismissed or withdrawn[48]. The Rules specify that the nominee must as soon as reasonably practicable gazette a notice of the coming into force of the moratorium, and may advertise the notice in such other manner as the nominee thinks fit[49]. The notice must specify the nature of the business of the company, that a moratorium under section 1A of IA 1986 has come into force, and the date on which it came into force[50]. Also, the nominee must deliver a notice of the coming into force of the moratorium and the date on which it came into force to any enforcement agent or other officer who, to the knowledge of the nominee, is charged with distress or other legal process against the company or its property, and any person who, to the nominee's knowledge, has distrained against the company or its property[51].

12.15 A moratorium may be extended or further extended to a day not later than the end of the period of two months beginning with the day after the last day of the period mentioned in Schedule A1 paragraph 8(3) of IA 1986 (the period mentioned in paragraph 8(3) is the initial period of 28 days, beginning with the day on which the moratorium comes into force). The meeting of the company may resolve that the moratorium be extended, or further extended, with or without conditions. The creditors may, by a qualifying decision procedure decide to extend, or further extend the moratorium, with or without conditions[52]. By Schedule A1 paragraph 36(2) of IA 1986, the decision to extend the moratorium will be effective if either both the company meeting and the creditors' decision approve the extension, or if the creditors have decided to extend the moratorium (thus giving the creditors the ultimate decision making power)[53]. If the moratorium is extended, the nominee must, as soon as reasonably practicable, file with the court and deliver to the registrar a notice of the decision. The notice must identify the company, give the name and address of the nominee, state the date on which the moratorium was extended or further extended, state the new expiry date of the moratorium and be authenticated and dated by the nominee[54].

12.16 Where it is proposed to extend (or further extend) the moratorium, the nominee must inform the meeting of the company or (as the case may be) inform the company's creditors before the decision to extend is taken:

(a) what the nominee has done to comply with his duty to monitor the company's affairs and the costs of his actions for the company; and

(b) what he intends to do to continue to comply with that duty if the moratorium is extended (or further extended) and the expected costs of his intended actions for the company[55].

---

48   Schedule A1 paragraph 10(1) and (2) of IA 1986 and Rule 2.15(4).
49   Rule 2.15(2) of the Rules.
50   Rule 2.15(3) of the Rules.
51   Rule 2.15(6) of the Rules.
52   Schedule A1 paragraph 32(1) and (2) of IA 1986, (as amended by Schedule 9 paragraph 9(21) and (22) of SBEEA 2015).
53   Schedule A1 paragraph 36(1) and (2) of IA 1986 (as amended by Schedule 9 paragraph 9(28) of SBEEA 2015).
54   Rule 2.17 of the Rules.
55   Schedule A1 paragraph 32(3) of IA 1986 (as amended by Schedule 9 paragraph 9(23) of SBEEA 2015).

Where the nominee informs a meeting of the company or informs the company's creditors of the expected costs of his intended actions, the meeting must resolve, or (as the case may be) the creditors by a qualifying decision procedure shall decide, whether or not to approve the expected costs[56]. If the meeting of the company and the creditors, or the company's creditors, resolve not to approve the expected costs of the nominee's intended actions, subject to any application by a member of the company to the court, which can order the decision of the company's meeting to have effect instead of the decision of the creditors or make such other order as it thinks fit, the moratorium comes to an end[57]. Where a moratorium has been extended or further extended, any subsequent meeting of the company and/or decision of the creditors or a decision of the creditors alone[58], may resolve to bring the moratorium to an end before the end of the period of the extension (or further extension)[59].

12.17   Amongst the conditions which may be imposed on a moratorium as extended (or further extended), is a requirement that the nominee be replaced by another person qualified to act as an insolvency practitioner or as a nominee in relation to the proposed voluntary arrangement[60]. Such person may only be appointed if he submits to the court a statement indicating his consent to act[61]. Where it is proposed to appoint such a replacement nominee, the provisions in relation to the information to be placed before the meeting of the company and before the creditors and the approval of the expected costs of the nominee's intended actions apply in respect of the proposed replacement nominee[62].

12.18   Where, in accordance with Schedule A1 paragraph 32 of IA 1986, a meeting of the company resolves, or the company's creditors decide, that the moratorium be extended (or further extended), the meeting may resolve, and the company's creditors may by a qualifying decision procedure decide, that a committee be established to exercise the functions conferred on it by the meeting or (as the case may be) by the company's creditors. The meeting may resolve that such a committee be established only if the nominee consents and the meeting approves an estimate of the expenses to be incurred by the committee in the exercise of the proposed functions. A decision of the company's creditors that such a committee be established is to be taken as made only if the nominee consents and the creditors by a qualifying decision procedure approve an estimate of the expenses to be incurred by the committee in the exercise of the proposed functions[63]. Any expenses thereafter incurred by the committee in the exercise of its functions, not exceeding the amount of the estimate, are required to be reimbursed by the nominee[64]. The committee ceases to exist when the

---

56   Schedule A1 paragraph 32(4) of IA 1986 (as amended by Schedule 9 paragraph 9(24) of SBEEA 2015).
57   Schedule A1 paragraphs 32(5) and 36 of IA 1986 (as amended by Schedule 9 paragraph 9(28) and (29) of SBEEA 2015).
58   Subject to an application by a member to the court, see Schedule A1 paragraph 36 of IA 1986. The time limit for any such application is as set out in **PARAGRAPH 12.15** *ante*.
59   Schedule A1 paragraph 32(6) of IA 1986 (subject to any application by a member of the company pursuant to Schedule A1 paragraph 36(3) of IA 1986) (as amended by Schedule 9 paragraph 9(25) and (29) of SBEEA 2015).
60   Schedule A1 paragraph 33(1) of IA 1986.
61   Schedule A1 paragraph 33(2) of IA 1986.
62   Schedule A1 paragraph 33(3) of IA 1986.
63   Schedule A1 paragraphs 35(1) and (2) of IA 1986 (as amended by Schedule 9 paragraph 9(27) of SBEEA 2015).
64   Schedule A1 paragraph 35(3) of IA 1986.

moratorium comes to an end[65]. If a decision taken by the creditors in respect of the establishment of a committee differs from the decision taken by the company, the decision by the creditors prevails, subject to any application by a member of the company to the court[66], which can order the decision of the company's meeting to have effect instead of the decision of the creditors or make such other order as it thinks fit.

12.19 The nominee is required to notify the registrar of companies and the court of any extension (or further extension) of the moratorium[67]. Where the extension (or further extension) results from an order of the court, the nominee is required to send an office copy of the order to the registrar of companies[68].

12.20 If, at the time a moratorium for a company under section 1A of IA 1986 comes to an end, no voluntary arrangements has effect in relation to the company, that fact is itself a ground upon which the court may wind up the company[69]. However, a petition to wind up the company on that ground can only be presented by one or more creditors[70].

EFFECTS OF A MORATORIUM

12.21 Schedule A1 paragraph 12 of IA 1986, as amended, provides that during the period for which a moratorium is in force for a company:

(a) no petition may be presented for the winding up of the company;

(b) no meeting of the company may be called or requisitioned except with the consent of the nominee or the leave of the court and subject (where the court gives leave) to such term as the court may impose;

(c) no resolution may be passed or order made for the winding up of the company;

(d) no administration application may be made in relation to the company and no administrator of the company may be appointed under Schedule B1 paragraph 14 or 22 of IA 1986;

(e) no administrative receiver of the company may be appointed;

(f) no landlord or other person to whom rent is payable may exercise any right of forfeiture by peaceful re-entry in relation to premises let to the company in respect of a failure by the company to comply with any term or condition of its tenancy of such premises, except with the leave of the court and subject to such terms as the court may impose;

(g) no other steps may be taken to enforce any security over the company's property, or to repossess goods in the company's possession under any hire-purchase agreement[71], except with the leave of the court and subject to such terms as the court may impose[72];

---

65   Schedule A1 paragraph 34(4) of IA 1986.
66   See Schedule A1 paragraph 36 of IA 1986. The time limit for any such application is as set out in **PARAGRAPH 12.15** *ante*.
67   Schedule A1 paragraph 34(1) of IA 1986; Rule 2.17 of the Rules.
68   Schedule A1 paragraph 34(2) of IA 1986; Rule 2.18 of the Rules.
69   Section 122(1)(fa) of IA 1986.
70   Section 122(3A) of IA 1986.
71   Hire-purchase agreement for this purpose includes a conditional sale agreement, a chattel leasing agreement and a retention of title agreement, see Schedule A1 paragraph 1 of IA 1986.
72   Compare **PARAGRAPH 2.7**ff *ante*.

(h) no other proceedings and no execution or other legal process may be commenced or continued, and no distress may be levied, against the company or its property, except with the leave of the court and subject to such terms as the court may impose.

12.22 However, the restrictions upon presenting a petition for the winding up of the company do not apply to 'excepted petitions'[73], that is to say:

(a) a petition under sections 124A or 124B of IA 1986 to wind up a company in the public interest;

(b) a petition under section 72 of the Financial Services Act 1986 to wind up an authorised person or appointed representative on the just and equitable ground;

(c) a petition under section 92 of the Banking Act 1987 to wind up an authorised institution or former authorised institution on a just and equitable ground;

(d) a petition under section 367 of FSMA 2000 to wind up a body which is or was an authorised person or an appointed representative or which is or has been carrying on a regulated activity in contravention of the general prohibition[74].

Further, where an excepted petition has been presented before the beginning of or during a moratorium, the restrictions upon calling meetings of the company and on making an order to wind up the company do not apply in relation to proceedings on the petition[75].

12.23 Where a winding up petition, other than an excepted petition, has been presented before the beginning of the moratorium, the provisions of section 127 of IA 1986 invalidating dispositions of the company's property, transfers of shares or alterations in the status of the company's members do not apply in relation to such dispositions, transfers or alterations made during the moratorium or at any time before the end of the period of 28 days beginning with the first day upon which each of the reports to the court required by Schedule A1 paragraph 30(3) of IA 1986 has been made (the report of the result of the company's meeting, or the report of the decision of the company's creditors) or at any time when an application under paragraph 38 or an appeal in respect of such an application is pending, or at any time in the period within which such an appeal may be brought[76].

12.24 In addition, the moratorium, whilst in force, prevents a floating charge from crystallising or restrictions being imposed upon the disposal of any of the company's property. Where there is an uncrystallised floating charge on the property of a company for which a moratorium is in force, the holder of the floating charge cannot give a notice whilst the moratorium is in force causing the crystallisation of the floating charge or imposing any restrictions on the disposal of the company's property. If otherwise entitled to do so, however, the holder can instead give such a notice as soon as practicable after the moratorium has come to an end[77]. Similarly, if an event occurs whilst the moratorium is in force which

---

73   Schedule A1 paragraph 12(4) of IA 1986. For the equivalent provisions in relation to an administration, see **PARAGRAPH 2.2** *ante*.
74   Schedule A1 paragraph 12(5) of IA 1986.
75   Schedule A1 paragraph 12(4) of IA 1986.
76   Schedule A1 paragraph 12(2) of IA 1986; paragraph 37(5) (as amended by Schedule 9 paragraph 9(31) of SBEEA 2015).
77   Schedule A1 paragraph 13(2) and (4) of IA 1986.

would otherwise cause the crystallisation of the floating charge or the imposition of any restrictions on the disposal of the company's property, then the event does not have the effect in question at that time but, if notice to that effect is given to the company by the holder of the floating charge as soon as is practicable after the moratorium has come to an end, the event is to be treated as if it had occurred when the notice was given[78]. There is a further express prohibition on applying for leave to enforce security over the company's property, or to repossess goods in its possession, or to commence or to continue proceedings, execution or other legal process or to levy distress with a view to obtaining the crystallisation of the floating charge or the imposition of any such restriction[79]. To counterbalance the above provisions, Schedule A1 paragraph 14 of IA 1986 provides that security granted by a company at a time when the moratorium is in force in relation to the company may only be enforced if, at the time it was granted, there were reasonable grounds for believing that the grant of the security would benefit the company.

12.25 The restrictions discussed in **PARAGRAPHS 12.21 TO 12.24** *ante* have effect in relation to the creditors of the company in relation to which a moratorium is in force. In addition, Schedule A1 paragraphs 16 to 23 of IA 1986 impose a series of restrictions which have effect in relation to the company itself. These provisions are discussed below. However, at the outset, it should be noted that the fact that a company enters into a transaction in contravention of such provisions[80] does not, of itself, render the transaction void or to any extent unenforceable against the company[81]. By implication, however, the company itself may be unable to enforce a transaction entered into by it in contravention of the provisions in question[82]. Furthermore, the transaction may be open to challenge on other grounds. Thus, for instance, a disposition of charged property in contravention of Schedule A1 paragraph 20 of IA 1986 may take effect but may be subject to the rights of the chargee.

12.26 Under Schedule A1 paragraph 16 of IA 1986, all invoices, orders for goods and business letters issued by or on behalf of the company or on which the company's name appears must also contain the nominee's name and a statement that a moratorium is in force for the company. Breach of this provision constitutes a criminal offence on the part of the company and any officer of the company who, without reasonable excuse, authorises or permits the default[83].

12.27 Under Schedule A1 paragraph 17 of the IA 1986, the company may not obtain credit to the extent of £250 or more from a person who has not been informed that a moratorium is in force in relation to the company[84]. For this purpose, obtaining credit includes obtaining the supply of goods under a hire purchase or conditional sale agreement or obtaining payment in advance for the supply of goods or services[85]. Contravention of this provision constitutes an

---

78 Schedule A1 paragraph 13(3) and (4) of IA 1986.
79 Schedule A1 paragraph 13(5) of IA 1986.
80 Excluding paragraph 23 for which express provision is made by Schedule A1 paragraph 23(3) of IA 1986; see **PARAGRAPHS 12.34 AND 12.35** *post*.
81 Schedule A1 paragraph 15(2) of IA 1986.
82 Contrast Schedule A1 paragraph 23(3) of IA 1986.
83 Schedule A1 paragraph 16(2) and (3) of IA 1986.
84 Schedule A1 paragraph 17(1) of IA 1986. The Secretary of State may, by order, increase or reduce the specified limit, see section 417A of IA 1986.
85 Schedule A1 paragraph 17(2) of IA 1986.

offence by the company and by any officer of the company who knowingly and willingly authorised or permitted the contravention[86].

12.28 During the moratorium the company may only dispose of any of its property or make a payment in respect of a debt or other liability of the company in existence before the beginning of the moratorium if there are reasonable grounds for believing the disposal or payment (as the case may be) will benefit the company and the disposal is approved by the committee, if any, established by the meetings of the company's creditors or, if there is no such committee, by the nominee[87]. The restriction does not apply, however, to the disposal of property by a company in the ordinary way of the company's business[88], or to a payment required to be made to a secured creditor under Schedule A1 paragraph 20(6) of IA 1986[89]. Nevertheless, directors who cause the company to trade during a moratorium may nevertheless be held liable for breach of duty, fraudulent trading or wrongful trading if the requirements for such liability are otherwise established. If the company makes a disposable payment in contravention of such expressed statutory prohibition, otherwise than in pursuance of an order of the court, the company and any officer of the company who without reasonable excuse authorised or permitted the contravention is guilty of an offence[90].

12.29 There are further express restrictions contained in Schedule A1 paragraphs 20 and 21 of IA 1986 applying to the disposal by a company subject to a moratorium of property which is subject to a security or of goods which are in the possession of the company under a hire-purchase agreement. For this purpose, a hire-purchase agreement includes a conditional sale agreement, a chattel leasing agreement or a retention of title agreement[91]. The provisions do not, however, apply in relation to any property which is subject to a market charge, a system charge or a collateral security charge[92].

12.30 In the case of property subject to a security (other than one which as created was a floating charge) or goods in the possession of the company subject to hire-purchase agreement, the company may dispose of the property or the goods as if, as the case may, they were not subject to the security or the rights of the owner under the hire-purchase agreement were vested in the company, provided that either the holder of the security or the owner of the goods consents or the court gives leave[93]. However, as a condition of any such consent or leave, the net proceeds of the disposal, together with any additional amount agreed or determined by the court to make good any amount by which the net proceeds are less than the net amount that would be realised on a sale of the property or goods in the open market by a willing vendor, must be applied in discharging the sums secured by the security or payable under the hire-purchase agreement[94]. Where there are two or more securities, such amounts are to be applied in discharging the sums secured by the securities in the order of their priorities[95]. The restriction

---

86   Schedule A1 paragraph 17(3) of IA 1986.
87   Schedule A1 paragraphs 18(1) and 19(1) of IA 1986.
88   Schedule A1 paragraph 18(2) of IA 1986.
89   Schedule A1 paragraph 19(2) of IA 1986; see **PARAGRAPH 12.30** *post.*
90   Schedule A1 paragraphs 18(3) and 19(3) of IA 1986 as amended.
91   Schedule A1 paragraph 1 of IA 1986. See also **PARAGRAPH 2.16** *ante.*
92   Schedule A1 paragraph 23(5) of IA 1986; see **CHAPTER 18** *post.*
93   Schedule A1 paragraph 20(1), (2) of IA 1986.
94   Schedule A1 paragraph 20(5) and (6) of IA 1986.
95   Schedule A1 paragraph 20(7) of IA 1986.

on making payments in respect of debts or liabilities in existence before the
beginning of the moratorium does not apply to such payments[96].

12.31   A company subject to a moratorium can also dispose of property subject
to a security which as created was a floating charge as if it was not subject to
the security provided that the holder of the security consents or the court gives
leave[97]. The fact that this power can only be exercised with consent or leave of
the court means that it is more restrictive than the power of an administrator
under Schedule B1 paragraph 70 of IA 1986[98]. Presumably, this is to provide
some protection for the holder of a floating charge whose ability to crystallise
his floating charge will have been restricted by Schedule A1 paragraph 13 of
IA 1986[99]. In such a case, the holder of the security has the same priority in
respect of any property of the company directly or indirectly representing the
property disposed of as he would have had in respect of the property subject to
the security[100].

12.32   If a court order is made for permission to dispose of property subject to
a security, or goods under a hire purchase agreement, the court must deliver two
sealed copies of the order to the company, and the company must deliver one of
them to the holder or owner as soon as reasonably practicable[101].

12.33   The provisions dealing with disposal of charged property or goods
subject to hire-purchase agreement are counterbalanced by provisions creating
criminal offences. If a company subject to a moratorium:

(a)   without the consent of the chargeholder or the leave of the court disposes of
any property which is subject to a security otherwise in accordance with the
terms of the security, or

(b)   without the consent of the owner or the leave of the court disposes of any
goods in the possession of the company under hire-purchase agreement
otherwise than in the terms of the agreement, or

(c)   fails to comply with any requirements imposed by Schedule A1 paragraph
20 or 21 of IA 1986,

it is liable to a fine[102]. Any officer of the company who without reasonable
excuse authorises or permits such a disposal or failure to comply is also guilty
of an offence[103].

12.34   In addition, Schedule A1 paragraph 23 of IA 1986 provides that the
company that is subject to a moratorium commits an offence if it:

(a)   enters into a market contract;

(b)   gives a transfer order;

(c)   grants a market charge or a system charge; or

(d)   provides any collateral security.

---

96   Schedule A1 paragraph 19(2) of IA 1986.
97   Schedule A1 paragraph 20(1) and (2) of IA 1986.
98   As to which, see **PARAGRAPH 5.14**ff *ante*.
99   See **PARAGRAPH 12.24** *ante*.
100   Schedule A1 paragraph 20(4) of IA 1986.
101   Rule 2.20 of the Rules.
102   Schedule A1 paragraph 22(1) of IA 1986.
103   Schedule A1 paragraph 22(2) of IA 1986.

An officer of the company who without reasonable excuse authorises or permits the company to enter into such a transaction is also guilty of an offence[104]. The various transactions referred to in Schedule A1 paragraph 23 of IA 1986 are considered in more detail in **CHAPTER 18** *post*. However, it should be noted that contravention of Schedule A1 paragraph 23 of IA 1986 does not render the transaction void or make it to an extent unenforceable either by or against the company[105]. Further, where a company during a moratorium enters into such a transaction, nothing done by or in pursuance of the transaction is to be treated as done in contravention of the provisions discussed in **PARAGRAPHS 12.21(g), 12.24 AND 12.26 TO 12.33** *ante*[106].

12.35 Finally, in this context, it should be noted that the provisions of section 233 of IA 1986 applying to public service suppliers of gas, electricity, water and telecommunications described in **CHAPTER 8** *ante* are extended to companies in respect of which a moratorium is in force by section 233(1)(ba) of IA 1986. Accordingly, if a request is made by or with the concurrence of the nominee after the date upon which the moratorium comes into force for the supply of gas, water, electricity or telecommunication services, a supplier to whom section 233 applies:

(a) may make it a condition that the nominee personally guarantees the payment of any charge in respect of the supply during the moratorium; but

(b) may not make a condition of the giving of the supply, or do anything which has the effect of making it a condition of the giving of the supply, that outstanding charges in respect of a supply to the company before the date of the moratorium came into force are paid[107].

NOMINEES

12.36 During the moratorium, the nominee is required to monitor the company's affairs for the purpose of forming an opinion as to whether:

(a) the proposed voluntary arrangement, with any proposed modifications, has a reasonable prospect of being approved and implemented; and

(b) the company is likely to have sufficient funding available to it during the remainder of the moratorium to enable it to carry on its business as the company proposes to carry it on during the remainder of the moratorium[108].

For this purpose, the directors are required to submit to the nominee any information necessary to enable him to comply with such duty as he requests[109]. In forming his opinion on the matters set out above, the nominee is entitled to rely upon the information submitted to him by the directors unless he has reason to doubt its accuracy[110].

---

104 Schedule A1 paragraph 23(1)(b) of IA 1986.
105 Schedule A1 paragraph 23(3) of IA 1986.
106 Schedule A1 paragraph 23(4) of IA 1986.
107 Section 233(2)(a) and (b) of IA 1986.
108 Schedule A1 paragraph 24(1) and (4) of IA 1986.
109 Schedule A1 paragraph 24(2) of IA 1986.
110 Schedule A1 paragraph 24(3) of IA 1986.

12.37   The nominee must withdraw his consent to act if at any time during the moratorium:

(a) he forms the opinion that:
   (i)   the proposed voluntary arrangement, together with any proposed modification, no longer has a reasonable prospect of being approved or implemented; or
   (ii) the company will not have sufficient funds available to it during the remainder of the moratorium to enable it to carry on its business as the company proposes to carry it on during the remainder of the moratorium;

(b) he becomes aware that on the date of filing, the company was not eligible for a moratorium; or

(c) the directors fail to supply him with information necessary to enable him to comply with his duty to monitor the company's affairs for the purpose mentioned in **PARAGRAPH 12.36** above which he requests from them[111].

Except in such circumstances, the nominee cannot withdraw his consent to act[112]. If he withdraws his consent to act, the moratorium comes to an end[113]. In such circumstances, the nominee must notify the court, the registrar of companies, the company and any creditor of the company of whose claim he is aware, of his withdrawal and the reason for it[114]. If he fails without reasonable excuse to give such a notification, he is liable to a fine[115].

12.38   Subject to the above, the nominee is required to summon a meeting of the company to consider the proposed voluntary arrangement and seek a decision from the company's creditors as to whether they approve the proposed voluntary arrangement[116]. The procedures for these processes and for the approval and implementation of the voluntary arrangement is considered in **CHAPTER 11** *ante*.

12.39   A creditor, director or member of the company or any other person affected by a moratorium who is dissatisfied by an act, omission or decision of the nominee during a moratorium is entitled to apply to the court either during the moratorium or after it has ended[117]. On such an application, the court may confirm, reverse or modify any act or decision of the nominee, give the nominee directions or make such other order as it thinks fit[118]. Such an order may, amongst other things, bring the moratorium to an end and make such consequential provision as the court thinks fit[119].

12.40   In addition, a creditor may apply to the court either during a moratorium or after it has ended where there are reasonable grounds for believing that, as a result of any act, omission or decision of the nominee during the moratorium,

---

111   Schedule A1 paragraph 25(2) and (3) of IA 1986.
112   Schedule A1 paragraph 25(1) of IA 1986. He can however apply to the court to be replaced, see **PARAGRAPH 12.41** *post*.
113   Schedule A1 paragraph 25(4) of IA 1986.
114   Schedule A1 paragraph 25(5) of IA 1986; Rule 2.21 of the Rules.
115   Schedule A1 paragraph 25(6) of IA 1986.
116   Schedule A1 paragraphs 29(1) and 31(1) of IA 1986 (as amended by Schedule 9 paragraph 9(7) of SBEEA 2015).
117   Schedule A1 paragraph 26(1) and (2) of IA 1986; under Rule 2.24 of the Rules, the nominee is entitled to at least five business days' notice of such application.
118   Schedule A1 paragraph 26(3) of IA 1986.
119   Schedule A1 paragraph 26(4) of IA 1986.

the company suffered loss but the company does not intend to pursue any claim it may have against the nominee[120]. On such an application, the court must have regard to the interests of the members and creditors of the company generally, and, unless it is satisfied that the act, omission or decision of the nominee was in all the circumstances reasonable, may:

(a) order the company to pursue any claim against the nominee;

(b) authorise any creditor to pursue such a claim in the name of the company; or

(c) make such other order with respect to such a claim as it thinks fit[121].

Such an order may:

(i) impose conditions on any authority given to pursue such a claim,

(ii) direct the company to assist in the pursuit of a claim,

(iii) give directions with respect to the distribution of anything received as a result of the pursuit of the claim, or

(iv) bring the moratorium to an end and make such consequential provision as the court thinks fit[122].

12.41 The court also has express power to direct the nominee to be replaced by another person qualified to act as an insolvency practitioner, or authorised to act as a nominee, in relation to the proposed voluntary arrangement[123]. The power may be exercised:

(a) on the application of the directors where the nominee has failed to comply with any duty imposed on him by Schedule A1 to IA 1986 or has died; or

(b) on the application of the directors or the nominee himself where it is impractical or inappropriate for the nominee to continue to act[124].

A person may only be appointed as replacement nominee if he submits to the court a statement indicating his consent to act[125]. Where a person is appointed as replacement nominee, he must give notice of his appointment as soon as reasonably practicable to the registrar of companies and to the former nominee[126].

12.42 To safeguard further the rights of members and creditors, Schedule A1 paragraph 40 of IA 1986 provides that the member or creditor may apply to the court either during or after the moratorium on the grounds:

(a) that the company's affairs, business and property are being or have been managed by the directors in a manner which is unfairly prejudicial to the interest of its creditors or members generally, or some part of its creditors or members (including at least the applicant); or

(b) that any actual or proposed act or omission of the directors would be so prejudicial[127].

---

120 Schedule A1 paragraph 27(1) and (2) of IA 1986; under Rule 2.24 of the Rules, the nominee is entitled to at least five business days' notice of such application.

121 Schedule A1 paragraph 27(3) and (5) of IA 1986.

122 Schedule A1 paragraph 27(4) of IA 1986.

123 Schedule A1 paragraph 28 of IA 1986. Five business days' notice of any application is required by Rule 2.22 of the Rules.

124 Schedule A1 paragraph 28(1) of IA 1986.

125 Schedule A1 paragraph 28(2) of IA 1986; Rule 2.22(3) of the Rules.

126 Rule 2.23 (1) of the Rules.

127 Schedule A1 paragraph 40(1), (2) and (3) of IA 1986. For the equivalent provisions in an administration (in which the jurisdiction arises where the administrator is acting or has acted so as unfairly to harm his interests), see **CHAPTER 14** *post*.

Where the appointment of an administrator has effect in relation to a company and the appointment took effect before the moratorium came into force, or the company is being wound up in pursuance of a petition presented before the moratorium came into force, such an application cannot be made by members or creditors but must be made by the administrator or liquidator (as the case may be)[128].

12.43   On such an application, the court may:

(a)   make such order as it thinks fit for giving relief in respect of the matters complained of;

(b)   adjourn the meeting conditionally or unconditionally; or

(c)   make an interim or any other order that it thinks fit[129].

In particular, such an order may:

(i)   regulate the management by the directors of the company's affairs, business and property during the remainder of the moratorium;

(ii)   require the directors to refrain from doing or continuing an act complained of by the petitioner or to do an act which the petitioner has complained that they have omitted to do;

(iii)   require the summoning of a meeting of creditors or members of the company for the purpose of considering such matters as the court may direct;

(iv)   bring the moratorium to an end and make such consequential provision as the court thinks fit[130].

In making such an order, the court is required to have regard to the need to safeguard the interests of persons who have dealt with the company in good faith and for value[131].

OFFENCES

12.44   In addition to the specific matters giving rise to offences already mentioned, Schedule A1 paragraphs 41 and 42 of IA 1986 create certain criminal offences in relation to moratoriums[132]. Thus, an officer of the company, which term includes a shadow director, commits an offence if, within the period of 12 months ending with the day on which the moratorium came into force or during the moratorium itself he does any of the following, namely:

(a)   concealing any part of the company's property to the value of £500[133] or more, or concealing any debt due to or from the company;

---

128   Schedule A1 paragraphs 40(7) and (8) of IA 1986 (as inserted by Schedule 17 paragraph 37(4) of the Enterprise Act 2002). Cf though that if the appointment of an administrator has effect in relation to a company, the company is ineligible for the moratorium procedure; see Schedule A1 paragraph 4(1)(a) of IA 1986.

129   Schedule A1 paragraph 40(4) of IA 1986.

130   Schedule A1 paragraph 40(5) of IA 1986.

131   Schedule A1 paragraph 40(6) of IA 1986.

132   Schedule A1 paragraph 41(5) of IA 1986.

133   The £500 minimum value may be increased or reduced by order of the Secretary of State; section 417A of IA 1986.

(b) fraudulently removing any part of the company's property to the value of £500[134] or more;

(c) concealing, destroying, mutilating or falsifying any book or paper affecting or relating the company's property or affairs;

(d) making any false entry in any book or paper affecting or relating to the company's property or affairs;

(e) fraudulently parting with, altering or making any omission in any document affecting or relating to the company's property or affairs; or

(f) pawning, pledging or disposing of any property of the company which has been obtained on credit and has not been paid for (unless the pawning, pledging or disposal was in the ordinary way of the company's business)[135].

An officer of the company, including a shadow director[136], also commits an offence if, within such 12-month period or during the moratorium itself, he is privy to the doing by others of any of the matters mentioned in sub-paragraphs (c), (d) or (e) above[137].

12.45 In respect of the matters mentioned in sub-paragraphs (a) and (f) in **PARAGRAPH 12.44** above, it is a defence for a person charged to prove that he had no intent to defraud[138]. In respect of the matters mentioned in sub-paragraphs (c) and (d), it is a defence for the person charged to prove that he had no intent to conceal the state of affairs of the company or to defeat the law[139].

12.46 Where such an offence is committed by pawning, pledging or disposing of property of the company which has been obtained on credit and has not been paid for, every person who takes in pawn or pledge, or otherwise receives the property also commits an offence if he knew it to be pawned, pledged or disposed of in circumstances which amount to an offence or would amount to an offence if a moratorium were obtained for the company within 12 months[140].

12.47 In addition, if for the purpose of obtaining a moratorium, or an extension of a moratorium, an officer of the company, including the shadow director[141], makes any false representation or fraudulently does, or omits to do anything, he also commits an offence[142]. Such an offence is committed even if no moratorium or extension is obtained[143].

FUNCTIONS OF THE FINANCIAL CONDUCT AUTHORITY AND PRUDENTIAL REGULATION AUTHORITY IN RELATION TO MORATORIUMS

12.48 Various specific rights are conferred on the Financial Conduct Authority and the Prudential Regulation Authority with regard to moratoriums in relation

---

134 The £500 minimum value may be increased or reduced by order of the Secretary of State; section 417A of IA 1986.
135 Schedule A1 paragraph 41(1), (2)(a), (3) and (4) of IA 1986.
136 Schedule A1 paragraph 41(5) of IA 1986.
137 Schedule A1 paragraph 44(1), (2)(b), (3) and (4) of IA 1986.
138 Schedule A1 paragraph 41(6)(a) of IA 1986.
139 Schedule A1 paragraph 41(6)(b) of IA 1986.
140 Schedule A1 paragraph 41(7) of IA 1986.
141 Schedule A1 paragraph 42(3) of IA 1986.
142 Schedule A1 paragraph 42(1) of IA 1986.
143 Schedule A1 paragraph 42(2) of IA 1986.

to a regulated company which is, or has been an authorised person within the meaning given by section 31 of FSMA 2000, or is, or has been, an appointed representative within the meaning given by section 39 of that Act, or is carrying on, or has carried on, a regulated activity, within the meaning given by section 22 of that Act, in contravention of the general prohibition contained in section 19 of that Act. In summary, by Schedule A1 paragraph 44 of IA 1986:

(a) any notice or document required to be sent to a creditor of a regulated company must also be sent to the appropriate regulator;

(b) the appropriate regulator is entitled to be heard on any application to the court for permission for the disposal of charged property of the company;

(c) the appropriate regulator may apply to the court to challenge any act, omission or decision of the nominee under Schedule A1 paragraph 26 of IA 1986;

(d) if any person other than the appropriate regulator applies to the court under Schedule A1 paragraph 26 of IA 1986, the regulator is entitled to be heard on that application;

(e) the appropriate regulator must be given notice of any qualifying decision procedure by which a decision of the company's creditors is sought for the purposes of Schedule A1 to IA 1986, and the appropriate regulator, or a person appointed by the appropriate regulator, may in the way provided by the rules participate in (but not vote in) any qualifying decision procedure by which a decision of the company's creditors is sought for the purposes of Schedule A1 to IA 1986[144];

(f) the appropriate regulator is entitled to be heard on any application to the court where a decision taken by the creditors differs from one taken at the company meeting;

(g) the appropriate regulator may challenge the acts or omissions of the directors of the company during moratorium under Schedule A1 paragraph 40 of IA 1986;

(h) if a person other than the appropriate regulator applies to the court to make such a challenge, the regulator is entitled to be heard on that application[145].

144 Schedule A1 paragraph 44(8) and (9) of IA 1986 (as amended and substituted by Schedule 9 paragraph 9(45) and (46) of SBEEA 2015).
145 Schedule A1 paragraph 44(15) and (16) of IA 1986.

13 Schemes of arrangement

INTRODUCTION

13.1 Part 26 of the Companies Act 2006 allows a compromise or arrangement to be proposed between a company and its creditors, or any class of them, or its members or any class of them[1]. The statute permits a scheme to be proposed not just by the company or its creditors or members, but also (where the company is in administration) by its administrator[2], and Schedule B1 of IA 1986 specifically contemplates that the promotion of a scheme is capable of being included amongst the administrator's proposals.[3] The concepts of compromise or arrangement are separate concepts and an arrangement need not involve a compromise or be confined to a case of dispute or difficulty.

13.2 The word 'arrangement' has a very broad meaning. A compromise implies some element of accommodation on each side, and an arrangement implies some element of give and take, but beyond that it is neither necessary nor desirable to attempt a definition of 'arrangement'[4]. The court can look at the totality of restructuring arrangements in determining whether a proposed scheme is an arrangement or compromise (rather than being confined to look only at the terms of the scheme document itself)[5]. Whatever the precise meaning of a compromise or arrangement, it must be proposed with creditors or members of a company. It is implicit that it must be made with them in their capacity as creditors or members and that it must at least concern their position as creditors or members of the company[6].

---

1 Section 895 of CA 2006. Part 26 of CA 2006 has a long history, going back to section 136 of the Companies Act 1862, section 2 of the Joint Stock Companies Arrangements Act 1870 and section 24 of the Companies Act 1900 (all which restricted compromises or arrangements to a company in winding up), and afterwards section 38 of the Companies Act 1907, section 120 of the Companies (Consolidation) Act 1908, section 153 of the Companies Act 1929, section 206 of the Companies Act 1948 and then section 425 of the Companies Act 1985 (all of which allowed a company to make a compromise or arrangement with members or creditors or any class, and jettisoned the original requirement that a company had to be in winding up).

2 Section 896(2)(d) of CA 2006.

3 Schedule B1 paragraph 49(3)(b) of IA 1986.

4 *Re T&N Ltd (No 4)* [2006] EWHC 1447 (Ch) (paragraphs 43–47) (cf *Re Lehman Brothers International (Europe) (in administration) (No 2)* [2009] EWCA Civ 1161 (paragraphs 62 ff where the Court of Appeal cited *T&N* with approval). See also *Mercantile Investment and General Trust Co v International Co of Mexico* [1893] 1 Ch 484n and *Mercantile Investment and General Trust Co v River Plate Trust, Loan and Agency Co* [1894] 1 Ch 578, and *Sneath v Valley Gold Ltd* [1893] 1 Ch 477 at 491n.

5 *Re Bluebrook Ltd* [2009] EWHC 2114 (Ch) (paragraphs 72–75). See also *Re Uniq plc* [2011] EWHC 749 (Ch) (paragraphs 24–25).

6 *Re T&N Ltd (No 4)* [2006] EWHC 1447 (Ch) (paragraph 45).

13.3   A scheme of arrangement which does no more than expropriate the interest of a member or creditor would not be a compromise or arrangement. However, it is not a necessary element of an arrangement that it should alter the rights existing between the company and the creditors or members with whom it is made. No doubt in most cases it will alter those rights. But, provided that the context and content of the scheme are such as properly to constitute an arrangement between the company and the members of creditors concerned, then it will fall within Part 26. An arrangement between a company and its members or creditors may alter the rights of the members or creditors as against a third party, provided the alteration is necessary or essential to the arrangement or compromise[7]. A scheme of arrangement under Part 26 may compromise or arrange the rights of secured creditors (whether debenture holder or otherwise) of a company[8] or a preferential creditor (subject to class issues), whereas a company voluntary arrangement under Part 1 of the Insolvency Act 1986 may not affect the right of a secured creditor to enforce his security except with the concurrence of the creditor concerned[9] and a CVA cannot be approved unless the preferential creditor rights are preserved[10]. A scheme of arrangement cannot be used to arrange or compromise assets held on trust by a company[11].

13.4   If a scheme of arrangement is proposed under Part 26 of CA 2006 between a company and its creditors, it is not necessary to hold a meeting of members for the arrangement or compromise to take effect, whereas with a CVA a members' meeting is required[12]. A single CVA can compromise creditors' rights in a differing way by way of the compromise, provided the compromise is not unfairly prejudicial[13], whereas in a scheme of arrangement creditors with sufficiently differing rights must be classed in separate meetings for the vote at the creditors' meetings (see further below), so that those with sufficiently similar rights vote together to amend or vary such rights.

13.5   A scheme of arrangement can be proposed and approved even where it overrides contractual provisions for amendment by unanimity or majority, as the whole purpose of Part 26 of CA 2006 is to be able to require all lenders or members to be bound by a scheme of arrangement which would not otherwise be possible[14]. If passed by the appropriate majorities and in accordance with the statutory procedures, a scheme of arrangement is binding upon all creditors or members (or a particular class of them), whether or not they voted at the meetings convened to consider the scheme[15].

---

7   See *Re T&N Ltd (No 4)* [2006] EWHC 1447 (Ch) (paragraphs 50–55). And see *Re Lehman Brothers International (Europe) (in administration) (No 2)* [2009] EWCA Civ 1161 (paragraphs 62–65).

8   *Re Alabama, New Orleans, Texas and Pacific Junction Railway Company* [1891] 1 Ch 213, CA.

9   Section 4(3) of IA 1986.

10   Section 4(4) of IA 1986.

11   *Re Lehman Brothers International (Europe) (in administration) (No 2)* [2009] EWCA Civ 1161.

12   Section 2(2) of IA 1986.

13   Section 6(1)(a) of IA 1986, and see *Sisu Capital Fund Ltd v Tucker* [2005] EWHC 2170 (Ch); [2005] EWHC 2321 (Ch).

14   *Re NEF Telecom Company BV* [2012] EWHC 2944 (Comm).

15   Section 899(3) of CA 2006. Also, there is no requirement stated in section 899 that creditors or members of the relevant class will only be bound if they received notice of the meeting, albeit the court at the convening stage and at the sanction stage will be alert to ensure that proper notice is given to those affected by the proposed scheme. For a discussion on appropriate notifications and consideration by the court of purported criticisms (in the event

13.6   The definition of 'company' within section 895(2) of CA 2006 provides that 'company' means any company liable to be wound up under IA 1986, and thus includes unregistered companies and foreign companies[16]. This definition of 'company' is different to the definition of a 'company' as provided in Schedule B1 paragraph 111(1A). The latter confines the jurisdiction as to when an administration order may be granted, or an administrator appointed, to:

- a company registered under CA 2006 in England and Wales;

- a company incorporated in an EEA State other than the United Kingdom;

- a company not incorporated in an EEA State but having its centre of main interests in a member state other than Denmark.

13.7   Before proposing a scheme of arrangement, the administrator will wish to clarify to what extent the scheme compromise will be effective abroad, in so far as there are foreign assets or foreign creditors outside England and Wales. Where a scheme compromise is effected within an administration, then formal recognition is provided for the compromise within European Union states (other than Denmark) by the terms of Article 25(1) of the EC Insolvency Regulation without further formality[17]. The effectiveness otherwise of the compromise outside England and Wales will depend on whether the contractual rights compromised are governed by English law, whether the relevant creditors concerned are subject to the powers of the English court, and/or whether the relevant local courts where the assets or the creditors are located would recognise the compromise (which will necessitate local law advice)[18].

THE THREE STAGES

13.8   The process by which a scheme of arrangement comes into effect involves three stages. First, there must be an application to the court under section 896(1) of CA 2006 for an order that a meeting or meetings of the class or classes of creditor be summoned in such manner as the court directs (and it ought to be at this first stage that the proper constitution of classes is determined). This is known as the scheme directions hearing or the convening hearing.

13.9   At the second stage (after circulation of the explanatory statement, the proposed scheme terms and other notification documents), the proposed scheme terms are put to the meeting or meetings held in accordance with the order which is made, and they must be approved by the requisite majority in number and value of those present and voting in person or by proxy.

rejected) of notifications given, see *Re British Aviation Insurance Co* [2005] EWHC 1621 (Ch) (paragraphs 77–79 (re notification of the convening hearing) and 98 (whether notice of the creditors meetings properly given)).

16   The prohibitions which prevent the English court making administration orders or winding up orders in respect of an EEA insurer or an EEA credit institution do not prevent the proposal of a scheme of arrangement, save that appropriate notifications to certain persons are required: see regulations 4 and 5 of the Insurers Regulations and regulations 3 and 4 of the Credit Institutions Regulations. See also **CHAPTER 22.**

17   Article 25(1) of Council Regulation (EC) No 1346/2000; and see Article 32(1) of Council Regulation (EU) 2015/848.

18   See *Re Sompo Japan Insurance Inc* [2007] EWHC 146 (Ch) (paragraphs 17–26) and *Re Magyar Telecom BV* [2013] EWHC 3800 (Ch) (paragraph 16).

13.10   If approved by the required majorities, then at the third stage, a further application is made to the court under section 899 of CA 2006 to obtain the court's sanction to the compromise or arrangement (known as the sanction hearing).

13.11   If the court sanctions the compromise or arrangement, the compromise or arrangement then becomes binding on the company and all its creditors (or all those creditors within the relevant class or classes of creditors with which the compromise or arrangement is made) pursuant to section 899(3) of CA 2006, and pursuant to section 899(4) of CA 2006 it becomes effective when a sealed copy of the order sanctioning the scheme is delivered to the registrar of companies.

FIRST STAGE: THE PRACTICE STATEMENT LETTER AND THE CONVENING HEARING

13.12   Pursuant to section 896(1) of CA 2006, where any compromise or arrangement is proposed between a company and its creditors, or any class of them, the court may order a meeting of the creditors or class of creditors (as the case may be) to be summoned in such manner as the court directs. As mentioned above, under section 896(2)(c) of CA 2006, an administrator may make an application for the proposal of a scheme[19]. The application is made by a Part 8 claim form supported by evidence[20]. The claim form must comply with CPR Rule 8.2, and the administrator must file any written evidence on which he intends to rely when he files the claim form[21]. At the first stage the court determines class issues, and any other determinative jurisdictional questions if they can be resolved at this stage.

13.13   Every person who has any pecuniary claim against the company, whether actual or contingent, can be a creditor for the purposes of section 895 of CA 2006[22]. Option holders may be considered to be creditors[23], as are life assurance policyholders[24]. 'Creditors' for the purpose of Part 26 of CA 2006 are not restricted to creditors with provable debts in bankruptcy or liquidation[25].

13.14   Prior to the convening hearing, unless there are good reasons for not doing so, the applicant should take all steps reasonably open to it, by the issue of a Practice Statement letter, to notify any person affected by the scheme that it is being promoted, the purpose which the scheme is designed to achieve, the meetings of creditors which the applicant considers will be required and their composition. It is the responsibility of the applicant to determine whether more than one meeting of creditors is required by a scheme and if so to ensure

---

19   An administrator may include in his proposals to creditors pursuant to Schedule B1 paragraph 49 of IA 1986 a proposal for a compromise or arrangement to be sanctioned under Part 26 of CA 2006: Schedule B1 paragraph 49(3)(b) of IA 1986.

20   See paragraphs 5 and 15 of CPR Practice Direction 49A Applications under the Companies Act and Related Legislation.

21   CPR Rule 8.5(1).

22   See Knox J in *Re Cancol Ltd* [1996] 1 All ER 37 at 45; *Re Midland Coal, Coke and Iron Co* [1895] 1 Ch 267.

23   *Re Compania de Electricidad de la Provincia de Buenos Aires Ltd* [1980] Ch 146.

24   *Re Equitable Life Assurance Society* [2002] EWHC 140 (Ch).

25   *Re T&N Ltd (No 4)* [2006] EWHC 1447 (Ch) (paragraph 70).

that those meetings are properly constituted by a class of creditor so that each meeting consists of creditors whose rights against the company are not so dissimilar as to make it impossible for them to consult together with a view to their common interest[26]. Where a creditor issue is drawn to the attention of the court it will also consider whether to give directions for the resolution of that issue including if necessary directions for the postponement of meetings of creditors until that resolution has been achieved. If the administrator wishes the court at the convening hearing to determine other jurisdictional issues, then proper notice of these issues must be given to the scheme creditors within the Practice Statement letter[27].

13.15 Creditors are expected to raise objections, if any, at the convening hearing (rather than at the sanction hearing, where if they appear to object they will have to explain why they did not raise a creditor issue at the earlier stage). The purpose of this practice is to avoid, if possible, the waste of costs and court time as illustrated in *Re Hawk Insurance Co Ltd*[28]. However, the court's function at the convening hearing is still relatively limited. In *Re Telewest Communications plc (No 1); Re Telewest Finance (Jersey) Ltd (No 1)*[29] David Richards J said:

> 'it is important to keep in mind the function of the court at this stage. This is an application by the companies for leave to convene meetings to consider the schemes. It is emphatically not a hearing to consider the merits and fairness of the schemes. Those aspects are among the principal matters for decision at the later hearing to sanction the schemes, if they are approved by the statutory majorities of creditors. The matters for consideration at this stage concern the jurisdiction of the court to sanction the scheme if it proceeds. There is no point in the court convening meetings to consider the scheme if it can be seen now that it will lack the jurisdiction to sanction it later. This is principally a matter of the composition of classes. Under s 425, the court will have no jurisdiction to sanction the scheme if the classes have been incorrectly constituted.'

13.16 As to jurisdiction, section 895(2) of CA 2006 provides that 'In this Part .... "company" ... means any company liable to be wound up under the Insolvency Act 1986'. Under section 117(1) of IA 1986 'The High Court has jurisdiction to wind up any company registered in England and Wales'. Section 220 of IA 1986 allows for the winding up of unregistered companies (such as foreign companies) and subsection (1) provides:

> 'For the purposes of this Part, "unregistered company" includes any association and any company, with the exception of a company registered under the Companies Act 2006 in any part of the United Kingdom.'[30]

Since in the case of a scheme being proposed by an administrator, the provisions of Schedule B1 section 111(1A) will have been satisfied, this will mean that the court is likely to be satisfied in any event that the company is a company liable to be wound up under IA 1986 (section 895(2)(b) of CA 2006), and that

26 Practice Statement (Companies: Schemes of Arrangement) [2002] 1 WLR 1345.
27 *Re Van Gansewinkel Groep BV* [2015] EWHC 2151 (Ch) (paragraphs 32 and 56).
28 [2001] EWCA Civ 241; Practice Statement (Companies: Schemes of Arrangement) [2002] 1 WLR 1345.
29 [2004] EWHC 924 (paragraph 14).
30 The interpretation sections for the First Group of Parts for IA 1986 are at sections 247–251 and add nothing to section 220 as regards unregistered companies.

the court will be satisfied that the company has a sufficient connection with the jurisdiction for a scheme of arrangement to be proposed[31].

13.17 Where the company is not in administration and even if the centre of main interests is outside England and Wales, and even if it is a foreign company, the English court could still exercise jurisdiction in respect of a proposed scheme, provided there is a sufficient connection with the jurisdiction, because:

1   The three conditions[32] for winding up foreign unregistered companies go to the discretion of the court, and not to jurisdiction. Accordingly, such conditions do not have to be satisfied before the court will exercise its jurisdiction to sanction a scheme, although as a matter of discretion the court will not do so unless a sufficient connection to the jurisdiction is established[33].

2   Where the obligations or covenants to be arranged or compromised are governed by a single facility agreement which is governed by English law and which contains an English law jurisdiction clause, this gives rise to a sufficient connection to the jurisdiction[34]. This includes cases where the governing law has been validly changed to English law pursuant to the contractual variation provisions contained in the relevant indenture or governing contractual deed[35]. Also, in an appropriate case, the establishment of a new co-obligor may provide a sufficient connection[36].

3   The EC Insolvency Regulation does not apply to schemes of arrangement (proposed outside an insolvency process), nor does the Judgments Regulation[37] limit the original jurisdiction of the English court[38].

At the scheme directions hearing, the court also considers the proposed class of creditors for any meeting, as required by Practice Statement (Companies: Schemes of Arrangement)[39], and pursuant to section 896(1) of CA 2006 the

---

31   *Re Drax Holdings Ltd* [2003] EWHC 2743 (Ch).
32   Ie that (1) there must be a sufficient connection with England which may, but does not necessarily have to, consist of assets within the jurisdiction; (2) there must be a reasonable possibility, if a winding up order is made, of benefit to those applying for the winding up order; and (3) one or more persons interested in the distribution of assets of the company must be persons over whom the court can exercise jurisdiction.
33   *Re Drax Holdings Ltd* [2003] EWHC 2743 (Ch) (paragraphs 22–27, and see also paragraphs 30–34). See also *Re Rodenstock GmbH* [2011] EWHC 1104 (Ch) (paragraphs 20–31, 54–56, 63 and 64–68) and *Re Primacom Holding GmbH* [2011] EWHC 3746 and [2012] EWHC 164 (Ch).
34   *Re Rodenstock GmbH* [2011] EWHC 1104 (Ch) (paragraph 68); *Re Primacom Holding GmbH* [2011] EWHC 3746 (paragraphs 18 and 61–64).
35   See *Re Apcoa Parking (UK) Ltd* [2014] EWHC 1867 (Ch) (change of governing law from German law to English law); *Re DTEK Finance BV* [2015] EWHC 1164 (Ch) (change of governing law from New York law to English law); *Re TORM A/S* [2015] EWHC 1749 (Ch) (change of governing law from Danish law to English law); *Re Yuksel Insaat AS* (9 Nov 2015, unreported, Barling J) (change of governing law from New York law to English law). See also Article 3 of Regulation (EC) No 593/2008 of the European Parliament and of the Council of 17 June 2008 on the law applicable to contractual obligations (Rome I) (OJ L177, 04/07/2008, 6–16).
36   *Re A I Scheme Ltd* [2015] EWHC 1233 (Ch) and [2015] EWHC 2038 (Ch); *Re Codere Finance (UK) Ltd* [2015] EWHC 3778 (Ch).
37   Council Regulation (EC) No 44/2001.
38   *Re Rodenstock GmbH* [2011] EWHC 1104 (Ch) (paragraphs 54, 61 and 63); *Re Primacom GmbH* [2011] EWHC 3746 (Ch) (paragraph 61).
39   [2002] 1 WLR 1345.

court is required to provide the method and manner in which the meeting is to be summoned and held.

13.18   The test for what constitutes a class of creditors was examined in detail by Chadwick LJ in *Re Hawk Insurance Co Ltd*. He confirmed the long-standing principle that 'a class "must be confined to those persons whose rights are not so dissimilar as to make it impossible for them to consult together with a view to their common interest"'[40].

13.19   The constitution of classes is a fact-specific exercise. In each case the answer to the question of the appropriate class or classes will depend upon analysis (i) of the rights which are to be released or varied under the scheme, and (ii) of the new rights (if any) which the scheme gives, by way of compromise or arrangement, to those whose rights are to be released or varied. It is in the light of that analysis that the test formulated by Bowen LJ in *Sovereign Life Assurance Co v Dodd*[41] in order to determine which creditors fall into a separate class (that is to say a class must be confined to those persons whose rights are not so dissimilar as to make it impossible for them to consult together with a view to their common interest) has to be applied[42]. As regards class constitution, a broad approach is to be taken, and the differences may be material, certainly more than *de minimis*, without leading to separate classes[43].

13.20   In *Re UDL Holdings Ltd*[44] Lord Millett summarised the relevant principles to be applied:

'(2) Persons whose rights are so dissimilar that they cannot sensibly consult together with a view to their common interest must be given separate meetings. Persons whose rights are sufficiently similar that they can consult together with a view to their common interest should be summoned to a single meeting.

(3) The test is based on similarity or dissimilarity of legal rights against the company, not on similarity or dissimilarity of interests not derived from such legal rights. The fact that individuals may hold divergent views based on their private interests not derived from their legal rights against the company is not a ground for calling separate meetings.

(4) The question is whether the rights which are to be released or varied under the scheme or the new rights which the scheme gives in their place are so different that the scheme must be treated as a compromise or arrangement with more than one class.'

---

40   [2001] EWCA Civ 241 (paragraph 30).
41   [1892] 2 QB 573.
42   *Re Hawk Insurance Co Ltd* [2001] EWCA Civ 241 (paragraph 30).
43   *Re Telewest Communications plc (No 1)* [2004] EWHC 924 (Ch) (paragraph 37); see also *Re Primacom Holding GmbH* [2011] EWHC 3746 (paragraphs 52–53 (interest rate differentials between a maximum of 4.25% and a minimum of 2.25% among creditors held not to fragment the class proposed) and 56–57 (a consent fee accepted by only some of the creditors in a class of 0.75% was *de minimis* and thus did not fragment the class)); see also *Re DX Holdings Ltd* [2010] EWHC 1513 (Ch) (where a 0.5% and a further 2% consent fee was proposed and was held *de minimis* and not such as to fragment the class proposed). Similar reasoning was applied in *Re Global Garden Products SpA* [2016] EWHC 1884 (Ch) as regards a work fee. Provided the proposed fee is disclosed to all creditors in the explanatory statement, is offered to all relevant creditors and is not so large as to influence a vote in a particular manner, then there is nothing in principle objectionable about such fees: *Re PrivatBank* [2015] EWHC 3299; *Re Global Garden Products SpA* [2016] EWHC 1884 (Ch).
44   [2002] 1 HKC 172 (paragraph 27).

13.21   Chadwick LJ in *Re Hawk* set out the analysis to apply as regards class rights[45]:

'When applying Bowen LJ's test to the question "are the rights of those who are to be affected by the scheme proposed such that the scheme can be seen as a single arrangement; or ought it to be regarded, on a true analysis, as a number of linked arrangements" it is necessary to ensure not only that those whose rights really are so dissimilar that they cannot consult together with a view to a common interest should be treated as parties to distinct arrangements – so that they should have their own separate meetings – but also that those whose rights are sufficiently similar to the rights of others that they can properly consult together should be required to do so; lest by ordering separate meetings the court gives a veto to a minority group. The safeguard against majority oppression is that the court is not bound by the decision of the meeting. It is important Bowen LJ's test should not be applied in such a way that it becomes an instrument of oppression by a minority.'

13.22   The focus on rights (rather than interests) enables the court 'to take a far more robust view as to what the classes should be and to determine a far less fragmented structure than if interests were taken into account'[46]. Nevertheless, there remains some uncertainty where, although there is a difference in interest as opposed to strict legal rights, the difference in interest derives from those rights[47]. Furthermore, the court will have regard and consider the overall restructuring as a whole in determining the proper composition of class, and the applicant has a duty of utmost candour with the court to disclose all matters relevant to both class composition and the application in respect of the proposed scheme[48].

13.23   If there are questions of doubt, it is appropriate to allow the creditors to meet to consult together and to review the position at the sanction hearing[49]. However, if a review at the sanction stage, where permitted by the court, results in a decision that the class constitutions were wrongly determined, sanction will become unavailable as a matter of jurisdiction[50].

13.24   In determining appropriate class constitution, the court will need to identify the appropriate comparator[51]. Where a scheme is proposed in the context of a formal insolvency process, as is likely to be the case where an administrator has been appointed, the existing rights to which the court will have regard are

---

45   [2001] EWCA Civ 241 (paragraph 33).
46   *Re Primacom Holding GmbH* [2011] EWHC 3746 (Ch) (paragraph 45).
47   *Re UDL Holdings Ltd* [2002] 1 HKC 172 (paragraph 27 at subparagraph (3)) and *Re Apcoa Parking Holdings GMBH* [2014] EWHC 3849 (Ch) (paragraphs 46–55).
48   In *Re Uniq plc* [2011] EWHC 749 (Ch) and in *Re Stemcor Trade Finance Ltd* [2015] EWHC 2662 (Ch), the court considered the overall restructuring as a whole in reaching its decision about the appropriate classes for meetings purposes. In *Re Global Garden Products SpA* [2016] EWHC 1884 (Ch), Snowden J requested applicants to provide the court with a table setting out the rights and interests granted by the proposed scheme to each creditor, so that the court could consider the overall impact of the proposed re-structuring pursuant to the scheme. In *Re Indah Kiat International Finance Company BV* [2016] EWHC 246 (Ch), Snowden J pointed out (paragraph 40) that 'the scheme jurisdiction can only work properly and command respect internationally if parties invoking the jurisdiction exhibit the utmost candour with the court.'
49   See *Re NRG Victory Reinsurance Ltd* [2006] EWHC 679 (Ch) (paragraph 15).
50   See *Re British Aviation Insurance Co Ltd* [2005] EWHC 1621.
51   *Re British Aviation Insurance Co Ltd* [2005] EWHC 1621 (Ch) (paragraph 88).

those to which the creditors will be entitled in that process[52]. In contrast, if the appropriate comparator is ongoing solvent trading, then creditors' rights must be assessed in that scenario[53].

13.25 The administrator is free to select the creditors to whom a scheme should be put, provided that the rights of the creditors and the effect of the scheme on those rights are not so dissimilar as to make it impossible for those creditors to consult together with a view to acting in their common interest. In *Sea Assets Ltd v Garuda*[54] the court decided that this was a sufficient meaning for the phrase a 'class of creditors' within section 895(1)(a) of CA 2006, and it was permissible for a company to select only some of the members of a particular class for inclusion in the arrangement if there were good commercial reasons for taking that course. However, the company concerned should not be encouraged to make an arbitrary selection of a particular body of creditors[55]. Thus it may, for example, enter into a scheme with its financial creditors, but leave trade creditors unaffected by the scheme. On the same principle, a company is entitled to exclude from a scheme creditors or liabilities which would otherwise be within the ambit of the scheme, provided that the exclusion is not arbitrary but is bona fide and for appropriate commercial or other reasons. Such exclusions have been approved by the court in two insurance company cases[56].

13.26 The proposer of the scheme of arrangement will be required to put before the court at the convening hearing a draft copy of the proposed scheme of arrangement, as proposed to be circulated to creditors, and a draft copy of the proposed explanatory statement pursuant to section 896 of CA 2006 as proposed to be circulated to creditors. This is so the court can see the terms of the proposed compromise to allow it to make class determinations by analysis of what scheme creditors receive pursuant to the terms of the proposed scheme.

13.27 Section 897(1) of CA 2006 provides that where a meeting is summoned under section 896 every notice summoning the meeting that is sent to a creditor must be accompanied by a statement complying with section 897 and every notice summoning the meeting given by advertisement must either include such a statement or state where and how creditors entitled to attend the meeting may obtain copies of such statement. By section 897(2), the explanatory statement must explain the effect of the compromise or arrangement, and in particular state any material interests of the directors of the company (whether as directors or as members or as creditors of the company or otherwise) and the effect on those interests of the compromise or arrangement in so far as it is different from the effect on the like interests of other persons. By section 897(3), where the compromise or arrangement affects the rights of debenture holders of the company, the statement must give the like explanation as respects

---

52   *Re Hawk Insurance Co Ltd* [2001] EWCA Civ 241 (paragraph 42). *Re Telewest Communications plc (No 1)* [2004] EWHC 924 (Ch) (paragraph 29), *Re British Aviation Insurance Company Ltd* [2005] EWHC 1621 (Ch) (paragraphs 61 and 62) and *Re Cortefiel SA* [2012] EWHC 2998 (Ch) (paragraphs 6–13).
53   See *Re British Aviation Insurance Co Ltd* [2005] EWHC 1621 (Ch) (paragraphs 88–97).
54   [2001] EWCA Civ 1696 (paragraphs 23 and 51).
55   See also *Re SAB Miller plc* [2016] EWHC 2153.
56   *Tower Insurance Ltd (known as the Dunedin Pool)* (2002) and *Seven Provinces Insurance Co Ltd* (2002) (both unreported). See also *Marconi Corpn plc v Marconi plc* [2003] EWHC 663 (Ch) (paragraph 20), Lindsay J, at the convening stage: the scheme was subsequently sanctioned.

the trustees of any deed for securing the issue of the debentures as it is required to give as respects the company's directors. In an administration, it is unlikely that a scheme of arrangement proposed with creditors would affect directors interests, but the point should nevertheless be clarified in accordance with section 897(2)(b).

13.28 The extent of the information required to be disclosed in the explanatory statement will depend upon the nature of the scheme and the circumstances of the case. In *Re Heron International NV*[57], Sir Donald Nicholls V-C stated that the explanation of the effect of the scheme requires that if a person called to vote on it is to be able to exercise a reasoned judgment on whether the scheme is in his interests or not, there must be an explanation of how the scheme will affect him commercially.

13.29 Another guiding principle is that, in addition to explaining the terms and meaning of the scheme, scheme creditors should be given all information which could reasonably be regarded as material in deciding whether or not to vote in favour of the scheme. In *Heron*, although the information provided to creditors was considered to be inadequate, the scheme was still sanctioned because, when further information was provided, it was considered that any creditor who had consented to the scheme would not have changed his mind had he been in possession of that further information from the start. It is clearly unwise to rely on this sort of outcome and safer to provide as much information as possible in the statement.

13.30 In another case[58], although the scheme itself was considered by the court to be fair and reasonable, the court directed that further meetings of the creditors concerned be convened, on the grounds that the circular was insufficient, misleading in certain respects, and omitted relevant information[59].

13.31 If at the convening hearing the court is satisfied that convening relief should be granted, it will ordinarily give directions for the class or classes of meetings to be convened[60]. There is jurisdiction to order a separate class meeting even if only one person is capable of falling within the class[61]. The court will give directions as to the date of the meeting and the place of the meeting, and will appoint the proposed chairman of the meeting, and it will give directions for the calling of the meeting and the circulation of the notice calling the meeting, the explanatory statement, the scheme and voting and proxy forms[62] and any other consequential directions. The chairman of the meeting will be directed to report the result of the meeting to the court (to be considered at the third stage, the sanction hearing). If it is proposed to have a number of schemes applying identically to companies within a group where, pursuant to the relevant financing

---

57 [1994] 1 BCLC 667. Criticisms of the explanatory statement made in *Re British Aviation Insurance Co* [2005] EWHC 1621 (Ch) were dismissed by the court as unfounded criticisms (see paragraphs 99–101).

58 *Re Dorman, Long & Co Ltd* [1934] Ch 635; *South Durham Steel and Iron Co Ltd* [1933] All ER Rep 460.

59 See also *Re Primacom Holding GmbH* [2011] EWHC 3746 (Ch) (paragraph 35) where Hildyard J commented that modifications to a proposal would not be supported by a court if the modification had the effect of falsifying the explanatory statement or making it irrelevant.

60 The meeting may be held abroad if that is most convenient in the circumstances: *Re RMCA Reinsurance Ltd* [1994] BCC 378.

61 *Re RMCA Reinsurance Ltd* [1994] BCC 378; *Re Altitude Scaffolding Ltd* [2006] EWHC 1401.

62 Whether by postal notice and, if appropriate, advertisement, or as is more often the case nowadays notification by website and email.

agreements (and borrowing covenants and cross guarantee clauses), all creditors of each of the relevant companies have claims identical in value against each of the proposed scheme companies, then a composite single meeting is permissible. However, as regards the poll to be taken, the chairman will be required to take separate polls for each of the notional meetings between each company and its respective creditors, so as to allow for a sufficient degree of separation to comply with the CA 2006 provisions, while also providing a convenient method of convening creditors[63].

SECOND STAGE: THE MEETING

13.32 The purpose of the second stage is to ensure that the proposals are acceptable to the requisite statutory majority. At this stage the meeting or meetings are held as directed by the court[64]. The requisite majority is a majority in number[65], representing three-fourths in value, of those who, being entitled to do so, take the opportunity of being present, in person (or, if a company, by representative) or by proxy, at the meeting or meetings and vote[66]. Where the creditors fall into more than one class, it must be approved by the same majority (ie a majority in number, representing three-fourths in value, of those who take the opportunity of being present, in person (or, if a company, by representative) or by proxy, and vote) at the meeting of each class.

13.33 Those responsible for convening the meeting should ensure that a suitable venue is chosen. The venue must be large enough to accommodate all those who are likely to attend, but without incurring the unnecessary additional cost of hiring a venue which proves to be out of proportion to those who actually attend. If, as events develop, the chosen venue seems likely to prove to be too small for all those who are expected to attend to be accommodated in one room, it may be possible, with suitable audio-visual links, to make arrangements for the use of more than one hall on the same premises, provided that all those who are present in each of the halls can hear, and preferably also see, what is happening in the other hall. If that fails, there will be no alternative but to adjourn the meeting, in which case it would almost certainly be necessary to incur the expense of giving notice of a revised date and venue to all those to whom notice of the original meeting was given (and possibly also to advertise the adjourned meeting)[67]. This could be substantially more expensive than arranging for a sufficiently large venue in the first place. Within reason, it is clearly safer to err on the side of caution and hire a venue large enough for all foreseeable requirements.

13.34 The notice of the meeting, and the accompanying documents, will give particulars of how and where proxy (and, where necessary, voting) forms should be submitted. Voting will always be by means of a poll[68]. Since the requisite

---

63   *Re Hills Motorway Ltd* [2002] NSWSC 897 (paragraphs 20–23).

64   Section 896(1) of CA 2006.

65   It is not permissible to manipulate creditor holdings to achieve or block the majority requirement: *Re PCCW Ltd* [2009] 3 HKC 292, *Re Dee Valley Group plc* [2017] EWHC 184 (Ch).

66   Section 899(1) of CA 2006.

67   *Byng v London Life Association Ltd* [1989] 1 All ER 560.

68   Section 899(1) of CA 2006, which requires a calculation of those voting by number and by value. See also *Re Hills Motorway Ltd* [2002] NSWSC 897 (where composite meetings were allowed, but separate polls for each meeting were required to calculate properly the votes).

majority includes a majority by reference to value as well as number, a show of hands will never be sufficient. For this reason, voting forms[69] are usually sent out with the notice of the meeting(s), the proxy forms and the other scheme documents. The voting form will require creditors wishing to vote to provide sufficient information, supported where appropriate by relevant documentation, to enable the chairman of the meeting and his staff to verify claims against the company's records[70]. Creditors who wish to vote will usually be required to return the voting forms, duly completed, whether or not they wish to appoint a proxy. The voting form particulars are usually incorporated in the same document as the proxy form. The appointment of a proxy will not prevent the creditor from attending and voting in person.

13.35   Since in many cases it is not so straightforward a task to ascertain and to verify who are creditors, and for what amounts, as it is to verify who are shareholders and how many shares they hold (where all that is required is to compare the proxy forms and, where members vote in person, the poll cards with the share register), it is usual for the terms of the convening order of the court to require that voting forms, with or without completed proxy forms, with appropriate details of the indebtedness claimed, be submitted in advance of the meeting in order for creditors to vote (although proxy and voting forms submitted at or before the vote is taken will usually be accepted)[71]. It will in any event usually be necessary to verify the amounts for which those claiming to be creditors seek to vote, and if the proxy and voting forms are not submitted sufficiently in advance of the meeting, this may delay the process of verifying claims after the vote is taken. Since the majority in percentage terms is assessed by reference not only to the number of those voting, but also to the value, it is important[72] that creditors vote for the correct amounts, as this will affect not only the value of the individual votes but also the total value of the votes cast and hence the relevant percentages[73].

13.36   Where claims against the company have not been agreed, it is usual to permit creditors to vote for the amounts for which they estimate that the company is liable to them, provided such amounts appear reasonable. If there is an obvious error (for example, if a creditor of an insurance company has claimed for 100 per cent of his loss whereas under the policy the company is only liable for a percentage of the risk, or if the conversion from one currency to another results in what is obviously the wrong amount, either because the wrong rate

---

69   What is known as a voting form is not the form used for the actual vote. As the vote will have to be by poll, poll cards are used for the voting at the meeting. The voting form is the form which creditors are required to use in order to give particulars of their estimates of the value of their debts, ie the amounts for which they will be entitled to vote.

70   Voting forms will almost always be required in the case of insurance companies, particularly non-life companies.

71   Cf *Re Philip Alexander Securities & Futures Ltd* [1999] 1 BCLC 124 (where the court held that proxies which had been lodged before the vote at a creditors meeting for a company in administration were valid (Neuberger J)).

72   This is perhaps less significant if the vote is obviously overwhelmingly in favour, or it is clear that on any basis a sufficient majority has not been attained, but if the amounts are not rigorously checked this should be reported to the court at the sanction stage.

73   If an insolvency is the appropriate comparator, and a creditor seeks to vote pursuant to its rights under a guarantee given by the relevant scheme company, then ordinarily the chairman would admit the creditor's right to vote at full value on the assumption that in an insolvency the guarantee claim would be provable at full value: *Re Kaupthing Singer & Friedlander Ltd* [2011] UKSC 48 (paragraph 11) (double dips permissible).

has been used or because it has been incorrectly calculated) the chairman of the meeting will correct the figure and admit it for the corrected amount. If he believes that a claim is totally groundless, he may reject a claim altogether. If he believes that the amount claimed is excessive, he may reduce it to what he believes to be a reasonable estimate. In any such case the creditor would be informed and, if the figure for which the claim is admitted for voting purposes will be material in deciding whether or not the statutory majority has or has not been obtained, the creditor would have the right to object, at the hearing for sanction, to the amount for which his claim is admitted by the chairman of the meeting for voting purposes. The chairman of the meeting is not expected to be an adjudicator of disputed claims and if there is real doubt as to whether the person claiming to be a creditor is a creditor, or as to the amount for which he claims the company is liable to him, which cannot be resolved by agreement with the creditor, the chairman of the meeting should admit the vote but mark it as objected to, so that if it becomes necessary, the court may adjudicate upon the issue[74]. Acceptance of the estimate at this stage is invariably for voting purposes only, and does not bind either the company or the creditor when it comes to admission of claims for the purpose of paying dividends to creditors.

13.37 Where more than one class meeting is held, it is often convenient for all the meetings to be held simultaneously[75]. So far as the informal part of the meetings is concerned (ie the chairman's introduction explaining the purpose of the meeting and the procedures to be adopted for voting, and answering any questions from the floor), this poses no problem. When it comes to the formal part of the meetings, ie the actual voting, persons who are not members of the class concerned may be permitted to be present at the meeting provided those who are members of the relevant class consent, but at each meeting only those eligible to vote at the particular meeting may actually vote[76].

13.38 A slightly different procedure, having effectively the same result, was approved in *Re Equitable Life Assurance Society*[77]. This involved all the discussions being held in the context of the first meeting. The first meeting is then adjourned without the poll having been taken and the second meeting is formally opened. The second meeting would not proceed to anything other than formal business, because all the discussion will have taken place, but the first meeting will have been adjourned, for the purpose of taking the poll, to the end of the second meeting. Thus, after a short period to explain to those present the precise procedure, the poll is taken and the votes are then counted separately. Both these procedures depend upon none of those whose meeting it is having any objection to the presence of others at their meeting[78].

13.39 The chairman's powers for conducting the meeting are ordinarily spelled out in the convening order. To ensure the vote of the creditors is not impugned at the sanction stage, the chairman ought to conduct the meeting in accordance with the procedure laid down by the court at the convening hearing. The chairman's decision at the meeting could also be impeached if the chairman did not act honestly, or if he acted perversely by reaching a decision which no

---

74 Cf in the case of a voluntary arrangement *Re a Debtor (No 222 of 1990), ex p Bank of Ireland* [1992] BCLC 137.
75 *Re Hills Motorway Ltd* [2002] NSWSC 897.
76 See *Carruth v Imperial Chemical Industries Ltd* [1937] AC 707.
77 [2002] EWHC 140 (Ch), [2002] BCC 319 at 327.
78 See *Carruth v Imperial Chemical Industries Ltd* [1937] AC 707.

reasonable chairman could have reached[79]. By the terms of the convening order, the chairman ordinarily is given the power to value the claims of creditors. This means he is required to value claims by way of going through a process which shows he has exercised whatever discretions or powers are given to him by the court convening order; and even where he is unsure of the value he must do his best to come to a genuine best estimate value rather than simply arbitrarily valuing the claim at £1 (unless the court convening order gives him the power to value claims at £1 in certain circumstances, such as he does not know the value and cannot find out)[80].

THIRD STAGE: THE SANCTION HEARING

13.40 Once a scheme has been approved by the requisite majority (or majorities) of creditors at the meeting (or meetings) convened for the purpose, the Part 8 claim form is then restored before the court for the hearing known as the 'sanction hearing' at an application by the proposer of the scheme under section 899(1) of CA 2006 for the court to sanction the compromise or arrangement. The scheme must be sanctioned by the court in order for it to be binding upon all persons who are the members of the relevant class convened. The sanction of the court is not a formality[81]. The role of the court in such circumstances was set out in *Buckley on the Companies Acts*, and the following passage has been approved by the courts[82]:

'Function of the court. In exercising its power of sanction the court will see, first, that the provisions of the statute have been complied with[83], second, that the class was fairly represented by those who attended the meeting and that the statutory majority are acting bona fide and are not coercing the minority in order to promote interests adverse to those of the class whom they purport to represent, and thirdly, that the arrangement is such as an intelligent and honest man, a member of the class concerned and acting in respect of his interest, might reasonably approve. The court does not sit merely to see that the majority are acting bona fide and thereupon to register the decision of the meeting, but, at the same time, the court will be slow to differ from the meeting, unless either the class has not been properly consulted, or the meeting has not considered the matter with a view to the interests of the class which it is empowered to bind, or some blot is found in the scheme.'

13.41 This statement derives from Court of Appeal authority from the end of the nineteenth century, and was later followed by Plowman J in *Re National Bank Ltd*. The passage has been cited, referred to, and applied by the courts

---

79 *Re British Aviation Insurance Co Ltd* [2005] EWHC 1621 (Ch) (paragraphs 66 and 67).

80 See *Re British Aviation Insurance Co Ltd* [2005] EWHC 1621 (Ch) (paragraphs 107–112 and 124–125) which concerned a situation where the chairman had admitted IBNR votes at an arbitrary value of £1 which led the judge at the sanction hearing to decide that the votes of IBNR claims as opposing creditors had not been properly treated and thus the vote was irregular.

81 *Kempe v Ambassador Insurance Co* [1998] 1 WLR 271 at 276, per Lord Hoffmann PC.

82 See for example *Re Telewest Communications plc (No 2)* [2004] EWHC 1466 (paragraph 20) where David Richard J recites and approves the passage from *Buckley on the Companies Acts* (13th ed, 1957, p.409).

83 For example, that all meetings have voted in favour of the scheme by the requisite statutory majority: *Re Dorman Long & Co Ltd* [1934] Ch 635.

at hearings for sanction of proposed compromises and arrangements pursuant to Part 26 of CA 2006 (previously section 425 of CA 1985 and its statutory predecessor) on numerous occasions[84].

13.42 The same approach is reflected in other cases. Thus in *Re English, Scottish and Australian Chartered Bank*[85], Lindley LJ said:

'If the creditors are acting on sufficient information and with time to consider what they are about, and are acting honestly, they are, I apprehend, much better judges of what is to their commercial advantage than the court can be. I do not say it is conclusive, because there might be some blot in a scheme which had passed that had been unobserved and which was pointed out later'

and a little later:

'the court ought to be slow to differ from [the necessary majority of the creditors who have voted in favour of the scheme]. It should do so without hesitation if there is anything wrong; but it ought not to do so, in my judgment, unless something is brought to the attention of the court to show that there has been some material oversight or miscarriage.'

13.43 David Richards J in *Re Telewest Communications plc (No 2)*[86] continued (after citing the passage from *Buckley on the Companies Act*):

'This formulation in particular recognises and balances two important factors. First, in deciding to sanction a scheme under s 425, which has the effect of binding members or creditors who have voted against the scheme or abstained as well as those who voted in its favour, the court must be satisfied that it is a fair scheme. It must be a scheme that "an intelligent and honest man, a member of the class concerned and acting in respect of his interest, might reasonably approve." That test also makes clear that the scheme proposed need not be the only fair scheme or even, in the court's view, the best scheme. Necessarily there may be reasonable differences of view on these issues. ...

[22] The second factor recognised by the above cited passage is that in commercial matters members or creditors are much better judges of their own interests than the courts. Subject to the qualifications set out in the second paragraph, the court "will be slow to differ from the meeting".'

13.44 As regards the sanction of a scheme for a foreign company, assuming the court is satisfied that there is sufficient connection between the foreign

---

84   *Re Alabama, New Orleans, Texas and Pacific Junction Rly Co* [1891] 1 Ch 213 at 239, per Lindley LJ; *Re English, Scottish and Australian Chartered Bank* [1893] 3 Ch 385 at 408, per Lindley LJ; *Edinburgh American Land Mortgage Co v Lang's Trustees* 1909 SC 488; *Re Anglo-Continental Supply Co Ltd* [1922] 2 Ch 723 at 736; *Re Dorman, Long & Co Ltd* [1934] Ch 635 at 657, per Maugham J; *Re National Bank Ltd* [1966] 1 All ER 1006 at 1012, where Plowman J quoted this and the next paragraph with approval; *Re NFU DevelopmentTrust Ltd* [1973] 1 All ER 135; *Re Hellenic & GeneralTrust Ltd* [1976] 1 WLR 123; *Re Heron International NV* [1994] 1 BCLC 667; and *Re Osiris Insurance Ltd* [1999] 1 BCLC 182 at 189 (Neuberger J). These three points were approved by Jonathan Parker J in *Re BTR plc* [1999] 2 BCLC 675 at 680. See also *Re RAC Motoring Services Ltd* [2000] 1 BCLC 307 (Neuberger J) and *Re Allied Domecq plc* [2000] 1 BCLC 134; *Re Equitable Life Assurance Society* [2002] EWHC 140 (Ch) (paragraph 66). In *Re BTR plc* [2000] 1 BCLC 740 at 747 Chadwick LJ emphasised that the court would not sanction a scheme if those voting in favour of it had done so with a special interest to promote which differs from the interests of an independent and objective shareholder.

85   [1893] 3 Ch 385 at 409.

86   [2004] EWHC 1466 (Ch) (paragraphs 21 and 22).

company and the English jurisdiction, then the court will ordinarily also need to see foreign law advice to the effect that the scheme will be effective in the relevant local jurisdiction, which is normally the jurisdiction where the foreign company is incorporated or registered (but could be another jurisdiction where there is a likelihood or danger of scheme creditors attempting to enforce their rights against the scheme company). This is not a jurisdictional test, but is to be factored into the court's decision-making process as a matter of discretion because the court will generally not act in vain. So if a creditor may take foreign local proceedings to enforce its original uncompromised debt against the scheme company, then an English scheme may not have the practical effect intended, despite the scheme being effective in the English jurisdiction. The legal test for the court at the sanction hearing is that it only has to be shown that the scheme will have some utility and it does not have to be proved that the scheme will in fact have universal effect[87].

13.45 The statute provides that once the scheme is sanctioned and a copy of the order sanctioning the scheme is delivered to the English registrar of companies, it becomes binding on all creditors or the class of creditors (as the case may be)[88]. By effect of the statute, after sanction, the scheme is statutorily imposed upon the creditors or the class of creditors (even upon a creditor who did not attend the meeting to vote) and cannot be altered merely by agreement of the parties[89].

COSTS

13.46 If the application for sanction of a scheme of arrangement is opposed, and the opposition fails but was not frivolous, the court will generally order the successful applicant to pay the costs of the unsuccessful opposing creditors if their arguments were of assistance to the court[90]. In a case where the presence of an objector is necessary for the proper testing of a proposed scheme so that the court can be satisfied that the proposals are fair, and where there is a public interest in the result of the case which involves a novel scheme of reorganisation, the objector's grounds are known in advance and he could be said to be performing a public service to the company in objecting and testing the scheme, the court may make a pre-emptive order for costs, but this is likely to be subject to an upper limit so that the company would only bear the costs of making appropriate arguments[91]. If the scheme is supported by some creditors and not others and it fails, the court will not usually order those who supported the scheme to bear the costs of those who opposed it. The opposers' costs should be borne from the company's assets[92].

---

87 See *Sompo Japan Insurance Inc v Transfercom Ltd* [2007] EWHC 146 (Ch) and *Magyar Telecom BV* [2013] EWHC 3800 (Ch).
88 Section 899(3) of CA 2006.
89 *Kempe v Ambassador Insurance Co* [1998] 1 WLR 271 at 276, per Lord Hoffmann PC; *Srimati Premila Devi v People's Bank of Northern India Ltd (in liquidation)* [1938] 4 All ER 337.
90 As in *Re National Bank Ltd* [1966] 1 WLR 819 at 830; *Re British Leyland Motor Corpn Ltd* (1 August 1975, unreported, Templeman J); see also *Re Thomas de la Rue & Co Ltd* [1911] 2 Ch 361.
91 *Re AXA Equity & Law Life Assurance Society plc and AXA Sun Life plc* [2001] 2 BCLC 447.
92 *Re Esal (Commodities) Ltd* [1985] BCLC 450.

COLLATERAL RELEASES

13.47 In *Re Lehman Brothers International (Europe) (in administration) (No 2)*[93], Patten LJ said:

'It seems to me that an arrangement between a company and its creditors must mean an arrangement which deals with their rights *inter se* as debtor and creditor. That formulation does not prevent the inclusion in the scheme of the release of contractual rights or rights of action against related third parties necessary in order to give effect to the arrangement proposed for the disposition of the debts and liabilities of the company to its own creditors. But it does exclude from the jurisdiction rights of creditors over their own property which is held by the company for their benefit as opposed to their rights in the company's own property held by them merely as security.'

Although the case concerned whether a scheme of arrangement could be used to compromise the rights of creditors as regards assets held on trust for them by the company, this passage in the Court of Appeal's judgment confirms that rights such as creditors' rights against a third party guarantor can be released or compromised by a term in the scheme made between the scheme company and the creditors (to which the guarantor is not a party)[94].

MODIFICATIONS

13.48 The ordinary form of the convening order usually provides for the creditors to meet to consider and, if thought fit, approve '(with or without modification)' the scheme proposed to be made between the scheme company and the scheme creditors. Since many creditors will be likely to submit proxies in support of the proposed scheme as circulated to them prior to the meeting, and actual attendance at the meeting is sparse, as a practical matter it may be impossible to modify a scheme without adjourning the meeting, re-circulating the modifications and re-convening the relevant meetings, so that all creditors who are entitled to attend the meeting know exactly what scheme proposals they are voting upon. In *Re Primacom Holding GmbH*[95], Hildyard J briefly considered a modification power. The judge said:

'It is difficult from this position to be able to determine with certainty and, in the absence of a very extended review of authorities, how broad a modification power would be permitted. It was accepted on all sides that at least three boundaries to the modification power could be discerned: first the court would be anxious to ensure that the scheme was not so different from the scheme which was before the scheme creditors at the class meetings that their votes would really not be on that scheme at all. Second, the court would be against modification if it would alter the class compositions; and, thirdly, the court would be against modification if, thereby, the explanatory statement would be falsified or proven irrelevant.'[96]

---

93 [2009] EWCA Civ 1161 (at paragraph 65).
94 See for example *Re La Seda de Barcelona SA* [2010] EWHC 1364 (Ch).
95 [2011] EWHC 3746 (Ch).
96 If extensive or radical modification is required between the convening hearing and the creditors meeting it is sometimes sensible to return to court for new or supplemental convening directions so that the procedure for the three required stages is clearly and transparently followed.

13.49 Scheme terms often contain an authority given by the creditors to the scheme company to allow the scheme company to consent on behalf of the scheme creditors to any modification of or addition to the scheme or to any terms or conditions that the court may think fit to approve or impose, save that if any such modification or addition is likely to have a material adverse effect on the interests of any scheme creditor, it may not consent without the prior written consent of that scheme creditor[97]. In *Re Hawk Insurance Co Ltd*[98], Chadwick LJ cautioned as regards modifications to be imposed by the court, saying:

> 'The court should be cautious before rewriting a scheme to accord with its own notions of proper draftsmanship. If the change is merely cosmetic, it is unnecessary; if it is more than cosmetic, then the scheme as sanctioned is not the scheme that has been approved by the meeting of creditors.'[99]

Save for the power to make such minor modifications, the court either sanctions the scheme in its entirety or refuses to sanction it. Unless the scheme itself allows this, the court cannot sanction parts of the scheme, because that is not what the creditors voted on[100].

HUMAN RIGHTS

13.50 In *Re Equitable Life Assurance Society*[101], Lloyd J said that the approval of the scheme (there under section 425 of CA 1985), so as to bind dissentients, did not breach the rights afforded by Article 1 of the First Protocol[102] because the scheme involved the exchange of rights and did not constitute a confiscation of rights. It does not follow from this that the Convention is not engaged at all, because an order under Part 26 of CA 2006 could still constitute an interference with a person's peaceful enjoyment of his possessions under Article 1 of the First Protocol, and the state is involved because the scheme can only become effective as a result of an action by an organ of the state and because it has provided a power to sanction a scheme.

13.51 Schemes of arrangement frequently contain some form of procedure for resolving disputes in the determination of a creditor's claim. Some incorporate the relevant provisions of the Rules, others provide for some form of independent expert determination in default of agreement. If some procedure of the latter kind is to be workable, it must, at least to the extent permitted by law, be final and binding. Two issues arise here. The first is whether the court should, as a matter of discretion, sanction a scheme which purports to make such a determination final and binding and to exclude all recourse to the courts. There is no difficulty if such determination is binding only to the extent that it relates to valuation of claims. Care must be taken in the drafting, so that it does not purport to exclude,

---

97 The limitations of any modification power were stressed in *Re Equitable Life Assurance Society* [2002] EWHC 140 (Ch) (paragraph 102).
98 [2001] EWCA Civ 241.
99 At first instance ([2001] BCC 57 at 77 and 78), Arden J had found that certain minor modifications were required to the drafting to avoid an apparent ouster of the jurisdiction of the court: see below. These modifications formed part of the scheme when it was sanctioned by the Court of Appeal, so were in the event left untouched by the Court of Appeal.
100 Cf also *Re Telewest Communications plc (No 2)* [2004] EWHC 1466 (Ch) (paragraph 21) (the legal test for sanctioning a scheme makes clear that the scheme proposed need not be the only fair scheme or even in the court's view the best scheme).
101 [2002] EWHC 140 (Ch).
102 Now set out in Schedule 1 to the Human Rights Act 1998.

for example, the right to apply to the court if the expert made a material error in carrying out his instructions, so that a party could apply to court on the grounds that the decision was not binding because the expert had not done what he was appointed to do[103]. This will be the case even if in the course of his work the expert may have to determine a point of law[104]. With suitable drafting, making it clear that a decision of the adjudicator would be final and binding only so far as the law permitted, such a provision would be acceptable[105].

13.52   The second issue relates to Article 6 of the European Convention on Human Rights[106], which provides that in the determination of his civil rights, every person has a right to a fair and public hearing within a reasonable time by an independent and impartial tribunal established by law. It was suggested in *Hawk* that the adjudication provisions in the scheme, providing for the determination of an independent expert to be final and binding, might infringe this right. On this point, it was held that the adjudication provisions did not infringe Article 6, because there was a difference between voluntary and compulsory arbitration, and this scheme was in the nature of voluntary arbitration. Every creditor had the opportunity of voting for or against the scheme and appearing at the sanction hearing to object, but all those who voted were in favour and none did object[107].

BAR DATES

13.53   In appropriate schemes, a bar date can be used to force creditors to prove their claims by a particular date, failing which their claim is barred. The court will allow the use of bar dates, provided sufficient notification to creditors is provided for, and provided creditors are given a proper and reasonable time to submit their claims[108]. The mechanisms to value creditors' claims, if some form of proof process is established by the scheme, must provide for a clear basis for treating all creditors alike[109] (and would normally in any event mirror the proof of debt rules in a liquidation or administration).

REVERSION TO RUN OFF

13.54   Insurance schemes often used to contain clauses allowing the insurance company to revert to run off if, in its discretion, it considered this was desirable. Lewison J refused to allow such a clause in *Re British Aviation Insurance Co Ltd*[110] because in his view a compromise by its very essence ought to be binding on both sides, whereas the relevant clause allowing the company a discretion to revert to run off gave the company a power to bring the compromise to an end more or less at will.

---

103   See *Jones v Sherwood Computer Services plc* [1992] 1 WLR 277 at 287.
104   See *Nikko Hotels (UK) Ltd v MEPC Ltd* [1991] 2 EGLR 103 at 109; *R E Brown v GIO Insurance Ltd* (1998) Ll Rep (IR) 201 at 206 and 208.
105   *Re Hawk Insurance Company Ltd* [2001] BCC 57 per Arden J at 74.
106   Set out in Schedule 1 to the Human Rights Act 1998.
107   Set out in Schedule 1 to the Human Rights Act 1998. See also on this issue, *Re Pan Atlantic Insurance Co Ltd* [2003] EWHC 1696 (Ch) in which the limited exclusion of a right of access to the court was regarded as proportionate. See also *Re British Aviation Insurance Co Ltd* [2005] EWHC 1621 (Ch) (paragraphs 129–133).
108   *Re British Aviation Insurance Co Ltd* [2005] EWHC 1621 (Ch) (paragraph 127).
109   *Re British Aviation Insurance Co Ltd* [2005] EWHC 1621 (Ch) (paragraphs 128 and 142(ii)).
110   [2005] EWHC 1621 (Ch) (paragraphs 134–137 and 142(iii)).

CREDITORS' COMMITTEES, SCHEME ADMINISTRATORS AND APPOINTMENT OF A FOREIGN AUTHORISED REPRESENTATIVE

13.55 Where a scheme does not involve a single lump sum payment to creditors or a single transaction or a once-and-for-all reorganisation effecting the grant of the new rights but is intended to be implemented over a considerable time, whilst assets are realised and payments made to creditors over a period, it has become usual practice that there should be a creditors' committee. This tends to mirror the existence of a creditors' committee in an administration or liquidation. If there is to be a creditors' committee, the scheme must contain provisions relating to the constitution, powers, functions and duties of such a committee. It is common practice for provisional liquidators and administrators to create an informal creditors' liaison committee to assist them in the development of the scheme proposals. The membership of such a committee is usually intended to be representative of the creditors as a whole. In a provisional liquidation, unless there are special provisions to that effect in the order appointing the provisional liquidator, or there is a further order dealing with the point, such a committee would have no legal standing. In an administration there is statutory authority for the existence of such a committee. Nevertheless, the views of such an informal committee are usually found helpful in the promotion of any scheme.

13.56 When a scheme is proposed by an insolvent company (which is likely to be the case where a scheme is used as the exit route from administration or from provisional liquidation) it is usual to have a scheme administrator who will be responsible for administering the terms of the scheme, or, less frequently, to supervise the directors of the company in administering the scheme. Since acting in that capacity does not constitute acting as an insolvency practitioner for the purposes of section 388 of IA 1986, there is no requirement for such a person to be a licensed insolvency practitioner[111]. Nevertheless, the following three points should be borne in mind. First, where a company is insolvent, the market generally would expect the scheme administrator to be a licensed insolvency practitioner. Secondly, where the company is an insolvent insurance company, the Financial Conduct Authority would be most unlikely to permit anybody to be appointed as the scheme administrator unless he were not only a licensed insolvency practitioner, but also experienced in insurance insolvency. Thirdly, if the company is solvent, then whether it is an insurance company or not, there is no objection in principle to the directors being responsible for administering the scheme.

FOREIGN REPRESENTATIVE FOR UNCITRAL MODEL LAW PURPOSES

13.57 If there is any need for application to be made to a foreign court for recognition of an English scheme of arrangement and recognition is available, normally under the UNCITRAL Model Law, then the English court will be

---

111 A person qualified to act as an insolvency practitioner is the wording used in sections 388 and 389 of IA 1986.

willing to appoint an appropriate person as the authorised representative of the scheme company to make such application abroad[112].

INSURANCE COMPANY SCHEMES: THE POSITION OF REINSURERS

13.58   Where a scheme is proposed by an insurance company, the scheme will be between the company and its creditors or a class of them. The scheme is not with reinsurers and cannot bind reinsurers, at least in their capacity as debtors. There is an issue, on which there appears to be no authority, as to whether a provision in a scheme, purporting to bind reinsurers, would be binding to the extent to which the reinsurer would be a net creditor, or possibly up to a nil balance either way, but not beyond, or possibly not binding at all. Nevertheless, when crafting what is known as a cut-off or valuation scheme, under which all unmatured claims are required to be valued, those promoting a scheme for an insurance company, whether solvent or not, usually have informal discussions with reinsurers to see whether the reinsurers are comfortable with the fact that liabilities of the company which might be the subject of reinsurance claims are to be ascertained or valued in the manner contemplated by the scheme. Careful consideration is likely to be necessary as regards the position of creditors if they are also reinsurers, both in determining the proper constitution of classes, and in considering whether the court is likely to sanction the proposed scheme of arrangement after proper consideration of the question whether the votes cast are properly representative of the relevant class[113].

---

112   *Re Telewest Communications plc (No 1)* [2004] EWHC 924 (Ch) (paragraphs 60–61).
113   See *Re British Aviation Insurance Co Ltd* [2005] EWHC 1621 (Ch) (paragraphs 93–96 and 118–123).

14 Protection of interests of creditors and members

UNFAIR HARM

14.1   Any creditor or member of the company may apply to the court claiming that the administrator is acting or has acted so as unfairly to harm his interests (whether alone or in common with some or all other members and creditors) or that the administrator is proposing so to act[1]. Any creditor or member of a company may also apply to the court claiming that the administrator is not performing his functions as quickly or as efficiently as is reasonably practicable[2]. In addition, in the case of an existing or former authorised person or appointed representative or a person who is carrying on or has carried on a regulated activity in contravention of the general prohibition[3], the Financial Conduct Authority or the Prudential Regulation Authority can also make such an application[4]. It is also thought that Article 32(3) of the EC Insolvency Regulation is wide enough to give any member state liquidator the right to make such an application, because he is thereby entitled to participate in an administration 'on the same basis as a creditor'. Under the former law it was plain that the application had to be made when the administration order was in force[5], thereby suggesting that any application for discharge of the order should be adjourned pending the hearing of any application under what was then section 27 of IA 1986[6]. Under the present law, the wording is different, and a court may grant relief for a claim brought under Schedule B1 paragraph 74 of IA 1986 after the administration has come to an end, provided any discharge order has reserved the position as regards the paragraph 74 application[7].

---

1   Schedule B1 paragraph 74(1) of IA 1986. It should be noted that action includes inaction: Schedule B1 paragraph 111(3) of IA 1986.
2   Schedule B1 paragraph 74(2) of IA 1986.
3   Within the meaning of section 19 of the Financial Services and Markets Act 2000 (cf the Financial Services Act 2012 which replaced the Financial Services Authority with the Financial Conduct Authority and the Prudential Regulation Authority).
4   See section 362(4) of the Financial Services and Markets Act 2000, as amended by Schedule 17 paragraph 57 of the Enterprise Act 2002 and the Financial Services Act 2012.
5   Section 27(1) of IA 1986 (now repealed).
6   See eg *Re Charnley Davies Business Services Ltd* (1987) 3 BCC 408 at 409.
7   *Re Coniston Hotel (Kent) LLP* [2013] EWHC 93 (Ch) (paragraph 28). Cf Schedule B1 paragraph 98 which provides for discharge of the administrator, and paragraph 98(4) which states that discharge applies to liability accrued before the discharge takes effect, and does not prevent the exercise of the court's powers under paragraph 75, albeit permission of the court is required (Schedule B1 paragraph 75(6)).

14.2 *Prima facie*, all creditors[8] and members[9] have standing to apply to the court under Schedule B1 paragraph 74 of IA 1986. The legislation does, however, provide that where the complaint is that the administrator is acting or proposing to act so as unfairly to harm some part of the company's members or creditors, the interests of the applicant personally should have been unfairly harmed[10]. This provision constitutes a statutory recognition of the principle that an applicant should have a tangible interest in the outcome of his application[11]. In the case of a member state liquidator, it is presumably the case that he must show unfair harm to some, at least, of the creditors claiming in the insolvency proceedings in which he has been appointed.

14.3 Accordingly, it will be a rare case in which a member will be able to seek relief unless he can show either that the company is solvent or that the company would be solvent but for the act or omission of which complaint is made. Similarly, a creditor who is fully secured is unlikely to be able to demonstrate an interest unless the complaint relates to a dealing with property over which he holds his security. Even then, where the act or omission is alleged to relate to property subject to a security other than security which was a floating charge on its creation, the complaint will initially be dealt with under the procedures contained in Schedule B1 paragraph 71 of IA 1986[12], although it should be noted that Schedule B1 paragraph 74(5) of IA 1986 expressly contemplates that there may be cases in which the court has made an order enabling the administrator to dispose of property subject to a fixed charge, but the chargee has a sustainable claim for relief that the effect of the order is to cause him unfair harm within the meaning of Schedule B1 paragraph 74(1) of IA 1986. Where, however,

---

8   Including presumably contingent, prospective and secured creditors.
9   As regards 'members', Schedule B1 paragraph 111 (1A) provides that 'company' means a company registered under the Companies Act 2006 in England and Wales or in Scotland, or a company incorporated in an EEA state other than the United Kingdom, or a company not incorporated in an EEA state but having its centre of main interests in a member state other than Denmark. By section 112 of the Companies Act 2006, as regards a company formed and registered under that Act, the members of a company are the subscribers to the company's memorandum who are deemed to have agreed to become members, and on the company's registration become members and must be entered as such in its register of members, and thereafter members include every other person who agrees to become a member of the company, and whose name is entered in its register of members. By section 250 of IA 1986 a person who is not a member of a company but to whom shares in the company have been transferred, or transmitted by operation of law, is to be regarded as a member of the company. As regards overseas companies where the centre of main interests of the company is in England and Wales, and an administration order is made pursuant to Schedule B1, the question of who is a member of the company will be a matter for the relevant local foreign company law.
10 Schedule B1 paragraph 74 (1)(a) and (b) of IA 1986. *Re Coniston Hotel (Kent) LLP* [2013] EWHC 93 (Ch) (paragraphs 33–35). Except where the petitioner is one of the authorised bodies acting under powers conferred by section 362(4) and (4A) of FSMA 2000, in which case there is the requirement to show that the administrator's act or omission to act has harmed the interests of some or all members or creditors (s.362(4A) of the Financial Services and Markets Act 2000).
11 See eg *Re Rica GoldWashing Co* (1879) 11 Ch D 36, *Re Chesterfield Catering Co Ltd* [1977] Ch 373, *Re Chelmsford City Football Club (1980) Ltd* [1991] BCC 133, *Re Land and Property Trust Co plc* [1991] BCLC 845, *Re J E Cade & Son Ltd* [1992] BCLC 213 and *Re Pimlico Capital Ltd* [2002] EWHC 878 (Ch), [2002] 2 BCLC 544 at 554.
12 See eg the procedure adopted in *Re ARV Aviation Ltd* [1989] BCLC 664, *Re Newman Shopfitters (Cleveland) Ltd* [1991] BCLC 407 and *O'Connell v Rollings* [2014] EWCA Civ 639, and the parties intentions in *Arthur D Little Ltd (in administration) v Ableco Finance LLC* [2002] EWHC 701 (Ch). See also *Capitol Films Ltd* [2010] EWHC 3223 (Ch) where unreasonable conduct by administrators of a Schedule B1 paragraph 71 application led to adverse costs sanctions rather than an application under Schedule B1 paragraph 74 of IA 1986.

the chargee is prevented from realising his security, the more appropriate procedure will be to apply for permission under Schedule B1 paragraph 43(2) of IA 1986[13]. On the other hand, the holder of a security which was a floating charge on its creation, may be seriously harmed by the acts or omissions of an administrator, thereby rendering resort to Schedule B1 paragraph 74 of IA 1986 more appropriate. There may also be cases in which it is appropriate for relief to be sought under Schedule B1 paragraphs 43 and 74 at the same time[14].

14.4 It is not thought that acts or omissions need to be unlawful or tortious in order unfairly to harm; nor does the fact that they are unlawful or tortious bring them within Schedule B1 paragraph 74 of IA 1986[15]. In *Four Private Investment Funds v Lomas*[16], Blackburne J posed the question of what was meant by 'unfairly harm' and continued:

> 'Two things are apparent. First, the action complained of must be shown to have caused the complainant to suffer harm to his interests or, in the case of a proposed action of the administrator, would cause the complainant to suffer harm. In short, the applicant must show that the action complained of is or will be causative of harm to its interests.
>
> ...
>
> The second aspect of the statutory requirement is that the harm must be "unfair"; harm alone is not enough.'

14.5 The judge continued to consider the concept of unfair prejudice as set out in section 994 of CA 2006 (formerly section 459 of the Companies Act 1985), but pointed out that the context of an administration is different because of the obligations upon the administrator as set out in Schedule B1 paragraphs 3(1), 3(2), 4, 59(1), 68(1) and 68(2) of IA 1986 and in this context the judge dismissed the application made for further information to be provided by the administrators in the circumstances before the court. In *Re Coniston Hotel (Kent) LLP*[17], Norris J commented that it was plain that for the purposes of Schedule B1 paragraph 74 of IA 1986, the application is brought by reference to the applicant's standing as a creditor or member and is directed to the protection of his interests as such, and that the primary relief is directed to regulating the conduct of the administration itself. Although the judge accepted there was an argument that compensation might be ordered under Schedule B1 paragraph 74 of IA 1986 (but declined to decide the point) he held that paragraph 74 does not exist to enable individually disgruntled creditors to pursue administrators for compensation because the focus of paragraph 74 is unfair harm, which 'will ordinarily mean unequal or differential treatment to the disadvantage of the applicant (or applicant class) which cannot be justified by reference to the interests of the creditors as a whole or to achieving the objective of the administration'. The test of whether or not a particular act or omission is unfair is an objective one[18]; accordingly, lack of

---

13   Eg *Air Ecosse Ltd v Civil Aviation Authority* (1987) 3 BCC 492, *Royal Trust Bank v Buchler* [1989] BCLC 130, *Bristol Airport plc v Powdrill* [1990] Ch 744, *Re Atlantic Computer Systems plc* [1992] Ch 505 and *Re Hamlet International plc; Trident International Ltd v Barlow* [1999] 2 BCLC 506.
14   Cf *London Flightline Centre (Stansted) Ltd v Osprey Aviation Ltd* [2002] BPIR 1115.
15   For the position under the former law, see *Re Charnley Davies Ltd (No 2)* [1990] BCLC 760 at 783d, where the applicable concept was one of unfair prejudice.
16   [2008] EWHC 2869 (Ch) (paragraphs 34–37).
17   [2013] EWHC 93 (Ch).
18   Cf *Re Guidzone Ltd* [2000] 2 BCLC 321.

bona fides by the administrator is not required[19]. An act of the administrator that may be harmful to one particular creditor (for example, procuring the termination of a contract) may not be harmful to the wider class of creditors and thus may not be within the category of unfair harm when considering the proper context of the purposes of the administration[20]. The court, by Schedule B1 paragraph 74(3) and (4) of IA 1986 has very wide powers to interfere where the administrator's acts are harmful to the applicant and are unfair in the context in which the administration order was made. It is suggested that that context will include factors such as the extent of the company's insolvency, the nature of its business, the objective with which the administrator is performing his functions and the nature of the complainant's relationship with the company.

14.6 A claim which is in essence one against an administrator for breach of fiduciary or other duty in relation to the company should not be brought by way of application under Schedule B1 paragraph 74 of IA1986[21] as such a claim does not seek relief from mismanagement of the company's affairs. A case based on unfair harm is different to a case centred on breach of fiduciary or other duty (which ought to be brought under Schedule B1 paragraph 75 of IA 1986)[22]. In such circumstances, the more appropriate course would be for the court to exercise its powers under Schedule B1 paragraph 75 or for the company to be placed into liquidation and a claim to be initiated by a liquidator, being an individual other than the administrator of whose acts and omissions complaint is made[23].

14.7 The procedure on an application under Schedule B1 paragraph 74 of IA 1986 is similar to any other application under IA 1986 or the Rules and, in England and Wales, is governed by Rule 1.35 of the Rules. Unless the case is one of urgency, the application should be returnable before the registrar in the first instance[24] (when directions for the future progress of the case would ordinarily be given).

14.8 On an application under Schedule B1 paragraph 74 of IA 1986, the court may grant relief, dismiss the application, adjourn the hearing conditionally or unconditionally, make an interim order or make any other order it thinks appropriate[25]. It is difficult to think of a wider form of words to describe the court's jurisdiction, but the court is also specifically empowered[26] to make orders regulating the administrator's exercise of his functions, requiring the administrator to do or not do a specified thing[27], requiring a creditors' meeting to be held for a specified purpose, providing for the appointment of an administrator

---

19 Cf the much stricter test applied on an application under section 168(5) of IA 1986 to confirm, reverse or modify the acts or decisions of a liquidator: *Re Edennote Ltd* [1996] 2 BCLC 389, *Mitchell v Buckingham International plc* [1998] 2 BCLC 369 and *Mohamed v Morris* [2000] 2 BCLC 536. As to the distinction see *Hockin v Marsden* [2014] EWHC 763 (Ch) (paragraph 15).
20 Cf *Zegna III Holdings Inc (In Administration); BLV Realty* [2009] EWHC 2994 (Ch).
21 *Re Charnley Davies (No 2)* [1990] BCLC 760 at 782b.
22 *Coniston Hotel (Kent) LLP* [2013] EWHC 93 (Ch) (paragraphs 33–39).
23 *Re Charnley Davies Ltd (No 2)* [1990] BCLC 760 at 784d–h. See also *MTI Trading Systems Ltd v Winter* [1998] BCC 591 at 595.
24 Practice Direction: Insolvency Proceedings, paragraph 3.1.
25 Schedule B1 paragraph 74(3) of IA 1986.
26 Schedule B1 paragraph 74(4) of IA 1986.
27 Such as the payment of tax falling due during the course of an administration: *IRC v Lawrence* [2001] 1 BCLC 204 (per Jules Sher QC at 213).

to cease to have effect[28] and making consequential provision. It may be that, in an appropriate case, the court has jurisdiction to award compensation or damages and grant declaratory relief[29]. Furthermore, the court can grant relief on a claim made under Schedule B1 paragraph 74 of IA 1986 whether or not the act of which complaint is made is within the administrator's powers and whether or not it was taken in reliance on an order made under Schedule B1 paragraph 71 or 72 of IA 1986[30].

14.9   The court is prohibited[31] from making any order under Schedule B1 paragraph 74 of IA 1986 which impedes or prevents the implementation of a voluntary arrangement once it has been approved[32], or a compromise or arrangement once it has been sanctioned[33], or the administrator's proposals or a revision to them more than 28 days after the date of their approval. There are alternative means by which an aggrieved member or creditor can seek relief for unfair harm caused by the approval of a voluntary arrangement or scheme:

(a)   where the complaint is that a voluntary arrangement is itself unfairly prejudicial, an aggrieved creditor or member is able to apply for relief under section 6 of IA 1986[34];

(b)   unfairness is a consideration for the court when sanctioning a compromise or arrangement[35].

APPLICATIONS FOR DIRECTIONS

14.10   The only provision in the legislation which permits the court to give general directions on the conduct of the administration is Schedule B1 paragraph 63 of IA 1986. This jurisdiction has been used to great effect in the Lehman administration for the purpose of raising a wide range of legal issues, even where declarations of substantive right are sought[36]. At first sight the jurisdiction would appear to be limited to cases in which the administrator himself seeks the guidance of the court. In *Re Mirror Group (Holdings) Ltd*[37], however, Sir Donald Nicholls V-C held that the court has a general power to give directions to its officers on the way in which particular aspects of the administration should be conducted, irrespective of whether or not the applicant is the administrator. The flexibility of this approach is one which is to be welcomed, but, save for exceptional circumstances, it is thought that the courts will be wary of attempts by individual creditors (and others) to intervene in the conduct of the administration. In the normal case, it remains likely that the court will need to

---

28   In such an event, the administrator is required, within 14 days, to send a copy of the order to the registrar of companies: Schedule B1 paragraph 86 of IA 1986.
29   Cf under the former law, *Re Charnley Davies Ltd (No 2)* [1990] BCLC 760 at 773i–774a, but see *Re Coniston Hotel (Kent) LLP* [2013] EWHC 93 (Ch) (paragraphs 35 and 36).
30   Ie an order enabling the administrator to dispose of (a) property subject to a fixed charge as if it were not subject to that security; or (b) goods in the company's possession under a hire-purchase agreement as if all the rights of the owner were vested in the company.
31   By Schedule B1 paragraph 74(6) of IA 1986.
32   Under section 4 of IA 1986.
33   Under Part 26 of CA 2006.
34   See eg *Re Primlaks (UK) Ltd (No 2)* [1990] BCLC 234.
35   Under Part 26 of CA 2006.
36   Eg *In re Lehman Brothers International (Europe) (in administration) (No 4)* [2014] EWHC 704 (Ch) and on appeal at [2015] EWCA Civ 485.
37   [1993] BCLC 538.

be satisfied that the interests of the applicant are being unfairly harmed and will expect an application to be made under Schedule B1 paragraph 74 of IA 1986 accordingly.

14.11   As is the case with all insolvency office-holders, the court will be extremely reluctant to interfere with any commercial decision made by an administrator[38]. Where it is not possible to characterise the conduct as giving rise to unfair harm to the applicant, the correct approach is that reflected by decisions in the context of winding up and bankruptcy, ie the court will only interfere if the complainant can show that the office-holder has acted in a way that is utterly unreasonable or absurd, ie perversely[39], and there is no room for any sort of *Wednesbury* reasonableness test[40]. The test is very different, however, where the court is being asked to decide whether or not a particular power should be exercised in a manner which might have the consequences of unfairly harming the interests of a particular creditor or class of creditors. The question then is one for the court: how should the discretion be exercised in all the circumstances of the case[41]?

MISFEASANCE

14.12   Where the issue is misconduct by the administrator, rather than mismanagement, the only remedy provided under the former law was to apply for his removal, combined, where appropriate, with an application to discharge the administration order and place the company in liquidation. Schedule B1 paragraph 75 of IA 1986 introduces a new remedy (derived from section 212 of IA 1986), which gives the court power to examine into the conduct of any existing, purported or former administrator of the company[42] and order him to repay, restore or account for money or property, to pay interest and to pay a sum to the company's property by way of compensation for breach of duty or misfeasance[43]. The power is only exercisable on the application of the official receiver, the administrator of the company, the liquidator of the company[44], or a creditor or contributory of the company[45]. The application must allege that the administrator:

(a)   has misapplied or retained money or other property of the company;

(b)   has become accountable for money or other property of the company;

---

38   *MTI Trading Systems Ltd v Winter* [1998] BCC 591, *Re C E King Ltd* [2000] 2 BCLC 297 and *Re T&N Ltd* [2004] EWHC 2361 (Ch) (paragraph 76).

39   *Re Edennote Ltd* [1996] 2 BCLC 389, *Re Broome (a debtor)* [1999] 1 BCLC 356 and *Bramston v Haut* [2012] EWCA Civ 1637. However, it is important to stress that, where unfair harm can be alleged, there is no need to show perversity as well – the tests are different: *Hockin v Marsden* [2014] EWHC 763 (Ch).

40   *Bramston v Haut* [2012] EWCA Civ 1637.

41   *Re Greenhaven Motors Ltd* [1999] 1 BCLC 635 and *Mitchell v Buckingham International plc (No 2)* [1998] 2 BCLC 369.

42   Schedule B1 paragraph 75(1) of IA 1986. Where a former administrator has been discharged under Schedule B1 paragraph 98, an application against him may only be made with the permission of the court (Schedule B1 paragraph 75(6) of IA 1986).

43   Schedule B1 paragraph 75(4) of IA 1986.

44   Schedule B1 paragraph 75(2)(c) of IA 1986, which will only apply once the company has ceased to be in administration.

45   Schedule B1 paragraph 75(2) of IA 1986.

(c)   has breached a fiduciary or other duty in relation to the company; or

(d)   has been guilty of misfeasance[46].

The structure of paragraph 75 is unusual in that it gives the court power to conduct the examination where a mere allegation is made (although presumably no examination would be ordered if the allegation could be shown to be without substance). If, from the examination, it appears that the allegation was well founded, the court then has a discretion as to whether or not it should grant any relief.

14.13   As with section 212 of IA 1986, it seems that Schedule B1 paragraph 75 does not introduce a new cause of action[47]. It simply introduces a procedural mechanism by which a defaulting administrator or former administrator can be ordered to compensate the company for loss caused by his defaults. Thus, where the claim is for breach of a duty of care[48], and notwithstanding the broad language of paragraph 75(4), the court's discretion can only be exercised so as to order such compensation as it could have awarded by way of damages for breach of duty if the company had proceeded against the administrator by way of ordinary action[49]. Likewise, the discretion to order compensation for misfeasance and breach of fiduciary duty cannot properly be exercised so as to award the company a windfall. It should also be noted that the discretionary nature of the relief available under Schedule B1 paragraph 75(4) of IA 1986 means that the court can take into account exculpatory considerations which might be relevant to a claim for relief under section 1157 of CA 2006[50], whether or not that section is strictly applicable or pleaded[51]. Whatever the underlying complaint, however, the jurisdiction available under Schedule B1 paragraph 75 of IA 1986 gives a remedy which can be exercised without the company being required to go into liquidation, although there will be few cases in which proceedings will be feasible against an administrator without him first being removed. The existence of this statutory cause of action, which is a class remedy and which replaces section 212 of IA 1986[52], is one of the reasons why an individual unsecured creditor does not have his own freestanding cause of action for breach of duty[53].

---

46   Schedule B1 paragraph 75(3) of IA 1986.

47   Cf *Re City Equitable Fire Insurance Co Ltd* [1925] Ch 407, *Coniston Hotel (Kent) LLP* [2013] EWHC 93 (Ch) (paragraph 38).

48   As occurred in *Re D'Jan of London Ltd* [1994] 1 BCLC 561. An argument that section 212 of IA 1986 was not wide enough to cover mere negligence was rejected in *Kyrris v Oldham* [2003] EWCA Civ 1506.

49   *Cohen v Selby* [2001] 1 BCLC 176 at 183.

50   Ie to grant relief to an officer of the company where he has acted honestly and reasonably and ought fairly to be excused. Section 1157 of CA 2006 was formerly s.727 of the Companies Act 1985.

51   *Kenburg Investments (Northern) Ltd v Minton* [2000] 1 Lloyd's Rep PN 736.

52   See the amendments to section 212 of IA 1986 introduced by Schedule 17 paragraph 18 of the Enterprise Act 2002.

53   *Kyrris v Oldham* [2003] EWCA Civ 1506 (paragraph 148), although when this case was decided, section 212 was the applicable provision and it was necessary for the company to be placed in liquidation first.

15 Payments and distributions

PAYMENTS IN PERFORMANCE OF AN ADMINISTRATOR'S FUNCTIONS

15.1 An administrator has power to make any payment which is necessary or incidental to the performance of his functions[1]. Thus, he is empowered to make payments, *inter alia*, to employees in order to secure their continued services and to suppliers in order to obtain continued supplies in the course of an administration. Schedule B1 paragraph 66 of IA 1986 also empowers an administrator to make any payment, otherwise than in accordance with his Schedule 1 power to make any payment necessary or incidental to the performance of his functions, if he thinks it likely to assist the achievement of the purpose of administration[2]. It is difficult to think of circumstances in which a payment would be likely to achieve the purpose of administration, but would not be at least incidental to the performance by the administrator of his functions. Be that as it may, it is plain that Parliament intended that an administrator should have the very widest powers to make payments directed towards the achievement of the purpose for which he was appointed[3]. In particular, the power to make payments to creditors enables the administrator to make such payments notwithstanding that the payment may be made in respect of unsecured liabilities of the company incurred prior to the time at which the company entered administration or under a contract entered into by the company prior to that time.

15.2 The power to pay pre-administration liabilities where to do so would be for the general benefit of the administration has been considered in a number of reported cases. It has been considered in the context of a debate as to the proper mechanism for bringing an administration to an end[4], the power to make a general distribution of the company's assets through the mechanism of a quasi-liquidation and generally as to the proper approach to determining what is capable of being a proper payment[5]. It has also been used[6] to justify the

---

1 Schedule B1 paragraph 60 of IA 1986 and Schedule 1 paragraph 13 of IA 1986.
2 As to the requirement that the payment is thought to be likely to assist the purpose of administration, see *In re Portsmouth City FC Ltd* [2012] EWHC 3088 (Ch) (paragraph 102) per Morgan J, whose judgment was approved by the Court of Appeal at [2013] EWCA Civ 916 (see in particular paragraph 41). See also *Re Lune Metal Products Ltd* [2006] EWCA Civ 1720 (paragraph 19).
3 This passage in the 2nd edition of this work was approved in *Re MG Rover Espana SA* [2006] EWHC 3426 (Ch) (paragraph 14).
4 See the discussion in **CHAPTER 17** *post* and *Re Lune Metal Products Ltd* [2006] EWCA Civ 1720.
5 Eg *Re TXU UK Ltd* [2002] EWHC 2784 (Ch).
6 *Re MG Rover Espana SA* [2006] EWHC 3426 (Ch), *Re Collins & Aikman Europe SA* [2006] EWHC 1343 (Ch) and *In Re Nortel Networks (UK) Ltd* [2015] EWHC 2506 (Ch).

making of payments where it has been necessary for administrators to agree to do so in order to avoid creditors taking steps to initiate secondary proceedings under Article 3(2) of the EC Insolvency Regulation[7]. The means by which the power is exercised may involve the administrator being directed by the court to make payments to creditors of the company as expenses of the administration[8] (or authorise the incurring of obligations which would give priority to the person to whom the obligation was incurred[9]), but there will be many cases in which he can exercise the power without the need for any such direction. The court also has power to direct the administrator to honour earlier assurances that such payments will be made, where the effect of those assurances was to facilitate the achievement of the purpose of administration[10]. It should be noted that the administrator might be directed to incur and pay costs which cannot be said to be necessary for the achievement of the purpose of administration[11], but it is thought that the cost must at least be incurred as a necessary part of the management of the affairs, business or property of the company, otherwise it could not be said to be incidental to the performance by him of his functions or likely to assist the achievement of the purpose of administration[12].

DISTRIBUTIONS

15.3 Before the introduction of distributing administrations, it was held[13] that an administrator had power, if the assets of the company permitted him to do so, to pay off preadministration creditors in full in order to ensure the survival of the company as a going concern and as a prelude to applying for the administration order to be discharged and the directors resuming control of the company. However, in *Re St Ives Windings Ltd*[14], which was decided shortly after IA 1986 came into force, it was also held provisionally by Harman J that, in the case of a company whose liabilities exceeded the value of its assets, which the administrator, in substance, had already realised, an administrator had no power to make a partial distribution to creditors so as to bind dissentient creditors other than by means of a voluntary arrangement under Part 1 of IA 1986 or a scheme of arrangement under section 425 of CA 1985. The provisional view reached by Harman J appears to have been followed, albeit without contrary argument, in *Re British and Commonwealth Holdings plc (No 3)*[15].

---

7   Regulation No 1346/2000, repealed and replaced with effect from 26 June 2017 by Regulation 2015/848/EU.
8   See, *inter alia, Re Atlantic Computer Systems plc* [1992] Ch 505.
9   *Centre Reinsurance International Co v Freakley* [2006] UKHL 45 (paragraph 65).
10   *Re Collins & Aikman Europe SA* [2006] EWHC 1343 (Ch), in which case the assurances were given to avoid the institution of secondary proceedings which would have been disruptive to the achievement of the purpose of administration.
11   Eg in the administration of the company's pension scheme, where no provision is made for the costs to be paid out of the scheme itself: *Polly Peck International plc v Henry* [1999] 1 BCLC 407.
12   *In re Portsmouth City FC Ltd* [2012] EWHC 3088 (Ch) (paragraph 102) per Morgan J and [2013] EWCA Civ 916 (paragraph 41).
13   *Re John Slack Ltd* [1995] BCC 1116.
14   *Re St Ives Windings Ltd* (1987) 3 BCC 634. In *Re Polly Peck International plc (No 4)* [1998] 2 BCLC 185, the Court of Appeal referred to the administrators being bound to distribute the assets of PPI among its creditors in accordance with the statutory scheme, but it should be noted that in that case, a scheme of arrangement permitting the payment of dividends to pre-administration creditors had been approved.
15   [1992] 1 WLR 672, see per Vinelott J at 674E–G.

15.4 In *Re Business Properties Ltd*[16] it was held, also by Harman J, that (under the old law) an administrator could not make a distribution to members[17]. This was on the basis that administration was a short-term process which was not designed to be terminal, and the position may have changed with the introduction of Schedule B1. However, on the assumption that such a power exists, and this may be clearer if a term to this effect is contained in a voluntary arrangement, a company in administration will still only be able to effect a distribution to its members if it has complied with the distribution of capital provisions contained in Part 23 of CA 2006. Section 829(2)(d) of CA 2006, which excludes a distribution of assets to members of a company on its winding up from the distribution restrictions contained in Part 23, does not exclude any distribution to members of a company during the course of its administration[18].

15.5 Notwithstanding the above authorities, in *Re Mount Banking plc*[19] it was held by Ferris J that pending the administrators' attempts to achieve the purposes for which they were appointed, which in that case included the survival of the company and the whole or part of its banking undertaking as a going concern, the administrators did have power to make a payment on account to depositors. The amount of the payment on account was calculated so as not to exceed the amount the depositors would have received in the event of a liquidation of the company, and the payment was to be made on terms that the depositors undertook that in any subsequent liquidation they would bring the payments received by them from the administrators into account and hold any dividends received by them in any such liquidation on trust for other creditors so far as necessary to ensure that other creditors were not prejudiced by the payment on account. The payment on account was justified on the basis that it was necessary to preserve the goodwill of the company's business pending the attempt to achieve the survival of the company and its business. The facts of that case were somewhat special, but it was eventually decided under the former law that the court could always give directions for a similar course to be adopted in any case in which it was plainly in the interests of the company's unsecured creditors for it to be done (in any event so long as it could be said to be necessary or incidental to the purpose for which the administrator was appointed[20]), although it remained a most unusual direction to be given[21]. Furthermore, a direction would not have been appropriate unless the court was satisfied that the recipient of the payment was being treated no more advantageously than he would be on a liquidation[22]. In the normal case in which the company was insolvent, the proper course was for the administrator to apply for the administration order to be discharged to enable

---

16   (1988) 4 BCC 684.
17   (1988) 4 BCC 684 per Harman J at 686.
18   *Re TXU Europe Group plc* [2011] EWHC 2072 (Ch).
19   (25 January 1993, unreported) discussed in *Re MG Rover Espana SA* [2006] EWHC 3426 (Ch) (paragraph 15).
20   *Re The Designer Room Ltd* [2004] EWHC 720 (Ch), *Re Lune Metal Products Ltd* [2006] EWCA Civ 1720 (paragraph 19).
21   *Re WBSL Realisations 1992 Ltd* [1995] 2 BCLC 576 in which Knox J discussed the width of the power under Schedule 1 paragraph 13 of IA 1986 in support of his conclusion, followed by Pumfrey J in *Rolph v A Y Bank Ltd* [2002] BPIR 1231. In both cases, the equivalent passage in the first edition of this work was cited with approval.
22   *Rolph v A Y Bank Ltd* [2002] BPIR 1231 at 1241. Pumfrey J also pointed out that a cautious approach was desirable because administrators did not then have power to determine provable debts, a deficiency which has been rectified by the introduction of the provisions contained in what is now Rule 14.7 of the Rules.

the company to go into liquidation so that the liquidator would then be able to make a distribution[23].

15.6 The restrictive nature of the jurisdiction to distribute was inconvenient and, in many cases, led to greater expense than was necessary or desirable, by reason of the additional costs caused by the need for the company to be placed in liquidation or made subject to a voluntary arrangement before a distribution could be made. In order to deal with this inconvenience, Schedule B1 paragraph 65 of IA 1986 introduced a power which gives to the administrator a general discretion to make a distribution to any creditor of the company[24], although, where the distribution is to be made to a creditor who is neither secured nor preferential, he may not do so unless the court gives permission[25]. Where this process has begun it is usual to refer to the administration as a distributing administration[26], and there will be some contractual contexts in which it will be right to treat it as equivalent to a winding-up[27]. Schedule B1 of IA 1986 gives no further guidance as to the circumstances in which the grant of permission to distribute might be appropriate. The most obvious situation is the case in which liquidation is unnecessary, because the effect of the administration has also been to wind up the company's affairs, but there are assets available for distribution to the company's unsecured creditors. In such a case, it will not be difficult to conclude that a distribution by the administrator is in the best interests of the company's creditors as a whole, and it will therefore be appropriate for permission to be granted[28]. In *Re MG Rover BeLux SA*[29] the court identified a number of relevant factors to be taken into account when deciding whether to grant permission: (a) the matter is to be judged at the time when permission is sought, at which time the court must be satisfied that the proposed distribution is conducive to the achievement of the objectives of the administration; (b) the court must be satisfied that the distribution is in the interests of the company's creditors as a whole; (c) the court must be satisfied that proper provision has been made for secured and preferential creditors; (d) the court must consider the realistic alternatives to the proposed distribution and assess whether the proposed distribution adversely affects the entitlement of others; (e) the court must take into account the basis on which the administration has been conducted (including the proposals) and the creditors' views on the proposed distribution; (f) the court must consider the nature and terms of the distribution and its impact on any proposed exit route. This approach has been considered and applied in a number of subsequent cases[30]. More generally, the Supreme Court confirmed in the *Nortel* case that paragraph 65 was intended to apply where the payment in question is necessary or desirable to achieve one of the administrator's statutory

---

23 The mere fact that an administration distribution would have been cheaper and more convenient than one effected through the mechanism of a liquidation did not give the court jurisdiction to grant permission for one to be made; it could not be said to be necessary or incidental to the performance by the administrators of their functions as such: *Re The Designer Room Ltd* [2004] EWHC 720 (Ch).

24 For these purposes, the structure of Part 14 of the Rules makes clear that the distributions with which Schedule B1 paragraph 65 is concerned are distributions to creditors with provable debts.

25 Schedule B1 paragraph 65(3) of IA 1986.

26 *In re Lehman Brothers (Europe) (No 4)* [2015] EWCA Civ 485 (paragraph 6) per Lewison LJ.

27 *In re Kaupthing Singer & Friedlander Ltd (in administration)* [2010] EWHC 316 (Ch).

28 *In re GHE Realisations Ltd* [2005] EWHC 2400 (Ch) (paragraphs 8, 9 and 11).

29 [2006] EWHC 1296 (Ch) (paragraph 7).

30 *Re M F Global (Overseas) Ltd* (5 June 2013, unreported), per David Richards J and *In re Nortel Networks (UK) Ltd* [2015] EWHC 2506 (Ch) (paragraphs 20–22) per Snowden J.

functions under Schedule B1 paragraph 3 of IA 1986. It was not intended to give the court a roving commission to change the statutory priorities in a particular case simply because it does not like the consequences of those priorities[31].

15.7   There will be circumstances in which particular categories of creditor may be adversely or beneficially affected by a distribution in an administration as opposed to a liquidation. In such cases, the court may be faced with a difficult decision as to what is in the best interests of the company's creditors as a whole, being the primary test which the court should apply in deciding whether to grant permission[32]. Thus the rules relating to interest[33] may alter the amount of the provable debt depending on whether the distribution is to be made in a liquidation or an administration. It may also be the case that the court's jurisdiction to give permission to distribute is limited to the circumstances in which it can also give directions under Schedule B1 paragraph 68(2) of IA 1986[34]. It is thought, however, that the jurisdiction is not circumscribed in that way because the grant of permission for a specific statutory power is different in concept from a general direction in connection with any aspect of the management of the company's affairs, business or property. Doubtless, however, it will require exceptional circumstances for permission to distribute to be granted when such permission would be inconsistent with the approved proposals and there has been no material subsequent change of circumstance.

PROCEDURES FOR MAKING A DISTRIBUTION

15.8   In the normal course a distribution under Schedule B1 paragraph 65 of IA 1986 will involve payment of a dividend to all of a company's creditors, or to all of a particular class or category of a company's creditors, and the relevant procedures are directed at the means by which that can be achieved in accordance with the *pari passu* rule as now codified in Rule 14.12 of the Rules. However, paragraph 65 also contemplates that a distribution might be made to a single creditor, and this is what occurred with the court's permission in *Re HPJ UK Ltd*[35]. This was an unusual case in which the administrator's power of compromise was being used, and it seems as if the payment may also have been justified under either Schedule B1 paragraph 66 of IA 1986 or Schedule 1 paragraph 13 of IA 1986. Having referred to the width of the power under paragraph 65, the court concluded that the power to distribute was wide enough to permit a distribution to a single creditor, where a compromise which involved

---

31   *In re Nortel GmbH (in administration)* [2013] UKSC 52 (paragraph 120). This statement of principle is consistent with the approach to paragraph 65 which had been adopted by Morgan J in *In re Portsmouth City FC Ltd* [2012] EWHC 3088 (Ch) (paragraphs 101–105) to the effect that the paragraph was not intended to promote creditors above their status as unsecured creditors, in the absence of some special reason (connected with the administration) for doing so. This judgment was approved by the Court of Appeal without further analysis: *In Re Portsmouth City FC Ltd* [2012] EWHC 3088 (Ch).

32   *In re GHE Realisations Ltd* [2005] EWHC 2400 (Ch) and Schedule B1 paragraph 3(1)(b2) of IA 1986.

33   See Rule 14.23 of the Rules and section 189(2) of IA 1986. See also *Re Lehman Brothers International (Europe) (No 4)* [2015] EWCA Civ 485 (paragraphs 102–111).

34   The court can normally only give directions where no proposals have been approved, or where the directions are consistent with the approved or revised proposals, or where the court thinks that the direction is required to reflect a change of circumstances since that approval or in the case of misunderstandings about the proposals (Schedule B1 paragraph 68(3) of IA 1986).

35   [2007] BCC 284.

the resolution of a disputed claim and the making of such a distribution facilitated the further conduct of the administration in the interests of the company's creditors as a whole. This approach is consistent with what Lord Neuberger said in the *Nortel* case[36] when, in dealing with an argument based on *Ex parte James; In re Condon*[37], he explained that paragraph 65 was intended to apply where the payment in question is necessary or desirable to achieve one of the administrator's statutory functions under Schedule B1 paragraph 3 of IA 1986.

15.9 Part 14 of the Rules now deals with distributions in administration and winding up together. If the court does give permission to distribute, this Part of the Rules makes detailed provision for the procedures to be adopted and the principles to be applied in making that distribution. The distributions with which Part 14 is concerned are distributions to creditors, but it should be noted that a member state liquidator appointed in main or secondary proceedings in another EU state is also entitled to lodge a claim in an English administration of the same company[38]. This claim operates as a proof of the claims lodged in the proceedings being administered by that member state liquidator. Where, however, the creditor whose debt is lodged under Article 45 also seeks to make his own claim by proof in his own right, payment of a distribution may only be made to the creditor as opposed to the member state liquidator[39]. The giving of notice to declare a dividend or make a distribution under Rule 14.29 of the Rules is the act which initiates the process. It must be given to the creditors in the administration[40] and to any member state liquidator appointed in relation to the company[41]. The notice must also be gazetted[42] and (if the administrator thinks fit) advertised in some other manner[43], unless the distribution is only to preferential creditors in which event the administrator has a discretion whether to do so[44]. Where the intended dividend is only for preferential creditors, the notice need only be delivered to them[45], and where it is to unsecured creditors as well it must state the value of the prescribed part (if applicable)[46]. It must specify a last date for proving which must be not less than 21 days from the date of the notice[47].

15.10 As is to be expected, the overriding principle in any distribution is that the company's unsecured debts rank equally between themselves and after the preferential debts[48]. The primary obligation to make prior payment to the company's preferential creditors is imposed by Schedule B1 paragraph 65(2) of IA 1986 which applies section 175 of IA 1986 to any distribution made in

---

36   *In re Nortel GmbH (in administration)* [2013] UKSC 52 (paragraph 120).
37   (1874) LR 9 Ch App 609.
38   Article 45 of the EC Insolvency Regulation.
39   Rule 14.32(4) of the Rules.
40   Rule 14.29(1)(a) of the Rules. Where the distribution is only to preferential creditors, the administrator is not obliged to give notice of a proposed distribution to the company's other creditors (Rule 14.29(2) of the Rules).
41   Rules 21.8(1) and 21.8(2)(a)(v) of the Rules.
42   Rule 14.28(1) of the Rules.
43   Rule 14.28(3) of the Rules.
44   Rule 14.28(2) of the Rules.
45   Rule 14.29(2) of the Rules.
46   Rule 14.29(3) of the Rules. For the administrator's duty in relation to the prescribed part, see below.
47   Rule 14.30(c) of the Rules.
48   Rule 14.12(2) of the Rules.

an administration. The effect of this provision is to impose on the administrator a statutory duty to pay those preferential creditors before he makes any distribution to the unsecured creditors[49]. For these purposes, the company's preferential creditors are now limited to unpaid contributions to occupational pension schemes, employees' remuneration, certain levies on coals and steel production and debts owed in relation to the Financial Services Compensation Scheme[50]. The relevant date, ie the date on which the period for calculating the preferential creditor's claim ends, will be the date on which the company entered administration[51]. As is also to be expected, the preferential debts themselves rank after the expenses of the administration[52]. There is a more detailed treatment of what constitutes an expense and the means by which expenses are paid later in this chapter, but the only place in which they are dealt with in Part 14 of the Rules is Rule 14.38, which provides that, where the dividend is a sole or final dividend, before making payment, the administrator is obliged to pay:

(a) any outstanding expenses of any liquidation or provisional winding up which preceded the administration;

(b) any amounts already payable in accordance with Schedule B1 paragraph 99 of IA 1986 (ie including the administrator's remuneration and expenses)[53]; and

(c) any amount outstanding (including debts or liabilities and the administrator's own remuneration and expenses) which would be payable under Schedule B1 paragraph 99 of IA 1986 if he were to cease to be administrator of the company[54].

15.11 For the purposes of identifying whether a claim qualifies as a provable debt, the draftsman of the Rules has introduced the concept of a 'relevant date', which is either the date that the company entered administration or (in the unusual case of a company being in liquidation immediately before the time that it entered administration) the date the company went into liquidation. It is then provided[55] that the company's debts are any debt or liability:

(a) to which the company is subject at the relevant date, or

(b) to which it may become subject thereafter by reason of any obligation incurred before that date, and

(c) any provable interest.

---

49 Presumably any breach is actionable at the suit of a preferential creditor in the same way as any breach by a liquidator or receiver of the equivalent duty, as to which see *IRC v Goldblatt* [1972] Ch 498. See also *Re BHT (UK) Ltd; Duckworth v Nat West Finance Ltd* [2004] EWHC 201 (Ch), for a case in which a liquidator failed in a restitutionary claim against a chargee which had received distributions from administrative receivers which should have been paid to the preferential creditors.

50 Section 386(1) and Schedule 6 to IA 1986.

51 Section 387(3A) of IA 1986. This will also be the relevant date where the distribution is to be effected in the course of a voluntary arrangement approved after the company has entered administration. If the distribution is to be made through a voluntary arrangement without an administration, the relevant date will be the date on which it takes effect and where a Schedule A1 moratorium is in force the relevant date will be the date of filing: section 387(2A) of IA 1986.

52 Schedule B1 paragraph 65(2) applying section 175 of IA 1986.

53 This is to cover the unusual circumstance in which an unpaid amount became payable under Schedule B1 paragraph 99 of IA 1986 at the time at which a predecessor administrator ceased to hold office.

54 Rule 14.38(1)(b) of the Rules.

55 By Rule 14.1(3) of the Rules,.

15.12 *Payments and distributions*

It is immaterial whether the debt or liability is present or future, certain or contingent, fixed or liquidated or capable of being ascertained by fixed rules or as a matter of opinion[56]; in all such cases the liability is capable of being a debt for the purposes of receiving a distribution. The basis for the liability, whether it be contract, statute or tort is also immaterial[57].

15.12 The question of what constitutes a contingent liability, and more particularly whether a debt is one to which the company may become subject after the relevant date by reason of any obligation incurred before that date, has been the subject of detailed consideration by the Supreme Court *In re Nortel GmbH* (in administration)[58]. In the *Nortel* case, the court was concerned with the question of whether a company's liability under a financial support direction (FSD) issued by the Pensions Regulator under the Pensions Act 2004, or a contribution notice subsequently imposed under the same legislation, was provable in its administration, even though the FSD was not issued until after the relevant date. The resolution of this issue involved analysing what was capable of constituting the obligation out of which any particular liability arises. As Lord Neuberger explained, where the source of the liability is a contract there is no particular difficulty. In so far as the contract imposes actual or contingent liabilities on a company, the incurred obligation is to be found in the relevant contract, and if that contract was entered into before the relevant date the liability will be a provable debt within what is now Rule 14.1(3)(b) of the Rules[59]. The position is more complex where the liability arises other than under a contract, and more particularly where it does so pursuant to a statute which was in force before the relevant date. Lord Neuberger's conclusion was that, in any such case, the company will normally have incurred an obligation if it has taken or been subjected to some step or combination of steps (a) which had some legal effect, and (b) which resulted in it being vulnerable to the specific liability such that there was a real prospect of that liability being incurred. Where that is the case it is also relevant to consider (c) whether it would be consistent with the regime under which the liability is imposed to conclude that the steps gave rise to an obligation under the Rule[60]. In deciding that the application of this test meant that any FSDs which might be imposed on the Nortel companies would give rise to provable liabilities, the Supreme Court swept away a significant part of the old case law dealing with the characteristics of a contingent liability[61]. It stressed that what was important was to identify the nature of the relationship between the parties arising out of the statutory scheme or body of rules as at the relevant date[62]. If a liability might then arise from the scheme, that is sufficient to point to the existence of an incurred obligation at the relevant date. This approach is both consistent with the existence of a contingent liability in other contexts[63] and

---

56 Rule 14.1(5) of the Rules.
57 *Secretary of State for Trade and Industry v Frid* [2004] UKHL 24 (paragraph 19). Liability means a liability to pay money or money's worth, including any liability under an enactment, any liability for breach of trust, any liability in contract, tort or bailment and any liability arising out of an obligation to make restitution: Rule 14.1(6) of the Rules.
58 [2013] UKSC 52.
59 *In Re Nortel GmbH* [2013] UKSC 52 (paragraph 75).
60 *In Re Nortel GmbH* [2013] UKSC 52 (paragraph 77).
61 Six cases were overruled including four decisions of the Court of Appeal (*In re British Gold Fields of West Africa* [1899] 2 Ch 7, *In re A Debtor (No 68 of 1911)* [1911] 2 KB 652, *Glenister v Rowe* [2000] Ch 76 and *R (Steele) v Birmingham City Council* [2005] EWCA Civ 1824).
62 On this aspect of the reasoning see also Lord Sumption at [2013] UKSC 52 (paragraps 178 and 179).
63 *In re Sutherland, decd* [1963] AC 235.

with a more general legislative policy leading to the progressive widening of the definition of provable debts[64].

15.13 In England and Wales, the Rules also make detailed provision for the machinery by which a creditor must prove his debt. The claim must be in writing, but need not be in any particular form[65]. It must, however, be authenticated by the creditor or someone authorised on his behalf[66] and it must state a number of specific matters[67]. These are the creditor's name and address, the total amount of the claim at the date of administration less any payments made after that date in relation to the claim, any deduction for trade and other discounts and any adjustment for set-off, whether the claim includes any uncapitalised interest, and particulars of how and when the debt was incurred. The claim must also give particulars of any security held, the date on which it was given, the value which the creditor puts on his security and details of any reservation of title in respect of goods to which the debt relates. If there are any documents by which the debt can be substantiated details of them must be specified in the proof, but they do not need to be attached to it unless the administrator requests them to be produced where he thinks that their production is necessary for the purpose of substantiating the whole or part of the claim made in the proof[68]. Unless the court orders otherwise, the creditor's own costs of proving his debt (including the production of documents) are born by himself, while the administrator's own costs of estimating the claim are payable as an expense of the administration[69]. Any creditor who has proved his debt and any contributory is entitled to inspect the proofs at all reasonable times on any business day[70]. Once it has been submitted, a creditor's proof may at any time be withdrawn or (by agreement between himself and the administrator) varied as to the amount claimed[71].

15.14 Debts can be admitted for dividend either in whole or in part, but if the whole or any part of the claim is rejected the administrator is required to prepare a written statement of his reasons for doing so and to send it as soon as reasonably practicable to the creditor[72]. In making his decision, it is presumably the case that the administrator is acting in a quasi-judicial capacity[73]. It is also thought that, as would be the case in a liquidation or a bankruptcy[74], he will be justified in going behind a judgment debt, if, but only if, it is necessary to avoid a miscarriage of justice in the sense that, if there had been a properly concluded judicial process it is likely that there would have been a finding that the debt was not in fact due to the claimant[75]. In that context, fresh evidence is admissible[76]. On receipt of

---

64   *In Re Nortel GmbH* [2013] UKSC 52 (paragraph 90) per Lord Neuberger.
65   Rule 14.3(1) of the Rules. The word 'proof' is defined by Rule 1.2(2) of the Rules.
66   Rule 14.4(1)(a) of the Rules. Where the proof is signed by a person other than the creditor that person's name, address and authority must be stated in the proof (Rule 14.4.(1)(k) of the Rules).
67   They are listed in Rule 14.4(1) of the Rules.
68   Rules 14.4(3) of the Rules.
69   Rule 14.5 of the Rules.
70   Rule 14.6 of the Rules, an entitlement which extends also to a member state liquidator (Rule 21.8(2)(a)(i) and (iv)).
71   Rule 14.10 of the Rules.
72   Rule 14.7 of the Rules.
73   *Re Menastar Finance Ltd* [2002] EWHC 2610 (Ch), [2003] 1 BCLC 338 at 347.
74   *Re Van Laun, ex p Chatterton* [1907] 2 KB 23.
75   *McCourt v Baron Meats Ltd* [1997] BPIR 114, *Re Menastar Finance Ltd* [2002] EWHC 2610 (Ch) and *International Brands USA Inc v Goldstein, Re Shruth Ltd* [2005] EWHC 1293 (Ch).
76   *Re Trepca Mines Ltd* [1960] 1 WLR 1273.

a statement of rejection, the creditor may apply to the court for the decision to be reversed or varied so long as he does so within 21 days of receipt[77]. Any member, contributory or other creditor of the company who is dissatisfied with the administrator's decision (whether to admit in full or to reject in whole or in part) may also apply to the court to reverse it and in his case the application must be made within 21 days of the time he becomes aware of the administrator's decision[78]. The period of time within which a challenge to the administrator's decision on a proof must be brought can be extended, but the court will only do so if good reason is shown, and in determining an extension application the court will have regard to the factors listed in CPR Rule 3.9 and the need for certainty in a collective insolvency process[79]. On the substantive challenge, the burden of proof is on the creditor seeking to reverse the administrator's decision[80]. The court conducts a hearing *de novo*[81] and in an appropriate case it will use all of the case management powers available to it[82] to determine the proper amount of the company indebtedness to the creditor concerned. The administrator himself may apply to the court for an order excluding a proof or reducing the amount claimed where he thinks that the proof has been improperly[83] admitted or ought to be reduced[84]. On such an application, the court has a discretion; thus, once it has been established on the burden of probabilities that the proof ought not to have been admitted, normal principles on the exercise of the discretion, such as the expiry of time and the balance of prejudice, will be applied to determine whether the relief ought to be granted[85].

PROOFS OF DEBT: THE VALUATION RULES

15.15 The rules, which relate to the estimation and valuation of claims proved for a distribution are based on those which apply in a liquidation. In any case in which the debt does not bear a certain value, the starting point is that the administrator is under a statutory duty to estimate its value[86]. He is then given a discretion to revise any estimate previously made by reference to any change of circumstance or to information becoming available to him[87]. In the ordinary course, a dissatisfied creditor should check that he does not wish to exercise that

---

77 Rule 14.8 of the Rules.
78 Rule 14.8(3) of the Rules. This entitlement also extends to any case in which the member, contributory or other creditor is dissatisfied with the administrator's decision to revalue a creditor's security under Rule 14.15 of the Rules.
79 *In Re Lehman Brothers International (Europe) (in administration) (No 5)* [2014] EWHC 1687 (Ch) and *In Re Legal Equitable Securities, Beller v Linton* [2010] EWHC 2046 (Ch).
80 *Bellmex International Ltd v British American Tobacco Ltd* [2001] 1 BCLC 91 at 97.
81 *Re Trepca Mines Ltd* [1960] 1 WLR 1273.
82 Including (for example) the power to order cross-examination of deponents (*Re Bank of Credit and Commerce International SA (No 6)* [1994] 1 BCLC 450) and the power to order further information and disclosure under Rule 12.27 of the Rules and CPR Parts 18 and 31.
83 The use of this word does not carry any moral opprobrium (*Re Globe Legal Services Ltd* [2002] BCC 858 at 862).
84 Rule 14.11 of the Rules. If the administrator declines to interfere, an application can be made by a member, contributory or creditor: Rule 14.11(1)(b) of the Rules. Any application must be made on notice to the creditor whose proof is in issue and (where not made by him) to the administrator: Rule 14.11(3) of the Rules.
85 *Re Globe Legal Services Ltd* [2002] BCC 858.
86 Rule 14.14(1) of the Rules.
87 Rule 14.14(2) of the Rules.

discretion before launching a challenge to the admission or rejection of the proof as the case may be[88]. The administrator's estimate of a claim for the time being is deemed to be the amount provable in the administration[89].

15.16 There are then a number of specific valuation rules. The first is that there must be deducted from a claim all trade and other discounts which would have been available to the company but for its administration except any discount for immediate or early settlement[90]. The second is that any proof for a debt incurred or payable in a foreign currency must state the amount of the debt in that foreign currency, but the administrator is then required to convert it into sterling at the single rate for each currency determined by reference to the rate prevailing on the relevant day[91]. Any creditor is entitled to challenge the rate selected by the administrator on the grounds of unreasonableness[92]. It should be noted that, unlike the position which existed up until 2005[93], the definition of 'relevant date'[94] means that there is no exchange rate differential between distributions in an administration and distributions in a succeeding liquidation of the same company – in both cases the relevant date at which the conversion must be made is the commencement of the administration[95]. The third relates to rent and other payments of a periodical nature. A creditor with such a claim may prove for any amounts due and unpaid up to the relevant date (normally the date when the company entered administration), applying an appropriate apportionment as if it had been accruing from day to day[96]. Thereafter, and for so long as any lease remains on foot, the landlord will be entitled to prove for instalments of rent as they fall due[97]. The fourth rule is that where a creditor has proved for a debt of which payment was not yet due on the date of the declaration of a dividend, he is entitled to a dividend equally with the other creditors but subject to a discount on his admitted proof in accordance with a statutory formula to reflect early receipt[98].

15.17 There is then a complex provision dealing with interest. The basic rule is that, where a debt bears interest, the interest is provable as part of the debt, except in so far as it is payable in respect of a period after the company entered administration[99]. So far as other debts are concerned, the right to prove for

---

88   For applications challenging an administrator's decision on a proof see Rule 14.8 of the Rules.
89   Rule 14.14(4) of the Rules.
90   Rule 14.20 of the Rules.
91   Rule 14.21 of the Rules. Rule 14.21 is modified in its application to financial collateral arrangements by regulation 14 of FCAR 2003.
92   Rule 14.21(4) of the Rules.
93   When what was then Rule 2.86 of the former Rules was amended by the Insolvency (Amendment) Rules 2005 (SI 2005 No 527).
94   Rule 14.1(3) of the Rules.
95   The position is similar in the unusual case in which a liquidation is succeeded by an administration; in that circumstance the relevant date is the date the company went into liquidation, being the earlier of the formal insolvency processes to which the company was subjected.
96   Rule 14.22 of the Rules.
97   *In Re Park Air Services plc* [2000] 2 AC 172 at 187 and *Jervis v Pillar Denton Ltd* [2014] EWCA Civ 180 (paragraph 15).
98   Rule 14.44 of the Rules. The adjustment is to be made in accordance with a formula which has been redrafted to deal with the criticisms of the original version made in *Re Park Air Services* [2000] 2 AC 172 at 187–188, per Lord Millett.
99   Rule 14.23(1) of the Rules.

interest is restricted to two circumstances in which interest is provable at the Judgments Act rate[100]:

(a) from the date at which any unpaid debt payable by virtue of a written instrument was payable; or

(b) from the date at which any other debt was demanded in writing with notice given that interest would be payable from the date of demand, in each case until the relevant date (normally being the date on which the company entered administration)[101].

15.18 It is also provided that post-administration interest is payable out of any surplus after payment of the proved debts[102]. The rate at which interest is payable out of the surplus is the greater of the Judgments Act rate[103] and the rate applicable to the debt apart from the administration[104]. This rule generated a great deal of litigation in the administration of a number of companies in the Lehman group, in which a number of points of construction of the former rules were determined. In summary, those points were as follows (although at the time of writing a number of these determinations were subject to appeal):

(a) the surplus out of which statutory interest is payable is the surplus after the payment of all proved debts, which may not extend to all of the company's liabilities[105];

(b) the rule constitutes a direction to the administrators to apply the surplus in a particular manner and imposes a statutory liability on the company to pay statutory interest[106];

(c) the rule operates as a complete code for the payment of post-administration interest on proved debts[107];

(d) the rule does not contemplate a re-allocation of dividends previously paid so as to treat those dividends as having been applied first in payment of interest[108];

(e) the rate applicable to the debt apart from the administration includes not just contractual interest but also interest payable under a foreign judgment obtained before the relevant date – it does not however extend to interest payable under judgments obtained thereafter[109];

---

100 Section 17 of the Judgments Act 1838. At present 8%: see Judgment Debts (Rate of Interest) Order 1993 (SI 1993 No 564).

101 Rule 14.23 of the Rules.

102 Rule 14.23(7) of the Rules.

103 Payable on a simple, not a compound basis: *Re Lehman Brothers International (Europe) (in administration)* [2015] EWHC 2269 (Ch) (paragraph 18).

104 Rule 14.23(7)(c) of the Rules. In considering which is the greater, it is necessary to take into account the total amounts of interest that would be payable based on each method of calculation, and also to take into account not just the numerical percentage but also the mode of calculating the rate (ie compounding): *Re Lehman Brothers International (Europe) (in administration)* [2015] EWHC 2269 (Ch) (paragraphs 22 and 28).

105 *In re Lehman Brothers International (Europe) (in administration)* [2014] EWHC 704 (Ch).

106 *In re Lehman Brothers International (Europe) (in administration) (No 4)* [2015] EWCA Civ 485.

107 *Re Lehman Brothers International (Europe) (in administration)* [2015] EWHC 2269 (Ch) (paragraph 164).

108 *Re Lehman Brothers International (Europe) (in administration)* [2015] EWHC 2269 (Ch) (paragraph 154) declining to apply the principle in *Bower v Marris* (1841) Cr & Ph 351.

109 *Re Lehman Brothers International (Europe) (in administration)* [2015] EWHC 2269 (Ch) (paragraph 183).

(f)   statutory interest is payable from the relevant date on debts which were future or contingent as at the relevant date[110];

(g)   statutory interest payable under Rule 14.23(7) is not 'yearly interest' within the meaning of section 874 of the Income Tax Act 2007, and so payment can be made gross without the deduction of basic rate income tax[111].

PROOFS OF DEBT: SET-OFF

15.19   The rule which deals with set-off in an administration[112] is similar but not identical to the rule which applies in a liquidation and only applies where, being authorised to do so, the administrator has given notice of proposed distribution pursuant to Rule 14.29 of the Rules. Many of the issues which have arisen in relation to the equivalent rule in a liquidation also now arise in the context of an administration distribution. Rule 14.24(2) of the Rules requires the administrator to take an account as at the date of the notice of proposed distribution[113] of what is due from the company and a creditor to each other in respect of their mutual dealings[114]. The language is slightly different from the words used in relation to liquidation set off but in both cases the mutual dealing must be with a person described as a creditor proving or claiming to prove in the administration or liquidation[115]. This means that the claim against the company must satisfy the test for provability already described above, and must therefore amount to a debt or liability to which the company is subject at the date the company entered administration or it must arise after that date by reason of an obligation incurred before that date[116]. The use of the word 'due' does not mean that the debt must be presently payable. This is clear from Rule 14.24(7) of the Rules which provides that a sum is to be treated as being due to[117] or from the company whether it is payable at present or in the future, whether the obligation by virtue of which it is payable is certain or contingent and whether its amount is fixed or liquidated or is capable of being ascertained by fixed rules or as a matter of opinion. The sums due from one party must then be set off against the sums due from the other[118]. Where the balance is owed by the company it is provable in the administration[119]. Where the balance is owed to the company it must be paid to the administrator as part of the assets, save to the extent that it results from a contingent or prospective debt owed by the creditor, in which event it must be paid in full without discount under Rule 14.44

---

110   *Re Lehman Brothers International (Europe) (in administration)* [2015] EWHC 2269 (Ch) (paragraph 225).

111   *Re Lehman Brothers International (Europe) (In administration)* [2016] EWHC 2492 (Ch).

112   Rule 14.24 of the Rules. This rule is modified in its application to financial collateral arrangements by regulation 12 of FCAR 2003.

113   Ie the notice given under Rule 14.29.

114   Rule 14.24 of the Rules.

115   Rules 14.24(6) and 14.25(6) of the Rules. See also Rule 14.25(1) of the Rules. It is long established that, although the Rules refer to a creditor who has submitted a proof, the true meaning is a creditor entitled to submit a proof whether or not he does so: *Stein v Blake* [1996] AC 243 at 253.

116   Rule 14.1(3) of the Rules, although there are also other bases on which it may be excluded from the account as further described below.

117   There has been a change in the Rules since *Stein v Blake* [1996] AC 243, so Lord Hoffmann's explanation (at 253A) of the quantification of contingent or unascertained claims by the company against the creditor is no longer good law.

118   Rule 14.24(2) of the Rules.

119   Rule 14.24(3) of the Rules.

of the Rules if and when it becomes due and payable[120]. As with its liquidation equivalent, the provisions of Rule 14.24 of the Rules are mandatory and cannot be excluded by agreement[121]. Furthermore, the set-off is self-executing[122] in the sense that its operation is automatic and is not dependent on the option of either party[123]. The principal distinction between administration and winding up is that in administration the automatic operation of the set-off takes effect as at the date of the notice of proposed distribution under Rule 14.29 of the Rules[124], whilst in winding up it takes effect as at the time of introduction of the formal insolvency process (viz the time at which the company goes into liquidation).

15.20 There are also special rules, which apply to the quantification of the claims by and against the company for the purposes of taking the set-off account. Thus, the estimation provisions contained in Rule 14.14 of the Rules are applied to obligations which do not bear a certain value[125], and it is thought that this is intended to apply to obligations on both sides of the account[126]. As to sums payable in a foreign currency, sums of a periodical nature and sums which bear interest, the relevant Rules which apply to proof of such sums against the company[127] are explicitly applied to that part of the set off account which quantifies sums due to the company[128]. Presumably it was thought that there was no need to make explicit that Rules 14.21 to 14.23 applied to sums owed by the company because they would be applied anyway to the quantification of any inbound provable claim. Finally, those provisions of the Rules which require a discount to be applied for the purposes of paying a dividend on a proof for a debt payment of which was not due at the date of declaration[129], are applied to the quantification of future sums due to and from the company for the purposes of the set-off account[130]. The discount is, however, limited to the set off, and so is not applicable to any balance owing to the company once the set off has been calculated[131].

---

120 Rule 14.24(4) and (5) of the Rules. The explicit reference to an exclusion of the discount provisions of Rule 14.44 of the Rules is statutory confirmation of the conclusion reached by the Court of Appeal in *In re Kaupthing Singer & Friedlander Ltd (in administration)* [2010] EWCA Civ 518 on the true construction of the former Rules.

121 Cf the liquidation case of *National Westminster Bank Ltd v Halesowen Presswork and Assemblies Ltd* [1972] AC 785. The mandatory nature of administration set off was confirmed by David Richards J in *In Re Lehman Bros International (Europe) (in administration)* [2014] EWHC 704 (Ch) (paragraphs 227, 243 and 246) (see also on appeal at [2015] EWCA Civ 485 at paragraph 236).

122 For the position in bankruptcy and winding up see: *Stein v Blake* [1996] AC 243 at 256D, *Orion Finance Ltd v Crown Financial Management Ltd (No 2)* [1996] 2 BCLC 382 at 387f–g and *Re Bank of Credit and Commerce International SA (No 8)* [1998] AC 214, 223B. The fact that administration set-off is also self-executing was accepted as clear by Briggs LJ in *In Re Lehman Bros International (Europe) (in administration) (No 4)* [2015] EWCA Civ 485 (paragraph 152).

123 *Stein v Blake* [1996] AC 243 at 254E and *Re Bank of Credit and Commerce International SA (No 8)* [1998] AC 214 at 233B.

124 *Revenue and Customs Commissioners v Football League Ltd* [2012] EWHC 1372 (Ch) (paragraph 84).

125 Rule 14.24(8)(a) of the Rules.

126 This was spelt out in the former Rules (Rule 2.85(5)), but the new drafting is not so clear cut.

127 Ie rules 14.21, 14.22 and 14.23 of the Rules.

128 Rule 14.24(8)(b) of the Rules.

129 Rule 14.44 of the Rules.

130 Rule 14.24(8)(c) of the Rules.

131 Rule 14.24(5) of the Rules, which clarifies that the discount provisions of Rule 14.44 of the Rules are only applied by Rule 14.24(8) for the purposes of the set-off itself, thereby giving statutory confirmation to the conclusion reached by the Court of Appeal in *In re Kaupthing Singer & Friedlander Ltd (in administration)* [2010] EWCA Civ 518.

15.21 It might be thought that the consequence of imposing a mandatory set-off with effect from the giving of notice under Rule 14.29 of the Rules is that debtors of the company can freely acquire set-off rights during the period between the commencement of the administration and the date of notice of intention to distribute. This potential problem has been mitigated by excluding from the definition of the mutual dealings to be brought into the statutory account debts[132] which arise out of obligations incurred after the company entered administration, after an immediately preceding winding up, or after a time when the creditor was on notice that an administration or an immediately preceding winding up was pending[133]. Rule 14.25 of the Rules also provides that in cases in which a liquidation was immediately preceded by an administration, the equivalent restriction on acquiring rights of set off relates back to the time at which the first steps were taken to place the company into administration[134]. It should also be noted that the set-off account taken on a distribution in an administration must exclude debts acquired by a creditor whether by assignment or otherwise under an agreement entered into after the date that steps were first taken to place it into administration (or an immediately preceding liquidation)[135]. These provisions prevent debtors from acquiring rights of set off against the company after the first steps have been taken to place it into administration, whether the distribution is made in the administration or a succeeding liquidation. Accordingly, the right to a set off will only be available if and to the extent that it could have been asserted if a formal insolvency had not intervened[136] and in the context either of legal proceedings[137] or the exercise of a remedy of self-help, ie outside the process of an administration distribution. It follows that third parties dealing with a company in administration will need to look to their position as an expense creditor for payment of post-administration credit if and to the extent that they are not paid before the company ceases to trade and notice to distribute has been given. Once the company has ceased trading and notice to distribute has been given, set-off will no longer be available.

THE POSITION OF SECURED CREDITORS

15.22 Schedule B1 to IA 1986 uses the word 'distribution' to describe payments made by the administrator not just to unsecured and preferential creditors but also to describe payments made to secured creditors out of assets charged to them[138]. From 2010, however, it was clear that the predecessor provisions to Part 14 of the Rules did not apply a proving process to the mechanism by which a secured creditor establishes his debt and receives payment out of the assets charged to him[139]. A distribution to which what was then Rule 2.68(1) of the

---

132 The use of the word 'debt' would appear to indicate that the exclusion is not intended to extend to sums owed to the company (see the definition in Rule 14.1(3) which limits the word debt to debts or liabilities owed by the company). This may be the legislative intent, but amounts to a change in the law from the form of Rule 2.85(4) of the Rules which was originally enacted in 2003.

133 Rule 14.24(6)(a)–(d) of the Rules.

134 Rule 14.25(6) of the Rules.

135 Rule 14.24(6)(e) of the Rules.

136 *Isovel Contracts Ltd v ABB Building Technologies Ltd* [2002] 1 BCLC 390.

137 For which permission to proceed might be required.

138 Schedule B1 paragraphs 3(1)(c) and 65(3) of IA 1986. See also section 176A(2)(b) of IA 1986.

139 The exclusion of distributions to secured creditors from Part 2 Chapter 10 of the former Rules was made explicit by an amendment to rule 2.68(1) of the former Rules made by the Insolvency (Amendment) Rules 2010 (SI 2010 No 686).

Rules referred, was limited to a payment made by an administrator out of the assets of the company[140], save to the extent that floating charge assets were being distributed by him to preferential creditors[141] and to unsecured creditors pursuant to the operation of the prescribed part[142]. The approach now taken by Part 14 of the Rules is to apply certain aspects of the proving regime to secured creditors[143], but to exclude them from the distribution provisions contained in Part 14 Chapter 3 of the Rules. This has the effect of treating them in the same manner as secured creditors in a winding up.

15.23 Furthermore, it is not the case that the only mechanism by which a secured creditor can recover the debt due to him is by asserting his rights to payment at a time notice to distribute is given. Thus, the realisation of a fixed charge asset can only be on terms (either imposed by the court, or more commonly agreed) that the proceeds of realisation shall be applied towards discharging the sums secured[144]. Alternatively, the secured creditor may have obtained the consent of the administrator or the permission of the court to enforce the security himself[145]. It is not thought, in either of these cases, that the application of a realisation in whole or partial discharge of the secured debt will constitute a distribution for the purposes of the Rules. The position is probably the same where a secured creditor seeks to procure the discharge of his debt out of the proceeds of assets charged by way of floating charge, whether or not a disposal by the administrator has been effected in reliance on his powers under Schedule B1 paragraph 70 of IA 1986. In any such case, the secured creditor's rights attach to the proceeds of the realisation, but rank after the preferential creditors, the expenses and the application of the prescribed part. It is thought that, while the preferential creditors and unsecured creditors will have to prove under Part 14 of the Rules to be entitled to a distribution out of the floating charge assets under section 175 or 176A of IA 1986, as the case may be, that is not the case for the holder of the floating charge himself. A secured creditor's entitlement to recovery is as the holder of a proprietary security interest in the relevant asset[146], not as a creditor proving for a share of a fund, although it may, of course, be necessary for him to come in and prove in respect of the unsecured element of his claim[147].

15.24 The Rules deal in detail with the position of secured creditors proving for a distribution in respect of the unsecured element of their claim. If a secured creditor has realised his security, whether prior to the administration or pursuant to the court's permission or the consent of the administrator under Schedule B1 paragraph 43(2) of IA 1986, he is entitled to prove for the balance of his debt after deducting the amount realised[148]. If he voluntarily surrenders his security

---

140 This is consistent with the fact that, in the context of liquidations, the rules for proving debts and paying dividends have only ever applied to distributions out of assets of the company. They have not applied to payments made to secured creditors out of charged assets, which fall outside the winding up altogether: see *Buchler v Talbot* [2004] UKHL 9.
141 Section 175 of IA 1986 as applied to an administration distribution by Schedule B1 paragraph 65(2) of IA 1986.
142 Section 176A of IA 1986.
143 Part 14 Chapter 2 of the Rules.
144 Schedule B1 paragraph 71(3) of IA 1986.
145 Schedule B1 paragraph 43 of IA 1986.
146 *Buchler v Talbot* [2004] UKHL 9.
147 See in particular Rules 14.4(1)(g), 14.15–14.19 and 14.41 of the Rules.
148 Rule 14.19 of the Rules.

for the general benefit of creditors, he is entitled to prove for his whole debt as if it were unsecured[149]. A secured creditor should have included in his proof the value which he puts on his security[150]; if he omits to disclose his security altogether, he is obliged to surrender it for the general benefit of creditors unless the court relieves him from the application of the relevant rule on the grounds that his omission was inadvertent or the result of an honest mistake[151]. Where the proof does disclose a value for the security, the creditor may, with the agreement of the administrator or the permission of the court, alter the value at any time[152]. If, however, he was the applicant for the administration order or the appointor of the administrator and has put a value on his security in the application or notice of appointment as the case may be, or if he has voted in respect of the unsecured balance of his debt, he can only revalue with the agreement of the administrator if he delivers a notice of the revaluation to the creditors within five business days of that agreement[153]. As part of the proving process, the administrator may redeem the security at the value put upon it in the creditor's proof[154] and if he does so the cost of transferring it is payable out of the assets[155]. Before exercising the power to redeem, the administrator must give 28 days notice that he proposes to do so. Once notice has been given, the creditor then has 21 days within which he must revalue his security, applying for the consent of the administrator or the leave of the court as the case may be[156]. If the administrator is dissatisfied with the value which a secured creditor puts on his security (whether or not pursuant to a re-valuation under Rule 14.15 of the Rules) he may require any property comprised in the security to be offered for sale and the terms of the sale will be as agreed or as directed by the court[157].

DECLARING AND PAYING A DIVIDEND

15.25   In the notice of proposed distribution under Rule 14.29 of the Rules, the administrator is required to identify a last date for proving which must be not

---

149   Rule 14.19(2) of the Rules.
150   Rule 14.4(1)(g) of the Rules.
151   Rule 14.16(1) of the Rules, as to which the onus is on the creditor (*In Re Safety Explosives Ltd* [1904] 1 Ch 226, 233). It should be noted that the obligation to surrender a security is subject to a secured creditor's rights under Article 5 of the EC Insolvency Regulation (Rule 14.16(3) of the Rules). Presumably, this means that where a creditor has the benefit of security situated in another member state, his omission to disclose that security in his proof of debt in an English administration will not cause it to be surrendered under Rule 14.16(1) of the Rules.
152   Rule 14.15(1) of the Rules. Rule 14.41 of the Rules explains what is to occur when a secured creditor re-values his security at a time when a dividend has been declared, including a provision that dividends declared (whether or not distributed) cannot be disturbed. It should be noted that where a creditor who has valued his security subsequently realises it, the net amount realised shall be substituted for the value previously put by him on the security and that amount shall be treated in all respects as an amended valuation made by him (Rule 14.19 of the Rules). Cf the discussion in *Whitehead v Household Mortgage Corpn plc* [2002] EWCA Civ 1657 and *Evans v Finance-U-Ltd* [2013] EWCA Civ 869.
153   Rule 14.15(3) of the Rules.
154   Rule 14.17(1) of the Rules. A secured creditor can call on the administrator to elect whether or not he will exercise this power and the administrator then has three months to do so or to determine not to exercise the power (Rule 14.17(5) of the Rules).
155   Rule 14.17(4) of the Rules.
156   Rule 14.17(2) of the Rules.
157   Rule 14.18 of the Rules. If the sale is by auction, the administrator (on behalf of the company) and the secured creditor may both appear and bid (Rule 14.18(3) of the Rules).

less than 21 days from the date of the notice[158]. He is then obliged, within 14 days of the last date for proving, to admit, reject or make appropriate provision for all proofs not already dealt with[159], and, within two months of the last date of proving, to declare a dividend to the specified class or classes of creditor[160]. He may not declare a dividend so long as there is pending any application to the court to reverse or vary a decision on a proof or to exclude a proof or reduce the amount claimed[161]. Notice of the declaration of the dividend must be given to all creditors who have proved their debts and to any member state liquidator appointed in relation to the company[162]. The distribution of the dividend can be made at the same time as the declaration notice[163]. There are also provisions which permit the court to disqualify a creditor from receiving a dividend on the grounds of contravention of any provision of IA 1986 or the Rules relating to the valuation of securities[164] and which provide a mechanism by which creditors can require the administrator to pay the dividend to a third party[165]. With the permission of the creditors or the creditors' committee, the administrator may divide the property in its existing form according to its estimated value (what used to be called a distribution in specie), so long as the property to be distributed cannot be readily or advantageously sold[166].

APPLICATION OF THE PRESCRIBED PART

15.26 Where a charge which is a floating charge on its creation relates to the property of a company in administration, the administrator is obliged to make a prescribed part of that company's net property available for the satisfaction of unsecured debts[167], a phrase which does not include the unsecured element of a secured creditor's claim[168]. He is also under a duty not to distribute that prescribed part to the holder of the floating charge except in so far as it exceeds the amount required for the satisfaction of the unsecured debts[169]. For these purposes, the company's net property is the amount which would, but for the operation of section 176A of IA 1986, be available for satisfaction of the claims of holders of a floating charge[170]. It seems to follow from this definition that the unsecured creditors' entitlement to a prescribed part of the floating charge assets ranks after the preferential creditors, because the amount available for satisfaction of the claims of holders of a floating charge is only such amount as is left after payment of the preferential creditors. Presumably, on the same basis, it also ranks after the sums payable out of floating charge assets under Schedule B1 paragraph 99 of IA 1986. The part of the company's net property which has

---

158 Rule 14.30(c) of the Rules.
159 Rule 14.32(1) of the Rules.
160 Rules 14.30(a) and 14.34(1) of the Rules.
161 Rule 14.34(2) of the Rules.
162 Rules 14.35(1) and 21.8(2)(a)(ii) of the Rules, the former of which also sets out the particulars which must be included in the declaration notice.
163 Rule 14.35(2) of the Rules.
164 Rule 14.42 of the Rules.
165 Rule 14.43 of the Rules.
166 Rule 14.13 of the Rules.
167 Section 176A(1) and (2)(a) of IA 1986.
168 *In re Airbase Services (UK) Ltd; Thorniley v Revenue and Customs Commissioners* [2008] EWHC 124 (Ch).
169 Section 176A(2)(b) of IA 1986.
170 Section 176A(6) of IA 1986.

been prescribed for the purposes of this provision is 50 per cent of amounts up to £10,000, plus 20 per cent of all amounts in excess of £10,000 subject to a maximum value available for the satisfaction of unsecured debts of £600,000[171].

15.27 These provisions do not apply if the company's net property is less than £10,000 and the administrator thinks that the costs of making a distribution would be disproportionate to the benefits[172] and they can be disapplied by the terms of a voluntary arrangement or a compromise agreed under Part 26 of CA 2006[173]. They do not apply to financial collateral arrangements[174]. They also have no application if the court orders that they should not do so in any case in which the administrator applies for an order disapplying section 176A(2) of IA 1986 on the grounds that the costs of making a distribution would be disproportionate to the benefits[175]. It is established that the court should not be too ready to disapply the provisions of section 176A(2) simply because the dividend would be small, and the courts have been at pains to stress that disapplication of section 176A(2) should be the exception not the rule[176]. It should also be noted that the court has no power to disapply section 176A(2) in relation to some only of the creditors[177]. The expenses associated with the prescribed part must be paid out of the prescribed part[178].

15.28 Section 176A of IA 1986 includes two quite separate duties. The first is a positive duty to make property available for the satisfaction of unsecured debts, the second is a negative duty not to distribute that property to the holder of a floating charge unless the unsecured creditors have been paid in full. Where the only possibility of a distribution to unsecured creditors is through an application of the prescribed part, it may be that an administration distribution[179] is the most efficient mechanism for making that property available for the satisfaction of unsecured debts. It is not thought, however, that section 176A of IA 1986 requires the administrator to make an actual payment to unsecured creditors simply because a prescribed part is payable. It is thought that, in cases in which an administration distribution is an unsuitable mechanism for paying dividends to unsecured creditors, the administrator will still comply with his obligation to make the net property 'available for the satisfaction' of unsecured debts if he ensures that the prescribed part is paid over to a subsequently appointed liquidator to be distributed in that liquidation, in any event so long as that distribution is then made. The obligation to make an asset available for satisfaction of a debt

---

171 Insolvency Act 1986 (Prescribed Part) Order 2003 (SI 2003 No 2097).
172 Section 176A(3) of IA 1986.
173 Section 176A(4) of IA 1986. In any such case the remedy of a disappointed unsecured creditor would be an unfair prejudice application under section 6 of IA 1986 or opposition to the company's application for sanction of the scheme under s.899 of Companies Act 2006.
174 Regulation 10 of the Financial Collateral Arrangements (No 2) Regulations 2003 (SI 2003 No 3226) and *Gray v G-T-P Group Ltd* [2010] EWHC 1772 (Ch) (paragraph 46).
175 Section 176A(5) of IA 1986. There are specific provisions set out in Rule 12.14 of the Rules for the material to be put before the court on any such application. The material must include a summary of the company's financial position and information substantiating the administrator's view that the cost of making such a distribution would be disproportionate to the benefits. For an example of such a case, see *Re Hydroserve Ltd* [2007] EWHC 3026 (Ch).
176 *Re International Sections Ltd* [2009] EWHC 137 (Ch), *Stephen & Hill (Administrators of QMD Hotels Ltd)* [2010] CSOH 168 and *Joint Administrators of Re Castlebridge Plant Ltd* [2015] CSOH 165.
177 *In re Courts plc* [2008] EWHC 2339 (Ch).
178 Rule 3.50(2) of the Rules. In the Rules, 'prescribed part' has the same meaning as it does in section 176A(2) of IA 1986: Rule 1.2(2) of the Rules.
179 In accordance with the procedures described above.

is different from an obligation to make a payment[180], particularly where there is a subsequent procedure administered by another (a liquidator) through which it may be the case that the payment can most effectively be made. It remains the case, however, that the administrator is under the primary obligation to make the prescribed part available and so might be in breach of his own duty if a liquidator fails to comply with an assurance that he will distribute it. It follows that, where a prescribed part is to be distributed by a liquidator in these circumstances, it would be prudent for the administrator to receive an indemnity from the liquidator against any failure to pay. Furthermore, the administrator ought to disclose that fact to the court or creditors as the case may be on any application for his discharge from liability[181] once he has ceased to be the administrator.

ADMINISTRATION COSTS AND EXPENSES

15.29 An administrator is not normally personally liable under contracts entered into by him as agent on behalf of the company unless it is apparent from the circumstances that the administrator intended to incur personal liability. Notwithstanding the absence of any such personal liability, the court has power to direct the administrator as its officer to make immediate payment in full of costs and expenses incurred by him and debts arising under contracts entered into by him as an expense of the administration[182]. Furthermore, there will be many cases in which an administrator considers it to be in the best interests of the company for a cost, expense or debt to be discharged forthwith and, in those cases, he will procure the company to make such payment without further directions from the court[183]. He will do so because it is well understood that administrators will normally pay expenses of the administration including salaries and other payments to employees as they arise during the continuance of the administration[184]. The position in relation to sums which he does not consider it appropriate to discharge or which have not in fact been discharged at the time he ceases to hold office is more complex. Furthermore, the legislation distinguishes between liabilities arising out of contracts entered into by an administrator and his other costs and expenses, notwithstanding that there will be many instances in which it would be proper to characterise a specific liability as both.

15.30 The effect of Schedule B1 paragraph 99(4) and (5) of IA 1986 is that upon a person ceasing to be administrator, sums payable in respect of debts and liabilities arising out of contracts entered into[185] and certain liabilities[186]

---

180 Cf the receiver's and liquidator's duty to pay preferential creditors (section 40 and 175 of IA 1986) and the administrator's duty to do so where he makes a distribution (Schedule B1 paragraph 65(2) of IA 1986).

181 As to which, see Schedule B1 paragraph 98 of IA 1986.

182 *Barclays Mercantile Business Finance Ltd v Sibec Developments Ltd* [1992] 1 WLR 1253.

183 *Re Salmet International Ltd* [2001] BCC 796 at 804A.

184 *Powdrill v Watson* [1994] 2 All ER 513 at 522, in which Dillon LJ also said 'There is no need to wait until the end, and it would be impossible as a practical matter to do that'.

185 This does not extend to a contract unless it comes into existence in the course of an administration by virtue of a positive and conscious act by the administrator: *In re PGL Realisations plc; Laverty v British Gas Trading Ltd* [2014] EWHC 2721 (Ch) (paragraph 64).

186 This is limited by paragraph 99(5)(c) to 'wages or salary', a phrase which does not include the statutory liabilities for redundancy or unfair dismissal, nor does it includes damages for unfair dismissal: *In Re Leeds United AFC Ltd* [2007] EWHC 1761 (Ch) and *In re Allders Department Stores Ltd* [2005] EWHC 172 (Ch).

arising under[187] contracts of employment adopted by him or a predecessor of his are charged on and payable out of any property of the company in his custody or under his control immediately prior to cessation[188] in priority both to any sums secured by any security over such property which was a floating charge on its creation and to the administrator's remuneration and expenses. The priority afforded to sums payable under contracts entered into or employment contracts adopted by an administrator is accordingly greater than the priority afforded to the administrator's remuneration and other expenses. Careful thought should therefore be given by an administrator before causing the company to enter into contracts or adopting employment contracts. This means that an employee or contracting counter-party will have an independent claim under Schedule B1 paragraph 99 of IA 1986 for payment and enforcement of the charge; a claim which arises at the end of the administration[189]. The nature of the charge has been given some consideration in the authorities[190], from which it is clear that the charge is a special statutory security with its own incidents. There is no statutory mechanism for its enforcement, but there is no doubt that the court has power to enforce it either by an order for sale or the appointment of a receiver[191]. It seems that the involvement of the court will normally be necessary[192], although, as the Court of Appeal pointed out in *In Re Hellas Telecommunications (Luxembourg) II SCA*[193], the question of how a paragraph 99 statutory charge can be enforced has not yet been the subject of a full decision. The statutory charge applies notwithstanding that, upon the administrator ceasing to act, control of the assets subject thereto passes to the official receiver or to another insolvency practitioner[194]. Where such control passes, the subsequently appointed office holder (whether a liquidator or a replacement administrator) will normally be able to pay out of that asset, the costs and expenses incurred in administering it (by application of the *Berkeley Applegate*[195] principle)[196].

15.31 The administrator's expenses are dealt with in a similar way. Thus, subject to the priority afforded to sums payable under contracts entered into or contracts of employment adopted by an administrator, where any person

---

187 For the significance of the word 'under' see *Re Huddersfield Fine Worsteds Ltd* [2005] EWCA Civ 1072 (paragraph 17), a case whose *ratio* is no longer relevant in the light of the repeal of Schedule B1 paragraph 99(6)(d) of IA 1986 by s.19 of the Deregulation Act 2015.

188 In *Re MK Airlines Ltd* [2012] EWHC 1018 (Ch), Sir Andrew Morritt C had to consider whether certain unrealized refunds later recovered by a liquidator fell within the ambit of the statutory charge. He held (at paragraph 23) that the legal test was whether a legal entitlement to the refunds had arisen at the time of cessation regardless of whether any steps had then been taken to recover them. See also the discussion in *Walker v National Westminster Bank plc* [2016] EWHC 315 (Ch) (paragraph 31).

189 *Re Maxwell Fleet and Facilities Management Ltd* [1999] 2 BCLC 721. The limitation period is six years on the obligation to pay and twelve years on the claim to enforce the charge. Furthermore, as that cause of action is only complete when the administrator vacates office, the limitation period will run from that point in time.

190 In *Re MK Airlines Ltd* [2012] EWHC 1018 (Ch), Morritt C said (at paragraph 25) that the statute makes no provision as to its effect and consequences and (at paragraph 44) that it does not fit the description of a fixed or floating charge.

191 *In re Hotel Company 42 The Calls Ltd* [2013] EWHC 3925 (Ch) (paragraph 12) and *In Re MK Airlines Ltd* [2012] EWHC 1018 (Ch) (paragraph 26).

192 *Walker v National Westminster Bank plc* [2016] EWHC 315 (Ch) (paragraph 28).

193 [2016] EWCA Civ 474 (paragraph 33).

194 *Re Sheridan Securities Ltd* (1988) 4 BCC 200 per Mervyn Davies J at 202–3. This will be the case both where the company goes into liquidation and where the administrator is replaced by another insolvency practitioner upon his vacating office.

195 *In re Berkeley Applegate (Investment Consultants) Ltd* [1989] Ch 32.

196 *In re Sports Betting Media Ltd* [2007] EWHC 2085 (Ch) (paragraph 11).

ceases to be administrator of a company, his remuneration and expenses are charged on and payable out of any property of the company which is then in his custody or under his control[197]. Further, the sums thereby secured in favour of the administrator have priority over sums secured by any security over the company's property which was a floating charge on its creation[198]. The nature of this statutory charge under Schedule B1 paragraph 99(3) of IA 1986 is the same as the charge imposed by paragraph 99(4) and (5). It would therefore appear to be capable of being invoked by third parties who have provided goods or services in an administration and remain unpaid, notwithstanding that the administrator is under no personal liability towards them.

15.32 Under the former law, the only reference in the legislation to the expenses of the administration was contained in the statutory predecessor to Schedule B1 paragraph 99(3) of IA 1986[199] and it was established that, in those circumstances, there was no room in administrations for what the Court of Appeal has called the hard-and-fast liquidation expenses principle[200]. It was held that, in an administration, Parliament intended there to be a more flexible approach to the question of whether a particular cost or liability should rank as an expense[201]. The statutory position has now changed. The administrator's expenses are not only charged on and payable out of the property of the company when his appointment ceases to have effect[202], they must also be defrayed on the making of a distribution by way of a sole or final dividend ahead of the preferential and unsecured creditors to whom that distribution is to be made[203]. Furthermore, the Rules also make provision for an order of priority in which what are described as the expenses of the administration are payable[204], a rule which is applicable whether or not a distribution is made[205]. This gives rise to the question of whether the flexible approach to payment of administration expenses described in *Re Atlantic Computer Systems plc*[206] is still applicable. In considering this question, it is important to appreciate that, unlike the commencement of a winding up, the mere fact that a company enters administration does not impose a statutory scheme for the distribution of the company's assets. Thus in a voluntary liquidation, part of the statutory distribution scheme (section 115 of IA 1986) obliges the liquidator to pay the expenses both out of the company's assets and in priority to all other claims[207]. This scheme applies with effect from the commencement of the liquidation[208], ie to all of the assets which are collected by the liquidator. There is no such general equivalent in an administration; indeed there are many cases in which the imposition of such a distribution scheme

---

197 Schedule B1 paragraph 99(3) of IA 1986.
198 Schedule B1 paragraph 99(3) of IA 1986 referring to Schedule B1 paragraph 70. For the definition of a floating charge, see Schedule B1 paragraph 111(1) of IA 1986.
199 Section 19(4) of IA 1986.
200 *Re Atlantic Computer Systems plc* [1992] Ch 505 at 527 a reference to the principle that the court will direct payment of outgoings on property the possession of which is retained for the purposes of the winding up.
201 *Re Atlantic Computer Systems plc* [1992] Ch 505 at 528.
202 Schedule B1 paragraph 99(3) of IA 1986.
203 Rule 14.38(1)(b) of the Rules. See also section 175 of IA 1986 as applied by Schedule B1 paragraph 65 of IA 1986.
204 Rule 3.51(2) of the Rules. The structure of the Rule is similar to Rule 7.108 of the Rules (the liquidation equivalent) but there are a number of differences.
205 Rules 3.50–3.52 of the Rules are in Part 3 of the Rules.
206 [1992] Ch 505.
207 See *Re Toshoku Finance UK plc* [2002] UKHL 6, [2002] 1 WLR 671 at 674.
208 *Buchler v Talbot* [2002] UKHL 9 (paragraph 28) per Lord Hoffmann.

from the outset would be inconsistent with the purpose of administration. In an administration, the statutory distribution scheme is only applied once the administrator has given notice of proposed distribution under Rule 14.29 of the Rules[209], an event which will often not occur. Accordingly, it is not thought that Rule 3.50 of the Rules affects the administrator's discretion to pay expenses in such order and at such time as he considers appropriate before notice of proposed distribution is given[210], although the discretion must, of course be exercised on settled principles and with proper regard both to the interests of the company and the achievement of the purpose of administration. That discretion is also, of course, subject to the court's jurisdiction to direct that a particular payment should be made whether on a creditor's application for permission to proceed or pursuant to its general power to give directions to its officers[211]. Its exercise will also be informed by the fact that, if an expense cannot ultimately be discharged out of the company's assets, the administrator will be exposed to proceedings for breach of duty[212].

15.33 Under the former law it was held that the class of expenses referred to in what was then section 19(4) of IA 1986 extended to any entitlement by the administrator to recover sums from the company which did not fall within what was then section 19(5) of IA 1986[213]. Rule 3.51 of the Rules now provides for what must be treated as an expense[214]. The reference to 'expenses of the administration' in Rule 3.51(2) is intended to encompass the same categories of expense as are covered by the concept of 'the former administrator's expenses' as that expression is used in Schedule B1 paragraph 99(3) of IA 1986[215]. It follows that, if an item qualifies as an expense within the meaning of Rule 3.51(2), it will be payable in the order of priority laid down by that rule both at the time of cessation[216] and at the stage of a distribution; to that extent there is no discretion[217]. Rule 3.51 of the Rules will also assist the administrator in assessing what is proper to be paid as an expense during the course of the

---

209 Although section 175 of IA 1986 is applied to an administration distribution (Schedule B1 paragraph 65(2)), it is not applied in an administration unless a distribution is effected under that paragraph. In *Re Polly Peck International plc (No 4)* [1998] 2 BCLC 185 at 201 Mummery LJ referred to administration as statutory scheme under which Parliament had sanctioned a *pari passu* distribution. In that case, however, the company was subject to a scheme of arrangement under section 425 of CA 1985, pursuant to which the administrators (as scheme supervisors) were distributing the company's assets.

210 Cf *Re Salmet International Ltd* [2001] BCC 796 at 803–804.

211 *Barclays Mercantile Business Finance Ltd v Sibec Developments Ltd* [1992] 1 WLR 1253.

212 Schedule B1 paragraph 75 of IA 1986.

213 Ie sums payable in respect of debts or liabilities incurred under contracts entered into by him or his predecessor in the carrying out of their functions. See *Re a Company (No 005174 of 1999)* [2000] 1 BCLC 593.

214 There is much in Rule 3.51 which is equivalent to Rule 7.108 of the Rules (the rule applicable in a liquidation). The comments of Blackburne J in *Re Salmet International Ltd* [2001] BCC 796 at 803G, to the effect that there is good reason for there being no administration equivalent to the predecessor to Rule 7.108 of the Rules, continue to hold good if it is recognised that, unlike its liquidation equivalent, Rule 3.51 does not apply a mandatory code from the commencement of the administration. It applies for the purpose of assessing expenses payable either at the moment of cessation or at the time of notice of proposed distribution.

215 Rule 3.50(4) of the Rules.

216 Pursuant to Schedule B1 paragraph 99(3) of IA 1986.

217 If something counts as an expense, it must be treated as such; ie there is no judicial discretion to say that it is not (cf *Re Toshuku Finance UK plc* [2002] UKHL 6, [2002] 1 WLR 671 at 682), a passage considered with approval in the context of administration expenses by Lord Neuberger in *In re Nortel GmbH* [2013] UKSC 52 (paragraph 117). That does not mean that it will be enforceable as such throughout the administration.

administration, but without (it is thought) requiring him to do so at any particular point in time. The order of priorities can be varied by the court where there is a shortfall[218]. It is difficult to see that this power to vary will ever be relevant in the case of a distribution because, if there is a shortfall for the expenses, it will not be appropriate for the administrator to give notice to distribute under Rule 14.29 of the Rules. The power to vary may, however, be more relevant where the issue is the priority of expenses charged at the time of cessation[219]. The listed expenses are as follows:

(a) expenses properly incurred by the administrator in performing his functions;

(b) the costs of any security provided by the administrator in accordance with IA 1986 or the Rules[220];

(c) the costs of the application for an administration order;

(d) the costs and expenses of an out of court appointment;

(e) any amount payable to a person in respect of assistance in the preparation of a statement of affairs or statement of concurrence[221];

(f) any allowance made, by order of the court, towards costs on an application for release from the obligation to submit a statement of affairs or statement of concurrence[222];

(g) any necessary disbursements by the administrator in the course of the administration (including any expenses incurred by members of the creditors' committee or their representatives and allowed for by the administrator under Rule 17.24, but not including any payment of corporation tax);

(h) the remuneration or emoluments of any person who has been employed by the administrator to perform any services for the company, as required or authorised under the Act or the Rules;

(i) the remuneration of the administrator agreed under Part 18 of the Rules and any unpaid pre-administration costs approved under Rule 3.52; and

(j) the amount of any corporation tax on chargeable gains accruing on the realisation of any asset of the company (irrespective of the person by whom the realisation is effected[223]).

15.34 It is important to appreciate that the mere fact that a liability is provable does not necessarily mean that it will not also constitute an administration expense[224]. In this context two of the categories of expense described in the Rules, ie category (a) expenses properly incurred by the administrator in performing his functions and category (g) any necessary disbursements by the administrator in the course of the administration warrant further explanation. Both of these categories of expense track the equivalent wording in relation to

---

218 By use of its powers under Rule 3.51(3) of the Rules.
219 Pursuant to Schedule B1 paragraph 99(3) of IA 1986.
220 See further, section 390(3) of IA 1986.
221 Presumably, a reference to the expenses described in Rule 3.34(1) of the Rules.
222 Rule 3.33 of the Rules.
223 Presumably therefore including not just the administrator, but also any secured creditor, or receiver or manager appointed to deal with a security, as was made explicit in the former version of the Rules.
224 *In re Nortel GmbH* [2013] UKSC 52 (paragraph 57). But in the normal case it will be one or the other: eg *In re PGL Realisations plc; Laverty v British Gas Trading Ltd* [2014] EWHC 2721 (Ch).

expenses of a liquidation[225]. As to expenses properly incurred, the concept is lifted from the former section 19(4) of IA 1986[226]. This form of words covers all liabilities properly incurred by or on behalf of the administrator personally[227] in the course of acting as such, including sums which as an officer of the court he has been or could have been directed to pay. The better view is that it does not extend any wider than this, despite the *obiter* comments to contrary effect by HHJ Purle QC in *Goldacre Offices Ltd v Nortel Networks UK Ltd*[228] in which it was suggested that the words were wide enough to cover all expenses incurred by an administrator (whether or not personally) in performing his functions. On the other hand, the court is likely to refuse to allow an administrator to reimburse or indemnify himself out of the assets of the company for expenses or liabilities incurred by him, where the court takes the view that although such expenses or liabilities were incurred by the administrator so as to make himself personally liable, they were not incurred properly[229].

15.35 As to necessary disbursements, this concept will cover any expense, which it is necessary for the administrator to pay during the administration. This category received authoritative consideration from the Supreme Court in *In re Nortel GmbH*[230], in which Lord Neuberger explained that the word 'necessary' carried with it a legal obligation to pay, although that is somewhat circular as it leaves open the very question which has to be decided, viz whether the liability imposed on the company is one which the administrator must pay[231]. The formulation which Lord Neuberger laid down with was that:

'a disbursement falls within [Rule 3.51(2)(g)] if it arises out of something done in the administration (normally by the administrator or on the administrator's behalf), or if it is imposed by a statute whose terms render it clear that the liability to make the disbursement falls on an administrator as part of the administration—either because of the nature of the liability or because of the terms of the statute.'

15.36 In the context of a liquidation, the phrase 'necessary disbursement' has been held to cover community charge and tax[232]. It will also include the other

---

225 Rule 7.108(4)(r) of the Rules in relation to expenses properly incurred (although the wording in winding up is 'properly chargeable') and Rule 7.108(4)(m) in relation to necessary disbursements. It is to be noted that the two categories rank differently in administration from where they rank in winding up, but it has been held on a number of occasions that the approach to what constitutes a liquidation expense and what constitutes an administration expense is the same: *Exeter City Council v Bairstow* [2007] EWHC 400 (Ch) (paragraphs 79–80), *In re Nortel GmbH* [2013] UKSC 52 (paragraph 117) and *In re Portsmouth City FC Ltd* [2012] EWHC 3088 (Ch) (paragraph 47) per Morgan J, whose judgment was approved by the Court of Appeal at [2013] Bus LR 1152 (see in particular paragraph 41).

226 The concept of an expense being 'properly incurred' no longer appears in section 19(4)'s statutory successor (viz Schedule B1 paragraph 99(3) of IA 1986).

227 *Exeter City Council v Bairstow* [2007] EWHC 400 (Ch) (paragraph 52), applying the approach adopted in *Freakley v Centre Re* [2006] UKHL 45.

228 [2009] EWHC 3389 (Ch) (paragraph 9). Although this point was not explicitly dealt with by the Court of Appeal in *Jervis v Pillar Denton Ltd* [2014] EWCA Civ 180, the fact that *Goldacre* was overruled weakens the authority of this *dictum* in any event.

229 Cf *Barclays Mercantile Business Finance Ltd v Sibec Developments Ltd* [1992] 1 WLR 1253 at 1260A–B.

230 [2013] UKSC 52 (paragraphs 97–114).

231 [2013] UKSC 52 (paragraph 99).

232 *Re Toshuku Finance UK plc* [2002] UKHL 6, [2002] 1 WLR 671 at 683 (in the case of community charge overruling *Re Kentish Homes Ltd* [1993] BCLC 1375).

side's costs of legal proceedings where the company is unsuccessful[233] and may even extend to costs incurred in respect of the period prior to the appointment of administrators[234]. It is now clear that this category also encompasses certain outgoings on property used for the benefit of the administration, including such items as rates[235] accruing due during the period of the administration[236]. It should be noted, however, that the true rationale for this is that the liability is one which was imposed on the company notwithstanding the administration[237]. The same principle will be applicable in relation to any statutory provision where it is possible to discern that there was a legislative decision to impose a liability that is to rank ahead of provable debts[238]. This was not established by a utility supplier seeking payment for the costs of electricity and gas supplied under deemed contracts following the time at which the relevant premises were no longer being used by the companies for the purposes of the administration[239]. The need to analyse both the source of the underlying liability, and its interaction with the terms of the insolvency legislation, is illustrated by the authorities on liabilities arising out of contracts of employment. Because the legislature has made special provision for the treatment of liabilities to employees both as preferential creditors, and under adopted contracts of employment, there is no room to treat further categories of employee liability as a necessary disbursement[240].

15.37 The position in relation to rent is slightly different. In a liquidation, the rule, which has hardened from the original exercise of a discretion into a rule of principle[241], is that such items should normally be paid as an expense, but not because they are an expense 'incurred by the liquidator' within the meaning of Rule 7.108 of the Rules. The obligation to pay rent arises out of a pre-insolvency event contract (in the form of a lease), but the court will still interpret the expenses rules as being applicable. The basis of the principle is that, where the property has continued to be occupied for the beneficial purpose of the winding up, the rent ought to be paid in full as a matter of equity[242]. The position in an administration has now been explained in the judgment of Lewison LJ in *Jervis v Pillar Denton Ltd*[243], which was a case concerned with the apportionment of

---

233 For a discussion of the invariable practice applicable in liquidation, see *Re Bank of Hindustan, China and Japan, ex p Smith* (1868) 3 Ch App 125 at 130, *Re Trent and Humber Shipbuilding Co, Bailey and Leatham's case* (1869) LR 8 Eq 94, *Re London Metallurgical Co* [1895] 1 Ch 758 at 764 and *Norglen Ltd v Reeds Rains Prudential* [1999] 2 AC 1 at 20.

234 See the liquidation cases of *Re London Drapery Stores* [1898] 2 Ch 684 and *Re Wenborn & Co* [1905] 1 Ch 413.

235 This does not apply to unoccupied property rates, in respect of which the *obiter* conclusion of David Richards J in *Exeter City Council v Bairstow* [2007] EWHC 400 (Ch) (paragraph 87) has now been reversed by Regulation 4(1) of the Non-Domestic Rating (Unoccupied Property) (England) Regulations 2008 (SI 2008 No 386).

236 *Exeter City Council v Bairstow* [2007] EWHC 400 (Ch) and *Jervis v Pillar Denton Ltd* [2014] EWCA Civ 180 (paragraphs 72–75). The rates cases were considered in the context of deemed contracts for the supply of gas and electricity in *In re PGL Realisations plc; Laverty v British Gas Trading Ltd* [2014] EWHC 2721 (Ch).

237 See *In re Nortel GmbH* [2013] UKSC 52 (paragraphs 102–104).

238 *In re Nortel GmbH* [2013] UKSC 52 (at para 111).

239 *In re PGL Realisations plc; Laverty v British Gas Trading Ltd* [2014] EWHC 2721 (Ch).

240 *Exeter City Council v Bairstow* [2007] EWHC 400 (Ch) (paragraphs 74–77), considering *In re Allders Department Stores Ltd* [2005] EWHC 172 (Ch). See also *In re Leeds United AFC Ltd* [2007] EWHC 1761 (Ch).

241 See *Re Toshuku Finance UK plc* [2002] UKHL 6, [2002] 1 WLR 671 at 680C.

242 For a discussion of the law see Lord Hoffmann's speech in *Re Toshuku Finance UK plc* [2002] UKHL 6, [2002] 1 WLR 671 at 677F–681C.

243 [2014] EWCA Civ 180.

rent payable in advance. This judgment contains a comprehensive explanation of the circumstances in which rent arising under a pre-administration lease will be payable as an administration expense and the conclusion is summarised at the end of his judgment as follows[244]:

'The true extent of the principle, in my judgment, is that the office holder must make payments at the rate of the rent for the duration of any period during which he retains possession of the demised property for the benefit of the winding up or administration (as the case may be). The rent will be treated as accruing from day to day. Those payments are payable as expenses of the winding up or administration. The duration of the period is a question of fact and is not determined merely by reference to which rent days occur before, during or after that period.'

15.38 Where the costs, charges and expenses of any person are payable out of the assets of the company in administration, it is always open to the administrator to agree the amount at which they are to be paid. In the absence of agreement between the administrator and the person entitled to payment, such costs, charges and expenses are required to be decided by detailed assessment in the court to which the administration is allocated[245]. The administrator may require taxation by notice in writing requiring the person entitled to commence detailed assessment proceedings under CPR Part 47[246]. Further, if the creditors' committee resolves that any such costs, charges and expenses should be decided by detailed assessment, the administrator is bound to require it[247]. Where a detailed assessment is required, the administrator is not precluded from making payments on account to the person seeking payment but that person must provide an undertaking to repay immediately any money which may prove to have been overpaid, with interest at the rate specified in section 17 of the Judgments Act 1838 on the date payment was made and for the period from the date of payment to that of repayment[248]. However, it was held by the Court of Appeal in *In Re Hellas Telecommunications (Luxembourg) II SCA*[249] that, once those costs charges and expenses had been agreed by the administrator, they could not subsequently be subjected to assessment proceedings under the predecessor to Rule 12.42 of the Rules at the suit of a liquidator. Any subsequent challenge by a liquidator would have to be pursued by misfeasance proceedings or an unfair prejudice application[250]. Furthermore to the extent that any costs charges and expenses had not already been paid at the time the administrator went out of office, enforcement of their payment under the statutory charge might be at risk[251].

15.39 Before making a detailed assessment of the costs in England and Wales of any person employed by the administrator in an administration, the costs officer must obtain a certificate of employment, endorsed on the bill of costs and signed by the administrator, setting out the name and address of the person employed, details of the functions carried out under the employment and a note of any

244 *Jervis v Pillar Denton Ltd* [2014] EWCA Civ 180 (paragraph 101).
245 Rule 12.42 of the Rules.
246 Rule 12.42(2) of the Rules.
247 Rule 12.42(2)(b) of the Rules.
248 Rule 12.42(4) of the Rules.
249 [2016] EWCA Civ 474 (paragraph 33).
250 Under Schedule B1 paragraph 74 of IA 1986.
251 *In Re Hellas Telecommunications (Luxembourg) II SCA* [2016] EWCA Civ 474 (paragraph 37).

special terms of remuneration agreed[252]. Every person whose costs are required to be decided by detailed assessment must commence detailed assessment proceedings in accordance with CPR Part 47 on being required in writing by the administrator to do so[253]. If within a period of three months thereafter, or such further time as the court may allow, he fails to commence detailed assessment proceedings, the administrator is entitled to deal with the insolvent estate without regard to any claim by that person whose claim is forfeited[254]. If the administrator is personally liable for such costs, charges and expenses, the claim against the administrator is also forfeited in such circumstances[255].

REMUNERATION

15.40 The administrator is entitled to receive remuneration for his services as such[256] and that remuneration, if properly fixed, can be drawn from time to time during the course of the administration[257]. Furthermore, as noted above, the remuneration as fixed is payable out of the assets of the company and, upon the administrator ceasing to act, is charged on and is to be paid out of the assets of the company in his custody or under his control at that time in priority to any sums secured by a security over such property which, as created, was a floating charge[258]. The amount of that remuneration is fixed either:

(a)   as a percentage of the value of the property with which he has to deal; or

(b)   by reference to the time properly given by the administrator and his staff in attending to matters arising in the administration; or

(c)   as a set amount[259].

15.41 The remuneration may be fixed as a combination of these bases and different bases or percentages may be fixed for different things done by the administrator[260]. Where the administrator proposes to take his remuneration on the basis of time properly given, he must deliver to the creditors a fees estimate and details of the expenses, which he considers will be incurred[261]. He must also give the same details of anticipated expenses, together with information relating to the work he proposes to undertake, before the determination of the basis on which he is to receive remuneration is made[262]. Concern has been expressed as to whether or not a fixing by reference to time given contemplates a two stage process – once to fix the basis and then a second approval to confirm that the time was properly given[263], but it is thought the wording of Rule 18.16

---

252   Rule 12.43(1) and (2) of the Rules.
253   Rule 12.43(3) of the Rules.
254   Rule 12.43(4) of the Rules.
255   Rule 12.43(5) of the Rules.
256   Rule 18.16(1) of the Rules. The entitlement does not extend to work done after the administrator's duties as such ceased, eg because the company went into liquidation: *In Re Brilliant Independent Media Specialists Ltd* [2015] BCC 113.
257   *Re Salmet International Ltd* [2001] BCC 796.
258   Schedule B1 paragraph 99(3) of IA 1986.
259   Rules 18.16(2) and 18.16(8) of the Rules. A set amount was introduced as one of the bases for fixing remuneration in 2010. Where this is the applicable basis, there are detailed provisions for apportioning the set amount in the event that the administrator ceases to hold office before the time has elapsed in respect of which the amount was set: Rule 18.32 of the Rules.
260   Rule 18.16(3) of the Rules.
261   Rule 18.16(4) of the Rules.
262   Rules 18.16(6) and 18.16(7) of the Rules.
263   *In re World Design and Trade Co Ltd* [2015] Lex Cit 250, Chief Registrar Baister.

of the Rules contemplates that the approval of a time-given fixing is for the basis of the remuneration, not the actual amount. If any creditor then wishes to challenge the amount actually charged in accordance with a time-given fixing, his remedy is to do so in accordance with Rule 18.34 of the Rules on the grounds that the remuneration actually charged is excessive (as to which see further below). Where there are joint administrators, it is for them to agree between themselves as to how the remuneration payable should be apportioned[264]. Any dispute arising between them may be referred to the creditors' committee or to the creditors (for settlement by a decision procedure[265]) or to the court, for settlement by order[266].

15.42 It is for the creditors' committee (if there is one) to determine the basis of the administrator's remuneration[267]. In determining the matter, the committee is required to have regard to the following matters:

(a) the complexity (or otherwise) of the case;

(b) any respects in which, in connection with the company's affairs, there falls on the administrator any responsibility of an exceptional kind or degree;

(c) the effectiveness with which the administrator appears to be carrying out, or to have carried out, his duties as such; and

(d) the value and nature of the property with which he has to deal[268].

15.43 If there is no creditors' committee, or the committee fails to make the requisite determination, the administrator's remuneration may be fixed by decision of the creditors, using a decision procedure[269]. The matters the committee is required to consider in reaching its determination apply equally to a determination by the creditors[270]. Where the administrator has made a statement in the proposals that he thinks the company has insufficient property to enable a distribution to be made to unsecured creditors other than by virtue of section 176A(2)(a) of IA 1986[271], the basis of the administrator's remuneration may be fixed by the consent of each secured creditor and, in a case in which the administrator has made or intends to make a distribution to preferential creditors, with the consent of each of the secured creditors and a decision of the preferential creditors given in a decision procedure[272]. It should be noted that the requirement for the unanimous approval of the secured creditors only applies where there are no free assets (apart from the prescribed part). It should also be noted that, even where the unsecured creditors (or the members of the creditors' committee) have no economic interest in the amount of the administrator's remuneration, a resolution may still be passed by them for the remuneration to be fixed in this way. It follows that it will usually be sensible to have a creditors' committee to fix remuneration, even though there may be no

---

264 Rule 18.17 of the Rules.
265 The procedure prescribed by Part 15 of the Rules.
266 Rule 18.17 of the Rules.
267 Rule 18.18(2) of the Rules.
268 Rule 18.16(9) of the Rules.
269 Rule 8.18(3) of the Rules. The reference to a decision procedure is a reference to the procedure prescribed by Part 15 of the Rules.
270 Rule 18.16(9) of the Rules.
271 Ie a statement under Schedule B1 paragraph 52(1)(b) of IA 1986 that unsecured creditors will only receive a distribution out of the prescribed part.
272 Rule 18.18(4) of the Rules. The reference to a decision procedure is a reference to the procedure prescribed by Part 15 of the Rules.

free assets from which a distribution to those creditors might be made. Likewise, if the administrator's remuneration has been fixed by the creditors' committee, and he considers the rate or amount to be insufficient, he may request that it be increased by the creditors[273], acting in accordance with procedures provided for by Rules 18.25 to 18.27 of the Rules. In essence this gives the decision to the creditors to approve the request by a decision procedure, unless there will be no distribution to the unsecured creditors other than out of the prescribed part[274] in which case the request must be approved by all of the secured creditors and, if a distribution is to be made to them, the preferential creditors (also acting by a decision procedure).

15.44 If not fixed by the creditors' committee or by the creditors, the administrator's remuneration is required, on his application, to be fixed by the court, although it is specifically provided that he must first seek to have it fixed by the committee or the creditors before he adopts this course[275]. Likewise, if the administrator considers that the remuneration fixed for him, whether by the creditors' committee or by the creditors, is insufficient, he may apply to the court for an order increasing its amount or rate[276]. Applications to the court for the fixing and approval of an administrator's remuneration are governed by Part 6 of Practice Direction: Insolvency Proceedings[277], which itself was the successor to Practice Statement: The Fixing and Approval of the Remuneration of Appointees[278] which came into force on 1 October 2004. The genesis of these practice directions, set against a general perception that costs in insolvency cases had reached an unacceptably high level and were subject to little effective control or supervision, is set out in some detail in the judgment of the Court of Appeal (delivered by David Richards J) in *Brook v Reed*[279]. The objective is to ensure that the remuneration which is fixed and approved by the court is fair, reasonable and commensurate with the nature and extent of the work properly undertaken by the administrator, an objective which is intended to be achieved by the application of eight guiding principles, which take the form of matters to be taken into account by the court on the application[280].

15.45 The administrator must give at least 14 days' notice of his application to the members of the creditors' committee[281]; and the committee may nominate one or more members to appear or to be represented, and to be heard, on the application[282]. If there is no creditors' committee, the administrator's notice of his application must be sent to such one or more of the company's creditors as the court may direct, which creditors may nominate one or more of their number to appear or be represented[283]. The application will normally be determined

273 Rule 18.24(a) of the Rules.
274 And the administrator has therefore made a statement under Schedule B1 paragraph 52(1)(b) of IA 1986.
275 Rule 18.23 of the Rules. See eg *Re Charnley Davies Business Services Ltd* (1987) 3 BCC 408, *Re Brooke Marine Ltd* [1988] BCLC 546 and *Re Sheridan Securities Ltd* (1988) 4 BCC 200.
276 Rules 18.24(b) and 18.28 of the Rules.
277 [2014] BCC 502.
278 [2004] BCC 912.
279 [2011] EWCA Civ 331.
280 They are listed in paragraph 21.2.3 of Practice Direction [2014] BCC 502 as: justification, the benefit of the doubt, professional integrity, the value of the services rendered, fair and reasonable, proportionality, professional guidance and timing of application.
281 Rule 18.28(6) of the Rules.
282 Rule 18.28(7) of the Rules.
283 Rules 18.28(6)(a)(ii) and 18.28(7) of the Rules.

summarily by the registrar sitting alone, but in cases of complexity the matter can be determined by a judge sitting with an expert assessor or costs judge[284]. The Practice Direction lists in some detail the matters which are to be put before the court on the application, distinguishing between applications for fixing and approval on the basis of time properly spent and applications for fixing and approval on some other basis[285]. If it appears to be a proper case, the court may order the costs of the administrator's application, including the costs of any member of the creditors' committee appearing or being represented on it, or any creditor so appearing or being represented, to be paid as an expense of the administration[286]. Paragraph 21.4.8 of the Practice Direction[287] indicates that these costs will be paid as an expense of the administration.

15.46 Any creditor of the company may, either with the concurrence of at least 10 per cent in value of the creditors (including himself) or with the permission of the court, apply to the court for an order that the administrator's remuneration be reduced on the grounds that it is, in all the circumstances, excessive, or that the basis is inappropriate or that the expenses were excessive[288]. An application to the same effect may also be made by a secured creditor. The former Practice Statement[289] was applicable to applications to challenge remuneration to the same extent as applications by an administrator under the equivalent of Rule 18.23 of the Rules[290]; it is clear from the definition of 'remuneration application' in the 2014 Practice Direction[291] that the position is unchanged. In cases in which the court's permission was not required, if the court thinks that no sufficient cause is shown for the application, the court may dismiss it without giving notice to any party other than the applicant[292]. If the application is not dismissed, or if the court gives permission for the application, the court fixes a venue for the application to be heard[293]. At least 14 days before the hearing, the applicant must send the administrator a notice stating the venue, together with copies of the application and of any evidence on which the applicant intends to rely[294]. If the court considers the application to be well founded, it is required to make an order fixing the remuneration at a reduced amount or rate and it can also change the basis of the remuneration, direct that all or some part of the remuneration be treated as not being an expense, and order repayment of any excess[295]. Unless the court otherwise orders, the costs of any such application are payable by the applicant and are not payable as an expense of the administration[296].

---

284 Paragraph 21.3.2 of Practice Direction [2014] BCC 502. Cf *Re Independent Insurance Co Ltd* [2003] EWHC 51 (Ch) (a case in which the court fixed the remuneration of a provisional liquidator, for which there was no statutory provision for fixing by the creditors).

285 [2014] BCC 502 (paragraph 21.4). The administrator should provide a succinct narrative of the work done which should not be expensive or require a disproportionate amount of time to produce: *In Re Brilliant Independent Media Specialists Ltd* [2015] BCC 113.

286 Rule 18.28(8) of the Rules.

287 [2014] BCC 502.

288 Rule 18.34 of the Rules. The application must be made within eight weeks of the time that the remuneration or expenses were first reported to creditors (Rule 18.34(3) of the Rules as to which see also *Justice Capital Ltd v Murphy; Re Calibre Solicitors Ltd* (12 November 2014, unreported, Registrar Jones).

289 [2004] BCC 912.

290 *Brook v Reed* [2011] EWCA Civ 331 (paragraph 42).

291 See [2014] BCC 502 at paragraph 1.1(11)(c).

292 Rule 18.37(1) of the Rules.

293 Rules 18.36(2) and 18.37(2) of the Rules.

294 Rules 18.36(3) and 18.37(3) of the Rules.

295 Rules 18.36(4) and 18.37(4) of the Rules.

296 Rules 18.36(6) and 18.37(6) of the Rules.

15.47 *Payments and distributions*

15.47 Although the administrator's remuneration will normally be payable out of the company's assets, there will be cases in which it is appropriate for assets in fact belonging to others (eg trust assets) to bear some part of that remuneration[297], where the work has benefited the administration of those assets. The jurisdiction to order such costs to be paid out of trust assets also extends to the costs of administering client money held by a company in administration[298], but is unlikely to be applicable where the relevant work was done for the benefit of the unsecured creditors as opposed to the trust beneficiaries[299]. The jurisdiction is also available whenever a subsequently appointed office holder (whether a liquidator or a replacement administrator) incurs time in administering an asset of the company which has been transferred to his control subject to the statutory charge imposed by Schedule B1 paragraph 99 of IA 1986[300]. In all of these categories of case, those of the Rules which deal with the fixing of remuneration will not apply.

---

297 *Tom Wise Ltd v Fillimore* [1999] BCC 129 discussing in an administration context the principles developed in *Re Berkeley Applegate (Investment Consultants) Ltd* [1989] Ch 32, *Re Eastern Capital Futures Ltd* (1989) 5 BCC 223 and *Re Tellsure Ltd* [1997] BCC 580.

298 *Allanfield Property Insurance Services Ltd v Aviva Insurance Ltd* [2015] EWHC 3721 (Ch) (paragraphs 146 and 147), *In re Lehman Bros International (Europe) (in administration)* [2012] UKSC 6 (paragraph 101).

299 *Gillan v Hec Enterprise Ltd* [2016] EWHC 3179 (Ch) (paragraph 102).

300 *In re Sports Betting Media Ltd* [2007] EWHC 2085 (Ch) (paragraph 11).

16 Partnerships and limited liability partnerships

PARTNERSHIP ADMINISTRATION

16.1   Until the coming into force of the Insolvent Partnerships Order 1994[1], an insolvent partnership could be wound up as an unregistered company under Part V of IA 1986, but there was no jurisdiction to make an administration order in relation to it, nor was there any provision for a voluntary arrangement to be entered into between a partnership and its creditors. It appears to have been assumed that a combination of the winding-up provisions and the insolvency procedures available in respect of the individual partners was sufficient. The introduction of partnership administration and partnership voluntary arrangements was a welcome development. It reflects the fact that in commerce, if not in law, partnerships are regarded as independent entities with a life of their own. Businesses owned and managed by partnerships are, by that fact, no less worthy of the full range of rescue procedures available under IA 1986 than businesses owned and managed by companies. The principal difficulties in applying the administration and voluntary arrangement procedures to partnerships are the technical ones which flow from the fact that, despite the commercial reality, a partnership has no legal existence independent of that of its partners. The affairs, business and property to be managed by the administrator are the affairs, business and property of the partnership[2] rather than the affairs, business and property of an individual partner, even though the property of an individual partner may be available to satisfy the claims of individual creditors.

16.2   Although the 1994 Order is an improvement on its predecessor[3], it is still a piece of legislation that is difficult to use and construe. Its approach is to apply the relevant provisions of IA 1986 to a partnership as if it were a company, making, in the process, such modifications as are necessary. Initially, the 1994 Order was unaffected by the Enterprise Act 2002[4], with the consequence that a partnership could only enter administration by order of the court. The position changed with effect from 1 July 2005[5], so that the provisions now contained

---

1   SI 1994 No 2421 (referred to in this chapter as the 1994 Order).
2   Article 3(2) of the 1994 Order. Partnership property has the same meaning as in the Partnership Act 1890 (article 2 of the 1994 Order).
3   Insolvent Partnerships Order 1986 (SI 1986 No 2142).
4   By article 3(3)(a) of the Enterprise Act 2002 (Commencement No 4 and Transitional Provisions and Savings) Order 2003 (SI 2003 No 2093), it was provided that the former administration provisions were to continue to apply insofar as was necessary to give effect to the 1994 Order.
5   The relevant amendments were introduced by the Insolvent Partnerships (Amendment) Order 2005 (SI 2005 No 1516).

in Schedule B1 to IA 1986 have been applied to insolvent partnerships, with appropriate modifications. The structure adopted is that Schedule 1 to the 1994 Order[6] sets out a modified form of Part I of IA 1986 (voluntary arrangements) and Schedule A1 to IA 1986 (small company moratorium) while Schedule 2 to the 1994 Order[7] applies Schedule B1 to IA 1986 with appropriate modifications and reading all references to the company as if they were a reference to the partnership[8]. The Insolvency Rules 1986 are applied for the purpose of giving effect to those parts of IA 1986 which are applicable to insolvent partnerships, with such modifications as the context requires[9]. The purpose of this chapter is to draw attention to those parts of the legislation in which insolvent partnership are treated differently from companies.

THE ABILITY OF A PARTNERSHIP TO ENTER ADMINISTRATION

16.3   A partnership may only go into administration if it is a partnership which the courts of England and Wales have jurisdiction to wind up[10]. For the court to have jurisdiction to wind up a partnership, it must be recognised as such as a matter of English law[11], which presumably means that it must be a partnership within the meaning of section 1 of the Partnership Act 1890[12]. The High Court has jurisdiction to wind up an insolvent partnership as an unregistered company if it has, or had, a principal place of business in England and Wales or a place in England and Wales at which business has been carried on in the course of which the debt arose which forms the basis for the relevant petition[13] or if its centre of main interest is in the United Kingdom[14]. The county court also has jurisdiction to wind up an insolvent partnership, such proceedings to be commenced in the county court hearing centre serving the area in which any such place of business is or was located[15]. The court only has jurisdiction to wind up an insolvent

---

6   In the form in which it has been replaced by Schedule 1 to the Insolvent Partnerships (Amendment) (No 2) Order 2002 (SI 2002 No 2708).
7   In the form introduced by the Insolvent Partnerships (Amendment) Order 2005 (SI 2005 No 1516).
8   Articles 3 and 6(1) of the 1994 Order.
9   Article 18 and Schedule 10 to the 1994 Order. At the time of writing, Schedule 10 has not been amended to include the Rules in place of the Insolvency Rules 1986.
10   Article 1(2) of the 1994 Order. The courts of England and Wales have no jurisdiction to wind up a partnership which has its principal place of business in Scotland unless it had a principal place of business in England and Wales at any time in the preceding year: section 117(4) of IA 1986, as modified by Schedule 3 paragraph 6 of the 1994 Order.
11   *Re Senator Hanseatische Verwaltungsgesellschaft mbH* [1996] 2 BCLC 562, 582e–f.
12   Which will include a limited partnership formed in the manner and subject to the conditions provided by the Limited Partnerships Act 1907.
13   This second ground for jurisdiction will not apply if the application is made by the members of the partnership in their capacity as such.
14   Section 117(1) and (7) of IA 1986, as modified by Schedule 3 paragraph 6 of the 1994 Order. As to the case in which a partnership's centre of main interest is in the United Kingdom, see Article 3 of the EC Insolvency Regulation and Schedule 3 paragraph 6(7) of the 1994 Order as inserted by paragraph 5 of the Insolvent Partnerships (Amendment) Order 2002 (SI 2002 No 1308). The EC Insolvency Regulation has been repealed with effect from 26 June 2017 by Regulation (EU) 2015/848 of the European Parliament and of the Council of 20 May 2015 on insolvency proceedings (OJ L141, 05/06/2015, 19–72) (the 'recast Insolvency Regulation'), but the essential substance of most of the EC Insolvency Regulation has been retained.
15   Section 117(2) of IA 1986, as modified by Schedule 3 paragraph 6 of the 1994 Order and rule 2 of the Insolvency (Commencement of Proceedings) and Insolvency Rules 1986 (Amendment) Rules 2014 (SI 2014 No 817).

partnership if the business of the partnership has been carried on in England and Wales at any time in the period of three years ending on the day on which the petition was presented[16]. Where a partnership's principal place of business is in Scotland or Northern Ireland, the courts in England and Wales have no jurisdiction to wind it up unless the principal place of business has been in England and Wales during the period of one year before the presentation of the petition (in the case of Scotland) and during the period of three years before the presentation of the petition (in the case of Northern Ireland)[17].

APPOINTMENT OF A PARTNERSHIP ADMINISTRATOR

16.4   Before 1 July 2005, the only means by which it was possible to obtain the appointment of an administrator of a partnership was by the making of a partnership administration order under the original provisions of Part II of IA 1986, which continued to apply to partnerships for almost three years after the coming into force of Schedule B1 of IA 1986 in relation to companies[18]. This changed when the 1994 Order was amended with effect from 1 July 2005[19] so as to apply a modified version of Schedule B1 of IA 1986 to the administration of insolvent partnerships, with the consequence that it is now possible for an administrator of an insolvent partnership to be appointed not just by order of the court, but also out of court by the holder of a qualifying agricultural floating charge in respect of partnership property[20], or by the members of the partnership in their capacity as such[21]. In broad terms, the circumstances in which and the procedures by which directors and a qualifying floating chargeholder can appoint an administrator of a company are reflected in the circumstances in which and the procedures by which members[22] and a qualifying agricultural floating chargeholder[23] (as the case may be) can appoint an administrator of a partnership.

16.5   An agricultural floating charge is a floating charge created under section 5 of the Agricultural Credits Act 1928[24], being a charge that was such a floating charge on its creation[25]. This is a special form of security by which a farmer can create in favour of a bank a charge on his farming stock[26] or other agricultural

---

16   Section 117(3) of IA 1986, as modified by Schedule 3 paragraph 6 of the 1994 Order: this is subject to Article 3 of the EC Insolvency Regulation (s.117(7) of IA 1986 as inserted by paragraph 5(2) of the Insolvent Partnerships (Amendment) Order 2002 (SI 2002 No 1308)) and so it is theoretically possible that a partnership may have its centre of main interests in England but has not carried on business in England and Wales during the previous three years.

17   Section 117(4) of IA 1986, as modified by Schedule 3 paragraph 6 of the 1994 Order.

18   Article 6 of the 1994 Order, as originally enacted.

19   Insolvent Partnerships (Amendment) Order 2005 (SI 2005 No 1516).

20   Partnership property has the same meaning as in the Partnership Act 1890 (article 2 of the 1994 Order), ie all property and rights and interests in property originally brought into the partnership stock or acquired on account of the partnership or for the purposes and in the course of the partnership business: section 20 of the Partnership Act 1890.

21   Schedule B1 paragraph 2 of IA 1986, as modified by Schedule 2 paragraph 2 of the 1994 Order.

22   Schedule B1 paragraph 22 of IA 1986, as modified by Schedule 2 paragraph 9 of the 1994 Order.

23   Schedule B1 paragraph 14 of IA 1986, as modified by Schedule 2 paragraph 7 of the 1994 Order.

24   Article 6 of the 1994 Order.

25   Schedule B1 paragraph 111(1) of IA 1986, as modified by Schedule 2 paragraph 41 of the 1994 Order.

26   Ie including crops, livestock, and agricultural machinery.

assets belonging to him. Its relevance in the case of insolvent partnerships is that it is the only material form of floating security which is capable of being effective when granted over goods and other assets by an unincorporated trader[27]. For an agricultural floating charge to qualify, the instrument by which it was created must fulfil one of three requirements which are very similar to those which apply in relation to a qualifying floating charge granted by a company[28]. The instrument must either state that Schedule B1 paragraph 14 of IA 1986 applies to the floating charge, or it must purport to empower the holder to appoint an administrator, or it must purport to empower the holder to make an appointment which would constitute the appointment of an agricultural receiver[29]. It follows that existing agricultural charges empowering the holder to appoint a receiver who would be an agricultural receiver will now empower the holder to appoint an administrator. A person is the holder of a qualifying agricultural floating charge if he holds one or more charges of the partnership secured by one or more qualifying agricultural floating charges which alone or together relate to the whole or substantially the whole of the partnership property. He is also the holder of a qualifying floating charge if he is the holder of one or more different forms of security which together relate to the whole or substantially the whole of the partnership property, so long as at least one of them is a qualifying agricultural floating charge[30].

16.6 Unlike the position in relation to a company, a partnership administration order can only be made if the court is satisfied that the partnership is in fact unable to pay its debts: the mere likelihood of insolvency is insufficient[31]. Likewise any notice of intention to appoint administrators by the members of a partnership, and any appointment by them, must contain a statutory declaration that the partnership is in fact unable to pay its debts[32]. The requirement to demonstrate insolvency does not, however, apply to an out-of-court appointment by the holder of a qualifying agricultural floating charge, nor does it apply in the unusual instance of an application to court made by the holder of a qualifying agricultural floating charge[33]. The definition of insolvency is also amended and is now defined by a modified version of those parts of IA 1986 which define the insolvency of an unregistered company[34]. There is deemed insolvency where, notwithstanding the service on a partnership of a statutory demand in the

---

27 See the registration requirements of the Bills of Sale Act (1878) Amendment Act 1882, the provisions of which are excluded by section 8(1) of the Agricultural Credits Act 1928.
28 Schedule B1 paragraph 14 of IA 1986, as modified by Schedule 2 paragraph 7 of the 1994 Order.
29 Ie a receiver appointed under an agricultural charge: article 2 of the 1994 Order.
30 Schedule B1 paragraph 14(3) of IA 1986, as modified by Schedule 2 paragraph 7 of the 1994 Order.
31 Schedule B1 paragraph 11 of IA 1986, as modified by Schedule 2 paragraph 52 of the 1994 Order.
32 Schedule B1 paragraph 27 of IA 1986, as modified by Schedule 2 paragraph 12 of the 1994 Order and Forms 1A and 1B inserted into Schedule 9 of the 1994 Order by article 10 of the Insolvent Partnerships (Amendment) Order 2006 (SI 2006 No 622).
33 Schedule B1 paragraph 35 of IA 1986, as modified by Schedule 2 paragraph 14 of the 1994 Order, so long as the applicant makes a statement that the application is made in reliance on Schedule B1 paragraph 35, and satisfies the court that it could have appointed an administrator under Schedule B1 paragraph 14 (ie out of court).
34 Schedule B1 paragraph 111(1) of IA 1986, as modified by Schedule 2 paragraph 41 of the 1994 Order applying sections 222 and 223 of IA 1986, as modified by Schedule 3 paragraphs 4 and 5 of the 1994 Order and section 224 of IA 1986.

prescribed form[35], requiring the partnership to pay any sum due (in excess of £750), it neglects to pay or secure for such sum within three weeks[36]. There is also deemed insolvency where proceedings have been instituted against a member of the partnership for any debt due or claimed to be due from the partnership or from him in his character as a member, and the partnership does not within three weeks of service of notice on it, pay or secure the debt, procure the proceedings to be stayed or indemnify the defendant member against the proceedings and all costs and damages incurred by him because of those proceedings[37]. In both instances, service is effected by leaving the demand or notice at the partnership's principal place of business in England and Wales, or at a place of business in England or Wales at which there is carried on the business in the course of which the debt arose or by delivering it to an officer[38] of the partnership[39]. In addition to these demand and notice provisions, section 224(1) of IA 1986 is applied so that a partnership is deemed insolvent on the return unsatisfied of any execution and on any other proof to the satisfaction of the court that the partnership is unable to pay its debts as they fall due[40]. Section 224(2) of IA 1986 also deems a partnership unable to pay its debts if the value of its assets is less than the amount of its liabilities, taking into account its contingent and prospective liabilities. For this purpose, the assets of individual partners are left out of account, even though they are available to satisfy the claims of individual creditors[41].

16.7   The statutory objectives for which a partnership administrator must perform his functions are similar but not identical to those for which the administrator of a company must perform his functions, and each of them amounts to the purpose of administration[42]. Unlike under the former law, the statutory objectives are capable of application to the administration of a partnership notwithstanding that it is not a legal entity in its own right. The first objective is rescuing the partnership as a going concern[43]. Unlike the position between 1994 and 2005[44], there would appear now to be a requirement for the rescue of the partnership itself, as well as sufficient of its undertaking to amount to a going concern. The consequence of this is that a partnership administration order can only be made on the basis of the first statutory purpose if there is a real prospect of both the partnership itself and a going concern being saved, although it is presumably sufficient for that going concern to be only a small part of the totality of the partnership's business. The second objective is achieving a

---

35 The form is contained in Schedule 9 to the 1994 Order, as amended by the Schedule to the Insolvent Partnerships (Amendment) Order 2002 (SI 2002 No 1308).

36 Section 222 of IA 1986, as modified by Schedule 3 paragraph 4 of the 1994 Order.

37 Section 223 of IA 1986, as modified by Schedule 3 paragraph 5 of the 1994 Order.

38 Defined by article 2(1) of the 1994 Order to mean a member of a partnership (which itself includes any person liable as a partner within the meaning of section 14 of the Partnership Act 1890) and any person who has management or control of the partnership business.

39 Section 222(2) of IA 1986, as modified by Schedule 3 paragraph 4 of the 1994 Order.

40 For this purpose the court will presumably apply the test established in *BNY Corporate Trustee Services Ltd v Eurosail-UK 2007-3BL plc* [2013] UKSC 28 to the effect that debts falling due in the reasonably near future will to be taken into account.

41 *H S Smith & Son* ((1999) Times, 6 January) per Park J.

42 Schedule B1 paragraphs 3 of IA 1986 as applied by articles 3(2) and 6(1) of the 1994 Order and Schedule B1 paragraph 111(1) of IA 1986, as modified by Schedule 2 paragraph 41 of the 1994 Order.

43 Schedule B1 paragraph 3(1)(a) of IA 1986 as applied by articles 3(2) and 6(1) of the 1994 Order.

44 See the form of section 8(3)(a) of IA 1986 in force in relation to partnerships by operation of the original versions of article 6 and Schedule 2 to the 1994 Order.

better result for the partnership's creditors as a whole than would be likely if the partnership were first to be wound up[45]. The third objective is realising property in order to make a distribution to one or more secured or preferential creditors[46]. It is presumably the case that, where this is relied on as the statutory objective, the relevant property is partnership property[47], for which purpose article 2(1) of the 1994 Order adopts the meaning used in the Partnership Act 1890[48]. Although there are these minor differences between the partnerships' jurisdiction and the companies' jurisdiction, it is thought that the approach that should be taken on an application for a partnership administration order (including the way in which the discretion should be exercised[49]) is essentially the same as the approach to be taken on an application for an administration order in relation to a company. In the case of out-of-court appointments, the equivalent requirement is that the proposed administrator must state in writing that in his opinion the purpose of administration is reasonably likely to be achieved[50].

16.8 An administrator of a partnership cannot be appointed after an order has been made to wind it up as an unregistered company nor can he be appointed after an order has been made under article 11 of the 1994 Order (ie where the members of a partnership jointly present a petition for the winding up of the partnership and the administration of its property in conjunction with an application for the bankruptcy of each of them as partners without the partnership being wound up as an unregistered company)[51]. This is the equivalent of the prohibition against a company going into administration after it has gone into liquidation. There is also a prohibition against the making of an administration order against a partnership which has permission under Part 4 of FSMA 2000 to effect or carry out contracts of insurance in the United Kingdom[52] and a partnership that continues to have a liability in respect of a deposit which it accepted in accordance with the Banking Act 1979 or the Banking Act 1987, but is not an authorised deposit taker[53]. There is no prohibition against making administration

---

45   Schedule B1 paragraph 3(1)(b) of IA 1986 as applied by articles 3(2) and 6(1) of the 1994 Order.
46   Schedule B1 paragraph 3(1)(c) of IA 1986 as applied by articles 3(2) and 6(1) of the 1994 Order.
47   Unlike the former law (see the form of section 8(3)(c) of IA 1986 in force in relation to partnerships by operation of the original versions of article 6 and Schedule 2 to the 1994 Order), this is not spelt out in the legislation but, as the powers of a partnership administrator are limited to dealing with partnership property, it is presumably the case that the statutory purpose is limited to the same extent.
48   Ie all property and rights and interests in property originally brought into the partnership stock or acquired on account of the partnership or for the purposes and in the course of the partnership business: section 20 of the Partnership Act 1890.
49   For two examples, see *Re Kyrris* [1998] BPIR 103 and *Re Greek Taverna* [1999] BCC 153.
50   This pre-condition applies whether the appointment is made by the holder of a qualifying agricultural floating charge (as to which see Schedule B1 paragraph 18(3)(b) of IA 1986 as applied by articles 3(2), 6(1) and 6(3)(b) of the 1994 Order) or by the members (as to which see Schedule B1 paragraph 29(3)(b) of IA 1986, as modified by Schedule 2 paragraph 13 of the 1994 Order).
51   Schedule B1 paragraph 8 of IA 1986, as modified by Schedule 2 paragraph 4 of the 1994 Order.
52   Schedule B1 paragraph 9(2) of IA 1986 as applied by articles 3(2) and 6(1) of the 1994 Order. However, the *prima facie* prohibition has been reversed by the Financial Services and Markets Act 2000 (Administration Orders Relating to Insurers) Order 2010 (SI 2010 No 3023), which applies to insurers, whether they are companies or partnerships. See also the Financial Markets and Services Act 2000 (Insolvency) (Definition of 'Insurer') Order 2001 (SI 2001 No 2634).
53   Schedule B1 paragraph 9(1) of IA 1986 as applied by articles 3(2) and 6(1) of the 1994 Order. The Banks (Former Authorised Institutions) (Insolvency) Order 2006 (SI 2006 No 3107) discussed in **CHAPTER 19** *post* does not apply to partnerships.

orders in relation to other partnerships which are or were authorised deposit takers, and the special administration regimes described in **CHAPTER 19** are also applicable to partnerships.

16.9 An application for a partnership administration order is by application in a prescribed form[54] presented either by the members of the partnership in their capacity as such or by a creditor or creditors (including any contingent or prospective creditors) or by all or any of those persons[55]. There is a potential difficulty if it is not possible to obtain the consent of all members for the presentation of a members' administration application. In the case of companies, it is established that a directors' application does not require the consent of all directors. It simply requires a resolution of the board properly passed, at which stage it is the duty of all directors to implement it whether they voted in favour or against[56]. Although the point is undecided in the context of partnerships, it is likely that a similar approach would be adopted and the court would only require to be satisfied that there had been a proper resolution of the members passed in accordance with the terms of the relevant partnership deed. Where the deed makes no provision for voting or the passing of resolutions (and more especially where there is no deed at all), the making of an application on the instruction of one or more partners would appear to be a right in relation to the partnership to be determined in accordance with the rules set out in section 24 of the Partnership Act 1890. Applying those rules[57], it is not clear whether the making of an administration application requires only a majority (as an ordinary matter connected with the partnership business) or unanimity (as a change made in the nature of the partnership business).

16.10 The circumstances in which and procedures by which the members of a partnership and the holder of a qualifying agricultural floating charge can appoint a partnership administrator out of court reflect the similar circumstances in which the directors of a company and the holder of a qualifying floating charge can take the same step to appoint an administrator of a company[58]. So far as an appointment by the members is concerned, the only relevant difference is that identified above in relation to applications for the making of an administration order. So far as concerns an appointment by the holder of a qualifying agricultural floating charge, there is an additional restriction where there is a prior qualifying agricultural floating charge to the one on which he relies. For these purposes, one floating charge is prior to another if it was created first in accordance with the provisions of section 8(2) of the Agricultural Credits Act 1928[59], which

---

54 Form 1 in Schedule 9 to the 1994 Order, as amended by the Schedule to the Insolvent Partnerships (Amendment) Order 2002 (SI 2002 No 1308).

55 Schedule B1 paragraph 12(1) of IA 1986, as modified by Schedule 2 paragraph 6 of the 1994 Order. The power given by section 87A of the Magistrates' Courts Act 1980 and Schedule B1 paragraph 12(1)(d) of IA 1986 to the clerk of a magistrates' court to apply for an administration order as part of an attempt to recover a fine from a company does not apply to partnerships.

56 *Re Equiticorp International plc* [1989] BCLC 597. See also now Schedule B1 paragraph 105 of IA 1986, although this does not obviate the need also to comply with a company's rules of internal management: *485 Minmar (929) Ltd v Khalastchi* [2011] EWHC 1159 (Ch).

57 See, in particular, section 24(8) of the Partnership Act 1890. For a case in which there was a partnership dispute as to whether a partnership should go into administration, although in the event the petition was presented by a creditor, see *Barclays Bank plc v Davidson* (8 February 2000, unreported), CA.

58 As to which see **CHAPTER 1** *ante*.

59 Schedule B1 paragraph 15(2) of IA 1986, as modified by Schedule 2 paragraph 8 of the 1994 Order.

provides for priority in accordance with the times of their registration under that act. Where there is such a prior qualifying agricultural floating charge, the person proposing to make an appointment under Schedule B1 paragraph 14 of IA 1986 may only do so if:

(a)   he has first given at least two business days' written notice to the holder of any such prior charge; or

(b)   the holder of any such prior charge has consented in writing to the making of the appointment[60].

16.11   As with the case of companies, this provision is to ensure that the holder of a prior qualifying agricultural floating charge is given an opportunity to make his own appointment should he choose to do so. In cases involving the appointment of administrators of companies by their directors, the requirements of Schedule B1 paragraph 26 of IA 1986 have caused some difficulty, because of failures to notify all of the prescribed persons of the directors' notice of intention to appoint[61]. This difficulty does not arise in precisely the same way in relation to a partnership, but it remains the case that service of the correct forms on all of the prescribed persons is likely to be a pre-condition to the validity of the appointment[62]; the formalities must be strictly complied with in relation to any out-of-court appointment[63].

THE INTERIM MORATORIUM

16.12   Schedule B1 paragraph 44 of IA 1986[64] provides that, during the period beginning with the making of an application for a partnership administration order and ending with the making of such an order or the dismissal of the petition, a statutory moratorium shall be in effect. The same moratorium applies from the time when a copy of notice of intention to appoint an administrator by the holder of a qualifying agricultural floating charge[65] or by the members of an insolvent partnership[66] is filed at court until such time as the appointment takes effect or the relevant time period expires[67]. This moratorium, which is similar

---

60   Schedule B1 paragraph 15(1) of IA 1986, as modified by Schedule 2 paragraph 8 of the 1994 Order.

61   For a summary of the law and the previous cases, see *Re M F Global Overseas Ltd* [2012] EWHC 1091 (Ch), reviewing the conflicting lines of authority represented by *Hill v Stokes* [2010] EWHC 3726 (Ch) and *Minmar (929) Ltd v. Khalastchi* [2011] EWHC 1159 (Ch).

62   *National Westminster Group plc v Msaada Group* [2011] EWHC 3423 (Ch) (a partnership case where the form was not served on the supervisor of a CVA).

63   In *Re Kaupthing Capital Partners II Master LP Inc (in administration)* [2010] EWHC 836 (Ch), Proudman J ruled that an out-of-court appointment over a foreign partnership with its COMI in England was invalid because it was mistakenly treated as if it were a company, and so the wrong forms were used.

64   As applied by articles 3 and 6(1) of the 1994 Order. Paragraph 44 itself applies the moratorium provisions of Schedule B1 paragraphs 42 and 43 of IA 1986 (as modified by Schedule 2 paragraphs 17 and 18 of the 1994 Order) to this interim period.

65   Schedule B1 paragraph 14 of IA 1986, as modified by Schedule 2 paragraph 7 of the 1994 Order.

66   Schedule B1 paragraphs 22 and 27 of IA 1986, as modified by Schedule 2 paragraphs 9 and 12 of the 1994 Order.

67   Schedule B1 paragraph 44 of IA 1986 as applied by article 6 of the 1994 Order. The relevant time period is five days in the case of a notice by the holder of a qualifying agricultural floating charge and ten days in the case of a notice filed by the members of a partnership.

to the moratorium imposed in respect of companies, imposes the following restrictions:

(a) no order may be made for the winding up of the insolvent partnership[68], no order can be made under article 11 of the 1994 Order[69] and no order may be made under section 35 of the Partnership Act 1890 in relation to the partnership[70];

(b) no steps may be taken to enforce any security over the partnership property, or to repossess goods in the partnership's possession, under any hire purchase agreement[71] of one or more of the officers of the partnership in their capacity as such[72], except with the permission of the court and subject to such condition or requirement in connection with any transaction as the court may impose;

(c) a landlord may not exercise a right of forfeiture by peaceable re-entry in relation to premises forming part of the partnership property or let to one or more officers of the partnership in their capacity as such except with the permission of the court and subject to such condition or requirement as the court may impose; and

(d) no legal process, (including legal proceedings, distress, execution, distress and diligence may be commenced or continued against the partnership or the partnership property except with the permission of the court and subject to such to such condition or requirement in connection with any transaction as the court may impose[73].

16.13 As in the case of a company, there are limitations upon the extent and effect of the moratorium. First, it does not come into effect where at the time of making the application there is an agricultural receiver[74] of the partnership and the person by or on whose behalf the agricultural receiver was appointed has not consented to the making of an administration order, unless and until that person so consents[75]. It follows that where an agricultural receiver has been appointed there may be room for doubt as to whether the restrictions imposed by Schedule B1 paragraph 42 of IA 1986 have come into effect. Secondly, nothing in Schedule BI paragraph 44 of IA 1986[76] requires the permission of the court for the appointment of an agricultural receiver of the partnership or for the carrying

---

68 Except for a petition presented on public interest grounds under section 124A of IA 1986 or by the FCA or the PRA under section 367 of FSMA 2000.
69 Ie an order on the petition of the members of a partnership for the winding up of the partnership and the administration of its property in conjunction with an application for the bankruptcy of each of them as partners without the partnership being wound up as an unregistered company.
70 Ie an order for dissolution of the partnership on any of the grounds set out in that section.
71 A term which includes conditional sale agreements, chattel leasing agreements and retention of title agreements: Schedule B1 paragraph 111(1) of IA 1986, as modified by Schedule 2 paragraph 41 of the 1994 Order.
72 Defined by article 2(1) of the 1994 Order to mean a member of a partnership (a word which itself includes any person liable as a partner within the meaning of section 14 of the Partnership Act 1890) and any person who has management or control of the partnership business.
73 Schedule B1 paragraphs 43 and 44 of IA 1986, as modified by Schedule 2 paragraphs 17 and 18 of the 1994 Order.
74 Ie a receiver appointed under an agricultural charge within the meaning of the Agricultural Credit Act 1928 (article 2(1) of the 1994 Order).
75 Schedule B1 paragraph 44(6) of IA 1986 as applied by article 6 of the 1994 Order.
76 As applied by article 6 of the 1994 Order.

out by such receiver (whenever appointed) of any of his functions[77]. Thirdly, nothing in Schedule B1 paragraph 44 of IA 1986 requires the permission of the court for the presentation of a petition for the winding up of the partnership presented on public interest grounds under section 124A of IA 1986 or by the FCA or the PRA under section 367 of FSMA 2000[78].

PROCEDURE AND THE HEARING OF A PARTNERSHIP ADMINISTRATION APPLICATION

16.14 The procedure for service of a partnership administration application is very similar to that adopted on an application for the appointment of an administrator of a company[79]. Where service is required to be made on the partnership, it should be made on its last known principal place of business in England and Wales. The requirement to give notice of the application forthwith to any person who has appointed or is or may be entitled to appoint an administrative receiver is replaced by an obligation to give notice forthwith to any person who has appointed, or is or may be entitled to appoint, an agricultural receiver[80]. Notification must also be given to any person who is or may be entitled to appoint an administrator of the partnership in his capacity as a holder of a qualifying floating charge[81]. In addition, service must be effected on any agricultural receiver of the partnership, the petitioner in any pending winding-up petition and any provisional liquidator, any member state liquidator appointed in main proceedings relating to the partnership, on the partnership itself (where the administration petition is presented by anyone other than the members), on any supervisor of a CVA in relation to the partnership[82] and on the proposed as administrator[83].

16.15 The court's powers on the hearing of a partnership administration application are similar to those on the hearing of an administration application

---

77 Schedule B1 paragraph 44(7)(c) and (d) of IA 1986 as applied by article 6 of the 1994 Order. In the case of agricultural charges, there is no provision similar to instruments conferring the right to appoint an administrative receiver of a company created before 29 December 1986, in respect of which Schedule 11 paragraph 1 of IA 1986 deems the conditions precedent to the exercise of that right to include the presentation of an application for the making of an administration order in relation to the company.

78 Schedule B1 paragraph 44(7)(a) of IA 1986 as applied by article 6 of the 1994 Order. This paragraph was not modified by Schedule 2 of the 1994 Order to refer to the modified form of Schedule B1 paragraph 42, but it is tolerably clear that paragraph 44(7)(a) ought to be read as cross-referring to Schedule B1 paragraph 42(5) (in its modified form) not paragraph 42(4). It is therefore thought that permission is required to commence proceedings to wind up or dissolve a partnership on any other grounds.

79 At the time of writing, article 18 and Schedule 10 to the 1994 Order have not been amended to include the Rules as the applicable subordinate legislation and so the Insolvency Rules 1986 continue to apply to partnership administrations. It is not known whether this omission is deliberate.

80 Schedule B1 paragraph 12(2)(a) and (b) of IA 1986, as modified by Schedule 2 paragraph 63 of the 1994 Order.

81 Schedule B1 paragraph 12(2)(c) of IA 1986, as modified by Schedule 2 paragraph 6 of the 1994 Order.

82 For a partnership case in which this requirement was not followed, see *National Westminster Group plc v Msaada Group* [2011] EWHC 3423 (Ch).

83 Rule 2.6 of the Insolvency Rules 1986 as applied by article 18 of the 1994 Order. Rule 3.8 of the Rules makes provision in similar form for service of an application for an administration order to be made against a company, and may be applied (as appropriately modified by the 1994 Order) to applications for a partnership administration order in due course.

in relation to a company[84], replacing references to an administrative receiver with references to an agricultural receiver. Thus the prior appointment of an administrator by the holder of an agricultural floating charge or the members of the partnership in their capacity as such prevents the court from making an administration order[85]. The court is also required to dismiss the application if an agricultural receiver is in office, unless his appointor consents to the making of an order, or the courts thinks that the charge under which he was appointed is liable to challenge or avoidance under section 238, 239 or 245 of IA 1986[86]. This enables the holder of a qualifying floating charge to appoint his own administrator (or agricultural receiver) at any time before the order is made unless the relevant charge is liable to challenge as a preference, transaction at an undervalue or on the grounds of non-registration[87]. In particular, on hearing the application the court may make an administration order, dismiss the application, or adjourn the hearing conditionally or unconditionally, or make an interim order or any other order that it thinks fit[88]. Where the court makes an interim order pending the final disposal of the petition, it may restrict the powers of the officers of the partnership[89] in the same manner and to the same effect as it may restrict the powers of a company's directors[90]. The eligibility of a person to act as an administrator of an insolvent partnership is governed by the same provisions as apply to the eligibility of a person to act as an administrator of a company[91], because Part XIII of IA 1986, which governs insolvency practitioners and their qualification, is applied to partnership administrators by article 6(5) of the 1994 Order, replacing the word 'company' where it appears with the word 'partnership'[92].

THE EFFECT OF A PARTNERSHIP ENTERING ADMINISTRATION

16.16 Many of the consequences which flow from a partnership being in administration are the same as those that flow from a company entering

---

84   As to which, see **CHAPTER 1** *ante*. Much of the discussion in that chapter is applicable to an application for a partnership administration order.
85   Ie Schedule B1 paragraph 7 of IA 1986, as modified by Schedule 2 paragraph 3 of the 1994 Order.
86   Schedule B1 paragraph 39(1) of IA 1986, as modified by Schedule 2 paragraph 15 of the 1994 Order.
87   Schedule B1 paragraph 39(2) of IA 1986, as modified by Schedule 2 paragraph 15 of the 1994 Order.
88   Schedule B1 paragraph 13 of IA 1986 as applied by article 6 of the 1994 Order. The court may also treat the application as if it was a winding up petition and make any order which it could make under section 125 of IA 1986 (ie a winding up order: see the form of section 125 modified by Schedule 4 paragraph 9 of the 1994 Order).
89   Defined by article 2(1) of the 1994 Order to mean a member of a partnership (which itself includes any person liable as a partner within the meaning of section 14 of the Partnership Act 1890) and any person who has management or control of the partnership business. This requires the word 'directors' in the unmodified version of Schedule B1 paragraph 13(3) of IA 1986 to be read as 'officers' for the purposes of its application to partnership administration. There is no specific provision to this effect but it is consistent with the previous law (see the old modified version of section 9(5)) and is justified by the general provisions of article 3(4) of the 1994 Order.
90   Schedule B1 paragraph 13(3) of IA 1986, as modified by Schedule 2 paragraph 3 of the 1994 Order.
91   As to which, see **CHAPTER 1** *ante*.
92   Article 3 of the 1994 Order.

administration[93]. The adapted version of Schedule B1 of IA 1986[94] provides that any petition for the winding up of the insolvent partnership[95] must be dismissed where a partnership administration order is made and must be suspended while the partnership is in administration pursuant to an appointment by the holder of a qualifying agricultural floating charge. This restriction continues throughout the duration of the administration because, during the period for which the administration order is in force, no order may be made for the winding up of the partnership and no order may be made under article 11[96]. In addition, no order may be made under section 35 of the Partnership Act 1890[97]. Where a partnership administration order is made, an agricultural receiver shall vacate office[98]. Any receiver of part of the partnership property must vacate office on being required to do so by the administrator[99], but he is not automatically obliged to do so[100]. During the course of an administration the appointment of an agricultural receiver is prohibited[101] and no other form of receiver may be appointed as part of the process of enforcing security over the partnership property without the consent of the administrator or the permission of the court[102]. It follows that administration is incompatible with a winding up of the partnership, but it is not necessarily incompatible with all forms of receivership.

16.17 Equivalent provisions to those discussed in **CHAPTER 2** *ante* apply to the payment of any remuneration and expenses properly incurred by an agricultural receiver who vacates office on the partnership entering administration by an administrator, which includes any indemnity to which he is entitled out of the partnership property[103]. The entitlement is charged on and is to be paid out of any partnership property which was in his custody or under his control immediately before he vacated office[104]. There is an odd omission in that the statutory

---

93 As to which see **CHAPTER 2** *ante* which deals, with Schedule B1 paragraphs 40 to 43 of IA 1986.

94 Schedule B1 paragraph 40(1) of IA 1986 as applied by article 6 of the 1994 Order.

95 Presumably including any petition for an order under any of articles 7–10 of the 1994 Order.

96 Schedule B1 paragraph 42 of IA 1986, as modified by Schedule 2 paragraph 17 of the 1994 Order. An order under article 11 is an order on the petition of the members of a partnership for the winding up of the partnership and the administration of its property in conjunction with an application for the bankruptcy of each of them as partners without the partnership being wound up as an unregistered company.

97 Ie an order for dissolution of the partnership. Schedule B1 paragraph 42(4) of IA 1986, as modified by Schedule 2 paragraph 17 of the 1994 Order.

98 Schedule B1 paragraph 41(1) of IA 1986, as modified by Schedule 2 paragraph 16 of the 1994 Order. This is not the case in relation to out-of-court appointments because no administrator can be appointed when an agricultural receiver is in office: Schedule B1 paragraph 17(b) and 25(c) of IA 1986, as applied by article 6 of the 1994 Order.

99 Schedule B1 paragraph 41(2) of IA 1986, as modified by Schedule 2 paragraph 16 of the 1994 Order.

100 Thus a receiver of part of the partnership property and an administrator can co-exist. There is a rather odd lacuna in relation to a receiver of all of the partnership property who is not also an agricultural receiver. The legislation does not seem to entitle an administrator to require him to vacate office, but it is difficult to see why he should be entitled to remain in office once the partnership has entered administration. It is thought that the statutory intention was that he too can be required to vacate office.

101 Schedule B1 paragraph 43(6) of IA 1986, as modified by Schedule 2 paragraph 18 of the 1994 Order.

102 Schedule B1 paragraph 43(2) of IA 1986, as modified by Schedule 2 paragraph 18 of the 1994 Order.

103 Schedule B1 paragraph 41(4) of IA 1986, as modified by Schedule 2 paragraph 16 of the 1994 Order.

104 Schedule B1 paragraph 41(3) of IA 1986, as modified by Schedule 2 paragraph 16 of the 1994 Order.

charge granted by the modified Schedule B1 paragraph 41(3) of IA 1986 is not drafted in such a way that it applies to a receiver of the whole or any part of the partnership property, where the receiver is not an agricultural receiver. There is little justification for this omission, because it is thought that the true statutory intention is that any such receiver can be obliged to vacate office if required to do so by the administrator (and this is clearly the case in relation to a receiver of part of the partnership property) and, if he does so, there is little justification for not protecting his remuneration, expenses and right to an indemnity to the same extent as those of an agricultural receiver[105].

16.18   The remaining parts of the statutory moratorium apply to partnerships as they apply to companies and apply to partnership property as they apply to the property of the company[106]. Thus:

(a)   no steps may be taken to enforce any security over the partnership property, or to repossess goods in the partnership's possession under any hire purchase agreement[107], except with the consent of the administrator or the permission of the court (subject to such conditions or requirements as the court may impose)[108];

(b)   a landlord, or other person to whom rent is payable[109], may not exercise a right of forfeiture by peaceable re-entry in relation to premises forming part of the partnership property or let to one or more officers[110] of the partnership in their capacity as such except with the consent of the administrator or the permission of the court (subject to such conditions or requirements as the court may impose)[111]; and

(c)   no legal process (including legal proceedings, execution, distress and diligence) may be instituted or continued against the partnership or the partnership property except with the consent of the administrator or the permission of the court (subject to such conditions or requirements as the court may impose)[112].

16.19   There has been a minor change in that part of the moratorium which relates to the prohibition against repossessing goods. Prior to 2005 the moratorium related to goods in the possession of one or more officers of the partnership in their capacity as such, rather than goods in the possession of

---

105   An even stranger aspect of this omission is that before the law was changed to permit the appointment of a partnership administrator by the members and the holder of a qualifying agricultural floating charge, the remuneration of a receiver of part of the partnership property was protected by the modified form of section 11(4) of IA 1986: see the original version of Schedule 2 to the 1994 Order.

106   There is a detailed description of their effect in **CHAPTER 2** *ante*.

107   Which includes a conditional sale agreement, a chattel leasing agreement and a retention of title agreement: Schedule B1 paragraph 111(1) of IA 1986, as modified by Schedule 2 paragraph 41 of the 1994 Order.

108   Schedule B1 paragraphs 43(2) and 43(3) of IA 1986, as modified by Schedule 2 paragraph 18 of the 1994 Order.

109   Schedule B1 paragraph 43(8) of IA 1986, as modified by Schedule 2 paragraph 18 of the 1994 Order.

110   Defined by article 2(1) of the 1994 Order to mean a member of a partnership (which itself includes any person liable as a partner within the meaning of section 14 of the Partnership Act 1890) and any person who has management or control of the partnership business.

111   Schedule B1 paragraph 43(4) of IA 1986, as modified by Schedule 2 paragraph 18 of the 1994 Order.

112   Schedule B1 paragraph 43(5) of IA 1986, as modified by Schedule 2 paragraph 18 of the 1994 Order.

the partnership[113]. It now refers to goods in the possession of the partnership, which will normally lead to the same result as would have applied under the former law.

POWERS OF A PARTNERSHIP ADMINISTRATOR

16.20 The provisions dealing with the powers of an administrator of a partnership are almost identical to the law applicable to the administrator of a company. Thus his powers are contained in a modified Schedule 1 to IA 1986[114] and they are exercised by him as agent of the members of the partnership in their capacity as such[115]. The structure is the same as is applicable to the powers of an administrator of a company, and the modified Schedule 1 includes powers drafted in exactly the same way. Like an administrator of a company he has power to apply to the court for directions[116]. The principal differences between the powers of a partnership administrator and those of the administrator of a company are that:

(a) in the modified Schedule B1 paragraph 61 of IA 1986, the power to remove and appoint directors of the company is replaced by a power to prevent any person from taking part in the management of the partnership business and to appoint any person to be a manager of the partnership business[117];

(b) the restriction on the exercise by the company or its officers of any power which could be exercised in such a way as to interfere with the exercise by the administrator of his powers is replaced by a similar restriction on partnership and the officers[118] of the partnership[119];

(c) all references in the modified form of Schedule 1 to property of the company are replaced by references to partnership property[120]; and

(d) the administrator's power to bring or defend legal proceedings, to do acts or execute documents, to draw, accept and endorse bills of exchange and to make arrangements or compromises extends to both the partnership itself and to any member of the partnership in his capacity as such[121].

---

113 Presumably because goods held under a hire purchase agreement are not partnership property as they will not have been 'been brought into the partnership stock or acquired' within the meaning of section 20 of the Partnership Act 1890.
114 Modified by Schedule 2 paragraph 43 of the 1994 Order.
115 Schedule B1 paragraph 69 of IA 1986, as modified by Schedule 2 paragraph 24 of the 1994 Order.
116 Schedule B1 paragraph 63 of IA 1986, as applied by article 6(1) of the 1994 Order.
117 Schedule B1 paragraph 61 of IA 1986, as modified by Schedule 2 paragraph 22 of the 1994 Order.
118 Defined by article 2(1) of the 1994 Order to mean a member of a partnership, any person liable as a partner within the meaning of section 14 of the Partnership Act 1890 and any person who has management or control of the partnership business.
119 Schedule B1 paragraph 64 of IA 1986, as applied by articles 3 and 6 of the 1994 Order.
120 Partnership property has the same meaning as in the Partnership Act 1890 (article 2 of the 1994 Order), ie all property and rights and interests in property originally brought into the partnership stock or acquired on account of the partnership or for the purposes and in the course of the partnership business: section 20 of the Partnership Act 1890.
121 These powers are set out in the modified Schedule 1 to IA 1986 at paragraphs 5, 8, 9 and 17. For a case in which the court was asked to consider whether an administrator had the power to continue or compromise proceedings by reference to the issue of whether they related to partnership property, see *Re Kyrris (No 2)* [1998] BPIR 111.

16.21 An administrator of a partnership also has similar powers to an administrator of a company to dispose of or exercise his powers in relation to charged property as if that property were not subject to a security[122], and reading the phrase 'floating charge' wherever it appears as 'agricultural floating charge'[123]. There is one important protection given to the members of a partnership against which a partnership administration order has been made. Unless he otherwise consents, an officer of the partnership is not personally liable for the debts and obligations of the partnership incurred during the period when the administration order is in force[124].

16.22 An administrator of a partnership also has all of the powers granted to administrators of a company by Part VI of IA 1986[125]. Thus he has the powers granted by section 234 to get in the partnership property, the power to apply for relief under section 236 of IA 1986 and the right to seek orders under section 241 of IA 1986 on the grounds that the partnership has entered into a transaction at an undervalue (within the meaning of section 238 of IA 1986) or given a preference (within the meaning of section 239 of IA 1986). In each case the relevant provision is applied by article 6(5) of the 1994 Order, construing references to the company as references to the partnership[126]. These powers do not extend to getting in the property of the members of the partnership, or to challenging antecedent transactions relating to their personal property. The reason for this is that, even though the partners' personal property may ultimately be susceptible to execution for the purpose of discharging their personal liabilities arising out of their role as partners, a partnership administrator is only appointed to manage the affairs, business and property of the partnership. The 1994 Order also introduces the jurisdiction under section 426 of IA 1986 which makes provision for co-operation between courts exercising an insolvency jurisdiction both in different countries and in different parts of the United Kingdom[127].

THE CONDUCT OF A PARTNERSHIP ADMINISTRATION: MISCELLANEOUS PROVISIONS

16.23 The remaining modifications to Schedule B1 to IA 1986 apply to the conduct of the administration of an insolvent partnership but the differences are minor. Those parts of Schedule B1 to IA 1986 which relate to statements of affairs, proposals to creditors and revisions of those proposals are applied to partnership administration by the 1994 Order with very little change. The only differences are that the persons who can be required to make a statement of affairs (as a relevant person) are any person who has been an officer of the partnership or who took part in its formation during the period of one year prior to the administration or who was an employee of the partnership or who was an officer

---

122   These powers are granted by Schedule B1 paragraphs 70, 71 and 72 of IA 1986 as applied by article 6(1) of the 1994 Order.
123   Article 6(3)(b) of the 1994 Order; ie one created under section 5 of the Agricultural Credits Act 1928 (article 6(6) of the 1994 Order).
124   Schedule B1 paragraph 69(2) of IA 1986 as modified by Schedule 2 paragraph 24 of the 1994 Order.
125   Article 6(4) and 6(5) of the 1994 Order.
126   Article 3(2) of the 1994 Order.
127   See article 6(3)(f) of the 1994 Order.

or employee of an officer of the partnership[128]. As to the proposals, the only difference is that they must be filed with the court rather than registered with the registrar of companies[129]. There is also a modification to the obligation to hold an initial creditors' meeting for the purpose of considering the proposals to reflect the fact that the obligation under section 176A of IA 1986 to make a prescribed part of the company's net assets available for the payment of unsecured debts does not apply in a partnership administration[130]. This same modification affects the means by which a partnership administrator can exercise his power to make a distribution or payment in accordance with Schedule B1 paragraphs 65 and 66 of IA 1986. There is no obligation imposed on a partnership administrator to deal with the prescribed part in accordance with section 176A of IA 1986, but subject to this, the means by which he is required to effect any distribution is the same as the means by which the administrator of a company is required to carry out the same task.

16.24   The general duties of the partnership administrator are in the same form as those imposed on the administrator of a company by Schedule B1 paragraphs 67 and 68 of IA 1986[131]. He is also under the same specific duty to summon a creditors' meeting in the circumstances described in Schedule B1 paragraph 56 of IA 1986[132]. Most of the provisions relating to the ending of administration[133] also apply without material modification, although the right to move from administration to creditors' voluntary liquidation is excluded[134] for obvious reasons. The process by which a partnership moves from administration to dissolution is also different, in that the relevant notice under Schedule B1 paragraph 84 of IA 1986 is filed with the court (rather than sent to the registrar of companies) and the dissolution takes effect three months after filing[135]. The law relating to his removal from office, resignation and the vacation of his office, together with that dealing with vacancies and substitution also reflects the equivalent provisions that relate to administrators of a company, although where an appointment was made out of court, the relevant notices must of course be given to the relevant appointor, ie the members of the partnership or the holder of a qualifying agricultural floating charge as the case may be[136]. The law relating to the imposition of a statutory charge in relation to (a) the administrator's costs and remuneration, and (b) sums payable in respect of debts or liabilities incurred under contracts entered into by him and contracts of employment adopted by him on his ceasing to hold office, is also in the same form as it is for companies[137].

---

128   Schedule B1 paragraph 48 of IA 1986, as modified by Schedule 2 paragraph 19 of the 1994 Order.
129   Schedule B1 paragraph 49(4) of IA 1986, as modified by Schedule 2 paragraph 20 of the 1994 Order.
130   Schedule B1 paragraph 52(1) of IA 1986, as modified by Schedule 2 paragraph 21 of the 1994 Order.
131   Taking custody and control of all the property to which he thinks the partnership is entitled and the management of the affairs, business and property of the partnership.
132   Ie where requested to do so by 10 per cent of the partnership's creditors or directed to do so by the court.
133   Schedule B1 paragraph 76–82 of IA 1986.
134   Schedule 2 paragraph 27 of the 1994 Order.
135   Schedule B1 paragraph 84 of IA 1986, as modified by Schedule 2 paragraph 28 of the 1994 Order.
136   Schedule B1 paragraphs 87–98 of IA 1986, as modified by Schedule 2 paragraphs 29–37 of the 1994 Order.
137   Schedule B1 paragraph 99 of IA 1986, as applied by article 6 of the 1994 Order.

PARTNERSHIP VOLUNTARY ARRANGEMENTS AND MORATORIUMS

16.25 The 1994 Order also applies to insolvent partnerships both the voluntary arrangement provisions contained in Part I of IA 1986 and the small company moratorium provisions contained in Schedule A1 to IA 1986[138]. In substance, the law is the same as that which relates to companies, but there are some specific differences between the procedure as it relates to companies and the procedure as it relates to partnerships which are identified in a modified version of Part I of IA 1986 set out in Schedule 1 Part I of the 1994 Order. The differences can be summarised as follows:

(a) In the case of a partnership, a voluntary arrangement is proposed by the members of the partnership in replacement for the directors of a company (so long as the partnership is not then in administration, being wound up or subject to an order under article 11 of the 1994 Order)[139]. It may also be proposed by any liquidator or administrator of the partnership and also by any trustee of the partnership where an order has been made under article 11 of the 1994 Order[140].

(b) The meetings to be held to approve the voluntary arrangement are meetings of the creditors and members of the partnership[141].

(c) The nominee's report must state whether there are in existence any insolvency proceedings not just relating to the partnership itself but also relating to its members[142].

(d) On approval of a partnership voluntary arrangement, in addition to the stay of any winding up and providing for the appointment of any administrator to cease to have effect, the court may also stay any proceedings under an order made pursuant to article 11 of the 1994 Order and any related proceedings of a member of the partnership in his capacity as such[143].

(e) A partnership voluntary arrangement may be challenged on the grounds of unfair prejudice or material irregularity by any trustee of the partnership where an order has been made under article 11 of the 1994 Order[144].

(f) The offence of making a false representation for which provision is made by section 6A of IA 1986 is extended to both officers of the partnership (ie members or persons with management or control of the partnership business[145]) and officers, including shadow directors of any corporate member of the partnership[146].

---

138 Article 4(1) of the 1994 Order. The drafting technique which has been adopted is to read all references in Part I of IA 1986 to companies as if they were references to insolvent partnerships (article 3(1) of the 1994 Order) and all expressions appropriate to companies as references to the corresponding persons, officers documents or organs as the case may be appropriate to a partnership (article 3(4) of the 1994 Order).

139 Section 1(1) of IA 1986, as modified by Schedule 1 Part I of the 1994 Order.

140 Sections 1(3) and 3 of IA 1986, as modified by Schedule 1 Part I of the 1994 Order. Where the proposal is made by a trustee, the procedure is the same as where a proposal is made by a liquidator or administrator.

141 Section 2(2) and 3 of IA 1986, as modified by Schedule 1 Part I of the 1994 Order.

142 Section 2(3) of IA 1986, as modified by Schedule 1 Part I of the 1994 Order.

143 Section 5(3) of IA 1986, as modified by Schedule 1 Part I of the 1994 Order.

144 Section 6(2)(d) of IA 1986 as modified by Schedule 1 Part I of the 1994 Order.

145 Article 2(1) of the 1994 Order.

146 Although the reporting provisions under section 7A of IA 1986 extend to possible offences committed by officers of the partnership, they do not extend to possible offences committed by officers of a corporate member.

16.26 The small company moratorium procedure, for which provision is made by Schedule A1 to IA 1986[147], is also applied[148] to partnerships which meet certain financial qualifying criteria. The specific differences between the procedure as it relates to companies and the procedure as it relates to partnerships are identified in a modified version of Schedule A1 to IA 1986, which is set out in Schedule 1 Part II of the 1994 Order. They can be summarised as follows:

(a) The method for computing the financial qualifying conditions is similar but not identical to the method to be used in the case of an insolvent company, in that it is spelt out in the 1994 Order itself rather than being identified by cross-reference to the qualifying condition for small companies provided for in section 382 of CA 2006[149]. The consequence of this is that, although the qualifying condition for companies has increased on a regular basis[150], the qualifying condition for partnerships has not.[151]

(b) An insolvent partnership is ineligible for a moratorium where an agricultural receiver has been appointed or where an order has been made under article 11 of the 1994 Order[152].

(c) On the coming into force of the moratorium, the stay extends to prevent the calling or requisitioning of any meeting of the members of the partnership except with the consent of the nominee or the leave of the court[153]. It also extends to prevent the appointment of an agricultural receiver except with leave of the court[154] and to the presentation of a petition or making of an order by virtue of article 11 of the 1994 Order[155] and to the making of an application or an order under section 35 of the Partnership Act 1890[156].

(d) The property in respect of which the moratorium stay prevents the exercise of rights of re-entry, the enforcement of security, the repossession of goods and the commencement or continuation of proceedings, execution or other legal process extends to the partnership property and, in the case of re-entry

---

147 Introduced by section 1 and Schedule 1 to IA 2000. See further, **Chapter 12** *ante* in which the provisions as they apply to companies are explained.
148 Article 4 and Schedule 1 Part II of the 1994 Order. The drafting technique which has been adopted is to read all references in Schedule A1 to companies as if they were references to insolvent partnerships (article 3(1) of the 1994 Order) and all expressions appropriate to companies as references to the corresponding persons, officers documents or organs as the case may be appropriate to a partnership (article 3(4) of the 1994 Order).
149 Schedule A1 paragraph 3 of IA 1986, as modified by Schedule 1 Part II of the 1994 Order.
150 It is now turnover of not more than £10.2 million and aggregate assets of not more than £3.26 million.
151 At the date of writing it is still the figures which were inserted in 2005, namely turnover of not more than £5.2 million and assets of not more than £2.8 million.
152 Schedule A1 paragraph 4(1)(c) and 4(1)(h) of IA 1986, as modified by Schedule 1 Part II of the 1994 Order.
153 Schedule A1 paragraph 12(1)(b) of IA 1986, as modified by Schedule 1 Part II of the 1994 Order.
154 Schedule A1 paragraph 12(1)(e) of IA 1986, as modified by Schedule 1 Part II of the 1994 Order, although, unlike the case of an administrative receiver, an agricultural receiver can be appointed by leave of the court and subject to such terms as the court may impose.
155 Schedule A1 paragraph 12(1)(i) of IA 1986, as modified by Schedule 1 Part II of the 1994 Order. If a petition has been presented before the moratorium comes into effect, it must be dismissed on the approval of a voluntary arrangement: Schedule A1 paragraph 37(4) of IA 1986, as modified by Schedule 1 Part II of the 1994 Order.
156 Ie an order for dissolution of the partnership on any of the grounds set out in that section: Schedule A1 paragraph 12(1)(j) of IA 1986, as modified by Schedule 1 Part II of the 1994 Order.

to premises or repossession of goods, extends to premises let to and goods in the possession of one or more officers of the partnership in their capacity as such[157].

(e) The partnership's power to dispose of charged property[158] is modified from the position in relation to a company so as to extend to partnership property and goods in the possession of one or more officers of the partnership in their capacity as such under a hire purchase agreement[159].

(f) The provisions of Schedule A1 paragraph 40 of IA 1986 which relate in the context of a small company moratorium to the acts or omissions of the directors are applied in the case of an insolvent partnership to the acts or omissions of the officers of the partnership[160]. The restriction on the making of any application under this provision where a company is in administration or being wound up is extended in the case of an insolvent partnership to cases in which an order is made under article 11 of the 1994 Order[161].

(g) The offence of making a false representation for which provision is made by Schedule A1 paragraph 42 of IA 1986 is extended to both officers of the partnership (ie members or persons with management or control of the partnership business[162]) and officers, including shadow directors of any corporate member of the partnership[163].

LIMITED LIABILITY PARTNERSHIPS

16.27　With effect from 6 April 2001, there has been a new legal entity known as a limited liability partnership ('LLP')[164]. Unlike a partnership governed by the provisions of the Partnership Act 1890, an LLP is a body corporate with legal personality separate from that of its members. It is incorporated by registration at the Companies Registry[165]. The mutual rights and obligations of the LLP itself and its members are governed by agreement between them and, in the absence of agreement on any particular matter, by regulations[166]. Save where express provision is made to the contrary, the law relating to partnerships[167]

157　Schedule A1 paragraphs 12(1)(f), (g) and (h) of IA 1986, as modified by Schedule 1 Part II of the 1994 Order.

158　Schedule A1 paragraph 20 of IA 1986, as modified by Schedule 1 Part II of the 1994 Order.

159　These powers are similar to those given to the administrator of an insolvent partnership. The expression 'floating charge' is limited to a floating charge created under section 5 of the Agricultural Credits Act 1928: Schedule A1 paragraph 20(8) of IA 1986, as modified by Schedule 1 Part II of the 1994 Order.

160　Defined by article 2(1) of the 1994 Order to mean a member of a partnership, any person liable as a partner within the meaning of section 14 of the Partnership Act 1890 and any person who has management or control of the partnership business.

161　Ie in such a case, an application can only be made by the administrator, liquidator or trustee as the case may be: Schedule A1 paragraph 40(7) of IA 1986, as modified by Schedule 1 Part II of the 1994 Order.

162　Article 2(1) of the 1994 Order.

163　Schedule A1 paragraph 42 of IA 1986, as modified by Schedule 1 Part II of the 1994 Order.

164　Section 1(1) of the Limited Liability Partnerships Act 2000. For commencement provisions, see Limited Liability Partnerships Act 2000 (Commencement) Order 2000 (SI 2000 No 3316).

165　Section 3 of the Limited Liability Partnerships Act 2000.

166　Section 5 of the Limited Liability Partnerships Act 2000. The relevant regulation is regulation 7 of the Limited Liability Partnerships Regulations 2001 (SI 2001 No 1090).

167　Eg the 1994 Order.

does not apply to an LLP[168] and in many respects this new form of entity has more in common with a limited company than it does with a partnership. The legislation contemplates that the members of an LLP fulfil similar functions to those of a company's directors and officers[169]. Some or all of the members may be what are called designated members[170], who seem to be closer in concept to the executive directors of a company and on whom certain specific statutory duties are imposed.

16.28 By section 14(1) of the Limited Liability Partnerships Act 2000, provision is made for regulations to deal with the insolvency of an LLP by application or incorporation of certain parts of IA 1986, including those that deal with administration and voluntary arrangements. In England and Wales, the regulations which identify those parts of IA 1986 to be applied to LLPs are the Limited Liability Partnerships Regulations 2001[171]. The structure that has been adopted is to apply the relevant Parts of IA 1986[172] reading references to a company as including references to an LLP, references to a director, officer or shadow director of a company as including references to a member or shadow member of an LLP and references to a company's memorandum and articles of association as including references to the limited liability partnership agreement[173]. The relevant parts of IA 1986 include all of the Parts of IA 1986 which deal with corporate insolvency, except those that deal with winding up unregistered companies[174]. The Limited Liability Partnerships Regulations 2001 also provide for a series of detailed modifications (which are set out in Schedule 3) and include a sweep-up provision which gives the court the ability to read such further modifications into IA 1986 as the context may require for the purpose of giving effect to IA 1986 as applied by the Regulations[175]. As with the 1994 Order, the Limited Liability Partnerships Regulations 2001 were originally unaffected by the Enterprise Act 2002[176], although the provisions of Schedule B1 to IA 1986 were eventually applied to insolvent LLPs with effect from 1 October 2005[177].

16.29 Much of the law is the same as applies to the administration of a company, and it can be seen from the limited number of cases in this area that the court's

---

168 Section 1(5) of the Limited Liability Partnerships Act 2000.

169 See eg regulations 4(1)(g) and 5(2)(b) of the Limited Liability Partnerships Regulations 2001.

170 Section 8 of the Limited Liability Partnerships Act 2000.

171 SI 2001 No 1090, amended by the Financial Services and Markets Act 2000 (Consequential Amendments) Order 2004 (SI 2004 No 355) in relation to insurers and deposit takers.

172 Regulation 5(1) of the Limited Liability Partnerships Regulations 2001.

173 Regulation 5(2) of the Limited Liability Partnerships Regulations 2001.

174 Thus the restriction on appointing an administrative receiver of a company for which provision is made by section 72A of IA 1986 also applies to an LLP: *Feetum v. Levy* [2005] EWCA Civ 1601.

175 It should be noted that the Rules and the other subordinate legislation made under IA 1986 relevant to administration and voluntary arrangements is applied to LLPs by regulation 10(1)(b) and Schedule 6 Part II of the Limited Liability Partnerships Regulations 2001. See also Rule 3(b) of the Insolvency (England and Wales) Rules 2016 (Consequential Amendments and Savings) Rules 2017 (SI 2017 No 369) which provides that the Insolvency Rules 1986 continue to have effect for the purposes of the application of the Limited Liability Partnerships Regulations 2001.

176 Article 3(3)(b) of the Enterprise Act 2002 (Commencement No 4 and Transitional Provisions and Savings) Order 2003 (SI 2003 No 2093).

177 Limited Liability Partnerships (Amendment) Regulations 2005 (SI 2005 No 1989).

approach to issues arising in the administration of an LLP will be very similar[178]. The principal detailed differences in the law applicable to the administration of an LLP and the approval of a voluntary arrangement in relation to an LLP seem to be as follows:

(a) The county court for the district in which the LLP has its registered office has unlimited jurisdiction to make an administration order in relation to an LLP[179].

(b) Schedule B1 paragraph 2(c) of IA 1986 has been modified to replace the reference to the company or its directors with a reference only to the LLP. It seems to follow from this that there is no power for an administration application to be made by the members of an LLP[180]. Likewise, the powers of the directors of a company, and of the company itself, to make an appointment out of court under Schedule B1 paragraph 22 of IA 1986 is replaced by a power of the LLP itself, but not its members[181]. There are consequential modifications to the provisions by which replacement administrators are appointed[182].

(c) The statutory moratorium for which provision is made by Schedule B1 paragraph 42 of IA 1986 replaces the prohibition against passing a resolution to wind up with a prohibition against making a determination for the winding up of the LLP. A determination to wind up is the simplified procedure equivalent to those procedures by which a company may commence its voluntary liquidation[183].

(d) The administrator's power to remove and appoint directors is replaced by a power to prevent any person from taking part in the management of the business of the LLP and to appoint any person to be such a manager[184]. Accordingly, the focus is not on a person's status as a member of the LLP (from that position he cannot be removed), rather it is on a person's role in the management of the business. Presumably the reason for this is that, although a member of an LLP might have a role equivalent to that of a director[185], he will not necessarily fulfil all the functions of a director of a limited company.

---

178 An example is *Clydesdale Financial Services Ltd v Smailes* [2009] EWHC 1745 (Ch), where administrators of an LLP were removed in circumstances in which the same approach would have been taken to a removal application against administrators of a company.

179 Court is defined to mean the court having jurisdiction to wind up the partnership: sections 117(2) and 251 of IA 1986 as modified by Schedule 3 to the Limited Liability Partnerships Regulations 2001.

180 It is not envisaged that an LLP will operate other than by determination of its members in accordance with the terms of the limited liability partnership agreement. There is no equivalent to the distinction between a company acting through its members in general meeting and the directors of a company resolving (as such) that a particular course of action should be pursued.

181 Schedule B1 paragraph 22(1) of IA 1986, as modified by Schedule 3 to the Limited Liability Partnerships Regulations 2001.

182 Schedule B1 paragraphs 87, 89, 91, 94, 95 and 97 of IA 1986, as modified by Schedule 3 to the Limited Liability Partnerships Regulations 2001.

183 Section 84 of IA 1986 as modified by Schedule 3 to the Limited Liability Partnerships Regulations 2001. Throughout the statutory scheme, a determination by the members of an LLP is treated as the equivalent of a resolution by a company in general meeting.

184 Schedule B1 paragraph 61 of IA 1986 as modified by Schedule 3 to the Limited Liability Partnerships Regulations 2001.

185 Unlike a member of a company, the basic rule is that a member of an LLP acts as agent for and can bind the limited liability partnership: section 6 of the Limited Liability Partnerships Act 2000.

(e) The administrator's powers to call up uncalled capital are replaced with a power to enforce any rights that the LLP has against the members under the terms of the LLP agreement[186].

(f) Of particular relevance to those parts of IA 1986 that deal with the statutory rights and remedies available to administrators, there is a new definition of associate, so that a member of an LLP is an associate of that LLP and of every other member and of the husband, wife or relative of every other member of that LLP[187].

(f) The only person entitled to propose a voluntary arrangement apart from a liquidator or administrator is the LLP itself; it cannot also be proposed by the equivalent of a director (viz a member of the LLP)[188]. In any such case, the conduct of the proposal is given to the designated members of the LLP[189]. Where a moratorium is also proposed, the role of the directors under section 1A of IA 1986 is fulfilled by the eligible LLP itself[190].

(g) Where a voluntary arrangement in relation to an LLP is proposed by the LLP itself, there is a requirement only for a meeting of the LLP's creditors to be held. In the case of a proposal made by a liquidator or administrator, the meeting of the company's members is replaced by a meeting of the members of the LLP[191].

186 Schedule 1 paragraph 19 of IA 1986, as substituted by Schedule 3 to the Limited Liability Partnerships Regulations 2001.

187 Section 435 of IA 1986, as modified by Schedule 3 to the Limited Liability Partnerships Regulations 2001.

188 Section 1(1) of IA 1986, as modified by Schedule 3 to the Limited Liability Partnerships Regulations 2001.

189 Sections 2(3) and 2(4) of IA 1986, as modified by Schedule 3 to the Limited Liability Partnerships Regulations 2001. The LLP's designated members are identified on incorporation or by subsequent agreement; in some cases all of the members will be designated members (see further, section 8 of the Limited Liability Partnerships Act 2000).

190 Section 1A(1) of IA 1986, as modified by Schedule 3 to the Limited Liability Partnerships Regulations 2001.

191 Section 2(2) of IA 1986, as modified by Schedule 3 to the Limited Liability Partnerships Regulations 2001 (separately in relation to each of the alternative cases).

17 Termination of administration proceedings and removal and replacement of an administrator

17.1 One of the more significant practical changes introduced by the Enterprise Act 2002 was that, in the absence of an extension of time granted by the court or by the consent of the creditors, the appointment of an administrator automatically ceases to have effect at the end of the period of one year beginning with the date on which it originally took effect[1]. Before that time, the administrator may procure that the administration shall cease to have effect by filing a notice at court if he thinks that the purpose of administration has been sufficiently achieved[2]. The court may also provide for the administration to cease to have effect either on the application of the administrator himself or of any creditor[3]. Where an administrator has been appointed by the court, his appointment can also be brought to an end by a successful appeal against the making of the administration order or by its rescission. An administrator may cease to hold office upon his removal by order of the court, upon his death or resignation, or upon his ceasing to be qualified to act as an insolvency petitioner in relation to the company[4]. This chapter examines the circumstances in which administration proceedings can be brought to an end or an administrator may cease to hold office and discusses the consequences which may follow either eventuality.

AUTOMATIC CESSATION

17.2 Schedule B1 paragraph 76 of IA 1986 provides for the appointment of an administrator (ie any administrator howsoever appointed) to cease to have effect at the end of the period of one year beginning with the date on which the appointment takes effect[5]. This provision reflects the administrator's duty to conduct his functions as quickly and efficiently as is reasonably practicable[6] and expresses a parliamentary assumption that in the normal case one year is a sufficient period of time within which to do so.

---

1   Schedule B1 paragraph 76(1) of IA 1986.
2   Schedule B1 paragraph 80 of IA 1986.
3   Schedule B1 paragraphs 79 and 81 of IA 1986.
4   Schedule B1 paragraphs 87, 88 and 89 of IA 1986.
5   In *Re Property Professionals + Ltd* [2013] EWHC 1903 (Ch), Judge Purle QC held that the period of one year should be calculated from the time at which the administration order was made.
6   Schedule B1 paragraph 4 of IA 1986.

351

17.3   There will, of course, be cases in which one year is not long enough for the administrator to complete the effective conduct of his functions and so the legislation makes express provision for the granting of extensions of time in an appropriate case. Thus, an administrator's term of office may be extended by the court for a specified period, but only on the application of the administrator himself[7]. The court may order an extension where the administrator's term of office has already been extended (whether by order or consent), but the court may not order an extension once the administrator's term of office has expired[8]. Under the pre-Enterprise Act 2002 law, it was not unusual for the court to make effective provision for the extension of an administration which was limited at the outset, even after the order had expired. This was achieved by a variation of the original order, but it is not a mechanism which is available to extend the one-year period of an administration under the present law, even where the original appointment was made by the court. Thus, administrators will have to be especially diligent to ensure that they make any extension application in time for an order extending the administration to be made before the expiry of their appointment, otherwise they may be found to have acted beyond their powers. An application to court for an extension of administration must state the reasons why the administrator is seeking an extension[9]. The requirement under the Insolvency Rules 1986 that the application must be accompanied by a progress report has been dispensed with; however, the details of the extension must be included in the next progress report after the date on which the extension is granted[10]. There is no express statutory guidance as to the circumstances in which an extension might be granted. In the unreported case of *Re Trident Fashions plc*[11], the court accepted a submission that the relevant test was similar to that applied when an application for an administration order was made, that is, would an extension of the administrators' appointments be reasonably likely to achieve the purposes of the administration[12]; in practice, this is the approach now taken by the courts. Any application for an extension should be made at least one month before the end of the administration or, in the absence of special circumstances, the costs of the application may be disallowed[13].

17.4   The administrator's term of office may also be extended by consent for a specified period not exceeding one year[14]. Unlike an application to the court for an extension of time, the consent procedure may only be used once and it may not be used after an administrator's term of office has already been extended by

---

7   Schedule B1 paragraph 76(2)(a) of IA 1986.
8   Schedule B1 paragraph 77(1)(b) of IA 1986. In *Re Frontsouth (Witham) Ltd* [2011] EWHC 1668 (Ch), Henderson J held that Rule 7.55 of the Insolvency Rules 1986 could not be used to cure a defective extension of an administration by consent and that he was therefore unable to make an order granting a further extension of the administration because the administrators' appointments had already expired. However, the court has jurisdiction to grant an extension so long as the application is actually made (even if not issued or heard) before the expiry date: *In re TT Industries Ltd* [2006] BCC 372.
9   Rule 3.54(2) of the Rules.
10   Rule 18.3(5) of the Rules.
11   (13 September 2004, unreported).
12   See P Ridgway and R Beckwith, 'Administrations: one year on' [2005] 18(2) Insolv Int 27–28. For the test on an application for an administration order see Schedule B1 paragraph 11 of IA 1986.
13   Practice Direction: Insolvency Proceedings [2014] BCC 502 (paragraph 10).
14   Schedule B1 paragraph 76(2)(b) of IA 1986, as amended by section 127 of the Small Business, Enterprise and Employment Act 2015.

the court[15]. Like an application to the court for an extension of time, the consent procedure may not be used after the administrator's term of office has expired[16]. For these purposes, there are detailed provisions dealing with the meaning of consent[17]. In summary, consent must be obtained from each secured creditor of the company and, if the company has unsecured debts, the unsecured creditors of the company[18]. However, if the administrator has made a statement under Schedule B1 paragraph 52(1)(b) that the company has insufficient property to enable a distribution to be made to creditors other than by virtue of the prescribed part, then the administrator need only obtain the consent of each secured creditor and, if he thinks that a distribution may be made to the preferential creditors of the company, the consent of the preferential creditors[19]. Whether the company's unsecured creditors or preferential creditors consent to an extension is to be determined by the administrator seeking a decision from those creditors[20]. The request for consent must be made by a notice delivered to creditors, which must state the reasons why the administrator is seeking an extension[21].

17.5   Where the administrator's term of office is extended, whether by order or consent, he must as soon as reasonably practicable, notify the registrar of companies[22] and the company's creditors[23]. Where the extension is by consent, he must also file notice of the extension with the court[24]. If he fails without reasonable excuse to give notice to the court or the registrar of companies as the case may be, the administrator commits an offence[25]. Notice must also be given to any member state liquidator appointed in relation to the company[26].

17.6   Where the appointment of an administrator ceases to have effect by reason of the expiry of the one-year period or any extension of it, the administrator is under a duty, as soon as reasonably practicable and in any event within five business days of cessation, to file with the court and deliver to the registrar of companies a notice of the automatic end of administration, accompanied by a final progress report[27]. The notice and final progress report must also be sent as soon as reasonably practicable to the directors of the company and to all other

---

15 Schedule B1 paragraph 78(4) of IA 1986.
16 Schedule B1 paragraph 78(4) of IA 1986.
17 Schedule B1 paragraph 78(1), (2), (2A) and (3) of IA 1986. Cf Schedule B1 paragraph 108 of IA 1986.
18 Schedule B1 paragraph 78(1) of IA 1986.
19 Schedule B1 paragraph 78(2) of IA 1986.
20 Schedule B1 paragraph 78(2A) of IA 1986. The decision may be made under the decision procedures set out at Part 15 of the Rules.
21 Rule 3.54 of the Rules. As with applications to court for an extension of an administration, there is no longer any need for a request to creditors for their consent to an extension to be accompanied by a progress report, but Rule 18.3(5) of the Rules requires details of the extension of an administrator's appointment to be included in the next progress report after the date the extension is granted.
22 Schedule B1 paragraphs 77(2) and 78(5)(b) of IA 1986.
23 Rule 3.54(5) and (6) of the Rules. Where the extension has been by consent, the administrator need not deliver a notice to creditors if Rule 3.54(3) of the Rules applies, which provides that the request for consent may contain or be accompanied by a notice that, if the extension is granted, a notice of the extension would be made available for viewing or downloading on a website and that no other notice will be delivered to creditors.
24 Schedule B1 paragraph 78(5)(a) of IA 1986.
25 Schedule B1 paragraphs 77(3) and 78(6) of IA 1986.
26 Rule 21.7 of the Rules.
27 Rule 3.55(2) of the Rules.

persons to whom notice of the administrator's appointment was delivered[28]. The final progress report must contain the information set out in Rule 18.3 of the Rules and must also include a summary of the administrator's proposals, any major amendments to or deviations from those proposals, the steps taken during the administration and the outcome[29]. Quite apart from his formal filing duties, an administrator should always takes steps to ensure that there is a proper plan made for the continuing management of the company's affairs once his time in office has come to an end. The circumstances in which it might be appropriate for the company to be restored to the control of its directors are considered in **PARAGRAPH 17.12** *post*, but if that is not the appropriate way forward, an administrator should always ensure that he has put in place a procedure for liquidation or dissolution before he ceases to hold office[30].

TERMINATION ON ACHIEVEMENT OF OBJECTIVE

17.7   Where an administrator appointed out of court (whether by the holder of a qualifying floating charge[31], by the company or by its directors[32]) thinks that the purpose of administration has been sufficiently achieved in relation to the company, he may cause his appointment to cease to have effect by filing a prescribed form of notice[33] with the court and the registrar of companies[34]. This procedure is not available where an administration order was made, because in any such case that order will have to be discharged. It is, however, plainly intended to be the standard procedure in any case in which an out-of-court appointment has led to the achievement of the purpose of administration, whether that be rescue, a better result for creditors or simply a distribution to the company's secured and preferential creditors[35]. Even in such a case, the administrator can still make an application to court if further relief is needed as part of the termination process (eg the making of a winding-up order)[36]. Three copies of the notice, which must be authenticated by the administrator and dated[37], must be filed with the court, each of which will be endorsed with the date and time of filing, and they must be accompanied by a final progress report[38]. Once endorsed, the administrator will receive back two of the sealed copies, one of which he must send to the registrar of companies[39].

---

28   Rule 3.55(6) of the Rules.
29   Rule 3.53 of the Rules.
30   Cf *Re Barrow Borough Transport Ltd* [1990] Ch 227 at 234e–f approved by the Court of Appeal in *Oakley Smith v Greenberg* [2002] EWCA Civ 1217, [2003] BPIR 709 at 721.
31   Under Schedule B1 paragraph 14 of IA 1986.
32   Under Schedule B1 paragraph 22 of IA 1986.
33   Rule 3.56(1) and (2) of the Rules sets out the information that the notice must contain.
34   Schedule B1 paragraph 80 of IA 1986.
35   In *Joint Administrators of Station Properties* [2013] CSOH 120 (paragraph 25), Lord Hodge held that an administrator appointed by a floating charge holder or by the company had the power to decide whether the company had been rescued as a going concern and was not required to apply to court under Schedule B1 paragraph 79 of IA 1986 before exercising his power under Schedule B1 paragraph 80 of IA 1986 to bring the administration to an end.
36   As to which, see Schedule B1 paragraph 79 of IA 1986 and **PARAGRAPH 17.9FF** *post*.
37   Rule 3.56(3) of the Rules.
38   Rule 3.56(4), (5) and (6) of the Rules.
39   Rule 3.56(6) of the Rules. The obligation to file with the court and the registrar of companies means that the same documents must be sent to any member state liquidator appointed in relation to the company: Rule 21.7 of the Rules.

17.8   Once the administration has terminated by notice that the purpose has been sufficiently achieved, the administrator is required, as soon as reasonably practicable and in any event within five business days, to send a copy of the notice and final progress report to every creditor of the company of whose claim and address he is aware[40] and to all other persons to whom notice of the administrator's appointment was delivered[41]. He can comply with the obligation to notify creditors by publishing a notice undertaking to provide a copy of the notice of termination within five business days of the filing at court[42], although this mechanism for compliance does not apply to the obligation to notify other persons who were notified of his appointment. The notice must be published in the *London Gazette* and may be advertised in such other manner as the administrator thinks fit[43]. The notice must state that the administration has ended and the date on which it ended, an undertaking that the administrator will provide a copy of the notice of the end of the administration to any creditor of the company who applies in writing and an address to which such creditors can write[44]. A failure without reasonable excuse to comply with the requirement to notify creditors means that the administrator commits an offence[45].

ADMINISTRATOR'S APPLICATION FOR CESSATION

17.9   Irrespective of the method by which the company went into administration, the administrator of a company may at any time apply to the court[46] for the appointment of an administrator to cease to have effect from a specified time. The administrator is bound to make such an application if he thinks that the purpose of administration cannot be achieved or if he thinks that the company should not have entered administration or if the company's creditors decide that he must make such an application[47]. Where an administration order has been made, the administrator must also make such an application if he thinks that the purpose of the administration has been sufficiently achieved in relation to the company[48], but this requirement is not imposed where the administrator was appointed out of court presumably because it is then open to him to file a notice of termination under Schedule B1 paragraph 80 of IA 1986[49]. An administrator's application to court for an order ending the administration must be accompanied by a progress report[50] covering the period since the last progress

40   Schedule B1 paragraph 80(4) of IA 1986 and Rule 3.56(7) and (8) of the Rules.
41   Rule 3.56(9) of the Rules.
42   Schedule B1 paragraph 80(5) of IA 1986 and Rule 3.56(10) of the Rules.
43   Rule 3.56(11) of the Rules.
44   Rule 3.56(10) of the Rules. Although the wording of the Rule means that the point is not free from doubt, it is thought that an administrator should also send to such creditors a copy of the final progress report.
45   Schedule B1 paragraph 80(6) of IA 1986.
46   Under Schedule B1 paragraph 79(1) of IA 1986. There is no limitation on the circumstances in which it may be appropriate for such an order to be made: *Re TM Kingdom Ltd* [2007] EWHC 3272 (Ch).
47   Schedule B1 paragraph 79(2) of IA 1986. Where the administrator has been required to make the application by a creditors' meeting, he must attach a statement to the application indicating (with reasons) whether or not he agrees with the creditors' requirement for him to make the application: Rule 3.57(1)(c) of the Rules.
48   Schedule B1 paragraph 79(3) of IA 1986.
49   As to which, see **PARAGRAPHS 17.7 and 17.8** *ante*.
50   As to the form which such a report must take, see Rule 18.3 of the Rules.

report (if any) or the date the company entered administration and a statement indicating what the administrator thinks should be the next steps for the company (if applicable)[51]. Whenever an application is made other than because of a requirement by a decision of the creditors, the administrator must give notice in writing to the applicant for the order by which he was appointed or the person by whom he was appointed (as the case may be) and to the creditors of his intention to apply[52]. Notice must be given at least five business days before the time at which the application is made and there must be attached to the application itself a statement that he has notified the creditors and copies of any responses to that notification[53]. If any application is made under Schedule B1 paragraph 79 of IA 1986 in conjunction with a petition to wind up the company, the administrator must also notify the creditors whether he intends to seek appointment as liquidator[54]. Article 31 of the EC Insolvency Regulation imposes a specific obligation on an administrator to communicate to a member state liquidator appointed in relation to the company any information relevant to measures aimed at terminating the proceedings. This obligation presumably imposes a duty on an administrator to give a member state liquidator proper notice of any application under Schedule B1 paragraph 79 of IA 1986 but even if it does not, Rule 21.7(2) of the Rules imposes such a duty on the administrator.

17.10 Depending on the precise circumstances, it may be prudent for an administrator appointed by the court either to apply for directions or to apply for an order under Schedule B1 paragraph 79 of IA 1986, where there has been a fundamental change of circumstance since the administration order was granted, although this will not necessarily lead to an order for cessation and discharge being made[55]. It should also be remembered that administration is designed to be a short-term process primarily aimed at maximising realisations for creditors in the context of a continuation of a company's business[56]. Once the business has been disposed of, a continuation of the administration will normally only be justified where it can be shown to be a more effective process for the achievement of a better result for creditors (eg because the extra costs of a liquidation are unnecessary and it is proposed that the company should move straight from administration to dissolution)[57].

17.11 There will be cases in which it may be appropriate for the court to make an order terminating the administration even though the administrator's proposals have not yet been presented to the company's creditors. Thus, in a case decided under the pre-Enterprise Act 2002 law, *Re Charnley Davies Business Services Ltd*[58], the court, on the application of the administrator, discharged administration orders relating to 13 separate companies where the statutory purposes for which the orders had been made either had been achieved to the extent possible or had proved incapable of achievement, notwithstanding that

---

51 Rule 3.57(1) of the Rules. This requirement is directed at the question of whether the company needs to be placed into liquidation or restored to the control of its directors.
52 Rule 3.57(2) of the Rules.
53 Rule 3.57(2) of the Rules.
54 Rule 3.57(3) of the Rules. The court's power to appoint him as liquidator is contained in section 140 of IA 1986.
55 Cf *Re C E King Ltd* [2000] 2 BCLC 297 and *Sisu Capital Fund Ltd v Tucker* [2005] EWHC 2170 (Ch) (paragraph 85), per Warren J.
56 See eg Schedule B1 paragraph 4 of IA 1986.
57 See also, **PARAGRAPH 17.3** *ante*.
58 (1987) 3 BCC 408.

the administrator had failed to place his proposals before the creditors pursuant to what was then section 23 of IA 1986 and that no creditors' meeting had taken place to consider the proposals. Following the modifications introduced by the Enterprise Act 2002, express provision was made for the situation where the administrator intended to take steps to terminate the administration before his proposals had been sent to creditors[59]. While this provision is not replicated in Chapter 7 of Part 3 of the Rules, it is thought it that the law will remain consistent with the approach taken in *Re Charnley Davies Business Services Ltd.*

17.12 If it is intended to return the company to its directors in a case in which the original appointment was made out of court, this will normally be achievable without the intervention of the court by use of the procedure under Schedule B1 paragraph 80 of IA 1986. Where, however, the court made the original appointment, this procedure cannot be used and the issue will arise as to the further directions if any which the court may be minded to make. It is enough that the company's short-term solvency has been restored; it is not a pre-condition that the company's medium- or long-term solvency should be assured. Put another way, it is enough that the proposals for the company's future stand a fair chance of success and are in the interests of the company and its creditors generally[60]. However, where the company remains insolvent, the court will not terminate the administration or discharge any administration order (and an administrator should not file notice under Schedule B1 paragraph 80 of IA 1986) unless proper proposals are put forward to achieve the realisation of the company's remaining assets, if any, and the distribution of the proceeds of any realisations amongst the creditors through a liquidation[61]. This result can be achieved through the exercise by the administrator of his power[62] to present a petition for the winding up of the company so that immediately following the order for the administrator's appointment to cease to have effect, a winding-up order can be made[63]. Any such petition presented by the administrator is the petition of the company acting by the administrator[64]. It should contain an application for termination of the administrator's appointment under Schedule B1 paragraph 79(2) of IA 1986[65]. For procedural purposes, such a petition is treated similarly to a petition filed

---

59 Rule 2.33(6) of the Insolvency Rules 1986, introduced by the Insolvency (Amendment) Rules 2003 (SI 2003 No 1730).
60 *Re Olympia &York Canary Wharf Holdings* [1993] BCC 866.
61 *Re Barrow Borough Transport Ltd* [1990] Ch 227 per Millett J at 234e–f approved by the Court of Appeal in *Oakley Smith v Greenberg* [2002] EWCA Civ 1217, [2003] BPIR 709 at 721. Where all that remains to be done is a distribution of the company's assets, an application for permission to do so under Schedule B1 paragraph 65 of IA 1986 may be the more appropriate course.
62 See Schedule B1 paragraph 60 and Schedule 1 paragraph 21 of IA 1986. This will not be necessary if a winding up petition was suspended pursuant to Schedule B1 paragraph 40(1)(b) of IA 1986. In such a case, the petition can be restored for hearing once the administration ceases to have effect: see what ocurred in *In re Portsmouth City FC Ltd* [2012] EWHC 3088 (Ch) (paragraph 8). See also *Re J Smiths Haulage Ltd* [2007] BCC 135.
63 See eg *Re Charnley Davies Business Services Ltd* (1987) 3 BCC 408. The petition must be presented to the court having jurisdiction for the administration (Rule 7.8(2) of the Rules), which will be the court where the administration order was made and in the case of an out-of-court appointment, will presumably be the court where the notice of appointment was filed.
64 Rule 7.27(1) of the Rules.
65 Rule 7.27(2)(e) of the Rules. There is no specific obligation on the applicant to include an application for discharge of any administration order, although if the court makes an order terminating the administration it is required to discharge the administration order: Schedule B1 paragraph 85 of IA 1986. It follows that it would be good practice to seek such relief in the petition.

by contributories[66] although, in practice, and unlike a contributories' petition, it is not normally returnable in chambers for directions, but is listed for hearing in open court from the outset[67]. Further, it has been held that on an application made under Schedule B1 paragraph 79 of IA 1986, the court may make a winding up order without a petition having been presented[68]. Where a winding-up order is made immediately upon the appointment of an administrator ceasing to have effect, the court has power to appoint as liquidator of the company the person whose appointment as administrator has ceased to have effect[69]. These provisions give valuable protection to the rights of creditors upon the discharge of an administration order and allow continuity in the administration of its affairs. The court, however, may hesitate before exercising its power to appoint the former administrator as liquidator where his performance as administrator may give ground for legitimate complaint[70]. Where, therefore, the administrator seeks appointment as liquidator, not less than nine business days before the return day for the winding-up petition, he must notify creditors of the company, either in writing or at a meeting of the creditors, of the intention to seek his appointment as liquidator and, not less than two business days before the return day, file in court a report including particulars of the date on which creditors were so notified and details of any response from creditors to that notification, including any objections to his proposed appointment[71].

17.13 On the hearing of an application by the administrator, the court has wide powers to grant other relief apart from an order under Schedule B1 paragraph 79(1) of IA 1986 providing for the appointment of an administrator to cease to have effect. Thus, it may adjourn the hearing conditionally or unconditionally or dismiss the application or make an interim order or make any other order it thinks appropriate (whether in addition to, in consequence of or instead of the order applied for)[72]. Under the pre-Enterprise Act 2002 law, it was established that the court had jurisdiction to make a conditional order discharging the administration order[73] or, alternatively, an immediate order for discharge coupled with an order restraining the presentation of a winding-up petition against the company without the prior leave of the court over the period which would have elapsed prior to a conditional order taking effect[74]. The equivalent point under the present law is now dealt with by the wording of Schedule B1 paragraph 79(1) of IA 1986 which expressly permits the court to provide for the appointment to cease to have effect from a specified time, a form of words which appears to contemplate both a future time certain and a time identifiable by reference to some future event. Where the court provides

---

66 Cf Rule 7.27(2) of the Rules. It should not therefore be advertised without the court's prior direction.
67 Cf Rule 7.29(3)(b) of the Rules.
68 *Re Graico Property Management Company Ltd* [2016] EWHC 2827 (Ch) in which a liquidation was appropriate in order to enable a leasehold interest to be disclaimed.
69 Section 140(1) of IA 1986; see eg *Re Charnley Davies Business Services Ltd* (1987) 3 BCC 408, *Re Exchange Travel (Holdings) Ltd* [1992] BCC 954 and *Re Angel Group Ltd* [205] EWHC 3624 (Ch).
70 Cf *Re Charnley Davies Business Services Ltd* (1987) 3 BCC 408 per Harman J at 412–413. The court has no power under section 140(1) of IA 1986 to appoint as liquidator anyone other than a former administrator: see *Re Exchange Travel (Holdings) Ltd* [1992] BCC 954 at 958h–959a.
71 Rule 7.30 of the Rules.
72 Schedule B1 paragraph 79(4) of IA 1986.
73 *Re Norditrack (UK) Ltd* [2000] 1 BCLC 467 and *Re Oakhouse Property Holdings Ltd* [2003] BPIR 469.
74 *Re Moran Holdings plc* (6 July 1993, unreported, Harman J).

for the appointment of an administrator appointed by order of the court to cease to have effect, it must also discharge the administration order[75]; presumably the order of discharge should take effect from the moment of cessation. Where the court makes an order to end the administration, the administrator must notify the registrar of companies as soon as is reasonably practicable[76], and in any event within 14 days[77] attaching copies of the court order and his final progress report[78]. The administrator must also deliver a copy of the order and of his final progress report to the directors of the company and all other persons to whom notice of the administrators appointment was delivered as soon as is reasonably practicable[79].

CREDITOR'S APPLICATION FOR CESSATION

17.14 A creditor of the company may also apply to the court[80] for an order that the appointment of an administrator ceases to have effect from a specified time. Any such application must allege an improper motive on the part of the applicant for any administration order or on the part of the person who made the appointment as the case may be[81]. This means that the court can only grant substantive relief on any such application if the allegation of improper motive is established[82], because otherwise there would be no point in the requirement that the allegation be made. The wording of this provision is, however, unfortunate. The test appears to require an examination of the subjective state of mind of the person concerned, a fact which will often be difficult to prove. In *Cursitan v Keenan*[83], which concerned a virtually identical provision at Schedule 1 paragraph 82 of the Insolvency (Northern Ireland) Order 2005[84], McCloskey J suggested that an improper motivation would be a motive incompatible with the statutory objective of the administration. A similar approach was taken in *Thomas v Frogmore Real Estate Partners GP1 Ltd*[85], where the court held that it would be sufficient to invoke the jurisdiction if there was a motive that is not in harmony with the statutory purpose of the administration and was causative of the decision to appoint; however, it is immaterial whether the improper motive was the applicant or appointor's sole motive, provided that it was causative of the decision to appoint. The court has a discretion under Schedule B1 paragraph 81(1) of IA 1986 and if the statutory purpose of the administration is likely to be achieved then an application for cessation is likely to be dismissed, notwithstanding the motives which may have underpinned the initiation of the process at the outset.

---

75 Schedule B1 paragraph 85 of IA 1986.
76 Rule 3.59 of the Rules. The obligation to notify the registrar of companies means that the same documents must be sent to any member state liquidator appointed in relation to the company: Rule 21.7 of the Rules.
77 Schedule B1 paragraph 86 of IA 1986. If the administrator fails without reasonable excuse to send a copy of the order to the registrar of companies within 14 days he commits an offence: Schedule B1 paragraph 86(3) of IA 1986.
78 Rule 3.59 of the Rules.
79 Rule 3.59 of the Rules.
80 Under Schedule B1 paragraph 81(1) of IA 1986.
81 Schedule B1 paragraph 81(2) of IA 1986.
82 *Thomas v Frogmore Real Estate Partners GP1 Ltd* [2017] EWHC 25 (Ch) (paragraph 48).
83 [2011] NI Ch 23.
84 SI 2005 No 1455.
85 [2017] EWHC 25 (Ch) (paragraph 50).

17.15 A copy of the application must be served on the administrator and the person who either made the application for the administration order or made the appointment[86]. Service must be effected no later than five business days before the date fixed for the hearing[87]. In cases in which the holder of the floating charge by which the appointment was made is no longer the same as the person who made the appointment (which will be the case if the charge has been assigned), the holder of the charge must be served as well as the original appointor[88]. In addition to the jurisdiction to provide for the appointment of an administrator to cease to have effect from a specified time, the court is given express power to adjourn the hearing unconditionally, to dismiss the application, to make an interim order and to make any order it thinks appropriate, whether in addition to, in consequence of or instead of the order applied for[89]. Presumably, these powers can be exercised whether or not the allegation of improper motive is established.

17.16 If the court is minded to make an order terminating the administrator's appointment on the application of a creditor, it must also satisfy itself that the position of the company is adequately protected for the future. Thus, many of the factors to which the court will have regard on an administrator's application will also be relevant to a creditor's application[90]. In particular, the court will wish to be satisfied that if the company is insolvent, steps will be taken to place it into liquidation. To that end it will often be necessary for a winding-up petition to be presented (for which the consent of the administrator or permission of the court will be required[91]) so that the court can make a winding-up order immediately after the appointment of an administrator ceases to have effect. If the court makes an order under Schedule B1 paragraph 81 of IA 1986 that the appointment of an administrator shall cease to have effect, it must also discharge any administration order made in relation to the company[92]. Where the court makes an order to end the administration, the court must send a copy of the order to the administrator[93] and he must notify the registrar of companies as soon as is reasonably practicable[94], and in any event within 14 days[95] attaching copies of the court order and his final progress report[96]. The administrator must also deliver a copy of the order and of his final progress report to the directors of the company and all other persons to whom notice of the administrator's appointment was delivered as soon as is reasonably practicable[97].

---

86   Rule 3.58(1) of the Rules.
87   Rule 3.58(1) of the Rules.
88   Rule 3.58(1) of the Rules.
89   Schedule B1 paragraph 81(3) of IA 1986.
90   As to which see **PARAGRAPH 17.9**FF *ante*.
91   Schedule B1 paragraph 43(6) of IA 1986.
92   Schedule B1 paragraph 85 of IA 1986.
93   Rule 3.58(3) of the Rules.
94   Rule 3.59 of the Rules. The obligation to notify the registrar of companies means that the same documents must be sent to any member state liquidator appointed in relation to the company: Rule 21.7 of the Rules.
95   Schedule B1 paragraph 86 of IA 1986. If the administrator fails without reasonable excuse to send a copy of the order to the registrar of companies within 14 days he commits an offence: Schedule B1 paragraph 86(3) of IA 1986.
96   Rule 3.59 of the Rules.
97   Rule 3.59 of the Rules.

RESCISSION OF AN ADMINISTRATION ORDER

17.17 In *Cornhill Insurance plc v Cornhill Financial Services Ltd*[98], the Court of Appeal affirmed the decision of the judge at first instance that, pursuant to the general power conferred by Rule 7.47 of the Insolvency Rules 1986[99] to review, rescind or vary orders made in the exercise of insolvency jurisdiction, the court by which an administration order has been made had power to rescind that order. It may well be the case that the powers now available to a creditor to make an application under Schedule B1 paragraph 81 of IA 1986 mean that there will be little need for the general rescission jurisdiction to be invoked, but there may still be some rare cases in which this is the proper method of bringing an administration to an end. Thus, an order for the rescission of an administration order may be made on the application of any party aggrieved[100] and, therefore, can be made not just on the application of a creditor[101] but also, in an appropriate case, on the application of a member of the company concerned[102]. As with the statutory jurisdiction under Schedule B1 paragraph 81 of IA 1986, the creditor or member concerned can apply whether or not he was represented before the court on the original application for the administration order.

17.18 The circumstances in which the court will exercise the power to rescind an administration order has not been considered in many reported cases, but presumably the power is exercisable not only where, at the time of making the administration order, the court was not fully appraised of the relevant factual background[103], but also where it has proceeded on the basis of some error or misapprehension as to the facts. Whether the power should also be exercised where it can subsequently be demonstrated that the administration order is likely to operate oppressively or unfairly against the interest of a particular creditor or group of creditors or of creditors or members generally is more open to question. In most cases in which the operation of the order is oppressive or unfair to a creditor or member, the proper course is for the administrator to be asked to apply for directions under Schedule B1 paragraph 63 of IA 1986 or cessation under Schedule B1 paragraph 79 and, if he does not do so, for an unfair harm application to be made under Schedule B1 paragraph 74. Even where the court may have been misled at the original hearing, an application to rescind based on a failure to make full and frank disclosure, is unlikely to succeed if it can be seen that administration is in the best interests of the company or its creditors[104]. Although the discretion under Rule 7.47(1) of the Insolvency Rules 1986 (and presumably under Rule 12.59 of the Rules) is a broad one, it seems that the

---

98 [1993] BCLC 914.

99 The equivalent provision under the present law is at Rule 12.59 of the Rules.

100 [1993] BCLC 914 per Dillon LJ at 963. At first instance, HHJ Micklem held, at 931, that the creditor concerned could apply to be joined to the administration proceedings pursuant to RSC Ord 15, rule 6(2)(b)(ii) as applied by Rule 7.51 of the Insolvency Rules 1986. See now, CPR Part 19.2(2)(b) and Rule 12.1(1) of the Rules.

101 Eg *Cornhill Insurance plc v Cornhill Financial Services Ltd* [1993] BCLC 914.

102 Subject to demonstrating a tangible interest in the company, cf *Re Chelmsford City Football Club (1980) Ltd* [1991] BCC 133.

103 See eg *Re Sharps of Truro Ltd* [1990] BCC 94 and *Cornhill Insurance plc v Cornhill Financial Services Ltd* [1993] BCLC 914.

104 *Re MTI Trading Systems Ltd* [1998] BCC 400, in which the Court of Appeal refused an application to rescind even though the evidence indicated that the petitioner may not have had *locus standi* to proceed.

court will only rescind an administration order in exceptional circumstances[105]. Since an administration order not only imposes a statutory moratorium upon the company's creditors but confers rights and duties upon the administrator, any application for rescission ought to be brought before the court without delay[106]. It is thought that the rescission of an administration order amounts to an order ending the administration within the meaning of Rule 3.59 of the Rules and that an administrator will therefore come under a duty to send a copy of the rescission order and a copy of his final progress report to the registrar of companies, the directors of the company and all other persons to whom notice of his appointment was delivered[107].

TERMINATION FOLLOWED BY CREDITORS' VOLUNTARY LIQUIDATION

17.19 In a number of cases under the pre-Enterprise Act 2002 law, it was sought to avoid the cost and expense of a compulsory liquidation and to have a voluntary liquidation instead following the discharge of an administration order[108]. Since a resolution for the winding up of a company could not be passed whilst the administration order remained in force it was necessary in such circumstances that the administration order should first be discharged[109]. However, even where a resolution to wind up the company was passed immediately after discharge of the administration order, there was no comparable provision to that applicable in a compulsory winding up to enable preferential creditors to be determined other than by reference to the date of the resolution to wind up the company[110] and, unless the winding-up resolution was passed immediately after the discharge of the administration order, the onset of insolvency for the purposes of sections 238 and 239 of IA 1986 (transactions at an undervalue and preferences) was deemed to be the date of the resolution to wind up rather than the date of presentation of the petition for the making of the administration order[111].

17.20 As a result, a number of techniques were developed to ensure that the date of presentation of the petition for the making of an administration order was

---

105 *Fitch v Official Receiver* [1996] 1 WLR 242, which concerned the equivalent provision in personal insolvency: section 375 of IA 1986; see also *Re Switch Services Ltd* (22 December 2011, unreported).

106 See eg *Barclays Bank plc v Davidson* (8 February 2000, unreported, CA) and *Re Switch Services Ltd* (22 December 2011, unreported) (paragraph 274).

107 Rule 3.59 of the Rules. Any member state liquidator would also have to be notified: Rule 21.7 of the Rules. Although Rule 3.59 is founded on Schedule B1 paragraph 86 of IA 1986 and is primarily dealing with orders made pursuant to the specific statutory powers to terminate (ie Schedule B1 paragraphs 79, 81, 82 and 83 of IA 1986), it is wide enough to cover a rescission order and there is an obvious policy reason for imposing such an obligation whenever a registered appointment comes to an end.

108 The fees payable under the Insolvency Fees Order 1986 (SI 1986 No 2030) (as amended) were substantially less in a voluntary liquidation than in a compulsory liquidation. In addition, there was a significant timing difference, of nearly six months, as regards the dates by which a compulsory liquidator and a voluntary liquidator were required to make payments into the Insolvency Services Account; cf regulation 5(1) and (2) of the Insolvency Regulations 1994 (SI 1994 No 2507). Since 1 April 2004, the obligation of a liquidator in a voluntary winding up to make payments into the Insolvency Services Account has been abolished altogether by the Insolvency (Amendment) Regulations 2004 (SI 2004 No 472).

109 Section 11(3)(a) of IA 1986 in its original form. The position remains the same: Schedule B1 paragraph 42(2) of IA 1986.

110 Cf section 387(3)(a) and (c) of IA 1986.

111 Cf section 240(3)(a) and (b) of IA 1986.

preserved as the date of the onset of insolvency for the purposes of sections 238 and 239 of IA 1986. One such technique was to have the shareholders of the company concerned present at court on the application for discharge of the administration order and to make the order for the discharge of the administration order conditional upon the shareholders' undertaking immediately thereafter to pass a resolution to wind up the company. A refinement of this procedure, of greater utility where there were a number of shareholders, was to make the order for the discharge of the administration order conditional upon, but to take effect immediately prior to, the passing of a resolution to wind up the company[112]. The alternative approach, involving the passing of a conditional resolution to wind up, the condition being the subsequent discharge of the administration order[113], was ultimately disapproved on the grounds that a resolution for voluntary winding up cannot be passed conditionally on another event[114].

17.21 Furthermore, and in order to protect the position of creditors whose claims would have been preferential in a compulsory liquidation which immediately followed the discharge of the administration order, orders were frequently made directing the administrator to pay such creditors the amount of such claims prior to the discharge of the administration order. Alternatively, arrangements were made to establish a trust fund for the benefit of such creditors. This established practice was not considered in a reasoned decision until the case of *Re Powerstore (Trading) Ltd, Re Homepower Stores Ltd*[115] when Lightman J concluded (with regret) that the court had no power to make such orders because they related to payments which were not being made for the purposes of the administration[116]. The manifest inconvenience of this decision meant that it was not long before it was challenged and in the case of *Re Mark One (Oxford St) plc*[117], Jacob J declined to follow *Powerstore* and sanctioned the old practice of directing payment to be made to (and in trust for) preferential creditors before the resolution to wind up took effect. Throughout these developments there was no case in which the court was asked to discharge an administration order to enable a company to go into voluntary liquidation in a case where creditors, whose claims would have been preferential in a compulsory winding up, would be adversely affected by a voluntary liquidation, but where no protection was offered to them[118]. In such a case, it would always have been

---

112 This was the route adopted in *Re Norditrack (UK) Ltd* [2000] 1 BCLC 467 and *Re Oakhouse Property Holdings Ltd* [2003] BPIR 469.
113 The route adopted in *Re Mark One (Oxford St) plc* [1999] 1 WLR 1445.
114 *Re Norditrack Ltd (UK) Ltd* [2000] 1 BCLC 467 and *In Re UCT (UK) Ltd* [2001] 1 WLR 436 at 439.
115 [1997] 1 WLR 1280.
116 Lightman J's reasoning was not dissimilar to the view expressed in the first edition of this work, viz that it may be difficult to justify such an order as being necessary or incidental to the achievement of the purposes specified in the administration order.
117 [1999] 1 WLR 1445, subsequently followed, although adopting a slightly different process of reasoning, by Arden J in *Re UCT (UK) Ltd* [2001] 1 WLR 436 and *Re Wolsey Theatre Co Ltd* [2001] BCC 486. For a case in which these authorities were reviewed in the slightly different context of an application for leave to distribute prior to the making of a winding-up order, see *Re Designer Room Ltd* [2004] EWHC 720 (Ch).
118 An alternative means of protecting the interests of preferential creditors was approved by Neuberger J in *Re Philip Alexander Securities & Futures Ltd* [1999] 1 BCLC 124 (a case decided between the decisions in *Re Powerstore (Trading) Ltd* and *Re Mark One (Oxford St) plc*). In that case, it was anticipated that certain non-preferential creditors would be prepared to accept a reduced dividend to ensure that the preferential creditors would receive the amount to which they would have been entitled if a winding-up order had been made.

open to the creditors concerned to present a winding-up petition and then to oppose the discharge of the administration order pending the determination of the winding-up petition.

17.22   The position was simplified by the introduction of Schedule B1 paragraph 83 of IA 1986. Under this provision, the administrator can send to the registrar of companies a notice that the paragraph applies[119]. On registration of the notice the appointment of the administrator ceases to have effect[120] and the company is wound up as if a resolution for winding up under section 84 of IA 1986 was passed on the day of registration[121]. The administrator is empowered to adopt this procedure where he thinks[122] that the total amount which each secured creditor of the company is likely to receive has been paid to him or set aside for him and that a distribution will be made to unsecured creditors, if there are any, which is not a distribution by virtue of section 176A(2)(a)[123]. It follows that the procedure would not seem to be appropriate if it is still necessary to make realisations from the charged assets in order to make a distribution to secured creditors[124], nor will it be permitted if there is no surplus for payment to unsecured creditors[125]. In the latter case, a distribution to the unsecured and preferential creditors in the administration, followed by a dissolution may be the more appropriate procedure. Where this procedure is adopted there is no need for the administrator to make a separate application to court under Schedule B1 paragraph 79 of IA 1986[126]. The administrator must, as soon as reasonably

---

119 Schedule B1 paragraph 83(3) of IA 1986. The notice must contain identification details for the proceeds, the name of the person who made the appointment or the administration application and the name and IP number of the proposed liquidator: Rule 3.60(2) of the Rules. The notice must be accompanied by a final progress report attached: Rule 3.60(3) of the Rules. The final progress report must contain the information set out in Rule 18.3 of the Rules and must also include a summary of the administrator's proposals, any major amendments to or deviations from those proposals, the steps taken during the administration and the outcome: Rule 3.53 of the Rules.

120 Schedule B1 paragraph 83(6)(a) of IA 1986 and see also *Re Globespan Airways Ltd* [2012] EWCA Civ 1159 and *Re Synergi Partners Ltd* [2015] EWHC 964 (Ch). The registrar's duty to register is spelled out in Schedule B1 paragraph 83(4) of IA 1986.

121 Schedule B1 paragraph 83(6)(b). It is expressly provided that any such winding up will be deemed to commence at the beginning of the date of registration of the notice: Schedule B1 paragraph 83(8)(b) of IA 1986. Notwithstanding this notional commencement date (a) the effect of section 387(3)(ba) of IA 1986 is to preserve the position of preferential creditors as at the date the company entered administration, and (b) the effect of section 240(3)(d) of IA 1986 is to retain that date as the onset of insolvency for the purposes of sections 239 and 293 of IA 1986.

122 The administrator must reach this conclusion through a rational thought process but he is not subject to any objective standard: *Unidare v Cohen* [2005] EWHC 1410 (Ch) (paragraph 71).

123 Schedule B1 paragraph 83(1) of IA 1986.

124 It may be that setting aside an unrealised charged asset is sufficient to give an administrator power to use this jurisdiction, but, if that were to be the case, Schedule B1 paragraph 83(1)(a) of IA 1986 has little purpose.

125 A difficulty arises if the administrator is only able to 'think' that there 'may' be a distribution to unsecured creditors, but is unable to 'think' that such a distribution 'will' be made. In cases of doubt, and where the administrator is only able to conclude that a distribution is a mere possibility, resort to the former procedure (see **PARAGRAPH 17.21** *ante*) will be the safer course. In such a case, the court can make an order that the appointment of an administrator shall cease to have effect immediately prior to the passing of a resolution to wind up (Schedule B1 paragraph 79(1) of IA 1986 and **PARAGRAPH 17.13** *ante*). Presumably, the court would require any unpaid preferential creditors to be given appropriate protection (as to which, see **PARAGRAPH 17.21** *ante*), because in such a case their preferential status will not have been preserved by the insertion of the new section 387(3)(ba) of IA 1986.

126 *Re Ballast plc* [2004] EWHC 2356 (Ch) (paragraph 15).

practicable after sending notice to the registrar of companies, file a copy of the notice with the court and send a copy of the notice to each creditor of the company of whose claim and address he is aware[127] and to all those who received notice of his appointment[128]. The procedure cannot be used to enable the company to go into members' voluntary winding up[129] and there are a number of detailed modifications made in relation to the conduct of the winding up itself[130].

17.23 Where this procedure is used, the liquidator will either be a person nominated by the creditors of the company or, where no such nomination is made, will be the administrator[131]. The procedure for nominating a voluntary liquidator is somewhat cumbersome and takes the following form. An administrator's proposals must state how it is envisaged that the administration shall end and, if a creditors' voluntary liquidation is proposed, details of the proposed liquidator must be provided[132]. Doubtless, it will often be the case that the administrator will propose himself as the putative voluntary liquidator, but sometimes this will be inappropriate. The proposals must also state that the creditors may nominate a different person for the purposes of Schedule B1 paragraph 83(7) of IA 1986, so long as the nomination is made before the proposals are approved[133]. Similar requirements are imposed where a proposed revision of the proposals relates to the ending of an administration by a creditors' voluntary liquidation[134]. Thereafter, the effective act of appointment is traced back to the approval of the proposals or revised proposals, whether in the form originally presented by the administrator, or in the modified form (eg by the approval of another putative liquidator nominated by the creditors)[135]. It follows that the creditors' first opportunity to vote on the identity of a voluntary liquidator comes immediately before and at the time of approval of the proposals. If it subsequently becomes apparent that the proposed liquidator (whether or not the same person as the administrator) no longer has the confidence of the creditors to act as such, the only mechanism for nominating an alternative would seem to be by a revision of the proposals promulgated by the administrator[136]. Presumably, in an extreme case it is open to the court to direct the administrator to propose a revision to his proposals for the purpose of enabling the creditors to nominate an alternative voluntary liquidator[137]. If, however, the administration has become so contentious that

---

127 Schedule B1 paragraph 83(5) of IA 1986. This means that the administrator must also serve notice on any member state liquidator appointed in relation to the company: Rule 21.7 of the Rules.
128 Rule 3.60(4) of the Rules. It is thought that the obligation to send copies to anyone notified of his appointment is a reference to those formally notified in accordance with an obligation under IA 1986 or the Rules. It is not intended to refer to others (such as suppliers, etc) who will have received notice of his appointment in the ordinary course of the company's business.
129 Because section 89 of IA 1986 is disapplied by Schedule B1 paragraph 83(8)(c) of IA 1986.
130 Schedule B1 paragraph 83(8) of IA 1986 and Rule 6.1(2) of the Rules.
131 Schedule B1 paragraph 83(7) of IA 1986.
132 Rule 3.35(1)(j)(ii)(aa) of the Rules.
133 Rule 3.35(1)(j)(ii)(cc) of the Rules.
134 Rule 3.42(2)(f) of the Rules.
135 Rule 3.60(6) of the Rules.
136 The reason for this is that the creditors of the company can only nominate a person to be liquidator in the prescribed manner and within the prescribed period: Schedule B1 paragraph 83(7)(a) of IA 1986. The only manner and period so prescribed is that set out above.
137 One of the circumstances in which the court can give directions which are inconsistent with the proposals is where there has been a change of circumstance: Schedule B1 paragraph 68(3)(c) of IA 1986.

such an application might be necessary, there will be real doubts as to whether the procedure under Schedule B1 paragraph 83 is appropriate[138].

MOVING FROM ADMINISTRATION TO DISSOLUTION

17.24 If the administrator thinks that the company has no property which might permit a distribution to its creditors[139], he then comes under a duty[140] to send a notice[141] to that effect, accompanied by a final progress report[142] to the registrar of companies[143]. The registrar is under a duty to register the notice[144] whereupon the appointment of an administrator ceases to have effect[145]. Where this procedure is followed, the administrator does not have to make a separate application to court under Schedule B1 paragraph 79 of IA 1986[146]. Where a notice is sent to the registrar under Schedule B1 paragraph 84(1) of IA 1986, the administrator is then under a duty as soon as reasonably practicable to file a copy of the notice with the court and send a copy of the notice[147] to each creditor of whose claim and address he is aware (other than an opted-out creditor)[148] and to all those who received notice of the administrator's appointment[149]. If an administrator fails without reasonable excuse to comply with the obligation to file at court and notify creditors he commits an offence[150]. This duty will arise in two distinct categories of case. The first is where it transpires that the company has no property available for distribution to creditors. The second is where distributions have been made by the administrator in exercise of his powers under Schedule B1 paragraph 65 of IA 1986 and there is no further distribution to be made, whether through the medium of the administration or a liquidation[151]. On application by the administrator, the court is

---

138 Cf *Hobbs v Gibson* [2010] EWHC 3676 (Ch).
139 The procedure under Schedule B1 paragraph 84 of IA 1986 is not limited to cases where the company never had any assets that might have enabled a distribution to creditors: *Re GHE Realisations Ltd* [2005] EWHC 2400 (Ch).
140 The duty is imposed by Schedule B1 paragraph 84(1) of IA 1986.
141 The notice must identify the proceedings: Rule 3.61(2) of the Rules.
142 The final progress report must contain the information set out in Rule 18.3 of the Rules and must also include a summary of the administrator's proposals, any major amendments to or deviations from those proposals, the steps taken during the administration and the outcome: Rule 3.53 of the Rules.
143 This means that the administrator must also serve notice on any member state liquidator appointed in relation to the company: Rule 21.7 of the Rules.
144 Schedule B1 paragraph 84(3) of IA 1986.
145 Schedule B1 paragraph 84(5) of IA 1986.
146 *Re Ballast plc* [2004] EWHC 2356 (Ch) (paragraph 19). In *Re Hellas Telecommunications (Luxembourg) II SCA* [2011] EWHC 3176 (Ch), the administrators were directed not to serve notice under Schedule B1 paragraph 84 of IA 1986, but instead to apply for the administration to cease to have effect under paragraph 79, and petition for the company to be wound up.
147 The copy of the notice should have the final progress report attached to it: Rule 3.61(4) of the Rules.
148 A creditor can opt out of receiving certain documents: Rules 1.37–1.39 of the Rules.
149 Schedule B1 paragraph 84(5) of IA 1986 and Rule 3.61(3) of the Rules. It is thought that the obligation to send copies to anyone notified of his appointment is a reference to those formally notified in accordance with an obligation under IA 1986 or the Rules. It is not intended to refer to others (such as suppliers, etc) who will have received notice of his appointment in the ordinary course of the company's business.
150 Schedule B1 paragraph 84(9) of IA 1986.
151 This passage was cited and followed by Rimer J in *Re GHE Realisations Ltd* [2005] EWHC 2400 (Ch) (paragraphs 21–23). Where the company at no time had any property then it is

empowered[152] to disapply paragraph 84(1), which presumably means that it can relieve the administrator from the obligation to send notice to the registrar, even though he may think that the company has no property which might permit a distribution to creditors. This procedure provides a convenient mechanism for terminating a company's existence where a winding up is not required[153].

17.25 Where a notice is registered under Schedule B1 paragraph 84 of IA 1986, the company will then be deemed to be dissolved at the end of the period of three months beginning with the date of registration[154]. On an application made by the administrator or any other interested person[155], the court can extend the three-month period, or it can suspend the period, or it can disapply Schedule B1 paragraph 84(6) of IA 1986 altogether so that the company is not deemed dissolved at all notwithstanding the registration of a notice[156]. Where the court makes any such order[157], the administrator is under a duty as soon as is reasonably practicable to notify the registrar of companies[158]. It is unclear whether this power can be exercised after the company has been dissolved[159], but if a retrospective order cannot be made, it is presumably open to any person interested to make an application for the restoration of the company to the register under section 1029 of CA 2006[160]. Normally such an application can be justified if an asset was overlooked during the administration or the company needs to be resurrected so that a creditor can make a claim against it, for example for the purposes of pursuing the company's insurers under the Third Parties (Rights against Insurers) Act 2010[161].

unlikely that it should have entered administration. In those circumstances, Rimer J considered that it would be more appropriate to terminate the administrator's appointment by way of an application under Schedule B1 paragraph 79(2) of IA 1986 rather than through the dissolution procedure at Schedule B1 paragraph 84 of IA 1986.

152 By Schedule B1 paragraph 84(2) of IA 1986.
153 It goes some way towards meeting the concerns expressed in the Northern Ireland case of *Re Review Publishing Ltd* [2002] NI Ch 5 that there was no convenient method for procuring the striking off of a company once an administration had been completed.
154 Schedule B1 paragraph 84(6) of IA 1986.
155 The concept of an 'interested person' does not appear elsewhere in Schedule B1 of IA 1986 and appears to be derived from section 651 of CA 1985 and sections 201 and 205 of IA 1986, in which context it has been held normally to relate to a pecuniary or proprietary interest (see the review of cases in *Re Philip Powis Ltd* [1998] 1 BCLC 440) although there are cases in which it may extend further: *Re Townreach Ltd* [1995] Ch 28.
156 Schedule B1 paragraph 84(7) of IA 1986.
157 If the application is made by a person other than the administrator, the court must give a copy of the order to the administrator: Rule 3.61(5) of the Rules.
158 Schedule B1 paragraph 84(8) of IA 1986. He must deliver a copy of the order to the registrar of companies with the notice: Rule 3.61(6) of the Rules. This obligation means that the administrator must also notify any member state liquidator appointed in relation to the company: Rule 21.7 of the Rules.
159 Compare the rather different wording used in sections 201(3) and 205(3) of IA 1986, which are clearer in their terms and only give the court power to defer a dissolution at the end of a winding up, before the dissolution actually takes effect.
160 Section 1029 of CA 2006 does not give an administrator the power available to a former liquidator to make an application under that section, but there may be cases in which he does qualify as 'a person appearing to the court to have an interest in the matter' within the meaning of section 1029(2), although that will not automatically be the case: *Barclays Bank plc v Registrar of Companies* [2015] EWHC 2806 (Ch).
161 See *Stanhope Pension Trust Ltd v Registrar of Companies* [1994] 1 BCLC 628 at 632, a case under the Third Parties (Rights Against Insurers) Act 1930, per Hoffmann LJ.

TERMINATION: MISCELLANEOUS CASES

17.26 The court also has power to provide that the appointment of an administrator shall cease to have effect from a specified time where the administrator has reported to the court under Schedule B1 paragraph 53 that the company's creditors have failed to approve the administrator's proposals or has reported to the court under Schedule B1 paragraph 54 that the company's creditors have failed to approve any revision of the administrator's proposals[162]. The court has a similar power where a voluntary arrangement has been approved by the company and its creditors[163] or on an unfair harm application under Schedule B1 paragraph 74 of IA 1986[164]. Presumably, the court could also direct an administrator to apply for an order that his appointment shall cease to have effect on an application for directions under Schedule B1 paragraph 63 of IA 1986[165] or on an application by a creditor for permission under Schedule B1 paragraph 43 or on any other application by any member or creditor of the company[166]. The court may also provide that the appointment of an administrator shall cease to have effect where it makes a winding-up order on a petition presented by the Secretary of State under section 124A of IA 1986 or by the FCA or the PRA under section 367 of FSMA 2000[167].

17.27 The final mechanism for bringing an administration to an end is where an administrator has been appointed in territorial proceedings opened before the opening of main proceedings in another EU member state[168]. In any such case, the liquidator in the main proceedings is entitled to apply under Article 37 of the EC Insolvency Regulation for the administration to be converted into a winding up. He can make such an application if it is in the interests of the creditors in the main proceedings and, on one reading of Article 37[169], if he does so, the English court has no discretion: it must then make a conversion order. It is submitted, however, that the court is at least able to decline the conversion request if it is not satisfied that conversion is in the interests of creditors in the main proceedings. The reason for this is that the court must be able to examine whether the request has been properly made in accordance with the article. It may also be the case that the court has a more general discretion, even where it is satisfied that the interests of the creditors in the main proceedings require a conversion[170], but

---

162 See Schedule B1 paragraph 55(2)(a) of IA 1986.
163 See section 5(3)(a) of IA 1986.
164 See Schedule B1 paragraph 74(4)(d) of IA 1986.
165 The direction would have to be available to the court in the light of the provisions of Schedule B1 paragraph 68(3) of IA 1986.
166 See *Re Mirror Group (Holdings) Ltd* [1993] BCLC 538 at 543.
167 Schedule B1 paragraph 82(3)(a) of IA 1986. There is no obligation to make a termination order, because the legislation contemplates that there may be some cases in which it is appropriate for a winding up based on public interest grounds to co-exist with an administration.
168 Where a company's centre of main interests is in another EU member state, it is only possible for it to go into administration if it has an establishment in the United Kingdom and even then only if the administration commences before the commencement of main insolvency proceedings in that other state: Article 3(2) of the EC Insolvency Regulation (see also Article 3(4)).
169 See the use of the word 'shall'.
170 Compare *Hughes v Hannover Rückversicherungs AG* [1997] 1 BCLC 497 at 517 (a case on section 426 of IA 1986) and see also Rule 21.3 of the Rules, which states that on hearing an application for conversion 'the court may, subject to Article 37 of the EC Insolvency Regulation, make such order as it thinks just'.

the circumstances in which that discretion might be exercised against making a conversion order would have to be wholly exceptional. The application must be supported by a witness statement[171], both of which must be served on both the company and the administrator[172]. The witness statement must be made by or on behalf of the member state liquidator[173] and it must state:

(a) that main proceedings have been opened in relation to the company in another member state;

(b) the deponent's belief that conversion would prove to be in the interests of the creditors in the main proceedings;

(c) the deponent's opinion as to whether the company ought to enter voluntary winding up or be wound up by the court;

(d) all other matters that, in the opinion of the member state liquidator, would assist the court in deciding whether to make such an order and, if the court were to do so, in considering the need for any consequential provision that would be necessary or desirable[174].

On the application, the court is empowered (subject to Article 37 of the EC Insolvency Regulation) to make such order as it thinks just[175]. If the court makes a conversion order it may also include in the order such consequential provisions as the court thinks just, including, in the case of a voluntary winding up, an order that the company be wound up as if a resolution under section 84 of IA 1986 were passed on the day on which the order is made[176].

RESIGNATION OF AN ADMINISTRATOR

17.28   The administrator of a company may, in the prescribed circumstances set out in the Rules, resign his office[177]. The Rules provide that an administrator may give notice of his resignation on grounds of ill-health or because he intends ceasing to be in practice as an insolvency practitioner, or because there is some conflict of interest or change in personal circumstances, which prevents or makes impracticable the further discharge by him of the duties of administrator[178]. The Rules also provide that an administrator may, with the permission of the court, give notice of his resignation on other grounds[179]. Before resigning or making an application for permission to do so, the administrator must give at least five business days' notice of his intention to any continuing administrator of the company, to any creditors' committee and, if there is no such administrator and no such creditors' committee, to the company and its creditors[180]. He must also

---

171   Rule 21.2(2) of the Rules.
172   Rule 21.2(4) of the Rules.
173   Rule 21.2(2) of the Rules.
174   Rule 21.2(3) of the Rules.
175   Rule 21.3(1) of the Rules.
176   Rule 21.3(2) and (3) of the Rules.
177   Schedule B1 paragraph 87(1) of IA 1986.
178   Rule 3.62(1) of the Rules. It is not impracticable for an administrator further to discharge his duties merely because it is undesirable or inexpedient for him to do so: *Re Alt Landscapes* [1999] BPIR 459 at 461.
179   Rule 3.62(2) of the Rules.
180   Rule 3.63 of the Rules. The notice must contain the identification details for the proceedings, the date of appointment of the administrator, the name of the person who made the appointment or the administration application, the date with effect from which the administrator intends to resign and, where the administrator was appointed by administration order, the date on

notify any member state liquidator appointed in relation to the company[181]. Where he was appointed out of court, the administrator must also give notice of intention to resign to his appointor and to the holder of any qualifying floating charge[182]. These notification provisions are designed to ensure that appropriate steps[183] can be taken by parties interested to apply for or to make an appointment to fill the vacancy. The resignation itself is then effected by the administrator giving notice in writing[184] to the court where he was appointed by an administration order, to the holder of the charge by which he was appointed[185] where he was appointed under Schedule B1 paragraph 14 of IA 1986 and to the directors or the company where he was appointed under Schedule B1 paragraph 22 of IA 1986[186]. Copies of the notice of resignation must also be sent to the registrar of companies and all those to whom notice of intention to resign was sent[187]. Where he was appointed out of court, the administrator must also file his notice of resignation with the court[188]. It should be noted that the resignation of the administrator does not mean that the company thereby ceases to be in administration[189], although in any such case a resigning administrator should normally take steps to ensure that he is replaced immediately after his resignation takes effect[190].

REMOVAL OF AN ADMINISTRATOR BY THE COURT

17.29 An administrator, however appointed, may also be removed from office by order of the court[191]. Unlike the removal of a liquidator, the statute does not use the expression 'on cause shown' as a qualification to the power of the court to remove an administrator. Although the statutory discretion is very wide[192] the applicant will have to show good or sufficient cause to justify such an order[193]; however the grounds relied upon need not involve misconduct, personal unfitness or imputation against the integrity of the administrator[194]. By analogy with the

---

which the administrator intends to file with the court an application for permission to resign: Rule 3.63(2) and (3) of the Rules.

181 Rule 3.63(4)(d) of the Rules.
182 Rule 3.63(4)(e) and (f) of the Rules.
183 As to which, see **PARAGRAPH 17.35FF** *post*.
184 The notice must contain the identification details for the proceedings, the date of appointment of the administrator, the name of the person who made the appointment or the administration application, the date with effect from which the resignation is to have effect and, where the resignation is by permission of the court, the date on which the permission was given: Rule 3.64(2) and (3) of the Rules.
185 This may not be the same as the person who appointed him where the charge has been transferred.
186 Schedule B1 paragraph 87(2) of IA 1986.
187 Rule 3.64(1) of the Rules. These copies must be delivered within five business days of the delivery of the notice under Schedule B1 paragraph 87(2) of IA 1986.
188 Rule 3.64(1)(c) of the Rules. This copy must be filed within five business days of the delivery of the notice under Schedule B1 paragraph 87(2) of IA 1986.
189 Schedule B1 paragraph 1(2)(d) of IA 1986.
190 As to which, see **PARAGRAPH 17.35FF** *post*.
191 Schedule B1 paragraph 88 of IA 1986. The extra-judicial substitution of an administrator appointed out of court is considered in **PARAGRAPHS 17.37–17.39** *post*.
192 In consequence, there is only limited scope for setting aside a decision on an application under Schedule B1 paragraph 88 of IA 1986 on appeal: *Re St George's Property Services (London) Ltd* [2011] EWCA Civ 858 (paragraph 32).
193 *Re St George's Property Services (London) Ltd* [2011] EWCA Civ 858 (paragraph 33).
194 *Clydesdale Financial Services v Smailes* [2009] EWHC 1745 (Ch) (paragraph 14), referring to the judgment of Warren J in *Sisu Capital Fund Ltd v Tucker* [2005] EWHC 2170 (Ch) (paragraphs 82–90).

position of liquidators, such an order might be made where the administrator was in a position of conflict of interest or duty[195], where he had been guilty of misconduct[196], where he failed to carry out his duties with sufficient vigour[197], where there is a well-founded perception of bias[198], or where he had acted or was acting contrary to the wishes of creditors. The court will be entitled to take into account the impact which the removal and replacement will have on the general conduct of the administration, particularly in relation to additional cost and delay[199]. Where an administrator has been appointed out of court, he may be removed if his appointment was invalid[200]. The court also has a jurisdiction to remove an administrator wherever the circumstances are such that it is no longer practicable for him to carry out his functions, irrespective of whether his conduct can be said to be blameworthy[201]; the issue for the court is what is in the best interests of the insolvent estate. This question most often arises where an administrator moves firm and the day-to-day conduct of the administration is conducted by employees of the firm in which the administrator is a partner. The court will look at all the circumstances of the case in order to determine the appropriate relief; it will also sometimes require the views of creditors to be canvassed[202].

17.30 As in the case of an application to remove a liquidator for cause shown[203], the statute does not impose an express limitation on the class of persons able to apply for the removal of an administrator. It is thought, however, that the courts will apply the conventional approach of limiting the categories of potential applicants to those who have a legitimate interest in the identity of the administrator. Thus, an unsecured creditor may have difficulty in securing an administrator's removal where there is no prospect of a return to unsecured creditors, although the position may be different if the reason for the shortfall is alleged to be a default by the administrator. This would also exclude those regarded as strangers to the administration and those with an interest adverse to that of the insolvent estate[204]. It should be noted that different principles apply where removal of an administrator is sought because he has retired or been expelled from his partnership. In such a case, his former partners have a sufficient interest, in any event where they and their staff have the day-to-day

---

195 Cf *Re Corbenstoke Ltd (No 2)* [1990] BCLC 60, approved by the Privy Council in *Deloitte &Touche AG v Johnson* [1999] 1 WLR 1605. See also *Sisu Capital Fund v Tucker* [2005] EWHC 2170 (Ch) and *Beattie v Smailes* [2011] EWHC 1563 (Ch).

196 It will often be sufficient to show that there may well be a case of misfeasance or incompetence: *Shepheard v Lamey* [2001] BPIR 939.

197 Cf *Re Keypak Homecare Ltd* [1987] BCLC 409.

198 *Re Gordon & Breach Science Publishers Ltd* [1995] 2 BCLC 189, a case on whether a winding-up order should be made against a company already in voluntary liquidation, but on this point the principles are similar. However, it is not necessarily unfair for an administrator to treat creditors differently: *BLV Realty Organization Ltd v Batten* [2009] EWHC 2994 (Ch).

199 *Re C E King Ltd* [2000] 2 BCLC 297 and *AMP Enterprises Ltd v Hoffman* [2002] EWHC 1899 (Ch).

200 *National Westminster Bank v Msaada* [2011] EWHC 3423 (Ch).

201 *Re A & C Supplies Ltd* [1998] 1 BCLC 603. In most cases the problem can be dealt with by resignation, as to which see **PARAGRAPH 17.28** *ante*.

202 Compare the different approaches of Chadwick J in *Re Sankey Furniture Ltd* [1995] 2 BCLC 594 and Blackburne J in Re A & C Supplies Ltd [1998] 1 BCLC 603. See also *Re Alt Landscapes* [1999] BPIR 459 and *Re Equity Nominees Ltd* [1999] 2 BCLC 19.

203 Sections 108(2), 171(2) and 172(2) of IA 1986.

204 *Deloitte &Touche AG v Johnson* [1999] 1 WLR 1605.

conduct of the administration[205], although it should be noted that in any such case there will be a difficulty in filling the vacancy because the court only has jurisdiction to fill a vacancy on the application of certain defined persons[206], which do not include an administrator's former partners.

17.31 Where an application for removal of an administrator is made under Schedule B1 paragraph 88 of IA 1986, the application must state the grounds on which the request is made[207]. It must be served on the administrator, the person who made the application for the administration order or made the appointment[208] as the case may be, the creditors' committee if there is one, any joint administrator, and where there is no creditors' committee and no joint administrator, on the company and all the creditors including any floating charge holders[209]. If an order removing the administrator is made, the court must give a copy to the applicant who must, as soon as reasonably practicable, and in any event within five business days, send it to the administrator[210] and within five business days send a copy to all those to whom notice of the application was sent and to the registrar of companies[211]. The removal of an administrator does not mean that the company thereby ceases to be in administration[212], although in any such case the applicant should normally take steps to ensure that a replacement can take office as soon as any order takes effect[213].

AUTOMATIC VACATION OF OFFICE

17.32 An administrator vacates office if he ceases to be qualified to act as an insolvency practitioner in relation to the company[214], in which event he vacates office automatically without further act on his part[215]. Where he vacates office in these circumstances, he is required to give notice to the registrar of companies[216]. He must also notify the court where he was appointed by an administration order, to the holder of the charge by which he was appointed where he was appointed under Schedule B1 paragraph 14 of IA 1986 and to the directors or the company where he was appointed under Schedule B1 paragraph 22[217]. Whether an administrator vacates office for this reason or by reason of his

---

205   *Re A & C Supplies Ltd* [1998] 1 BCLC 603.
206   See further **PARAGRAPH 17.35FF** *post*. In many cases this problem can be overcome if an application is made by a continuing joint administrator.
207   Rule 3.65(1) of the Rules.
208   Where the floating charge by virtue of which an appointment was made under Schedule B1 paragraph 14 of IA 1986 is no longer held by the appointor, service must be effected on the holder.
209   Rule 3.65(2) of the Rules.
210   Rule 3.65(4)(a) of the Rules.
211   Rule 3.65(4)(b) of the Rules. It must also be sent to any member state liquidator appointed in relation to the company (Rule 21.7 of the Rules), although it would seem that there is no obligation to notify him of the application.
212   Schedule B1 paragraph 1(2)(d) of IA 1986.
213   As to which, see **PARAGRAPH 17.35FF** *post*.
214   Schedule B1 paragraph 89(1) of IA 1986.
215   Cf *Re AJ Adams (Builders) Ltd* [1991] BCLC 359. Thus, an application to remove in such circumstances will be unnecessary: *Re Stella Metals Ltd* [1997] BCC 626.
216   Rule 3.66 of the Rules. Notice should also be given to any member state liquidator appointed in relation to the company: Rule 21.7 of the Rules.
217   Schedule B1 paragraph 89(2) of IA 1986. If he fails without reasonable excuse to notify he commits an offence: Schedule B1 paragraph 89(3) of IA 1986.

death, the company does not thereby cease to be in administration[218], although, in such a case, steps should be taken by the appropriate person to ensure that a replacement is appointed as soon as possible[219].

17.33   Where an administrator has died, notice of the fact and date of his death must be given to the court as soon as reasonably practicable by a surviving administrator, by a member of the deceased administrator's firm, by an officer of the deceased administrator's company or by a personal representative of the deceased administrator[220]. If notice has not been filed within 21 days following the administrator's death, then any other person may file the notice[221]. The person who files the notice must also give notice to the registrar of companies[222].

ADMINISTRATOR'S DUTIES ON VACATING OFFICE

17.34   Where an administrator is removed, resigns or ceases to be qualified to act as an insolvency practitioner in relation to the company, he is under a duty[223], as soon as reasonably practicable, to deliver up to the person succeeding him as administrator the assets of the company, the records of the administration including correspondence, proofs and other documents relating to the administration and the company's records[224]. If the administrator makes default in complying with this duty he is liable to a fine[225]. It should be noted that the duty to file a final progress report which arises on the company ceasing to be in administration[226], does not arise where an administrator is removed, resigns, ceases to be qualified to act or dies.

REPLACEMENT OF AN ADMINISTRATOR

17.35   Where an administrator dies, resigns, is removed from office by the court or vacates office on ceasing to be qualified to act as an insolvency practitioner in relation to the company, there are a series of complex provisions dealing with his replacement[227]. In broad terms, the person who made the original appointment is the person who is entitled to appoint the replacement. Thus, if the original appointment was made by the court, only the court may replace the administrator and, in the normal course, the company, the directors or the

---

218   Schedule B1 paragraph 1(2)(d) of IA 1986.
219   As to which, see **PARAGRAPH 17.35FF** *post.*
220   Rule 3.67(1) and (2) the Rules.
221   Rule 3.67(3) of the Rules.
222   Rule 3.67(4) of the Rules. The notice must contain identification details for the proceedings, the name of the person who appointed the administrator or made the administration application, the date of the appointment of the administrator and the fact and date of the administrator's death. It must also be sent to any member state liquidator appointed in relation to the company: Rule 21.7 of the Rules.
223   Rule 3.70(1) of the Rules.
224   The distinction drawn between the records of the administration and the records of the company may mean that an administrator vacating office in these circumstances must deliver up all his own working papers if they relate to the administration, irrespective of whether or not they can properly be characterised as records of the company.
225   Rule 3.70(2) of the Rules.
226   Rules 3.55, 3.56, 3.59, 3.60 and 3.61 of the Rules.
227   Schedule B1 paragraphs 90–95 of IA 1986.

appointing qualifying floating charge holder (as the case may be) will be the person entitled to appoint the replacement of an out-of-court appointee.

17.36   Where the administrator was appointed by the court, only the court may make an order replacing him. The application may be made by any creditors' committee, by the company, by the directors of the company, by one or more creditors of the company or by any joint administrator who remains in office[228]. In the normal case, the application must be made by the creditors' committee or any continuing administrator, because it is expressly provided that the other potential applicants are only permitted to make a replacement application where there is no creditors' committee, or the court is satisfied that the creditors' committee or continuing administrator is not taking reasonable steps to make a replacement or that it is right for some other reason for the application to be made[229]. It follows that administrations are different from liquidations in that IA 1986 imposes an express limitation on the categories of person entitled to apply for an order filling a vacancy. The application to appoint a replacement administrator must be accompanied by the proposed replacement administrator's consent to act[230], and must be delivered to the persons listed in Rule 3.68(2) of the Rules. The provisions relating to the hearing and the content and notification of any order contained in Rules 3.12, 3.13 and 3.15(1) and (2) of the Rules are applied, with any necessary modifications, to an application for a replacement order[231]. Once a replacement administrator has been appointed, his appointment must be notified, advertised and identified, with certain modifications as in the case of an original appointment[232] and the replacement administrator is required to send notice of his appointment to the registrar of companies[233].

17.37   Where the original appointment was made by the holder of a qualifying floating charge under Schedule B1 paragraph 14 of IA 1986, the holder of that charge (whether or not he made the original appointment) may replace the administrator[234]. The notification requirements at Rules 3.17, 3.24, 3.25, 3.26 and 3.27 (with certain modifications) apply to the appointment of a replacement administrator[235]. Once it has been made, the replacement administrator is required to deliver notice of his appointment to the registrar of companies[236]. In such a case, the court is also empowered to replace the administrator, but only on the application of the creditors' committee (if there is one), the company, the directors of the company, one or more creditors of the company or any joint administrator who remains in office[237]. Furthermore, in any such case, the

---

228   Schedule B1 paragraph 91(1) of IA 1986.

229   Schedule B1 paragraph 91(2) of IA 1986.

230   Rule 3.68(1) of the Rules. The consent to act must be authenticated and dated by the proposed appointee and must contain the information set out at Rule 3.2(2) of the Rules.

231   Rule 3.68(4) of the Rules.

232   Rule 3.69(a) of the Rules.

233   Rule 3.69(b) of the Rules. The notice of appointment must therefore also be sent to any member state liquidator appointed in relation to the company: Rule 21.7 of the Rules.

234   Schedule B1 paragraph 92 of IA 1986. It should be noted that the power to replace only arises on an administrator's death, resignation, removal from office by the court or vacation on ceasing to be qualified to act as an insolvency practitioner: Schedule B1 paragraph 90 of IA 1986.

235   Rule 3.69 of the Rules.

236   Rule 3.69 of the Rules. Notice must therefore also be given to any member state liquidator appointed in relation to the company: Rule 21.7 of the Rules.

237   Schedule B1 paragraphs 91(1) and 95 of IA 1986.

court's power can only be exercised if it is satisfied that the holder of the relevant qualifying floating charge is not taking reasonable steps to make a replacement or that for some other reason it is right for the court to make the appointment[238]. Where an application to appoint a replacement administrator is made under this power, it must be accompanied by a witness statement setting out the applicant's belief that the holder of the relevant qualifying floating charge is not taking reasonable steps to make a replacement or that for some other reason it is right for the court to make the appointment[239]. The same hearing provisions, with any necessary modifications, apply as are applicable to the replacement of an administrator originally appointed by the court[240]. Furthermore, once a replacement administrator has been appointed, whether by the holder of a qualifying floating charge or the court, his appointment must be notified, advertised and identified, with certain modifications, as in the case of an original appointment[241].

17.38 Where the original appointment was made by the company or its directors under Schedule B1 paragraph 22 of IA 1986, the original appointor may replace the administrator[242]. The replacement administrator is required to send notice of his appointment to the registrar of companies[243]. In this situation, however, a replacement may only be made with the consent of each person who is the holder of a qualifying floating charge in relation to the property of the company or, where consent is withheld, with the permission of the court[244]. The court's power to give permission only arises where consent has been withheld, which indicates that consent must at least be sought from each relevant charge holder before an application for permission is made. Presumably, in the normal case, the court will also require the charge holders to be served with the application for permission. As with the case in which the original appointment was made by the holder of a qualifying floating charge, the court is also empowered to replace the administrator on the application of the same group of interested persons[245]. In this case as well, the court's own power to appoint can only be exercised if it is satisfied that the person primarily entitled to appoint (viz the company or the directors) is not taking reasonable steps to make a replacement or that for some other reason it is right for it to make the appointment[246]. The same formalities apply in relation to the application, the hearing and notification of any replacement as are described in **PARAGRAPH 17.36** *ante*. Furthermore, once a replacement administrator has been appointed, whether by the company, the directors or the court, his appointment must be notified, advertised and identified, with certain modifications, as in the case of an original appointment[247].

---

238 Schedule B1 paragraph 95(a) and (b) of IA 1986.
239 Rule 3.68(3) of the Rules.
240 Rule 3.68(4) of the Rules and **PARAGRAPH 17.36** *ante*.
241 Rule 3.69 of the Rules.
242 Schedule B1 paragraphs 93 and 94 of IA 1986. It should be noted that the power to replace only arises on an administrator's death, resignation, removal from office by the court or vacation on ceasing to be qualified to act as an insolvency practitioner: Schedule B1 paragraph 90 of IA 1986.
243 Rule 3.69(b) of the Rules. The notice of appointment must therefore also be sent to any member state liquidator appointed in relation to the company: Rule 21.7 of the Rules.
244 Schedule B1 paragraphs 93(2) and 94(2) of IA 1986.
245 Schedule B1 paragraphs 91(1) and 95 of IA 1986. See further **PARAGRAPH 17.37** *ante*.
246 Schedule B1 paragraph 95(a) and (b) of IA 1986.
247 Rule 3.69 of the Rules.

SUBSTITUTION OF AN ADMINISTRATOR

17.39 There are two further circumstances in which Schedule B1 provides for an administrator to be removed and replaced. The first is where he has been appointed by the holder of a qualifying floating charge under Schedule B1 paragraph 14 of IA 1986[248]. In any such case, the holder of a prior floating charge[249] may apply to the court for the original administrator to be replaced by his own appointee[250]. As the holder of a prior floating charge should have been given the opportunity to make his own appointment when he was notified of the original intention to appoint[251], it is thought that there will not be many circumstances in which any such substitution is appropriate. In the normal case, the holder of a prior floating charge should decide whether he wishes to make his own appointment at the outset rather than waiting to make an application under Schedule B1 paragraph 96 of IA 1986, with the likely delays and consequential increases in cost that such an order would entail[252]. The other circumstance in which substitution of an administrator is possible is where the company or the directors have made an appointment under Schedule B1 paragraph 22 of IA 1986 and there is no holder of a qualifying floating charge in respect of the company's property[253]. In any such case, the administrator may be replaced by a decision of the creditors made by a qualifying decision procedure[254]. Where this procedure is used, the written consent of the new administrator to act must be obtained before the decision is made[255]. This power is a valuable check on the ability of a company to make an appointment which is unacceptable to its creditors without the expense of an application to the court. In both forms of substitution, the replacement appointment must, with certain modifications, be notified, advertised and identified as in the case of an original appointment[256] and the new administrator is required to send notice of his appointment to the registrar of companies[257]. Presumably, the requirements of Rule 3.70 of the Rules[258] also apply to a substitution under these provisions.

APPOINTMENT OF AN ADDITIONAL ADMINISTRATOR

17.40 Under the pre-Enterprise Act 2002 law there was no express power to appoint an additional administrator. Thus, in the case of *Polly Peck*

---

248 Schedule B1 paragraph 96(1) of IA 1986.
249 Ie a charge which was created first or is to be treated as having priority in accordance with an agreement to which the holder of each floating charge was party: Schedule B1 paragraph 96(3) of IA 1986.
250 Schedule B1 paragraph 96(2) of IA 1986.
251 Schedule B1 paragraph 15(1)(a) of IA 1986.
252 The most likely situation is where the holder of a prior floating charge was in fact unaware of the proposed appointment and moves quickly to apply for his own appointee as soon as he becomes aware of what has occurred. Even then, however, the court will require to be satisfied that the prima facie right of the prior charge holder to have his own appointee is not outweighed by the extra cost and disruption which will be caused by a substitution.
253 Schedule B1 paragraph 97(1) of IA 1986.
254 Schedule B1 paragraph 97(2) of IA 1986. The qualifying decision procedures are set out at Rule 15.3 of the Rules.
255 Schedule B1 paragraph 97(3) of IA 1986.
256 Rule 3.69(a) of the Rules.
257 Rule 3.69(b) of the Rules. The notice of appointment must therefore also be sent to any member state liquidator appointed in relation to the company: Rule 21.7 of the Rules.
258 The duties to deliver up are described in **PARAGRAPH 17.34** *ante*.

International plc[259], the appointment of an additional administrator was made by Chadwick J by a variation of the original order[260], while in *Clements v Udal*[261], Neuberger J, recognising that there was no express power, took the view that the court had an inherent jurisdiction to appoint an additional administrator pending the substantive determination of an application to remove and replace the original administrator. Under the present law, there is an express statutory power to appoint an additional administrator[262], although in each case, for sound practical reasons, it can only be exercised with the consent of the existing appointees[263]. On appointment, the additional administrator is required to send notice of his appointment to the registrar of companies[264].

17.41 Where the company entered administration by an administration order, only the court can appoint an additional administrator, and it can only do so on the application of one of the persons who did or could have applied for that order or on the application of the existing administrator[265]. Where the original administrator was appointed by the holder of a qualifying floating charge under Schedule B1 paragraph 14 of IA 1986, an additional appointment can only be made by the holder of that charge or by the court on the application of the existing administrator[266]. Where the original administrator was appointed by the company or its directors under Schedule B1 paragraph 22 of IA 1986, an additional appointment can only be made:

(a) by the court on the application of the existing administrator; or

(b) by the company or directors depending on which of them made the original appointment[267].

17.42 An additional appointment by the company or the directors can only be made with the consent of each person who is the holder of a qualifying floating charge in relation to the property of the company or, where consent is withheld, with the permission of the court[268]. As with the appointment of a replacement administrator under Schedule B1 paragraphs 93 and 94 of IA 1986[269], the court's power to give permission only arises where consent has been withheld, which indicates that consent must at least be sought from each relevant charge holder before an application for permission is made[270]. Once an additional administrator has been appointed, his appointment must, with certain modifications, be notified, advertised and identified as in the case of an initial appointment[271].

---

259 (20 May 1994, unreported).
260 Similar relief was also granted by Jacob J in *Cyma Petroleum Ltd v Cyma Holdings Ltd* (22 December 2000, unreported).
261 [2002] 2 BCLC 606.
262 Schedule B1 paragraph 103(1) of IA 1986.
263 Schedule B1 paragraph 103(6) of IA 1986.
264 Rule 3.69(b) of the Rules. The notice of appointment must therefore also be sent to any member state liquidator appointed in relation to the company: Rule 21.7 of the Rules.
265 Schedule B1 paragraph 103(2) of IA 1986.
266 Schedule B1 paragraph 103(3) of IA 1986.
267 Schedule B1 paragraphs 103(4) and (5) of IA 1986.
268 Schedule B1 paragraphs 103(4)(b) and 103(5)(b) of IA 1986.
269 See paragraph 17.38 *ante*.
270 Presumably, in this case as well, the court will normally require the charge holders to be served with the application for permission.
271 Rule 3.69 of the Rules.

VACATION OF OFFICE: DISCHARGE FROM LIABILITY

17.43   Where a person ceases to be the administrator of a company whether through resignation, death, removal from office or because his appointment ceases to have effect, he is discharged from liability in respect of any action of his as administrator. This discharge takes effect from the following time[272]:

(a)   in the case of an administrator who has died, on the filing with the court of notice of his death;

(b)   in the case of an administrator appointed out of court under Schedule B1 paragraphs 14 or 22 who has not made a statement under paragraph 52(1) (b), at a time appointed by resolution of the creditors' committee or, if there is no committee, by decision of the creditors;

(c)   in the case of an administrator appointed out of court under Schedule B1 paragraphs 14 or 22 who has made a statement under paragraph 52(1)(b), at a time decided by the relevant creditors[273]; or

(d)   in any case, at a time specified by the court[274].

17.44   Where the administrator has made a statement under Schedule B1 paragraph 52(1)(b) of IA 1986 (ie that the company has insufficient property to enable a distribution to be made to unsecured creditors other than by virtue of section 176A(2)(a) (the prescribed part provisions)), the relevant creditors who may decide the time of discharge are defined by Schedule B1 paragraph 98(3) as each secured creditor of the company or, if the administrator has made a distribution to preferential creditors or thinks that a distribution may be made to preferential creditors, each secured creditor of the company and preferential creditors whose debts amount to more than 50 per cent of the company's preferential debts, disregarding the debts of any creditor who does not respond to an invitation[275].

17.45   The discharge does not prevent the exercise of the court's powers under Schedule B1 paragraph 75 of IA 1986, whereby the court may examine the conduct of and grant relief against an actual or purported administrator or former administrator who is found to have misapplied or retained, or to have become accountable for any money or other property of the company, or to have been guilty of any misfeasance or breach of fiduciary or other duty in relation to the company[276]. Where, however, the administrator has been granted his discharge, an application against him under Schedule B1 paragraph 75 of IA 1986 can only be made with the permission of the court[277]. The applicable test for permission is the same as that under sections 212 and 304 of IA 1986, namely whether there is a reasonably meritorious cause of action and whether granting permission is reasonably likely to benefit the estate[278]. It also appears that the release does

---

272   The list of times is set out in Schedule B1 paragraph 98(2) of IA 1986.
273   Thus, the court can always grant a discharge, even in a case in which discharge can also be granted by the creditors' committee or creditors.
274   Schedule B1 paragraph 98(3) of IA 1986.
275   Schedule B1 paragraph 98(3)(b) of IA 1986. The obligation to disregard the failure of non-responding preferential creditors to give their approval or disapproval does not apply to secured creditors.
276   Schedule B1 paragraph 98(4)(b) of IA 1986.
277   Schedule B1 paragraph 75(6) of IA 1986.
278   *Katz v Oldham* [2016] BPIR 83 (paragraphs 5–7).

not affect the duty of the official receiver, where a winding-up order is made in England and Wales, to investigate, if the company has failed, the causes of the failure and generally the promotion, formation, business, dealings and affairs of the company and to make such report, if any, to the court as he thinks fit. Where a company is being compulsorily wound up, the power of the official receiver to apply to the court for the public examination of anyone who has acted as administrator of the company also remains unaffected[279].

17.46 Although the court was always able to grant the administrator his release (the word used under the pre-Enterprise Act 2002 law) immediately upon discharge of the administration order[280], the usual practice where a liquidation of the company was to follow, was to postpone the release for some time after the discharge of the administration order so as to allow any necessary investigations into the conduct of the administration to take place and to allow, if appropriate, an application to be made to postpone the date upon which the release would otherwise take effect[281]. It was also usual to postpone the release until such time as the administrator had delivered his receipts and payments account up to the date upon which the administration order was discharged, or the administrator ceased to act as such, if different[282]. The practice, however, was not an invariable one[283]. Where there was a proper claim outstanding against an administrator, the court would not grant the administrator a release to take effect prior to the claim being determined[284]. It was also held that the court had power to grant a partial release excepting certain defined categories of claim[285]. A similar approach has been adopted under the present law where the discharge is granted by the court; the usual practice is that an administrator will be granted his discharge 28 days after he has sent out his final progress report[286]. In *Re Angel Group Ltd*[287], where the proposed liquidators wished to investigate the administrators' conduct, Rose J discharged the administrators from liability with effect from 21 days after the filing of their final progress report save in respect of claims made in proceedings issued by a liquidator of the company within six months of the date of liquidation; this latter time limit was imposed to ensure that the liquidators carried out their investigations promptly and efficiently.

---

279   See sections 132 and 133 of IA 1986; *Re Exchange Travel (Holdings) Ltd* [1992] BCC 954 at 960f–g.

280   *Re Brooke Marine Ltd* [1988] BCLC 546 and *Re Olympia & York Canary Wharf Holdings* [1993] BCC 866. Under the former law, a release was the equivalent to a discharge from liability under Schedule B1 paragraph 98 of IA 1986.

281   *Re Sheridan Securities Ltd* (1988) 4 BCC 200, *Re Exchange Travel (Holdings) Ltd* [1992] BCC 954 and *Re Oakhouse Property Holdings Ltd* [2003] BPIR 469.

282   The standard period was 28 days after delivery of the receipts and payment account: see eg *Re UCT (UK) Ltd* [2001] 1 WLR 436.

283   See eg *Re Olympia &York Canary Wharf Holdings* [1993] BCC 866, although in that case control of the relevant companies was restored to their respective boards of directors upon a successful conclusion of the administrations.

284   *Barclays Mercantile Business Finance Ltd v Sibec Developments Ltd* [1992] 1 WLR 1253. See also eg the course adopted in *Re Philip Alexander Securities & Futures Ltd* [1999] 1 BCLC 124; cf *IRC v Hoogstraten* [1985] QB 1077.

285   *Re Powerstore (Trading) Ltd* [1997] 1 WLR 1280 at 1286 and see also the order referred to in *Kyrris v Oldham* [2003] EWCA Civ 1506 (paragraph 17).

286   See *Re Hellas Telecommunications (Luxembourg) II SCA* [2011] EWHC 3176 (Ch) (paragraph 96). Sales J explained that it would usually be right to discharge an administrator from liability because he would no longer retain the assets of the company out of which he is entitled to meet any liability properly incurred by him; it is therefore unfair to leave the administrator on risk generally.

287   [2015] EWHC 3624 (Ch).

VACATION OF OFFICE: THE STATUTORY CHARGE

17.47 Where at any time a person ceases to be the administrator of the company[288], his remuneration and any expenses are charged on and payable out of property of which he had custody or control immediately before cessation in priority to any security which is a floating charge on its creation[289]. In addition, any sum payable in respect of a debt or liability arising out of a contract entered into or a contract of employment adopted by him or a predecessor of his before cessation, are charged on and payable out of any such property in priority to any claim by the administrator for his remuneration and expenses[290]. These provisions have already been considered in **CHAPTERS 5, 7 AND 15** *ante*.

---

288 Whether through vacation of office through resignation, death or otherwise, because he is removed from office or because his appointment ceases to have effect: Schedule B1 paragraph 99(1) of IA 1986.
289 Schedule B1 paragraph 99(3) of IA 1986.
290 Schedule B1 paragraph 99(4) and (5) of IA 1986.

18 Administrations and the financial markets

INTRODUCTION

18.1 Part VII of the Companies Act 1989 ('CA 1989'), the principal provisions of which, subject to certain savings, came into force on 25 April 1991[1], introduced various modifications to the general law of insolvency, including that relating to administrations, for the purpose of safeguarding the operation of certain financial markets in the event of an insolvency[2]. Additional provision has also been made by the Financial Markets and Insolvency Regulations 1996[3] ('FMIR 1996') and the Financial Markets and Insolvency (Settlement Finality) Regulations 1999[4] ('the Settlement Finality Regulations'). This chapter discusses the impact of the provisions of Part VII of CA 1989 and the subordinate legislation made thereunder, as subsequently amended as they specifically apply to administrations. This chapter also considers the impact on administrations of the Financial Collateral Arrangements (No 2) Regulations 2003 ('FCAR 2003')[5], which implements the EU Directive on financial collateral arrangements[6] with effect from 26 December 2003.

MARKET CONTRACTS

18.2 The provisions of Part VII of CA 1989 apply to 'market contracts' connected with an investment exchange or clearing house which has been recognised under FSMA 2000[7].

---

1 Companies Act 1989 (Commencement No 10 and Savings Provisions) Order 1991 (SI 1991 No 878).
2 Section 154 of CA 1989.
3 SI 1996 No 1469.
4 SI 1999 No 2979.
5 SI 2003 No 3226, replacing the revoked Financial Collateral Arrangements Regulations 2003 (SI 2003 No 3112).
6 Directive 2002/47/EC of the European Parliament and of the Council of 6 June 2002 on financial collateral arrangements (OJ L168, 27/6/2002, 43).
7 Sections 155(1) and 190(1) of CA 1989. The recognition of investment exchanges and clearing houses is governed by the provisions of Part XVIII of FSMA 2000 and the Financial Services and Markets Act 2000 (Recognition Requirements for Investment Exchanges and Clearing Houses) Regulations 2001 (SI 2001 No 995). The following UK investment exchanges are recognised: ICE Futures Europe, London Stock Exchange plc (The Stock Exchange), LIFFE Administration and Management (LIFFE), The London Metal Exchange Ltd (LME), NEX Exchange, CME Europe Ltd, BATS Trading Ltd and Euronext London Ltd. The following UK clearing houses are recognised: CME Clearing Europe Ltd, ICE Cleaar Europe Ltd, LCH Clearnet Ltd, LME Clear Ltd and Euroclear UK & Ireland Ltd.

18.3   In relation to a recognised investment exchange, market contracts are:

(a) contracts entered into by a member or designated non-member of the exchange, but not of an overseas exchange[8], with a person other than the exchange which is either a contract made on the exchange[9] or a contract in the making of which the member or designated non-member concerned was subject to the rules of the exchange[10];

(b) contracts entered into by the exchange, in its capacity as such with a member of the exchange or with a recognised clearing house or with another recognised investment exchange for the purpose of enabling the rights and liabilities of that member or clearing house or other investment exchanged under a transaction to be settled; and

(c) contracts entered into by the exchange with a member of the exchange or with a recognised clearing house or with another recognised investment exchange for the purpose of providing central counterparty clearing services to that member or clearing house or other investment exchange[11].

A designated non-member means a person in respect of whom action may be taken under the default rules of the exchange but who is not a member of the exchange[12]. Default rules are those rules (of a recognised investment exchange or recognised clearing house) which provide for the taking of action in the event of a person[13] appearing to be unable, or likely to become unable, to meet his obligations in respect of one or more market contracts connected with the exchange or clearing house[14].

18.4   In relation to a recognised clearing house which is a recognised central counterparty[15], market contracts are:

(a) contracts between a recognised central counterparty and a clearing member[16] recorded in the accounts of the recognised central counterparty as a position held for the account of the clearing member ('clearing member house contracts');

---

8   Section 155(2A) of CA 1989; an 'overseas exchange' is one which has its head office outside the United Kingdom: see section 190(1) of CA 1989.
9   Alternatively, of an exchange to whose undertaking the exchange has succeeded either by amalgamation, merger or otherwise.
10 Alternatively, of an exchange to whose undertaking the exchange has succeeded either by amalgamation, merger or otherwise.
11 Section 155(2) of CA 1989.
12 Section 155(2) of CA 1989.
13 Including another recognised investment exchange or recognised clearing house.
14 Section 188(1) of CA 1989.
15 Section 285(1) of FSMA 2000 defines a recognised clearing house as either a recognised central counterparty or a recognised clearing house providing clearing services in the UK without doing so as a central counterparty. A central counterparty is defined in Article 2(1) of Regulation (EU) No 648/2012 of the European Parliament and of the Council of 4 July 2012 on OTC derivatives, central counterparties and trade repositories ('EMIR Level 1 Regulation') as 'a legal person that interposes itself between the counterparties to the contracts traded on one or more financial markets, becoming the buyer to every seller and the seller to every buyer'.
16 'Clearing member' has the meaning given by Article 2(14) of the EMIR Level 1 Regulation: 'an undertaking which participates in a [central counterparty] and which is responsible for discharging the obligations arising from that participation': section 190(1) of CA 1989.

(b) contracts between a recognised central counterparty and a clearing member or a client[17] or an indirect client[18] which is recorded in the accounts of the recognised central counterparty as a position held for the account of a client, an indirect client or a group of clients or indirect clients ('clearing member client contracts');

(c) contracts between two or more of a clearing member, a client or an indirect client which corresponds to a clearing member client contract ('client trades') except where the clearing member which is a party to the clearing member client contract (or, if the client trade was entered into by a client in the course of providing indirect clearing services to an indirect client, the client) defaults and the clearing member client contract is not transferred to another clearing member within the period specified in the default rules of the recognised central counterparty[19]; and

(d) contracts entered into by the recognised central counterparty with a recognised investment exchange or a recognised clearing house for the purpose of providing central counterparty clearing services to the exchange or clearing house[20].

18.5 Central counterparty clearing services are those services provided by a recognised investment exchange or a recognised clearing house to:

(a) the parties to a transaction in connection with contracts between each of the parties and investment exchange or clearing house (in place of, or as an alternative to, a contract directly between the parties); or

(b) a recognised clearing house or a recognised investment exchange in connection with the contracts between them[21].

18.6 In relation to a recognised clearing house, which is not a recognised central counterparty, market contracts are:

(a) contracts entered into by the clearing house, in its capacity as such, with a member of the clearing house or with a recognised investment exchange or with another recognised clearing house for the purpose of enabling the rights and liabilities of that member or investment exchange or other clearing house under a transaction to be settled; and

(b) contracts entered into by the clearing house with a member of the clearing house or with a recognised investment exchange or with another recognised clearing house for the purpose of providing central counterparty clearing service to that member or investment exchange or other clearing house[22].

---

17 'Client' has the meaning given by Article 2(15) of the EMIR Level 1 Regulation: 'an undertaking with a contractual relationship with a clearing member of a [central counterparty] which enables that undertaking to clear its transactions with that [central counterparty]': section 190(1) of CA 1989.

18 'Indirect client' has the meaning given by Article 1(a) of Commission Delegated Regulation (EU) No 149/2013 of 19 December 2012 ('EMIR Level 2 Regulation'): 'a client of a client of the clearing member': section 190(1) of CA 1989.

19 Section 155(2C) and (2D) of CA 1989. Where it is the client that has defaulted, if no period for transferring the clearing member client contract is specified in the default rules of the recognised central counterparty, then the relevant period is 14 days beginning with the day on which proceedings are commenced in respect of the client's insolvency. The beginning of insolvency proceedings is defined at section 155(3B) and (3C) of CA 1989.

20 Section 155(1), (1A) and (2B) of CA 1989.

21 Section 155(3A) of CA 1989.

22 Section 155(3A) of CA 1989.

MODIFICATIONS TO THE LAW OF INSOLVENCY WITH RESPECT TO MARKET CONTRACTS

18.7   Section 158(1) of CA 1989 provides that, subject to the provisions of sections 159 to 165, the general law of insolvency[23] has effect in relation to market contracts and certain action taken under the rules of a recognised investment exchange or recognised clearing house with respect to such contracts. Sections 159 to 165 of CA 1989, which are designed to protect the integrity of the market settlement process in the event of an insolvency, are specifically limited in their application[24] to:

(a)   insolvency proceedings in respect of a defaulter[25];

(b)   insolvency proceedings in respect of a recognised investment exchange or a member or designated non-member[26] of a recognised investment exchange;

(c)   insolvency proceedings in respect of a recognised clearing house or a member of a recognised clearing house; and

(d)   insolvency proceedings in respect of a party to a market contract[27] (other than a client trade) begun, in the case of administration proceedings, by the application for an administration order[28], after a recognised investment exchange or recognised clearing house has taken action under its default rules in relation to a person party to the contract as a principal; for this purpose, an application for an administration order includes the filing with the court, by a floating charge holder, the company or its directors, of a copy notice of intention to appoint an administrator under Schedule B1 paragraph 14 or 22 of IA 1986 or, where no such notice is filed, the appointment under paragraph 14 or 22 itself[29].

Sections 159 to 165 do not therefore apply to other insolvency proceedings notwithstanding that rights or liabilities arising from market contracts fall to be dealt with in the proceedings[30].

18.8   Where applicable, the following provisions of sections 159 to 165 of CA 1989 have particular reference to administration proceedings:

(a)   The powers of the administrator and the powers of the court under IA 1986 are not to be exercised in such a way as to prevent or interfere with:

   (i)   the settlement[31] in accordance with the rules of a recognised investment exchange or recognised clearing house (which is not a recognised

---

23   See section 190(6) of CA 1989.
24   By section 158(2) of CA 1989.
25   Defined by section 188(2) of CA 1989 as meaning a person in respect of whom action has been taken by a recognised investment exchange or recognised clearing house under its default rules, whether by declaring him to be a defaulter or otherwise: see also **PARAGRAPH 18.2FF** *ante*.
26   See **PARAGRAPH 18.2FF** *ante*.
27   Unless the context otherwise requires, a person may be a party to a market contract as either a principal or an agent: section 187(2) of CA 1989. If a person enters into market contracts in more than one capacity, the provisions of Part VII of CA 1989 apply as if the contracts entered into in each different capacity were entered into by different persons: section 187(1) of CA 1989; see also regulation 16 of FMIR 1991.
28   Section 158(3)(b) of CA 1989.
29   Section 158(3A) of CA 1989.
30   Section 158(2) of CA 1989.
31   'Settlement' means the discharge of the rights and liabilities of the parties to the contract concerned whether by performance, compromise or otherwise: section 190(2) of CA 1989.

central counterparty) of a market contract not dealt with under its default rules;

(ii) any action taken under the default rules of such an exchange or clearing house;

(iii) the transfer of a clearing member client contract or the settlement of a clearing member client contract or a clearing member house contract, in accordance with the default rules of a recognised central counterparty, or any action to give effect to such a transfer;

(iv) where a clearing member client contract transferred in accordance of a recognised central counterparty was entered into by the clearing member or client as principal, the transfer of a client trade or group of client trades corresponding to that clearing member contract, or any action to give effect to such a transfer;

(v) the transfer of a qualifying collateral arrangement[32] in conjunction with a transfer of a clearing member client contract or client trade as mentioned in sub-paragraphs (a)(iii) and (iv) above, or any action to give effect to such a transfer; or

(vi) any action to give effect to a qualifying property transfer[33].

Subject, however, to the provisions of section 165 of CA 1989[34], the court is not prevented from afterwards making an order or decree in relation to any transaction which constitutes a transaction at an undervalue, a preference or a transaction defrauding creditors[35].

(b) It is the duty of any person, including an administrator, who has or had control of any assets of a defaulter or of any document[36] of or relating to a defaulter to give a recognised investment exchange or recognised clearing house such assistance as it may reasonably require for the purposes of its default proceedings[37]. Such a person cannot however be required to provide information or to produce any document which he would be entitled to refuse to provide or to produce on grounds of legal professional privilege in proceedings[38]. The exchange or clearing house must return any original documents so supplied to it forthwith after the completion of the relevant default proceedings and must in the meantime allow reasonable access to the person by whom they were supplied and to any person who would be

---

32 A 'qualifying collateral arrangement' means any contracts or contractual obligations for, or arising out of, the provision of property as margin where: (i) the margin is provided to a recognised central counterparty and is recorded in the accounts of the recognised counterparty as an asset held for the account of a client or group of clients (direct or indirect); or (ii) the margin is provided to a client or clearing member for the purpose of providing cover for exposures arising out of present or future client trades: section 155A of CA 1989.

33 Sections 159(2) and 189(1)(b) of CA 1989; note also that if an exchange or clearing house takes action under its default rules in respect of a defaulter, all subsequent proceedings under its rules for the purposes of or in connection with the settlement of market contracts to which the defaulter is a party are to be treated as done under its default rules: section 188(4) of CA 1989. As to what constitutes a 'qualifying property transfer', see section 155A of CA 1989.

34 See **SUB-PARAGRAPHS (h) AND (i)** *post.*

35 Section 159(2) of CA 1989.

36 'Document' includes information recorded in any form: section 160(6) of CA 1989.

37 Section 160(1) of CA 1989: 'default proceedings' means proceedings taken by a recognised investment exchange or recognised clearing house under its default rules: section 188(3) of CA 1989.

38 Section 160(2) of CA 1989.

entitled to have access to them if they were still in control of the person by whom they were supplied[39]. The expenses[40] of an administrator in giving such assistance are recoverable as part of the expenses incurred by him in the discharge of his duties[41]. Further, an administrator cannot be required to take any action which involves expenses which cannot be recovered as an expense of the administration, unless the exchange or clearing house undertakes to meet them[42].

(c)   The moratorium provisions contained in Schedule B1 paragraphs 42 and 43 (including paragraph 43(6) as applied to interim moratoriums by paragraph 44) of IA 1986 do not apply to restrict any action taken by an exchange or clearing house for the purpose of its default proceedings[43]12.

(d)   On completion of proceedings under its default rules, a recognised exchange or recognised clearing house must report to the appropriate regulator[44] on such proceedings, stating, in respect of each creditor or debtor, the sum certified by them to be payable from or to the defaulter, or, as the case may be, the fact that no sum is payable[45]. The report need not deal with a clearing member client contract which has been transferred in accordance with the default rules of a recognised central counterparty[46].

The exchange or clearing house may either make a single report or may make reports from time to time as proceedings are completed with respect to the transactions affecting particular persons[47]. The exchange or clearing house must supply a copy of its report or reports to the defaulter and to, *inter alios*, any administrator acting in relation to the defaulter[48]. There are further provisions relating to the publication of notice of the receipt of such reports by the appropriate regulator and for the inspection of reports by and the provision of copies thereof to creditors and debtors of the defaulter[49].

(e)   A debt or other liability arising out of a market contract which is the subject of default proceedings is not to be taken into account for purposes of any set-off until the investment exchange or clearing house has reported to the FCA or the Bank of England, as appropriate, stating the sum, if any, certified to be due to or from the creditor or debtor concerned[50].

(f)   If the court is satisfied on the application of, *inter alios*, an administrator who has been appointed in relation to a defaulter that a party to a market contract with the defaulter intends to dissipate or apply his assets so as to prevent the administrator from recovering such sums as may become

39   Section 160(3) of CA 1989.
40   An administrator's 'expenses' include such reasonable sums as he may determine in respect of time spent in giving the assistance: section 160(4) of CA 1989.
41   Section 160(4) of CA 1989.
42   Section 160(4) of CA 1989.
43   Section 161(4) of CA 1989.
44   The appropriate regulator is the FCA for recognised investment exchanges and recognised overseas investment exchanges and the Bank of England for recognised clearing houses and recognised overseas clearing houses: section 162(7) of CA 1989.
45   Section 162(1) of CA 1989. A recognised overseas investment exchange or clearing house is not required to make a report unless notified by the FCA or the Bank of England, as appropriate: section 162(1A).
46   Section 162(1B) of CA 1989.
47   Section 162(2) of CA 1989.
48   Section 162(3) of CA 1989.
49   Section 162(4), (5) and (6) of CA 1989.
50   Section 159(4) and (5) of CA 1989. Such a debt or liability may, however, be taken into account for voting purposes, see section 159(4A).

due upon completion of the default proceedings, the court may grant such interlocutory relief as it thinks fit[51].

(g) The court may on an application by, *inter alios*, an administrator, make such order as it thinks fit altering or dispensing from compliance with such of the duties of his office as are affected by the fact that default proceedings are pending or could be taken, or have been or could have been taken[52].

(h) No order under sections 238 (transactions at an under-value), 239 (preferences) or 423 (transactions defrauding creditors) of IA 1986 may be made in relation to:

(i)   market contracts to which a recognised investment exchange or recognised clearing house is a party or which is entered into under its default rules;

(ii) clearing member house contracts;

(iii) clearing member client contracts;

(iv) client trades;

(v) contracts entered into be a recognised central counterparty with a recognised investment exchange or a recognised clearing house for the purpose of providing central counterparty clearing services to that exchange or clearing house; or

(vi) dispositions of property in pursuance of such market contracts[53].

(i) Similarly, where, for whatever reason, no such order has been or could be made in relation to a market contract in relation to which margin has been provided, no such order may be made in relation to:

(i)   the provision of the margin;

(ii) a qualifying collateral arrangement;

(iii) any contract effected by the exchange or clearing house in question for the purpose of realising the property provided as margin; or

(iv) any disposition of property in accordance with the rules of the exchange or clearing house in question as to the application of property provided as margin[54].

(j) Further, no such order may be made in relation to:

(i)   the provision of default fund contribution from a recognised investment exchange or a recognised clearing house;

(ii) any contract effected by a recognised investment exchange or a recognised clearing house for the purpose of realising property provided as a default fund contribution;

(iii) any disposition of property in accordance with the rules of the recognised investment exchange or recognised clearing house as to the application of property provided as default fund contribution;

(iv) a transfer of a clearing member client contract, a client trade or a qualifying collateral arrangement; or

(v) a qualifying property transfer[55].

---

51   Section 161(1) of CA 1989.
52   Section 161(3) of CA 1989.
53   Section 165(1), (2) and (3) of CA 1989.
54   Section 165(4) of CA 1989.
55   Section 165(5) of CA 1989.

DISAPPLICATION OF MODIFICATIONS TO THE LAW OF INSOLVENCY WITH RESPECT TO MARKET CONTRACTS

18.9   Under section 166 of CA 1989, the FCA or the Bank of England, as appropriate[56], have wide powers to give directions to a recognised UK investment exchange or a recognised UK clearing house[57]:

(a) if it appears to the FCA or the Bank of England that the exchange or clearing house could take action under its default rules, to require it to do so; or

(b) if it appears to the FCA or the Bank of England that the exchange or clearing house is proposing to take or may take such action, to require it not to do so[58].

It is, however, expressly provided[59] that no direction may be given not to take action if, in relation to the person in question, *inter alios*, an administrator has been appointed. Further, on the appointment of, *inter alios*, an administrator, any previous direction not to take action ceases to have effect[60].

18.10   The FCA or the Bank of England, as appropriate, may also give a direction to, *inter alios*, an administrator appointed in respect of a defaulting clearing member to take any action or refrain from taking any action if the direction is given for the purposes of facilitating the transfer of a clearing member client contract, a client trade, a qualifying collateral arrangement, or a qualifying property transfer[61]. On receipt of such a direction, the administrator must comply with it, notwithstanding any duty on him under any enactment relating to insolvency unless the value of the clearing member's estate is unlikely to be sufficient to meet the administrator's reasonable expenses of complying[62].

18.11   Where, *inter alia*, an administrator is appointed in relation to a recognised investment exchange, a member or a designated non-member of a recognised investment exchange, a recognised clearing house, a member of a recognised clearing house or a client which is providing indirect clearing services to an indirect client ('the person in default'), and the exchange or clearing house has not taken action under its default rules in consequence of the order or the matters giving rise to it, the administrator may apply to the FCA or Bank of England, as appropriate, specifying the exchange or clearing house concerned and the grounds on which the application is made[63]. On receipt of the application the appropriate regulator is required to notify the exchange or clearing house. Unless, within three business days after the day on which the notice is received, either the exchange or clearing house takes action under its default rules or notifies the appropriate regulator that it proposes to do so forthwith, or the appropriate regulator gives

---

56   See section 166(9) of CA 1989.
57   Ie a recognised investment exchange or clearing house with its head office in the United Kingdom: section 190(1) of CA 1989.
58   Section 166(2) of CA 1989.
59   By section 166(6) of CA 1989.
60   By section 166(6) of CA 1989.
61   Section 166(3A) of CA 1989. The expenses of an administrator in complying with a direction under this section are recoverable as an expense in the administration: section 166(3C) of CA 1989.
62   Section 166(3B) of CA 1989.
63   Section 167(1), (1B) and (2) of CA 1989. This provision is extended to cases in which an administrator is appointed out of court under Schedule B1 paragraphs 14 and 22 of IA 1986, by section 167(1A) of CA 1989. The appropriate regulator is specified by section 167(6) of CA 1989.

the exchange or clearing house a direction to take action under its default rules[64], the provisions of sections 158 to 165 of CA 1989 are disapplied in relation to market contracts to which the person in default is a party and to anything done by the exchange or clearing house for the purposes of, or in connection with, the settlement of any such contract[65]. Where, within the three-day period mentioned above, the exchange or clearing house notifies the appropriate regulator that it proposes to take action under its default rules forthwith, it is under a duty to do so[66]. The duty to act is enforceable on the application of the appropriate regulator by injunction[67].

MARKET CHARGES

18.12 Subject to certain amendments and qualifications made by the Financial Markets and Insolvency Regulations 1991 ('FMIR 1991')[68], a market charge is defined by section 173(1) of CA 1989 as meaning a charge[69], whether fixed or floating, granted:

(a) in favour of a recognised investment exchange, for the purpose of securing debts or liabilities arising in connection with the settlement of market contracts; or

(b) in favour of the Stock Exchange[70] for the purpose of securing debts or liabilities arising in connection with short-term certificates[71]; or

(c) in favour of a recognised clearing house, for the purpose of securing debts or liabilities arising in connection with its ensuring the performance of market contracts; or

(d) in favour of a person[72] who agrees to make payments as a result of the transfer[73] or allotment of specified securities[74] made through the medium of a computer-based system established by the Bank of England and the Stock Exchange, for the purposes of securing debts or liabilities of the transferee or allottee arising in connection with such transfer or allotment[75].

---

64 Section 167(4) of CA 1989; no such direction may be given after the end of the three-day period.

65 Section 167(3) of CA 1989.

66 Section 167(5) of CA 1989.

67 Section 167(5) of CA 1989.

68 SI 1991 No 880.

69 'Charge' is widely defined as meaning any form of security, including a mortgage: section 190(1) of CA 1989.

70 Ie London Stock Exchange Ltd: section 190(1) of CA 1989.

71 A 'short-term certificate' is an instrument issued by the Stock Exchange undertaking to procure the transfer of property of a value and description specified in the instrument to or to the order of the person to whom the instrument is issued or his endorsee or to a person acting on behalf of either of them and also undertaking to make appropriate payments in cash, in the event that the obligation to procure the transfer of the property cannot be discharged in whole or in part: section 173(3) of CA 1989. Short-term certificates are issued by the Stock Exchange to enable member firms to borrow against securities standing to the credit of their trading account with the Stock Exchange.

72 Ie a Stock Exchange member firm's settlement bank which has undertaken to make payments under the assured payments system operated by the Central Gilts Office Service as a result of the transfer of specified securities.

73 'Transfer' means a transfer of the beneficial interest in specified securities: section 173(3) of CA 1989.

74 'Specified securities' means securities for the time being specified in the list in Schedule 1 to the Stock Transfer Act 1982 and includes any right to such securities: section 173(3) of CA 1989.

75 See **PARAGRAPHS 18.19 AND 18.20** *post.*

Where a charge is granted partly for the purposes specified above and partly for other purposes, it is a market charge so far as it has effect for the specified purposes[76].

18.13 To the above general definition, the FMIR 1991 have added a number of qualifications. The first, and probably most important, is that no charge, whether fixed or floating, is to be treated as a market charge to the extent that it is a charge on land or any interest in land[77]. However, a charge on a debenture forming part of an issue or series is not treated as a charge on land or any interest in land merely by reason of the fact that the debenture itself is secured by a charge on land or an interest in land[78].

18.14 Regulations 10 and 11 of FMIR 1991 introduce further qualifications upon the extent to which a charge granted in favour of a recognised investment exchange or a recognised clearing house is to be treated as a market charge. In the case of an exchange other than the Stock Exchange, a charge granted in its favour is only treated as a market charge to the extent that:

(a) it is a charge over property provided as margin in respect of market contracts entered into by the exchange for the purposes of or in connection with the provision of clearing services or over property provided as a default fund contribution;

(b) in the case of a UK exchange[79], it secures the obligation to pay to the exchange the net sum due from a defaulter under the exchange's default rules[80] in respect of market contract which were unsettled at the time of default; and

(c) in the case of an overseas exchange[81], it secures the obligation to reimburse the cost (other than fees and other incidental expenses) incurred by the exchange in settling unsettled market contracts in respect of which the charged property is provided as margin[82].

18.15 In the case of the Stock Exchange, a charge granted in its favour is treated as a market charge only to the extent that:

(a) it would be treated as a market charge in the case of any other recognised UK investment exchange[83]; or

(b) it is a Talisman charge[84] and secures:

 (i) the obligation of the chargor to reimburse the Stock Exchange for payments (including stamp duty and taxes but excluding Stock Exchange fees and incidental expenses arising from the operation by

---

76 Section 173(2) of CA 1989.
77 Regulation 8(1) of FMIR 1991.
78 Regulation 8(2) of FMIR 1991.
79 Ie an exchange whose head office is situate in the UK: section 190(1) of CA 1989.
80 The default rules must comply with provisions of paragraph 12 of the Schedule to the Financial Services and Markets Act 2000 (Recognition Requirements for Investment Exchanges and Clearing Houses) Regulation 2001 (SI 2001 No 995) (the 'Recognition Requirements Regulations').
81 Ie an exchange whose head office is situate outside the UK: section 190(1) of CA 1989.
82 Regulation 10(1) of FMIR 1991.
83 See **PARAGRAPH 18.14** *ante*.
84 A 'Talisman charge' means a charge granted in favour of the Stock Exchange over property credited to an account within the Talisman settlement system maintained in the name of the chargor in respect of certain property beneficially owned by the chargor: regulation 7 of FMIR 1991.

the Stock Exchange of settlement arrangements) made by the Stock Exchange in settling through Talisman, market contracts entered into by the chargor; and/or

(ii) the obligation of the chargor to reimburse the Stock Exchange the amount of any payment it has made pursuant to a short-term certificate[85].

18.16 In the case of a recognised clearing house, a charge granted in its favour is only treated as a market charge to the extent that:

(a) it is a charge over property provided as margin in respect of market contracts entered into by the clearing house or over property provided as a default fund contribution to the clearing house;

(b) in the case of a UK clearing house[86] which is a recognised central counterparty, it is a charge which secures the obligation to pay to the recognised central counterparty any sum due to it from a clearing member, a client, an indirect client, a recognised investment exchange or recognised clearing house in respect of unsettled market contracts to which the clearing member, client, indirect client, investment exchange or clearing house is a party;

(c) in the case of a UK clearing house which is not a recognised central counterparty, it secures the obligation to pay to the clearing house the net sum payable by a defaulter under the clearing house's default rules[87] in respect of market contracts which were unsettled at the time of the default; and

(d) in the case of an overseas clearing house[88], it secures the obligation to reimburse the costs (other than fees or other incidental expenses) incurred by the clearing house in settling unsettled market contracts in respect of which the charged property is provided as margin[89].

18.17 Regulations 12 and 13 of FMIR 1991 make provision in respect of the type of charge described in **PARAGRAPH 18.12(d)** *ante*, ie a Central Gilts Office ('CGO') service charge[90]. A CGO service charge is only treated as a market charge if:

(a) it is granted to a settlement bank[91] by a transferee or allottee for the purpose of securing debts or liabilities of the transferee or allottee arising in connection with the transfer or allotment of specified securities[92] incurred by the transferee or allottee through his use as a CGO service member[93] of the CGO computer-based system ('the CGO service') for the transfer or allotment of such securities; and

---

85 Regulation 10(2) and (3) of FMIR 1991; for the meaning of 'short-term certificate', see reg. 10(4) of FMIR and **PARAGRAPH 18.12** *ante*.

86 Ie a clearing house whose head office is situate in the United Kingdom, see section 190(1) of CA 1989.

87 The default rules must comply with the provisions of paragraph 12 of the Schedule to the Recognition Requirements Regulations.

88 Ie a clearing house whose head office is situate outside the United Kingdom, see section 190(1) of CA 1989.

89 Regulation 11 of FMIR 1991.

90 See regulation 7 of FMIR 1991.

91 Ie a person who has agreed to make payments as a result of the transfer or allotment of securities through the medium of the CGO service: see regulation 7 of FMIR 1991.

92 See **PARAGRAPH 18.12(d)** *ante*.

93 Ie a person entitled by contract with CRESTCo Ltd to use the CGO service: see regulation 7 of FMIR 1991.

(b) it contains provisions which refer expressly to the CGO Service[94].

18.18 Assuming that it satisfies the above requirements, a CGO service charge is treated as a market charge only to the extent that:

(a) it is a charge over any one or more of the following:

    (i) specified securities held within the CGO service to the account of a CGO service member or a former CGO service member[95],

    (ii) specified securities which were held as mentioned in sub-paragraph (i) *ante* prior to their being removed from the CGO service consequent upon the person in question becoming a former CGO service member,

    (iii) sums receivable by a CGO service member or former CGO service member representing interest accrued on specified securities held within the CGO service to his account or which were so held immediately prior to their being removed from the CGO service consequent upon his becoming a former CGO service member,

    (iv) sums receivable by a CGO service member or former CGO service member in respect of the redemption or conversion of specified securities which were held within the CGO service to his account at the time that the relevant securities were redeemed or converted or which were so held immediately prior to their being removed from the CGO service consequent upon his becoming a former CGO service member, and

    (v) sums receivable by a CGO service member or former CGO service member in respect of the transfer by him of specified securities through the medium of the CGO service; and

(b) it secures the obligation of a CGO service member or former CGO service member to reimburse a settlement bank for the amount due from him to the settlement bank as a result of the settlement bank having discharged or become obliged to discharge payment obligations in respect of transfers or allotments of specified securities made to him through the medium of the CGO service[96].

MODIFICATIONS TO THE LAW OF INSOLVENCY WITH RESPECT TO MARKET CHARGES

18.19 Subject to the provisions of section 175 of CA 1989, the general law of insolvency applies in full both to market charges and to action taken in enforcing them[97]. Section 175 of CA 1989 provides, however, that neither Schedule B1 paragraph 43(2) and (3) of IA 1986 (restrictions on enforcement of security), including those provisions as applied by Schedule B1 paragraph 44 (interim moratoriums), nor Schedule B1 paragraphs 70, 71 and 72 (power of administrator to deal with charged property) apply in relation to market charges[98]. Similarly,

---

94   Regulation 12 of FMIR 1991.
95   Ie a person whose entitlement to use the CGO service has been terminated or suspended: regulation 7 of FMIR 1991.
96   Regulation 13 of FMIR 1991.
97   Section 174(1) of CA 1989.
98   Section 175(1) of CA 1989.

Schedule B1 paragraph 41(2), pursuant to which the administrator can require a receiver of part of the company's property to vacate office, does not apply in the case of a receiver appointed under a market charge[99].

18.20 Where a market charge falls to be enforced after the making of an administration application under Schedule B1 paragraph 12 of IA 1986 or the appointment of an administrator under Schedule B1 paragraph 14 or 22 or the filing with the court of a copy notice of intention to appoint an administrator under paragraph 14 or 22, and there exists any other charge over some or any of the same property ranking in priority to or *pari passu* with the market charge, the court may order, on the application of any person interested, that such steps shall be taken after enforcement of the market charge as the court may direct for the purpose of ensuring that the chargee under the other charge is not prejudiced by the enforcement of the market charge[100]. The purpose of this latter provision, which appears to confer a wide discretion on the court, is to protect the other charge holder who may, of course, be subject to the provisions of Schedule B1 paragraphs 41, 43 or 44 and 70, 71 or 72 of IA 1986 and therefore, *prima facie*, unable to enforce his security. Presumably, in an appropriate case, the court can order the market charge holder to disgorge all or part of the proceeds of enforcement.

18.21 In relation to CGO service charges, the disapplication of Schedule B1 paragraph 43(2) and (3) of IA 1986, including those provisions as applied to interim moratoriums by paragraph 44, is qualified so that it has effect only to the extent necessary to enable there to be realised, whether through the sale of specified securities or otherwise, a sum equal to whichever is the less of the following:

(a) the total amount of payment obligations discharged by the settlement bank in respect of transfers and allotments of specified securities made during the qualifying period[101] to the relevant CGO service member or former CGO service member through the medium of the CGO service less the total amount of payment obligations discharged to the settlement bank in respect of transfers of specified securities made during the qualifying period by the relevant CGO service member or former CGO service member through the medium of the CGO service; and

(b) the total amount, if any, due to the settlement bank from the relevant CGO service member or former CGO service member as a result of the settlement bank having discharged or become obliged to discharge payment obligations in respect of transfers and allotments of specified securities made to such member or former member through the medium of the CGO service[102].

It follows that if the amount due to a settlement bank under (a) is less than the amount due to it under (b), a CGO service charge will be free from the

---

99 Section 175(1) of CA 1989.
100 Section 175(2) of CA 1989.
101 'Qualifying period' means the period commencing with the fifth business day before the day on which an application for the making of an administration order in respect of the relevant CGO service member or former member is presented and ending with the second business day after the day on which an administration order is made pursuant to the application. Where an appointment is made out of court under Schedule B1 paragraph 14 or 22 to IA 1986, the period begins five business days before the appointment or notice of intention to appoint as the case may be and ends with the appointment: regulation 14(1) and (1A) of FMIR 1991.
102 Regulation 14(2) of FMIR 1991.

restrictions contained in Schedule B1 paragraph 43(2) and (3), only to the extent necessary to realise the lesser sum.

18.22   Similarly, in relation to both CGO service charges[103] and Talisman charges[104], the disapplication of Schedule B1 paragraphs 70, 71 and 72 of IA 1986 is qualified in that it ceases to have effect after the end of the second business day after the day on which an administration order is made or an administrator is appointed under Schedule B1 paragraph 14 or 22 of IA 1986 in relation to the grantor of the charge in relation to property subject to it which:

(a)   in the case of a CGO service charge, is not, on the basis of the value of the property subject to the charge, required for the realisation of the lesser of the sums specified in **PARAGRAPH 18.21(a) AND (b)** *ante* due to the settlement bank at the close of business on the second business day after the making of the administration order or the appointment of an administrator as the case may be; and

(b)   in the case of a Talisman charge is not, on the basis of the value of the property subject to the charge, required to enable the Stock Exchange to reimburse itself for any payment it has made of the kind specified in **PARAGRAPH 18.15(b)(i) AND (ii)** *ante*[105].

18.23   For the purpose of ascertainment of the value of property subject to a CGO service charge or Talisman charge, the value of any investment for which a price for the second business day following the making of the administration order or the appointment of an administrator under Schedule B1 paragraph 14 or 22 of IA 1986 is quoted in the daily official list of the Stock Exchange is:

(a)   in a case in which two prices are so quoted, an amount equal to the average of those two prices, adjusted where appropriate to take account of any accrued interest; and

(b)   in a case in which one price is quoted, an amount equal to that price, adjusted where appropriate to take account of any accrued interest[106].

The value of any other property is taken to be such as may be agreed between the administrator on the one hand and the settlement bank or the Stock Exchange on the other[107].

18.24   The above provisions contain no guidance as to how particular items of property which are not so required by the holder of a CGO service charge or a Talisman charge are to be identified and appropriated. Presumably, in the absence of such guidance, the administrator is entitled to choose the assets in respect of which the disapplication of Schedule B1 paragraphs 70, 71 and 72 of IA 1986 is to cease to have effect although this, at least in theory, may have an adverse impact upon the charge holder in the event of a subsequent fall in value of those items of property which remain subject to the disapplication of paragraphs 70, 71 and 72[108]. Nor do the provisions contain any guidance as to

---

103   See **PARAGRAPHS 18.17 AND 18.18** *ante*.
104   See **PARAGRAPH 18.15** *ante*.
105   Regulation 15(1) and (1A) of FMIR 1991.
106   Regulation 15(3) of FMIR 1991.
107   Regulation 15(2) of FMIR 1991.
108   Where the property comprises of realisable investments, the charge holder will normally have realised his security, to the extent necessary or permitted, by the time the disapplication of Schedule B1 paragraphs 70, 71 and 72 of IA 1986 takes effect.

how any disagreement between the administrator and the charge holder as to the value of property, other than investments for which a price is quoted, is to be resolved.

ADDITIONAL PROVISIONS OF GENERAL APPLICATION AFFECTING ADMINISTRATIONS UNDER IA 1986

18.25 Where property (other than land) is held by a recognised investment exchange or a recognised clearing house as margin in relation to a market contract or as a default fund contribution, section 177(2) of CA 1989 provides that, so far as necessary to enable the property to be applied in accordance with the rules of the exchange or clearing house, it may be so applied notwithstanding any prior equitable interest or any right or remedy arising from a breach of fiduciary duty, unless the exchange or clearing house had notice of the interest, right or breach of duty at the time that the property was provided as margin or as default fund contribution. A person is taken to have notice of a matter if he deliberately failed to make enquiries as to that matter in circumstances in which a reasonable and honest person would have done so[109]. It is further provided that no right or remedy arising subsequent to such property being provided as margin or as default fund contribution may be enforced so as to prevent or interfere with the application of the property by the exchange or clearing house in accordance with its rules[110]. Where, by virtue of such provision an exchange or clearing house has power to apply property notwithstanding any such interest, right or remedy, a person to whom the exchange or clearing house disposes of the property in accordance with its rules takes free from that interest right or remedy[111].

18.26 In addition, section 179 of CA 1989 also provides that where property subject to an unpaid vendor's lien becomes subject to a market charge, the market charge has priority over the lien unless the chargee had actual notice of the lien at the time that the property became subject to the charge. It should be noted however that this provision does not apply to land or any interest in land[112]. It may also be open to doubt as to whether this provision extends to common law liens such as that exercised by an unpaid vendor of goods who remains in possession of the goods in question[113].

18.27 Property (other than land) which is held by a recognised investment exchange or a recognised clearing house as margin in relation to market contracts, or as a default fund contribution, or which is subject to a market charge is also protected against action by unsecured creditors. In particular, it is provided[114] that no execution or other legal process for the enforcement of a judgment or order may be commenced or continued (as the case may be), no distress may be levied[115] and the procedure for taking control of goods in Schedule 12 to the Tribunals, Courts and Enforcement Act 2007 may not be used against such

---

109 Section 190(5) of CA 1989.
110 Section 177(3) of CA 1989.
111 Section 177(4) of CA 1989.
112 By virtue of the provisions of regulation 8 of FMIR 1991: see **PARAGRAPH 18.15** *ante*.
113 See sections 39 and 41–43 of the Sale of Goods Act 1979.
114 By section 180(1) and (4) of CA 1989.
115 Presumably, these words bear a similar meaning to those appearing in Schedule B1 paragraph 43(6) of IA 1986.

property by a person not seeking to enforce any interest in or any security over the property[116], except with the consent of:

(a) in the case of property provided as cover for margin or as default fund contribution[117], the investment exchange or clearing house in question; or

(b) in the case of property subject to a market charge, the person in whose favour the charge was granted.

18.28 It is further provided[118] that where by virtue of such provision, a person would not be entitled to enforce a judgment or order against any property, any injunction or other remedy granted with a view to facilitating the enforcement of such judgment or order is not to extend to that property. This latter provision would appear to inhibit the grant of a freezing order against property held by a recognised investment exchange or recognised clearing house as margin in relation to a market contract or subject to a market charge. It would not appear to prevent the grant of such an injunction in relation to a defaulter's equity of redemption, if any, in such property.

18.29 Somewhat curiously, section 180(2) of CA 1989 provides that, where the investment exchange or clearing house or the person in whose favour the market charge was granted gives consent to an unsecured creditor under section 180(1) of CA 1989 to take 'proceedings' against the property concerned, the proceedings may be commenced or continued notwithstanding any provision of IA 1986. Presumably, the word 'proceedings' extends in this context to any execution, diligence, other legal process or distress as used in section 180(1) of CA 1989. In the context of an administration, there appears to follow the very odd result that where such consent is given an unsecured creditor will not, in relation to the property concerned, be subject to the restrictions imposed by paragraphs 43(6) or 44 of Schedule B1 to IA 1986 but a secured creditor, without the leave of the court or the consent of the administrator, if any, will be prevented from enforcing his security over such property.

18.30 Section 182A of CA 1989 provides that nothing in the law of insolvency shall enable the setting off against each other of:

(a) positions and assets recorded in an account at a recognised central counterparty and held for the account of a client, an indirect client or a group of clients or indirect clients in accordance with Article 39 of the EMIR Level 1 Regulation or Article 3(1) of the EMIR Level 2 Regulation;

(b) positions and assets recorded in an account at a clearing member and held for the account of a client, an indirect client or a group of clients or indirect clients in accordance Articles 4(2) and (3) of the EMIR Level 2 Regulation;

(c) positions and assets recorded in any other account at the recognised central counterparty or clearing member[119].

Thus in these circumstances insolvency set-off, which is ordinarily self-executing, will not apply.

---

116 Ie an unsecured creditor. The provision will apply to prevent any application for a charging order being made against such property, although, once a charging order has been obtained, it would be the provisions of section 177 of CA 1989 and of Schedule B1 paragraphs 43 and 44 of IA 1986 which would prevent enforcement of the charging order against property of a company in administration.

117 'Cover for margin' bears the same meaning as 'margin': section 190(3) of CA 1989.

118 By section 180(3) of CA 1989.

119 Section 182A of CA 1989.

18.31 Section 183(1) of CA 1989 provides that references to insolvency law in section 426 of IA 1986 (co-operation between courts exercising insolvency jurisdiction) include, in relation to a part of the United Kingdom, the provisions made by or under Part VII of CA 1989 and, in relation to a relevant country or territory, so much of the law of that country or territory as corresponds to any provision made by or under Part VII. The effect of section 426 of IA 1986, so far as it concerns administration proceedings, is considered in **CHAPTER 22** *post*. In this respect, however, the provisions of Part VII of CA 1989 as they apply in any part of the United Kingdom are treated as part of the general insolvency law of that part.

18.32 Finally, section 184 of CA 1989 contains a number of provisions protecting office holders, including administrators, recognised investment exchanges, recognised clearing houses and the officers, servants and members of the governing bodies of such exchanges and clearing houses from liability in respect of their actions. Of principal import for present purposes are the following:

(a) section 184(1), which provides that where a relevant office holder takes any action in relation to property of a defaulter which is liable to be dealt with in accordance with the default rules of a recognised investment exchange or recognised clearing house, and believes and has reasonable grounds for believing that he is entitled to take that action, he is not liable to any person in respect of any loss or damage resulting from his action except in so far as the loss or damage is caused by the office holder's own negligence[120]; and

(b) section 184(2), which provides that any failure by a recognised investment exchange or recognised clearing house to comply with its own rules in respect of any matter is not to prevent that matter being treated for the purposes of Part VII of CA 1989 as done in accordance with those rules[121] so long as the failure does not substantially affect the rights of any person entitled to require compliance with the rules.

Plainly, whether the rights of a person entitled to require compliance with the rules of an exchange or clearing house have been substantially affected in a particular case may be open to debate. The consequences of such a person's rights having been substantially affected, at least in the context of an administration, are not specified.

UNCERTIFICATED SECURITIES

18.33 The provisions of Part VII of CA 1989 are also applied by FMIR 1996[122], with certain modifications, to certain charges, referred to as 'system charges', granted in favour of settlement banks who undertake assured payment obligations in connection with the settlement of transactions through a system whose operation has been approved under the Uncertificated Security Regulations 2001[123]. Pursuant to the latter regulations, the Bank of England may

---

120 This provision appears to be a parallel provision to section 234(3) and (4) of IA 1986 and presumably is to be construed similarly.
121 Eg for the purposes of sections 159(2) and 161(4) of CA 1989, see **PARAGRAPH 18.8(a) AND (c)** *ante*.
122 SI 1996 No 1469.
123 SI 2001 No 3755.

approve operators of computer-based systems enabling title to units of security to be transferred without written instrument. Under such powers, Euroclear UK & Ireland Ltd (formerly CRESTCo Ltd) has been approved as the operator of the Crest system for the paperless transfer of shares and other securities listed on the Stock Exchange introduced by the Stock Exchange in July 1996.

18.34 The provisions of Part VII of CA 1989 applied are those relating to market charges, action taken to enforce market charges and property subject to market charges[124]. Specifically, they apply to system charges (and action taken to enforce such charges and property subject thereto) granted in favour of settlement banks for the purpose of securing debts or liabilities arising in connection with the transfer of, or agreement to transfer, uncertificated securities or interests in relation to such securities or the issue of such securities by means of the relevant system[125]. Such system charges must be granted either by a system-member[126] or by a system-beneficiary[127] and must expressly refer to the relevant system[128]. Part VII applies only to the extent that the relevant system charge is a charge over particular descriptions of property[129] and secures obligations of system-members, former system-members[130] or system-beneficiaries to reimburse the settlement bank arising in connection with transactions undertaken by means of the relevant system[131].

18.35 The disapplication of paragraph 43(2) and (3), including those provisions as applied to interim moratoriums by Schedule B1 paragraph 44 of IA 1986 (restriction on the enforcement of security rights) is limited to the extent necessary to enable there to be realised in the case of both system-members and system-beneficiaries maximum sums limited by reference to payment obligations discharged by or to the settlement bank in respect of transactions effected during what is described as the 'qualifying period'. This is a reference to the period beginning with the fifth business day before the day on which the application for the administration order was made, or the appointment of an administrator or filing with the court of notice of intention to appoint under Schedule B1 paragraph 14 or 22 of IA 1986 was effected (as the case may be) and ending on the second business day after the day on which the order was made or the administrator was appointed (as the case may be)[132]. Similarly, the disapplication of Schedule B1 paragraphs 70, 71 and 72 of IA 1986 (power of administrator to deal with charged property) ceases to have effect after the end of the second business day after the day on which the administration order is made or the administrator is appointed under Schedule B1 paragraph 14 or 22 of IA 1986, if the charge is not required for the realisation of such maximum sum[133].

---

124 Ie those referred to in **PARAGRAPHS 18.19, 18.20 AND 18.25** *ante*.

125 Regulation 3 of FMIR 1996.

126 Defined by regulation 2(1) of FMIR 1996 as a person who is permitted by an operator to transfer by means of the relevant system titled to uncertificated units of security held by him.

127 Defined by regulation 2(1) of FMIR 1996 as a person on whose behalf of a system-member or former system-member holds or held uncertificated units of security.

128 Regulation 4 of FMIR 1996.

129 Listed in regulation 5(a) of FMIR 1996.

130 Ie a person whose participation in the relevant system has been terminated or suspended; see regulation 2(1) of FMIR 1996.

131 Regulation 5 of FMIR 1996.

132 Regulations 6 and 7 of FMIR 1996.

133 Regulation 8 of FMIR 1996.

SETTLEMENT SYSTEMS

18.36 By way of implementation of the EU Directive on settlement finality in payment and securities systems[134], Part III of the Settlement Finality Regulations[135] contains similar provisions[136] to those described in **PARAGRAPHS 18.8(a), (e) AND (h), 18.19 AND 18.20** *ante* applying to transfer orders effected through designated payment or securities settlement systems and to collateral security[137]. A transfer order is an instruction by a participant in the designated system to place at the disposal of a recipient an amount of money by means of a book entry on the accounts of a credit institution, central bank or settlement agent, an instruction which results in the assumption or discharge of a payment obligation as defined by the rules of the system, or an instruction by a participant to transfer, the title to, or an interest in, a security by means of a book entry on a register or otherwise[138]. Collateral security for this purpose means any realisable assets, including money, provided under a charge, or a repurchase or similar agreement, for the purpose of securing rights and obligations potentially arising in connection with a designated system, or provided to a central bank, for the purpose of securing rights and obligations in connection with its operations or the carrying out of its functions as a central bank[139].

18.37 The provisions in question apply in relation to insolvency proceedings:

(a) in respect of a participant in a designated system, or of a participant which is an interoperable system in relation to that designated system;

(b) in respect of a provider of collateral security in connection with the functions of a central bank, insofar as the proceedings affect the rights of the central bank to the collateral security; and

(c) in respect of a system operator[140] of a designated system or of a system which is an interoperable system[141] to that designated system but not in relation to any other insolvency proceedings[142].

18.38 It is further provided that the provisions do not apply in relation to any transfer order given by a participant in a designated system which is entered into the system after the making of an administration order in respect of that participant, a participant in a system which is an interoperable system in relation to the designated system or a system operator which is not a participant in the

---

134 Directive 98/26/EC of the European Parliament and of the Council of 19 May 1998 on settlement finality in payment and securities settlement systems (OJ L166, 19/05/98, 45).

135 SI 1999 No 2979 as amended by paragraphs 74–76 of the Schedule to the Enterprise Act 2002 (Insolvency) Order 2003 (SI 2003 No 2096).

136 Regulations 13 to 26 of the Settlement Finality Regulations.

137 Ie a payment or securities settlement system that has been designated by the FCA or the Bank of England pursuant to Part II of the Settlement Finality Regulations; see regulations 2(1) and 3–12.

138 Regulation 2 of the Settlement Finality Regulations.

139 Regulation 2 of the Settlement Finality Regulations.

140 Regulation 2(1) of the Settlement Finality Regulations defines an interoperable system in relation to a system ('the first system') as 'a second system whose system operator has entered into an arrangement with the system operator of the first system that involves cross-system execution of transfer orders'.

141 Regulation 2(1) of the Settlement Finality Regulations defines a system operator as 'the entity or entities legally responsible for the operation of a system. A system operator may also act as a settlement agent, central counterparty or clearing house'.

142 Regulation 13(2) of the Settlement Finality Regulations.

designated system unless the transfer order is carried out on the same business day of the designated system that the administration order is made, and the system operator can show that it did not have notice of the making of the administration order at the time the transfer order became irrevocable[143]. For this purpose, the relevant system operator is to be taken to have notice of the making of the administration order if it deliberately failed to make enquiries as to the making of the order in circumstances in which a reasonable and honest person would have done so[144]. The court is required to notify both the system operator and the relevant designating authority forthwith of the making of an administration order in respect of a participant in a designated settlement system[145].

18.39 Part III of the Settlement Finality Regulations also makes provision:

(a) that where securities are provided as collateral security to a participant in a designated system, a system operator or a central bank, and a register, account or centralised deposit system located in a state which is a member of the European Economic Area ('EEA') legally records the entitlement of that person to the collateral security, the rights of that person as the holder of the collateral security are governed by the law of the state, or where appropriate, the law of the part of the state, where the register, account or centralised deposit system is located[146];

(b) that where insolvency proceedings are brought in any jurisdiction against a person who participates, or has participated, in a system which has been designated for the purposes of the EU directive[147], any question relating to the rights and obligations arising from or in connection with that participation falling to be determined in a court in England, Wales or in Scotland or the High Court in Northern Ireland is to be determined in accordance with the law governing that system[148];

(c) extending the references to insolvency law in section 426 of IA 1986 to the provisions of Part III of the Settlement Finality Regulations and the corresponding law of other relevant countries or territories within the meaning of section 426[149]; and

(d) applying the provisions of Part III to transfer orders and collateral security held in connection with settlement systems designated in other EEA states or Gibraltar[150].

FINANCIAL COLLATERAL ARRANGEMENTS

18.40 Since the coming into effect of the Settlement Finality Regulations, there has been further European legislation relating to the provision of collateral in the capital markets in the form of the EU Directive on Financial Collateral Arrangements[151]. This has been given effect by the Financial Collateral

---

143 Regulation 20(1) and (2) of the Settlement Finality Regulations.
144 Regulation 20(3) of the Settlement Finality Regulations.
145 Regulation 22(1) of the Settlement Finality Regulations.
146 Regulation 23 of the Settlement Finality Regulations.
147 Directive 98/26/EC.
148 Regulation 24 of the Settlement Finality Regulations.
149 Regulation 25 of the Settlement Finality Regulations.
150 Regulation 26 of the Settlement Finality Regulations.
151 Directive 2002/47/EC.

Arrangements (No 2) Regulations 2003 ('FCAR 2003')[152], Part 3 of which provides that certain provisions of insolvency law relating to administrations and company voluntary arrangements shall not apply to financial collateral arrangements. The purpose of FCAR 2003 is to facilitate the effectiveness and enforceability of financial collateral arrangements, more especially where a party to the arrangement has entered into a reorganisation procedure such as administration or a company voluntary arrangement. It follows that FCAR 2003 has a much wider application than the Settlement Finality Regulations, because they are not limited to the insolvency proceedings referred to in **PARAGRAPH 18.37** *ante*.[153]

18.41 A financial collateral arrangement is an agreement or arrangement[154], the purpose of which is to secure or otherwise cover obligations[155] owed to the collateral-taker. To qualify as a financial collateral arrangement[156], it must provide either:

(a) for the collateral-provider to create (or for there otherwise to arise) a security interest[157] in financial collateral to secure those obligations; or

(b) for the collateral-provider to transfer to the collateral-taker legal and beneficial ownership in financial collateral on terms that when those obligations are discharged the collateral-taker will transfer legal and beneficial ownership in equivalent financial collateral to the collateral provider.

It follows that the definition extends beyond what would normally be regarded in English law as security by way of a mortgage or charge. The collateral-provider and the collateral-taker must both be non-natural persons. Financial collateral means either cash[158] or financial instruments[159]. FCAR 2003 is therefore designed to facilitate the enforcement of security and other equivalent interests over cash and instruments tradeable in the capital markets, without regard to the question of whether any such interest is itself acquired as part of a transaction in the capital markets[160].

---

152 SI 2003 No 3226.
153 As to which, see regulation 13(2) of the Settlement Finality Regulations.
154 The only formality is that it should be evidenced in writing. It is also necessary that the agreement pursuant to which the collateral was provided was entered into on or after 26 December 2003: *Re Lehman Bros International (Europe) (in administration)* [2012] EWHC 2997 (Ch).
155 The obligations are defined in regulation 3 of FCAR 2003 as the obligations which are secured or otherwise covered by a financial collateral arrangement; this is a somewhat circular definition.
156 FCAR 2003 provides for two different types of financial collateral arrangement (viz title transfer financial collateral arrangements and security financial collateral arrangements).
157 Defined by regulation 3 of FCAR 2003 to include a pledge, mortgage, fixed charge, floating charge (so long as the financial collateral is in the possession or under the control of the collateral-taker) and a lien.
158 Which itself means money in any currency credited to an account or a similar claim for repayment: for the full definition see regulation 3 of FCAR 2003.
159 Financial instruments are defined by regulation 3 of FCAR 2003 to mean: (a) shares or equivalent securities, (b) bonds and other debt instruments if they are tradeable on the capital market, (c) any other securities which are normally dealt in and give the right to acquire any such shares, bonds or instruments, and (d) units of a collective investments scheme, eligible debt securities, money market instruments and any other claims to or rights in such instruments.
160 Although the stability of the financial system was the prime motivating factor for the legislation: see Recital (3) to Directive 2002/47/EC.

18.42 The following provisions of FCAR 2003 are of particular relevance to administrations and company voluntary arrangements:

(a) Sections 895A and 895H of CA 2006 shall not apply in relation to a security financial collateral arrangement or any charge created or otherwise arising under a security financial arrangement[161]. It follows that any such charge will not be void as against, *inter alios*, an administrator even if it is not registered under the relevant section.

(b) Neither Schedule B1 paragraph 43(2) nor Schedule B1 paragraph 44 of IA 1986 apply to any security interest created or otherwise arising under a financial collateral arrangement[162]. It follows that the moratorium on enforcement of security for which those paragraphs provide shall not apply in relation to a financial collateral arrangement[163].

(c) Schedule B1 paragraph 65(2) of IA 1986 does not apply to any security interest created or otherwise arising under a financial collateral arrangement. It follows that a company's preferential debts shall not be paid in priority to such a security interest arrangement[164].

(d) Schedule B1 paragraph 99(3) and (4) of IA 1986 does not apply to any security interest created or otherwise arising under a financial collateral arrangement. It follows that neither a former administrator's remuneration or expenses, nor sums payable in respect of debts or liabilities arising out of contracts into by a former administrator shall be charged over property subject to such a security interest[165].

(e) Schedule B1 paragraph 41(2) of IA 1986 does not apply to a receiver appointed under a charge created or otherwise arising under a financial collateral arrangement[166]. Accordingly, any such receiver cannot be required to vacate office by an administrator.

(f) Neither Schedule B1 paragraph 70 nor Schedule B1 paragraph 71 of IA 1986 apply to any security interest created or otherwise arising under a financial collateral arrangement[167]. It follows that the administrator has no power to deal with property charged by a financial collateral arrangement without the consent of the chargee.

(g) Section 176A of IA 1986 does not apply so as to require an administrator to make available any part of the property charged under a financial collateral arrangement as part of the prescribed part[168].

(h) Section 245 of IA 1986 does not apply to any charge created or otherwise arising under a financial collateral arrangement[169]. It follows that such a charge is not vulnerable to avoidance under that section[170].

---

161 Regulation 4(4) of FCAR 2003. A security financial collateral arrangement is one of the two types of financial collateral arrangement for which provision is made by FCAR 2003.
162 Regulation 8(1)(a) of FCAR 2003. The exclusion also applies to the predecessor provisions in sections 10 and 11 of IA 1986.
163 There is a similar provision (regulation 8(5) of FCAR 2003) in relation to Schedule A1 paragraphs 12(1)(g) and 20 of IA 1986 in relation to small company moratoriums.
164 Regulation 8(1)(aa) of FCAR 2003.
165 Regulation 8(1)(c) of FCAR 2003.
166 Regulation 8(2) of FCAR 2003. The exclusion also applies to the predecessor provision in section 11(2) of IA 1986.
167 Regulation 8(1)(b) of FCAR 2003. The exclusion also applies to the predecessor provisions in section 15 of IA 1986.
168 Regulation 10(3) of FCAR 2003.
169 Regulation 10(5) of FCAR 2003.
170 In essence any right of set-off, but see the wide definition in regulation 3 of FCAR 2003.

(i) Any 'close-out netting provision'[171] relating to a financial collateral arrangement will take effect in accordance with its terms notwithstanding that either party is subject to an administration or a company voluntary arrangement[172]. Rule 2.85(4)(a) of the Insolvency Rules 1986[173] is then disapplied, save for the circumstance in which the other party was aware or should have been aware that administration or company voluntary arrangement proceedings had commenced in relation to the company[174].

---

171 In *Gray v G-T-P Group Ltd* [2010] EWHC 1772 (Ch), Vos J held that the mere reference to floating charges at regulation 3 of FCAR 2003 did not mean that the EU Directive on financial collateral arrangements should automatically apply to floating charges as that term was understood under English law. It was necessary to prove that the floating charge under consideration fell within the definition of a security interest as defined at regulation 3 of FCAR 2003. Following Vos J's decision, a broad definition of possession was added at regulation 3(2) of FCAR 2003 by the Financial Markets and Insolvency (Settlement Finality and Financial Collateral Arrangements) (Amendment) Regulations 2010 (SI 2010 No 2993). In *Re Lehman Bros International (Europe) (in administration)* [2012] EWHC 2997 (Ch), Briggs J held that test for possession or control for an arrangement to be a security collateral financial arrangement could only be satisfied if the collateral provider parted with dominion over the collateral. This approach was endorsed by the CJEU in *Private Equity Insurance Group SIA v Swedbank AS: C-156/15* [2016] All ER (D) 116.

172 Regulation 12(1) of FCAR 2003.

173 The equivalent provision under the Rules is at Rule 14.24(7)(a) and FCAR 2003 will, presumably, be amended in due course to reflect this.

174 Regulation 12(4) of FCAR 2003.

19 Administrations and special administrations in the financial services sector

INTRODUCTION

19.1   There have always been special provisions for the administration of companies operating in the financial services sector. Thus, section 8(5) of IA 1986 (in its original form) and Schedule B1 paragraph 9 of IA 1986 both provide that an administrator may not be appointed of a company if:

(a) it effects or carries out contracts of insurance and is not exempt from the general prohibition; or

(b) it has continuing liabilities in respect of a deposit but is not an authorised deposit taker.

Those prohibitions have for some time been reversed by secondary legislation: in relation to insurers by what is now the Financial Services and Markets Act 2000 (Administration Orders Relating to Insurers) Order 2010[1] and in relation to banks by what is now the Banks (Former Authorised Institutions) (Insolvency) Order 2006[2]. These Orders do not give rise to separate or special administration regimes, but they do make special provision for how any administration should be conducted and in particular they give the regulators (the Financial Conduct Authority ('the FCA') and the Prudential Regulation Authority ('the PRA')) rights to participate in any administrations. Where the company or partnership concerned is an authorised or former authorised person or appointed representative within the meaning of FSMA 2000[3], the regulators also have similar rights of participation, which are set out in Part XXIV of FSMA 2000.

19.2   Quite separately from these enhanced rights, there a number of special administration regimes which have been introduced in the financial services sector, namely bank administration[4], building society administration[5]

---

1   SI 2010/3023, replacing the Financial Services and Markets Act 2000 (Administration Orders Relating to Insurers) Order 2002 (SI 2002 No 1242).
2   SI 2006/3107, revoking and replacing the Banks (Administration Proceedings) Order 1989 (SI 1989 No 1276).
3   Whether or not they are also an insurer of a former bank.
4   Under Part 3 of BA 2009, with the relevant procedures being prescribed by the Bank Administration (England and Wales) Rules 2009 (SI 2009 No 357).
5   Section 90C of the Buildings Societies Act 1986, as inserted by article 2 of the Building Societies (Insolvency and Special Administration) Order 2009 (SI 2009 No 805), with the

and investment bank special administration[6], with additional provision for investment banks which are deposit takers[7], and a regime (FMI administration[8]), which is not yet in force, but which will be dealt with briefly at the end of the chapter. So far as banks are concerned, following the financial crisis of 2008, the government considered that the provisions in Part XXIV of FSMA 2000 were insufficiently flexible to deal with the insolvency of a bank. Accordingly, the Banking Act 2009 ('BA 2009') introduced a special resolution regime ('the SRR') for banks, which it defined as entities incorporated or formed in the UK that have the permission to accept deposits[9]. Subsequent amendments to BA 2009 made investment firms[10], recognised central counterparties[11] and UK branches of foreign institutions[12] subject to a modified SRR. This chapter summarises the administration aspects of the SRR. It also describes the position of cooperative and community benefit societies.

AUTHORISED AND FORMER AUTHORISED PERSONS

19.3   Part XXIV of FSMA 2000, as amended by IA 2000, the Enterprise Act 2002 and the Financial Services Act 2012, confers a series of rights on the FCA and the PRA[13] in relation to insolvency proceedings relating to authorised persons or appointed representatives[14] or recognised investment exchanges[15] or persons who are or have carried on a regulated activity in contravention of the general prohibition contained in section 19 of FSMA 2000. The right to participate also extends to the scheme manager of the Financial Services Compensation Scheme where an administrator of a relevant person[16] is appointed[17]. So far as is relevant to the scope of this work, the rights in question are as follows:

(a)   The right to make application to the court under sections 6 and 7 of IA 1986 (challenge to decisions and implementation of proposals) with regard to

---

relevant procedures being prescribed by the Building Society Special Administration (England and Wales) Rules 2010 (SI 2010 No 2580).

6   Under article 4 of the Investment Bank Special Administration Regulations 2011 (SI 2011 No 245).

7   Special administration (bank insolvency) under Schedule 1 of the Investment Bank Special Administration Regulations 2011 (SI 2011 No 245) and special administration (bank administration) under Schedule 2 of the Investment Bank Special Administration Regulations 2011.

8   Under Part 6 of the Financial Services (Banking Reform) Act 2013.

9   Section 2 of BA 2009. Building societies (as defined by section 119 of the Building Societies Act 1986) and credit unions (as defined by section 31 of the Credit Unions Act 1979) are excluded from the definition but under section 84 of BA 2009 building societies are subject to a modified SRR and under section 89 of BA 2009, credit unions may be made subject to the SRR.

10   Section 89A of BA 2009.

11   Section 89B of BA 2009.

12   Section 89JA of BA 2009.

13   Sections 356 and 362 describe when each of the FCA and the PRA is to be treated as 'an appropriate regulator': for the purposes of the relevant provisions. One of these is inclusionary and the other is exclusionary, the rationale for which is not clear from the face of the provisions.

14   As defined in sections 31 and 39 of FSMA 2000. Some of the rights extend to former authorised persons and former appointed representatives.

15   As defined in section 285 of FSMA 2000.

16   Defined by section 213(9) of FSMA 2000 to mean a person who was an authorised person at the time the act or omission giving rise to the claim against him took place or an appointed representative at that time.

17   Section 215(3) and (3A) of FSMA 2000.

a voluntary arrangement in respect to a company or insolvent partnership which is an authorised person or a recognised investment exchange[18].

(b) The right to be heard on such an application made by a person other than the FCA or the PRA[19].

(c) The right[20] to make an administration application under Schedule B1 to IA 1986 in relation to a company or insolvent partnership which is or has been an authorised person or an appointed representative or a recognised investment exchange or which is carrying on, or which has carried on, a regulated activity in contravention of the general prohibition[21]. For this purpose, a company or partnership which is in default of an obligation to pay a sum due and payable under an agreement, the making of which constitutes part of the regulated activities carried on by the company or partnership, is treated as unable to pay its debts[22]. Similarly, for this purpose, an authorised deposit taker which is in default of an obligation to pay a sum due and payable in respect of a relevant deposit is also to be treated as unable to pay its debts[23].

(d) The right to be heard on the hearing of an administration application under Schedule B1 to IA 1986 made by a person other than the FCA or the PRA in relation to such a company or partnership, or on the hearing of any other application concerning the administration under Schedule B1 of such a company or partnership, including an administration following the appointment of an administrator under Schedule B1 paragraph 14 or 22 of IA 1986[24].

(e) The right to be sent all documents required to be sent to creditors and to attend any creditors' meeting or creditors' committee meeting[25].

(f) The right to apply to the court under Schedule B1 paragraph 74 of IA 1986 (protection of interests of creditors and members) in relation to such a company or partnership[26]. The FCA and the PRA do not have to show that their own interests were unfairly harmed by the act or omission of which complaint is made; it is sufficient if the interests of any creditor or member were so harmed[27].

(g) The right to apply to the court under sections 896 or 899 of CA 2006 (application to summon meetings of creditors and members or for sanction) where in the course of the administration of such a company, a compromise

---

18 Section 356(1) of FSMA 2000. If either regulator makes an application to the court under this provision in relation to a PRA-authorised person, the other regulator is entitled to be heard at any hearing relating to the application (section 356(5) of FSMA 2000).

19 Section 356(3) of FSMA 2000. The right is conferred on the 'appropriate regulator', which term is defined by section 356(4) of FSMA 2000.

20 Under section 359(1) of FSMA 2000 this right is conferred on the FCA. The PRA may only make an administration application in relation to a company or insolvent partnership that is a PRA-regulated person (section 356(1A) of FSMA 2000).

21 Ie that contained in section 19 of FSMA 2000.

22 Section 359(3) and (4) of FSMA 2000.

23 Section 359(3) and (4) of FSMA 2000.

24 Section 362(2) of FSMA 2000. The rights under sub-paragraphs (d), (e) and (f) in the text above are conferred on the 'appropriate regulator', which term is defined by section 362(5) of FSMA 2000. The rights under subparagraphs (d), (e) and (f) in the text above do not apply where the Company is in administration as a result of an administration application made by the FCA or the PRA (section 362(8) of FSMA 2000).

25 Sections 362(3) and 362(5) of IA 1986.

26 Section 362(4) of FSMA 2000.

27 Section 362(4A) of FSMA 2000.

or arrangement is proposed between the company and its creditors or any class of creditors[28].

(h) the right to apply for an order under section 423 of IA 1986 (transactions defrauding creditors) in relation to a debtor if, at the time the transaction at an undervalue was entered into, the debtor was carrying on a regulated activity and a victim of the transaction is or was party to an agreement with the debtor, the making or performance of which constituted or was part of a regulated activity carried on by the debtor[29].

19.4 Further to the above rights:

(a) Where any company or partnership is in administration within the meaning of Schedule B1 to IA 1986 other than in consequence of an administration application made by the FCA or the PRA, if the administrator thinks that the company or partnership is carrying on, or has carried on, a regulated activity in contravention of the general prohibition or a credit-related regulated activity in contravention of section 20 of FSMA 2000, the administrator is required to report the matter to the appropriate regulator without delay[30].

(b) Various further rights are conferred on the FCA and the PRA with regard to moratoriums and company voluntary arrangements under Schedule A1 and Part 1 of IA 1986 in relation to companies which are or have been authorised persons or appointed representatives or which are carrying on or have carried on regulated activities in contravention of the general prohibition. The rights in question are set out in section 356 of FSMA 2000, Schedule A1 paragraph 44 of IA 1986 and section 4A(5) of IA 1986 as amended. They are considered in **CHAPTERS 11 AND 12** *ante*.

19.5 In addition to the regulators' rights of participation, there are also restrictions on the ability of such companies to enter administration out of court without the regulators' consent. Section 362A of FSMA 2000 provides that an administrator of a company, which is or has been an authorised person or a recognised investment exchange or an appointed representative or which is carrying on, or which has carried on, a regulated activity in contravention of the general prohibition, cannot be appointed by the company or its directors under Schedule B1 paragraph 22 of IA 1986 without the written consent of the PRA if the company is a PRA-regulated body or, in any other case, the FCA[31], which consent must be filed with the court along with any copy of the notice of intention to appoint under Schedule B1 paragraph 27 of IA 1986. If no such notice of intention is required, the written consent of the PRA or the FCA, as applicable, must be filed along with the notice of the appointment under Schedule B1 paragraph 29 of IA 1986[32].

19.6 A similar structure has been introduced for certain banks and insurers, whether or not they continue to be authorised. Thus, in the case of any bank with

---

28 Section 362(6) of FSMA 2000.
29 Section 375 of FSMA 2000.
30 Section 361 of FSMA 2000. Section 361(2A) of FSMA 2000 defines the appropriate regulator as the FCA and the PRA where the regulated activity is a PRA-regulated activity and as the FCA in any other case.
31 Section 362A(2B) of FSMA 2000.
32 In *Re Ceart Risk Services Ltd* [2012] EWHC 1178 (Ch), Arnold J held that failure to obtain the prior consent of the regulator before the appointment of an administrator under Schedule B1 paragraph 22 of IA 1986 did not incurably invalidate the appointment but that the appointment did not take effect until the consent of the appropriate regulator was filed with the court.

continuing liabilities in respect of deposits but which does not have permission under FSMA 2000 to accept deposits, the starting point is that Schedule B1 paragraph 9(1) of IA 1986 provides that a person may not be appointed as administrator of any such company. However, this prohibition is subject to any order made pursuant to the power granted by section 422 of IA 1986, which authorises Part II of IA 1986 to be applied to any bank which is a former authorised institution[33]. The relevant order[34] applies Schedule B1 of IA 1986 with appropriate modifications[35] that are very similar to those for which specific provision is made by sections 362 and 362A of FSMA 2000 in respect of those companies and insolvent partnerships to which section 362(1) of FSMA 2000 applies. In particular, an application for an administration order must be served on the FCA and the PRA, and no such company can enter administration under Schedule B1 paragraph 22 of IA 1986 without their consent.

19.7 So far as insurers are concerned, the position is governed by the Financial Services and Markets Act 2000 (Administration Orders Relating to Insurers) Order 2010[36], which provides that Schedule B1 paragraph 9(2) of IA 1986 shall not preclude the making of an administration order in relation to an insurer[37]. However the disapplication of Schedule B1 in relation to companies which effect or carry out contracts of insurance, continues to apply so as to preclude an insurer from entering administration out of court, whether through an appointment by the company, its directors or the holder of a qualifying floating charge[38]. The Rules are also applied to the administration of insurers, but with a modification permitting the FCA (and if relevant the PRA) and the scheme manager of the FSCS to appear at the hearing for an administration order[39].

19.8 The modifications of Schedule B1 include an additional purpose of assisting the administration of the Financial Services Compensation Scheme and in the case of long-term insurance to secure continuity of insurance[40]. The way that this is drafted means that the administrator is under a mandatory obligation to carry on the insurer's long-term insurance business with a view to that business being transferred as a going concern to a person who may lawfully carry out the relevant contacts[41]. In carrying out that long-term business

---

33 Ie any person who has a liability in respect of a deposit accepted in accordance with the Banking Act 1979 or 1987, but which does not have permission under Part IV of FSMA 2000 to accept deposits.

34 Banks (Former Authorised Institutions) (Insolvency) Order 2006 (SI 2006 No 3107), enacted under the power given by section 422 of IA 1986 and revoking the earlier Banks (Administration Proceedings) Order 1989.

35 Set out in the Schedule to Banks (Former Authorised Institutions) (Insolvency) Order 2006 (SI 2006 No 3107).

36 SI 2010 No 3023, made pursuant to section 360 of FSMA 2000, replacing Financial Services and Markets Act 2000 (Administration Orders Relating to Insurers) Order 2002 (SI 2002 No 1242), save for cases in which an administrator of an insurer was appointed before 1 February 2011.

37 For these purposes 'insurer' is defined by article 2 of the Financial Services and Markets Act 2000 (Insolvency) (Definition of "Insurer") Order 2001 (SI 2001 No 2634).

38 Article 2 of the Financial Services and Markets Act 2000 (Administration Orders Relating to Insurers) Order 2010 (SI 2010 No 3023).

39 Article 3 of Financial Services and Markets Act 2000 (Administration Orders Relating to Insurers) Order 2010 (SI 2010 No 3023).

40 Schedule paragraph 1 of the Financial Services and Markets Act 2000 (Administration Orders Relating to Insurers) Order 2010 (SI 2010 No 3023), modifying Schedule B1 paragraph 3 of IA 1986.

41 Schedule B1 paragraph 3A of IA 1986, as inserted by Schedule paragraph 2(1) of the Financial Services and Markets Act 2000 (Administration Orders Relating to Insurers) Order 2010 (SI 2010 No 3023).

the administrator is not, however, permitted to enter into any new contracts without the approval of the PRA or the FCA as the case may be[42]. The court is empowered to appoint a special manager, to reduce contracts of long-term insurance and (on the application of the administrator, any special manager, the FCA or the PRA) to appoint an actuary to report on the long term business[43]. The modifications also give to the FCA, the PRA and the scheme manager of the FSCS rights of participation in the administration relating to the administrator's proposals and the ending of administration[44]. It also provides that the length of administration is extended from one year to 30 months[45]. There is also an expanded payment power[46] to make payments to any creditor 'the amount which the administrator reasonably considers that the creditor would be entitled to receive on a distribution of the insurer's assets in a winding up'.

THE SPECIAL RESOLUTION REGIME

19.9   As mentioned above, BA 2009 introduced a special resolution regime for banks, which it defined as entities incorporated or formed in the UK that have the permission to accept deposits[47]. Subsequent amendments to BA 2009 made investment firms[48], recognised central counterparties[49] and UK branches of foreign institutions[50] subject to a modified SRR. The SRR consists of five stabilisation options, a bank insolvency procedure and a bank administration procedure[51]. The five stabilisation options are[52] transfer to a private sector purchaser[53], transfer to a bridge bank[54], transfer to an asset management vehicle[55], the bail-in option[56] and transfer to temporary public-sector ownership[57].

---

42   Schedule B1 paragraph 3A(3) of IA 1986, as inserted by Schedule paragraph 2(1) of the Financial Services and Markets Act 2000 (Administration Orders Relating to Insurers) Order 2010 (SI 2010 No 3023).

43   Schedule B1 paragraph 3A(4)–(10) of IA 1986, as inserted by Schedule paragraph 2(1) of the Financial Services and Markets Act 2000 (Administration Orders Relating to Insurers) Order 2010 (SI 2010 No 3023).

44   Schedule paragraphs 3, 4, 5, 8 and 9 of the Financial Services and Markets Act 2000 (Administration Orders Relating to Insurers) Order 2010 (SI 2010 No 3023), modifying Schedule B1 paragraphs 49, 53, 54, 79 and 91 of IA 1986.

45   Schedule paragraphs 6 and 7 of the Financial Services and Markets Act 2000 (Administration Orders Relating to Insurers) Order 2010 (SI 2010 No 3023), modifying Schedule B1 paragraph 76 of IA 1986.

46   Inserted into Schedule 1 of IA 1986 by Schedule paragraph 10 of the Financial Services and Markets Act 2000 (Administration Orders Relating to Insurers) Order 2010 (SI 2010 No 3023).

47   Section 2 of BA 2009. Building societies (as defined by section 119 of the Building Societies Act 1986) and credit unions (as defined by section 31 of the Credit Unions Act 1979) are excluded from the definition but under section 84 of BA 2009 building societies are subject to a modified SRR and under section 89 of BA 2009, credit unions may be made subject to the SRR.

48   Section 89A of BA 2009.

49   Section 89B of BA 2009.

50   Section 89JA of BA 2009.

51   Section 1(2) of BA 2009.

52   Section 1(3) of BA 2009.

53   Section 11 of BA 2009.

54   Section 12 of BA 2009.

55   Section 12ZA of BA 2009.

56   Section 12A of BA 2009.

57   Section 13 of BA 2009.

19.10 The stabilisation options are to be achieved through the exercise of one or more stabilisation powers which include the powers to compel the transfer of the subject bank's shares, securities or property[58]. Before a stabilisation power may be exercised in respect of a bank, the PRA must be satisfied that the bank is failing or likely to fail[59] and the Bank of England must be satisfied that in the circumstances it is not reasonably likely that action taken by the bank will avoid its failure or likely failure[60], that the exercise of the power is necessary having regard to the public interest in the advancement of one or more special resolution objectives[61] and that one of more of the special resolution objectives would not be met to the same extent by winding up the bank[62]. Before determining whether the first condition is met, the PRA must consult the Bank of England[63] and before determining whether the latter three conditions are met, the Bank of England must consult the PRA, the FCA and the Treasury[64]. In addition to these general conditions, specific conditions apply where the Bank of England is considering making a property transfer instrument[65] and where the Treasury has already provided financial assistance to a bank[66].

19.11 The bank insolvency procedure is set out at Part 2 of BA 2009. If a bank is unable, or is likely to become unable, to pay its debts, or if the winding up of the bank would be fair, the PRA may apply for a bank insolvency order[67]. Before it applies for a bank insolvency order, the PRA must be satisfied that the bank is failing, or is likely to fail and that the bank has depositors who are eligible for compensation under the Financial Services Compensation Scheme ('the FSCS')[68]. The PRA must also have been informed by the Bank of England that it is not reasonably likely that action will be taken in respect of the bank that will prevent it failing, or being likely to fail and the Bank of England must consent to the application[69]. The bank administration procedure is set out at Part 3 of BA 2009. This is the first of the special administration regimes with which this chapter is concerned. Substantially the same regime was then applied to building societies by section 90C of the Building Societies Act 1986 and article 3 of the Building Societies (Insolvency and Special Administration) Order 2009[70].

---

58 Section 1(4) of BA 2009.
59 Sections 7(1) and 7(2) of BA 2009. Section 7(5C) of BA 2009 sets out the circumstances in which this condition will be met. The PRA must treat this condition as met if it would be met but for financial assistance provided to the bank by the Treasury or the Bank of England, disregarding ordinary market assistance provided by the Bank of England on its usual terms (section 7(5A) of BA 2009).
60 Sections 7(1) and 7(3) of BA 2009. The Bank of England must treat this condition as met if it would be met but for financial assistance provided to the bank by the Treasury or the Bank of England, disregarding ordinary market assistance provided by the Bank of England on its usual terms (section 7(5B) of BA 2009).
61 Sections 7(1) and 7(4) of BA 2009. The special resolution conditions are set out at section 4 of BA 2009.
62 Sections 7(1) and 7(5) of BA 2009.
63 Section 7(5F) of BA 2009.
64 Sections 7(5G) and 7(5H) of BA 2009.
65 Section 8ZA of BA 2009. In determining whether these specific conditions have been met and, if so, how to react, the Bank of England must consult the PRA, the FCA and the Treasury (section 8ZA(4) of BA 2009).
66 Section 8 of BA 2009.
67 Section 96 of BA 2009.
68 Section 96(3)(b) of BA 2009.
69 Section 96(3)(a) of BA 2009.
70 SI 2009 No 805.

BANK AND BUILDING SOCIETY ADMINISTRATION

19.12   Bank administration is intended for the special circumstances in which the business of a bank is sold to a commercial purchaser[71] or transferred to a bridge bank[72] or in the case of certain multiple transfers under Part 1 of BA 2009. One of the principle features of bank administration is that the bank administrator is enabled and required to ensure that the non-sold or non-transferred part of the bank (described as 'the residual bank') provides services or facilities required to enable the commercial purchaser or the bridge bank to operate effectively[73].

19.13   A bank administration order is made by the court on the application of the Bank of England and appoints a bank administrator who may do anything necessary or expedient for the pursuit of the two statutory objectives[74]. The first objective is the supply to the private sector purchaser or bridge bank of such services and facilities as are required to enable it in the opinion of the Bank of England to operate effectively[75]. This objective ceases when the Bank of England notifies the bank administrator that the residual bank is no longer required in connection with the private sector purchaser or bridge bank[76]. The second objective is what is called 'normal' administration, being the rescue of the residual bank as a going concern and achieving a better result for the residual bank's creditors as a whole than would be likely if the residual bank were to be wound up without first being in bank administration[77]. The first objective takes priority over the second objective, but the bank administrator is required to work towards both objectives from the time of his appointment[78]. The two conditions which have to be met in order for the Bank of England to make the application are first that the Bank of England has made or intends to make a property transfer instrument[79] under sections 11(2) or 12(2) of BA 2009 and secondly that the residual bank is unable to pay its debts or is likely to become unable to do so as a result of the property transfer instrument which the Bank of England proposes to make[80].

19.14   The powers and duties of a bank administrator and the general processes and effects of bank administration are set out in two tables of applied provisions at the end of section 145 of BA 2009. Table 1 applies the relevant paragraphs of Schedule B1 of IA 1986 in modified form and Table 2 applies certain other provisions of IA 1986 in modified form. These include a modified version of the moratorium provisions. They also include a modified version of the obligation of the bank administrator to make a statement setting out his proposals for the achievement of the objectives which reflect participation of the Bank of England in the process, and the bank administrator must send a statement setting out his proposals to the PRA and send a copy of this statement to the FCA[81].

---

71   In accordance with section 11 of BA 2009.
72   In accordance with section 12 of BA 2009.
73   Section 136(2)(c) of BA 2009.
74   Sections 141(1), 142(1) and 145(1) of BA 2009.
75   Sections 137(1)(a) and 138 of BA 2009.
76   Section 139 of BA 2009.
77   Sections 137(1)(b) and 140 of BA 2009.
78   Section 137(2) of BA 2009.
79   Ie an instrument which provides for property, rights or liabilities of a specified bank to be transferred: section 33 of BA 2009.
80   Section 143 of BA 2009.
81   Section 147 of BA 2009. Where the bank is not regulated by the PRA, the statement need only be sent to the FCA (section157A of BA 2009).

There is also a modification of the bank administrator's powers (again to reflect the role of the Bank of England), a right of the Bank of England to participate in any application for directions and the processes for filling a bank administrator vacancy and terminating a bank administration. If the bank administrator makes an application to the court to end the administration under Schedule B1 paragraph 79 of IA 1986, he must send a copy to the PRA and the FCA[82]. There are also restrictions on the circumstances in which the administrator can make a distribution to creditors without Bank of England consent. These and a number of other powers are circumscribed where the bank administrator is still pursuing the first statutory objective. Indeed the whole structure of the legislation focuses on the application of the normal administration process to the extent, but only to the extent that it does not interfere with the achievement of the first statutory objective. Furthermore, once the first statutory objective has been achieved, the legislation contemplates that many of the powers available to a bank administrator while pursuing the second statutory objective can only be exercised having regard to the original achievement of the first statutory objective[83]. Further provision for the relevant procedure is made by the Bank Administration (England and Wales) Rules 2009[84].

INVESTMENT BANK SPECIAL ADMINISTRATION

19.15 The next regime, which was also authorised by BA 2009 but not introduced immediately, was that made available for investment banks by the Investment Bank Special Administration Regulations 2011[85]. This is the special administration regime which has had the most use and is the one in relation to which the courts have been required to give the most guidance[86]. The need for this regime was driven by the absence of an insolvency framework suitable for dealing with failed investment firms and more especially investment firms holding or controlling assets belonging to their clients. This had been thrown into sharp relief by the difficulties which were faced by the administrators of the principal English Lehman company, Lehman Brothers International (Europe), in returning client assets, and the absence of any mechanism for promulgating a scheme of arrangement which varied proprietary rights in those assets[87].

19.16 An investment bank is defined by section 232 of BA 2009 to mean an institution incorporated or formed in the United Kingdom, which has permission

---

82 Section 153 of BA 2009. Where the bank is not regulated by the PRA, the application need only be sent to the FCA (section 157A of BA 2009).

83 Table 2 to section 145 of BA 2009.

84 SI 2009 No 357. The relevant rules in relation to building societies are Building Society Special Administration (England and Wales) Rules 2010 (SI 2010 No 2580).

85 SI 2011 No 245, made under the delegated powers granted by sections 233 and 234 of BA 2009. They came into force on 8 February 2011.

86 *In re M F Global UK Ltd* [2015] EWHC 2319 (Ch); *In re M F Global UK Ltd (in special administration) (No 5)* [2014] EWHC 2222 (Ch); *In re M F Global UK Ltd (No 4)* [2013] EWHC 2556 (Ch); *In re M F Global UK Ltd (No 3)* [2013] EWHC 1655 (Ch); *In re M F Global UK Ltd (No 2)* [2013] EWHC 92 (Ch); *In re M F Global UK Ltd* [2012] EWHC 3068 (Ch); *In Re Worldspreads Ltd* [2015] EWHC 1263 (Ch); *In Re Worldspreads Ltd* [2015] EWHC 1719 (Ch); *In re Hartmann Capital Ltd* [2015] EWHC 1514 (Ch); *In re Hume Capital Securities plc* [2015] EWHC 3717 (Ch)

87 An attempt to promulgate a scheme under section 895 of CA 2006, relying on the clients' status as creditors, had failed for want of jurisdiction: *In re Lehman Brothers International (Europe) (in administration) (No 2)* [2009] EWCA Civ 1161.

to safeguard and administer investments or to deal in investments whether as principal or agent and which holds client assets[88]. Although the regime only applies to institutions incorporated in or formed under the law of any part of the United Kingdom, it covers different types of legal entity including partnerships[89] and limited liability partnerships[90] as well as companies. 'Client assets' includes money, but does not (subject to certain exceptions) include anything which an institution holds for the purposes of carrying on an insurance mediation activity[91]. The holding of client assets is at the core of the definition of an investment bank, because one of the central purposes of the investment bank special administration regime is the introduction of a process which facilitates their return to clients when the investment bank is insolvent. The effect of these definitions is that any institution which provides investment services will be an investment bank if it holds client assets; for that reason, many of the institutions to which the regime has been applied[92] might more accurately be described as investment firms.

19.17 An investment bank special administration order is an order of the court appointing an insolvency practitioner to be an investment bank administrator[93] who is required to pursue the special administration objectives in accordance with the proposals approved by creditors, clients and (in some circumstances) the relevant regulator, ie the FCA or the PRA[94]. The three special administration objectives are[95] to ensure the return of client assets as soon as is reasonably practicable, to ensure timely engagement with market infrastructure bodies and the authorities[96] and either to rescue the investment bank as a going concern, or to wind it up in the best interests of the creditors. The concept of a return of client assets includes the transfer of those assets to another institution[97], although the Investment Bank Special Administration Regulations 2011 do not make explicit provision for a mechanism to facilitate any such transfers. This is an omission

---

88 'Client assets' means assets which an institution has undertaken to hold for a client (whether or not on trust and whether or not the undertaking has been complied with): section 232(4) of BA 2009.

89 Regulation 25 and Schedule 4 of the Investment Bank Special Administration Regulations 2011 (SI 2011 No 245).

90 Regulation 24 and Schedule 3 of the Investment Bank Special Administration Regulations 2011 (SI 2011 No 245).

91 Section 232(5A) of BA 2009 and article 2 of the Investment Bank (Amendment of Definition) Order 2011 (SI 2011 No 239).

92 In the FCA's Discussion Paper (DP16/2) on the Special Administration Regime Review, it listed the following SAR appointments as at March 2016: M F Global UK Ltd (broker dealers), Pritchards Stockbrokers Ltd (stockbroker), Worldspreads Ltd (spread betting), Fysche Horton Finney Ltd (stockbroker), City Equities Ltd (stockbroker), Hartmann Capital Ltd (stockbroker), Alpari (UK) Ltd (FX broker), LQD Markets (UK) Ltd (FX broker), Boston Prime Ltd (FX and CFD prime broker), Hume Capital Securities plc (stockbroker), Maple Securities (UK) Ltd (securities broker/dealer) and Avalon Investment Services Ltd (investment administrator for ISAs and SIPPs). Since then, European Pensions Management Ltd (SIPP provider) and Solo Capital Partners LLP (investment services) have entered special administration.

93 Regulation 4 of the Investment Bank Special Administration Regulations 2011 (SI 2011 No 245).

94 Regulation 3(2) of the Investment Bank Special Administration Regulations 2011 (SI 2011 No 245).

95 Regulation 10 of the Investment Bank Special Administration Regulations 2011 (SI 2011 No 245).

96 The Bank of England, the Treasury, the FCA and the PRA: regulation 2(1) of the Investment Bank Special Administration Regulations 2011 (SI 2011 No 245).

97 Section 233(4) of BA 2009.

which was discussed in the Bloxham review of the Investment Bank Special Administration Regulations 2011[98], and the government has indicated that the law will amended to deal with the point.

19.18 An investment bank special administration order can be made by the court on the application of the same categories of person who can make an application for a normal administration order under Schedule B1 paragraph 12 of IA 1986, together with a contributory of the company[99], the Secretary of State, the FCA and the PRA[100]. The FCA and (where appropriate) the PRA are entitled to be heard on the application and notice must be given to the investment bank itself (if not the applicant), the proposed special administrator, any person who has notified the FCA or the PRA that it is seeking the commencement of insolvency proceedings, and any supervisor of a CVA[101]. The grounds for applying for a special administration order are one of the following:

(a) that the investment bank is or is likely to become unable to pay its debts[102];

(b) that it would be fair to put the investment bank into special administration; or

(c) that it is expedient in the public interest to put the investment bank into special administration[103].

Where the fairness ground is relied on by members of the investment bank as contributories, there is a provision[104] which appears to draw on section 125(2) of IA 1986, so as to restrict the making of a special administration order where an alternative remedy is available and they are acting unreasonably in not pursuing it.

19.19 There are restrictions on the following steps being taken in relation to an investment bank, each of which is designed to ensure that full consideration can be given to whether special administration is the appropriate way forward before any other form of insolvency procedure is implemented:

(a) the making of an application for an administration order;

(b) the presentation of a petition to wind up;

(c) the passing of a resolution to wind up; and

(d) the appointment of an administrator.

---

98 Final Review of the Investment Bank Special Administration Regulations 2011 by Peter Bloxham presented to Parliament pursuant to section 236 of BA 2009 in January 2014.

99 Subject to the limitations in regulation 5(7) of the Investment Bank Special Administration Regulations 2011 (SI 2011 No 245).

100 Regulation 5(1) of the Investment Bank Special Administration Regulations 2011 (SI 2011 No 245).

101 Regulation 5(4) of the Investment Bank Special Administration Regulations 2011 (SI 2011 No 245) and Rule 10 of the Investment Bank Special Administration (England and Wales) Rules 2011 (SI 2011 No 1301).

102 Within the meaning of section 123 of IA 1986: section 117(5) of the Financial Services (Banking Reform) Act 2013.

103 Regulation 6(1) of the Investment Bank Special Administration Regulations 2011 (SI 2011 No 245). Ground (a) can be relied on by any applicant apart from the Secretary of State, ground (b) can be relied on by any applicant, and ground (c) can only be relied on by the Secretary of State, taking the same approach as he would take if seeking a winding up order on public interest grounds under section 124A of IA 1986.

104 Regulation 7(3) of the Investment Bank Special Administration Regulations 2011 (SI 2011 No 245).

None of these steps can be taken unless the FCA or the PRA has been given notice of the preliminary step in relation to the relevant procedure, that notice has been filed in court, a period of two weeks has expired with the FCA or the PRA consenting to the procedure, and no application for a special administration order is pending[105]. The FCA or the PRA (as the case may be) is then required to inform the applicant whether or not it consents to the relevant insolvency procedure, or whether it proposes to apply itself for that procedure or some other insolvency procedure, or whether it intends to apply for a special administration order[106].

19.20 Regulation 11 of the Investment Bank Special Administration Regulations 2011 makes provisions for facilitating the achievement of the first objective (namely the expeditious return of client assets), and in particular for the setting of a bar date by which claims to ownership of, and security interests in, client assets are to be submitted[107]. Reasonable notice of the bar date must be given so as to enable claimants sufficient time to calculate and submit their claims, and Part 5 of the Investment Bank Special Administration (England and Wales) Rules 2011 then provides for the mechanism of returning client assets after the bar date has passed, including in particular the drawing up of a distribution plan which must be approved by any creditors' committee and the court[108]. Late claims can be made, but there is to be no disruption to client assets already returned and the recipient obtains good title as against the late claimant[109]. It should be noted that although the objective of returning client assets extends to client monies, the bar date provisions do not[110]. This gave rise to difficulties in *MF Global*[111], and the Bloxham review[112] recommended that the law should be changed, a recommendation which the government has accepted in principle but which has not yet been implemented. Although these bar date provisions do not apply to client monies[113], in *In re M F Global UK Ltd (No 3)*[114] the court exercised its inherent jurisdiction[115] and sanctioned a procedure to facilitate the return of client monies, which was based on the rules as they applied to bar dates for other client assets.

---

105 Regulation 8 of the Investment Bank Special Administration Regulations 2011 (SI 2011 No 245).

106 Regulation 8(6) of the Investment Bank Special Administration Regulations 2011 (SI 2011 No 245).

107 It should be noted that although the objective of returning client assets extends to client monies, the bar date provisions do not.

108 Rules 144–146 of the Investment Bank Special Administration (England and Wales) Rules 2011 (SI 2011 No 1301). For a case in which approval was given see *In re Hume Capital Securities Plc* [2015] EWHC 3717 (Ch).

109 Regulation 11(5) of the Investment Bank Special Administration Regulations 2011 (SI 2011 No 245), although this does not arise in the case of a return made in bad faith and where a recipient made a 'false claim'. Rule 147 of the Investment Bank Special Administration (England and Wales) Rules 2011 (SI 2011 No 1301).

110 Regulation 11(8) of of Investment Bank Special Administration Regulations 2011 (SI 2011 No 245).

111 *In re M F Global UK Ltd (No 3)* [2013] EWHC 1655 (Ch).

112 Final Review of the Investment Bank Special Administration Regulations 2011 by Peter Bloxham presented to Parliament pursuant to section 236 of BA 2009 in January 2014.

113 Regulation 11(8) of of the Investment Bank Special Administration Regulations 2011 (SI 2011 No 245). The Bloxham review recommended that the law should be changed, a recommendation which the government has accepted in principle but which has not yet been implemented.

114 *In re M F Global UK Ltd (No 3)* [2013] EWHC 1655 (Ch). See also *Re Worldspreads Ltd* [2015] EWHC 1719 (Ch).

115 Cf *In re Benjamin* [1902] 1 Ch 723.

19.21 Regulation 12 of the Investment Bank Special Administration Regulations 2011 then makes further provision for how the statutory objective of returning client assets is to be achieved where client assets are held in an omnibus account, and there is a shortfall in the amount available for distribution of securities of a particular description. In such a case, the special administrator is required to ensure that the shortfall is borne pro rata by all affected clients and, if there is a dispute as to how that is to be done which cannot be resolved by agreement, the affected securities may be lodged with the court, thereby discharging his obligation to achieve the first objective in respect of those securities. A client has what is called a shortfall claim against the investment bank in respect of any shortfall, the amount of which is based on the market price of the relevant securities on the date that the investment bank entered special administration.

19.22 The interrelationship between a client's claim to client assets and its claim as a creditor of the investment bank was considered in *In re M F Global UK Ltd (No 2)*[116] and *In re M F Global UK Ltd (in special administration) (No 4)*[117]. The issues arose in relation to client monies, as distinct from other forms of client asset. In the first of these decisions, it was held that as the client's underlying entitlement to client monies arose under Chapters 7 and 7A of the FCA's Client Assets Sourcebook, it was to be valued by reference to market value as at the date of the administrator's appointment[118], without the application of any hindsight. In the second decision[119] it was held that any distributions from the client money pool would reduce pro tanto the amount of the client's claim in its capacity as a creditor, whether that distribution took place before or after the time of the client's proof. The client would also have a shortfall claim for the difference between the client money entitlement and the amount in fact recovered from the client money pool. This was quantified by the extent to which the investment bank had defaulted in its obligation under CASS 7 and 7A to maintain the client money at the required level.

19.23 The powers and duties of a special administrator and the general processes and effects of investment bank administration are set out in two tables of applied provisions at the end of regulation 15 of the Investment Bank Special Administration Regulations 2011. As with bank administration, Table 1 applies the relevant paragraphs of Schedule B1 of IA 1986 in modified form and Table 2 applies certain other provisions of IA 1986 in modified form. The most important of these changes relate to the participation of clients and their entitlements in respect of client assets. They are entitled to receive information in the same way as creditors, to attend creditors' meetings and to receive the statement by which the special administrator sets out his proposals for the achievement of the objectives. The clients' voting rights at any meetings are prescribed by the rules and provide for the client to vote for the value of the relevant security or client asset, but claiming as a creditor in respect of any shortfall[120]. Detailed provisions for proving and valuation of claims for distribution purposes are contained in the Investment Bank Special Administration (England and Wales) Rules 2011. It should be noted that one of the differences between investment bank special administration and normal administration is that distributions can be made

---

116 [2013] EWHC 92 (Ch).
117 [2013] EWHC 2556 (Ch).
118 The time of the primary pooling event for the purposes of CASS 7 and 7A.
119 *In re MF Global UK Ltd (in special administration) (No 4)* [2013] EWHC 2556 (Ch).
120 Rules 90 and 91 of the Investment Bank Special Administration (England and Wales) Rules 2011 (SI 2011 No 1301).

without the leave of the court[121], although the consent of the Bank of England is required if a distribution is sought to be made before the return of client assets has been achieved[122].

19.24 Most of the other parts of Schedule B1 of IA 1986 which relate to normal administration orders are applied to investment bank special administration, and the court will normally adopt the same approach in applying the applicable principles[123]. Notwithstanding that fact, when an investment bank enters special administration under the 2011 Regulations, it does not enter administration under Part II of IA 1986; the regime is different[124]. Thus the special administrator's powers include the general power of compromise[125], which was exercised in the case of *MF Global* with the court's approval, so as to enable a compromise to be effected between the investment bank's general estate and the investment bank in its capacity as trustee of the client money trust[126].

19.25 Where the investment bank is also a bank in respect of which a bank administration order can be made under Part 3 of BA 2009[127], there is provision made by Regulation 9 and Schedule 2 of the Investment Bank Special Administration Regulations 2011 for the making of what is called a special administration (bank administration) order. This is designed to combine the objectives of a bank administration with the objectives of an investment bank administration in a manner which gives priority to the first objective of a bank administration[128] (ie the supply to the private sector purchaser of a bank's business, or bridge bank, of such services and facilities as are required to enable it in the opinion of the Bank of England to operate effectively[129]). There are a large number of detailed changes to the regime in those circumstances but the essential structure is that the approach for a normal investment bank special administration is applied with such modifications as are appropriate to reflect the preference given to the first objective of bank administration and an enhanced role for the Bank of England, the FCA and the PRA.

FMI ADMINISTRATION

19.26 The next relevant procedure is special administration for the operation of certain financial market infrastructure systems known as FMI administration. This was introduced by Part 6 of the Financial Services (Banking Reform)

---

121 Schedule B1 paragraph 65(3) is disapplied.
122 Rule 148(3) of the Investment Bank Special Administration (England and Wales) Rules 2011 (SI 2011 No 1301).
123 Thus one of the recent leading cases on the extra territorial effect of section 236 of IA 1986, as applied to investment bank administration by Table 2 is *In re MF Global UK Ltd (in special administration)* [2015] EWHC 2319 (Ch).
124 *In re Hartmann Capital Ltd (in special administration)* [2015] EWHC 1514 (Ch), and therefore the pre-LASPO provisions relating to conditional fee agreements in insolvency proceedings did not apply. The position is *a fortiori* when comparing the special administration regime to liquidation, as to which the essential characteristics are very different: *In re M F Global UK Limited (in special administration)* [2012] EWHC 3068 (Ch).
125 Schedule 1 paragraph 18 of IA 1986 as applied by regulation 15 Table 1 of the Investment Bank Special Administration Regulations 2011 (SI 2011 No 245).
126 *In re M F Global UK Ltd (in special administration) (No 5)* [2014] EWHC 2222 (Ch).
127 As to which see the section on Bank Administration above.
128 Schedule 2 paragraph 3 of the Investment Bank Special Administration Regulations 2011 (SI 2011 No 245).
129 Sections 137(1)(a) and 138 of BA 2009.

Act 2013 with provision for the relevant procedure to be made by the Financial Market Infrastructure Administration (England and Wales) Rules 2017[130]. At the time of writing the primary legislation has been enacted but is not yet in force and the Rules are still in draft. The companies to which it is applied are the operators of recognised inter-bank payment systems and securities settlement systems together with other companies providing services to such operators where HM Treasury is satisfied that an interruption in the provision of those services would have a serious adverse effect on the effective operation of the recognised inter-bank payment system or securities settlement system in question[131]. For the purposes of the legislation, these companies are called infrastructure companies.

19.27 An FMI administration order is intended to be an order of the court which directs that during the period for which it is in force the affairs, business and property of the infrastructure company are to be managed by an FMI administrator so as to achieve the objectives set out in section 115 of the Financial Services (Banking Reform) Act 2013[132]. The objectives will be:

(a) to secure that the system[133] is and continues to be maintained and operated as an efficient and effective system;

(b) that where the operator of the system is also a clearing house, to ensure that the protected activities[134] continue to be carried on; and

(c) that it becomes unnecessary for the FMI administration order to remain in force for that purpose[135].

19.28 The means by which the objectives are to be achieved are the rescue of the company as a going concern and/or a transfer as a going concern to another company of so much of that undertaking as it is appropriate to transfer for the purpose of achieving the objective[136]. The means by which transfers may be effected include, in particular, a hive-down to a subsidiary of the infrastructure company and a transfer of shares in the hive-down company[137]. A transfer is only to be effected where a rescue as a going concern is not reasonably practicable[138], where the rescue of that company as a going concern will not achieve the objective[139], or where such transfer would produce a result for the company's creditors as a whole that is better than the result that would be produced without it[140].

19.29 An FMI administration order can only be made in relation to an infrastructure company by the court on the application of the Bank of England[141]. Notice will have to be given to the infrastructure company[142]. The draft

---

130   In draft at the time of writing.
131   Section 112(2) of the Financial Services (Banking Reform) Act 2013.
132   Section 114(3) of the Financial Services (Banking Reform) Act 2013.
133   Ie the recognised inter-bank payment systems and securities settlement system: section 113(1) of the Financial Services (Banking Reform) Act 2013.
134   Designated as such by the Bank of England.
135   Section 115(1) of the Financial Services (Banking Reform) Act 2013.
136   Section 115(4) of the Financial Services (Banking Reform) Act 2013.
137   Section 115(6) of the Financial Services (Banking Reform) Act 2013.
138   Or is not reasonably practicable without such transfers.
139   Or will not do so without such transfers.
140   Section 115(7) of the Financial Services (Banking Reform) Act 2013.
141   Section 116(1) of the Financial Services (Banking Reform) Act 2013.
142   Section 116(3) of the Financial Services (Banking Reform) Act 2013.

Financial Market Infrastructure Administration (England and Wales) Rules 2017[143] also require notice of an application to be given to the proposed FMI administrator, any person entitled to appoint an administrator, any petitioner seeking a winding up order, the infrastructure company itself, any applicant for an administration order and any person seeking to enforce security over property of the infrastructure company[144]. The conditions which will have to be satisfied before an FMI administration order can be made are one of the following:

(a) that the company is or is likely to become unable to pay its debts[145]; or

(b) that on a petition by the Secretary of State it would otherwise be just and equitable for the company to be wound up on public interest grounds, and the Secretary of State has given a certificate to that effect[146].

19.30 There is to be a prohibition against:

(a) the making of a winding up order against an infrastructure company on a petition by any person other than the Bank of England,

(b) the passing by an infrastructure company of a resolution to wind up without permission of the court, and

(c) the making of an administration order under Part II of IA 1986,

in each case without first giving to the Bank of England at least 14 days' notice of the petition, the application for leave or the application for an administration order as the case may be[147]. It seems that the purpose behind these provisions is to give the Bank of England sufficient time to determine whether it wishes to make an application for an FMI administration order under section 116 of the Financial Services (Banking Reform) Act 2013. Unlike the companies to which a number of other special administration regimes apply, the Act does not appear to prevent an infrastructure company from entering administration out of court (pursuant to Schedule B1 paragraph 14 or 21 of IA 1986)[148], nor does it contain any restrictions on out-of-court appointment when an application for an FMI administration order is outstanding, nor does it require prior notice of any appointment to be given to the Bank of England. There is however a prohibition against any person enforcing any security over the property of an FMI company except where that person has served 14 days' notice of his intention to take that step on the Bank of England[149], which may extend to any out-of-court appointment by the holder of a qualifying floating charge.

19.31 An FMI administrator will be an officer of the court, will act as the agent of the infrastructure company and will have to exercise his powers for the purpose of achieving the statutory objective as quickly and efficiently as possible and (so far as consistent with that objective) in a manner which best protects the interests of the company's creditors as a whole[150]. The relevant

---

143 Rule 7.

144 So long as notified to the Bank of England.

145 Within the meaning of section 123 of IA 1986: section 117(5) of the Financial Services (Banking Reform) Act 2013.

146 Section 117(1) and (2) of the Financial Services (Banking Reform) Act 2013.

147 Sections 122 and 123 of the Financial Services (Banking Reform) Act 2013.

148 Section 249(1) of the Enterprise Act 2002, which replaced the original Part II of IA 1986 with Schedule B1, does not list infrastructure companies as one of the categories of excluded entity.

149 Section 124 of the Financial Services (Banking Reform) Act 2013.

150 Section 118 of the Financial Services (Banking Reform) Act 2013 and subject to that the interests of the company's members as a whole.

parts of Schedule B1 of IA 1986 which relate to a normal administration are also to be applied to the conduct of an FMI administration with appropriate modifications[151]. The principal changes are to enable the Bank of England to participate in the FMI administration and in particular to enable it to receive the administrator's proposals and to participate in and be notified of the ending of the FMI administration. There are also detailed provisions which are beyond the scope of this work, but which empower the Treasury to make loans and give indemnities to an infrastructure company in FMI administration[152].

19.32 As with a number of the public sector special administration regimes, section 121(2) and Schedule 7 of Financial Services (Banking Reform) Act 2013 make provision for transfer schemes to be made by the infrastructure company (acting through the FMI administrator), for the purpose of giving effect to a proposed transfer intended to achieve the objective of FMI administration. Such a scheme can transfer property rights and liabilities at a time appointed by the court, but that time must not be appointed by the court unless the scheme has been approved by the Bank of England[153]. In approving the transfer scheme the Bank of England is required to consult with the Treasury, and to have regard to the public interest and the effect which the scheme is likely to have on third parties (amongst whom it is to be expected that creditors will feature prominently)[154]. The categories of property, rights and liabilities which are capable of transfer are broadly defined, and include property located anywhere in the world, rights and liabilities governed by any law, and property rights and liabilities which would not otherwise be capable of transfer, and whether or not consent by third parties would otherwise require to be given[155]. Schedule 7 paragraphs 6 to 10 of the Financial Services (Banking Reform) Act 2013 contain widely drafted provision for the effectiveness of the transfer.

COOPERATIVE AND COMMUNITY BENEFIT SOCIETIES

19.33 The administration of cooperative and community benefit societies is governed by the Co-operative and Community Benefit Societies and Credit Unions (Arrangements, Reconstructions and Administration) Order 2014[156], which applies Parts 1 and 2 of IA 1986 to such societies, with certain modifications[157]. The 2014 Order also applies section 176A of IA 1986 to the administration of a society[158] together with the whole of Parts 6, 7 and 12 to 19 of IA 1986 as if it were a company[159]. There are also a number of provisions of FSMA 2000, dealing with the rights of the Financial Services Compensation Scheme and the relevant regulator (either FCA or PRA) to participate in the

---

151 Section 121(1) and Schedule 6 of the Financial Services (Banking Reform) Act 2013.
152 Sections 125 and 126 of the Financial Services (Banking Reform) Act 2013.
153 Schedule 7 paragraph 4 of the Financial Services (Banking Reform) Act 2013.
154 Schedule 7 paragraph 4(7) and (8) of the Financial Services (Banking Reform) Act 2013.
155 Schedule 7 paragraph 5 of the Financial Services (Banking Reform) Act 2013.
156 SI 2014 No 229 made pursuant to section 255(1)(a) of the Enterprise Act 2002.
157 Article 2 and Schedule 1 of the Co-operative and Community Benefit Societies and Credit Unions (Arrangements, Reconstructions and Administration) Order 2014 (SI 2014 No 229).
158 Thus, where a society goes into administration, the prescribed part must be made available out of the society's net assets in the same way as would occur if a society were a company.
159 Article 4 of of the Co-operative and Community Benefit Societies and Credit Unions (Arrangements, Reconstructions and Administration) Order 2014 (SI 2014 No 229).

administration[160], including also the right to apply to the court for the appointment of a replacement administrator[161]. These specific modifications to Parts 1 and 2 of IA 1986 are relatively minor, and are all concerned with ensuring that the procedures for a voluntary arrangement or administration of a cooperative and community benefit society reflect the difference in characteristics between such a society and the companies to which those Parts were enacted to apply.

19.34 The main modification to the voluntary arrangement provisions is that the members of a society are treated as creditors in respect of their members' share, where the society is an authorised deposit taker and the amount is owed in respect of a deposit[162]. Otherwise the only change is that the FCA has a role in the prosecution of delinquent officers under section 7A of IA 1986. So far as the Schedule A1 moratorium provisions are concerned, the main difference is that the phrase 'floating charge' is defined to mean both floating charges registered under section 59 of the Cooperative and Community Benefit Societies Act 2014 and floating charges created by a debenture registered under section 9 of the Agricultural Credits Act 1928[163].

19.35 These modifications are also reflected in the modifications made to Schedule B1 of IA 1986 in its application to the administration of a cooperative and community benefit society. Thus, the members of a society owed any amount in respect of a deposit fall within the class of a society's 'creditors as a whole'[164], and the administrator is empowered[165] to make a distribution to members of any society which is a deposit taker where the proposed distribution is in respect of any amount owed in respect of a deposit. In the same vein, the administrator's proposals must be put before a meeting of members, and there are a number of modifications to Schedule B1 of IA 1986 which reflect the principle that in some respects it is appropriate to treat the members of a society in the same manner as the creditors of a company[166]. Likewise, members are treated as creditors for the service of notice of termination where the objective of administration has been achieved, or where the society is to move from administration to dissolution[167]. The definition of a floating charge is also modified in

---

160 Articles 5–10 of the Co-operative and Community Benefit Societies and Credit Unions (Arrangements, Reconstructions and Administration) Order 2014 (SI 2014 No 229).

161 Schedule 1 paragraph 32 of the Co-operative and Community Benefit Societies and Credit Unions (Arrangements, Reconstructions and Administration) Order 2014 (SI 2014 No 229), modifying Schedule B1 paragraph 91 of IA 1986.

162 Schedule 1 paragraphs 3 and 4 of the Co-operative and Community Benefit Societies and Credit Unions (Arrangements, Reconstructions and Administration) Order 2014 (SI 2014 No 229).

163 The forms of floating security which are capable of being effective when granted over goods and other assets by a society, because the registration requirements of the Bills of Sale Act (1878) Amendment Act 1882 are excluded: see section 59(2) of the Cooperative and Community Benefit Societies Act 2014 and section 8(1) of the Agricultural Credits Act 1928. For further details on agricultural floating charges see **CHAPTER 16** *ante*.

164 For the purposes of a modified Schedule B1 paragraph 3 of IA 1986: Schedule 1 paragraph 11 of the Co-operative and Community Benefit Societies and Credit Unions (Arrangements, Reconstructions and Administration) Order 2014 (SI 2014 No 229).

165 By a modified Schedule B1 paragraph 65 of IA 1986: Schedule 1 paragraph 29 of the Co-operative and Community Benefit Societies and Credit Unions (Arrangements, Reconstructions and Administration) Order 2014 (SI 2014 No 229).

166 Schedule 1 paragraphs 18–25 of the Co-operative and Community Benefit Societies and Credit Unions (Arrangements, Reconstructions and Administration) Order 2014 (SI 2014 No 229).

167 Schedule B1 paragraphs 80 and 84 of IA 1986, as modified by Schedule 1 paragraphs 30 and 31 of the Co-operative and Community Benefit Societies and Credit Unions (Arrangements, Reconstructions and Administration) Order 2014 (SI 2014 No 229).

exactly the same manner as that described above in relation to the Schedule A1 moratorium[168]. There are then a number of changes which reflect the involvement of the relevant regulator; this is consistent with the application of the relevant FSMA 2000 provisions described above. Thus the administrator's proposals can include provision for an amendment of the society's rules, but only if the FCA states that it would be prepared to register an amendment in the terms proposed. Not surprisingly the proposals cannot include anything which is contrary to the provisions of the society's governing legislation nor can provisions be included in any amendment to the rules if the intended effect is that the society will cease to be a registered society[169]. Finally there are some changes to the administrator's powers under Schedule 1 of IA 1986, to limit the administrator's power to borrow, to grant security, to establish subsidiaries and to transfer property to them, distinguishing between societies which are credit unions, and those which are not[170].

---

168 Schedule 1 paragraph 34(a) of the Co-operative and Community Benefit Societies and Credit Unions (Arrangements, Reconstructions and Administration) Order 2014 (SI 2014 No 229).
169 Schedule 1 paragraph 18 of the Co-operative and Community Benefit Societies and Credit Unions (Arrangements, Reconstructions and Administration) Order 2014 (SI 2014 No 229).
170 Schedule 1 paragraphs 35–40 of the Co-operative and Community Benefit Societies and Credit Unions (Arrangements, Reconstructions and Administration) Order 2014 (SI 2014 No 229).

20 Public sector special administration regimes

INTRODUCTION

20.1 Since the enactment of IA 1986, the legislature has introduced a number of special administration regimes for companies carrying out a statutory function of a public nature, where their functions are funded (anyway partially) by private sector finance. Where a company operates in that particular sector, it may be appropriate for an administrator to be appointed to manage its affairs, business and property, but the public interest may require the objectives with which he is required to act to be modified. In a number of these regimes, the furtherance of those objectives is facilitated by statutory provision for the making of a scheme, either for the reorganisation of rights interests and liabilities which are not otherwise capable of being reorganised by the procedures available more generally, or for the transfer of such assets, interest and liabilities to another person. The usual structure is that the special regime draws on some of the principles underpinning the administration regime which is available for companies generally, but includes additional purposes which will normally take priority over, or even replace altogether, the objectives for which an ordinary administrator is required to perform his functions. Those purposes will invariably include the transfer to another company as a going concern of so much of its undertaking as it is necessary to transfer in order to ensure that its statutory functions or activities may be properly carried on, together with the carrying on of those functions or activities pending such transfer. In most instances, the regime can only be initiated by the court making a special administration order, and the company concerned is not permitted to enter normal administration by any of the routes for which provision is made by Schedule B1 of IA 1986.

20.2 A detailed consideration of the structure of each of these special administration regimes is beyond the scope of this work, but the remainder of this chapter identifies each of the categories of activity to which such a regime applies, and summarises how it works. The regimes with which this chapter is concerned are those that have been introduced for water and sewerage undertakers[1], protected railways companies[2], public private partnership ('PPP') companies[3], licence companies providing air traffic services[4], protected energy

1   Sections 23–26 of the Water Industry Act 1991.
2   Sections 59–65 of the Railways Act 1993.
3   Sections 220–224 of the Greater London Authority Act 1999.
4   Sections 26–32 of the Transport Act 2000.

companies and energy supply companies[5], NHS foundation trusts[6] and universal postal service providers[7]. There are also a number of other regimes which are either on the statute book (but not yet in force) or in contemplation; brief reference will be made to them at the end of this chapter. They are health special administration, housing administration and further education administration.

SPECIAL ADMINISTRATION FOR WATER UNDERTAKERS

20.3   The first category of entity for which a special administration regime was introduced was companies holding an appointment under Part II Chapter I of the Water Industry Act 1991, ie as the water undertaker or sewerage undertaker for any area of England and Wales[8]. This jurisdiction was extended to a qualified licensed water supplier by the Water Act 2003[9]. The statutory purposes are the transfer to another company or companies, as a going concern, of so much of its undertaking as it is necessary to transfer in order to ensure that the functions which have been vested in the company by virtue of its appointment may be properly carried out, together with the carrying out of those functions pending the making of the transfer and the vesting[10].

20.4   A special administration order can only be made in relation to a water undertaker, a sewerage undertaker or a qualified licensed water supplier by the court on the petition of the Secretary of State or the Water Services Regulation Authority[11]. The grounds for making a special administration order include:

(a)   the actual or anticipated contravention of certain duties and enforcement orders;

(b)   that the company is or is likely to become unable to pay its debts[12]; and

(c)   that the Secretary of State has certified that it would otherwise be just and equitable for the company to be wound up on public interest grounds[13].

20.5   There is a provision[14] not yet in force to the effect that where a company is in special administration as a result of an order made on the grounds that it is or is likely to be unable to pay its debts, a purpose of the special administration order is to rescue the company as a going concern. To that end, the statutory purpose of effecting a transfer only applies if the special administrator thinks that it is not likely to be possible to rescue the company as a going concern, or the transfer is likely to secure more effective performance of the statutory

---

5   Sections 154–171 of the Energy Act 2004 and sections 94–101 of the Energy Act 2011.
6   Chapter 5A of the National Health Service Act 2006.
7   Sections 68–78 of the Postal Services Act 2011.
8   Section 23 of the Water Industry Act 1991.
9   Schedule 8 paragraph 8(2) of the Water Act 2003 amended by section 23 of the Water Industry Act 1991.
10   Section 23(2) of the Water Industry Act 1991. In the case of a qualified water supplier the transfer is of so much of the company's undertaking as it is necessary to transfer in order to ensure that activities relating to the introduction of water may be properly carried on: section 23(2A) of the Water Act 1991.
11   Where the petition is presented in respect of a qualified licensed water supplier the National Assembly for Wales must first be consulted and where it is presented by the Authority, the consent of the Secretary of State must first be obtained: section 24(1) and (1A) of the Water Industry Act 1991.
12   Within the meaning of section 123 of IA 1986: section 24(6) of the Water Industry Act 1991.
13   Section 24(2) of the Water Industry Act 1991.
14   Section 23(2B) and (2C) of the Water Industry Act 1991.

functions. A special administrator is then specifically authorised to propose a voluntary arrangement under Part 1 of IA 1986 or a scheme of arrangement under Part 26 of CA 2006 for the purpose of rescuing the company as a going concern[15].

20.6 There is a prohibition against the making of a winding up order against a water undertaker, a sewerage undertaker or a qualified licensed water supplier, but if a winding up petition is presented against such an entity, the court may make a special administration order on that petition if it is satisfied that it would otherwise have been appropriate to make a winding up order[16]. Where a company is a water undertaker, a sewerage undertaker or a qualified licensed water supplier it cannot be wound up voluntarily and no ordinary administration order can be made against it[17], nor can it enter administration under the regime introduced by Schedule B1 of IA 1986, because section 248 of Enterprise Act 2002 which replaced the original Part II of IA 1986 with Schedule B1 has no effect in relation to any such entity[18]. There is also a prohibition against any person enforcing any security over its property except where that person has served 14 days' notice of his intention to take that step on the Secretary of State and on the Water Services Regulation Authority[19].

20.7 These provisions were originally enacted before Schedule B1 was introduced into IA 1986, and in any event (as mentioned above), it has no effect in relation to any such entity[20]. As a result the drafting device used to apply the most appropriate parts of Part II of IA 1986 to the special administration regime was to enact a schedule to the Water Industry Act 1991 which applied sections 11 to 15, 17 to 23 and 27 of the original form of IA 1986 to the regime with appropriate modifications[21]. The principal changes were to enable the Secretary of State and the Water Services Regulation Authority to participate in the special administration and in particular to enable it to apply for the appointment of a new railway administrator on a vacancy, to receive the section 23 proposals and to give them locus to apply to court to secure achievement of the statutory purpose where the special administrator is not exercising his powers to that end[22]. Section 23(3) has now been amended to provide that Schedule B1 is to apply subject to regulations to be made by the Secretary of State, which may apply, disapply or modify the effect of any provision in IA 1986 or any other enactment about insolvency. This exceptionally wide power has not yet been exercised and so at the time of writing the modified provisions of the original Part II of IA 1986 continue to apply to water special administrations. Provision for the relevant procedure is made by the Water Industry (Special Administration) Rules 2009[23], which set out a complete procedural code modelled on the Insolvency Rules 1986. The 1986 Rules continue to have effect for the purposes of the application of the 2009 Rules[24].

15 Section 23(2D) of the Water Industry Act 1991, not in force at the time of writing.
16 Section 25 of the Water Industry Act 1991.
17 Section 26 of the Water Industry Act 1991.
18 Section 249(1)(a) and (aa) of the Enterprise Act 2002.
19 Section 26(1) of the Water Industry Act 1991. 'Security' and 'property' have the same meanings as they do in IA 1986, as to which see sections 248(b) and 436(1) of IA 1986.
20 Section 249(1)(a) and (aa) of the Enterprise Act 2002.
21 Section 23(3) and Schedule 3 of the Water Industry Act 1991.
22 Schedule 3 paragraphs 3, 9 and 10 of the Water Industry Act 1991.
23 SI 2009 No 2477.
24 Rule 3(f) of the Insolvency (England and Wales) Rules 2016 (Consequential Amendments and Savings) Rules 2017 (SI 2017 No 369), although in the light of rule 5(2) of Water Industry (Special Administration) Rules 2009, this saving provision has little practical impact.

RAILWAY ADMINISTRATION

20.8 The next category of entity for which a special administration regime was introduced was the making of a railway administration order in respect of a protected railway company within the meaning of section 59(6) of the Railways Act 1993. A protected railway company is a private sector operator which also holds one or more operating licences within the meaning of Part 1 of that Act[25]. A railway administration order is an order of the court which directs that during the period for which it is in force the affairs, business and property of the company are to be managed by a railway administrator for the achievement of the purposes of the order and in a manner which protects the respective interests of the members and creditors of the company[26]. A railway administration order may also be made against unregistered companies, including foreign companies as defined[27]. The statutory purposes are the transfer to another company or companies, as a going concern, of so much of the company's undertaking as it is necessary to transfer in order to ensure that the relevant activities may be properly carried on and the carrying on of those relevant activities pending the making of the transfer[28]. Those activities are the carriage of passengers by railway, or the management of a network, station or light maintenance depot, depending on the nature of the licence held by the company concerned[29].

20.9 A railway administration order can only be made in relation to a protected railway company by the court on the petition of the Secretary of State who (in England Wales) is also the appropriate national authority[30]. The grounds for making a railway administration order are:

(a) that the company is or is likely to become unable to pay its debts[31]; and

(b) that the Secretary of State has certified that it would otherwise be just and equitable for the company to be wound up on public interest grounds[32].

20.10 There is a prohibition against:

(a) the making of a winding up order against a protected railway company on a petition by any person other than the Secretary of State;

(b) the passing by a protected railway company of a resolution to wind up without leave of the court; and

(c) the making of an administration order under Part II of IA 1986, in each case without first giving the appropriate national authority at least 14 days' notice of the petition, the application for leave or the application for an administration order as the case may be[33].

In all such circumstances the appropriate national authority is then empowered to apply for a railway administration order, and the court may make a special

---

25 A passenger licence, a European licence which authorises the carriage of passengers by railway (or both), a network licence, a station licence or a light maintenance depot licence, all within the meaning of section 89 of the Railways Act 1993.
26 Section 59(1) of the Railways Act 1993.
27 Section 65 of the Railways Act 1993.
28 Section 59(2) of the Railways Act 1993.
29 Section 59(6)(b) of the Railways Act 1993.
30 Section 60(1A) of the Railways Act 1993.
31 Within the meaning of section 123 of IA 1986: section 60(6) of the Railways Act 1993.
32 Section 60(2) of the Railways Act 1993.
33 Sections 61(1), 62(1) and 62(5) of the Railways Act 1993.

administration order on that petition if it is satisfied that either of the two grounds identified in section 60(2) of Railways Act 1993 is satisfied[34]. This structure has been said to indicate a legislative preference that a protected railway company should not be wound up and that all or part of its undertaking should be transferred to another company as a going concern, its relevant activities having been carried on in the interim[35]. It is also to be noted that a protected railways company cannot enter administration under the regime introduced by Schedule B1 of IA 1986, because section 248 of Enterprise Act 2002, which replaced the original Part II of IA 1986 with Schedule B1, has no effect in relation to any such entity[36]. There is also a prohibition against any person enforcing any security over the property of a protected railway company except where that person has served 14 days' notice of his intention to take that step on the appropriate national authority[37].

20.11 These provisions were originally enacted before Schedule B1 was introduced into IA 1986, and in any event (as mentioned above), it has no effect in relation to any such entity[38]. As a result the drafting device used to apply the most appropriate parts of Part II of IA 1986 to the railway administration regime was to enact[39] a schedule to the Railways Act 1993 which applies sections 11 to 23 and 27 of the original form of IA 1986 to the regime with appropriate modifications[40]. The principal changes were to enable the appropriate national authority (and the Secretary of State) to participate in the special administration and in particular to enable it to apply for the appointment of a new railway administrator on a vacancy, to receive the section 23 proposals[41], to enable it to initiate a discharge of the special administration[42] and to give it locus to apply to court to secure achievement of the statutory purpose where the special administrator is not exercising his powers to that end[43]. The modified section 27 power also arises where there is a contravention of a licence, and the court is further empowered to order a discharge of the railway administration order in those circumstances. Creditor involvement is reduced because there is no meeting to consider the proposals and no provision for a creditors' committee[44]. Further provision for the relevant procedure is made by the Railway Administration Order Rules 2001[45], which are modelled on but contain many detailed differences from the Insolvency Rules 1986. To the limited extent that they have any application to a railway administration, the Insolvency Rules 1986 continue

---

34 Section 61(2), 62(3) and 62(6) of the Railways Act 1993.
35 Per Lord Woolf CJ in *Winsor v Bloom, In re Railtrack plc (in railway administration)* [2002] EWCA Civ 955 (paragraph 11).
36 Section 249(1)(b) of the Enterprise Act 2002.
37 Section 62(7) of the Railways Act 1993. 'Security' and 'property' have the same meanings as they do in IA 1986, as to which see sections 248(b) and 436(1) of IA 1986.
38 Section 249(1)(b) of the Enterprise Act 2002.
39 By section 59(3) (and see also section 60(4) and (5)) of the Railways Act 1993.
40 See Schedule 6 to the Railways Act 1993.
41 The modified section 23 does not require a meeting of creditors to consider the proposals: Schedule 6 paragraph 9 of the Railways Act 1993, and section 24 of IA 1986 is not one of the provisions applied by Schedule 6 in the first place.
42 As to which see Secretary of State for Transport v Railtrack plc [2002] EWHC 1995 (Ch).
43 Schedule 6 paragraphs 3, 9 and 10 of the Railways Act 1993.
44 Sections 24 and 26 of IA 1986 are not applied by Schedule 6.
45 SI 2001 No 3352. These Rules were made in a great rush on the day before the Secretary of State applied for an administration order in relation to Railtrack plc.

to have effect for the purposes of the application of the Railway Administration Order Rules 2001[46].

20.12 The other main difference from normal administration is that section 59(4) and Schedule 7 to the Railways Act 1993 make provision for transfer schemes to be made by the relevant protected railway company (for this purpose called the existing appointee), where it is proposed that another company (called the new appointee) should carry on the relevant activities of the existing appointee. Such a scheme can transfer property rights and liabilities at a time appointed by the court, but the scheme cannot have effect unless it has been approved by the appropriate national authority[47]. Consent must also be given by the new appointee and (in relation to matters affecting them) by persons described as other appointees[48], the identification of which caused difficulties in the Metronet PPP administration[49]. In approving the transfer scheme the appropriate national authority is required to ensure that any transfer provisions in the scheme allocate property rights and liabilities in such proportion as are appropriate in the context of the relevant activities[50]. The categories of property, rights and liabilities which are capable of transfer are broadly defined and include property located anywhere in the world, rights and liabilities governed by any law, property rights and liabilities which would not otherwise be capable of transfer, and whether or not consent by third parties would otherwise be required to be given[51].

20.13 Unlike some of the other special administration regimes, the railway administration regime has been tested. In October 2001, railway administrators were appointed in relation to Railtrack plc, the holder of a network licence for the ownership and operation of the UK's principal national railway network. The legal aspect of the administration which caused most trouble for the courts was the operation of the statutory stay on proceedings against Railtrack imposed by the modified section 11(3)(d) of IA 1986. In *In re Railtrack plc (in railway administration)*[52], the court confirmed[53] that criminal proceedings by the Health and Safety Executive were caught by the moratorium, but directed that the railway administrators be entitled to consent to the prosecution despite the prospect of the proceedings compromising their ability to achieve the statutory purpose. Rimer J concluded that the public interest in the prosecution (it arose out of the disastrous Ladbroke Grove rail crash) outweighed this consideration. A few months later, in *Winsor v Bloom, In re Railtrack Plc (in railway administration)*[54], the Court of Appeal was required to decide whether the procedures leading to a direction by the Rail Regulator to Railtrack to grant permission to another party to use part of the track for the purposes of operating trains also fell foul of the

---

46   Rule 3(a) of the Insolvency (England and Wales) Rules 2016 (Consequential Amendments and Savings) Rules 2017 (SI 2017 No 369), although in the light of rule 10.11 of the Railway Administration Order Rules 2001, this saving provision has little practical impact.
47   Schedule 7 paragraph 2(2) of the Railways Act 1993.
48   Schedule 7 paragraph 2(1) of the Railways Act 1993.
49   As to which see *In re Metronet Rail BCV Ltd* [2007] EWHC 2697 (Ch). Metronet was a PPP administration, not a railway administration, but similar principles applied.
50   Schedule 7 paragraph 2(6) of the Railways Act 1993.
51   Schedule 7 paragraph 3 of the Railways Act 1993.
52   [2002] EWHC 249(Ch).
53   Applying In re Rhondda Waste Disposal Ltd [2001] Ch 57.
54   [2002] EWCA Civ 955.

statutory moratorium. It concluded that these procedures were regulatory and administrative in their nature; they were different in their essence from the legal or quasi-legal proceedings (such as arbitrations) with which section 11(3)(d) is concerned, with the result that the statutory stay did not apply at all. In this instance, 'the national interest that the railways should continue to function as effectively as possible' was vindicated by a conclusion that one of the bulwarks of the normal administration regime did not apply at all to a regulatory process.

20.14 The other point of legal significance which came out of the *Railtrack* case is that the railway administration came to an end because it was no longer necessary for the purposes of the order to be achieved, not because the purpose was in fact achieved by the transfer of its undertaking as a going concern. The reason for this is that the continued operation of the railway was secured by a transfer of Railtrack's shares to a new holding company, itself owned by the newly established Network Rail. The decision to transfer the shares rather than the undertaking was highly political, and the discharge application was opposed on the bases that not all creditors were being treated equitably and that the court could not be satisfied that Railtrack would be solvent going forward[55]. The court was, however satisfied that the Secretary of State had made out a substantial case for discharge and made the order sought.

PPP ADMINISTRATION

20.15 The third category of special administration regime in point of time was the PPP administration order regime for which provision was made by Part IV of the Greater London Authority Act 1999[56]. This regime was introduced for any PPP company, an entity which was defined to mean any party to a public-private partnership agreement with London Regional Transport, Transport for London or one of their subsidiaries, by which the relevant company undertook to provide, construct, renew, improve or maintain a railway[57]. These agreements were authorised by Part IV Chapter VII of the Greater London Authority Act 1999 as a means of financing and carrying out the maintenance of the infrastructure of the underground network as part of the Mayor of London's transport strategy[58]. As with railway administration, the PPP administration regime has been used on a single occasion when companies in the Metronet group went into PPP administration in July 2007. The structure is very similar to railway administration, and is derived from it[59]. Thus a PPP administration order is an order of the court which directs that during the period for which it is in force the affairs, business and property of the company are to be managed by a PPP administrator for the achievement of the purposes of the order and in a manner which protects the respective interests of the members and creditors of the company[60]. A PPP administration order may also be made against unregistered companies, including foreign companies as defined[61]. The statutory

55   Secretary of State for Transport v Railtrack plc [2002] EWHC 1995 (Ch).
56   Sections 220 and 221 of the Greater London Authority Act 1999.
57   Section 210 of the Greater London Authority Act 1999.
58   *In re Metronet Rail BCV Ltd* [2007] EWHC 2697 (Ch) (paragraph 2).
59   *In re Metronet Rail BCV Ltd* [2007] EWHC 2697 (Ch) (paragraph 25).
60   Section 220(1) of the Greater London Authority Act 1999.
61   Section 224 of the Greater London Authority Act 1999.

purposes are the transfer to another company or companies, as a going concern, of so much of the company's undertaking as it is necessary to transfer in order to ensure that the relevant activities may be properly carried on and the carrying on of those relevant activities pending the making of the transfer[62]. Those activities are the activities carried out or to be carried out by the company in performing its obligations under the relevant PPP agreement[63].

20.16 A PPP administration order can only be made in relation to a PPP company by the court on the petition of the Mayor of London or Transport for London acting as his agent[64]. The grounds for making a PPP administration order are:

(a) that the company is or is likely to become unable to pay its debts[65]; and

(b) that the Secretary of State has certified that it would otherwise be just and equitable for the company to be wound up on public interest grounds[66].

20.17 There is a prohibition against:

(a) the making of a winding up order against a PPP company on a petition by any person other than the Mayor,

(b) the passing by a PPP company of a resolution to wind up without leave of the court, and

(c) the making of an administration order under Part II of IA 1986,

in each case without first giving the Mayor at least 14 days' notice of the petition, the application for leave or the application for an administration order as the case may be[67]. In all such circumstances the Mayor is then empowered to apply for a PPP administration order, and the court may make a PPP administration order on that petition if it is satisfied that either of the two grounds identified in section 221 of the Greater London Act 1999 is satisfied[68]. As with railway administration[69], it can properly be said that this structure indicates a legislative preference that a PPP company should not be wound up and that all or part of its undertaking should be transferred to another company as a going concern, its relevant activities having been carried on in the interim. It is also to be noted that a PPP company cannot enter administration under the regime introduced by Schedule B1 of IA 1986, because section 248 of the Enterprise Act 2002 which replaced the original Part II of IA 1986 with Schedule B1 has no effect in relation to any such entity[70]. There is also a prohibition against any person enforcing any security over the property of a PPP company except where that person has served 14 days' notice of his intention to take that step on the Mayor[71].

---

62 Section 220(2) of the Greater London Authority Act 1999.
63 Section 220(6) of the Greater London Authority Act 1999.
64 Section 221(1) and (7) of the Greater London Authority Act 1999.
65 Within the meaning of section 123 of IA 1986: section 221(6) of the Greater London Authority Act 1999.
66 Section 221(2) of the Greater London Authority Act 1999.
67 Sections 222(1), 223(1) and 223(5) of the Greater London Authority Act 1999.
68 Section 222(2), 223(3) and (6) of the Greater London Authority Act 1999.
69 Per Lord Woolf CJ in Winsor v Bloom, In re Railtrack plc (in railway administration) [2002] EWCA Civ 955 (paragraph 11).
70 Section 249(1)(d) of the Enterprise Act 2002.
71 Section 223(7) of the Greater London Authority Act 1999. 'Security' and 'property' have the same meanings as they do in IA 1986, as to which see sections 248(b) and 436(1) of IA 1986.

20.18 As with railway administration, these provisions were originally enacted before Schedule B1 was introduced into IA 1986 and, in any event (as mentioned above), it has no effect in relation to any such entity[72]. As a result the drafting device used to apply the most appropriate parts of Part II of IA 1986 to the PPP administration regime was to enact[73] a schedule to the Greater London Authority Act 1999 which applies sections 11 to 23 and 27 of the original form of IA 1986 to the regime with appropriate modifications[74]. The principal changes were to enable the Mayor to participate in the special administration and in particular to enable him to apply for the appointment of a new PPP administrator on a vacancy, to receive the section 23 proposals[75], to enable him to initiate a discharge of the special administration and to give him locus to apply to court to secure achievement of the statutory purpose where the PPP administrator is not exercising his powers to that end[76]. Creditor involvement is reduced because there is no meeting to consider the proposals and no provision for a creditors' committee[77]. Further provision for the relevant procedure is made by the PPP Administration Order Rules 2007[78], which are modelled on but contain many detailed differences from the Insolvency Rules 1986. To the limited extent that they have any application to a PPP administration, the Insolvency Rules 1986 continue to have effect for the purposes of the application of the PPP Administration Order Rules 2001[79].

20.19 The other main difference from normal administration is that section 220(4) and Schedule 15 to the Greater London Authority Act 1999 make provision for transfer schemes to be made by the relevant PPP company (for this purpose called the existing appointee), where it is proposed that another company (called the new appointee) should carry on the relevant activities of the existing appointee. Therefore, it is clear that a transfer scheme of this sort is intended to achieve the statutory purpose of transferring to another company as a going concern so much of its undertaking as it is necessary to transfer in order to ensure that the activities carried out or to be carried out by the company in performing its obligations under the relevant PPP agreement may be properly carried on[80]. Such a scheme can transfer property rights and liabilities at a time appointed by the court, but the scheme cannot have effect unless it has been approved by the Mayor[81]. Consent must also be given by the new appointee and (in relation to matters affecting them) persons described as

---

72 Section 249(1)(d) of the Enterprise Act 2002.
73 By section 220(3) (and see also sections 221(4) and 221(5)) of the Greater London Authority Act 1999.
74 See Schedule 14 to the Greater London Authority Act 1999.
75 The modified section 23 does not require a meeting of creditors to consider the proposals: Schedule 14 paragraph 9 of the Greater London Authority Act 1999 and section 24 of IA 1986 is not one of the provisions applied by Schedule 14 in the first place.
76 Schedule 14 paragraphs 3, 9 and 10 of the Greater London Authority Act 1999.
77 *In re Metronet Rail BCV Ltd* [2007] EWHC 2697 (Ch) (paragraph 12). Sections 24 and 26 of IA 1986 are not applied by Schedule 14.
78 SI 2007 No 3141. On this occasion, the relevant Rules were only made after the first appointment of PPP administartors (to the members of the Metronet group) had been made. At the outset the court was obliged to apply relevant provisions of the Insolvency Rules 1986 by analogy.
79 Rule 3(e) of the Insolvency (England and Wales) Rules 2016 (Consequential Amendments and Savings) Rules 2017 (SI 2017 No 369), although in the light of rule 125(2) of the PPP Administration Order Rules 2007, this saving provision has little practical impact.
80 *In re Metronet Rail BCV Ltd* [2007] EWHC 2697 (Ch) (paragraph 37).
81 Schedule 15 paragraph 2(2) of the Greater London Authority Act 1999.

other appointees[82], the identification of which caused difficulties in the Metronet PPP administration[83]. In approving the transfer scheme, the Mayor is required to ensure that any transfer provisions in the scheme allocates property rights and liabilities in such proportion as are appropriate in the context of the relevant activities[84]. The categories of property, rights and liabilities which are capable of transfer are broadly defined, and include property located anywhere in the world, rights and liabilities governed by any law, property rights and liabilities which would not otherwise be capable of transfer, and whether or not consent by third parties would otherwise be required to be given[85]. Schedule 21 paragraphs 7 and 8 of the Energy Act 2004 contain widely drafted provision for the effectiveness of the transfer.

20.20 Unlike the railway administration of Railtrack[86], the PPP administration of Metronet led to the formulation of a transfer scheme in accordance with Schedule 15 to the Greater London Authority Act 1999. An issue arose out of the fact that, while a statutory transfer scheme can transfer property rights and liabilities from the company in relation to which the PPP administration order has been made to a new appointee, not only must it be approved by the Mayor, it must also be consented to both by the new appointee and (in relation the matters affecting them) by any person who is an 'other appointee'. In *In re Metronet Rail BCV Ltd*[87], Patten J decided the phrase 'other appointee' only extended to other persons in whose favour a transfer scheme had also been made; it did not extend to sub-contractors or creditors whose consent would otherwise have been required to render the scheme effective. This is another example of the court taking an approach to the operation of special administration provisions which reflected the public interest for which the order was made, rather than giving undue weight to the interests of the creditors for whose benefit a normal administration regime is imposed.

AIR TRAFFIC ADMINISTRATION

20.21 The next form of special administration regime has not yet been used. It has introduced the concept of an air traffic administration order in relation to a company (called a 'licence company') which holds a licence granted under Chapter 1 of the Transport Act 2000, ie a licence authorising it to provide air traffic services[88]. The structure of the legislation is different to that which introduced the railway and PPP administration regimes, but many of the same points apply, albeit in a different form.

20.22 An air traffic administration order is an order of the court which directs that during the period for which it is in force the affairs, business and property of the company are to be managed by an air traffic administrator for the achievement of the purposes of the order and in a manner which protects

---

82 Schedule 15 paragraph 2(1) of the Greater London Authority Act 1999.
83 As to which see *In re Metronet Rail BCV Ltd* [2007] EWHC 2697 (Ch).
84 Schedule 15 paragraph 2(6) of the Greater London Authority Act 1999.
85 Schedule 15 paragraph 3 of the Greater London Authority Act 1999.
86 *Secretary of State for Transport v Railtrack plc* [2002] EWHC 1995 (Ch).
87 [2007] EWHC 2697 (Ch).
88 The air traffic control services defined by section 98 of the Transport Act 2000, which are carried out by NATS.

the respective interests of the members and creditors of the company[89]. The statutory purposes are the transfer to another company or companies, as a going concern, of so much of the company's undertaking as it is necessary to transfer in order to ensure that the licensed activities[90] may be properly carried on and the carrying on of those activities pending the transfer[91].

20.23 An air traffic administration order can only be made in relation to a licence company by the court on the petition of the Secretary of State or by the Civil Aviation Authority ('CAA') with his consent[92]. One of the following conditions has to be satisfied before an air traffic administration order can be made:

(a) the company is or is likely to become unable to pay its debts[93];

(b) the Secretary of State has certified that it would otherwise be just and equitable for the company to be wound up on public interest grounds; or

(c) there is an actual or apprehended contravention by the licence company of certain of its duties under the Transport Act 2000 and it is inappropriate for it to continue to hold the licence[94].

20.24 By section 27(5) of the Transport Act 2000, the Secretary of State and CAA may propose a person to manage the company's affairs, business and property while the air traffic administration order is in force, and if they do so the court must appoint that person. This is an oddly worded provision, given that the very essence of an air traffic administration order is for a person to be appointed to fulfil those functions and section 28 of the Transport Act 2000 gives the court a discretion to make such an order and the obligation to satisfy itself that one of the statutory conditions has been satisfied. It is thought that the purpose of section 28 is to remove any discretion that the court might otherwise have as to the identity of the air traffic administrator once the court is otherwise satisfied that such an order ought to be made.

20.25 There is an absolute prohibition against the passing by a licence company of a resolution to wind up and the making of an application for an administration order against it under Part II of IA 1986[95]. There is also a prohibition against the making of an application to wind up a licence company by any person other than the Secretary of State, without first giving the Secretary of State and the CAA at least 14 days' notice of an intention to do so[96]. In any case in which a winding up application is before the court, the court cannot make a winding up order (or appoint a provisional liquidator) but it may make an air traffic administration order if it is satisfied that it would be appropriate to make a winding up order if the company were not a licence company[97]. It is also to be noted that a licence company cannot enter administration under the regime introduced by Schedule B1 to IA 1986, because section 248 of the Enterprise Act 2002 which replaced the

---

89 Section 29(1) of the Transport Act 2000.
90 Ie the licence authorising it to provide air traffic services.
91 Section 29(2) of the Transport Act 2000.
92 Section 28(1) of the Transport Act 2000.
93 Within the meaning of section 123 of IA 1986: section 28(6) of the Transport Act 2000.
94 Section 28(2)–(5) of the Transport Act 2000.
95 Section 26(1) and (2) of the Transport Act 2000.
96 Section 26(4) of the Transport Act 2000.
97 Section 27(3) and (4) of the Transport Act 2000.

original Part II of IA 1986 with Schedule B1 has no effect in relation to any such entity[98]. There is also a prohibition against any person enforcing any security over the property of a licence company except where that person has served 14 days' notice of his intention to take that step on the Secretary of State and the CAA[99].

20.26 As with railway administration and PPP administration, these provisions were originally enacted before Schedule B1 was introduced into IA 1986 and, in any event (as mentioned above), it has no effect in relation to any such entity[100]. As a result the drafting device used to apply the most appropriate parts of Part II of IA 1986 to the air traffic administration regime was to enact[101] a schedule to the Transport Act 2000 which applies sections 11 to 23 and 27 of the original form of IA 1986 to the regime with appropriate modifications[102]. The principal changes were to enable the Secretary of State and the CAA to participate in the special administration and in particular to enable him to apply for the appointment of a new air traffic administrator on a vacancy, to receive the section 23 proposals[103], to enable him to initiate a discharge of the special administration and to give him locus to apply to court to secure achievement of the statutory purpose where the air traffic administrator is not exercising his powers to that end[104]. Creditor involvement is reduced because there is no meeting to consider the proposals and no provision for a creditors' committee[105].

20.27 The other main difference from normal administration is that section 30 and Schedule 2 of the Transport Act 2000 make provision for a scheme to be made by the existing licence company to secure that a new licence company carries out the relevant licensed activities. It must be consented to by the new licence company and will only take effect once approved by the Secretary of State acting in consultation with the CAA. In approving the scheme the Secretary of State is required to have regard to the need to ensure that the scheme allocates property rights and liabilities in such manner as is appropriate, taking into account the relevant activities and who will carry them on[106]. The categories of property, rights and liabilities which are capable of transfer are broadly defined, and include property located anywhere in the world, rights and liabilities governed by any law, property rights and liabilities which would not otherwise be capable of transfer, and whether or not consent by third parties would otherwise require to be given[107]. Schedule 2 paragraphs 8 to 11 of the Transport Act 2000 contain widely drafted provision for the effectiveness of the transfer.

---

98   Section 249(1)(c) of the Enterprise Act 2002.
99   Section 26(3) of the Transport Act 2000. 'Security' and 'property' have the same meanings as they do in IA 1986, as to which see sections 248(b) and 436(1) of IA 1986.
100 Section 249(1)(c) of the Enterprise Act 2002.
101 By sections 30(2) (and see also sections 30(3) and 30(4)) of the Transport Act 2000.
102 See Schedule 1 of the Transport Act 2000.
103 The modified section 23 does not require a meeting of creditors to consider the proposals: Schedule 1 paragraph 11 of the Transport Act 2000 and section 24 of IA 1986 is not one of the provisions applied by Schedule 1 in the first place.
104 Schedule 1 paragraphs 5, 11 and 12 of the Transport Act 2000.
105 Sections 24 and 26 of IA 1986 are not applied by Schedule 1 of the Transport Act 2000.
106 Schedule 2 paragraph 6 of the Transport Act 2000.
107 Schedule 2 paragraph 7 of the Transport Act 2000.

ENERGY ADMINISTRATION

20.28 The next category of entity for which a special administration regime was introduced was the making of an energy administration order[108] in respect of a protected energy company within the meaning of section 154(5) of the Energy Act 2004. A protected energy company is a company which holds an electricity transmission or distribution licence[109] or a gas transporter licence[110]. It can be a registered or an unregistered company, and for certain purposes the legislation uses the phrase 'non-GB company', to refer to a company incorporated outside Great Britain.

20.29 An energy administration order is an order of the court which directs that during the period for which it is in force the affairs, business and property of the protected energy company are to be managed by an energy administrator so as to achieve the objectives set out in section 155 of the Energy Act 2004[111]. The primary objective is to secure that the company's system[112] is and continues to be maintained and developed as an efficient, economical and (in the case of electricity distribution or transmission) coordinated system, and that it becomes unnecessary for the energy administration order to remain in force for that purpose[113]. The means by which this objective is to be achieved are the rescue of the company as a going concern and/or a transfer as a going concern to another company of so much of that undertaking as it is appropriate to transfer for the purpose of achieving the objective[114]. The means by which transfers may be effected include, in particular, a hive-down to a subsidiary of the protected energy company and a transfer of shares in the hive-down company[115]. A transfer is only to be effected where a rescue as a going concern is not reasonably practicable[116], where the rescue of that company as a going concern will not achieve the objective[117], where such transfer would produce a result for the company's creditors as a whole that is better than the result that would be produced without it or where such transfer would (without prejudicing the interests of the creditors as a whole) produce a result for the company's members as a whole that is better than the result that would be produced without it[118]. There is an additional administration objective for certain categories of protected energy company[119], namely to secure that their relevant functions are and continue to be carried out in an efficient and effective manner and that it becomes unnecessary, by the means already described, for the energy administration order to remain in force for that purpose[120].

---

108 Within the meaning of section 154 of the Energy Act 2004.
109 Within the meaning of section 6(1)(b) or (c) of the Electricity Act 1989. The jurisdiction does not extend to the holders of the other licences for which provision is made by section 6(1) (ie generation, supply, interconnector or smart meter communication licences).
110 Section 7 of the Gas Act 1986.
111 Section 154(3) of the Energy Act 2004.
112 Ie the system of electricity distribution or of electricity transmission, or the pipe-line system for the conveyance of gas as the case may be: section 155(6) of the Energy Act 2004.
113 Section 155(1) and (7) of the Energy Act 2004.
114 Section 155(2) and (3) of the Energy Act 2004.
115 Section 155(4) of the Energy Act 2004.
116 Or is not reasonably practicable without such transfers.
117 Or will not do so without such transfers.
118 Section 155(5) of the Energy Act 2004.
119 Those with functions conferred by Part 2 Chapter 2, 3 or 4 of the Energy Act 2013 or an order made under section 46 of the Energy Act 2013.
120 Section 155(9) of the Energy Act 2004.

20.30   An energy administration order can only be made in relation to a protected energy company by the court on the petition of the Secretary of State or by the Gas and Electricity Markets Authority ('GEMA') with his consent[121]. Notice must be given to any person who has appointed an administrative receiver or who is or may be entitled to appoint an administrative receiver or an administrator[122]. The Energy Administration Rules 2005[123] also require notice of an application to be given to any administrative receiver, the applicant for the making of any administration order or winding up order, any creditor who has served notice of intention to enforce their security, the proposed energy administrator, the protected energy company, the supervisor of any CVA and whichever of the Secretary of State or GEMA is not the applicant. One of the following conditions have to be satisfied before an energy administration order can be made:

(a)   the company is or is likely to become unable to pay its debts[124]; or

(b)   on a petition by the Secretary of State it would otherwise be just and equitable for the company to be wound up on public interest grounds, and the Secretary of State has given a certificate to that effect[125].

An energy administration order cannot be made against a protected energy company which is already in administration or being wound up[126].

20.31   There is a prohibition against:

(a)   the making of a winding up order against a protected energy company on a petition by any person other than the Secretary of State,

(b)   the passing by an energy company of a resolution to wind up without leave of the court, and

(c)   the making of an administration order under Part II of IA 1986,

in each case without first giving to GEMA at least 14 days' notice of the petition, the application for leave or the application for an administration order as the case may be[127]. In all such circumstances the Secretary of State and GEMA are then empowered to apply for an energy administration order, and the court may make an energy administration order under section 157 of the Energy Act 2004. Unlike the companies to which a number of other special administration regimes apply, a protected energy company can enter administration out of court (pursuant to Schedule B1 paragraph 14 or 21 of IA 1986)[128]. However, an out-of-court appointment cannot be made when an energy administration order has been made or an application for such an order is outstanding[129], and it only takes effect after 14 days' notice of the appointment has been given to both the Secretary of State and GEMA, and where no application for an energy administration order is outstanding and no energy administration order has

---

121   Section 156(1) of the Energy Act 2004.
122   Section 156(2) of the Energy Act 2004.
123   SI 2005 No 2483: rule 8.
124   Within the meaning of section 123 of IA 1986: section 157(8) of the Energy Act 2004.
125   Sections 157(2) and (3) of the Energy Act 2004.
126   Section 157(4) of the Energy Act 2004.
127   Sections 160–162 of the Energy Act 2004.
128   Section 249(1) of the Enterprise Act 2002, which replaced the original Part II of IA 1986 with Schedule B1, does not list protected energy companies as one of the categories of excluded entity.
129   Section 163(1) of the Energy Act 2004.

been made[130]. There is also a prohibition against any person enforcing any security over the property of a protected energy company except where that person has served 14 days' notice of his intention to take that step on both the Secretary of State and GEMA[131].

20.32 An energy administrator is an officer of the court, acts as the agent of the protected energy company and must exercise his powers for the purpose of achieving the statutory objective as quickly and efficiently as possible and (so far as consistent with that objective) in a manner which best protects the interests of the company's creditors as a whole[132]. The relevant parts of Schedule B1 of IA 1986 which relate to a normal administration are also applied to the conduct of an energy administration with appropriate modifications[133]. The principal changes are to enable the Secretary of State and GEMA to participate in the energy administration and in particular to enable them to receive the administrator's proposals[134], to participate in and be notified of the ending of the energy administration[135] and to give them locus to apply to court to secure achievement of the statutory objective where the energy administrator is not exercising his powers to that end[136]. There are also detailed provisions which are beyond the scope of this work, but which empower the Secretary of State to make grants and loans and give indemnities to a protected energy company in administration[137]. Schedule B1 paragraph 99 of IA 1986 is modified to add sums payable under those arrangements to the amounts payable out of and chargeable on the company's property in the hands of the energy administrator as at cessation[138]. Provision for the relevant procedure is made by the Energy Administration Rules 2005[139], which are modelled on but contain many detailed differences from the Insolvency Rules 1986. To the limited extent that they have any application to an energy administration, the Insolvency Rules 1986 continue to have effect for the purposes of the application of the Energy Administration Rules 2005[140].

20.33 The other main difference from normal administration is that section 159(2) and Schedule 21 of the Energy Act 2004 make provision for transfer schemes to be made by the protected energy company (acting through the energy administrator), for the purpose of giving effect to a proposed transfer intended to achieve the objective of energy administration. Such a scheme can transfer

---

130 Section 163 of the Energy Act 2004, and the interim moratorium under Schedule B1 paragraph 44 of IA 1986 does not apply to prevent the making of an application for an energy administration order: section 163(4) of the Energy Act 2004.
131 Section 164 of the Energy Act 2004.
132 Section 158 of the Energy Act 2004 and subject to that the interests of the company's members as a whole.
133 Section 159 and Schedule 20 to the Energy Act 2004.
134 Schedule B1 paragraph 49 of IA 1986 as modified by Schedule 20 paragraph 10 of the Energy Act 2004.
135 Schedule B1 paragraphs 79–91 of IA 1986 as modified by Schedule 20 paragraphs 18–24 of the Energy Act 2004.
136 There are detailed provisions in Schedule B1 paragraph 74 of IA 1986 as modified by Schedule 20 paragraph 16 of the Energy Act 2004.
137 Sections 165–169 of the Energy Act 2004.
138 Schedule B1 paragraph 99(4A) as inserted by Schedule 20 paragraph 26 of the Energy Act 2004.
139 SI 2005 No 2483.
140 Rule 3(d) of the Insolvency (England and Wales) Rules 2016 (Consequential Amendments and Savings) Rules 2017 (SI 2017 No 369), although in the light of rule 187 of the Energy Administration Rules 2005, this saving provision has little practical impact.

property rights and liabilities at a time appointed by the court, but that time must not be appointed by the court unless the scheme has been approved by the Secretary of State[141]. In approving the transfer scheme the Secretary of State is required to consult with GEMA, and to have regard to the public interest and the effect which the scheme is likely to have on third parties (amongst whom it is to be expected that creditors will feature prominently)[142]. The categories of property, rights and liabilities which are capable of transfer are broadly defined, and include property located anywhere in the world, rights and liabilities governed by any law, and property rights and liabilities which would not otherwise be capable of transfer, and whether or not consent by third parties would otherwise be required to be given[143]. Schedule 21 paragraphs 7 and 8 of the Energy Act 2004 contain widely drafted provision for the effectiveness of the transfer.

20.34 There is also a separate administration procedure for energy supply companies[144] within the meaning of the Energy Act 2011 for which procedural provisions have been introduced by the Energy Supply Company Administration Rules 2013[145], which are modelled on but contain many detailed differences from the Insolvency Rules 1986. To the limited extent that they have any application to an energy supply company administration, the Insolvency Rules 1986 continue to have effect for the purposes of the application of the Energy Supply Company Administration Rules 2005[146]. The objective of an energy supply company administration is to secure that energy supplies are continued at the lowest cost which it is reasonably practicable to incur, and that it becomes unnecessary for the administration order to remain in force for that purpose[147]. Otherwise the means by which the objective is to be achieved and the principles applicable to an energy supply company administration are very similar to those which apply to the administration of a protected energy company; the provisions of sections 156 to 167 and Schedules 20 and 21 to Energy Act 2004 are applied to an energy supply company administration *mutatis mutandis*[148].

TRUST SPECIAL ADMINISTRATION

20.35 The number of different regimes which have been introduced since the enactment of IA 1986 is considerable, and some of them are closer than others to a normal administration conducted in accordance with Schedule B1. One of the regimes which has been used[149], but which has little in common with normal administration (and is only mentioned here for completeness) is the appointment of a trust special administrator of an NHS trust or NHS foundation trust. It was introduced by section 16 of the Health Act 2009 which inserted a

---

141 Schedule 21 paragraph 3 of the Energy Act 2004.
142 Schedule 21 paragraph 3(7) and 3(8) of the Energy Act 2004.
143 Schedule 21 paragraph 4 of the Energy Act 2004.
144 Ie the holders of electricity supply licences granted under section 6(1)(d) of the Electricity Act 1989 and gas supply licences under section 7A(1)(a) or (b) of the Gas Act 1986.
145 SI 2013 No 1046.
146 Rule 3(i) of the Insolvency (England and Wales) Rules 2016 (Consequential Amendments and Savings) Rules 2017 (SI 2017 No 369), although in the light of rule 208 of the Energy Supply Company Administration Rules 2013, this saving provision has little practical impact.
147 Section 95 of the Energy Act 2011.
148 Section 96 of the Energy Act 2011.
149 Mid Staffordshire NHS Foundation Trust and South London Healthcare NHS Trust.

new Chapter 5A into Part 2 of the National Health Service Act 2006 and was subsequently amended by the Care Act 2014 and the Health and Social Care Act 2012. The purpose of the regime is to ensure the continued delivery of clinically and financially viable patient services which are essential to the local population. In the case of foundation trusts, this is expressed in the form of a statutory objective to secure:

(a) the continued provision of services of sufficient safety and quality and at such level, as the commissioners of those services determine; and

(b) that it becomes unnecessary for the order to remain in force for that purpose[150].

20.36 A trust special administrator of an NHS foundation trust can only be appointed by the regulator (known as Monitor) if it is satisfied that the foundation trust is, or is likely to become, unable to pay its debts as and when they are due and/or there is a serious failure by the foundation trust to provide services of sufficient quality[151]. Before making the order the regulator is required to consult with the Secretary of State, the foundation trust, NHS England, the CQC and appropriate commissioners. If the Care Quality Commission ('CQC') is satisfied that there has been a serious failure it may require Monitor to make such an appointment[152]. When an order is made, the trust special administrator is under a duty to manage the trust's affairs, business, and property so as to achieve the statutory objective as efficiently as is reasonably practicable[153]. The effect of such an order is to suspend from office the governors, chairman and executive and non-executive directors of the trust[154].

20.37 The main task of the trust special administrator is to prepare a draft report for Monitor (also to be laid before Parliament) stating the action which the administrator recommends that Monitor should take in relation to the trust and must publish a statement setting out the means by which the administrator will seek responses to the draft report. In preparing the draft report the trust special administrator is under a duty to consult the National Health Service Commissioning Board, any provider of goods and services whom the regulator directs him to consult and the CQC[155]. The draft report must be produced within 65 working days of the appointment[156]. There is then a period of consultation before the report is finalized and the final report must then be sent to Monitor who is required to publish it and lay it before Parliament[157]. The remainder of Part 2 Chapter 5A of the National Health Service Act 2006 then makes provision for the implementation by Monitor and the Secretary of State of the recommendations and the termination of the special administration, with or without the dissolution of the foundation trust.

---

150 Section 65DA(1) of the National Health Service Act 2006.
151 Section 65D of the National Health Service Act 2006. The Secretary of State has a wider power to appoint a trust special administrator to an NHS trust if he considers that it is the interests of the health service to do so.
152 Section 65D of the National Health Service Act 2006.
153 Section 65D(9) of the National Health Service Act 2006.
154 Section 65D(10) of the National Health Service Act 2006.
155 Section 65F of the National Health Service Act 2006.
156 Section 65F(1) of the National Health Service Act 2006, a time which can be extended by the Secretary of State under section 65J of the National Health Service Act 2006.
157 Sections 65H and 65I of the National Health Service Act 2006.

POSTAL ADMINISTRATION

20.38 The next category of entity for which a special administration regime has been introduced is the making of a postal administration order in respect of a universal service provider[158] within the meaning of section 68 of the Postal Services Act 2011. The purpose is to secure the continued provision of the universal postal service should a privately-owned Royal Mail (or any other universal service provider) be at risk of entering insolvency proceedings.

20.39 A postal administration order is an order of the court which directs that during the period for which it is in force the affairs, business and property of the company are to be managed by a postal administrator so as to achieve the objectives set out in section 69 of the Postal Services Act 2011[159]. The primary objective is to secure that a universal postal service is provided in accordance with the standards set out in the universal postal service order[160], and that it becomes unnecessary for the postal administration order to remain in force for that purpose[161]. The means by which this objective is to be achieved are the rescue of the company as a going concern and/or a transfer as a going concern to another company of so much of that undertaking as it is appropriate to transfer for the purpose of achieving the objective[162]. The means by which transfers may be effected include, in particular, a hive-down to a subsidiary of the company and a transfer of shares in the hive-down company[163]. A transfer is only to be effected where a rescue as a going concern is not reasonably practicable[164], where the rescue of that company as a going concern will not achieve the objective[165], where such transfer would produce a result for the company's creditors as a whole that is better than the result that would be produced without it or where such transfer would (without prejudicing the interests of the creditors as a whole) produce a result for the company's members as a whole that is better than the result that would be produced without it[166].

20.40 A postal administration order can only be made in relation to a company which is a universal service provider by the court on the petition of the Secretary of State or by OFCOM with his consent[167]. Notice must be given to any person who has appointed an administrative receiver or who is or may be entitled to appoint an administrative receiver or an administrator[168]. The Postal Administration Rules 2013[169] also require notice of an application to be given to any administrative receiver, the applicant for the making of any administration order or winding up order, any creditor who has served notice of intention to

---

158 Defined by section 35 of the Postal Services Act 2011.
159 Section 68 of the Postal Services Act 2011.
160 This is the order made by OFCOM under section 30 of the Postal Services Act 2011 to set out a description of the services that they consider should be provided in the UK as a universal postal service, and the standards with which those services are to comply: see the Postal Services (Universal Postal Service) Order 2012 (SI 2012 No 936).
161 Section 69 of the Postal Services Act 2011.
162 Section 69(2) of the Postal Services Act 2011.
163 Section 69(4) of the Postal Services Act 2011.
164 Or is not reasonably practicable without such transfers.
165 Or will not do so without such transfers.
166 Section 69(5) of the Postal Services Act 2011.
167 Section 70(1) of the Postal Services Act 2011.
168 Section 70(2) of the Postal Services Act 2011.
169 SI 2013 No 3208: rule 8.

enforce their security, the proposed postal administrator, the company, the supervisor of any CVA and whichever of the Secretary of State or OFCOM is not the applicant. One of the following conditions have to be satisfied before an energy administration order can be made:

(a) the company is or is likely to become unable to pay its debts[170]; or

(b) on a petition by the Secretary of State it would otherwise be just and equitable for the company to be wound up on public interest grounds, and the Secretary of State has given a certificate to that effect[171].

A postal administration order cannot be made against a company which is already in administration or being wound up[172].

20.41 There is a prohibition against:

(a) the making of a winding up order against a company which is a universal service provider on a petition by any person other than the Secretary of State,

(b) the passing by a company which is a universal service provider of a resolution to wind up without leave of the court, and

(c) the making of an administration order under Part II of IA 1986,

in each case without first giving to the Secretary of State and OFCOM at least 14 days' notice of the petition, the application for leave or the application for an administration order as the case may be[173]. In all such circumstances the Secretary of State and OFCOM are then empowered to apply for a postal administration order, and the court may make such an order under section 71 of the Postal Services Act 2011. Unlike the companies to which a number of other special administration regimes apply, a company which is a universal services provider can enter administration out of court (pursuant to Schedule B1 paragraph 14 or 21 of IA 1986)[174]. However, an out-of-court appointment cannot be made when a postal administration order has been made or an application for such an order is outstanding[175] and it only takes effect after 14 days' notice of the appointment has been given to both the Secretary of State and OFCOM, and where no application for a postal administration order is outstanding and no such order has been made[176]. There is also a prohibition against any person enforcing any security over the property of a company which is a universal services provider except where that person has served 14 days' notice of his intention to take that step on both the Secretary of State and OFCOM[177].

20.42 A postal administrator is an officer of the court, acts as the agent of the company and must exercise his powers for the purpose of achieving the statutory

---

170 Within the meaning of section 123 of IA 1986: section 71(8) of the Postal Services Act 2011.
171 Sections 71(2) and (3) of the Postal Services Act 2011.
172 Section 71(4) of the Postal Services Act 2011.
173 Sections 74–76 of the Postal Services Act 2011.
174 Section 249(1) of the Enterprise Act 2002, which replaced the original Part II of IA 1986 with Schedule B1, does not list companies which are universal service providers as one of the categories of excluded entity.
175 Section 77(2) of the Postal Services Act 2011.
176 Section 76 of the Postal Services Act 2011, and the interim moratorium under Schedule B1 paragraph 44 of IA 1986 does not apply to prevent the making of an application for a postal administration order: section 76(4) of the Postal Services Act 2011.
177 Section 78 of the Postal Services Act 2011.

objective as quickly and efficiently as possible and (so far as consistent with that objective) in a manner which best protects the interests of the company's creditors as a whole[178]. The relevant parts of Schedule B1 of IA 1986 which relate to a normal administration are also applied to the conduct of a postal administration with appropriate modifications[179]. The principal changes are to enable the Secretary of State and OFCOM to participate in the postal administration and in particular to enable them to receive the administrator's proposals[180], to participate in and be notified of the ending of the postal administration[181] and to give them locus to apply to court to secure achievement of the statutory objective where the postal administrator is not exercising his powers to that end[182]. There are also detailed provisions which are beyond the scope of this work, but which empower the Secretary of State to make grants and loans and give indemnities to a company in postal administration[183]. Schedule B1 paragraph 99 of IA 1986 is modified to add sums payable under those arrangements to the amounts payable out of and chargeable on the company's property in the hands of the postal administrator as at cessation[184]. The procedural aspects of this regime are governed by the Postal Administration Rules 2013[185], which are modelled on but contain many detailed differences from the Insolvency Rules 1986. To the limited extent that they have any application to a postal administration, the Insolvency Rules 1986 continue to have effect for the purposes of the application of the Postal Administration Rules 2005[186].

20.43 The other main difference from normal administration is that section 71(2) and Schedule 11 of the Postal Services Act 2011 make provision for transfer schemes to be made by a company which is a universal service provider (acting through the postal administrator), for the purpose of giving effect to a proposed transfer intended to achieve the objective of postal administration. Such a scheme can transfer property rights and liabilities at a time specified in the scheme[187]. The scheme must be approved by the Secretary of State and consented to by both transferor and transferee[188]. In approving the transfer scheme the Secretary of State is required to consult with OFCOM, and to have regard to the public interest and the effect which the scheme is likely to have on third parties (amongst whom it is to be expected that creditors will feature prominently)[189]. The categories of property, rights and liabilities which are capable of transfer are broadly defined, and include property located anywhere in the world, rights and

---

178 Section 72 of the Postal Services Act 2011, and subject to that the interests of the company's members as a whole.
179 Section 73 and Schedule 10 to the Postal Services Act 2011.
180 Schedule B1 paragraph 49 of IA 1986 as modified by Schedule 10 paragraph 8 of the Postal Services Act 2011.
181 Schedule B1 paragraphs 79–91 of IA 1986 as modified by Schedule 10 paragraphs 17–24 of the Postal Services Act 2011.
182 There are detailed provisions in Schedule B1 paragraph 74 of IA 1986 as modified by Schedule 10 paragraph 15 of the Postal Services Act 2011.
183 Sections 79–83 of the Postal Services Act 2011.
184 Schedule B1 paragraph 99(4A) as inserted by Schedule 10 paragraph 25 of the Postal Services Act 2011.
185 SI 2013 No 3208.
186 Rule 3(j) of the Insolvency (England and Wales) Rules 2016 (Consequential Amendments and Savings) Rules 2017 (SI 2017 No 369), although in the light of rule 210 of the Postal Administration Rules 2013, this saving provision has little practical impact.
187 This is different from energy administration where the time is specified by the court.
188 Schedule 11 paragraph 3 of the Postal Services Act 2011.
189 Schedule 11 paragraph 4(5) and 4(6) of the Postal Services Act 2011.

liabilities governed by any law, and property rights and liabilities which would not otherwise be capable of transfer, and whether or not consent by third parties would otherwise require to be given[190]. Schedule 11 paragraphs 7 to 23 of the Postal Services Act 2011 contain widely drafted provision for the effectiveness of the transfer.

FUTURE DEVELOPMENTS

20.44 The introduction of a special administration regime for entities which both provide an essential public service and fund their activities with private sector finance continues to be popular. There are a number of further areas in which special regimes have been proposed either by legislation which is enacted, but not yet brought into force, or is contained in draft legislation which at the time of writing is not yet on the statute book.

Health special administration

20.45 The first is health special administration for relevant providers under the Health and Social Care Act 2012[191]. A relevant provider is a company which holds a licence to provide a health care service for the purposes of the NHS. Health care is defined by section 65 of the Health and Social Care Act 2012 to mean all forms of health care provided for individuals, and includes adult social care. This regime was therefore intended to apply to independent providers of NHS-funded services and its objective was to provide an alternative corporate insolvency procedure to ensure that patients receive an uninterrupted service if the provider becomes insolvent, that objective to be achieved either through a rescue or through the statutory transfer of all or part of the company's undertaking as a going concern[192]. It had been intended that regulations would be introduced to make further provision for health administration orders, but in April 2014 the government announced that for the time being the risks associated with not having a health special administration regime were manageable. Accordingly, an ordinary administration remains the appropriate insolvency procedure for companies providing health care services, so long as they satisfy the jurisdictional requirements of Schedule B1 to IA 1986 for entering administration.

Housing administration

20.46 The second regime not yet in force is housing administration for registered providers of social housing (housing associations) under the Housing and Planning Act 2016. At the time of writing the government has announced that the draft regulations contemplated by section 102 will shortly be laid before Parliament. A housing administration order[193] will be capable of extending not just to a company but also to a registered cooperative and community benefit

---

190 Schedule 11 paragraph 6 of the Postal Services Act 2011.
191 The intention was that the court would make orders under section 128 of the Health and Social Care Act 2012.
192 Section 129 of the Health and Social Care Act 2012.
193 Within the meaning of section 95 of the Housing and Planning Act 2016.

society[194] and a charitable incorporated organisation[195]. There are two statutory objectives[196]; the first is what is described as normal administration[197] and the second is to ensure that the registered provider's social housing remains in the regulated housing sector[198]. The first objective takes priority over the second, but the housing administrator must work towards both objectives[199]. As with most other special administration regimes in the public sector, a registered provider will only be able to go into administration by order of the court and the court will only be able to make an order on the application of the Secretary of State or the regulator (being the Regulator of Social Housing)[200]. The court will have to be satisfied that the registered provider is unable or likely to become unable to pay its debts within the meaning of section 123 of IA 1986[201], but there is no requirement for the court to be satisfied that the order is reasonably likely to achieve one of those objectives[202], presumably because it is assumed that as applications have to be made by the Secretary of State or regulator, there is no need for any such filter to be included. There are the usual restrictions on the making of an order where the provider is already in administration or liquidation. In most other respects the proposed regime is similar or identical to normal administration. In particular, section 102 and Schedule 5 to the Housing and Planning Act 2016 introduces an amended version of Schedule B1 of IA 1986 to the conduct of the special administration regime which, in its essentials, provides for the application of all of the provisions of a normal administration, save for those which are only relevant to appointments out of court.

Education administration

20.47   The third intended regime relates to further education. The Technical and Further Education Bill, which is going through Parliament at the time of writing, will provide (if and when enacted) for the making of an education administration order in relation to further education bodies, including further education corporations or sixth form college corporations established under the Further and Higher Education Act 1992. As with all other special administration regimes, it is proposed that the procedure will only be available pursuant to a court order to be made on the application of the Secretary of State where the further education body is or is unlikely to become unable to pay its debts. There are special objectives for an education administration, namely to avoid or minimise disruption to the studies of the existing students or the further education body as a whole and to ensure that it becomes unnecessary for the body to remain in education administration for that purpose. The means by which it is proposed that the education administrator may achieve that objective

---

194 Within the meaning of the Co-operative and Community Benefit Societies Act 2014.
195 See Part 11 of the Charities Act 2011.
196 Section 96 of the Housing and Planning Act 2016.
197 Ie the same as the objectives provided for by Schedule B1 paragraph 3 of IA 1986: section 97 of the Housing and Planning Act 2016.
198 Section 98 of the Housing and Planning Act 2016.
199 Section 96 of the Housing and Planning Act 2016. Initially the government had proposed that the prioritisation should be the other way around, but this was changed after pressure from lenders.
200 Section 99(1) of the Housing and Planning Act 2016.
201 Section 100(2) of the Housing and Planning Act 2016.
202 Cf Schedule B1 paragraph 11(b) of IA 1986.

are by rescuing the further education body as a going concern, by transferring some or all of its undertaking to another body, by keeping it going until existing students have completed their studies, and by making arrangements for existing students to complete their studies at another institution. It is proposed that the process will be governed by a modified version of Schedule B1 to IA 1986 and a schedule which will make provision for transfer schemes to be approved by the Secretary of State, which will facilitate the transfer of property, rights and liabilities which could not otherwise be transferred.

21 Court practice and procedure

21.1 The court plays an important role in many administrations. In some cases it will determine whether the company ought to go into administration in the first place and, if so, the identity of the individual to be appointed as its officer[1]. There will also be many other cases in which the court will be required to consider applications for the appointment of an administrator to cease to have effect as well as numerous other different types of application during the course of an administration, ranging from applications for directions[2] to unfair harm applications[3] and applications for permission to proceed under Schedule B1 paragraph 43 of IA 1986. The court also plays a role in some voluntary arrangements under Part I of IA 1986, whether or not the arrangement is promulgated by an administrator. Some of these applications will be contentious and adversarial in form, whilst others will be of a more administrative and technical nature. In England and Wales, however, it is to the Rules, rather than the Civil Procedure Rules that an applicant must turn in the first instance to establish the appropriate procedure[4]. This chapter considers the more detailed provisions applicable in England and Wales.

21.2 For the purposes of construing IA 1986, the court means the court having jurisdiction to wind up the company[5]. The High Court has jurisdiction to wind up any company registered in England and Wales[6], as has the county court, so long as the amount of its share capital paid up or credited as paid up does not exceed £120,000[7]. In the case of the county court, proceedings must be commenced in the county court hearing centre serving the area in which the company's registered office is situate[8].

APPLICATIONS TO THE COURT

21.3 Any applications in the administration (whether under IA 1986, the Rules or the court's inherent jurisdiction) should be made to the court which

---

1 See eg *Re Maxwell Communication Corpn plc* [1992] BCLC 465 and *Re World Class Homes Ltd* [2004] EWHC 2906 (Ch).
2 Schedule B1 paragraph 63 of IA 1986, *Re Mirror Group (Holdings) Ltd* [1993] BCLC 538 and *Re Nortel Networks UK Ltd* [2014] EWHC 2614 (Ch).
3 Schedule B1 paragraph 74 of IA 1986.
4 See Rule 12.1 and generally Part 12 of the Rules.
5 Section 251 of IA 1986.
6 Section 117(1) of IA 1986.
7 Section 117(2) of IA 1986.
8 Rule 12.3(1) and (2) and Schedule 6 of the Rules. If there is any doubt, applications should be made to the High Court.

made the administration order or with which an appointment under Schedule B1 paragraph 14 or 22 was filed, even though there may have been another court[9] which would have had jurisdiction to wind up the company. The court which made the administration order or with which the notice of appointment was filed will retain the records of (and the file relating to) the administration[10] and it is that court of which the administrator will be an officer. A similar practice should be adopted in relation to voluntary arrangements; thus an application to challenge a decision of a creditors' meeting under section 6 of IA 1986 should be made to the same court to which the nominee's report was submitted. It should, however, be noted that many county courts have little or no experience of administration procedure and it is normally desirable for administration applications to be made to the High Court[11]. The High Court may order insolvency proceedings which are pending in that court to be transferred to a specified hearing centre and a judge in the High Court may order insolvency proceedings pending in the county court to be transferred to the High Court[12]. The county court may order insolvency proceedings which are pending in a hearing centre to be transferred either to the High Court or another hearing centre[13].

21.4 Anything to be done under or by virtue of IA 1986 or the Rules by, to or before the court may be done by, to or before a judge, district judge or a registrar[14]. In London, the jurisdiction of the High Court is exercised by the judges of the Chancery Division[15] and by the registrars; in practice there is a single judge, usually the applications judge, assigned to hear Companies Court business from time to time and one of the registrars acts as the Companies Court registrar. Outside London, the district registries of Birmingham, Bristol, Cardiff, Leeds, Liverpool, Manchester, Newcastle-upon-Tyne and Preston have insolvency jurisdiction and the functions of the registrar are exercised by the district judge. Where a matter is proceeding in a district registry, applications before the judge are listed to be heard by either a judge of the Chancery Division[16] or one of the circuit judges designated to hear Chancery High Court business. In the county court, the functions of the registrar are exercised by the officer of the court whose duty it is to exercise the functions which in the High Court are exercised by a registrar[17].

21.5 Except where inconsistent with the Rules, the CPR and the practice and procedure of the High Court or the county court (including any practice direction) apply to insolvency proceedings in the High Court or the county court as the case may be[18]. In fact, a large number of procedural matters are given specific consideration by the Rules. Where a matter is given specific consideration by the Rules, the equivalent CPR provisions are not incorporated at all. It should be noted that all insolvency proceedings (including those relating to an administration and company voluntary arrangement) are automatically

---

9   Eg the county court.
10   See Part 7 Chapter 5 of the Rules.
11   Either in London or an appropriate District Registry.
12   Rule 12.30(1) and (3) of the Rules.
13   Rule 12.30(2) of the Rules.
14   Rule 12.2(1) of the Rules
15   See section 61 and Schedule 1 paragraph 1 of the Senior Courts Act 1981.
16   Eg the Vice-Chancellor of the County Palatine of Lancaster who sits in the North of England.
17   Ie a district judge.
18   Rule 12.1 of the Rules.

allocated to the multi-track and so those parts of the CPR which provide for allocation questionnaires and track allocation do not apply[19].

21.6 Applications for administration orders are heard by a judge[20]. Interim applications and applications for directions or case management after any proceedings have been referred to the judge should also be made direct to the judge[21]. There will also be other instances in which a party makes an application to the court to give, under its inherent jurisdiction, directions to the administrator[22], in which an application direct to the judge may be justified, but they will be rare unless it is an application for urgent interlocutory relief where the registrar is not available. Occasionally, there are substantial matters (such as the Lehman, M F Global and Nortel administrations) in which a judge has been assigned to the administration, in which event that judge will hear every application, unless it is released by him to some other judge or registrar. All other applications in an administration or a company voluntary arrangement should normally be made to the registrar or district judge in the first instance[23].

21.7 The procedure applicable to the issue and hearing of an application for an administration order is described in **CHAPTER 1**. It is worth noting that Part 12 Chapter 3 of the Rules does not apply to applications for an administration order[24]. The procedural requirements are contained in Schedule B1 paragraphs 12 and 13 of IA 1986 and Part 3 Chapter 2 of the Rules. Apart from the application for an administration order, all other applications in an administration are made by way of ordinary application[25] in the administration proceedings. The mere fact that proceedings are commenced by an administrator or a company in administration does not, of course, mean that they are applications to which Part 12 of the Rules apply. Although Rule 12.6 of the Rules is no longer explicit on this point[26], it is thought that for Part 12 to apply at all, the application must be under IA 1986 or the Rules and even that form of words does not cover applications for relief under those parts of the Act to which the rule-making power does not apply, being in particular any claim under section 423 of IA 1986[27].

21.8 All applications should be made in the proceedings initiated by the application on which the administrator was appointed or which were opened by the filing of notice of appointment, as the case may be. Accordingly, as such an application will not be an originating process, it should be by way of ordinary application bearing the title and number of the relevant order or notice of appointment[28]. The form of the application itself is provided for by Rule 1.35(2) of the Rules; it must include the names of the parties, the nature of the relief sought, the names and addresses of the persons (if any) on whom it is intended

---

19   Rule 12.1(2) of the Rules.
20   Practice Direction: insolvency proceedings [2014] BCC 502 (paragraph 3.2(2)).
21   Practice Direction: insolvency proceedings [2014] BCC 502 (paragraph 3.2(5)).
22   See eg *Re Mirror Group (Holdings) Ltd* [1993] BCLC 538 and *Re Nortel Networks UK Ltd* [2014] EWHC 2641 (Ch).
23   Practice Direction: insolvency proceedings [2014] BCC 502 (paragraph 3.4).
24   Rule 12.6(a) of the Rules.
25   See Rule 1.35 of the Rules.
26   Compare Rule 7.1 of the Insolvency Rules 1986.
27   *TSB Bank plc v Katz* [1997] BPIR 147, *Jyske Bank Ltd v Spjednaes* [1998] 95(40) LSG 37, Evans-Lombe J, referred to at [1999] 2 BCLC 101 at 124 and *Banca Carige SpA v Banco Nacional de Cuba* [2001] 1 WLR 2039.
28   Rule 1.35 of the Rules.

to serve the application, the names and addresses of all persons on whom the application is required to be served and the applicant's address for service. It must be signed by the applicant (if he is acting in person) and otherwise by or on behalf of his solicitor[29]. Although an ordinary application is not required to state the grounds on which the applicant claims to be entitled to the relief sought, in most cases the grounds of the application will be apparent from an accompanying witness statement.

SERVICE

21.9   On the filing of an application[30] with the court, the court will fix a venue[31] for the application to be heard. In a normal case where there is no urgency, the application will be listed for hearing not less than 14 days after the date of filing to enable the applicant to serve the application on all respondents[32]. In an urgent case, an application can be made for short service[33], and if necessary the court can hear the matter immediately[34]. With certain exceptions, the provisions as to service contained in CPR Part 6 apply to the service of applications and indeed other documents in proceedings in the administration or the company voluntary arrangement[35]. Part 6 of the CPR applies to the service of any document, including an application, out of the jurisdiction[36].

21.10   In an appropriate case, the court is empowered to hear an application without notice. The Rules make express provision for this power to be exercised in cases of urgency[37] and in any case in which neither IA 1986 nor the Rules require the application to be served on any other person[38]. Applications in an administration can take a wide variety of forms and there is rarely provision for service on specified persons. The court may, of course, direct that particular parties with an interest in the outcome of the application should be served[39] but, in general, an applicant should anticipate the identity of persons whom the court will regard as having a legitimate interest in being heard and take steps to have them served in time for the first hearing.

EVIDENCE

21.11   In the ordinary case, where IA 1986 or the Rules require evidence, such evidence may be given by witness statement verified by a statement of truth unless the court directs otherwise[40], although, where there are no respondents, an administrator may (unless the court otherwise directs) support his application

---

29   Rule 1.35(3) of the Rules.
30   An application filed with the court in hard-copy must be accompanied by at least one additional copy plus sufficient copies for service: Rule 12.7 of the Rules.
31   Rule 12.8 of the Rules.
32   This must be done not less than 14 days before the hearing: Rule 12.9(3) of the Rules.
33   Rule 12.10(2) of the Rules.
34   Rule 12.10(1) of the Rules.
35   Schedule 4 paragraph 1 of the Rules.
36   Schedule 4 paragraph 1(8) of the Rules.
37   Rule 12.10 of the Rules.
38   Rule 12.12 of the Rules.
39   Rule 12.11 of the Rules.
40   Rules 12.28 of the Rules. Where the statement is made by an administrator it must comply with Rule 12.29(1) of the Rules.

with an unsworn report[41]; this will then be treated as if it were a witness statement[42]. The court may order any maker of a witness statement to attend for cross-examination. If such an order is made, and the maker does not attend, the witness statement may not be used in evidence without the leave of the court[43]. Witness statements to be used by the applicant on the first hearing of the application must be filed in court and served on the respondents not less than 14 days before the date of the hearing[44] and any respondent seeking to rely on written evidence in answer must file and serve it not less than five business days before the hearing[45]. In practice, compliance with these time limits is often relaxed and, where an application is not urgent, the first hearing is often used for the obtaining of directions.

DISCLOSURE

21.12 In a proper case, the court will order further information in accordance with CPR Part 18 and disclosure in accordance with CPR Part 31[46], although such orders are not automatic and the very nature of most applications in an administration or a company voluntary arrangement is such that they will often be inappropriate. As with other categories of case, disclosure will only be ordered in insolvency proceedings to the extent that it is proportionate to the issues in dispute. Applications seeking relief under Schedule B1 paragraphs 74 and 75 of IA 1986 are the types of proceeding in which disclosure and further information are most likely to be ordered. The court is expressly empowered to make an order for further information or disclosure without notice to any respondent[47], but it is thought that such relief will rarely be granted.

COURT RECORDS

21.13 The court keeps a record of all steps taken and documents filed with the court in the administration or the company voluntary arrangement and the court's decision in relation to each such step[48]. The administrator or supervisor (as the case may be), any duly authorised officer of the Secretary of State, any person stating himself in writing to be a creditor of the company and any director, officer or member of the company each has the right at all reasonable times to inspect the court's file[49]. The right of inspection may also be exercised by any person duly authorised by any of the foregoing[50] and the court has a general discretion to give any person special leave to inspect[51]. The approach of the court under the old Rules consisted of two stages:

1   The starting point is a strong presumption in favour of access to documents read by the court.

---

41   Rule 12.29(3) of the Rules. This right is not given to the supervisor of a voluntary arrangement.
42   Rule 12.29(4) of the Rules.
43   Rule 12.28(3) and (4) of the Rules.
44   Rule 12.28(2)(a) of the Rules.
45   Rule 12.28(2)(b) of the Rules.
46   Rule 12.27 of the Rules.
47   Rule 12.27(2) of the Rules.
48   Rule 12.39(1) of the Rules.
49   Rule 12.39(3) and (8) of the Rules.
50   Rule 12.39(5) of the Rules.
51   Rule 12.39(6) of the Rules.

2   The presumption could be departed from when there were countervailing reasons operating against it[52].

The court will want to be sure that the application is not simply a fishing expedition and that there is a genuine and legitimate interest on the part of the applicant.

21.14 Notwithstanding these rights to inspect, the court may direct that the file, a document (or part of it) or a copy of a document (or a part of it) must not be made available without permission of the court. This direction can be made at the suit of the administrator himself or any person interested; it is a particularly useful power where there is documentation which is of a commercially sensitive nature[53], or which may, for example, relate to the conduct of proceedings to which the company is a party. Under the former law, it was not unusual for such an order to be made in relation to all or part of the independent report prepared in support of the petition for an administration order.

COSTS

21.15 In general, CPR Parts 44 and 47 apply to applications for costs in proceedings in an administration or company voluntary arrangement[54]. Reference should be made to those parts of the CPR for their detailed provisions. There are, however, a number of specific provisions in the Rules which relate to the recovery of costs in insolvency proceedings[55]. It is with those specific provisions that this part of the chapter is concerned.

21.16 It is not unusual for the court to direct that the costs of some or all of the parties to proceedings in or arising out of an administration or company voluntary arrangement should be paid out of the company's assets. In such a case, the administrator or supervisor (as the responsible insolvency practitioner) can agree the amount of the costs or, if agreement cannot be reached, he can require (by notice in writing) the party entitled to costs to commence detailed assessment proceedings in accordance with CPR Part 47[56]. In any case, detailed assessment is required where a creditors' committee formed in relation to the administration resolves so or the court orders so[57]. Presumably, the power of the court to require a detailed assessment can be exercised on the application of a person entitled to his costs out of the assets, where the administrator or supervisor is being obdurate in agreeing an appropriate figure yet is himself refusing to require an assessment.

21.17 Where a person is required to have his costs decided by detailed assessment, he must commence detailed assessment proceedings in accordance with CPR Part 47 and it must be commenced in the court to which the insolvency proceedings are allocated, or, where in relation to a company there is no such

---

52   *Times Newspapers v McNamara* [2013] BPIR 1092.
53   Rule 12.39(9) and (11) of the Rules. As to which see eg *Astor Chemicals Ltd v Synthetic Technology Ltd* [1990] BCLC 1 at 7.
54   Rule 12.41 of the Rules.
55   See generally, Part 12 Chapter 8 of the Rules.
56   Rule 12.42(1) and (2) of the Rules.
57   Rule 12.42(2)(b) and (5) of the Rules.

court, any court having jurisdiction to wind up the company[58]. If the person does not do so within three months (or such further time as the court on application may allow), the estate may be dealt with without regard to his claim, which is thereupon forfeited[59]. The same applies to any claim which any person may have against the administrator or supervisor personally in addition to his claim to be paid out of the company's assets[60].

21.18 The court has a general discretion to make orders for costs, notwithstanding that the application was not made at the time of the particular proceeding to which the application relates[61]. However, if any person seeks to rely on this provision, he will not be entitled to his costs of the further application, unless the court is satisfied that it could not have been made at the time of the original proceeding[62].

ENFORCEMENT PROCEDURES

21.19 Orders made in administration proceedings are enforced as if they were judgments to the same effect[63]. Where a county court makes an order in administration proceedings, it may be enforced by any other hearing centre, whether or not it is a hearing centre in which such proceedings could have been commenced[64]. The court may, on application by the administrator, make such orders as it thinks necessary for the enforcement of obligations on a person to submit a statement of affairs[65].

REVIEWS AND APPEALS

21.20 Any court exercising jurisdiction in the administration of a company or in relation to a company voluntary arrangement has power to review, rescind or vary any order made by it in the exercise of that jurisdiction[66]. It may exercise its power on the application of any person aggrieved and whether or not they were or should have been parties to the original application[67]. The exercise of this power is not restricted to cases in which the order has not been drawn up, although it may be that the longer the delay, the less likely it is that a review will be granted. This power is one which is expressed in very general terms[68],

58 Rule 12.42(3) and 12.43(3) of the Rules.
59 Rule 12.43(4) of the Rules.
60 Rule 12.43(5) of the Rules.
61 Rule 12.48(1) of the Rules.
62 Rule 12.48(5) of the Rules.
63 Rule 12.51(1) of the Rules.
64 Rule 12.51(2) of the Rules.
65 Rule 12.52(1)(a) and (2)(a) of the Rules.
66 Rule 12.59(1) of the Rules. Although the rule refers to courts having jurisdiction to wind up companies and makes no reference to administration proceedings or to proceedings under Part I of IA 1986, it must be remembered that the court is only vested with jurisdiction in relation to an administration or company voluntary arrangement by reason of the fact that it has jurisdiction to wind up the company.
67 *Cornhill Insurance plc v Cornhill Financial Services Ltd* [1993] BCLC 914 and *Re Dianoor Jewels Ltd* [2001] 1 BCLC 450 at 455.
68 *Calmex Ltd v C Lila Ltd* [1989] 1 All ER 485 at 486j, approved by the CA in *Mond v Hammond Suddards* [2000] Ch 40 at 49 and *Credit Lucky Ltd and Gui Hui Dong v National Crime Agency* [2014] EWHC 83 (Ch). See *Wilson v Specter Partnership* [2007] EWHC 133 (Ch) for limitations on the jurisdiction.

but in practice the court will be reluctant to accede to an application for review or rescission where there has been no change of circumstance since the original order was made. In particular, where an application to review is in substance to be regarded as an appeal, and the time for appealing has expired, the court will not generally exercise its review jurisdiction unless there are special circumstances which make it proper to hear an application[69]. It is inappropriate, save in the most exceptional circumstances for a judge to substitute his own decision for that of another judge of co-ordinate jurisdiction reached on the same material after full consideration of the arguments[70]. However, unlike the position on appeal[71], the court may be prepared to admit fresh evidence on a review, even where that evidence was available when the matter was originally heard[72]. If the complaint is simply that the court making the original order was in error, the appropriate course is to appeal. On the other hand, particularly where the application is made by a party who was not represented on the original hearing[73], the court may be prepared to exercise the jurisdiction to review its previous order where it is demonstrated that at the time of the order the court was not fully appraised of the relevant facts or proceeded on the basis of some error or misapprehension or that the order is likely to operate oppressively or unfairly against the interest of the applicant[74]. An application to review a decision of a registrar should be made to a registrar and not to a single judge of the High Court whose jurisdiction in relation to decisions of the registrar is an appellate one[75].

21.21 Appeals from decisions of the county court and registrars of the High Court lie to a single judge of the High Court and appeals from a judge of the High Court lie to the Court of Appeal[76]. An appeal against a decision at first instance may be brought only with the permission of the court which made the decision or of the court that has jurisdiction to hear the appeal[77]. The Insolvency Practice Direction makes provision for the court centre in which the appeal is to be filed depending on the court which made the original decision[78]. An appellant must file an appellant's notice within 21 days after the date of the decision of the court that the appellant wishes to appeal[79].

---

69 *Re Jeavons, ex p Brown* (1874) 9 Ch App 304, *Re May, ex p May* (1884) 12 QBD 497, *Re Cohen* [1950] 2 All ER 36 and *Re Debtors (Nos VA7 and VA8), ex p Stevens* Lindsay J (27 October 1992, unreported). See also *Re Piccadilly Property Management Ltd* [1999] 2 BCLC 145.

70 *Mond v Hammond Suddards* [2000] Ch 40 at 49D–E.

71 As to which see *Ladd v Marshall* [1954] 1 WLR 1489.

72 *Re a Debtor (No 32/SD/1991)* [1993] 1 WLR 314, cited with approval in *Mond v Hammond Suddards* [2000] Ch 40 at 49F.

73 For an unusual case in which an application to review an administration order was made by a person (the estranged wife of one of the company's directors) not present at the original hearing, see *Re Dianoor Jewels Ltd* [2001] 1 BCLC 450.

74 See *Cornhill Insurance plc v Cornhill Financial Services Ltd* [1993] BCLC 914 and *Re W & A Glaser Ltd* [1994] BCC 199. Even in those circumstances the jurisdiction will be approached with great caution: *Re Thirty-Eight Building Ltd (No 2)* [2000] 1 BCLC 201.

75 *Re SN Group plc* [1994] 1 BCLC 319.

76 Rule 12.59(2) of the Rules. See also *Re Probe Date Systems Ltd (No 3)* [1992] BCLC 405 and *Re Tasbian Ltd (No 2)* [1991] BCLC 59.

77 Rule 12.61(1) of the Rules.

78 Practice Direction: insolvency proceedings [2014] BCC 502 (paragraphs 20.5–20.8).

79 Rule 12.61(2) of the Rules.

21.22 CPR Part 52 and Practice Directions 52A, 52B and 52C apply to appeals under Part 12 Chapter 10 of the Rules[80]. The appeal to a single judge of the High Court is a true appeal and is not treated as a hearing *de novo*[81]. Accordingly, the judge will not interfere with the exercise of a discretion, unless the court below took into account irrelevant considerations, failed to take into account relevant considerations, misdirected itself in law or reached a decision which is plainly wrong[82].

---

80 Rule 12.58 of the Rules and Practice Direction: insolvency proceedings [2014] BCC 502 at paragraph 2.9.
81 *Re Probe Data Systems Ltd (No 3)* [1991] BCLC 586 (at first instance) and *Re Tasbian Ltd (No 3)* [1991] BCLC 792: see also *Re Busytoday Ltd* [1993] BCLC 43.
82 See eg *The Abidin Daver* [1984] AC 398 per Lord Brandon at 420A–B and *Re MTI Trading Systems Ltd* [1998] BCC 400.

22 International aspects

POWERS OF AN ADMINISTRATOR TO ACT EXTRA-TERRITORIALLY

22.1 In relation to companies incorporated in England and Wales, the powers conferred on an administrator by IA 1986 do not appear to be limited territorially[1]. An administrator is required to manage the affairs, business and property of the company to which he is appointed[2]. The word 'affairs' is not defined by IA 1986, but 'business' is defined as including a trade or profession and 'property' as including 'money, goods, things in action, land and every description of property wherever situated'[3]. The use of the words 'wherever situated' means that the administrator's duties extend to property wherever in the world it may be[4], and it would therefore appear that an administrator's authority as regards assets situate abroad is, as a matter or English law, at least as extensive as that of a liquidator[5] and that *prima facie* his powers are fully exercisable in relation to such property to the extent necessary or desirable for the achievement of the purposes for which he was appointed[6].

22.2 Nevertheless, there is a distinction to be drawn between the authority of an administrator under IA 1986 to act extra-territorially on behalf of the company and his ability to do so effectively and without incurring liability under the law of the place where such acts are carried out. For instance, under English law, title to immovable property is governed by the law of the place where the immovable is situate[7]. Similarly, under English law, the validity of a transfer of a tangible movable is generally governed by the *lex situs* of the property in question[8]. Thus, notwithstanding the appointment of an administrator, English law may recognise the validity and effect of a foreign attachment of property

---

1   The effect of the EC Regulation on Insolvency Proceedings, which came into force on 31 May 2002, is considered *post*.
2   Schedule B1 paragraph 1(1) of IA 1986.
3   By section 436 of IA 1986.
4   *Bloom v Harms Offshore AHT 'Taurus' GmbH & Co KG* [2009] EWCA Civ 632 (paragraph 23).
5   Cf eg *Re Oriental Inland Steam Co* (1874) 9 Ch App 557 and *Stichting Shell Pensioenfonds v Krys* [2014] UKPC 41 (pargaraphs 14 and 15).
6   Schedule B1 paragraph 3(1) of IA 1986.
7   Dicey, Morris and Collins *The Conflict of Laws* (15th edn) Rule 132 (p.1330).
8   Dicey, Morris and Collins *The Conflict of Laws* (15th edn) Rule 133 (p.1336).

situate abroad[9] which an administrator may have therefore no option but to accept[10].

22.3 Similarly, in exercising his powers to deal with charged and other property under IA 1986, an administrator may find that, where the property in question is situate abroad, the courts of the place where the property is situate may decline to give effect to his powers under Schedule B1 paragraph 70 of IA 1986, in relation to property the subject of a security which, as created, was a floating charge, or to recognise or give effect to an order of the English courts under Schedule B1 paragraph 71, in relation to property subject to any other security, or under Schedule B1 paragraph 72, in relation to property subject to a hire-purchase agreement, conditional sale agreement, chattel leasing agreement or retention of title agreement. Indeed, where the property in question is situate abroad, the English courts may decline to make an order under Schedule B1 paragraph 71 or 72, particularly where the holder of the security has not submitted to the jurisdiction or is only incidentally present within and therefore subject to the jurisdiction, for example through the presence of a branch office, and where there is evidence that the courts of the country where the property is situate would not recognise or give effect to such an order[11]. In such circumstances, in order to act effectively, the administrator may be obliged to institute proceedings before the foreign court, either under the foreign equivalent of section 426 of IA 1986, by seeking relief under the UNCITRAL Model law or by instituting formal insolvency proceedings in respect of the company in the foreign court.

22.4 Nor are an administrator's specific powers as an office holder necessarily exercisable extra-territorially. Thus, the court, in the exercise of its powers under section 236 of IA 1986 (enquiry into the company's dealings), cannot summon before it on the application of an administrator a person beyond its territorial jurisdiction[12], although there are a number of other statutory powers which do have extra-territorial application[13]. Of equal significance is the fact that, even if the exemption from liability conferred on an office holder by section 234(3) and (4) of IA 1986, (where he seizes or disposes of property which is not the

9   Cf in the context of a liquidation, *Banco de Portugal v Waddell* (1880) 5 App Cas 161 especially per Lord Blackburn at 175 and *Minna Craig Steamship Co v Chartered Mercantile Bank of India, London and China* [1897] 1 QB 460; cf *Re Suidair International Airways Ltd* [1951] Ch 165.

10   An alternative course might be to commence insolvency proceedings in respect of the company in the country where the attachment took place: see eg *Barclays Bank plc v Homan* [1993] BCLC 680. Compare also *Re Buckingham International plc* [1997] 1 BCLC 673 and *Re Buckingham International plc (No 2)* [1998] 2 BCLC 369, where provisional liquidators, who were later appointed full liquidators, commenced ancillary proceedings in the United States under section 304 of the United States Bankruptcy Code with a view to restraining a judgment creditor from proceeding with writs of garnishment in the United States.

11   Cf *Re Paramount Airways Ltd* [1993] Ch 223 and *Barclays Bank plc v Homan* [1993] BCLC 680; see also *Re Vocalion (Foreign) Ltd* [1932] 2 Ch 196.

12   See *Re Tucker (a Bankrupt)* [1990] Ch 148. The court does have jurisdiction to order the examination of such a person outside the jurisdiction pursuant to section 237(3) of IA 1986 but will not normally exercise such jurisdiction unless the courts of the place where any such examination is to take place will act so as to compel the examination: *Re Tucker (a Bankrupt)* [1990] Ch 148. The law and authorities in this area were recently reviewed by David Richards J in *Re M F Global UK Ltd (in special administration) (No 7)* [2015] EWHC 2319 (Ch), who concluded that he was bound by the decision in *Re Tucker (a Bankrupt)*.

13   See the judgments of the Supreme Court in *Bilta (UK) Ltd v Nazir (No 2)* [2015] UKSC 23 (paragraphs 10, 53 110 and 214) approving the decisions of the Court of Appeal in *Re Seagull Manufacturing Co Ltd* [1993] Ch 345 and *Re Paramount Airways Ltd* [1993] Ch 223 to the effect that sections 133, 238 and 239 of IA 1986 have extra-territorial effect.

property of the company but at the time of such seizure or disposal believes on reasonable grounds that he is entitled to seize or dispose of the property) does, under IA 1986, have extra-territorial effect[14], it by no means follows that a foreign court would give effect thereto. Similar considerations would appear to apply to the statutory unenforceability of liens on the company's books, papers and other records pursuant to section 246 of IA 1986, to the extent that such books, papers and records are held outside the jurisdiction.

22.5 On the other hand, where the court is requested to make an order under section 236 of IA 1986 requiring a person within the territorial jurisdiction of the court to produce documents, there is no requirement that exceptional circumstances must be demonstrated before that person can be ordered to produce documents which are themselves held outside the jurisdiction[15]. In *Mid East Trading Ltd*[16], the Court of Appeal held that in so far as the making of an order under section 236 of IA 1986 involves an assertion of sovereignty, it is an assertion which the legislature must have intended the courts to make in an appropriate case. Whilst, in determining whether there was a proper case for the order to be made, the court would give weight to any real risk that compliance with the order would or might subject the examinee's claims for breach of confidence or criminal penalties in the jurisdiction in which the documents were held, there was no special hurdle of exceptional circumstances that had to be overcome. In *Re Omni Trustees Ltd (No 2)*[17], HHJ Hodge QC relied on *Mid East Trading Ltd* in reaching his conclusion[18] that section 236 did have extra-territorial application, although there was a difference in approach to be adopted where the relief sought was an examination as opposed merely to the disclosure of documents.

EXTRA-TERRITORIAL EFFECT OF THE STATUTORY MORATORIUM

22.6 A further question is the extent to which the courts will regard the provisions of Schedule B1 paragraphs 43 to 44 of IA 1986, by which the statutory moratorium is imposed on creditors, as having extra-territorial effect. In the context of a compulsory liquidation, the courts have held that the provisions now contained in section 130(2) of IA 1986, which provides that when a winding-up order has been made or a provisional liquidator has been appointed no action or proceeding may be proceeded with or commenced against the company or its property, except by the leave of court and subject to such terms as the court may impose, do not apply to actions or proceedings proceeded with or commenced outside the United Kingdom[19]. It does not follow that the courts will construe

---

14 Given that an administrator's powers may be exercised abroad, it is submitted that, as a matter of English law, the exemption from liability does have extra-territorial effect.

15 *Re Mid East Trading Ltd* [1998] 1 BCLC 240 (followed in *Re Casterbridge Properties Ltd* [2003] EWHC 1731 (Ch)).

16 [1998] 1 BCLC 240.

17 [2015] EWHC 2697 (Ch).

18 Contrary to that of David Richards J in *Re M F Global UK Ltd (in special administration) (No 7)* [2015] EWHC 2319 (Ch).

19 See *Oriental Inland Steam Co* (1874) 9 Ch App 557 affirming (1874) 30 LT 317 and *Re Vocalian (Foreign) Ltd* [1932] 2 Ch 196; cf *Re International Pulp and Paper Co* (1876) 3 Ch D 594, *Re Middlesbrough Firebrick Co Ltd* (1885) 52 LT 98 and *Re Dynamics Corpn of America* [1973] 1 WLR 63. See also *Hughes v Hannover Rückversicherungs AG* [1997] 1 BCLC 497 at 519a–d.

Schedule B1 paragraphs 43 and 44 of IA 1986 in the same way[20], although in *Bloom v Harms Offshore AHT 'Taurus' GmbH & Co KG*[21], Stanley Burnton LJ clearly thought that the territorial limitation given to the phrase 'action or proceeding' in section 130(2) of IA 1986 ought also to apply to the phrase 'legal proceedings' in Schedule B1 paragraph 43(6) of IA 1986. In the event the Court of Appeal concluded that it did not need to decide the point because of the existence of the jurisdiction to grant *in personam* injunctive relief in any event[22], but it is submitted that the provisional view expressed in the *Harms* case is correct.

22.7   Schedule B1 paragraphs 43 and 44 of IA 1986 are not confined in their application to the prohibition of actions or other legal proceedings against the company but extend so as to inhibit the taking by creditors of extra-judicial actions, including the taking of steps to enforce security over the company's property and the repossession of goods in its possession as well as to the levying of distress over its property. As already noted, the word 'property' is given a wide meaning by section 436 of IA 1986 and extends to 'every description of property' wherever situated. The statutory moratorium is imposed in order to assist the achievement of statutory purposes for which the company enters administration. The achievement of those purposes is capable of being jeopardised by action against the company or its property or goods in its possession either within or outside the United Kingdom. It is therefore submitted that the court should interpret Schedule B1 paragraphs 43 and 44 of IA 1986 as widely as possible[23].

22.8   The difficulty which arises is that while, in an appropriate case[24], there is a well-established jurisdiction in the English courts to restrain litigants from suing in a foreign jurisdiction, there is a very strong presumption that Parliament does not legislate to interfere with proceedings in foreign courts[25]. Acting in breach of Schedule B1 paragraphs 43 and 44 of IA 1986 is capable of being a contempt of court[26]; on one view it would be a surprising conclusion if a non-resident alien (not subject to the English court's *in personam* jurisdiction)

---

20   Cf *Re a Debtor (No 1 of 1987)* [1989] 1 WLR 271, per Nicholls LJ at 276G–277B approved by the House of Lords in *Smith (A Bankrupt) v Braintree District Council* [1990] 2 AC 215.

21   [2009] EWCA Civ 632 (paragraphs 21 and 22).

22   In *Kaupthing HF v Kaupthing Singer & Friedlander Ltd (in administration)* [2012] EWHC 2235 (Ch), Sir Andrew Morritt C decided (at paragraph 39) that the statutory moratorium in the administration of a credit institution to which the Credit Institutions (Reorganisation and Winding up) Regulations 2004 (SI 2004 No 1045) applies does extend to legal proceedings in another EEA member state.

23   It is a matter of regret that the English courts have not always been prepared to give effect to the worldwide operation of the statutory moratoria of foreign insolvency jurisdictions; cf *Felixstowe Dock and Rly Co v United States Lines Inc* [1989] QB 360. The *Felixstowe* case does not properly represent the approach of the UK courts to the recognition of foreign statutory moratoria. For a different approach, see *Banque Indosuez SA v Ferromet Resources Inc* [1993] BCLC 112 at 117i, approved by Lord Collins in *Rubin v Eurofinance SA* [2012] UKSC 46 (paragraph 29). See also *Re OJSC Ank Yugraneft v Sibir Energy plc* [2008] EWHC 2614 (Ch) (paragraph 48).

24   *Re Distin* (1871) 24 LT 197, *Re Tait & Co* (1872) LR 13 Eq 311, *Re North Carolina Estate Co Ltd* (1889) 5 TLR 328, *Re Vocalion (Foreign) Ltd* [1932] 2 Ch 196, *South Carolina Insurance Co v Assurantie Maatschappij de Zeven Provincien NV* [1987] AC 24, *Société Nationale Industrielle Aerospatiale v Lee Kui Jak* [1987] AC 871 and *Bank of Tokyo Ltd v Karoon* [1987] AC 45n.

25   See eg Mellish LJ in *Re Oriental Inland Steam Co* (1874) 9 Ch App 557 at 560 and the reasoning of Maugham J in *Re Vocalion (Foreign) Ltd* [1932] 2 Ch 196.

26   See eg *Sabre International Products Ltd* [1991] BCC 694.

were to be guilty of contempt of the English court because he had sued in his own place of domicile a company in administration in England. The solution to this difficulty is that while the English courts have jurisdiction to grant *in personam* relief restraining litigants from suing in a foreign jurisdiction, it should only be exercised in an appropriate case. The courts have stressed that relief in this form will not often be granted[27], but, although vexatious or oppressive conduct (or sharp practice) by the creditor will justify such relief, it is not necessary for this to be established[28]. The jurisdiction flows from the court's ability to grant, against persons subject to its jurisdiction, such relief as may be appropriate to prevent interference with the achievement by the administrator of the purposes for which the administrator has been, or is to be, appointed[29]. Put another way, the court has power to grant such relief as may be necessary in any particular case to enable the administrators to exercise their statutory functions and to fulfil their statutory duties[30].

22.9   Thus, as regards creditors subject to the jurisdiction or who seek to prove in a voluntary arrangement or compromise or scheme of arrangement entered into in the course of an administration, it is submitted that the court has jurisdiction to restrain such creditors from taking action outside its jurisdiction which would interfere with the achievement by the administrator of the purposes for which he has been appointed or to disgorge or to give credit for assets recovered outside the jurisdiction as a result of such action[31]. The fact that a particular creditor may be outside the jurisdiction of the court, and accordingly able to take such action with impunity, ought not to deflect the courts from adopting a wide purposive interpretation of Schedule B1 paragraphs 43 and 44 of IA 1986 or to cause the courts to deny their jurisdiction to grant relief against those subject to their territorial jurisdiction[32].

22.10   Of course, the court is not bound to grant relief in a particular case, merely because actions taken, or proposed to be taken, abroad would interfere with the achievement by the administrator of the purposes for which he has been appointed. The court may decline to grant injunctive relief or to require the disgorgement of assets recovered abroad where, on an application duly made, it would grant, or would have granted permission to the creditor concerned to take the proposed action abroad. Similarly, in the case of a foreign domiciled creditor temporarily within the jurisdiction or a foreign incorporated or foreign resident

---

27   For an appropriate case see *Bloom v Harms Offshore AHT 'Taurus' GmbH & Co KG* [2009] EWCA Civ 632 in which the Court of Appeal stressed that injunctive relief restraining foreign proceedings will always be exceptional even where it is in aid of an English insolvency.

28   *Stichting Shell Pensioenfonds v Krys* [2014] UKPC 41 (paragraph 24).

29   Cf the analysis of Robert Goff LJ in *Bank of Tokyo Ltd v Karoon* [1987] AC 45 at 60B–H and the judgment of the Privy Council in *Société Nationale Industrielle Aerospatiale v Lee Kui Jak* [1987] AC 871 at 892G–893B. In this context, it is clear that administration forms part of the statutory scheme under IA 1986 designed to achieve a fair distribution of an insolvent company's property among its unsecured creditors; see *Re Polly Peck International plc (No 4)* [1998] 2 BCLC 185 per Mummery LJ at 201b–e.

30   *Bloom v Harms Offshore AHT 'Taurus' GmbH & Co KG* [2009] EWCA Civ 632 (paragraph 27).

31   See, *inter alia*, *Re Distin* (1871) 24 LT 197, *Re North Carolina Estate Co Ltd* (1889) 5 TLR 328, *ReTait & Co* (1872) LR 13 Eq 311 and *Banco de Portugal v Waddell* (1880) 5 App Cas 161.

32   *Stichting Shell Pensioenfonds v Krys* [2014] UKPC 41 in which the Privy Council concluded that allowing proceedings which would put the claimant at an advantage over other comparable claimants was not conducive to the ends of justice. See also *Re Buckingham International plc (No 1) Mitchell v Carter* [1997] 1 BCLC 673.

company whose dealings with the company have taken place abroad, but which incidentally has a branch office within the jurisdiction, the court in the exercise of its discretion may decline to grant relief[33], particularly where the grant of such relief would amount to an indirect interference with the processes of a foreign court[34]. Further, the court may decline to enjoin an English domiciled or resident creditor from taking action abroad where there are foreign creditors not subject to the jurisdiction of the court who in any event are likely to take similar action abroad. In such circumstances, by granting an injunction, the English court might simply be favouring foreign creditors at the expense of English creditors[35]. In each case, the court is likely to consider critically what is 'likely to be more conducive to substantial justice'[36]. However, the possibility of the court taking such discretionary considerations into account, and declining injunctive relief in particular circumstances, does not negate the existence of jurisdiction to grant such relief[37].

TRANSACTIONS PRE-DATING THE ADMINISTRATION

22.11 As considered in **CHAPTER 8** *ante*, an administrator is given extensive powers to attack transactions at an undervalue and preferences (or, in Scotland, gratuitous alienations and unfair preferences), extortionate credit transactions and transactions defrauding creditors. As a matter of construction of IA 1986, each of these powers is exercisable with respect both to persons resident outside the territorial jurisdiction of the court and to transactions involving property situate outside the jurisdiction[38]. In each case, however, the power of the court to grant relief to the administrator is discretionary[39]. It should also be noted that, as the better view is that administrations are excluded by the bankruptcy exception from the scope of the Brussels Regulation[40], its jurisdiction, recognition and enforcement provisions are unlikely to be applicable to applications made by administrators to attack transactions on the basis of any of the foregoing powers[41].

---

33   See *Re Vocalion (Foreign) Ltd* [1932] 2 Ch 196 especially per Maugham J at 204–5 and 210–11; cf *Moor v Anglo-Italian Bank* (1879) 10 Ch D 681.

34   Cf *Barclays Bank plc v Homan* [1993] BCLC 680 especially per Hoffmann J at 686d–g, per Glidewell LJ at 700g–701b and per Leggatt LJ at 706a–d.

35   See *Re Vocalion (Foreign) Ltd* [1932] 2 Ch 196 especially per Maugham J at 205.

36   See the dictum of Lord Cranworth LC in *Carron Iron Co v Mclaren* (1855) 5 HL Cas 416 at 439 applied in *Re Vocalion (Foreign) Ltd* [1932] 2 Ch 196 at 208. See also *Stichting Shell Pensioenfonds v Krys* [2014] UKPC 41 (paragraph 38).

37   *Bloom v Harms Offshore AHT 'Taurus' GmbH & Co KG* [2009] EWCA Civ 632.

38   See *Re Paramount Airways Ltd* [1993] Ch 223 approved in *Bilta (UK) Ltd v Nazir (No 2)* [2015] UKSC 23 (paragraphs 10, 53 110 and 214).

39   See sections 238(3), 239(3), 242(4), 243(4), 244(2) and 423(2) of IA 1986.

40   Regulation (EC) 44/2001 on jurisdiction and the recognition and enforcement of judgments in civil and commercial matters, as recast in Regulation (EU) 1215/2012 of the European Parliament and of the Council on jurisdiction and the recognition and enforcement of judgments in civil and commercial matters.

41   As to section 238 see *Byers v Yacht Bull Corp* [2010] EWHC 133 (Ch) (paragraph 23). See also *UBS AG v Omni Holding AG* [2000] 2 BCLC 310 (a Swiss liquidation in which the analogous exclusion in the Lugano Convention was under consideration). Cf *Jyske Bank (Gibraltar) Ltd v Spjeldnaes* [1999] 2 BCLC 101 where it was held by Evans-Lombe J at 123 that a claim by a creditor under section 423 of IA 1986 (not made in the course of formal insolvency proceedings) fell within the scope of what was then the Brussels Convention. See also *Fondazione Enasarco v Lehman Brothers Finance SA, Anthracite Rated Investments (Cayman) Ltd* [2014] EWHC 34 (Ch).

22.12 In *Re Paramount Airways Ltd*[42], Sir Donald Nicholls V-C in delivering the judgment of the Court of Appeal, stated that the court's discretion was wide enough to enable the court, if justice required, to make no order and that if a foreign element was involved the court would need to be satisfied that, in respect of the relief sought against him, the defendant was sufficiently connected with the forum for it to be just and proper to make the order against him despite the foreign element[43]. The Vice-Chancellor continued[44]:

'This connection might be sufficiently shown by the residence of the defendant. If he is resident in England, or the defendant is an English company, the fact that the transaction concerned moveable or even immoveable property abroad would by itself be unlikely to carry much weight. Likewise if the defendant carries on business here and the transaction related to that business. Or the connection might be shown by the situation of the property, such as land, in this country. In such a case, the foreign nationality or residence of the defendant would not *by itself* normally be a weighty factor against the court exercising its jurisdiction under the sections. Conversely, the presence of the defendant in this country, either at the time of the transaction or when the proceedings were initiated, will not necessarily mean that he has sufficient connection with this country in respect of the relief sought against him. His presence might be coincidental or unrelated to the transaction. Or the defendant may be a multinational bank, carrying on business here, but all the dealings in question may have taken place at an overseas branch.

Thus in considering whether there is a sufficient connection with this country the court will look at all the circumstances, including the residence and place of business of the defendant, his connection with the insolvent, the nature and purpose of the transaction being impugned, the nature and locality of the property involved, the circumstances in which the defendant became involved in the transaction or received a benefit from it or acquired the property in question, whether the defendant acted in good faith, and whether under any relevant foreign law the defendant acquired an unimpeachable title free from any claims even if the insolvent had been adjudged bankrupt or wound-up locally. The importance to be attached to these factors will vary from case to case. By taking into account and weighing these and any other relevant circumstances, the court will ensure that it does not seek to exercise oppressively or unreasonably the very wide jurisdiction conferred by the sections.'

It follows that the court has a very wide discretion to decline to grant relief against foreign residents in respect of transactions involving property situate abroad[45].

22.13 The court's discretionary powers are also relevant when considering whether or not to grant permission under CPR Part 6[46] to serve process outside the jurisdiction on a respondent who is abroad. In determining whether or not to grant such permission, the court will take into account, *inter alia*, the

---

42   [1993] Ch 223.
43   [1993] Ch 223 at 239H–240A. This principle was applied by Lightman J in *Re Banco Nacional de Cuba* [2001] 1 WLR 2039 at 2058.
44   [1993] Ch 223 at 240A–F.
45   For an example, see *Jyske Bank (Gibraltar) Ltd v Spjeldnaes* [1999] 2 BCLC 101 where an order was made under section 423 of IA 1986 setting aside a contract between two Irish companies, made and to be performed in Ireland, governing the disposition of land in Ireland.
46   As applied by Schedule 4 paragraph 1(8) of the Rules.

strength or weakness of the administrator's claim[47], and in particular the apparent strength or weakness of the administrator's claim that the defendant has a sufficient connection with the jurisdiction in respect of the relief sought in the proceedings[48]. The administrator must establish first, that the claim has a reasonable prospect of success[49], or a real issue between him and the prospective respondent which the court may reasonably be asked to try[50]. Secondly, the court must take account of the fact that the prospective respondent is abroad and should not be required to answer claims in the UK unless there is good reason why the UK is the proper place for those claims to be litigated[51]. If the court is not satisfied that there is a sufficient connection with the jurisdiction, it will refuse the administrator permission to serve process abroad. The fact that the Inland Revenue is a major, or, indeed, the only creditor in the relevant insolvency proceedings is not, however, a ground for declining permission[52].

22.14 As previously mentioned, charges created by a company may be void against an administrator under section 859H of CA 2006 for nonregistration or invalid under section 245 of IA 1986. Once again, these provisions are capable of applying with respect both to chargeholders resident and charged property situate outside the jurisdiction, although no discretion arises under either section 859H of CA 2006 or, if the requirements thereof are satisfied, under section 245 of IA 1986. Nor indeed does the operation of these sections depend upon an order of the court, although it does not follow, particularly where the charge is not governed by English law and extends to property situate outside the jurisdiction, that their effect will necessarily be recognised by the courts of the foreign country where the charged property is situate[53].

22.15 Nevertheless, in so far as the above-mentioned statutory provisions are capable of having effect as against persons not capable of being served with the process within the jurisdiction, similar discretionary considerations as those discussed above may be relevant to the question of whether or not leave should be granted under CPR Part 6 to serve process upon a proposed respondent outside the jurisdiction. In each case the court asked to grant leave must determine that the case is a proper one for service out of the jurisdiction[54]. Thus, where a foreign chargeholder is seeking to enforce or has enforced against property of a company in administration situate outside the jurisdiction a charge, particularly one not governed by English law, granted pursuant to dealings between the company and the chargeholder which took place outside the jurisdiction, but which nevertheless may be capable of attack under section 859H of CA 2006 or section 245 of IA 1986, the court may not necessarily grant leave for service out of the jurisdiction[55].

---

47 Taking into account the insolvency context: *Hosking v Apax Partners LLP* [2016] EWHC 558 (Ch).
48 *Re Paramount Airways Ltd* [1993] Ch 223 per Sir Donald Nicholls V-C at 241E–H. See also *In Re Banco Nacional de Cuba* [2001] 1 WLR 2039 where the issue arose in the context of an application for permission to serve out of the jurisdiction proceedings commenced by a creditor under section 423 of IA 1986.
49 The test articulated in Practice Direction: insolvency proceedings [2014] BCC 502 at paragraph 6.6.
50 *Re Howard Holdings Inc* [1993] BCC 549 per Chadwick J at 553D–554B.
51 *Re Sahaviriya Steel Industries UK Ltd* [2015] EWHC 2877 (Ch).
52 *Miller v Bain* [2002] BCC 899.
53 Cf *Galbraith v Grimshaw and Baxter* [1910] AC 508.
54 See *Re Paramount Airways Ltd* [1993] Ch 223 per Sir Donald Nicholls V-C at 241E–H.
55 Cf *Re Vocalion (Foreign) Ltd* [1932] 2 Ch 196 especially per Maugham J at 205–206.

CO-OPERATION BETWEEN COURTS EXERCISING JURISDICTION IN RELATION TO INSOLVENCY

22.16 Pursuant to section 426(1) of IA 1986, an order made in the course of administration proceedings by a court in England and Wales is enforceable in any other part of the United Kingdom[56] as if it were made by a court exercising the corresponding jurisdiction in that other part. However, the provision does not, of itself, oblige a court in any part of the United Kingdom to enforce, in relation to property situate in that part, any order made by a court in any other part of the United Kingdom[57].

22.17 In addition, pursuant to section 426(4) of IA 1986, the courts having jurisdiction in relation to insolvency law in any part of the United Kingdom are required to assist the courts having the corresponding jurisdiction in any other part of the United Kingdom or any relevant country or territory. The relevant countries and territories currently comprise the Channel Islands and the Isle of Man[58] or any of the following[59]: Anguilla, Australia, the Bahamas, Bermuda, Botswana, Brunei Darussalam, Canada, Cayman Islands, Falkland Islands, Gibraltar, Hong Kong, the Republic of Ireland, Malaysia, Montserrat, New Zealand, St Helena, South Africa, Turks and Caicos Islands, Tuvalu and the Virgin Islands.

22.18 It is, accordingly, open to a court in England and Wales or Scotland to request the assistance of the courts of any other part of the United Kingdom, and in particular to request such other court to apply the insolvency law of the requesting court. The court to which the request is addressed must give effect thereto by applying either the insolvency law of the requesting court applicable to comparable matters within its own jurisdiction, if so requested, or its own insolvency law applying to comparable matters within its jurisdiction[60]. *Prima facie*, the court to which the request is addressed should give effect to such request, notwithstanding that it relates to property situate within its own jurisdiction[61].

22.19 Where a request is made to a UK court pursuant to section 426(4) of IA 1986, the request is authority for the court to which the request is made to apply, in relation to the matters specified in the request, the insolvency law[62] which is applicable by either the requesting court or the court to which the request is made in relation to comparable matters falling within its jurisdiction[63]. Section 426(5) provides that in exercising its discretion under section 426(4) the court must have regard in particular to the rules of private international law[64].

---

56 Ie Scotland and Northern Ireland.
57 Section 426(2) of IA 1986.
58 Section 426(11)(a) of IA 1986.
59 Section 426(11)(b) and the Co-operation of Insolvency Courts (Designation of Relevant Countries and Territories) Orders 1986 (SI 1986 No 2123), 1996 (1996 No 253) and 1998 (1998 No 2766) (as modified by SI 2001 No 1090).
60 Section 426(5) of IA 1986.
61 Cf section 426(2) of IA 1986.
62 As defined in section 426(10) of IA 1986.
63 Section 426(5) of IA 1986. It has been held that 'comparable matters' include matters in which the facts are the same as specified in the request apart from the foreign element: see *Re Dallhold Estates (UK) Pty Ltd* [1992] BCLC 621 at 626f–g, approved in *Hughes v Hannover Rückversicherungs AG* [1997] 1 BCLC 497 per Morritt J at 516h–517e.
64 See the last sentence of section 426(5) of IA 1986.

The wording of this requirement has been described as 'slightly mystifying'[65], 'obscure and ill-thought out'[66] and 'difficult and obscure'[67]; it is not even clear which court is being referred to – is it the requesting court or the receiving court? In *Re Dallhold Estates (UK) Pty Ltd*[68], Chadwick J held that section 426(5) referred to the discretion of the court in making the request, but in *Re Bank of Credit and Commerce International Ltd*[69], Rattee J expressed the view that the requirement was directed at the discretion of the court to which the request was addressed to apply its own law or the law of the requesting court to the matters specified in the request[70]. In the light of the decision of the House of Lords in *In re HIH Casualty and General Insurance Ltd; McGrath v Riddell*[71] the latter view is to be preferred so that, for example, the English court would retain a discretion to refuse to apply English insolvency law to a preference claim to be brought against an English resident pursuant to a request under section 426(4) of IA 1986, even though the foreign court had requested the English court to apply English law, where the events giving rise to the alleged preference all occurred in the foreign country where the insolvent company was incorporated.

22.20 Once a request complying with the provisions of section 426 is made to it, a UK court will, in normal circumstances, give effect thereto either by applying the provisions of its own insolvency law, whether procedural or substantive, or by applying the provisions of the foreign insolvency law which, in either case, would be applicable to comparable matters falling within the respective jurisdictions of the respective courts[72]. For the purposes of section 426 of IA 1986, insolvency law is widely defined as meaning, in relation to England and Wales, provision made by or under IA 1986 or under certain sections of the Company Directors Disqualification Act 1986 extending to England and Wales and, in relation to Scotland, provision made by or under IA 1986, the same sections of the Company Directors Disqualification Act 1986, Part XVIII of CA

---

65 *In re HIH Casualty and General Insurance Ltd; McGrath v Riddell* [2008] UKHL 21 (paragraph 82) per Lord Neuberger.

66 *Re Television Trade Rentals Ltd* [2002] EWHC 211 (Ch) (paragraph 17).

67 *Rubin v Eurofinance SA* [2012] UKSC 46 (paragraph 147) per Lord Collins. See also *Singularis Holdings Ltd v PwC* [2014] UKPC 36 (paragraph 47) and *In re HIH Casualty and General Insurance Ltd; McGrath v Ridell* [2008] UKHL 21 (paragraphs 55 and 77).

68 [1992] BCLC 621 per Chadwick J at 626g–h.

69 [1993] BCC 787.

70 [1993] BCC 787 at 801G. This appears to have been the view also of Morritt LJ in *England v Smith* [2001] Ch 419 at 432D–E. See also *Re Television Trade Rentals Ltd* [2002] EWHC 211 (Ch) where Lawrence Collins J expressed the view that the court should take into account the foreign elements, such as the respective connections of the parties with England and the foreign country, in deciding what law to apply.

71 [2008] UKHL 21 (see in particular paragraph 30 per Lord Hoffmann in which he explained that the primary rule of international law which was to be applied by the English court was the principle of modified universalism).

72 *Re Dallhold Estates (UK) Pty Ltd* [1992] BCLC 621 per Chadwick J at 626b–h and 627c–628d, where an administrator order was made in relation to a company incorporated outside the UK. See also *Re Business City Express Ltd* [1997] 2 BCLC 510 where Rattee J at the request of the Irish High Court applied to English creditors Irish law as to the binding effect on creditors of an Irish scheme of arrangement and *Re Trading Partners Ltd* [2002] 1 BCLC 655 where Patten J made an order recognising the status as liquidators within the English jurisdiction of joint liquidators of a company incorporated in the British Virgin Islands who had been appointed by the courts of that jurisdiction. In *Re Television Trade Rentals Ltd* [2002] EWHC 211 (Ch), Lawrence Collins J made an order directing that the provisions of Part I of IA 1986 relating to company voluntary arrangements should apply to two Isle of Man incorporated companies. He declined, however, to order that the provisions should apply with retrospective effect.

1985 and the Bankruptcy (Scotland) Act 1985 extending to Scotland[73]. In relation to countries or territories outside the United Kingdom, however, insolvency law includes only so much of the law of that country or territory as corresponds to the insolvency laws of the countries forming the United Kingdom[74]. Difficulties may arise in future as to whether a particular provision of the law of a non-UK country or territory does in fact correspond to UK provisions.

22.21 In relation to incoming requests for assistance, it is made clear by the judgment of the Court of Appeal in *Hughes v Hannover Rückversicherungs AG*[75], that in providing assistance the courts of the UK have their usual jurisdiction and powers. Thus, there is available to the courts of England and Wales, or Scotland, when asked for assistance:

(a) their own general jurisdiction and powers; and either

(b) their own insolvency laws as specified in section 426(1) of IA 1986; or

(c) so much of the law of the relevant country as corresponds to that comprised in (b)[76].

In the case of (b) and (c), but not (a), the requested court is entitled to apply such law on the hypothesis that the matters specified in the request fall within the jurisdiction of the court whose insolvency law is to be applied in so far as 'comparable matters' not containing a foreign element would do so.

22.22 Notwithstanding the apparently mandatory terms of section 426(4) of IA 1986, which imposes a duty on the court to assist, the court, nevertheless, retains a residual discretion as to the extent of the assistance and the method by which such assistance should be given. Thus, assistance may be limited, or subject to conditions, or refused altogether, where to give effect to the request would conflict with concurrent domestic insolvency proceedings relating to the company[77] or where the foreign insolvency is effectively a tax-gathering exercise[78]. An example of such a refusal occurred in *Re Focus Insurance Co Ltd*[79] where the liquidators of a Bermudian company sought to apply section 426 to obtain orders for disclosure of assets by an English resident judgment debtor of the Bermudian company. The company had already obtained a bankruptcy order against the judgment debtor in England based upon the judgment. Sir Richard Scott V-C, holding that the court retained a discretion to refuse assistance where there was a good or compelling reason for not giving assistance[80], refused to give the assistance requested on the basis that to do so would be inconsistent with the scheme under IA 1986 for the administration of the judgment debtor's assets by his trustee in bankruptcy. However, absent this type of case, the English court

---

73 Section 426(10) of IA 1986.

74 Section 426(10) of IA 1986.

75 [1997] 1 BCLC 497.

76 On this point the conclusion of the Court of Appeal in *Hughes v Hannover* was approved by the House of Lords in *In re HIH Casualty and General Insurance Ltd; McGrath v Riddell* [2008] UKHL 21 (paragraph 26) per Lord Hoffmann.

77 Cf *Re Osborn, ex p the Trustee* [1931–2] B & CR 189 per Farwell J at 194 and *Re a Debtor, ex p the Viscount of the Royal Court of Jersey* [1981] Ch 384 per Goulding J. at 402, applying section 122 of the Bankruptcy Act 1914.

78 Cf *Government of India v Taylor* [1955] AC 491 and *Peter Buchanan Ltd and Macharg v McVey* [1955] AC 516n.

79 [1997] 1 BCLC 219.

80 Following dicta of Chadwick J in *Re Dallhold Estates (UK) Pty Ltd* [1992] BCLC 621 at 627e and of Rattee J in *Re Bank of Credit and Commerce International SA (No 9)* [1994] 2 BCLC 636 at 657h–658n.

will in an appropriate case exercise its discretion to accede to a request under section 426 even where compliance with the request will lead to assets being distributed in a manner that is inconsistent with the English statutory scheme[81].

22.23 The basis for a UK court refusing to give effect to a letter of request was considered by the Court of Appeal in *Hughes v Hannover Ruckversicherungs-AG*[82]. Morritt LJ pointed out that there was nothing in subsections (4) or (5) of section 426 of IA 1986 which required the UK courts merely to grant the assistance sought 'for sub-section (4) does not refer to the request and sub-section (5) does not require assistance to be given by reference to the request'. He went on to summarise the proper approach[83] of the requested court in the following terms:

> 'Accordingly the function of the court under s 426 must be to consider whether in accordance with the three sources of law I earlier identified as (a), (b) and (c) the assistance may properly be granted. If it may then it should be, thereby discharging the statutory duty imposed by s 426. But if it may not be properly granted then it should be withheld for it must be implicit in the fact that the duty is cast on a court that the duty is qualified by reference to what the court may properly do as a court. Of course if the court in England cannot do exactly what is sought then it should consider whether it can properly assist in some other way in accordance with any of the available systems of law. Thus the reasons for withholding assistance either as sought or in any other way are not limited to reasons of public policy. Of course public policy is a reason why assistance may be impossible under (a) and (b). But it is by no means the only reason. Further public policy might prevent assistance being given under (c) if the provision of the insolvency law of the country the court of which requested the assistance were contrary to the public policy recognised by the court in England. In my view the court must consider in all cases whether the assistance sought or any other comparable assistance may be properly granted in accordance with the laws the court is authorised to apply on the hypotheses likewise permitted.
>
> In some cases the assistance sought is, in accordance with the system [of] law (sc. (a), (b) and (c)) under which it is available, discretionary. Obviously the fact of the request for assistance is a weighty factor to be taken into account. Further the court in England may be expected, as Knox J did in this case, to accept without further investigation the views of the requesting court as to what was required for the proper conduct of the bankruptcy or winding up. But I do not think that the request can ever be conclusive as to the manner in which the discretion of the court should be exercised. It would be incompatible with the principle of the law which was being applied that the decision was one for the discretion of the court if the fact of the request was anything more than a factor however weighty.'[84]

Applying those principles, the Court of Appeal went on to refuse the request by the Bermudian courts for an injunction restraining a German-based reinsurer

---

81 *In re HIH Casualty and General Insurance Ltd; McGrath v Riddell* [2008] UKHL 21, where the liquidators in an English ancillary liquidation were directed to remit assets to Australia for distribution in the principal liquidation notwithstanding the existence in Australia of a class of preferential creditors who would not have priority in an English distribution.

82 [1997] 1 BCLC 497.

83 An approach that is consistent with the approach adopted by the House of Lords in *In re HIH Casualty and General Insurance Ltd; McGrath v Riddell* [2008] UKHL 21.

84 [1997] 1 BCLC 497 at 517h–518e.

with a place of business in England from commencing arbitration proceedings outside the UK against an insurance company in liquidation in Bermuda. In so doing, the Court of Appeal expressed the view that, as one of the factors to be taken into account, the weight to be attached to the request for assistance was reduced by a change in circumstances since the letter of request had been issued which had not been reconsidered by the requesting court.

22.24 It does not follow, however, that where a UK court is requested to apply the insolvency law of a foreign court, the English law should exercise its discretion in the same way that it would exercise its discretion in determining whether to exercise the jurisdiction conferred by a comparable provision of its own law. So, in *England v Smith*[85], on the application of the Australian liquidator of an Australian company being wound up in Australia, the Court of Appeal directed the private examination in England of an English-based accountant pursuant to section 596B of the Australian Corporation Law. The Court of Appeal held that the fact that the English courts would not in similar circumstances have made an order under section 236 of IA 1986 was not determinative of whether effect should be given to the letter of request[86]. Having made the decision under section 426(5) of IA 1986 to apply a provision of Australian law, the UK court was bound to apply the applicable principles in accordance with which the jurisdiction thereby conferred would be exercised by the Australian courts. Whilst the UK court retained discretion as to whether to accede to the letter of request, the request by the foreign court was a weighty factor to be taken into account, and given that the UK court was under duty to give assistance to the foreign court where that assistance could properly be given, it was appropriate in the circumstances to accede to the letter of request.

22.25 As regards the possibility of the recognition and the enforcement in EC member states under the Brussels Regulation[87] of court orders made in the course of an administration, the position would appear to be that since Article 1(2)(b) provides that the Regulation does not apply to, *inter alia*, 'proceedings relating to the winding up of insolvent companies ... judicial arrangements, compositions and analogous proceedings', administration proceedings as such are excluded. It will be noted that in his authoritative report on the predecessor Convention[88], the rapporteur MP Jenard stated that Article 1(2) excluded from the operation of the Convention proceedings which:

'depending upon the system of law involved, are based on the suspension of payments, the insolvency of the debtor or his inability to raise credit, and which involve the judicial authorities for the purpose either of compulsory and collective liquidation of the assets or simply of supervision'[89].

---

85 [2001] Ch 419.
86 The Court of Appeal held that the section 236 approach, which had been followed by both the judge below and the judge in *Re JN Taylor Finance Pty Ltd* [1999] 2 BCLC 25 (where the facts were similar), was flawed. *England v Smith* was subsequently followed in *Re Duke Group Ltd* [2001] BCC 144.
87 Regulation (EC) 44/2001 on jurisdiction and the recognition and enforcement of judgments in civil and commercial matters, as recast in Regulation (EU) 1215/2012 of the European Parliament and of the Council on jurisdiction and the recognition and enforcement of judgments in civil and commercial matters.
88 Which the courts were required to take into account when construing the Convention: section 3(3) of Civil Jurisdiction and Judgments Act 1982.
89 OJ 1979 No C59/1.

Administration proceedings would appear to fall within this definition. It does not, however, follow that proceedings to which a company in administration is party are necessarily excluded from the scope of the Regulation. The test is whether such proceedings are derived directly from the winding up or analogous proceedings[90]. A claim therefore by a company in administration to recover a debt due to it in the normal course of trading would not be excluded from the scope of the Brussels Regulation.

22.26 In addition to the provisions of section 426 of IA 1986, the Cross Border Insolvency Regulations 2006 ('CBIR')[91] have given the UNCITRAL Model Law ('the Model Law') the force of law in Great Britain in the form set out in Schedule 1 to the CBIR. The Model Law is primarily designed to deal with the circumstances in which assistance can be sought in Great Britain by a foreign court or a foreign representative, and assistance is sought in a foreign state in connection with British insolvency proceedings, including administrations and CVAs[92]. A foreign representative is a person or body authorised in a foreign proceeding to administer the reorganisation of the debtor's assets or affairs or to act as a representative of the foreign proceeding[93]. A foreign proceeding is a collective judicial or administrative proceeding in a foreign state pursuant to a law relating to insolvency in which proceeding the assets and affairs of the debtor are subject to control or supervision by a foreign court for the purpose of reorganisation or liquidation[94]. Schedule 2 to the CBIR then sets outs detailed procedural matters on how the Model Law is to be implemented in England and Wales. It is expressly provided[95] that to the extent of any conflict, the provisions of the EC Insolvency Regulation[96] shall prevail. A description of the Model Law is beyond the scope of this work, but there are a number of provisions which relate to the conduct of administration proceedings and CVAs, and which it is proposed to summarise.

22.27 So far as concerns the rights of an office holder in English insolvency proceedings[97], he is explicitly authorised by Article 5 of the Model Law to act in a foreign state on behalf of a proceeding under British insolvency law (ie the proceeding in which he is appointed) to the extent permitted by the applicable foreign law. This has the effect of authorising him to seek recognition elsewhere in the world and also to exercise such powers as the foreign law may permit him to use in furtherance of his statutory functions. He is also required, to the extent consistent with his other duties, and in the exercise of his functions, and subject to the supervision of the court, to cooperate to the maximum extent possible with foreign courts and foreign representatives[98]. He is also entitled to communicate directly with foreign courts and foreign representatives[99].

---

90 See *Gourdain v Nadler: Case 133/78* [1979] ECR 733, *Re Hayward* [1997] Ch 45 and *Re UBS AG v Omni Holding AG* [2000] 2 BCLC 310. See also *Ashurst v Pollard* [2001] Ch 595, *Byers v Yacht Bull Corp* [2010] EWHC 133 (Ch) and *Fondazione Enasarco v Lehman Brothers Finance SA, Anthracite Rated Investments (Cayman) Ltd* [2014] EWHC 34 (Ch).
91 SI 2006 No 1030. Made under the authority of s.14 of IA 2000.
92 Article 1(1) of the Model Law.
93 Article 2(j) of the Model Law.
94 Article 2(i) of the Model Law and for an analysis of the definition see *In re Stanford International Bank Ltd* [2010] EWCA Civ 137.
95 Article 3 of the Model Law.
96 Council Regulation (EC) No 1346/2000.
97 Which includes an administrator and the nominee or supervisor of a CVA: Article 2(b)(ii) of the Model Law and s.388(1) of IA 1986.
98 Article 26 of the Model Law; for the types of cooperation, see Article 27 of the Model Law.
99 Article 26(2) of the Model Law.

22.28 So far as concerns the rights of foreign representatives in Great Britain, Article 11 of the Model Law entitles him to apply to commence an English insolvency proceeding, which will include administration or a CVA if the conditions for commencing such a proceeding are otherwise met. This gives the foreign representative procedural standing in England and Wales to seek the appointment of an administrator under Schedule B1 paragraph 12 of IA 1986 or to propose a CVA, anyway in relation to the debtor in respect of which he acts as such. He is also entitled to seek an order recognising the foreign proceeding of which he is a foreign representative[100], and once he has done so he is then entitled to participate in any proceeding regarding the debtor under British insolvency law[101], and even to intervene in any other proceedings to which the debtor is a party[102]. On the recognition application, the foreign proceeding must be recognised as a foreign main proceeding (if the company has its centre of main interests in the relevant foreign state[103]) or a foreign non-main proceeding (if the company has an establishment in the relevant foreign state)[104].

22.29 In addition to the general right to participate, the effect of recognition of a foreign proceeding is to obtain a mandatory stay equivalent to the stay granted by section 130 of IA 1986 when a winding up order is made[105]. The court also has a discretion to grant a number of additional categories of relief. Those categories include provisions for the examination of witnesses and the delivery of information, entrusting the administration (and even the distribution) of assets to the foreign representative and granting all of the relief provided under Schedule B1 paragraph 43 of IA 1986[106]. Perhaps the most far-reaching of the additional rights given to a foreign representative (on recognition of his foreign proceeding) is the standing to make applications under a significant number of provisions of IA 1986, even where the debtor company is in administration in England[107]. In any such case the relevant provisions are modified in a number of respects to render them compatible with the fact that the applicant is not the English office holder, and the court must give directions to ensure that the interests of the creditors in Great Britain are adequately protected[108] and (in the case of a foreign non-main proceeding) be satisfied that any assets to which any application relates ought to be administered in that foreign proceeding[109]. Where the company is already in administration or subject to a CVA, the foreign

---

100 He is entitled to recognition if certain requirements, including those set out in Article 15 of the Model Law are met: Article 17 of the Model Law. The recognition application must be decided upon at the earliest possible time: Article 17(3) of the Model Law.
101 Article 12 of the Model Law. This will include any administration and any CVA.
102 Article 24 of the Model Law.
103 As to which see eg *American Energy Group Ltd v Hycarbex Asia Pte Ltd* [2014] EWHC 1091 (Ch).
104 Article 17(2) of the Model Law. This is a similar exercise to the one mandated by the EC Insolvency Regulation (Council Regulation (EC) No 1346/2000): *In re Stanford International Bank Ltd* [2010] EWCA Civ 137 (paragraph 36) and *Trustees of the Olympic Airlines SA Pension & Life Insurance Scheme v Olympic Airlines SA* [2013] EWCA Civ 643 (paragraphs 18 and 19).
105 Article 20 of the Model Law.
106 Article 21(1) of the Model Law, a course which was taken in *Re Transfield ER Cape Ltd* [2010] EWHC 2851 (Ch) and *Re Pan Oceanic Maritime Inc* [2010] EWHC 1734 (Comm).
107 Article 23(1) and (2) of the Model Law. The relevant sections are sections 238, 239, 242, 243, 244, 245 and 423 of IA 1986.
108 Article 23(7) of the Model Law.
109 Article 23(5) of the Model Law.

representative cannot make an application under Article 23 without first seeking the permission of the High Court[110].

CONCURRENT INSOLVENCIES

22.30 Apart from invoking the provisions of section 426 of IA 1986, or exercising his rights under the Model Law to the extent that its provisions are applicable in the relevant jurisdiction, an administrator may seek to secure control of assets situate outside the jurisdiction by instituting formal insolvency proceedings in the courts of the country where such assets are situate. Presumably, before doing so, an administrator should seek the directions of the court since submission to the jurisdiction of a foreign court may involve surrender, at least in part, of control of the company's affairs to the foreign court. However, this risk may be more limited where he is exercising his power under Article 5 of the Model Law. This is because, on the assumption that the foreign state has enacted the Model Law in the same terms as it has been enacted in Great Britain, the equivalent of Article 10 of the Model Law should mean that he will not thereby be treated as submitting to the jurisdiction of the foreign court for any purpose other than the relevant application. Alternatively, the administrator may find that without any action on his part, as a result of the action of directors of the company or of its creditors, the company to which he has been appointed may be already, or may become, subject to formal insolvency proceedings in a foreign country. In such circumstances, questions may arise as to the extent to which the administrator may seek to apply the provisions of the foreign insolvency law.

22.31 In *Barclays Bank plc v Homan*[111], the company was subject to an administration order in England and proceedings under Chapter 11 of the US Bankruptcy Code in New York. An English clearing bank sought to restrain the administrators from taking proceedings against it in New York under section 547 of the US Bankruptcy Code to recover a payment which had been made to the bank shortly prior to the making of the administration order and the commencement of the Chapter 11 proceedings. Hoffmann J, whose decision was upheld by the Court of Appeal, declined to grant the injunction. He held that since the company was subject to insolvency proceedings in New York in circumstances where, in a comparable case, an English court would regard itself as having jurisdiction over the company[112], and since on the facts the source of the repayment was the proceeds of sale of assets situate in the United States, a decision by the New York court to assert jurisdiction over the claim would not constitute so 'egregious' a claim of extra-territoriality that it should be prevented by injunction[113]. In the judge's view, in such circumstances the foreign court should be left to make its own decision as to whether proceedings before it should be continued or stayed and it was only in an exceptional case, where the institution or continuation of the foreign proceedings would be vexatious or oppressive to the defendant concerned, that the English court would intervene to prevent the prosecution of foreign proceedings by injunction[114]. In considering

---

110 Article 23(6) of the Model Law.
111 [1993] BCLC 680.
112 [1993] BCLC 680 per Hoffmann J at 684e–g.
113 [1993] BCLC 680 per Hoffmann J at 692d–e.
114 [1993] BCLC 680 per Hoffmann J at 686b–689a and 691d–692a; see also per Glidewell LJ at 701bff and 730g–704b. See also per Millett LJ in *Re Buckingham International plc* [1997] 1 BCLC 673 at 687e–g.

the question of vexation and oppression, Hoffmann J did not regard the fact that the defendant would be at a substantive disadvantage in defending the claim in the New York court[115] as rendering the foreign proceedings vexatious or oppressive[116]. More recently the courts have stressed that, although relief in this form will not often be granted[117], it is not necessary for vexatious or oppressive conduct to be established[118]. The jurisdiction flows from the court's ability to grant, against persons subject to its jurisdiction, such relief as may be appropriate to prevent interference with the achievement by the administrator of the purposes for which the administrator has been, or is to be, appointed[119], and the court has power to grant such relief as may be necessary in any particular case to enable the administrators to exercise their statutory functions and to fulfil their statutory duties[120].

22.32 A further reason given by Hoffmann J for reaching his decision was that the company was in any event subject to the jurisdiction of the New York court, that if the administrators did not authorise the institution of proceedings in New York, the New York court to which they owed fiduciary duties would authorise others to do so, and that the grant of an injunction would serve no purpose except to antagonise the New York court[121]. Earlier in his judgment, Hoffmann J had stressed the importance, in the absence of an international convention on cross-border insolvency, of the discretionary exercise of jurisdictional self-restraint so as to avoid jurisdictional conflicts in cross-border insolvencies but added that one could not expect every jurisdiction to exercise that discretion in the same way[122]. This part of Hoffmann J's judgment, with which, in the Court of Appeal, Mann and Leggatt LJJ appear to have agreed[123], suggests that, irrespective of the facts relating to the particular transaction in issue, an English court is unlikely to seek to restrain, even indirectly, the exercise by a foreign court of insolvency jurisdiction in relation to a company subject to English administration proceedings where, in a comparable case, the English court would regard itself as having jurisdiction over the company. Presumably, however, where compliance with such directions would not render the company or its administrator in breach of its obligations in concurrent foreign insolvency proceedings to which the UK courts regarded the company as properly subject, the court could give directions to an administrator, as its officer, as to in what jurisdiction proceedings against a particular respondent should be commenced.

---

115 By reason of the differences between the English and US laws on preferences.

116 See also per Glidewell LJ at 704g–705b.

117 For an appropriate case see *Bloom v Harms Offshore AHT 'Taurus' GmbH & Co KG* [2009] EWCA Civ 632 in which the Court of Appeal stressed that injunctive relief restraining foreign proceedings will always be exceptional even where it is in aid of an English insolvency.

118 *Stichting Shell Pensioenfonds v Krys* [2014] UKPC 41 (paragraph 24).

119 In this context, it is clear that administration forms part of the statutory scheme under IA 1986 designed to achieve a fair distribution of an insolvent company's property among its unsecured creditors, see *Re Polly Peck International plc (No 4)* [1998] 2 BCLC 185 per Mummery LJ at 201b–e.

120 *Bloom v Harms Offshore AHT 'Taurus' GmbH & Co KG* [2009] EWCA Civ 632 (paragraph 27).

121 [1993] BCLC 680 per Hoffmann J at 693a–e.

122 [1993] BCLC 680 at 691g–692a.

123 [1993] BCLC 680 at 705d–e and 705h–706e.

POWER TO MAKE ADMINISTRATION ORDERS IN RELATION TO FOREIGN INCORPORATED COMPANIES

22.33 It is settled that pursuant to a duly formulated request for assistance under section 426(4) of IA 1986, and subject to being satisfied as to the matters specified in Schedule B1 paragraph 11 of IA 1986, the English courts have jurisdiction to make an administration order in respect of a company incorporated outside the United Kingdom[124]. It also appears clear that only an English court can make an administration order in respect of an English incorporated company and only a Scottish court can make an administration order in respect of a Scottish incorporated company[125]. Similarly, it is clear that neither an English nor a Scottish court can make an administration order in relation to a company registered or incorporated in Northern Ireland[126].

22.34 In the first edition of this book[127], it was suggested that absent a request for assistance under section 426(4) of IA 1986, the English courts had no jurisdiction to make an administration order under Part II of IA 1986 as originally enacted in relation to a company incorporated outside the United Kingdom. Briefly, the reason for that conclusion was that in the absence of any definition of 'company' in IA 1986 itself as originally enacted, section 251 of IA 1986 provided that any expression for whose interpretation provision was made by Part XXVI of CA 1985 was to be construed in accordance with that provision. Part XXVI of CA 1985 defined 'company' as meaning a company formed and registered under CA 1985 or an existing company, ie a company formed and registered under the former Companies Acts, 'unless the contrary intention appears'[128]. *Prima facie* therefore, since on the face of it, no contrary intention appeared in Part II of IA 1986 itself relating to administration orders as originally enacted, it was submitted that there was no power, save pursuant to section 426 of IA 1986, to make an administration order in respect of a company incorporated outside the United Kingdom. However, whatever the position used to be, the law has now been clarified.

22.35 Schedule B1 paragraph 111(1A) of IA 1986 now provides that, in relation to Schedule B1, 'company' means:

(a)   a company registered under CA 2006 in England and Wales or Scotland;

(b)   a company incorporated in an EEA state other than the United Kingdom; or

(c)   a company not incorporated in an EEA state but having its centre of main interests in a member state other than Denmark[129].

---

124   See *Re Dallhold Estates (UK) Pty Ltd* [1992] BCLC 621.
125   Since, for the purpose of Schedule B1 paragraph 11 of IA 1986, the 'court' means the court having jurisdiction to wind up the company (s.251 of IA 1986) and since section 117 of IA 1986 gives the English courts jurisdiction to wind up companies registered in England and Wales and section 120 of IA 1986 gives the Scottish courts jurisdiction to wind up companies registered in Scotland. The EC Regulation on Insolvency Proceedings does not govern the allocation of jurisdiction within the UK; see Recital 15.
126   See section 441 of IA 1986.
127   **CHAPTER 18, PARAGRAPHS 18.26–18.33.**
128   Section 735 of CA 1985.
129   This formulation has now replaced a definition of company which was contained in Schedule B1 paragraph 111(1) until 2005 to the effect that the word 'company' included a company which may enter into administration by virtue of Article 3 of the EC Insovency Regulation, a definition that was considered in *Re The Salvage Association* [2003] EWHC 1028 (Ch).

It is also provided that the phrase 'centre of main interests' is to have the same meaning as in the EC Insolvency Regulation[130] and in the absence of proof to the contrary is presumed to be the place of its registered office[131]. Section 1(4) and (5) of IA 1986 makes similar provision in relation to company voluntary arrangements. The predecessor to Schedule B1 paragraph 111(1A) had led to the English courts holding that they had jurisdiction to make an administration order in relation to a company incorporated outside the UK, including a company incorporated outside the EU, provided that the company has its centre of main interests in England and Wales[132]. This remains the case under the new definition, because such a company will fall within subparagraph (c) above[133]. It should be noted, however, that there will often be practical problems if any foreign company enters administration other than by means of an order of the court. The reason for this is that there will have been no judicial determination that jurisdiction exists[134]. It must, though, have all of the attributes of an incorporated institution, otherwise it will not be a company at all[135].

THE EC REGULATION ON INSOLVENCY PROCEEDINGS

22.36 The EC Regulation on insolvency proceedings ('the EC Insolvency Regulation')[136] applies, *inter alia*, to administrations and corporate voluntary arrangements commenced in the United Kingdom after the coming into force of the EC Regulation on 31 May 2002[137]. It has been repealed with effect from 26 June 2017 by Regulation of the European Parliament and the Council on insolvency proceedings ('the recast Insolvency Regulation')[138], but the essential substance of most of the EC Insolvency Regulation has been retained. It provides for the international jurisdiction of the courts of EU member states in insolvency proceedings, the recognition and enforcement of such proceedings and orders made pursuant thereto in other EU member states and for the choice of law in such proceedings. For this purpose, the word 'court' is widely defined as meaning the judicial body or any competent body of a member state empowered to open insolvency proceedings or to take decisions in the course of such proceedings[139]. Thus in relation to a corporate voluntary arrangement, it appears that the creditors' meeting constitutes a 'court' for the purpose of the EC Insolvency Regulation[140]. The EC Insolvency Regulation does not apply in the UK to the extent that it is irreconcilable with obligations arising in relation to the winding up of insolvent companies from any arrangement with the Commonwealth existing at the date of entry into force of the EC Insolvency

---

130 Council Regulation (EC) No 1346/2000.
131 Schedule B1 paragraph 111(1B) of IA 1986.
132 See *Re BRAC Rent-A-Car International Inc* [2003] EWHC 128 (Ch), *Re Salvage Association* [2003] EWHC 1028 (Ch) and *Re Daiseytek-ISA Ltd* [2003] BCC 562.
133 *Mackellar v Griffin* [2014] EWHC 2644 (Ch).
134 For the disputes which can subsequently arise see *Re FREP (Knowle) Ltd* [2017] EWHC 25 (Ch).
135 *Panter v Rowellian Football Social Club* [2011] EWHC 1301 (Ch).
136 Council Regulation (EC) No 1346/2000.
137 Articles 43 and 47 of the EC Insolvency Regulation.
138 Regulation (EU) 2015/848 (the 'recast Insolvency Regulation').
139 Article 2(d) of the EC Insolvency Regulation and Article 2(6) of the recast Insolvency Regulation.
140 See *Re Salvage Association* [2003] EWHC 1028 (Ch), [2003] 3 All ER 246 per Blackburne J at 251–2.

Regulation[141]. Insolvency proceedings concerning insurance undertakings, credit institutions, investment undertakings holding funds or securities for third parties and collective investment undertakings are also excluded from the operation of the EC Insolvency Regulation[142].

22.37 It is beyond the scope of this work to enter into a full discussion of the terms and effect of the EC Insolvency Regulation which is not confined to administrations and other rescue procedures. What follows, therefore, is limited to a summary of the principal effects of the EC Insolvency Regulation as it applies to United Kingdom administrations and voluntary arrangements.

22.38 The EC Insolvency Regulation provides for main insolvency proceedings and secondary insolvency proceedings to be opened in member states. Insolvency proceedings are described in the EC Insolvency Regulation as collective insolvency proceedings which entail the partial or total divestment of a debtor and the appointment of a liquidator or other office-holder[143]. There is a more extensive description of the types of proceeding to which the recast Insolvency Regulation is intended to apply[144], namely public collective proceedings based on laws relating to insolvency in which, for the purposes of rescue, adjustment of debt, reorganisation or liquidation, one of three things occur. The first is that a debtor is totally or partially divested of its assets and an insolvency practitioner is appointed. The second is that the assets and affairs of a debtor are subject to control or supervision of a court. The third is that a temporary stay is granted to allow for negotiations between a debtor and its creditors provided suitable protective measures are introduced. The different types of insolvency proceedings and the different types of office-holder in the various member states are listed in Annexes A and C to the EC Insolvency Regulation and Annexes A and B to the recast Insolvency Regulation. They include, in the United Kingdom, administration (including by filing with the court[145]) and administrators and voluntary arrangements and their supervisors. For the purpose of the EC Insolvency Regulation, an administrator or supervisor constitutes a liquidator[146], but the recast Insolvency Regulation now uses the phrase 'insolvency practitioner' to describe the relevant office holder, including an administrator[147]. Main insolvency proceedings are to be opened in the member state where the debtor has the centre of his main interests which should correspond to the place where the debtor conducts the administration of his interests on a regular basis and is therefore ascertainable by third parties[148]. In the case of a company, there is a presumption that this is the place of its registered office, which can only be

---

141 Article 44(3)(b) of the EC Insolvency Regulation and Article 85(3)(b) of the recast Insolvency Regulation.

142 Article 1(2) of the EC Insolvency Regulation and the recast Insolvency Regulation. Separate provision has been made for insurance undertakings and credit institutions, see the EC Directives 2001/17 and 2001/24 enacted in the United Kingdom by the Insurers (Reorganisation and Winding Up) Regulations 2004 (SI 2004 No 353) and the Credit Institutions (Reorganisation and Winding up) Regulations 2004 (SI 2004 No 1045).

143 Article 1(1) of the EC Insolvency Regulation.

144 Article 1(1) of the recast Insolvency Regulation.

145 Ie appointments by directors, the company and the holders of a qualifying floating charge.

146 Article 2(b) of the EC Insolvency Regulation and Annex C.

147 Article 2(5) of the recast Insolvency Regulation and Annex B.

148 See Article 3(1) of the EC Insolvency Regulation and Recital 13. See also Article 3(1) of the recast Insolvency Regulation and Recitals 27–34. The leading case on the test for identifying the centre of main interests ('COMI') of a debtor is the decision of the CJEU in *Re Eurofood IFSC Ltd* [2006] Ch 508; see also *Re Interedil Srl* [2012] BCC 851.

rebutted if factors which are objective and ascertainable by third parties point to some other place[149]. There is a more detailed description of the centre of main interests concept in the Recitals in the recast Insolvency Regulation which makes clear that the reference to third parties is to creditors in particular. The determination is to be made at the time the proceedings are opened[150]. The EC Insolvency Regulation does not apply to proceedings where the centre of the debtor's main interests is located outside of the EU[151].

22.39   Where the centre of the debtor's main interests is situate in a member state, the courts of other member states only have jurisdiction to open insolvency proceedings against the debtor if he possesses an establishment within the territory of the other member state concerned[152]. In the EC Insolvency Regulation an establishment is defined to mean a place of operations where the debtor carries out a non-transitory economic activity with human means and goods[153]; in the recast Insolvency Regulation, the word 'goods' has been replaced with 'assets'[154]. The effects of such proceedings are restricted to the assets of the debtor situate in that other member state[155].

22.40   Where main insolvency proceedings have already been opened in a member state, any proceedings subsequently commenced in other member states are secondary proceedings. Under the EC Insolvency Regulation they must constitute winding-up proceedings[156], but this requirement is no longer included in the recast Insolvency Regulation. Winding-up proceedings are defined in the EC Insolvency Regulation as insolvency proceedings which involve realising the assets of the debtor and include proceedings which are closed by a composition or other measure or by reason of the insufficiency of the assets[157]. The different types of winding-up proceedings in the various member states are listed in Annex B to the EC Insolvency Regulation. Since administrations, though insolvency proceedings, do not constitute winding-up proceedings within the meaning of the EC Insolvency Regulation[158], it follows that it is not possible

---

149   Article 3(1) of the EC Insolvency Regulation. The presumption was rebutted in *Re Daisytek-ISA Ltd* [2003] BCC 562 (German and French incorporated companies), *Re Collins & Aikman Group* [2005] EWHC 1754 (Ch) (companies incorporated throughout Europe), *Re Parkside Flexibles SA* [2006] BCC 589, (a company incorporated in Poland), *Aim Underwriting Agencies (Ireland) Ltd* [2005] I L Pr 22 (company incorporated in Ireland) and *Re Kaupthing Capital Partners II Master LP Inc* (in administration) [2010] EWHC 836 (Ch) (a Guernsey partnership). For other cases in which the COMI of a company in administration was considered, see *Re Nortel Networks SA* [2009] EWHC 206 (Ch), *Mackellar v Griffin* [2014] EWHC 2644 (Ch) and *Re FREP (Knowle) Ltd* [2017] EWHC 25 (Ch).
150   *Shierson v Vlieland-Boddy* [2005] EWCA Civ 974.
151   See Recital 14 of the EC Insolvency Regulation and Recital 25 of the recast Insolvency Regulation. Denmark is excluded for this purpose: see Recital 33.
152   Article 3(2) of the EC Insolvency Regulation and of the recast Insolvency Regulation.
153   Article 2(h) of the EC Regulation. In *TeliaSonera AB v Hilcourt (Docklands) Ltd* [2002] EWHC 2377 (Ch), Park J held that the business premises in England of a Swedish debtor's UK subsidiary did not rank as an establishment of the Swedish debtor. For a review of the law on what is sufficient to constitute an 'establishment', see *Trustees of the Olympic Airlines SA Pension & Life Insurance Scheme v Olympic Airlines SA* [2013] EWCA Civ 643 and *Re Office Metro Ltd* [2012] EWHC 1191 (Ch).
154   Article 2(1) of the recast Insolvency Regulation.
155   Article 3(2) of the EC Insolvency Regulation and the recast Insolvency Regulation and see also Article 17(2) of the EC Insolvency Regulation.
156   Article 3(3) of the EC Insolvency Regulation.
157   Article 2(c) of the EC Insolvency Regulation.
158   Article 2(c) of the EC Insolvency Regulation and Annex B.

until 26 June 2017 to appoint an administrator where the centre of the company's main interests is situate in another member state and insolvency proceedings have already been commenced in the other member state. Nor will it be possible to put into effect a corporate voluntary arrangement where main insolvency proceedings relating to the debtor have been commenced in another member state in which the centre of the company's main interests is situate.

22.41 Further, even where insolvency proceedings have not already been commenced in another member state where the centre of the debtor's main interests is situate, it is not possible to appoint an administrator to, or to put into effect a corporate voluntary arrangement in relation to, a corporate debtor with an establishment in the United Kingdom unless either main insolvency proceedings cannot be opened because of conditions laid down by the law of the member state in which the centre of the debtor's main interests is situate or the opening of the proceedings is requested by a creditor who has his domicile, habitual residence or registered office within the United Kingdom or whose claims arise from the operations of the debtor's establishment within the United Kingdom[159]. In such circumstances the effect of the proceedings, which are referred as 'territorial proceedings', will be restricted to the assets of the debtor within the United Kingdom[160].

22.42 The appointment of an administrator or the putting into effect of a corporate voluntary arrangement in the exercise of the United Kingdom's international jurisdiction under the EC Insolvency Regulation will be recognised automatically in all the other member states[161]. However, even where the proceedings constitute main proceedings within the meaning of the EC Insolvency Regulation, such recognition does not preclude the opening of secondary proceedings within other member states[162]. The appointment of an administrator or the putting into effect of a corporate voluntary arrangement in proceedings which constitute main proceedings within the meaning of the EC Insolvency Regulation will produce the same effect in other member states as in the United Kingdom unless the EC Insolvency Regulation otherwise provides and as long as no secondary proceedings are opened in the other member state concerned[163]. Similarly, an administrator or the supervisor of a voluntary arrangement in main insolvency proceedings will have power to exercise all

---

159 Article 3(4) of the EC Insolvency Regulation and the recast Insolvency Regulation. It is somewhat difficult to envisage how the latter requirement could be satisfied in relation to a corporate voluntary arrangement.

160 Article 3(2) of the EC Insolvency Regulation and see Article 17(2). Article 3(2) of the recast Insolvency Regulation. The closing words of Article 17(2) of the EC Insolvency Regulation indicate that it is open to individual creditors to agree otherwise.

161 Article 16(1) of the EC Insolvency Regulation and see also Recital 22. Article 19(1) of the recast Insolvency Regulation. However, in *Klempka v ISA Daisytek SA* [2003] BCC 984, the French Court at first instance purported to make a French administrator order as main proceedings in respect of a French company notwithstanding that the English Courts had already made an administration order as main proceedings in respect of the company on the grounds that the company's centre of main interests was in England. This decision was reversed on appeal to the Court of Appeal of Versailles which held that English administration order was entitled to automatic recognition and that the French Court had no jurisdiction to make an administration order thereafter, a decision which was upheld by the Court of Cassation: *Klempka v ISA Daisytek SA* [2006] BCC 841. See also *Re Eurofood IFSC Ltd* [2004] BCC 383.

162 Article 16(2) of the EC Insolvency Regulation and Article 19(2) of the recast Insolvency Regulation.

163 Article 17(1) of the EC Insolvency Regulation and Article 20(1) of the recast Insolvency Regulation.

the powers conferred on him in other member states so long as no secondary proceedings have been opened in the other member state concerned and no preservation measure to the contrary has been taken there further to a request for the opening of such secondary proceedings[164]. Subject to Articles 5 and 7 of the EC Insolvency Regulation[165], the administrator or the supervisor in such circumstances will have power to remove the company's assets from the member state in which they are situated[166]. By contrast, Article 18(2) of the EC Insolvency Regulation[167] makes provision, in effect, for an administrator or supervisor appointed in territorial proceedings to reclaim, in another member state, movable property which was removed from the jurisdiction of the UK after the opening of the proceedings. A 'temporary administrator' appointed in main proceedings is empowered to request the imposition of preservation measures in another member state to secure and preserve the company's assets situate in the other member state[168].

22.43 Subject to Articles 5 and 7 of the EC Insolvency Regulation, a creditor who, after the opening of insolvency proceedings in the United Kingdom which constitute main proceedings within the meaning of the EC Insolvency Regulation, obtains by any means, in particular through enforcement, total or partial satisfaction of his claim on the assets belonging to the debtor situate in another member state, is required to return that which he has obtained to the office-holder concerned, including an administrator or supervisor[169]. However, where a third-party debtor in another member state pays or discharges an obligation owed to a company in administration or subject to a corporate voluntary arrangement in the United Kingdom (when he should have paid it to the administrator or the supervisor), he will be deemed to have discharged his obligation if he was unaware of the making of the opening of the proceedings[170]. The EC Insolvency Regulation further provides for rebuttable presumptions, depending upon whether or not publication has occurred within the member state concerned, to apply for the purpose of determining whether a third-party debtor was aware of the opening of the proceedings[171].

---

164 Article 18(1) of the EC Insolvency Regulation and Article 21(1) of the recast Insolvency Regulation.

165 Articles 8 and 10 of the recast Insolvency Regulation.

166 Article 18(1) of the EC Insolvency Regulation and Article 21(1) of the recast Insolvency Regulation. Article 2(g) of the EC Insolvency Regulation and Article 2(9) of the recast Insolvency Regulation set out rules for determining in which member states different types of property are situated.

167 Article 21(2) of the recast Insolvency Regulation.

168 Article 38 of the EC Insolvency Regulation and Article 52 of the recast Insolvency Regulation. In the context of a proposed administration, an interim manager or receiver appointed by the court would presumably qualify as a 'temporary administrator'. *Quaere* the position in relation to a proposed corporate voluntary arrangement or the proposed appointment of an administrator out of court.

169 Article 20(1) of the EC Insolvency Regulation and Article 23(1) of the recast Insolvency Regulation. These Articles refer to 'the opening of the proceedings'. However, in view of the fact that Article 2(f) of the EC Insolvency Regulation and Article 2(8) of the recast Insolvency Regulation define 'the time of the opening of proceedings' as meaning the time at which the judgment opening the proceedings becomes effective, it would seem that in the context of administrations the opening of the proceedings means the time at which the appointment of the administrator takes effect and, in the context of corporate voluntary arrangements, the approval of the arrangement by the creditors' meeting.

170 Article 24(1) of the EC Insolvency Regulation and Article 31(1) of the recast Insolvency Regulation.

171 Article 24(2) of the EC Insolvency Regulation and Article 31(2) of the recast Insolvency Regulation.

22.44 Where the appointment of an administrator or the putting into effect of a corporate voluntary arrangement is entitled to recognition under the EC Insolvency Regulation, further provision is also made for the automatic recognition and enforcement of further judgments concerning the course and closure of insolvency proceedings and compositions approved by the United Kingdom court concerned[172]. Similar recognition and enforcement is afforded to the judgments of other courts which derive directly from such administration proceedings and are closely linked with them[173]. However, member states are not obliged to recognise or enforce judgments which might result in a limitation of personal freedom or postal security[174], and they may refuse to recognise insolvency proceedings opened in another member state or to enforce a judgment made in such proceedings where the effect of such recognition or enforcement would be manifestly contrary to the state's public policy, in particular its fundamental principles or the constitutional rights and liberties of the individual[175].

22.45 Where an administrator or supervisor of a corporate voluntary arrangement has been appointed in main proceedings in the UK, the administrator or the supervisor and any other person or authority entitled to do so under the law of the member state concerned, may request the courts of another member state to commence secondary proceedings in respect of the company in that other member state[176]. It may be appropriate for an administrator to seek the permission of the English court before he exercises his power to make such a request[177]. There may also be cases in which it is appropriate for the English court to issue a letter of request to other EU courts asking for administrators appointed in English main proceedings to be notified of any request in their courts to open secondary proceedings[178]. The office-holder in the main proceedings and the relevant office-holder in the secondary proceedings in the other member state are duty bound to communicate with each other, and, subject to rules applicable in each proceedings, are bound to co-operate with each other[179]. The office-holder in the secondary proceedings is required to give an administrator or supervisor in the main proceedings an early opportunity of submitting proposals on the

---

172 In accordance with the 1968 Brussels Convention (Article 25(1) of the EC Insolvency Regulation) or the Brussels Regulation EU 1215/2012 (Article 32 of the recast Insolvency Regulation).
173 Article 25(1) of the EC Insolvency Regulation and Article 32(1) of the recast Insolvency Regulation.
174 Article 25(3) of the EC Insolvency Regulation. This provision is not included in the recast Insolvency Regulation.
175 Article 26 of the EC Insolvency Regulation and Article 33 of the recast Insolvency Regulation. It is well established that this is a very high hurdle: *Klempka v ISA Daisytek SA* [2006] BCC 841 and *Re Eurofood IFSC* [2006] Ch 508.
176 Articles 27 and 29 of the EC Insolvency Regulation and Articles 34 and 37 of the recast Insolvency Regulation. The courts of the other member state must have jurisdiction under Article 3(2) of the EC Insolvency Regulation or the recast Insolvency Regulation and any such proceedings are restricted to the assets of the company situate in the territory of the other member state. It is not entirely clear how the ability of, say, a creditor to open secondary proceedings pursuant to the EC Regulation is consistent with the moratorium preventing the institution of legal process against a company in administration, see Schedule B1 paragraph 43(6) of IA 1986. Presumably the EC Insolvency Regulation prevails.
177 *Re Nortel Networks SA (in administration) (No 2)* [2009] EWHC 1482 (Ch).
178 *Re Nortel Networks SA* [2009] EWHC 206 (Ch).
179 Article 31 of the EC Insolvency Regulation and Article 41 of the recast Insolvency Regulation.

liquidation or use of the assets in the secondary proceedings[180]. Creditors are entitled to lodge their claims both in the main proceedings and in any secondary proceedings[181]. Article 39 of the EC Insolvency Regulation[182] goes on to provide that any creditor who has his habitual residence, domicile or registered office in a member state other than the state of the opening of the proceedings, including tax authorities and social security authorities of member states[183], should have the right to lodge claims in insolvency proceedings, thereby abrogating, in the case of tax and social security authorities of other member states, the English common law rule preventing them from proving[184].

22.46 Article 33 of the EC Insolvency Regulation and Article 46(1) of the recast Insolvency Regulation provide that a court which has opened secondary proceedings shall stay the process of liquidation in whole or in part on receipt of a request from, *inter alia*, an administrator or supervisor in main insolvency proceedings in the United Kingdom. Such a court may require the administrator or the supervisor to take suitable measures to guarantee the interests of creditors in the secondary proceedings and individual classes of creditors. Such a request, however, may only be rejected if it is manifestly of no interest to the creditors in the main proceedings. Such a stay may be ordered for up to a period of three months and may be continued or renewed for similar periods. Such a stay may also be lifted at the request of the administrator or, of the court's own motion or at the request of a creditor or office-holder in the secondary proceedings, if it appears to the court of the other member state that the stay is no longer justified by the interests of creditors in the main proceedings or in the secondary proceedings.

22.47 An administrator or supervisor in main insolvency proceedings in the United Kingdom can also make a proposal for secondary proceedings in another member state to be closed without liquidation by a rescue plan, composition or other comparable measure[185]. Further, if by a liquidation of assets in the secondary proceedings it is possible to meet all claims allowed in those proceedings, the office-holder appointed in those proceedings is required to transfer any assets remaining to the office-holder in the main proceedings[186].

22.48 The provisions relating to the duty to co-operate, communication of information, exercise of creditor's rights, stay and termination of secondary proceedings and transfer of assets following liquidation all apply, insofar as the progress of the proceedings permits, to territorial proceedings commenced

---

180 Article 31(3) of the EC Insolvency Regulation and Article 41(2)(c) of the recast Insolvency Regulation.

181 Article 32(1) of the EC Insolvency Regulation and Article 45(1) of the recast Insolvency Regulation. Articles 32 and 45 go on to make provision for the lodging of claims by office-holders in main and secondary proceedings and their right to attend creditors' meetings in both the main and the secondary proceedings. For the many miscellaneous contexts in which a member state liquidator is to be treated as a creditor of the company in administration, see Rule 21.8 of the Rules.

182 Article 53 of the recast Insolvency Regulation.

183 In the recast Insolvency Regulation this result is achieved by the definition of foreign creditor contained in Article 2(12).

184 Cf *Government of India v Taylor* [1955] AC 491. Similar rules in other member states are also thereby abrogated.

185 Article 34(1) of the EC Insolvency Regulation and Article 47 of the recast Insolvency Regulation (provided that the law applicable to the secondary proceedings allows for such a closure).

186 Article 35 of the EC Insolvency Regulation and Article 49 of the recast Insolvency Regulation.

pursuant to Article 3(2) of the EC Insolvency Regulation prior to the opening of the main proceedings[187]. The office-holder in such main proceedings may also request that such earlier proceedings be converted into winding-up proceedings if this proves to be in the interests of creditors in the main proceedings, in which event the court having jurisdiction in the territorial proceedings is required to order conversion into winding-up proceedings[188]. So, where an administrator or the supervisor of a corporate voluntary arrangement has been appointed in territorial proceedings commenced in the United Kingdom prior to the opening of main proceedings in another member state, the office-holder in the main proceedings can request that the territorial proceedings are converted into winding-up proceedings and, on the face of the wording of the EC Insolvency Regulation, the United Kingdom court will be bound to so order if this is in the interests of creditors in the main proceedings. The Insolvency Rule introduced to give effect to this provision appear, however, to contemplate that the United Kingdom courts will retain a discretion whether to accede to the foreign office-holder's request[189].

22.49 In the case of both main proceedings and of territorial proceedings, Article 4 of the EC Insolvency Regulation and Article 7 of the recast Insolvency Regulation provide that save as otherwise provided, the law applicable to insolvency proceedings and their effects shall be that of the member state in which such proceedings are commenced and that such law shall determine the conditions for the opening of those proceedings, their conduct and their closure including, *inter alia*, the rules relating to the voidness, voidability and unenforceability of legal acts detrimental to all the creditors.

22.50 However, the opening of insolvency proceedings is expressed not to affect:

(a) the rights *in rem* of creditors or third parties in respect of tangible or intangible, movable or immovable assets, whether specific or changing from time to time, belonging to a debtor which are situate in another member state at the time of opening of the proceedings[190];

(b) the rights of creditors to demand the set-off of their claims against the claims of the debtor, where such a set-off is permitted by the law applicable to the insolvent debtor's claim[191];

(c) the rights of a seller based on reservation of title where, at the time of the opening of the proceedings, the asset is situate in another member state[192].

Such limitations do not preclude actions for voidness, voidability or unenforceability under the law of the court of the member state in which the insolvency proceedings are opened[193].

---

187 Article 36 of the EC Insolvency Regulation and Article 50 of the recast Insolvency Regulation.
188 Article 37 of the EC Insolvency Regulation. In the recast Insolvency Regulation this right to convert is to any other type of insolvency proceedings in Annex A: Article 51.
189 Rule 21.2 of the Rules.
190 Article 5 of the EC Insolvency Regulation and Article 8 of the recast Insolvency Regulation. The application of this Article to rights *in rem* over assets changing from time to time appears to cover a floating charge.
191 Article 6 of the EC Insolvency Regulation and Article 9 of the recast Insolvency Regulation.
192 Article 7 of the EC Insolvency Regulation and Article 10 of the recast Insolvency Regulation.
193 Articles 5(4), 6(2) and 7(3) of the EC Insolvency Regulation and Article 8(4), 9(2) and 10(3) of the recast Insolvency Regulation.

22.51   In addition, there are a number of specific choice of law rules to the following effect:

(a)   the effect of insolvency proceedings on contracts conferring the right to acquire or make use of immovable property is governed solely by the law of the member state where the immovable property is situate[194];

(b)   the effect of insolvency proceedings on the rights and obligations of parties to a payment or settlement system or to a financial market is governed solely by the law of the member state applicable to that system or market[195];

(c)   the effect of insolvency proceedings on employment contracts and relationships is governed solely by the law of the member state applicable to the contract of employment[196];

(d)   the effect of insolvency proceedings on the rights of a debtor in immovable property, a ship or an aircraft subject to registration in a public register is determined by the law of the member state under the authority of which the register is kept[197]; and

(e)   the effect of insolvency proceedings on a law suit pending concerning an asset or right of which the debtor has been divested is governed solely by the law of the member state in which that law suit is pending[198].

22.52   Finally, there are specific provisions:

(a)   that the law of a member state in which insolvency proceedings are opened relating to voidness, voidability and unenforceability of legal acts detrimental to all creditors shall not apply where a person who has benefited from the act proves that the act was subject to the law of another member state and that law does not allow any means of challenging that act in the relevant case[199];

(b)   that where, by an act concluded after the opening of insolvency proceedings, the debtor disposes for consideration of an immovable asset, a ship or aircraft subject to registration in a public register or securities whose existence pre-suppose registration in a register laid down by law, the validity of that act is governed by the law of the state in which the immovable asset is situated or under the authority of which the register is kept[200]; and

(c)   that Community patents, Community trade marks and similar rights established by Community law may be included only in main proceedings[201].

INSURANCE COMPANIES AND CREDIT INSTITUTIONS

22.53   The Insurers (Reorganisation and Winding Up) Regulations 2004[202] ('the Insurers Regulations'), revoking and replacing the Insurers (Reorganisation and

---

194   Article 8 of the EC Insolvency Regulation and Article 11 of the recast Insolvency Regulation.
195   Article 9 of the EC Insolvency Regulation and Article 12 of the recast Insolvency Regulation.
196   Article 10 of the EC Insolvency Regulation and Article 13 of the recast Insolvency Regulation.
197   Article 11 of the EC Insolvency Regulation and Article 14 of the recast Insolvency Regulation.
198   Article 15 of the EC Insolvency Regulation. The recast Insolvency Regulation has changed this slightly so that it covers the effect of insolvency proceedings on arbitral proceedings as well, and the assets concerned any asset or right forming part of the debtor's estate (Article 19 of the recast Insolvency Regulation).
199   Article 13 of the EC Insolvency Regulation and Article 16 of the recast Insolvency Regulation.
200   Article 14 of the EC Insolvency Regulation and Article 17 of the recast Insolvency Regulation.
201   Article 12 of the EC Insolvency Regulation and Article 15 of the recast Insolvency Regulation.
202   SI 2004 No 353.

Winding Up) Regulations 2003[203] give effect in the United Kingdom to the EC Directive on the Reorganisation and Winding Up of Insurance Undertakings[204]. It is beyond the scope of this work to give a detailed account of the Insurers Regulations. It should, however, be noted that the Insurers Regulations provide that as from 20 April 2003 an administrator cannot be appointed in respect of an EEA insurer or any branch of an EEA insurer[205]. Nor can a corporate voluntary arrangement have effect in relation to an EEA insurer if the decision to approve the arrangement was taken after 20 April 2003[206]. For this purpose, an EEA insurer means an undertaking, other than a UK insurer, pursuing the activity of direct insurance which has received authorisation from its home state regulator[207]. A UK insurer is a person who has permission under Part 4A of the FSMA 2000 to effect or carry out contracts of insurance unless that person carries on that activity exclusively in relation to reinsurance contracts[208]. Lloyd's is specifically excluded from the definition of UK insurer[209].

22.54 The position in relation to schemes of arrangement proposed under Part 26 of CA 2006 is, however, different. A United Kingdom court is not prevented from sanctioning such a scheme in relation to an EEA insurer, merely because regulation 4 of the Insurers Regulations prevents it from making a winding-up order[210]. Specific restrictions only apply where an EEA insurer or branch of an EEA insurer is subject to a reorganisation measure or winding-up proceedings, as defined in Article 2 of the Directive[211] (which was adopted, imposed or opened on or after 20 April 2003). In any such case, the EEA insurer or branch of an EEA insurer cannot be made the subject of a scheme of arrangement under section 899 of CA 2006 if the home liquidator or administrator or home administrative or judicial authorities object[212].

22.55 The Insurers Regulations proceed to make provision, in relation to the reorganisation and winding up of UK insurers, and third country insurers whose head office is outside the UK and the EEA but who have permission under FSMA 2000 to carry out contracts of insurance, for such matters as notification to EEA regulators, publication in the Official Journal of the EC, notifications to creditors, submission of claims, priority of payment of insurance claims and choice of law. Pursuant to the Directive, and the local laws of EEA member states giving effect thereto, United Kingdom reorganisation and winding-up

---

203 SI 2003 No 1102.
204 Directive 2001/17/EC.
205 Regulation 4(1)(c), (5) and (9) of the Insurers Regulations.
206 Regulation 4(6) and (9) of the Insurers Regulations.
207 Regulation 2(1) of the Insurers Regulations.
208 Regulation 2(1) of the Insurers Regulations. Where a company in fact only conducts reinsurance, although is authorised to carry on insurance business as well, the court's jurisdiction to make an administration order arises under Schedule B1 to IA 1986 and the EC Insolvency Regulation applies: *Re Indemnity Guarantee Assurance Ltd* [2015] EWHC 1493 (Ch).
209 See Regulation 3 of the Insurers Regulations.
210 Regulation 5(1) of the Insurers Regulations. The definition of company contained in section 895(2)(b) of CA 2006 means that the court is only permitted to sanction a scheme of arrangement under section 899 of CA 2006 in respect of a company liable to be wound up under IA 1986. In the absence of regulation 5(1), the wording of regulation 4(1)(a) would have meant that an EEA insurer or branch of an EEA insurer would not be liable to be wound up for the purposes of section 895(2)(b) of CA 2006 as well as for the purposes of section 221 of IA 1986. See also *Re DAP Holding NV* [2005] EWHC 2092 (Ch).
211 Directive 2001/17/EC.
212 Regulation 5 of the Insurers Regulations and the various definitions contained therein and in Article 2 of the Directive.

measures commenced after 20 April 2003 in relation to UK insurers, and third country insurers with branches in the United Kingdom and in no other EEA member states, are effective and are entitled to automatic recognition in other EEA member states.

22.56 The Credit Institutions (Reorganisation and Winding Up) Regulations 2004[213] ('the Credit Institutions Regulations') give effect in the United Kingdom to the EC Directive on the Reorganisation and Winding Up of Credit Institutions[214]. As with the Insurers Regulations it is beyond the scope of this work to give a detailed account of the Credit Institutions Regulations. It should, however, be noted that the Credit Institutions Regulations provide that as from 5 May 2004 an administrator cannot be appointed in respect of an EEA credit institution or any branch of an EEA credit institution[215]. Nor can a corporate voluntary arrangement have effect in relation to an EEA credit institution if the decision to approve the arrangement was taken after 5 May 2004[216]. For this purpose, an EEA credit institution means an undertaking, other than a UK credit institution, whose business is to take deposits or other repayable funds from the public and to grant credits for its own account[217]. A UK credit institution is a person whose head office is in the UK with permission under Part 4 of the Financial Services and Markets Act 2000 to accept deposits or to issue electronic money as the case may be, but excluding insurers and credit unions[218].

22.57 As with insurers, the position in relation to schemes of arrangement under Part 26 of CA 2006 is, however, different. A United Kingdom court is not prevented from sanctioning such a scheme in relation to an EEA credit institution, merely because regulation 4 of the Credit Institutions Regulations prevents it from making a winding-up order[219]. Specific restrictions only apply where an EEA credit institution or branch of an EEA credit institution is subject to a reorganisation measure or winding-up proceedings, as defined in Article 2 of the Directive[220] (which was adopted, imposed or opened on or after 5 May 2004). In any such case, the EEA credit institution or branch of an EEA credit institution cannot be made the subject of a scheme of arrangement under section 899 of CA 2006 if the home liquidator or administrator or home administrative or judicial authorities object[221].

22.58 The Credit Institutions Regulations proceed to make provision, in relation to the reorganisation and winding up of UK credit institutions, and third country credit institutions whose head office is outside the UK and the EEA but who have permission under FSMA 2000 to accept deposits, for such matters

---

213 SI 2004 No 1045.
214 Directive 2001/24/EC. For a review of the interaction between the Credit Institutions Regulations and the Directive see *Joint Administrators of Heritable Bank plc v Winding Up Board of Landsbanki Islands HF* [2013] UKSC 13.
215 Regulation 4(1)(c), (5) and (8) of the Credit Institutions Regulations.
216 Regulation 4(6) and (9) of the Credit Institutions Regulations.
217 Regulation 2(1) of the Credit Institutions Regulations, which applies the definitions in Article 4(1)(1) of Regulation (EU) No 575/2013 of the European Parliament and the Council of 26 June on prudential requirements for credit institutions and investment firms.
218 Regulation 2(1) of the Credit Institutions Regulations.
219 Regulation 4(1) of the Credit Institutions Regulations.
220 Directive 2001/24/EC.
221 Regulation 4 of the Credit Institutions Regulations and the various definitions contained therein and in Article 2 of the Directive.

as notification to EEA regulators, publication in the Official Journal of the EC, notifications to creditors, submission of claims, honouring of certain obligations and choice of law. Pursuant to the Directive, and the local laws of EEA member states giving effect thereto, United Kingdom reorganisation and winding-up measures commenced after 5 May 2004 in relation to UK credit institutions, and third country credit institutions with branches in the United Kingdom and in no other EEA member states, are effective and are entitled to automatic recognition in other EEA member states.

Appendix
The Insolvency Rules: Tables
of destination and derivation

GUIDE TO THE DERIVATION OF THE INSOLVENCY (ENGLAND AND WALES) RULES 2016 (SI 1024 NO 2016)

This table indicates the derivation of provisions in the 2016 Rules relating to corporate insolvency. The 2016 Rules broadly derive from the 1986 Rules and forms. However there is rarely an exact match as the structure of the 2016 Rules is different, the language has been modernised and there have been significant changes, in particular as a result of amendments to the primary legislation made by the Enterprise and Regulatory Reform Act 2013, the Deregulation Act 2015, and the Small Business, Enterprise and Employment Act 2015. Furthermore the information requirements previously contained in forms have now been imported into the relevant rule as specified content. Finally the new Rules try to avoid copying out of the primary legislation. Instead they contain many references to Insolvency Act 1986 to enable the user to connect individual rules with the relevant provisions of the Act that the Rules supplement.

2016 Rule heading	2016 Rule	1986 Rule
Introductory rules		
Citation and commencement	1	0.1
Revocations	2	N/A
Extent and application	3	0.3
Transitional and savings provisions	4	13.14
Power of Secretary of State to regulate certain matters	5	12.1
Punishment of offences	6	12.21, Sch. 5
Review	7	N/A
Part 1: Scope, interpretation, time and rules about documents		
Chapter 1: Scope of these Rules		
Scope	1.1	13.7

2016 Rule heading	2016 Rule	1986 Rule
Chapter 2: Interpretation		
Defined terms	1.2	0.2, Part 13
Calculation of time periods	1.3	12A.55
Chapter 3: Form and contents of documents		
Requirement for writing and form of documents	1.4	12A.7
Authentication	1.5	12A.9
Information required to identify persons and proceedings, etc.	1.6	N/A
Reasons for stating that proceedings are or will be main, secondary, etc. under the EC Regulation	1.7	N/A
Prescribed format of documents	1.8	N/A
Variation from prescribed contents	1.9	N/A
Chapter 4: Standard contents of Gazette notices and the Gazette as evidence, etc.		
Contents of notices to be gazetted under the Act or Rules	1.10	12A.33, 12A.36
Standard contents of all notices	1.11	12A.33, 12A.36
Gazette notices relating to a company	1.12	12A.34, 12A.36
Gazette notices relating to a bankruptcy	1.13	12A.35, 12A.36
The Gazette: evidence, variations and errors	1.14	12A.37
Chapter 5: Standard contents of notices advertised otherwise than in the Gazette		
Standard contents of notices advertised other than in the Gazette	1.15	12A.38, 12A.41
Non-Gazette notices relating to a company	1.16	12A.39, 12A.41
Non-Gazette notices relating to a bankruptcy	1.17	12A.40, 12A.41
Non-Gazette notices: other provisions	1.18	12A.41
Chapter 6: Standard contents of documents to be delivered to the registrar of companies		
Standard contents of documents delivered to the registrar	1.19	12A.42, 12A.43
Registrar of companies: covering notices	1.20	
Standard contents of all documents	1.21	12A.43
Standard contents of documents relating to the office of office-holders	1.22	12A.44
Standard contents of documents relating to other documents	1.23	12A.45
Standard contents of documents relating to court orders	1.24	12A.46

2016 Rule heading	2016 Rule	1986 Rule
Standard contents of returns or reports of decisions	1.25	12A.47
Standard contents of returns or reports of matters considered by company members by correspondence	1.26	12A.47
Documents relating to other events	1.27	12A.48
Chapter 7: Standard contents of notices for delivery to other persons, etc.		
Standard contents of notices to be delivered to persons other than the registrar of companies	1.28	N/A
Standard contents of all notices	1.29	N/A
Standard contents of notices relating to the office of office-holders	1.30	N/A
Standard contents of notices relating to documents	1.31	N/A
Standard contents of notices relating to court proceedings or orders	1.32	N/A
Standard contents of notices of the results of decisions	1.33	N/A
Standard contents of returns or reports of matters considered by company members by correspondence	1.34	N/A
Chapter 8: Applications to the court		
Standard contents and authentication of applications to the court under Parts 1 to 11 of the Act	1.35	7.3
Chapter 9: Delivery of documents and opting out (sections 246C, 248A, 379C and 383A)		
Application of this Chapter	1.36	N/A
Delivery to the creditors and opting out	1.37	4.44, 6.74. (but not opt-out)
Creditor's election to opt out	1.38	N/A
Office-holder to provide information to creditors on opting-out	1.39	N/A
Delivery of documents to authorised recipients	1.40	12A.5
Delivery of documents to joint office-holders	1.41	12A.15
Postal delivery of documents	1.42	12A.3
Delivery by document exchange	1.43	N/A
Personal delivery of documents	1.44	12A.2
Electronic delivery of documents	1.45	12A.10

2016 Rule heading	2016 Rule	1986 Rule
Electronic delivery of documents to the court	1.46	12A.14
Electronic delivery of notices to enforcement officers	1.47	12A.29
Electronic delivery by office-holders	1.46	12A.11
Use of website by office-holder to deliver a particular document (section 246B and 379B)	1.49	12A.12
General use of website to deliver documents	1.50	12A.13
Retention period for documents made available on websites	1.51	12A.12, 12A.13
Proof of delivery of documents	1.52	12A.8
Delivery of proofs and details of claims	1.53	4.54, 6.81
Chapter 10: Inspection of documents, copies and provision of information		
Right to copies of documents	1.54	12A.52
Charges for copies of documents provided by the office-holder	1.55	12A.53
Offence in relation to inspection of documents	1.56	12.18
Right to list of creditors	1.57	12A.54
Confidentiality of documents – grounds for refusing inspection	1.58	12A.51
Part 2: Company Voluntary Arrangements under Part 1 of the Act		
Chapter 1: Preliminary		
Interpretation	2.1	N/A
Chapter 2: the proposal for a CVA (section 1)		
Proposal for a CVA: general principles and amendment	2.2	1.3
Proposal: contents	2.3	1.3
Chapter 3: Procedure for a CVA without a moratorium		
Procedure for proposal where the nominee is not the liquidator or the administrator (section 2)	2.4	1.4
Information for the official receiver	2.5	1.10
Statement of affairs (section 2(3))	2.6	1.5
Application to omit information from statement of affairs delivered to creditors	2.7	1.56
Additional disclosure for assistance of nominee where the nominee is not the liquidator or administrator	2.8	1.6

2016 Rule heading	2016 Rule	1986 Rule
Nominee's report on proposal where the nominee is not the liquidator or administrator (section 2(2))	2.9	1.7
Replacement of nominee (section 2(4))	2.10	1.8
Chapter 4: Procedure for a CVA with a moratorium		
Statement of affairs (paragraph 6(1)(b) of Schedule A1)	2.11	1.37
Application to omit information from a statement of affairs	2.12	1.56
The nominee's statement (paragraph 6(2)(a) of Schedule A1)	2.13	1.38
Documents filed with the court to obtain a moratorium (paragraph 7(1) of Schedule A1)	2.14	1.39
Notice and advert of beginning of a moratorium	2.15	1.40
Notice of continuation of a moratorium where physical meeting of creditors is summoned (paragraph 8(3B) of Schedule A1)	2.16	N/A
Notice of decision extending or further extending a moratorium (paragraph 36 of Schedule A1)	2.17	1.41
Notice of court order extending or further extending or continuing or renewing a moratorium (paragraph 34(2) of Schedule A1)	2.18	1.41
Advertisement of end of a moratorium (paragraph 11(1) of Schedule A1)	2.19	1.42
Disposal of charged property, etc. during a moratorium	2.20	1.43
Withdrawal of nominee's consent to act (paragraph 25(5) of Schedule A1)	2.21	1.44
Application to the court to replace the nominee (paragraph 28(a) of Schedule A1)	2.22	1.45
Notice of appointment of replacement nominee	2.23	1.46
Applications to court to challenge nominee's actions, etc. (paragraphs 26 and 27 of Schedule A1)	2.24	1.47
Chapter 5 Consideration of the proposal by the company members and creditors		
Consideration of proposal – common requirements (section 3)	2.25	1.9, 1.11, 1.48
Members' consideration at a meeting	2.26	
Creditors' consideration by a decision procedure	2.27	

2016 Rule heading	2016 Rule	1986 Rule
Timing of decisions on proposal	2.28	1.13
Creditors' approval of modified proposal	2.29	N/A
Notice of members' meeting and attendance of officers	2.30	1.9, 1.11, 1.48
Requisition of physical meeting by creditors	2.31	N/A
Non-receipt of notice by members	2.32	12A.4
Proposal for alternative supervisor	2.33	1.22
Chair at meetings	2.34	1.14
Members' voting rights	2.35	1.18, 1.51
Requisite majorities of members	2.36	1.20, 1.53
Notice of order made under section 4A(6) or paragraph 36(5) of Schedule A1	2.37	1.22A
Report of consideration of proposal under section 4(6) and (6A)(a) or paragraph 30(3)(b) and (4) of Schedule A1	2.38	1.24
Chapter 6: additional matters concerning and following approval of CVA		
Hand-over of property, etc. to supervisor	2.39	1.23, 1.54
Revocation or suspension of CVA	2.40	1.25
Supervisor's accounts and reports	2.41	1.26A
Production of accounts and records to Secretary of State	2.42	1.27
Fees and expenses	2.43	1.28
Termination or full implementation of CVA	2.44	1.29
Chapter 10: Time recording information		
Provision of information	2.45	1.55
Part 3: Administration		
Chapter 1: Interpretation		
Interpretation for Part 3	3.1	2.33(2A)
Proposed administrator's statement and consent to act	3.2	Form 2.2
Chapter 2: Appointment of Administrator by court		
Administration application (paragraph 12 of Schedule B1)	3.3	Form 2.1
Administration application made by the directors	3.4	2.3(2)
Administration application by the supervisor of a CVA	3.5	2.2(4)
Witness statement in support of administration application	3.6	2.2, 2.3, 2.4
		2.11

2016 Rule heading	2016 Rule	1986 Rule
Filing of application	3.7	2.5
Service of application	3.8	2.6
Notice to enforcement agents charged with distress or other legal process, etc.	3.9	2.7
Notice of other insolvency proceedings	3.10	2.5
Intervention by holder of qualifying floating charge (paragraph 36(1)(b) of Schedule B1)	3.11	2.10
The hearing	3.12	2.12
The order	3.13	2.13, Form 2.4B
Order on an application under paragraph 37 of Schedule B1	3.14	2.13
Notice of administration order	3.15	2.14
Chapter 3: Appointment of administrator by holder of floating charge		
Notice of intention to appoint	3.16	2.15, Form 2.5B
Notice of appointment	3.17	2.16, Form 2.6B
Filing of notice with court	3.18	2.17
Appointment by floating charge holder after administration application made	3.19	2.18
Appointment taking place out of court business hours: procedure	3.20	2.19
Appointment taking place out of court business hours: content of notice	3.21	2.19(1) and Form 2.7B
Appointment taking place out of court business hours: legal effect	3.22	2.19(2)
Chapter 4: Appointment of administrator by company or directors		
Notice of intention to appoint	3.23	2.20 form 2.8B
Notice of appointment after notice of intention to appoint	3.24	2.23, 2.24 and Form 2.9B
Notice of appointment without prior notice of intention to appoint	3.25	2.25 and Form 2.8B
Notice of appointment: filing with the court	3.26	2.26
Chapter 5: Notice of administrator's appointment		
Publication of administrator's appointment	3.27	2.27
Chapter 6: Statement of affairs		
Interpretation	3.28	2.28(1)
Statement of affairs: notice requiring and delivery to the administrator (paragraph 47(1) of Schedule B1)	3.29	2.28 and form 2.13B
Statement of affairs: content (paragraph 47 of Schedule B1)	3.30	2.29 and form 2.14B
Statement of affairs: statement of concurrence	3.31	2.29(2) et seq

2016 Rule heading	2016 Rule	1986 Rule
Statement of affairs: filing	3.32	2.29(7)
Statement of affairs: release from requirement and extension of time	3.33	2.31
Statement of affairs expenses	3.34	2.32
Chapter 7: Administrator's proposals		
Administrator's proposals: additional content	3.35	2.33
Administrator's proposals: statement of pre-administration costs	3.36	2.33(2A), (2B)
Administrator's proposals: ancillary provisions about delivery	3.37	2.33
Seeking approval of the administrator's proposals	3.38	2.34
Invitation to creditors to form a creditors' committee	3.39	N/A
Notice of extension of time to seek approval	3.40	2.34
Notice of the creditors' decision on the administrator's proposals (paragraph 53(2))	3.41	2.46
Administrator's proposals: revision	3.42	2.45
Notice of result of creditors' decision on revised proposals (paragraph 54(6))	3.43	2.46
Chapter 8: Limited disclosure of statement of affairs and proposals		
Application of Chapter	3.44	2.30
Orders limiting disclosure of statement of affairs, etc.	3.45	2.30, 2.33A
Order for disclosure by administrator	3.46	2.30(4)
Rescission or amendment of order for limited disclosure	3.47	2.30(7)
Publication, etc. of statement of affairs or statement of proposals	3.48	2.30(8), (9) and (10)
Chapter 9: Disposal of charged property		
Disposal of charged property	3.49	2.66
Chapter 10: Expenses of the administration		
Expenses	3.50	2.67, 12.2
Order of priority	3.51	2.67
Pre-administration costs	3.52	2.67A
Chapter 11: Extension and ending of administration		
Interpretation	3.53	2.110
Application to extend an administration and extension by consent (paragraph 76(2)(a) of Schedule B1)	3.54	2.112

2016 Rule heading	2016 Rule	1986 Rule
Notice of automatic end of administration (paragraph 76 of Schedule B1)	3.55	2.111
Notice of end of administration when purposes achieved (paragraph 80(2) of Schedule B1)	3.56	2.113
Administrator's application for order ending administration (paragraph 79 of Schedule B1)	3.57	2.114
Creditor's application for order ending administration (paragraph 81 of Schedule B1)	3.58	2.115
Notice by administrator of court order	3.59	2.116
Moving from administration to creditors' voluntary winding up (paragraph 83 of Schedule B1)	3.60	2.117A
Moving from administration to dissolution (paragraph 84 of Schedule B1)	3.61	2.118
Chapter 12: Replacing the administrator		
Grounds for resignation	3.62	2.119
Notice of intention to resign	3.63	2.120
Notice of resignation (paragraph 87 of Schedule B1)	3.64	2.121
Application to court to remove administrator from office	3.65	2.122
Notice of vacation of office when administrator ceases to be qualified to act	3.66	2.123
Deceased administrator	3.67	2.124
Application to replace	3.68	2.125
Appointment of replacement or additional administrator	3.69	2.126, 2.127, 2.128
Administrator's duties on vacating office	3.70	2.129
Part 4: Receivership		
Chapter 1: Appointment of joint receivers or managers to whom Part 3 of the Act applies (other than those appointed under section 51 (Scottish receiverships))		
Receivers or managers appointed under an instrument: acceptance of appointment (section 33)	4.1	3.1
Chapter 2: Administrative receivers (other than in Scottish receiverships)		
Application of Chapter 2	4.2	N/A
Interpretation	4.3	N/A

2016 Rule heading	2016 Rule	1986 Rule
Administrative receiver's security	4.4	12A.56
Publication of appointment of administrative receiver (section 46(1))	4.5	3.2
Requirement to provide a statement of affairs (section 47(1))	4.6	3.3
Statement of affairs: contents and delivery of copy (section 47(2))	4.7	3.4(1) form 3.2
Statement of affairs: statement of concurrence	4.8	3.4(2)–(5)
Statement of affairs: retention by administrative receiver	4.9	3.4(6)
Statement of affairs: release from requirement and extension of time (section 47(5))	4.10	3.6
Statement of affairs: expenses	4.11	3.7
Limited disclosure	4.12	3.5
Administrative receiver's report to the registrar of companies and secured creditors (section 48(1))	4.13	3.8
Copy of report for unsecured creditors (section 48(2)(a))	4.14	3.8
Invitation to creditors to form a creditors' committee	4.15	N/A
Disposal of charged property (section 43(1))	4.16	3.31
Summary of receipts and payments	4.17	3.32
Resignation	4.18	3.33
Deceased administrative receiver	4.19	3.34
Other vacation of office	4.20	3.35
Notice to registrar of companies (section 45(4))	4.21	3.35(2)
Chapter 3: Non-administrative receivers and the prescribed part		
Application of Chapter 3	4.22	3.39
Report to creditors	4.23	3.39
Receiver to deal with prescribed part	4.24	3.40
Part 5: Members' voluntary winding up		
Chapter 1: Statutory declaration of solvency (section 89)		
Statutory declaration of solvency: requirements additional to those in section 89	5.1	Form 4.70
Chapter 2: The liquidator		
Appointment by the company	5.2	4.139

2016 Rule heading	2016 Rule	1986 Rule
Meetings in members' voluntary winding up of authorised deposit-takers	5.3	4.72
Appointment by the court (section 108)	5.4	4.140
Cost of liquidator's security	5.5	12A.56
Liquidator's resignation	5.6	4.142(3)
Removal of liquidator by the court	5.7	4.143
Removal of liquidator by company meeting	5.8	4.142
Delivery of draft final account to members (section 94)	5.9	4.126A
Final account prior to dissolution (section 94)	5.10	4.126A
Deceased liquidator	5.11	4.145
Loss of qualification as insolvency practitioner	5.12	4.146
Liquidator's duties on vacating office	5.13	4.148
Application by former liquidator to the Secretary of State for release (section 173(2)(b)(a))	5.14	4.144(3), 4.147
Power of court to set aside certain transactions entered into by liquidator	5.15	4.149
Rule against improper solicitation on or behalf of the liquidator	5.16	4.150
Chapter 3: Special manager		
Application for and appointment of special manager (section 177)	5.17	4.206
Security	5.18	4.207
Failure to give or keep up security	5.19	4.208
Accounting	5.20	4.209
Termination of appointment	5.21	4.210
Chapter 4: Conversion to creditors' voluntary winding up		
Statement of affairs (section 95(3))	5.22	4.34
Part 6: Creditors' voluntary winding up		
Chapter 1: Application of Part 6		
Application of Part 6	6.1	4.1(6)
Chapter 2: Statement of affairs and other information		
Statement of affairs made out by the liquidator under section 95(1A)	6.2	4.34, Form 4.18
Statement of affairs made out by the directors under section 99(1)	6.3	4.34, Form 4.19
Additional requirements as to statement of affairs	6.4	Form 4.18, Form 4.19

2016 Rule heading	2016 Rule	1986 Rule
Statement of affairs: statement of concurrence	6.5	4.34(5)
Order limiting disclosure of statement of affairs, etc.	6.6	4.35
Expenses of statement of affairs and decisions sought from creditors	6.7	4.38
Delivery of accounts to liquidator (section 235)	6.8	4.40
Expenses of assistance in preparing accounts	6.9	4.41
Chapter 3: Nomination and appointment of liquidators and information to creditors		
Application of the rules in this Chapter	6.10	N/A
Nomination of liquidator and information to creditors on conversion from members' voluntary winding up (section 96)	6.11	N/A
Creditors' decision on appointment other than at a meeting (conversion from members' voluntary winding up)	6.12	N/A
Information to creditors and contributories (conversion of members' voluntary winding up into creditors' voluntary winding up)	6.13	4.49
Information to creditors and appointment of liquidator	6.14	
Information to creditors and contributories (conversion from MVL)	6.14	4.49
Information to creditors and contributories	6.15	4.49-CVL
Further information where administrator becomes liquidator (paragraph 83(3) of Schedule B1))	6.16	4.49A
Report by director, etc.	6.17	4.53B
Decisions on nomination	6.18	4.63
Invitation to creditors to form a liquidation committee	6.19	N/A
Chapter 4: The liquidator		
Appointment by creditors or by the company	6.20	4.101
Power to fill vacancy in office of liquidator	6.21	4.101A
Appointment by the court (section 100(3) or 108)	6.22	4.103
Appointment to be gazetted and registered	6.23	4.106A
Cost of liquidator's security (section 390(3))	6.24	12A.56
Liquidator's resignation and replacement	6.25	4.108

2016 Rule heading	2016 Rule	1986 Rule
Removal of liquidator by creditors	6.26	4.117
Removal of liquidator by the court	6.27	4.120
Final account prior to dissolution (section 106)	6.28	4.126
Deceased liquidator	6.29	4.133
Loss of qualification as insolvency practitioner	6.30	4.135
Vacation of office on making of winding-up order	6.31	4.136
Liquidator's duties on leaving office	6.32	4.138
Application by former liquidator for release (section 173(2)(b))	6.33	4.122(3), Form 4.41
Power of court to set aside certain transactions	6.34	4.149
Rule against improper solicitation	6.35	4.150
Permission for exercise of powers by liquidator	6.36	4.184
Chapter 5: Special manager		
Application for and appointment of special manager (section 177)	6.37	4.206
Security	6.38	4.207
Failure to give or keep up security	6.39	4.208
Accounting	6.40	4.209
Termination of appointment	6.41	4.210
Chapter 6: Priority of payment of costs and expenses, etc.		
General rule as to priority	6.42	4.218, 12.2
Saving for powers of the court	6.43	4.220
Chapter 7: Litigation expenses and property subject to a floating charge		
Interpretation	6.44	4.218A
Requirement for approval or authorisation	6.45	4.218B
Request for approval or authorisation	6.46	4.218C
Grant of approval or authorisation	6.47	4.218D
Application to the court by the liquidator	6.48	4.218E
Part 7: Winding up by the court		
Chapter 1: Application of Part		
Application of Part	7.1	N/A
Chapter 2: The statutory demand (sections 123(1)(a) and 222(1)(a))		
Interpretation	7.2	4.4
The statutory demand	7.3	4.5, 4.6 and Form 4.1

2016 Rule heading	2016 Rule	1986 Rule
Chapter 3: Petition for winding-up order		
Application of this Chapter	7.4	N/A
Contents of petition	7.5	Form 4.2
Verification of petition	7.6	4.12
Petition: presentation and filing	7.7	4.7
Court to which petition is to be presented where the company is subject to a CVA or is in administration	7.8	4.7
Copies of petition to be served on company or delivered to other persons	7.9	4.10
Notice of petition	7.10	4.11
Persons entitled to request a copy of petition	7.11	4.13
Certificate of compliance	7.12	4.14
Permission for the petitioner to withdraw	7.13	4.15
Notice by persons intending to appear	7.14	4.16
List of appearances	7.15	4.17
Witness statement in opposition	7.16	4.18
Substitution of creditor or contributory for petitioner	7.17	4.19
Order for substitution of petitioner	7.18	N/A
Notice of adjournment	7.19	4.18A
Order for winding up by the court	7.20	N/A
Notice to official receiver of winding-up order	7.21	4.20 and form 4.13
Delivery and notice of the order	7.22	4.21
Petition dismissed	7.23	4.21B
Injunction to restrain presentation or notice of petition	7.24	4.6A
Chapter 4: Petition by a contributory or a relevant office-holder		
Interpretation and application of rules in Chapter 3	7.25	4.24
Contents of petition for winding-up order by a contributory	7.26	Form 4.14
Petition presented by a relevant office-holder	7.27	4.7
Verification of petition	7.28	Form 4.14
Presentation and service of petition	7.29	4.22
Request to appoint former administrator or supervisor as liquidator (section 140)	7.30	4.7
Hearing of petition	7.31	4.23

2016 Rule heading	2016 Rule	1986 Rule
Order for winding up by the court of a company in administration or where there is a supervisor of a CVA in relation to the company	7.32	4.20 and form 4.12
Chapter 5: Provisional liquidator		
Application for appointment of provisional liquidator (section 135)	7.33	4.25
Deposit by applicant	7.34	4.27
Order of appointment of provisional liquidator	7.35	4.26, form 4.15
Notice of appointment of provisional liquidator	7.36	4.25A
Security	7.37	4.28, 4.29
Remuneration	7.38	4.30
Termination of appointment	7.39	4.31
Chapter 6: Statement of affairs and other information		
Notice requiring statement of affairs (section 131)	7.40	4.32
Statement of affairs	7.41	Form 4.17
Statement of affairs: statement of concurrence	7.42	4.33
Order limiting disclosure of statement of affairs, etc.	7.43	4.35
Release from duty to submit statement of affairs: extension of time (section 131)	7.44	4.36
Statement of affairs: expenses	7.45	4.37
Delivery of accounts to official receiver	7.46	4.39
Further disclosure	7.47	4.42
Chapter 7: Reports and information to creditors and contributories		
Reports by official receiver	7.48	4.43, 4.45, 4.46
Reports by official receiver: estimate of prescribed part	7.49	4.43
Further information where winding up follows administration	7.50	4.49A
Notice of stay of winding up	7.51	4.48(2)
Chapter 8: The liquidator		
Choosing a person to be liquidator	7.52	4.50
Appointment of liquidator by creditors or contributories	7.53	4.100
Decisions on nomination	7.54	4.63

2016 Rule heading	2016 Rule	1986 Rule
Invitation to creditors and contributories to form a liquidation committee	7.55	
Appointment by the court	7.56	4.102
Appointment by Secretary of State	7.57	4.104
Cost of liquidator's security (section 390(3))	7.58	12A.56
Appointment to be gazetted and notice given to registrar of companies	7.59	4.106A
Hand-over of assets by official receiver to liquidator	7.60	4.107
Liquidator's resignation	7.61	4.108(4)
Notice to official receiver of intention to vacate office	7.62	4.137
Decision of creditors to remove liquidator	7.63	7.113
Procedure on removal by creditors	7.64	4.116
Removal of liquidator by the court (section 172(2))	7.65	4.119
Removal of liquidator by the Secretary of State	7.66	4.123
Deceased liquidator	7.67	4.132
Loss of qualification as insolvency practitioner	7.68	4.134
Application by liquidator for release (section 174(4)(b) or (d))	7.69	4.121
Release of official receiver	7.70	4.124
Final account prior to dissolution (section 146)	7.71	4.125
Relief from, or variation of, duty to report	7.72	4.125A
Liquidator's duties on vacating office	7.73	4.138
Power of court to set aside certain transactions	7.74	4.149
Rule against improper solicitation	7.75	4.150
Chapter 9: Duties and powers of liquidator		
General duties of liquidator	7.76	4.179
Permission for exercise of powers by liquidator	7.77	4.184
Enforced delivery up of company's property (section 234)	7.78	4.185
Chapter 10: Settlement of list of contributories		
Delegation to liquidator of power to settle list of contributories	7.79	4.195
Duty of liquidator to settle list (section 148)	7.80	4.196
Contents of list	7.81	4.197

2016 Rule heading	2016 Rule	1986 Rule
Procedure for settling list	7.82	4.198
Application to court for variation of the list	7.83	4.199
Variation of, or addition to, the list	7.84	4.200
Costs of applications to vary, etc. the list of contributories	7.85	4.201
Chapter 11: Calls on contributories		
Making of calls by the liquidator (sections 150 and 160)	7.86	4.202
Sanction of the liquidation committee for making a call	7.87	4.203
Application to court for permission to make a call (sections 150 and 160)	7.88	4.204, form 4.56
Order giving permission to make a call	7.89	Form 4.57
Making and enforcement of the call	7.90	4.205, form 4.58
Court order to enforce payment of call by a contributory	7.91	4.205, form 4.59
Chapter 12: Special manager		
Application of this Chapter and interpretation	7.92	
Appointment and remuneration of special manager (section 177)	7.93	4.206
Security	7.94	4.207
Failure to give or keep up security	7.95	4.208
Accounting	7.96	4.209
Termination of appointment	7.97	4.210
Chapter 13: Public examination of company officers and others (section 133)		
Applications relating to promoters, past managers, etc. (section 133(1)(c))	7.98	4.211
Request for a creditor for a public examination (section 133(2))	7.99	4.213
Request by a contributory for a public examination	7.100	4.213
Further provisions about requests by a creditor or contributory for a public examination	7.101	4.213(3), 4.213(4), 4.214(5)
Order for public examination	7.102	Form 4.61
Notice of the public examination	7.103	4.212
Examinee unfit for examination	7.104	4.214
Procedure at public examination	7.105	4.215
Adjournment	7.106	4.216
Expenses of examination	7.107	4.217

2016 Rule heading	2016 Rule	1986 Rule
Chapter 14: Priority of payment of costs and expenses, etc.		
General rule as to priority	7.108	4.218, 12.2
Winding up commencing as voluntary	7.109	4.219
Saving for powers of the court (section 156)	7.110	4.220
Chapter 15: Litigation expenses and property subject to a floating charge		
Interpretation	7.111	4.218A
Priority of litigation expenses	7.112	4.218A(2)
Requirement for approval or authorisation of litigation expenses	7.113	4.218B
Requests for approval or authorisation	7.114	4.218C
Grant of approval or authorisation	7.115	4.218D
Application to the court by the liquidator	7.116	4.218E
Chapter 16: Miscellaneous rules		
Sub-division A: Return of capital		
Application to court for order authorising return of capital	7.117	4.221
Procedure for return	7.118	4.222
Sub-division B: Dissolution after winding up		
Secretary of State's directions under sections 203 and 205 and appeal	7.119	4.224, 4.225
Part 12: Court procedure and practice		
Chapter 1: General, Application of the Civil Procedure Rules 1998		
Court rules and practice to apply	12.1	7.51A
Performance of functions by the court	12.2	7.6A
Chapter 2: Commencement of insolvency proceedings in the county court		
Commencement of insolvency proceedings under Parts 1 to 7 of the Act (corporate insolvency proceedings)	12.3	Rule 2 of SI 2014/817
Commencement of insolvency proceedings under Parts 7A to 11 of the Act (personal insolvency proceedings; bankruptcy)	12.4	Rule 3 of SI 2014/817
Allocation of proceedings to the London Insolvency District	12.5	7.10ZA
Chapter 3: Making applications to court: general		
Preliminary	12.6	7.1
Filing of application	12.7	7.4(1)
Fixing the venue	12.8	7.4(2)
Service or delivery of application	12.9	7.4(3–5)
Hearing in urgent case	12.10	7.4(6)

2016 Rule heading	2016 Rule	1986 Rule
Directions	12.11	7.10(3)
Hearing and determination without notice	12.12	7.5A
Adjournment of the hearing of an application	12.13	7.10(1–2)
Chapter 4: Making applications to court: specific applications		
Sub-division A: Applications in connection with section 176A (prescribed part)		
Applications under section 176A(5) to disapply section 176A	12.14	7.3A
Notice of application under section 176A(5)	12.15	7.4A
Notice of an order under section 176A(5)	12.16	12A.57
Sub-division B: Applications for private examination (sections 236, 251N and 366)		
Application of this sub-division and interpretation	12.17	9.1
Contents of application	12.18	9.2
Order for examination, etc.	12.19	9.3
Procedure for examination	12.20	9.4
Record of examination	12.21	9.5
Costs of proceedings under sections 236, 251N and 366	12.22	9.6
Sub-division C: persons unable to manage own property or affairs		
Application and interpretation	12.23	7.43
Appointment of another person to act	12.24	7.44
Witness statement in support of application	12.25	7.45A
Service of notices following appointment	12.26	7.46
Chapter 5: Obtaining information and evidence		
Further information and disclosure	12.27	7.60
Witness statements and reports	12.28	7.7A, 7.8
Evidence provided by the official receive, an insolvency practitioner or a special manager	12.29	7.9
Chapter 6: Transfer of proceedings		
Sub-division A: General		
General power of transfer	12.30	7.11
Proceedings commenced in the wrong court	12.31	7.12
Applications for transfer	12.32	7.13
Procedure following order for transfer	12.33	7.14
Consequential transfer of other proceedings	12.34	7.15
Sub-division B: Block transfer of cases where insolvency practitioner has died, etc.		
Interpretation	12.35	7.10A

2016 Rule heading	2016 Rule	1986 Rule
Power to make a block transfer order	12.36	7.10B
Application for a block transfer order	12.37	7.10C
Action following application for a block transfer order	12.38	7.10D
Chapter 7: The court file		
The court file	12.39	7.31A
Office copies of documents	12.40	7.61
Chapter 8: Costs		
Application of Chapter and interpretation	12.41	7.33A
Requirement to assess costs by the detailed procedure	12.42	7.34A
Procedure where detailed assessment is required	12.43	7.35
Costs of officers charged with execution of writs or other process	12.44	7.36
Petitions presented by insolvent companies	12.45	7.37A
Costs paid otherwise than out of the insolvent estate	12.46	7.38
Awards of costs against an office-holder, the adjudicator or the official receiver	12.47	7.39
Applications for costs	12.48	7.40
Costs and expenses of petitioners and other specified persons	12.49	7.41
Final costs certificate	12.50	7.42
Chapter 9: Enforcement procedures		
Enforcement of court orders	12.51	7.19
Orders enforcing compliance	12.52	7.20
Warrants (general provisions)	12.53	7.21
Warrants under sections 134 and 364	12.54	7.22
Warrants under sections 236, 251N and 366	12.55	7.23
Warrants under section 365	12.56	7.25
Execution overtaken by judgment debtor's insolvency	12.57	12A.28
Chapter 10: Appeals		
Application of Chapter	12.58	7.49A
Appeals and reviews of court orders in corporate insolvency	12.59	7.47
Appeals in bankruptcy by the Secretary of State	12.60	7.48
Procedure on appeal	12.61	7.49A

2016 Rule heading	2016 Rule	1986 Rule
Appeal against decisions of the Secretary of State or official receiver	12.62	7.50
Chapter 11: Court orders, formal defects and shorthand writers		
Court orders	12.63	N/A
Formal defects	12.64	7.55
Shorthand writers: nomination, etc.	12.65	7.16, 7.17
Part 13: Official receivers		
Official receivers in court	13.1	10.1
Persons entitled to act on official receiver's behalf	13.2	10.2
Application for directions	13.3	10.3
Official receiver's expenses	13.4	10.4
Official receiver not to be appointed liquidator or trustee	13.5	4.101B
Part 14: Claims by and distributions to creditors in administration, winding up and bankruptcy		
Chapter 1: Application and interpretation		
Application of Part 14 and interpretation	14.1	13.12
Chapter 2: Creditors' claims in administration, winding up and bankruptcy		
Provable debts	14.2	12.3
Proving a debt	14.3	2.72, 4.73, 6.96
Requirements for proof	14.4	2.72(3), 4.73, 4.75, 6.98
Costs of proving	14.5	2.74, 4.78, 6.100
Allowing inspection of proofs	14.6	2.75, 4.79, 6.101
Admission and rejection of proofs for dividend	14.7	2.77, 4.82, 6.104
Appeal against decision on proof	14.8	2.78, 4.83, 6.105
Office-holder not liable for costs under Rule 14.8	14.9	2.78(6), 4.83(6), 6.105(6)
Withdrawal or variation of proof	14.10	2.79, 4.84, 6.106
Exclusion of proof by the court	14.11	2.80, 4.85, 6.107
Administration and winding up by the court: debts of insolvent company to rank equally	14.12	2.69, 4.181
Administration and winding up: division of unsold assets	14.13	2.71, 4.183
Administration and winding up: estimate of value of debt	14.14	2.81, 4.86

2016 Rule heading	2016 Rule	1986 Rule
Secured creditor: value of security	14.15	2.90, 4.95, 6.115
Secured creditor: surrender for non-disclosure	14.16	2.91, 4.96, 6.116
Secured creditor: redemption by office-holder	14.17	2.92, 4.97, 6.117
Secured creditor: test of security's value	14.18	2.93, 4.98, 6.118
Realisation or surrender of security by creditor	14.19	2.83, 2.94, 4.88, 4.99, 6.119
Discounts	14.20	2.84, 4.89, 6.110
Debts in foreign currency	14.21	2.86, 4.91, 6.111
Payments of a periodical nature	14.22	2.87, 4.92, 6.112
Interest	14.23	2.88, 4.93, 6.113
Administration: mutual dealings and set-off	14.24	2.85
Winding up: mutual dealings and set-off	14.25	4.90
Chapter 3: Distributions to creditors in administration, winding up and bankruptcy		
Application of Chapter to particular class of creditors and to distributions	14.26	2.95(5)
Declaration and distribution of dividends in a winding up	14.27	4.180
Gazette notice of intended first dividend or distribution	14.28	11.2, 2.95, 4.182A
Individual notices to creditors, etc. of intended dividend or distribution	14.29	2.95, 11.2
Contents of notice of intention to declare dividend or make a distribution	14.30	2.95(4), 11.2
Further contents of notice to creditors owed small debts, etc.	14.31	
Admission or rejection of proofs following last date for proving	14.32	2.96, 11.3
Postponement or cancellation of dividend	14.33	2.96A, 11.4
Declaration of dividend	14.34	2.97, 11.5
Notice of declaration of a dividend	14.35	2.98, 2.99, 11.6
Last notice about dividend in a winding up	14.36	4.186
Contents of last notice about dividend (administration, winding up and bankruptcy)	14.37	2.100, 11.7
Sole or final dividend	14.38	2.68, 4.186
Administration and winding up: provisions as to dividends	14.39	4.182(1)
Supplementary provisions as to dividends and distributions	14.40	2.101, 4.182(2), 11.8

2016 Rule heading	2016 Rule	1986 Rule
Secured creditors	14.41	2.102, 6.109, 11.9
Disqualification from dividend	14.42	2.103, 11.10
Assignment of right to dividend	14.43	2.104, 11.11
Debt payable at future time	14.44	2.89, 2.105, 4.94, 6.114, 11.13
Administration and winding up: non-payment of dividend	14.45	2.70(3), 4.182(3)
Part 15: Decision making		
Chapter 1: Application of Part		
	15.1	N/A
Chapter 2: Decision procedures		
Interpretation	15.2	N/A
The prescribed decision procedures	15.3	N/A
Electronic voting	15.4	N/A
Virtual meetings	15.5	N/A
Physical meetings	15.6	N/A
Deemed consent (sections 246ZF and 379ZB)	15.7	N/A
Chapter 3: Notices, voting and venues for decisions		
Notices to creditors of decision procedure	15.8	1.9, 1.48, 2.34, 4.50, 4.51, 4.54, 5.17, 6.79, 6.81
Voting in a decision procedure	15.9	2.38, 3.11, 4.50, 4.51, 4.54, 6.79, 6.81
Venue for decision procedure	15.10	1.13, 2.35, 3.9, 4.60, 5.18, 6.86
Notice of decision procedures or seeking deemed consent: when and to whom delivered	15.11	1.9, 1.48, 2.35, 3.9, 4.50, 4.54, 5.17, 6.79, 6.81
Notice of decision procedure by advertisement only	15.12	2.37A, 4.59, 6.85
Gazetting and advertising of meeting	15.13	2.34, 4.50, 4.53C and D, 6.79
Notice to company officers, bankrupts, etc. in respect of meetings	15.14	1.16, 2.34(2), 4.58, 6.84
Non-receipt of notice of decision	15.15	12A.4
Decisions on remuneration and conduct	15.16	4.63, 6.88

2016 Rule heading	2016 Rule	1986 Rule
Chapter 4: Decision making in particular proceedings		
Decisions in winding up of authorised deposit-takers	15.17	4.72
Chapter 5: Requisitioned decisions		
Requisitions of decision	15.18	2.37, 4.57, 6.83
Expenses and timing of requisitioned decision	15.19	2.37, 4.57(2), 4.61(3, 5), 6.83(2), 6.87
Chapter 6: Constitution of meetings		
Quorum at meetings	15.20	12A.21
Chair at meetings	15.21	2.36, 3.10, 4.55, 4.56, 5.19, 6.82
The chair – attendance, interventions and questions	15.22	4.58, 6.84
Chapter 7: Adjournment and suspension of meetings		
Adjournment by chair	15.23	1.21, 1.53, 2.35, 3.14, 4.65(3), 5.24, 6.91
Adjournment of meetings to remove a liquidator or trustee	15.24	4.113, 4.114, 6.129
Adjournment in absence of chair	15.25	2.35(5), 4.65(6A), 6.91(4A)
Proofs in adjournment	15.26	2.35, 4.65(7), 6.91(5)
Suspension	15.27	1.21, 1.53, 2.35, 3.14, 4.65, 5.24, 6.90
Chapter 8: Creditors' voting rights and majorities		
Creditors' voting rights	15.28	1.17,1.49, 2.38, 3.11, 4.67, 4.68, 5.21, 6.93, 6.93A
Scheme manager's voting rights	15.29	Sch. 1, paras 2–4 and 6
Claim made in proceedings in other member States	15.30	2.38, 4.67, 6.93
Calculation of voting rights	15.31	1.17(2)–(3), 1.49(3), 1.52(3), 2.38(4), 2.40(2), 3.11(4), 5.21(2)–(3), 5.41(2), 6.93
Calculation of voting rights: special cases	15.32	2.42, Sch. 1

2016 Rule heading	2016 Rule	1986 Rule
Procedure for admitting creditors' claims for voting	15.33	1.17A, 1.50, 2.39, 4.70, 5.21(1)–(4), 5.22, 6.94(1) and (3)
Requisite majorities	15.34	1.19, 1.52, 2.43, 3.15, 4.63, 5.23, 6.88
Appeals against decisions under this Chapter	15.35	1.17A, 1.50, 1.52, 2.39, 3.12, 4.70, 5.22, 5.23, 5.42, 6.94
Chapter 9: Exclusions from meetings		
Action where person excluded	15.36	12A.23
Indication to excluded persons	15.37	12A.24
Complaint	15.38	12A.25
Chapter 10: Contributories' voting rights and majorities		
Contributories' voting rights and requisite majorities	15.39	4.63, 4.69
Chapter 10: Records		
Record of a decision	15.40	2.44A, 3.15, 4.71, 6.95
Chapter 12: Company meetings		
	15.41	2.49(5A)
Remote attendance: notification requirements	15.42	
Location of company meetings	15.43	12A.22
Action where person excluded	15.44	12A.23
Indication to excluded person	15.45	12A.24
Complaint	15.46	12A.25
Part 16: Proxies and corporate representation		
Application and interpretation	16.1	N/A
Specific and continuing proxies	16.2	8.1
Blank proxy	16.3	8.2
Use of proxies	16.4	8.2, 8.3
Use of proxies by the chair	16.5	1.15, 2.36, 4.64, 5.20, 6.89, 8.3(3)
Right of inspection and retention of proxies	16.6	8.4, 8.5
Proxy-holder with financial interest	16.7	8.6
Corporate representation: bankruptcy and IVA	16.8	8.7

2016 Rule heading	2016 Rule	1986 Rule
Instrument conferring authorisation to represent corporation	16.9	8.7
Part 17: Creditors' and liquidation committees		
Chapter 1: Introductory		
Scope and interpretation	17.1	N/A
Chapter 2: Functions of a committee		
Functions of a committee	17.2	2.52, 3.18
Chapter 3: Membership and formalities of formation of a committee		
Number of members of a committee	17.3	2.50, 3.16, 4.152, 6.150
Eligibility for membership of creditors' or liquidation committee	17.4	2.50, 3.16, 4.152, 6.150
Establishment of committees	17.5	2.51, 3.17, 4.153, 6.151
Liquidation committee established by contributories	17.6	4.154
Notice of change of membership of a committee	17.7	2.51, 3.17, 4.153, 6.151
Vacancies: creditor members of creditors' or liquidation committee	17.8	2.59, 3.25, 4.163, 6.160
Vacancies: contributory members of liquidation committee	17.9	4.164
Resignation	17.10	2.56, 3.22, 4.160, 6.157
Termination of membership	17.11	2.57, 3.23, 4.161, 6.158
Removal	17.12	2.58, 3.24, 4.162, 6.159
Cessation of liquidation committee in a winding up when creditors are paid in full	17.13	4.171A
Chapter 4: Meetings of committee		
Meetings of committee	17.14	2.52, 3.18, 4.156, 6.153
The chair at meetings	17.15	2.53, 3.19, 4.157, 6.154
Quorum	17.16	2.54, 3.20, 4.158, 6.155
Committee-members' representatives	17.17	2.55, 3.21, 4.159, 6.156
Voting rights and resolutions	17.18	2.60, 3.26, 4.165, 4.166, 6.161

2016 Rule heading	2016 Rule	1986 Rule
Resolutions by correspondence	17.19	2.61, 3.27, 4.167, 6.162
Remote attendance at meetings of committee	17.20	12A.26
Procedure for requests that a place for a meeting should be specified	17.21	12A.27
Chapter 5: Supply of information by the office-holder to the committee		
Notice requiring office-holder to attend the creditors' committee (administration and administrative receivership) (paragraph 57(3)(a) of Schedule B1 and section 49(2))	17.22	2.62, 3.28
Office-holder's obligation to supply information to the committee (winding up and bankruptcy)	17.23	4.155, 4.168, 6.152, 6.163
Chapter 6: Miscellaneous		
Expenses of members, etc.	17.24	2.63, 3.29, 4.169, 6.164
Dealings by committee members and others	17.25	4.170, 6.165
Dealings by committee members and others: administration and administrative receivership	17.26	2.64, 3.30
Formal defects	17.27	2.65, 3.30A, 4.172A
Special rule for winding up by the court and bankruptcy: functions vested in the Secretary of State	17.28	4.172, 6.166
Chapter 7: Winding up by the court following an administration		
Continuation of creditors' committee	17.29	4.173, 4.174A, 4.176, 4.178
Part 18: Reporting and remuneration of office-holders		
Chapter 1: Introductory		
Scope of Part 18 and interpretation	18.1	N/A
Chapter 2: Progress reports		
Reporting by the office-holder	18.2	N/A
Contents of progress reports in administration, winding up and bankruptcy	18.3	2.47, 4.49B, 4.49C, 6.78A
Information about remuneration	18.4	2.47, 4.49B, 4.49C, 6.78A
Information about pre-administration costs	18.5	2.67A
Progress reports in administration: timing	18.6	2.47(3) and (6)

2016 Rule heading	2016 Rule	1986 Rule
Progress reports in voluntary winding up: timing	18.7	4.49C
Progress reports in winding up by the court and bankruptcy: timing	18.8	4.49B, 6.78A(3)
Creditors' and members' requests for further information in administration, winding up and bankruptcy	18.9	2.48A, 4.49E, 6.78C
Administration, creditors' voluntary liquidation and compulsory winding up: reporting distribution of property to creditors under Rule 14.13	18.10	4.49F
Voluntary winding up: reporting arrangements under section 110	18.11	4.49F
Members' voluntary winding up: reporting distribution to members other than under section 110	18.12	4.49G
Bankruptcy proceedings: reporting distribution of property to creditors under section 326	18.13	6.78D
Chapter 3: Final accounts in winding up and bankruptcy		
Contents of final account (winding up) and final report (bankruptcy)	18.14	4.125, 4.126, 4.126A, 4.49D, 6.78B
Chapter 4: Remuneration and expenses in administration, winding up and bankruptcy		
Application of Chapter	18.15	
Remuneration: principles	18.16	2.106, 4.127, 4.148A, 6.138
Remuneration of joint office-holders	18.17	2.106(7), 4.128(2), 6.139(2)
Remuneration: procedure for initial determination in an administration	18.18	2.106, 2.106(5A)
Remuneration: procedure for initial determination in a members' voluntary winding up	18.19	4.148A
Remuneration: procedure for initial determination in a creditors' voluntary winding up or a winding up by the court	18.20	4.127
Remuneration: procedure for initial determination in a bankruptcy	18.21	6.138
Application for scale fees where creditors fail to fix the basis for the office-holder's remuneration	18.22	4.127A, 6.138A

2016 Rule heading	2016 Rule	1986 Rule
Remuneration: application to the court to fix the basis	18.23	2.106(6), 4.127(7), 4.148A(6)
Remuneration: administrator, liquidator or trustee seeking increase, etc.	18.24	2.107, 4.129A, 6.140A
Application for an increase, etc. in remuneration: the general rule	18.25	2.107(1), 4.129A, 6.140A
First exception: administrator has made a statement under paragraph 52(1)(b) of Schedule B1	18.26	2.107(2)
Second exception: administrator who had applied for increase, etc. under Rule 18.24 becomes liquidator	18.27	4.127(5A)
Remuneration: recourse by administrator, liquidator or trustee to the court	18.28	2.108, 4.130, 6.141
Remuneration: review at request of administrator, liquidator or trustee	18.29	2.109A, 4.131A, 6.142A
Remuneration: exceeding the fee estimate	18.30	2.109AB, 4.131AB, 6.142AB[1]
Remuneration: new administrator, liquidator or trustee	18.31	2.109B, 4.131B, 4.148D, 6.142B
Remuneration: apportionment of set fees	18.32	2.109C, 4.131C, 4.148E, 6.142C
Remuneration: variation of the application of Rules 18.29, 18.30 and 18.32	18.33	2.109D, 4.131D[2]
Remuneration and expenses: application to court by a creditor or member on grounds that remuneration or expenses are excessive	18.34	2.109, 4.131, 4.148C, 6.142
Remuneration and expenses: application to court by a bankrupt on grounds that remuneration or expenses are excessive	18.35	6.142
Applications under Rules 18.34 and 18.35 where the court has given permission for the application	18.36	2.109, 4.131, 4.148C, 6.142
Applications under Rule 18.34 where the court's permission is not required for the application	18.37	2.109, 4.131, 4.148C 6.142

---

1 Inserted into the Insolvency Rules 1986 by the Insolvency (Amendment) Rules 2015, to commence 1 October 2015.
2 Inserted into the Insolvency Rules 1986 by the Insolvency (Amendment) Rules 2015, to commence 1 October 2015.

2016 Rule heading	2016 Rule	1986 Rule
Remuneration in winding up and bankruptcy where assets are realised on behalf of charge holder	18.38	4.127B, 6.139

Part 19: Disclaimer in winding up and bankruptcy

2016 Rule heading	2016 Rule	1986 Rule
Application of this Part	19.1	4.187, 6.178
Notice of disclaimer (sections 178 and 315)	19.2	4.187, 6.178
Notice of disclaimer to interested persons (sections 178 and 315)	19.3	4.188, 6.179
Notice to disclaimer of leasehold property (sections 179 and 317)	19.4	4.188(2), 6.179(2)
Notice of disclaimer in respect of a dwelling house (bankruptcy) (section 318)	19.5	6.179(3)–(4)
Additional notices of disclaimer	19.6	4.189, 6.180
Records	19.7	4.190A, 6.181A
Application for permission to disclaim in bankruptcy (section 315(4))	19.8	6.182
Application by interested party for decision on disclaimer (sections 178(5) and 316)	19.9	4.191A, 6.183
Disclaimer presumed valid and effective	19.10	4.193, 6.185
Application for exercise of court's powers under section 181 (winding up) or section 320 (bankruptcy)	19.11	4.194, 6.186

Part 20: Debtors and their families at risk of violence: orders not to disclose current address

2016 Rule heading	2016 Rule	1986 Rule
Application of this Part and interpretation	20.1	5.67(2), 5A.18(1), 6.235B(2)
Proposed IVA (order for non-disclosure of current address)	20.2	5.67
IVA (order for non-disclosure of current address)	20.3	5.67
Debt relief application (order for non-disclosure of current address)	20.4	5A.18
Bankruptcy application (order for non-disclosure of current address)	20.5	6.50B
Bankruptcy and debt relief proceedings (order for non-disclosure of current address)	20.6	5A.18, 6.235B
Additional provisions in respect of order under Rule 20.6(4)	20.7	N/A

2016 Rule heading	2016 Rule	1986 Rule
Part 21: The EC Regulation		
Interpretation for this Part	21.1	N/A
Conversion into winding up proceedings or bankruptcy: application	21.2	1.31,1.32, 2.130, 2.131, 5.62, 5.63
Conversion into winding up proceedings or bankruptcy: court order	21.3	1.33, 2.132, 5.64
Confirmation of creditors' voluntary winding up: application	21.4	7.62(1)–(3)
Confirmation of creditors' voluntary winding up: court order	21.5	7.62(5)–(8)
Confirmation of creditors' voluntary winding up: notice to member State liquidator	21.6	7.63
Member state liquidator: duty to give notice	21.7	1.34, 2.133, 4.231, 5.65, 6.238, 6.239
Member state liquidator: rules on creditors' participation in proceedings	21.8	2.133, 4.231, 6.238, 6.239, 7.64, 8.8
Part 22: Permission to act as director, etc. of company with a prohibited name (section 216)		
Preliminary	22.1	4.226
Application for permission under section 216(3)	22.2	4.227A
Power of court to call for liquidator's report	22.3	4.227A(2)
First excepted case: business of insolvent company acquired under specified arrangements	22.4	4.228
	22.5	
Second excepted case	22.6	4.229
Third excepted case	22.7	4.230
Revocations	Sch. 1	N/A
Transitional and Savings Provisions	Sch. 2	N/A
Punishment of Offences under these Rules	Sch. 3	Sch. 5
Service of documents	Sch. 4	
● Service of documents	para. 1	12A.17, 12A.20
● Service of winding-up petitions	para. 2	4.8, 4.22
● Service of administration application (paragraph 12 of Schedule B1)	para. 3	N/A
● Service on joint office-holders	para. 3	12A.19

2016 Rule heading	2016 Rule	1986 Rule
• Service of orders staying proceedings	para. 4	7.56, 12A.18
• Certificate of service	para. 5	2.8, 2.9, 4.9A, 6.15A
CALCULATION OF TIME PERIODS	Sch. 5	12.55
INSOLVENCY JURISDICTION OF COUNTY COURT HEARING CENTRES	Sch. 6	Sch. 2 and SI 2014 No 817
INFORMATION TO BE PROVIDED IN THE BANKRUPTCY APPLICATION	Sch. 7	Sch. 2A
Part 1: Debtor's personal information		
Part 2: Additional personal information		
ADDITIONAL INFORMATION TO BE PROVIDED IN THE BANKRUPTCY APPLICATION	Sch. 8	Sch. 2B
INFORMATION TO BE GIVEN TO CREDITORS	Sch. 9	Sch. 2C
DESTINATION OF APPEALS FROM DECISIONS OF DISTRICT JUDGES IN CORPORATE INSOLVENCY MATTERS	Sch. 10	N/A
DETERMINATION OF INSOLVENCY OFFICE-HOLDER'S REMUNERATION	Sch. 11	Sch. 6

GUIDE TO THE DESTINATION OF THE INSOLVENCY RULES 1986 (SI 1986 NO 1925) IN THE INSOLVENCY RULES (ENGLAND AND WALES) 2016 (SI 2016 NO 1024)

This table indicates the destination of provisions in the 1986 Rules relating to corporate insolvency. The 2016 Rules broadly derive from the 1986 Rules. However there is rarely an exact match as the structure of the 2016 Rules is different, the language has been modernised and there have been significant changes, in particular as a result of amendments to the primary legislation made by the Enterprise and Regulatory Reform Act 2013, the Deregulation Act 2015, and the Small Business, Enterprise and Employment Act 2015. Furthermore the information requirements previously contained in forms have now been imported into the relevant rule as specified content. Finally the new Rules try to avoid copying out of the primary legislation. Instead they contain many references to the Insolvency Act 1986 to enable the user to connect individual rules with the relevant provisions of the Act that the Rules supplement.

1986 Rule heading	1986 Rule	2016 Rule
Citation and commencement	0.1	1
Construction and interpretation	0.2	2
Extent	0.3	3

1986 Rule heading	1986 Rule	2016 Rule
THE FIRST GROUP OF PARTS		
Part 1: Company voluntary arrangements		
Chapter 1: Preliminary		
Scope of this Part; interpretation	1.1	
Chapter 2: Proposal by directors		
Preparation of proposal	1.2	
Contents of proposal	1.3	2.2, 2.3
Notice to intended nominee	1.4	
Statement of affairs	1.5	2.6
Additional disclosure for assistance of nominee	1.6	2.8
Nominee's report on the proposal	1.7	2.9
Replacement of nominee	1.8	2.10
Summoning of meetings under section 3	1.9	2.25–2.28
Chapter 3: Proposal by administrator or liquidator (himself the nominee)		
Preparation of proposal.	1.10	2.3, 2.5
Summoning of meetings under section 3.	1.11	2.25–2.29, 2.31
Chapter 4: Proposal by administrator or liquidator (another insolvency practitioner the nominee)		
Preparation of proposal and notice to nominee.	1.12	2.3
Chapter 5: Proceedings on a proposal made by the directors, or by the administrator, or by the liquidator		
SECTION A: MEETINGS OF COMPANY'S CREDITORS AND MEMBERS		
Summoning of meetings	1.13	2.29, 15.8, 15.29
The chairman at meetings	1.14	15.21
The chairman as proxy-holder	1.15	16.5
Attendance by company officers	1.16	2.30, 15.14
SECTION B: VOTING RIGHTS AND MAJORITIES		
Voting rights (creditors)	1.17	15.7, 15.29
Procedure for admission of creditors' claims for voting purposes	1.17A	15.33
Voting rights (members)	1.18	2.35
Requisite majorities (creditors)	1.19	15.31
Requisite majorities (members)	1.20	2.36
Proceedings to obtain agreement on the proposal	1.21	Part 15

1986 Rule heading	1986 Rule	2016 Rule
SECTION C: IMPLEMENTATION OF THE ARRANGEMENT		
Resolutions to follow approval	1.22	2.33
Notice of order made under section 4A(6)	1.22A	2.37
Hand-over of property, etc. to supervisor	1.23	2.39
Report of meetings	1.24	2.38
Revocation or suspension of the arrangement	1.25	2.40
Supervisor's accounts and reports	1.26A	2.41
Production of accounts and records to Secretary of State	1.27	2.42
Fees, costs, charges and expenses	1.28	2.43
Completion of the arrangement	1.29	2.44
EC REGULATION--CONVERSION OF VOLUNTARY ARRANGEMENT INTO WINDING UP		
Application for conversion into winding up	1.31	21.2
Rule 1 32 Contents of witness statement	1.32	21. 2
Rule 1 33 Power of court	1.33	21. 3
EC REGULATION – MEMBER STATE LIQUIDATOR		
Rule 1 34 Interpretation of creditor and notice to member State liquidator	1.34	21.7, 21.8
OBTAINING A MORATORIUM PROCEEDINGS DURING A MORATORIUM		
NOMINEES CONSIDERATION OF PROPOSALS WHERE MORATORIUM OBTAINED		
SECTION A: OBTAINING A MORATORIUM		
Preparation of proposal by directors and submission to nominee	1.35	
Delivery of documents to the intended nominee, etc.	1.36	
Statement of affairs	1.37	2.11
The nominee's statement	1.38	2.13
Documents submitted to the court to obtain moratorium	1.39	2.14
Notice and advertisement of beginning of a moratorium	1.40	2.15
Notice of extension of moratorium	1.41	2.16, 2.17
Notice and advertisement of end of moratorium	1.42	2.18, 2.19
SECTION B: PROCEEDINGS DURING A MORATORIUM		
Disposal of charged property, etc. during a moratorium	1.43	2.18, 2.19

1986 Rule heading	1986 Rule	2016 Rule
SECTION C: NOMINEES		
Withdrawal of nominee's consent to act	1.44	2.20
Replacement of nominee by the court	1.45	2.22
Notification of appointment of a replacement nominee	1.46	2.23
Applications to court under paragraphs 26 or 27 of Schedule A1 to the Act	1.47	2.24
SECTION D: CONSIDERATION OF PROPOSALS WHERE MORATORIUM OBTAINED		
Summoning of meetings; procedure at meetings, etc.	1.48	2.25–2.28, 2.30, Part 15
Entitlement to vote (creditors)	1.49	15.28
Procedure for admission of creditors' claims for voting purposes	1.50	15.33
Voting rights (members)	1.51	2.35
Requisite majorities (creditors)	1.52	15.31
Requisite majorities (members) and proceedings to obtain agreement	1.53	2.36, 15.21, 15.25
Implementation of the arrangement	1.54	2.39
TIME RECORDING INFORMATION		
Provision by nominee or supervisor of information about time spent	1.55	2.45
OMISSION OF INFORMATION FROM STATEMENT OF AFFAIRS		
Omission of Information from Statement of Affairs	1.56	2.7, 2.12
PART 2 ADMINISTRATION PROCEDURE		
Chapter 1: Application for, and making of, the order		
Introductory and interpretation	2.1	N/A
Chapter 2: Appointment of administrator by court		
Witness statement in support of administration application	2.2	3.6
Form of application	2.3	3.3, 3.4, 3.5
Contents of application and witness statement in support	2.4	3.6
Filing of application	2.5	3.7, 3.10
Service of application	2.6	3.7, Sch. 4 para. 3
Notice to officers charged with execution of writs or other process, etc.	2.7	3.9
Manner in which service to be effected	2.8	Sch. 4
Proof of service	2.9	Sch. 4 para. 6

1986 Rule heading	1986 Rule	2016 Rule
Application to appoint specified person as administrator by holder of qualifying floating charge	2.10	3.11
Application where company in liquidation	2.11	3.5
The hearing	2.12	3.11
Contents of court order	2.13	3.13, 3.14
Notice of administration order	2.14	3.15
Chapter 3: Appointment of administrator by holder of floating charge		
Notice of intention to appoint	2.15	3.16
Notice of appointment	2.16	3.17
Filing notice with court	2.17	3.18
Appointment by floating charge holder	2.18	3.19
Appointment taking place out of court business hours	2.19	3.20, 3.21, 3.22
Chapter 4: Appointment of administrator by company or directors		
Notice of intention to appoint	2.20	3.23
Statutory declaration	2.21	3.23
Notice of intention to appoint	2.22	3.23
Notice of appointment	2.23	3.24
Statutory declaration	2.24	3.24
Accompanying documents	2.25	3.25
	2.26	3.27
Chapter 5: Process of administration		
Notification and advertisement of administrator's appointment	2.27	3.29
Notice requiring statement of affairs	2.28	3.27
Verification and filing	2.29	3.30, 3.31, 3.32
Limited disclosure	2.30	3.44, 3.45, 3.47
Release from duty to submit statement of affairs; extension of time	2.31	3.33, 3.37
Expenses of statement of affairs	2.32	3.34
Administrator's proposals	2.33	3.35, 3.36
Limited disclosure of paragraph 49 statement 15	2.33A	3.45
Chapter 6: Meetings and reports		
SECTION A: CREDITORS' MEETINGS		
Meetings to consider administrator's proposals	2.34	3.38, 15.7, 15.12, 15.13

1986 Rule heading	1986 Rule	2016 Rule
Creditors' meetings generally	2.35	15.8, 15.9, 15.10, 15.23, 15.24, 15.25
The chairman at meetings	2.36	15.21, 16.5
Meeting requisitioned by creditors	2.37	15.18, 15.19
Notice of meetings by advertisement only	2.37A	15.12
Entitlement to vote	2.38	15.28, 15.31, 15.34
Admission and rejection of claims	2.39	15.33, 15.35
Secured creditors	2.40	15.31
Holders of negotiable instruments	2.41	N/A
Hire-purchase, conditional sale and chattel leasing agreements	2.42	15.32
Resolutions	2.43	15.34
Minutes	2.44A	15.40
Revision of the administrator's proposals	2.45	3.42
Notice to creditors	2.46	3.43
Reports to creditors	2.47	18.6–18.10
Correspondence instead of creditors' meetings	2.48	N/A
Creditors' request for further information	2.48A	18.9
SECTION B: COMPANY MEETINGS		
Venue and conduct of company meeting	2.49	15.21, 15.25, 15.40, 15.41
Chapter 7: The creditors' committee		
Constitution of committee	2.50	17.3, 17.4
Formalities of establishment	2.51	17.5
Functions and meetings of the committee	2.52	17.2, 17.14
The chairman at meetings	2.53	17.15
Quorum	2.54	17.16
Committee-members' representatives	2.55	17.17
Resignation	2.56	17.10
Termination of membership	2.57	17.11
Removal	2.58	17.12
Vacancies	2.59	17.8
Procedure at meetings	2.60	17.18
Resolutions of creditors' committee otherwise than at a meeting	2.61	17.19
Information from administrator	2.62	17.22

1986 Rule heading	1986 Rule	2016 Rule
Expenses of members	2.63	17.24
Members' dealing with the company	2.64	17.25
Formal defects	2.65	17.27
Chapter 8: Disposal of charged property		
	2.66	3.49
Chapter 9: Expenses of the administration		
	2.67	3.51
Pre-administration costs	2.67A	3.52
Chapter 10: Distributions to creditors		
SECTION A: APPLICATION OF CHAPTER AND GENERAL		
	2.68	14.28, 14.27, 14.38
Debts of insolvent company to rank equally	2.69	14.12
Supplementary provisions as to dividend	2.70	14.39
Division of unsold assets	2.71	14.13
SECTION B: MACHINERY OF PROVING A DEBT		
Proving a debt	2.72	14.3, 14.4
Costs of proving	2.74	14.5
Administrator to allow inspection of proofs	2.75	14.6
New administrator appointed	2.76	3.70
Admission and rejection of proofs for dividend	2.77	14.7
Appeal against decision on proof	2.78	14.8, 14.9
Withdrawal or variation of proof	2.79	14.10
Expunging of proof by the court	2.80	14.11
SECTION C: QUANTIFICATION OF CLAIMS		
Estimate of quantum	2.81	14.14
Negotiable instruments, etc.	2.82	N/A
Secured creditors	2.83	14.19
Discounts	2.84	14.20
Mutual credits and set-off	2.85	14.24
Debt in foreign currency	2.86	14.21
Payments of a periodical nature	2.87	14.22
Interest	2.88	14.23
Debt payable at future time	2.89	14.44
Value of security	2.90	14.15
Surrender for non-disclosure	2.91	14.16
Redemption by administrator	2.92	14.17

1986 Rule heading	1986 Rule	2016 Rule
Test of security's value	2.93	14.18
Realisation of security by creditor	2.94	14.19
Notice of proposed distribution	2.95	14.26, 14.28, 14.29, 14.30
Admission or rejection of proofs	2.96	14.32
Postponement or cancellation of dividend	2.96A	14.33
Declaration of dividend	2.97	14.34
Notice of declaration of a dividend	2.98	14.35
Payments of dividends and related matters	2.99	14.35
Notice of no dividend, or no further dividend	2.100	14.37
Proof altered after payment of dividend	2.101	14.40
Rule 2102 Secured creditors	2.102	14.41
Disqualification from dividend	2.103	14.42
Assignment of right to dividend	2.104	14.43
Debt payable at future time	2.105	14.44
Chapter 11: The administrator		
Fixing of remuneration	2.106	18.16, 18.17, 18.18, 18.23
Recourse to meeting of creditors	2.107	18.24, 18.25
Recourse to the court	2.108	18.24–18.29
Creditors' claim that remuneration is or other expenses are excessive	2.109	18.34, 18.36, 18.37
Review of remuneration	2.109A	18.29
Remuneration of new administrator	2.109B	18.31
Apportionment of set fee remuneration	2.109C	18.32
Chapter 12: Ending administration		
Final progress reports	2.110	3.56, 18.3
Notice of automatic end of administration	2.111	3.55
Applications for extension of administration	2.112	3.54
Notice of end of administration	2.113	3.56
Application to court by administrator	2.114	3.57
Application to court by creditor	2.115	3.58
Notification by administrator of court order	2.116	3.59
Moving from administration to creditors' voluntary liquidation	2.117A	3.60
Moving from administration to dissolution	2.118	3.61
Chapter 13: Replacing administrator		
Grounds for resignation	2.119	3.62

1986 Rule heading	1986 Rule	2016 Rule
Notice of intention to resign	2.120	3.63
Notice of resignation	2.121	3.64
Application to court to remove administrator from office	2.122	3.65
Notice of vacation of office when administrator ceases to be qualified to act	2.123	3.66
Administrator deceased	2.124	3.67
Application to replace	2.125	3.68
Notification and advertisement of appointment of replacement administrator	2.126	3.69
Notification and advertisement of appointment of joint administrator	2.127	3.69
	2.128	3.69
Administrator's duties on vacating office	2.129	3.70
Chapter 14: EC Regulation: Conversion of administration into winding up		
Application for conversion into winding up	2.130	21.2
Contents of witness statement	2.131	21.2
Power of court	2.132	21.3
Chapter 15: EC Regulation: Member state liquidator		
Interpretation of creditor and notice to member State liquidator	2.133	21.8
Part 3: Administrative receivership		
Chapter 1: Appointment of administrative receiver		
Acceptance of appointment	3.1	4.1
Notice and advertisement of appointment	3.2	4.5
Chapter 2: Statement of affairs and report to creditors		
Notice requiring statement of affairs	3.3	4.6
Verification and filing	3.4	4.7, 4.8, 4.9
Limited disclosure	3.5	4.12
Release from duty to submit statement of affairs; extension of time	3.6	4.10
Expenses of statement of affairs	3.7	4.11
Report to creditors	3.8	4.13, 4.14
Chapter 3: Creditors' meeting		
Procedure for summoning meeting under section 48(2)	3.9	15.8, 15.9, 15.10
The chairman at the meeting	3.10	15.21
Voting rights	3.11	15.8, 15.28

1986 Rule heading	1986 Rule	2016 Rule
Contents of claim	3.11A	1.2
Admission and rejection of claim	3.12	15.31, 15.33
Adjournment	3.14	15.23
Resolutions and minutes	3.15	15.34, 15.40
Chapter 4: The creditors' committee		
Constitution of committee	3.16	17.3, 17.4
Formalities of establishment	3.17	17.5
Functions and meetings of the committee	3.18	17.14
The chairman at meetings	3.19	17.15
Quorum	3.20	17.16
Committee-members' representatives	3.21	17.17
Resignation	3.22	17.10
Termination of membership	3.23	17.11
Removal	3.24	17.12
Vacancies	3.25	17.8
Procedure at meetings	3.26	17.18
Resolutions by post	3.27	17.19
Information from receiver	3.28	17.22
Expenses of members	3.29	17.24
Members' dealings with the company	3.30	17.26
Formal defects	3.30A	17.27
Chapter 5: The administrative receiver (miscellaneous)		
Disposal of charged property	3.31	4.16
Abstract of receipts and payments	3.32	4.17
Resignation	3.33	4.18
Receiver deceased	3.34	4.19
Vacation of office	3.35	4.20, 4.21
Chapter 7: Section 176a The revised Part		
Report for creditors	3.39	4.22, 4.23
Receiver to deal with prescribed part	3.40	4.24
Part 4: Companies winding up		
Chapter 1: The scheme of this part of the rules		
Voluntary winding up; winding up by the court	4.1	6.1
Winding up by the court: the various forms of petition	4.2	
Time-limits	4.3	

1986 Rule heading	1986 Rule	2016 Rule
Chapter 2: The statutory demand (no CVL application)		
Preliminary	4.4	7.2
Form and content of statutory demand	4.5	7.3
Information to be given in statutory demand	4.6	7.3
Chapter 3: Petition to winding-up order (no CVL application) (no application to petition by contributories)		
Injunction to restrain presentation or advertisement of petition	4.6A	7.24
Presentation and filing of petition	4.7	7.7
Service of petition	4.8	Sch. 4 para. 2
Proof of service	4.9A	Sch. 4 para. 6
Other persons to receive copies of petition	4.10	7.9
Advertisement of petition	4.11	7.10
Verification of petition	4.12	7.6
Persons entitled to copy of petition	4.13	7.11
Certificate of compliance	4.14	7.12
Leave for petitioner to withdraw	4.15	7.13
Notice of appearance	4.16	7.14
List of appearances	4.17	7.15
Affidavit in opposition	4.18	7.16
Adjournment	4.18A	7.19
Substitution of creditor or contributory for petitioner	4.19	7.17
Notice and settling of winding-up order	4.20	7.21
Transmission and advertisement of order	4.21	7.22
Expenses of voluntary arrangement	4.21A	N/A
Petition dismissed	4.21B	7.23
Chapter 4: Petition by contributories (no CVL application)		
Presentation and service of petition	4.22	7.29, Sch. 4 para. 2
Return of petition	4.23	7.31
Application of Rules in Chapter 3	4.24	N/A
Chapter 5: Provisional liquidator (no CVL application)		
Appointment of provisional liquidator	4.25	7.33
Notice of appointment	4.25A	7.36
Order of appointment	4.26	7.35
Deposit	4.27	7.34
Security	4.28	7.37
Failure to give or keep up security	4.29	7.37

1986 Rule heading	1986 Rule	2016 Rule
Remuneration	4.30	7.38, 18.16, 18.20
Termination of appointment	4.31	7.39
Chapter 6: Statement of affairs and other information		
Notice requiring statement of affairs	4.32	7.40
Verification and filing	4.33	7.41
Statement of affairs	4.34	6.2, 6.3, 6.4, 6.5
Copy statement of affairs	4.34A	N/A
Limited disclosure	4.35	6.6, 7.43
Release from duty to submit statement of affairs; extension of time	4.36	7.44
Expenses of statement of affairs	4.37	7.45
Expenses of statement of affairs	4.38	6.7
Submission of accounts	4.39	7.46
Submission of accounts	4.40	6.8
Expenses of preparing accounts	4.41	6.9
Further disclosure.	4.42	7.47
Chapter 7: Information to creditors and contributories		
Reports by official receiver	4.43	7.48
Meaning of 'creditors'	4.44	1.37
Report where statement of affairs lodged	4.45	7.48
Statement of affairs dispensed with	4.46	7.48
General rule as to reporting	4.47	7.48
Winding up stayed	4.48	7.51, 7.52
Information to creditors and contributories	4.49	6.15
Further information where liquidation follows administration	4.49A	6.16, 7.50
Reports to creditors and members – winding up by the court	4.49B	18.3, 18.8
CVL Progress reports – voluntary winding up	4.49C	18.3, 18.7
Final report to creditors	4.49D	18.14
Creditors' and members' request for further information	4.49E	18.9
Arrangements under section 110 (acceptance of shares, etc., as consideration	4.49F	18.11
Other distributions to members in specie	4.49G	18.12
Chapter 8: Meetings of creditors and contributories		
SECTION A: RULES OF GENERAL APPLICATION		
First meetings	4.50	7.52, 15.8, 15.11

1986 Rule heading	1986 Rule	2016 Rule
First meeting of creditors	4.51	15.8
Business at first meetings in the liquidation	4.52	15.9
Business at meeting under section 95 or 98	4.53	N/A
Effect of adjournment on company meeting	4.53A	N/A
Report by director, etc.	4.53B	6.17
Additional contents of notices gazetted or advertised under section 95	4.53C	15.8
Additional contents of notices gazetted or advertised under section 98	4.53D	15.8
General power to call meetings	4.54	1.51, 15.3, 15.6
The chairman at meetings	4.55	15.21, 15.22
The chairman at meeting	4.56	15.21, 15.22
Requisitioned meetings	4.57	15.18, 15.19
Attendance at meetings of company's personnel	4.58	15.14, 15.22
Notice of meetings by advertisement only	4.59	15.12
Venue	4.60	15.10
Expenses of summoning meetings	4.61	15.19
Expenses of meeting under section 98	4.62	N/A
Resolutions	4.63	6.18, 15.34, 15.39
Resolutions by correspondence	4.63A	15.3
Chairman of meeting as proxy-holder	4.64	16.5
Suspension and adjournment	4.65	15.23, 15.25, 15.26
Entitlement to vote (creditors)	4.67	15.28
Chairman's discretion to allow vote	4.68	15.28
Entitlement to vote (contributories)	4.69	15.39
Admission and rejection of proof (creditors' meeting)	4.70	15.33
Record of proceedings	4.71	15.40
SECTION B: WINDING UP OF RECOGNISED BANKS, ETC		
Additional provisions as regards certain meetings	4.72	5.3, 15.17
Chapter 9: Proof of debts in a liquidation		
SECTION A: PROCEDURE FOR PROVING		
Meaning of 'prove'	4.73	1.2, 14.3
Supply of forms	4.74	N/A
Contents of proof	4.75	14.4
Particulars of creditor's claim	4.76	N/A

1986 Rule heading	1986 Rule	2016 Rule
Cost of proving	4.78	14.5
Liquidator to allow inspection of proofs	4.79	14.6
Transmission of proofs to liquidator	4.80	7.60
New liquidator appointed	4.81	7.73
Admission and rejection of proofs for dividend	4.82	14.7
Appeal against decision on proof	4.83	14.8, 14.9
Withdrawal or variation of proof	4.84	14.10
Expunging of proof by the court	4.85	14.11
SECTION B: QUANTIFICATION OF CLAIM		
Estimate of quantum	4.86	14.14
Negotiable instruments, etc.	4.87	N/A
Secured creditors	4.88	14.19
Discounts	4.89	14.20
Mutual credit and set-off	4.90	14.25
Debt in foreign currency	4.91	14.21
Payments of a periodical nature	4.92	14.22
Interest	4.93	14.23
Debt payable at future time	4.94	14.44
Chapter 10: Secured creditors		
Value of security	4.95	14.15
Surrender for non-disclosure	4.96	14.16
Redemption by liquidator	4.97	14.17
Test of security's value	4.98	14.18
Realisation of security by creditor	4.99	14.19
Chapter 11: The liquidator		
SECTION A: APPOINTMENT AND ASSOCIATED FORMALITIES		
Appointment by creditors or contributories	4.100	7.53
Appointment by creditors or by the company	4.101	6.20
Power to fill vacancy in office of liquidator	4.101A	6.21
Official Receiver not to be appointed liquidator	4.101B	N/A
Appointment by the court	4.102	7.56
Appointment by the court	4.103	6.22
Appointment by Secretary of State	4.104	7.57
Authentication of liquidator's appointment	4.105	N/A
Appointment to be gazetted and registered	4.106A	7.59
Hand-over of assets to liquidator	4.107	7.60

1986 Rule heading	1986 Rule	2016 Rule
SECTION B: RESIGNATION AND REMOVAL; VACATION OF OFFICE		
Creditors' meeting to receive liquidator's resignation	4.108	6.25, 7.61
Resignation (application under Rule 4.131)	4.108A	N/A
Action following acceptance of resignation	4.109	N/A
Action following acceptance of resignation	4.110	N/A
Leave to resign granted by the court	4.111	N/A
Advertisement of resignation	4.112	N/A
Meeting of creditors to remove liquidator	4.113	7.63
Meeting of creditors to remove liquidator	4.114	15.7(3)
Court's power to regulate meetings under Rules 4.113, 4.114-CVL	4.115	N/A
Procedure on removal	4.116	7.64
Procedure on removal	4.117	6.26
Advertisement of removal	4.118	N/A
Removal of liquidator by the court	4.119	7.65
Removal of liquidator by the court	4.120	6.27
Release of resigning or removed liquidator	4.121	7.69
Release of resigning or removed liquidator	4.122	6.33
Removal of liquidator by Secretary of State	4.123	7.66
SECTION C: RELEASE ON COMPLETION OF ADMINISTRATION		
Release of official receiver.	4.124	7.70
Final meeting	4.125	7.69, 7.71, 18.14
Rule as to reporting	4.125A	7.72
Final meeting	4.126	6.28. 18.14
Final meeting	4.126A	5.9, 5.10, 18.14
SECTION D: REMUNERATION		
Fixing of remuneration	4.127	18.16, 18.19, 18.20
Liquidator's entitlement to remuneration where it is not fixed under Rule 4.127	4.127A	18.22
Liquidator's remuneration where he realises assets on behalf of chargeholder	4.127B	18.38
Other matters affecting remuneration.	4.128	18.17
Recourse of liquidator to meeting of creditors	4.129A	18.24
Recourse to the court	4.130	18.23
Creditors' claim that remuneration is excessive	4.131	18.28, 18.34
Review of remuneration	4.131A	18.29

1986 Rule heading	1986 Rule	2016 Rule
Remuneration of new liquidator	4.131B	18.31
Apportionment of set fee remuneration	4.131C	18.32
SECTION E: SUPPLEMENTARY PROVISIONS		
Liquidator deceased	4.132	7.67
Liquidator deceased	4.133	6.29
Loss of qualification as insolvency practitioner	4.134	7.68
Loss of qualification as insolvency practitioner	4.135	6.30
Vacation of office on making of winding-up order	4.136	6.31
Notice to official receiver of intention to vacate office	4.137	7.62
Liquidator's duties on vacating office	4.138	6.32, 7.73
SECTION F: THE LIQUIDATOR IN A MEMBERS' VOLUNTARY WINDING UP		
Appointment by the company	4.139	5.2
Appointment by the court	4.140	5.4
Authentication of liquidator's appointment	4.141	N/A
Company meeting to receive liquidator's resignation	4.142	5.6, 5.8
Removal of liquidator by the court	4.143	5.7
Release of resigning or removed liquidator	4.144	5.14
Liquidator deceased	4.145	5.11
Loss of qualification as insolvency practitioner	4.146	5.12
Vacation of office on making of winding-up order	4.147	5.14
Liquidator's duties on vacating office	4.148	5.13
Remuneration of liquidator in members' voluntary winding up	4.148A	18.16, 18.19
Members' claim that remuneration is excessive	4.148C	18.34
Remuneration of new liquidator	4.148D	18.31
Apportionment of fixed fee remuneration	4.148E	18.32
SECTION G: RULES APPLYING IN EVERY WINDING UP, WHETHER VOLUNTARY OR BY THE COURT		
Power of court to set aside certain transactions	4.149	5.15, 6.34, 7.74
Rule against solicitation	4.150	5.16, 6.35, 7.75

1986 Rule heading	1986 Rule	2016 Rule
CHAPTER 12 THE LIQUIDATION COMMITTEE		
Preliminary	4.151	N/A
Membership of committee	4.152	17.3
Formalities of establishment	4.153	17.5
Committee established by contributories	4.154	17.6
Obligations of liquidator to committee	4.155	17.21
Meetings of the committee	4.156	17.12
The chairman at meetings	4.157	17.13
Quorum	4.158	17.14
Committee-members' representatives	4.159	17.15
Resignation	4.160	17.8
Termination of membership	4.161	17.9
Removal	4.162	17.10
Vacancy (creditor members)	4.163	17.8
Vacancy (contributory members)	4.164	17.9
Voting rights and resolutions	4.165	17.18
Voting rights and resolutions	4.166	17.18
Resolutions by post	4.167	17.19
Liquidator's reports	4.168	17.21
Expenses of members, etc.	4.169	17.24
Dealings by committee-members and others	4.170	17.25
Composition of committee when creditors paid in full	4.171A	17.13
Committee's functions vested in Secretary of State	4.172	17.28
Formal defects	4.172A	17.27
Chapter 13: The liquidation committee where winding up follows immediately on administration (no CVL application)		
Preliminary	4.173	17.29
Continuation of creditors' committee	4.174A	17.29
Liquidator's certificate	4.176	17.29
Obligations of liquidator to committee	4.177	17.23
Application of Chapter 12	4.178	17.29
Chapter 14: Collection and distribution of company's assets by liquidator		
General duties of liquidator	4.179	7.76
Manner of distributing assets	4.180	14.27
Debts of insolvent company to rank equally	4.181	14.12
Supplementary provisions as to dividend	4.182	14.39, 14.40, 14.45

1986 Rule heading	1986 Rule	2016 Rule
Distribution in members' voluntary winding up	4.182A	14.28
Division of unsold assets	4.183	14.13
General powers of liquidator	4.184	6.36, 7.77
Enforced delivery up of company's property	4.185	7.78
Final distribution	4.186	14.36, 14.37, 14.38
Chapter 15: Disclaimer		
Liquidator's notice of disclaimer	4.187	19.1, 19.2
Communication of disclaimer to persons interested	4.188	19.3, 19.4
Additional notices	4.189	19.6
Records	4.190A	19.7
Application to interested party under section 178(5)	4.191A	19.9
Interest in property to be declared on request	4.192	N/A
Disclaimer presumed valid and effective	4.193	19.10
Application for exercise of court's powers under section 181	4.194	19.11
Chapter 16: Settlement of list of contributories (no CVL application)		
Preliminary	4.195	7.79
Duty of liquidator to settle list	4.196	7.79, 7.80
Form of list	4.197	7.81
Procedure for settling list	4.198	7.82
Application to court for variation of the list	4.199	7.83
Variation of, or addition to, the list	4.200	7.84
Costs not to fall on official receiver	4.201	7.85
Chapter 17: Calls (no CVL application)		
Calls by liquidator	4.202	7.86
Control by liquidation committee	4.203	7.87
Application to court for leave to make a call	4.204	7.88, 7.99
Making and enforcement of the call	4.205	7.90, 7.91
Chapter 18: Special manager		
Appointment and remuneration	4.206	5.17, 6.37, 7.93
Security	4.207	5.18, 6.38, 7.94
Failure to give or keep up security	4.208	5.19, 6.39, 7.95
Accounting	4.209	5.20, 6.40, 7.96
Termination of appointment	4.210	5.21, 6.41, 7.97

1986 Rule heading	1986 Rule	2016 Rule
Chapter 19: Public examination of company officers and others		
Order for public examination	4.211	7.98, 7.102
Notice of hearing	4.212	7.103
Order on request by creditors or contributories	4.213	7.99, 7.100, 7.101
Witness unfit for examination	4.214	7.104
Procedure at hearing	4.215	7.105
Adjournment	4.216	7.106
Expenses of examination	4.217	7.107
Chapter 20: Order of payment of costs, etc., out of assets		
General rule as to priority.	4.218	6.42, 7.108
Litigation expenses and property subject to a floating charge – general provisions	4.218A	6.44, 7.111, 7.112
Litigation expenses and property subject to a floating charge – requirement for approval or authorisation	4.218B	6.45, 7.113
Litigation expenses and property subject to a floating charge – request for approval or authorisation	4.218C	6.46, 7.114
Litigation expenses and property subject to a floating charge – grant of approval or authorisation.	4.218D	6.47, 7.115
Litigation expenses and property subject to a floating charge – application to court by the liquidator	4.218E	6.48, 7.116
Winding up commencing as voluntary	4.219	7.109
Saving for powers of the court	4.220	6.43, 7.110
Chapter 21: Miscellaneous rules		
SECTION A: RETURN OF CAPITAL (NO CVL APPLICATION)		
Application to court for order authorising return	4.221	7.117
Procedure for return	4.222	7.118
SECTION C: DISSOLUTION AFTER WINDING UP		
Secretary of State's directions under section 203, 205	4.224	7.119
Procedure following appeal under section 203(4) or 205(4)	4.225	7.119
Chapter 22: Leave to act as director, etc., of company with prohibited name (section 216 of the act)		
Preliminary	4.226	22.1
Application for leave under section 216(3)	4.227A	22.3
First excepted case	4.228	22.4, 22.5

1986 Rule heading	1986 Rule	2016 Rule
Second excepted case	4.229	22.6
Third excepted case	4.230	22.7
Chapter 23: EC Regulation – Member state liquidator		
Interpretation of creditor and notice to member State liquidator	4.231	21.9, 21.10
THE THIRD GROUP OF PARTS		
Part 7: Court procedure and practice		
Chapter 1: Applications		
Preliminary	7.1	12.5
Form and contents of application	7.3	1.35
Application under section 176A(5) to disapply section 176A	7.3A	12.14
Filing and service of application	7.4	12.7, 12.9, 12.10
Notice of application under section 176A(5)	7.4A	12.15
Hearings without notice	7.5A	12.12
Hearing of application	7.6A	12.2(3)
Witness statements – general	7.7A	12.28
Filing and service of witness statements	7.8	12.28
Use of reports	7.9	12.28
Adjournment of hearing; directions	7.10	12.9, 12.13
Chapter 1ZA The London insolvency district		
Allocation of proceedings to the London insolvency district	7.10ZA	12.5
Chapter 1A Block transfer of cases where insolvency practitioner.		
Preliminary and interpretation	7.10A	12.35
Power to make a block transfer order	7.10B	12.36
Application for a block transfer order	7.10C	12.37
Action following application for a block transfer order	7.10D	12.38
Chapter 2 Transfer of proceedings between courts		
General power of transfer	7.11	12.30
Proceedings commenced in wrong court	7.12	12.31
Applications for transfer	7.13	12.32
Procedure following order for transfer	7.14	12.33
Consequential transfer of other proceedings	7.15	12.34
Chapter 3: Shorthand writers		
Nomination and appointment of shorthand writers	7.16	12.65

1986 Rule heading	1986 Rule	2016 Rule
Remuneration	7.17	12.65
Chapter 4: Enforcement procedures		
Enforcement of court orders	7.19	12.51
Orders enforcing compliance with the Rules	7.20	12.52
Warrants (general provisions)	7.21	12.53
Warrants under sections 134, 364	7.22	12.54
Warrants under sections 236, 366	7.23	12.55
Warrants under section 365	7.25	12.56
Chapter 5: Court records and returns		
Court file	7.31A	12.39
Chapter 6: Costs and taxation		
Application of Chapter	7.33A	12.41
Requirement to assess costs by the detailed procedure	7.34A	12.42
Procedure where detailed assessment required	7.35	12.43
Costs of officers charged with execution of writs or other process	7.36	12.44
Petitions presented by insolvents	7.37A	12.45
Costs paid otherwise than out of the insolvent estate	7.38	12.46
Award of costs against official receiver or responsible insolvency practitioner	7.39	12.47
Applications for costs	7.40	12.48
Costs and expenses of witnesses	7.41	12.49
Final costs certificate	7.42	12.50
Chapter 7: Persons who lack capacity to manage their affairs		
Introductory	7.43	12.23
Appointment of another person to act	7.44	12.24
Witness statement in support of application	7.45A	12.25
Service of notices following appointment	7.46	12.26
Chapter 8: Appeals in insolvency proceedings		
Appeals and reviews of court orders (winding up)	7.47	12.59
Appeals in bankruptcy	7.48	12.60
Procedure on appeal	7.49A	12.58, 12.61
Appeal against decision of Secretary of State or official receiver	7.50	12.62

1986 Rule heading	1986 Rule	2016 Rule
Chapter 9: General		
Principal court rules and practice to apply	7.51A	12.1
Right of audience	7.52	13.1(2)
Formal defects	7.55	12.65
Service of orders staying proceedings	7.56	Sch. 4 para. 5
Payment into court	7.59	N/A
Further information and disclosure	7.60	12.27
Office copies of documents	7.61	12.40
EC REGULATION – CREDITORS' VOLUNTARY WINDING UP – CONFIRMATION BY THE COURT		
Application for confirmation	7.62	21.4, 21.5
Notice to member state liquidator and creditors in member states	7.63	21.6
EC REGULATION – MEMBER STATE LIQUIDATOR		
Interpretation of creditor	7.64	N/A
Part 8: Proxies and company representation		
Definition of 'proxy'	8.1	16.2
Issue and use of forms	8.2	16.3, 16.4
Use of proxies at meeting	8.3	16.4, 16.5
Retention of proxies	8.4	16.6
Right of inspection	8.5	16.6
Proxy-holder with financial interest	8.6	16.7
Company representation	8.7	16.8
Interpretation of creditor	8.8	N/A
Part 9: Examination of persons concerned in company and individual insolvency		
Preliminary	9.1	12.17
Form and contents of application	9.2	12.18
Order for examination, etc.	9.3	12.19
Procedure for examination	9.4	12.20
Record of examination	9.5	12.21
Costs of proceedings under sections 236, 366	9.6	12.22
Part 10: Official receivers		
Appointment of official receivers	10.1	13.1

1986 Rule heading	1986 Rule	2016 Rule
Persons entitled to act on official receiver's behalf	10.2	13.3
Application for directions	10.3	13.4
Official receiver's expenses	10.4	13.5

Part 11: Declaration and payment of dividend (winding up and bankruptcy)		
Preliminary		N/A
Notice of intended dividend	11.2	14.28
Final admission/rejection of proofs	11.3	14.32
Postponement or cancellation of dividend	11.4	14.33
Decision to declare dividend	11.5	14.34
Notice of declaration	11.6	14.35
Notice of no, or no further, dividend	11.7	14.37
Proof altered after payment of dividend	11.8	14.40
Secured creditors	11.9	14.41
Disqualification from dividend	11.10	14.42
Assignment of right to dividend	11.11	14.43
Preferential creditors	11.12	14.28(2), 14.29(2)
Debt payable at future time	11.13	14.44

Part 12: Miscellaneous and general		
Power of Secretary of State to regulate certain matters	12.1	0.5
Costs, expenses, etc.	12.2	3.50, 6.42, 7.108, 10.147
Provable debts	12.3	14.2
False claim of status as creditor, etc.	12.18	1.56
Punishment of offences	12.21	0.6

Part 12A: Provisions of general effect		
THE GIVING OF NOTICE AND THE SUPPLY OF DOCUMENTS – GENERAL		
Application	12A.1	N/A
Personal delivery of documents	12A.2	1.44
Postal delivery of documents	12A.3	1.42
Non-receipt of notice of meeting	12A.4	N/A
Notice, etc. to solicitors	12A.5	1.40

1986 Rule heading	1986 Rule	2016 Rule
THE GIVING OF NOTICE AND THE SUPPLY OF DOCUMENTS BY OR TO OFFICE-HOLDERS		
Application	12A.6	N/A
The form of notices and other documents	12A.7	1.4
Proof of sending, etc.	12A.8	1.52
Authentication	12A.9	1.5
Electronic delivery in insolvency proceedings – general	12A.10	1.45
Electronic delivery by office-holders	12A.11	1.48
Use of websites by office-holder	12A.12	1.47, 1.49
Special provision on account of expense as to website use	12A.13	1.49, 1.50
Electronic delivery of insolvency proceedings to courts	12A.14	1.46
Notice, etc. to joint office-holders	12A.15	1.41
SERVICE OF COURT DOCUMENTS		
Application	12A.16	N/A
Application of CPR Part 6 to service of court documents within the jurisdiction	12A.17	Sch. 4, para. 1
Service of orders staying proceedings	12A.18	Sch. 4, para. 5
Service on joint office-holders	12A.19	Sch. 4 para. 4
Application of CPR Part 6 to service of court documents outside the jurisdiction	12A.20	Sch. 4, para. 1
MEETINGS		
Quorum at meeting of creditors or contributories	12A.21	15.20
Remote attendance at meetings of creditors	12A.22	15.6(6)
Action where person excluded	12A.23	15.36, 15.44
Indication to excluded person	12A.24	15.37, 15.45
Complaint	12A.25	15.38, 15.46
Remote attendance at meetings of creditors' committees and liquidation	12A.26	17.20
Procedure for requests that a place for a meeting should be specified 794	12A.27	17.21
EFFECT OF INSOLVENCY ON EXECUTION – SPECIFIC PROVISIONS FOR NOTICES TO ENFORCEMENT OFFICERS ETC		
Execution overtaken by judgment debtor's insolvency	12A.28	12.57
Notice to enforcement officers	12A.29	1.47
FORMS		

1986 Rule heading	1986 Rule	2016 Rule
Forms for use in insolvency proceedings	12A.30	N/A
Electronic submission of information instead of submission of forms	12A.31	N/A
Electronic submission of information instead of submission of forms	12A.32	N/A
GAZETTE NOTICES		
Contents of notices to be gazetted under the Act or Rules	12A.33	1.10
Gazette notices relating to companies	12A.34	1.12
Gazette notices relating to bankrupts	12A.35	1.13
Omission of unobtainable information	12A.36	1.10(2)
The Gazette – general	12A.37	1.14
NOTICES ADVERTISED OTHERWISE THAN IN THE GAZETTE		
Notices otherwise advertised under the Act or Rules	12A.38	1.15
Non-Gazette notices relating to companies	12A.39	1.16
Non-Gazette notices relating to bankrupts	12A.40	1.17
Non-Gazette notices – other provisions	12A.41	1.18
NOTIFICATIONS TO THE REGISTRAR OF COMPANIES		
Application of this Chapter	12A.42	1.19
Information to be contained in all notifications to the registrar	12A.43	1.20, 1.21
Notifications relating to the office of office-holders	12A.44	1.22
Notifications relating to documents	12A.45	1.23
Notifications relating to court orders	12A.46	1.24
Returns or reports of meetings	12A.47	1.25, 1.26
Notifications relating to other events	12A.48	1.27
Notifications of more than one nature	12A.49	1.19
Notifications made to other persons at the same time	12A.50	1.19
INSPECTION OF DOCUMENTS AND THE PROVISION OF INFORMATION		
Confidentiality of documents – grounds for refusing inspection	12A.51	1.58
Right to copy documents	12A.52	12.39, 12.40, 12.54
Charges for copy documents	12A.53	1.55
Right to have list of creditors	12A.54	1.57
COMPUTATION OF TIME AND TIME LIMITS		

1986 Rule heading	1986 Rule	2016 Rule
Time limits	12A.55	1.3, Sch. 5
SECURITY		
Insolvency practitioners' security	12A.56	4.4, 5.5, 6.24, 7.37, 7.58, 10.52, 10.69
NOTICE OF ORDER UNDER SECTION 176A(5)		
Notice of order under section 176A(5)	12A.57	12.15
Part 13: Interpretation and application		
Introductory.	13.1	N/A
'The court'; 'the registrar'	13.2	1.2
'Give notice', etc.	13.3	N/A
Notice, etc. to solicitors	13.4	N/A
Notice to joint liquidators, joint trustees, etc.	13.5	N/A
'Venue'	13.6	1.2
'Insolvency proceedings'	13.7	N/A
'Insolvent estate'	13.8	1.2
'Responsible insolvency practitioner', etc.	13.9	N/A
'Office holder'	13.9A	1.2
'Petitioner'	13.10	1.2
'The appropriate fee'	13.11	N/A
'Debt', 'liability' (winding up)	13.12	14.1
'Authorised deposit-taker and former authorised deposit-taker'	13.12A	1.2
Expressions used generally	13.13	1.2
Application	13.14	0.3
Application of Insolvency Act 1986 and Company Directors Disqualification Act 1986	13.15	N/A
Schedule 1 SCHEME MANAGER'S VOTING RIGHTS		15.29, 15.30, 15.31, 15.32
Schedule 2 ALTERNATIVE COUNTY COURT HEARING CENTRES		Sch. 6
Schedule 4 FORMS		N/A
Schedule 5 PUNISHMENT OF OFFENCES UNDER THE RULES		Sch. 3
Schedule 6 DETERMINATION OF INSOLVENCY OFFICE HOLDER'S REMUNERATION		Sch. 11

Index

All references are to paragraph number